HINDU SPIRITUALITY
Vedas through Vedanta

World Spirituality

An Encyclopedic History of the Religious Quest

1. Asian Archaic Spirituality
2. European Archaic Spirituality
3. African and Oceanic Spirituality
4. South and Meso-American Native Spirituality
5. North American Indian Spirituality
6. Hindu Spirituality: Vedas through Vedanta
7. Hindu Spirituality: Postclassical and Modern
8. Buddhist Spirituality: Indian, Sri Lankan, Southeast Asian
9. Buddhist Spirituality: Chinese, Tibetan, Japanese, Korean
10. Taoist Spirituality
11. Confucian Spirituality
12. Ancient Near Eastern Spirituality: Zoroastrian, Sumerian, Assyro-Babylonian, Hittite
13. Jewish Spirituality: From the Bible to the Middle Ages
14. Jewish Spirituality: From the Sixteenth-Century Revival to the Present
15. Classical Mediterranean Spirituality: Egyptian, Greek, Roman
16. Christian Spirituality: Origins to the Twelfth Century
17. Christian Spirituality: High Middle Ages and Reformation
18. Christian Spirituality: Post-Reformation and Modern
19. Islamic Spirituality: Foundations
20. Islamic Spirituality: Manifestations
21. Modern Esoteric Movements
22. Spirituality and the Secular Quest
23. Encounter of Spiritualities: Past to Present
24. Encounter of Spiritualities: Present to Future
25. Dictionary of World Spirituality

Board of Editors and Advisors

Volume 6 of
World Spirituality:
An Encyclopedic History
of the Religious Quest

HINDU SPIRITUALITY

VEDAS THROUGH VEDANTA

Edited by
Krishna Sivaraman

CROSSROAD • NEW YORK

1989
The Crossroad Publishing Company
370 Lexington Avenue, New York, NY 10017

World Spirituality, Volume 6
Diane Apostolos-Cappadona, Art Editor

Printed in the United States of America

Library of Congress Cataloging in Publication Data

Hindu spirituality.

(World spirituality ; v. 6)
Bibliography: p.
Includes index.
1. Hinduism—Doctrines. 2. Spiritual life (Hinduism)
I. Sivaraman, Krishna. II. Series.
BL1212.72.H55 1988 294.5 88-3714
ISBN: 0-8245-0755-X (v. 1)

अचिकित्वाञ्चिकितुषश्चिदत्र कविन् पृच्छामि विद्मने न विद्वान ॥

Ignorant, I ask the seers who
know, not as one knowing do I
ask for the sake of gaining
knowledge

(*Ṛg Veda* 1.164.6)

To the Seers and Sages,
Poets and Philosophers, Preceptors,
and followers of the traditions
that blazed the trail for posterity
to tread the path to immortal life.

Contents

Preface to the Series

THE PRESENT VOLUME is part of a series entitled World Spirituality: An Encyclopedic History of the Religious Quest, which seeks to present the spiritual wisdom of the human race in its historical unfolding. Although each of the volumes can be read on its own terms, taken together they provide a comprehensive picture of the spiritual strivings of the human community as a whole—from prehistoric times, through the great religions, to the meeting of traditions at the present.

Drawing upon the highest level of scholarship around the world, the series gathers together and presents in a single collection the richness of the spiritual heritage of the human race. It is designed to reflect the autonomy of each tradition in its historical development, but at the same time to present the entire story of the human spiritual quest. The first five volumes deal with the spiritualities of archaic peoples in Asia, Europe, Africa, Oceania, and North and South America. Most of these have ceased to exist as living traditions, although some perdure among tribal peoples throughout the world. However, the archaic level of spirituality survives within the later traditions as a foundational stratum, preserved in ritual and myth. Individual volumes or combinations of volumes are devoted to the major traditions: Hindu, Buddhist, Taoist, Confucian, Jewish, Christian, and Islamic. Included within the series are the Jain, Sikh, and Zoroastrian traditions. In order to complete the story, the series includes traditions that have not survived but have exercised important influence on living traditions—such as Egyptian, Sumerian, classical Greek and Roman. A volume is devoted to modern esoteric movements and another to modern secular movements.

Having presented the history of the various traditions, the series devotes two volumes to the meeting of spiritualities. The first surveys the meeting of spiritualities from the past to the present, exploring common themes that

A longer version of this preface may be found in Christian Spirituality: Origins to the Twelfth Century, *the first published volume in the series.*

can provide the basis for a positive encounter, for example, symbols, rituals, techniques. The second deals with the meeting of spiritualities in the present and future. Finally, the series closes with a dictionary of world spirituality.

Each volume is edited by a specialist or a team of specialists who have gathered a number of contributors to write articles in their fields of specialization. As in this volume, the articles are not brief entries but substantial studies of an area of spirituality within a given tradition. An effort has been made to choose editors and contributors who have a cultural and religious grounding within the tradition studied and at the same time possess the scholarly objectivity to present the material to a larger forum of readers. For several years some five hundred scholars around the world have been working on the project.

In the planning of the project, no attempt was made to arrive at a common definition of spirituality that would be accepted by all in precisely the same way. The term "spirituality," or an equivalent, is not found in a number of the traditions. Yet from the outset, there was a consensus among the editors about what was in general intended by the term. It was left to each tradition to clarify its own understanding of this meaning and to the editors to express this in the introduction to their volumes. As a working hypothesis, the following description was used to launch the project:

> The series focuses on that inner dimension of the person called by certain traditions "the spirit." This spiritual core is the deepest center of the person. It is here that the person is open to the transcendent dimension; it is here that the person experiences ultimate reality. The series explores the discovery of this core, the dynamics of its development, and its journey to the ultimate goal. It deals with prayer, spiritual direction, the various maps of the spiritual journey, and the methods of advancement in the spiritual ascent.

By presenting the ancient spiritual wisdom in an academic perspective, the series can fulfill a number of needs. It can provide readers with a spiritual inventory of the richness of their own traditions, informing them at the same time of the richness of other traditions. It can give structure and order, meaning and direction to the vast amount of information with which we are often overwhelmed in the computer age. By drawing the material into the focus of world spirituality, it can provide a perspective for understanding one's place in the larger process. For it may well be that the meeting of spiritual paths—the assimilation not only of one's own spiritual heritage but of that of the human community as a whole—is the distinctive spiritual journey of our time.

Ewert Cousins

Introduction

Krishna Sivaraman

> Different is the good and different, indeed, is the pleasant (or the pleasing). The two having different meanings (or ends) grasp a human being (binding him). Both (as it were) approach him. . . . The discerning ponders over them and discriminates (turning them all around). The unregenerate settles for the second (without a sense of discrimination) for the sake of comfort and cuddling (of worldly possessions enveloped as he or she is in a protecting world). (Katha U 2.1.1)

This oft-quoted verse sums up the spirit of the "turning around" that singularly dominates the early religious landscape of India: Hindu, Buddhist, and Jaina. It can be put in a simple theistic idiom as a turning around from facing the world to face God. Trans-theistically, it is turning around from the sphere of what presents itself not simply as actual but as real to reality itself, the "really real." In such turning consists the true spiritual vocation–turning from what serves one's temporal ends toward a growing insight into reality and a resulting fullness of life variously called life eternal or life divine or more simply life of the spirit. The spiritual journey is only an image of the turning around.

Throughout their long and variegated development, the religious traditions of India have never ceased to express their sense of commitment to what is often described in such negative terms as "renunciation" and "otherworldliness." It would, however, be more precise to use the term worldlessness, because "otherworldliness" was never the sole paradigm for the larger sphere of the Hindu cultural heritage. Those who do not make radical renunciation of the world, who live their lives in the matrix of outer relations called "the world," must nevertheless not become enmeshed in the world. For them, as well as for those who externally renounce the world, the "turning around" involves a liberation from the lack of freedom that characterizes life engulfed in the world. In this sense, for anyone who is in search of the meaning of his existence in the world, "worldlessness" embodies the greatest common denominator of the spiritual quest and represents the vocational symbol of India.

Worldlessness, then, is not "life-and-world negation" but reflects a spiritual mood and a sense of orientation that includes a positive and a negative disposition. Worldlessness is a disposition to live in the world, singly or collectively, not for its own sake, not as a goal in itself worthy of pursuit as a sufficient "human end," but as a means or medium to life "in God," as a condition of life in the spirit. Alternately expressed, life in the world is valued, but as an instrument and a condition of accomplishing "dwelling in oneself in ease" (*prasama*), becoming truly aware, as never possible before, of the basic worth of all beings and one's kinship with them. Achieving of an "integral orientation of life" (*samyak dṛṣṭi*) in and through but beyond life in the world is the mark of spirituality. It is what supplies to the human endeavor a new access to spiritual dynamism.

Worldlessness is used here as the term of contrast to worldliness and its existential correlate, egoism. It is not the world as such, but the world generated and reared by the ego, individual and corporate, appropriated and owned as "mine" that inhibits the expression of spirit. Spirit represents precisely that dimension which precludes the assertion of I as *against* you in any of its forms. True, the lure of worldliness and the thirst for life that it continually evokes also bespeak a vital urge of spirit, in response to the "pleasant (*preyas*) seizing upon a human being," but it has its source in a fundamental unwisdom, a primordial lack of insight into reality. One becomes aware that it is also an expression of spirit, though distorted and deflected and therefore not truly spiritual, but this awareness comes only in retrospect and again from the perspective of the turning around and the dawning of wisdom about reality that accompanies it.

The spiritual quest presented in this and the following volume is thus positive although expressed negatively in relation to the everyday world. To glimpse its contours one must focus on its true cutting edge, namely, a progressive and systematic diffusion of the ego-sense. The ego is, really speaking, the lever that lifts and sustains the whole weight of worldliness. It is the constitutive condition of our life in the world locking us in our cave of isolated existence, plunging into spiritual darkness, the "darkness thickening into greater darkness" (*tama āsit tamasā gūḍham*) (RV 10.129). This picturesque expression of the Veda means a falsehood compounded by an unredeemed deception by which the false is not only not unmasked but passionately held fast.

The religious literature of India, in effect, acclaims with a striking unanimity that the actor who dominates the stage of life is a "person," but in the etymological sense of one wearing a mask, a false self. I, as the person (the first person as grammar sanctifies it), is not the real "I" and much less the immortal spirit which I truly am by essence or affinity behind the veil of my nature. The ego is the mono-actor in the drama of a life of worldliness, being by definition what exists solely for itself even while feigning altruism, what isolates and separates from others while also ensconced in a web of relationship. The "I" of "I am" or "I do" is not spirit as such but the misdirected, deflected *dynamis* of the spirit element in the service of deception. In this deception I identify with my possessions which by a right I claim belong to me *but not to others.* I identify even less aware with my body, my senses, and even my "mind," which I presume without question to be necessarily, not contingently, myself or "mine." The "I" (*aham*) is thus understood as the edge of "mine" (*mama*), where "I am" is a mere function of an explicit or incipient "I have." Such is the nature of identity that is assumed in reply to the question "Who am I?" which one both asks and answers in every decision and in every cognitive endeavor. The subject-object split, which inhibits knowledge from realizing its destined goal of immediacy of "truth," is both a reflection of and a development through one's sense of identity as "I," vis-à-vis "mine."

The "I" as thus understood is severely castigated by the generality of Indian spiritual traditions, specially in view of the claim that it (the "I") makes in the name of the ego. The ego is, by definition, that which claims attention for itself, as the center, as it were, of the universe, endowing one with the imaginary royalty of the world. The real person—the spirit—calm, disinterested, and all-compassionate (What else can spirit be?) is what stands behind the ego letting itself be "confused."

> The locus where there is absent a sense of "I" and "mine" is the locus of spirit, its Holy feet even as the serenity of supreme blissfulness is its Holy Crown. (Kumaraguruparar, *Kantarkalivenpa,* line 11)

To renounce the ego by tracking it in its most far-reaching sweep is true renunciation, and to loosen it from its most insidious claim is true detachment. Conversely, any activity, to the extent that it entails liberation from the hold of the ego, even though seemingly an aspect of being-in-the-world, to that extent is "worldless" and is revelatory of spirit.

The story of the spiritual wisdom of India is the story of the concerted effort to contain the power and pretensions of the egoistic or self-asserting will. To efface egoism is prized not merely on moral grounds as an exhortation to be humble or meek. It is also an enhancement of value, of willpower and of "personality," if we remember not to understand these terms out of the context of the spiritual life. Through a discipline of mind and reason (*jñāna mārgam, saṃyak jñānam*), through heart and love (*bhakti mārgam, saṃyak darsánam*), and through will and power (*karma mārgam, saṃyak caritram*), what, incidentally, is accomplished is an enhancement or exaltation of life. These are not mere techniques of self-actualization but spiritual paths with redemptive enlightenment as their goal. Yoga, again, is not a mere technique but an exaltation of "excellence" (*kausalam*) cultivated as the art by which to apply the discipline toward a harmonic expression of the spirit. To recover real life, which is life "established in God" (*brahma niṣṭha*) or life of "supreme spiritual being" (*paramātman*) is to shun or turn away from the shadow of life. By losing oneself one is "awakened to the spirit" (*prabuddha ātmā*); by becoming united with the spirit of the universe, one finds oneself and with it the whole universe.

The Wide Spectrum of Hindu Spirituality

India's religious life in view of its bewildering complexity may well be described as itself providing a miniature World Spirituality Series. Because of its complexity, Hinduism may be viewed more as a locus for "meeting of traditions" than as a singular religious tradition. In the estimation of contemporary historians of religions, Hinduism to India is, most aptly, what comparative religion itself is to the world.

The term "Hindu" refers to the religious life of the people of India or, more correctly, of *Bhārata-varṣa*, the "world of Bharata." The latter expression is not merely the geographical equivalent of India in vogue before the advent of the English term (which etymologically means the land of the Indus River), but it signifies a single, though cumulatively diversified, cultural area like a pyramid inverted or, better, slanted on the side picturing its horizontal expansion. Hinduism, which again was indigenously named to mean "eternal religion" (*sanātana dharma*) or "revealed religion" (*vaidika dharma*), labels the religious quest of a people rooted in a single cultural soil. One may understand this feature by contrasting it with a case like Buddhism, which also was preeminently an "Indian" religion but was not determined by the circumstance of its rootedness in the culture of the area of its origin and unfolding. On the contrary, being essentially a homeless wisdom, a mendicant and missionary faith, it was as a movement *introduced* in historical time into the society where it made itself at home and into a culture whose coloring it readily took. Hinduism, in contrast, stands indistinguishable from the spiritual life of a culture and was not introduced or inaugurated as a movement at any assignable period of time. One may say the same about Jainism (see Part 3 below).

We began our account of "Hindu" spirituality with the attention rather on its "worldlessness," which it shared with the śrāmaṇic outlook. A "*śramana*" is one who treads the spiritual way of toil or existing (*śrm*) and describes, among others, preeminently the Jaina and the Buddhist. In contrast, however, stand the Hindu concern and preoccupation with the order of the world—cosmic, social, and the individual. The sacred order is not man-made but given in the nature of things. "The four-fold order was created by me" (BG 4.13). Likewise, the Hindu spiritual tradition sanctifies the life of the householder with his civic, social, and "cosmic" obligations while, at the same time, providing a path to inward liberation for those wholly absorbed in the spiritual quest.

The Hindu spiritual journey is typically the affirmative way: using things found in the realm of the many as means to affirming the one. The ascetic way of denial of the many as a means for realizing the unaffirmable One, surely, is accepted but only in spirit. "The day on which there is non-attachment (felt) renounce even on that very day" (*Jābāla upanisad* 4). For the very reason of its intrinsic importance, the ascetic way is sanctioned only in the light of an express requirement or a felt call as a special vocation—it is not prescriptive for everyone. The watchword here is "eligibility" (*adhikāra*). What this implies may be stated thus: The essential equality of all human lives in terms of the ability to will the spiritual good cuts across the institutionalizing of inequality in the name of social class and biological family. Everyone shall be enabled to become what one has in oneself to become. The options are perpetually open so that at the "right" time there will be the needed turning around for everyone.

The conflict and tension between the negative and the affirmative approaches of the religious quest should, nevertheless, not be understated. As earlier indicated, it underlies the story of the conflict and tension between the "orthodox" Hinduism on the one side and the traditions of Buddhism and Jainism, which espouse with varying emphases "homelessness" or ascetic withdrawal as the only *spiritual* option. Within Hinduism itself, it is present in a discursively unresolved manner between the rival demands of understanding spirit as subjectivity and inwardness or, alternatively, as holistic and integral. In a holistic view of spirit, what is without and what is within are valued alike. They are but the two sides of the same coin, so that no special significance is accorded to inwardness and interiority of life, except heuristically, and there is no exaltation of the ascetic vocation.

In Hinduism from the very moment of its initial formulation the conflict is present which looms into an ongoing and as yet unresolved "spiritual" difference for over a millennium within a common framework of Vedanta (see Parts 5 and 6 below).

In almost every generation and in every cultural, geographical unit of India from the time of her recorded history to the present day, there have been men and women who abiding away from the mainstream of life have borne witness to the power of the Spirit. Kings and commoners alike seek them out for guidance and often for experiencing "peace." From the point of practical spirituality mirrored in life as simply lived instead of being reflected upon, the holy personal presence itself is the eloquent example of what is spiritual, its meaning and its justification. The approach to spirituality, however, that is attempted through the essays of this volume, mostly draws from religious life and religious thought, from texts and their conflicting interpretations acclaimed alike as authoritative and from diversified intellectual and spiritual traditions and philosophies of India.

The negative and affirmative approaches may be seen to articulate different orders of evaluation of the central question of ego-consciousness in the Vedic heritage. The Vedas, specially in their crystallization as Vedanta, spell out the nonduality of Ātman, which is veiled by the I-consciousness, and Brahman, which lies hidden as the ground of the world. The Ātman/Brahman axis lends itself to all shades of interpretative analyses which determine the variety of religious denominations of the Hindu way of life.

The general Hindu conceptualization of spirit is done in terms of the upanisadic notion of *ātman* and its identity with the ground of being. Ātman, the true *theion* of Hindu spiritual tradition, is preeminently *not* will or dynamic spirit as such. Itself beyond the distinction of static and dynamic, *ātman* is rather the "ground" which provides for this and similar other distinctions. It is the manifesting source of everything that is, and, likewise, negatively speaking the condition of everything that is not. But when it is discovered or realized, it is realized rather as a fullness of the depth in which everything "of the surface" disappears. The Knower of the transcendent world of spirit, it is avowed, attains the highest (TU 2.1). But it is also avowed, paradoxically, that by knowing the *ātman* one knows the all (ChU 6.3). What this means may be stated thus: There is a certain looseness (or, more appropriately, one-sidedness) about the relation of spirit, and its manifestations in time, and a freedom about manifesting in diverse forms, including also the freedom of remaining without manifestation. Spirit itself, in other words, precedes the distinction of time and timelessness and therefore provides alike for life in the world and living "worldlessly."

The imagery of a tree is a commonplace of Indian religious literature. The tree in manifesting itself above ground inevitably relates to that which lies invisible underground as well as to the ground itself. The image, incidentally, vivifies the sense of the spectrum as applied to Hindu spirituality, its compactness and differentiation. Brahman, according to a Vedic text (*Sāṅkhayana Āraṇyaka* 11.2), is the great green tree that is spread out with its roots moistened. There is also the well-known upanisadic image (MU 6.4) of Brahman as root and branch of one and the same tree and indeed as rooted in the dark ground of the Axis of Brahman and as standing up and branching out in the manifested cosmos and the latter, therefore, as "inverted." There is again a description given of the Veda and the Upanisads themselves as the tree with branches, tender blades, foliage, flowers and fruits, the fruits being compared to Vedanta "the end of the Veda" (Upanisad). Life characterizes every stage of the tree's growth, and it is the same life that is more fully expressed in the fully grown tree than in the seedling or the plant, more again in the fruits than in the tender blade or flowers. The criterion for thus grading in terms of less and more is, of course, how the tree stands in relation to the needs of the beneficiary in fulfilling whom it also, as it were, fulfills itself.

The point of the imagery of significance for understanding spirituality, however, lies in how the tree is viewed in relation to its origin or source. Trees and plants, flowers and fruits manifest themselves above the surface in their luxurious proliferation but arise out of it, unfolding from the tiny, all but invisible nuclei hidden below the surface. In order, however, to elicit the more precise nature of "spirituality" (*ātmyam*) as outreaching and resisting identification with religious processes as such, we say that the spiritual is the soil or the ground, intrinsically prior to and beyond the forms of religion that are cognate with it, just as the soil is cognate with a seed or roots. Spirituality surrounds and underlies its religious expressions and is not reducible to the latter. What is unique about the Hindu notion of spirit (*ātman*), it may here be noted, is its intrinsic otherness in relation to its "expression" as the ethical, the political, the aesthetic, and even the religious. In their very midst spirit remains transcendent.

Understanding the spiritual more in terms of a neutral soil than as a seed which is continuous with the plant helps us to account for some of the features distinctive of the development of the Hindu religious tradition. To begin with, we can see that proliferations appear not as cancellations of each other's identities but as an enrichment of the whole spectrum. The questionings which reach toward *ātman* are subsumed under *Adhyātma-vidyā*, the science and art of realizing of spirit as such, and so pervade the entirety of religious consciousness either as its inarticulate overtone or as expressly countenanced as in the Vedanta.

The traditional Hindu religious notion of *adhyātma,* literally "pertaining to atman," plays almost the same pervasive role that the category "spiritual" does in the West. It is the name for the integrative function by which to unify the various aspects of existence. In this respect it is cognate to and paired with *adhibhūta,* implying unification on the objective side, and *adhideva,* meaning integration *in divinis. Adhyātma* is used for integrating the various aspects of subjectivity which is, again, simply existence contemplated from the inwardized vantage point of the self. *Adhyātman* functions like a symbol pointing beyond itself, opening up levels of reality which remain undisclosed without a corresponding opening up of levels of the human mind beyond the discursive and the sense-bound.

The integrative role of spirit under the name *adhyātman* was recognized by the great Vedic etymologist Yāska (fifth century B.C.), who states clearly:

> It is because of His great divisibility that they apply many names to him, one after another. The other Gods come to be submembers of the One spirit (*ekasya ātmānā*) . . . their becoming is a birth from one another, they are of one another's nature; they originate in function; the spirit is their origin. Spirit is even their chariot, their horse, their weapon, their arrows. Spirit is the whole of what God is (*ātmā sarvam devasya*). (*Nirukta,* 7.4)

Spirituality, thus understood as wisdom about the "way back into the ground" of pluralism of religious forms, serves as the rationale also for the infinite diversity in the way of one's being in the world. Spirituality in this specific sense also preeminently integrates the affirmative and the negative ways distinguished earlier. The foundational conceptual formulation of the tradition can be stated thus: *brahman* represents the highest state of existence, universal and transcendent, the ultimate source of all positivity from which all things originate, have their being, and into which all return; *saṃsāra,* that is, the "phenomenal or natural existence," refers to the human being's empirical situation governed by the law of necessity (*karma*) and consequent unfreedom and finitude. The scriptures inculcate and encourage cognitive, reflective disciplines (*vidyā*(s)), emphasizing negation in the sense of a turning away, a choosing of the "good" in the place of that which is pleasing.

The ultimate "good" in this case is liberation or "freedom of the spirit." The other goals described as life values in the picturesque scheme of "ends of human life" (*puruṣārtha*), one may say, are summed up under the rubric of the "pleasant" (*preyas*). The order of the pleasant includes the enjoyment of senses (*kāma*) and material comfort (*artha*), both, however, always to be determined by a sense of obligation to the "other" as against self-centeredness. The latter represents the sphere of *dharma,* which marks the transition from the pleasant to the good (see below pp. 140ff.). In general, all Hindu traditions accept this framework differing only in their interpretations of the concepts involved. The *summum bonum* (*śreyas*) of liberation or "freedom of the spirit," however, is the commonly cherished goal of life marking the attainment of fulfillment in life as well as beyond life. Consistent with its description as "spiritual," it marks both a process (*sādhana*) and its result (*sādhya*), as it were, coincidentally, as if saying that every point on the journey is also the arrival point. Seeking and finding are a dialectical continuum involving, in existential terms, an inner transformation of life. One may even stretch this continuum to encompass phenomenal or natural existence itself: spirituality, as an outlook, then, will be as explained in the beginning—a matter of winning an orientation or a sense of perspective and a wholeness or completeness which the ideal of "liberation" implies. Living in the presence of the ideal with such a perspective enables one to look in retrospect at "life in the world" and to see it as continuous with its transformation. This is spirituality and spiritual life. The natural man imperceptibly yields to the spiritual man; life values are transformed through a retrospective reorientation into spiritual values. When the distinction between the "should" or "must" and the "is" thus ceases to exist, the spiritual goal of "being free from" (*mukti, mokṣa*) overreaching the divide or distinction, humanly speaking, may be said to have been realized.

Content of the Hindu Volumes

The first Hindu volume of World Spirituality brings together the complex profiles of thought, belief, and practice beginning with their development from the archaic period of the Vedas and their early crystallization as Vedanta, "the end of the Veda." The latter marks the transition to what has been aptly termed in a global historical setting the advent of axial awareness[1] with the focus crystallizing on individual consciousness. Vedic spirituality, which includes as its culmination the emergence of Vedanta, is followed by accounts of Hindu beliefs and practices, philosophies and faiths, found reflected in its legal treatises, epics, and doctrinal literature in the forms of aphorisms and exegeses. All of these are accepted as "tradition" (*smṛti*) in addition to the Vedas, which are "revelation" (*śruti*). From the perspective of spirituality, the distinction may be restated as "re-collected" experience and "direct" experience. The Jaina religious quest, which is described also in this volume, likewise admits of a distinction between its direct, canonical representations and later reflections and re-collections. All these early developments, Hindu and the Jaina, the brāhmaṇic and the śrāmaṇic, may be described as marking the classical spirit. This description is analogous to the description of the "classical" period of Indian civilization. The one massive omission here is Buddhism, also "classical" in the above sense, which is treated elsewhere in separate volumes. Developing into the Maḥayana movement, Buddhism in India changed and in changing left its mark on Hinduism before disappearing from the country of its origin.

Postclassical Hinduism is treated in the next volume, which deals with ecstatic devotion, the cult of the temple and other popular expressions of piety and devotion, the Tantra with its sacramentalization of sex, latter-day rituals and practices, regional expressions and reorientations of the Hindu religious quest aiming at novel reconstructions and newer self-definitions of the classical spirit. The medieval religious climate of northern India was open to the spirit of popular devotional Hinduism from the south. In its turn it witnessed the rise of Sikhism, under the stimulus of the impact of Islam. This was followed by modern developments touched off by the impact of the Christian West and often treated under the rubric of Renascent Hinduism. The Ramakrishna movement, Tagore, and Gandhi, among others, highlight this phase, while no less significant as a spiritual movement is the shaping of Indian Christianity itself.

The two Hindu volumes accordingly are structured along this division between the classical and the postclassical. Although roughly chronological, their division is not strictly historical: the historical roots of what is called later Hinduism stretch back to dim antiquity, and some aspects of its culture and cultus are clearly traced even to pre-Vedic Harappa culture. Many of its other features, for example, Pauranic elements, which in their distinctive form surfaced later, are related almost by a straight line to Brahminical Hinduism; and even the Tantras, according to Hindu self-understanding, derive from Vedic texts presumably now lost to us. Incidentally, this feature of viewing new departures as still essentially in terms of rootedness "in the Veda," belittled by historians as anachronistic, throws some new light in retrospect on the meaning of the Vedas themselves: The "Veda" in the singular comprises not merely the four Vedas structured as hymns, rites, and doctrines, but all words that speak of "God," all utterances that are self-revealed and, therefore, partaking of the "word" (*Vāk*). The Vedic seer himself, it may be remembered, is, among other things, a medium to transmit to posterity the timeless and impersonal insights which he receives.

The term Hinduism is used here without the restricted sense in which historians employ it to refer to developments falling within a specific period of chronological history. Thus, Hinduism, according to an indologist of our times, *began* at the time when the Vedic framework was lost, which can be even dated as an occurrence between the sixth century and fourth B.C. (see below p. 40). In these volumes, however, the term Hinduism is used to mean an undifferentiated whole which includes the Vedas as the point of departure but has no assignable time of beginning. It is indeed used to mean both the archaic-classical Hinduism of the Veda and the Vedanta and its neoclassical and postclassical transformations inclusive of what has come to be called Renascent Hinduism. Using this single term does not, however, preclude discerning type differences that are significant for viewing Hinduism under the aspect of spirituality. Types, it is useful to remind oneself, do not quite exist in space and time, and therefore it follows that they can coexist across the stretches of history and geography. At any rate, the principle of division in organizing the material in these volumes rests on the dimensions of types, which can coexist without the implication of superseding and without being structured in a hierarchy of levels.

Thus, there is what may be termed a normative side to Hinduism presenting itself as "orthodoxy" or "orthopraxis" (translations of *āstika,* literally, "one who says yes"). This term implies an ideal norm while also allowing for variety as a matter of principle. The normative is what presents itself as both impersonal and timeless and is always operative as a subtle prescription infusing a character, invisible but nonetheless discernible, to the content of life. "Timeless rhythm" will aptly describe this character that is unique as a "Hindu" way of life. What is the "Hindu" character? One may say that it consists in making one live spiritually as if time were not "history." This is not the same as living without a sense of time or the change that time brings, as it is often caricatured. If anything, it bespeaks a sense of "history" or change but as enfolded in a timeless meaning. Time itself is a crucial category for Hinduism, as a coordinate of the journey of life in and through and beyond the world. As a metaphysical discipline in the form of Vedanta, in the broad sense Hinduism is, however, a severe judge of all notions of history and historical teleology that occidental historical awareness assumes as valid, and of all forms of evolution which, likewise, rest on the assumption of an all-too-easy identification of the good with the necessary.

The category of time may be seen to operate here in the process of a perpetual unfolding, in an ever-widening circle of spirituality, of the original inspirations of Veda. Sometimes norms are changed in practice and also in theory. Hinduism at times is manifest more in the mode of revivals, under different names and banners; reformations, as different and divergent movements; and even rejections, resulting in the rise of new religious forces in the course of history and in different parts of India. The interesting thing is that the two, the timeless nonform as well as the forms and stratifications that the tradition has undergone and still does in unpredictably diversified ways on the scales of time and space, are simultaneously operative in varied degrees in the life and thought of the spiritually sensitive Hindu.

Hindu spirituality is "traditional" in both senses of the term: it is "conservative," and it is also synthetically continuous. The ardent traditionalist as well as the iconoclastic reformer imbued with a zeal for change alike can avow the Hindu "tradition." In the same breath one can describe its growth as dialectical "advancing" through opposition and resolution and also as linear in some sense, as a case of widening with the flow of time but never in its farthest sweep moving out of a center. The tradition as it were espouses affirmation of co-existence of forms, resisting all pressures to coalesce into a homogeneity. While retaining a conservative core, it never ceases to envision unequivocally directions for new development conducive to the growth of spirit. This volume presents the eternal, timeless dimension of Hinduism, while the spiritual elements that are uniquely reflected in the unfolding of Hinduism as a widening circle are postponed for Volume 7.

Spirituality and the Issue of Hindu Scholarship

The writers of the articles in this and the subsequent volume were selected on the basis of their scholarly specialization as well as a certain sensibility which enables them to reflect on and out of the Indian tradition. The personal involvement is the criterion which meant choosing those who could speak spiritually from within the Hindu tradition. The issue is indeed not one of choosing "Hindu" scholars but concerns the type and temper of scholarship that is appropriate for the task. Scholarship becomes a moot problem in the general context of modern indological writing established by the labors of Western indologists. It becomes especially urgent in the present context, where the concern is spirituality and not the more objective aspects of religion and culture.

The development of the Hindu volumes, as well as that of the others in the series World Spirituality, has raised a deep issue which can be expressed in a twofold question: How convey in reflective language the spiritual experience that lies at the heart of the tradition? How assimilate into that expression the various dimensions of objective scholarship that have been developed in the past several centuries in the West: critical history, textual studies, sociology, anthropology, and psychology? This implies a further question: What relation do these new disciplines have to traditional scholarship? Do they supersede classical forms that are peculiar to each religious tradition, for example, the great commentary tradition of Hindu scholarship built around sacred texts composed by Hindu grammarians, philosophers, and theologians throughout the centuries? The position of the World Spirituality series has been to respect the traditional forms of scholarship as integral to the respective spiritual traditions and at the same time to assimilate in varying degrees the perspectives of the newer disciplines. The present and subsequent Hindu volumes accordingly are designed to reflect a whole spectrum ranging from examples of traditional methods to those reflecting varying degrees of assimilation of newer approaches.

Thus, chapter 2, "The Spirituality of Vedic Sacrifice" in this volume, may be taken as representative of the traditional synchronistic method without a concern for or an assimilation of the controls of critical Western academic scholarship. Of the other essays, those by Wayne Whillier and by Kenneth H. Post swing to the other end, remaining within the bounds of "scientific" indological research and often untroubled by the perception of the tradition itself. Others in different degrees utilize the spirit of the traditional approach combining it with historical, literary, and cultural aspects of objective scholarship. One of them even seeks to reconcile spirituality with the scientific world view. The articles, in other words, reflect the present state of mutual assimilation of traditional and objective modes of scholarship indicating an effort and the will to understand Hindu spirituality as something that can be appropriated even strictly on its own terms to the present, as integral to contemporary concerns.

After we state it thus, it becomes necessary, even at the risk of digressing, to pause and reflect on what is the real issue between traditional Hindu and modern Western scholarship. The issue is, to state it in its most simplified form, objectivism in interpretation. Objectivism, and with it a certain kind of historicism, one may generalize, colors the modern Western approach. Objectivism, which must be distinguished from objectivity, looks upon the past as object. It sees the past as a field of study, a field that lies, as it were, at one's feet while the observer stands above it as a "subject" that surveys the field. With objectivism goes hand in hand also a distorted notion of history: history is something that we make and indeed experience our freedom in making it. It is not something that we participate in. The past becomes what we learn about, not something we learn from. These modernist assumptions, when brought to bear on a study of Hindu sacred texts, ill accord with the tradition's claim of revelatory status for its scriptures and sacred writings derived therefrom. An objectivist approach to spirituality that would not recognize the reality of a living tradition or its claim becomes therefore questionable to those within the tradition.

This is not, however, to question the significance of modern scholarship or even critical history and their relevance for investigating Hindu spirituality. One can envisage the possibility of historical studies of the more imaginative kind contributing to an understanding of the spirituality of a tradition which itself may be avowedly a-historical, as in the case of

Hinduism. History and historical research can function as hermeneutics from within as well as an ordering of facts from an objective perspective from without. Likewise, thought even of the highest kind can be viewed as a function of a presupposed particularity of experienced circumstances without detriment to a perception of it as at the same time also disclosive of something nonparticular, as laying claim to a universal relevance. History thus can help in keeping the past alive in the present.

The Hindu conceptualization of tradition was expressed by a term which meant literally "memory" (*smrti*). Memory is the bridging of the past and the present in one's consciousness. Remembering and interpreting and recreating again and again as time goes by what was disclosed and what found utterance in a beginningless beginning—such is briefly the general self-understanding of the Hindu tradition. The meaning of Hindu spirituality as dynamic flow must then be sought in what may indeed be described as a historical unfolding of consciousness within the Hindu tradition. One can see in the Hindu mythic figure of Vyāsa the vision of the sense of tradition as a holding together of past and present. The Supreme who declares that he "comes into being from age to age" (BG 4.8) also says appropriately, "of the sages I am Vyāsa" (BG 10.37). Vyasa is the one who gathered and comprehended all Vedic texts (*śruti*), all the tomes of the Puranas as well as the *Mahabharata*, the grand epic of one hundred thousand verse (*smrti*).

An objective approach and history in the sense of interpretation may thus be seen as dimensions of a reflective awareness of a total experience within the Hindu tradition. Tradition is not something that stands like a mountain for exploration. It functions rather as an archetype in relation to spirituality so that the approach that is proper to it must be one of evoking it by an attitude of respect and "receiving," of appropriation and advance.[2]

There is a method of investigation that is integral to the content of Hindu spirituality specific to this volume. The Indian philosophical assumptions underlying its theories of meaning and methods of investigating texts show some striking consensus despite debates and discussions surrounding them. The Veda itself consists of inspired utterances as well as spiritual "reason" diving into the things of the beyond and coming up with inspired "thought." The latter—technically, *mīmāmsa*—is not mere logical reasoning but coordination of spiritual experiences or thoughts having an inner certitude and is, eminently, part of a process that culminates in meditative realization. The *mīmāmsa* method of interpretation subsequently became the established approach to the study of sacred texts. Scholarship, objectivity, and analytic clarity are conspicuous by their pervasive presence thanks to the collaboration of the disciplines of grammar (*Vyākaraṇa*), exegesis (*Pūrva*

Mīmāmsa), and logic (*Nyāya*), whose areas of specializations, respectively, are the word, sentence, and means or verifiers of valid knowledge. What is striking is that these objective features of study are combined with sensitivity, sympathy, and imagination as in perceiving hidden meanings and implied connections, the unsaid in between the sayings, the indirectly said in the very mode of a direct saying, seeing the text as a coherent whole from within in terms of an implicit content transmitted by the tradition. While the "letter" is analyzed in terms strictly of a logical and semantic rationality, the "spirit" of symbolic apprehension is never lost sight of. The interpretative responses, in fine, are "spiritual" rather than a literal, exoteric, external apperception of the meaning of words and syntax. "The letter kills but the spirit gives life," as a criterion of understanding, holds good with special force in the context of Hinduism.

The *mīmāmsa* method of investigation to which reference was made can be summed up in one or two sentences, in its most generalized form: Verbal meaning (which after all is the issue at stake in interpreting texts) should be explicable in terms purely of the linguistic system in which the texts operate, in this case of the Veda, and with the help of well-established principles of reasoning. They do not depend for their comprehension on such extraneous factors as the person addressed and who interprets it. It is not that these factors are ignored. In fact, one of the literary conventions that governs all writings, sacred as well as secular, is to provide in a preamble details about the name of the author, the name of the work, the literary antecedents of the work, and the scope of its reception and other details. But for construing the meaning of the text itself these are considered as purely extraneous.

The classical *mīmāmsaka* is a Vedic exegete concerned with the correct determination of the meaning of texts and with the settling of problematic passages in them. It accords with the traditional Western sense of hermeneutics as a *technē*, a practical discipline for dealing with difficult texts or obscure passages where understanding is blocked. This traditional sense, incidentally, is replaced in modern times under the dominance of science by the ideal of understanding as an objective knowledge verifiable and falsifiable and guaranteed by methodological self-control. The *mīmāmsa* method of investigation, however, in the way it is conceived resists the very possibility of becoming faulted. It, in the main, is determined by what it considers the axiom of interpretation, colored as it is by the avowed nature of the subject matter in whose service the "method" acquires its "methodical" function. These "axioms" of interpretation may be barely mentioned without elucidation, the object being merely to illustrate that there is a highly sophisticated and at the same time spiritually sensitive interpretive tradition at the very heart of the Hindu spirituality under consideration: The entire Vedic corpus is directed toward a unified sense (*ēkavakyatā*, "unified sentenceness"), lest the Veda become a house divided against itself, forfeiting its right to be deemed revelation, i.e., knowledge otherwise unobtainable. This is a formal rule, but in applying it to the Vedic exegesis the tradition becomes internally divided over the priority accorded to sections relating to ritual or to gnosis. Likewise, there is the principle of autonomy of verbal signs, according to which words convey meaning independently of any external authority and corroboration by another source of knowledge (cf. how this principle is utilized in Vedanta as integral to understanding the nature of Spirit vis-à-vis the authenticity of scripture [see below pp. 231ff.]). There is again the thesis that becomes the focus of sustained discussion, namely, the nonpersonal character of verbal knowledge and its inherent independence of any personal author who intends their meaning. The author(s) or the reader(s) do not play a significant part in the hermeneutical act. What the speaker intends and the listener understands are themselves but the function of the spoken word. While the Mīmāmsā as a philosophical tradition was sought to be modified and in certain respects even responded to with an emphatic no by other Hindu schools or traditions, it is nevertheless true to say that the *mīmāmsa* overview colors the generality of a methodological orientation that one can label as classical Hindu scholarship.

Plan of the Volume

The topics in the two volumes are grouped in such a way that each volume is designed to be self-contained and to meet the requirements of those interested either in the classical or the later developments of Hindu spirituality. The treatment does not aim at a chronological history and may be described as thematic and topical, although the overall design reflects the process of history in the sense of the development of ideas. The present volume is divided into parts that are arranged in an order which reflects the transitions from the Vedas (ca. 1500 B.C.) to the Upanisad (ca. 1200–600 B.C.), from the Vedic texts to the *Dharmasastra*(s) (ca. 400 B.C.) and the *Itihasa*(s), that is, the *Ramayana* and the *Mahabharata* (ca. 200 B.C.), from the times of Patañjali (ca. A.D. 200) to that of Sankara (A.D. 800), from Sankara to the post-Sankara Advaitins (ca. A.D. 900 to 1400) and to Rāmānuja (ca. A.D. 1100) and Madhva (ca. A.D. 1300), and to Srikanṭha and Appayya Dīkṣita (A.D. 1300–1500) bringing the account into the middle of the second millennium after Christ and representing the story of Hindu spiritual development spread over a period of more than two thousand years. To this are added contemporary affirmations of the classical spirit, which extend the story to an even longer period. No essay in the volume, however, addresses exclusively the development of thought as such, although many of them give biographical, textual, and sociocultural data. This is, however, done as incidental to the main task of presenting a synchronic picture of Hindu spirituality.

Part 1 of the volume, entitled "The Vedic Spirit," contains articles ranging from the vision of the Vedic seers concerning mysteries of the world of spirit to the wisdom of the sages of the Upanisads. Vedic literature begins with mantra, "words rising from the depths" (RV 4.3.16), presented as the *saṁhitā*(s) ("collections"), and a large body of ritual texts called the *Brahmaṇa*(s) ending with the Upanisads. As the manifestation of the *Vāk*, "the eternal Logos" of the Veda in human, linguistic form, the Upanisads describe themselves as representing the "end" of the Veda. If the entire volume under consideration represents the timeless rhythm of the classical spirit of early Hindu spirituality, the section on the Vedic spirit presents it in a miniature form. The polarity and complementarity between ritual and knowledge, between symbolism and rationalism, between heaven and liberation are characteristic of the Vedic heritage and are enduring features of later philosophical doctrines and religious practices.

The section begins with the essay "The Vision of the Vedic Seer" by Rajendra P. Pandeya, which sets the stage for the entire volume, highlighting the recurrent features of harmony and inclusiveness which, in general, both the brahminical and the śrāmaṇic spirituality exhibit. The Vedic seer, pure of mind and heart, embraces all aspects of human life or nature, harmonizing material-vital existence and psychical-intellectual life. The uniquely Vedic concept of *yajña,* "sacrificial rite," is the path to the knowledge of truth and everlasting happiness. These points of harmony are further brought out in *ṛta,* the universally unitary and obligatory principle which in turn leads to the realization of the unity of being, the cosmic and transcendent reality called the *puruṣa.* The Vedic sages discover this *puruṣa* in the very being of the human self.

Hridaya R. Sharma takes his point of departure here and focuses on the spiritual import of *yajña*(s), the Vedic "rite" *par excellence.* Through the sacrificial rite human beings play out their active and conscious participation in the gradual process of purification and upgrading. The mystic fire on the altar is a liberating force. The sacrifice spans cosmic, vital, and corporeal existence and brings about a "second birth" which is described as the fountainhead of the flow toward the final goal of all three modes of living. The essay concludes with the discerning observation about the spiritual import of *yajña* as a means for *brahmabhāva*, "state of brahman," a state truly unaffected by do's and don'ts, merit and sin, and such other pairs of opposites resulting from Necessity. Rite thus becomes itself transformed spiritually into an ascetic station of life. If Pandeya writes as a thinker and scholar, Sharma brings to bear his rich experience as a performing ritualist and teacher. His reflections are based on his study and application of the vast literature on the subject in original Sanskrit.

The essay "Truth, Teaching, and Tradition" by Wayne Whillier strikes a different note, looking at Vedic spirituality as it were from without. The author concurs with the general self-understanding of the Hindu tradition in viewing Vedism as its most ancient form and recognizes it as still a living force in Indian spirituality which conserves a unity of purpose in India's cultural homogeneity. There is a clearly discernible transition from Vedism to Hinduism, he observes at the outset, representing a triumph of caste ideology over contest ideology, the triumph of individual worship over the cult and of philosophy and the quest for intuitive truth over ritual performance. The triumph of caste ideology meant a new understanding of truth as private and personal, and a rigorous ordering of men and women on the basis of one's proximity to truth. The article also contains valuable information about the visionary poets of the Veda and development of *brahmodya* as a teaching device. It concludes with a note of spiritual import, indicating how at the core of ritual—the *raison d'être* of Vedism—lies the relationship of brahman as "power," "ritual," "powerful prayer and speech" as well as "participant." The great service of indology has been to stimulate a renaissance of Vedic studies, and Whillier's essay is representative of creative indological thinking in recent times.

Last in the section is "Spirit and Spiritual Knowledge in the Upaniṣads" by John G. Arapura. The Upanisads bequeath to Hindu spirituality a unique conception of spirit and spiritual knowledge, and therefore also of salvation. However, this does not mean, cautions Arapura, that the later tradition, particularly the classical Indian philosophical tradition, saw it with full clarity. Identity, which is the truth that resides at the center of the upanisadic approach to spiritual knowledge, is not a concept or an idea but "a fullness that makes everything full." Everything in the world as directed by the unseen logos—*Vāk* in the Vedic language—leads to that identity. Yet without the advantage of its light, it is not easy to see how things in the world, principles, relations, arrangement of concepts, inferences, and deductions themselves unaidedly could lead to it. If the spiritual journey is from ignorance to knowledge, then it is logos that puts us on the way. Logos enacts the directional movement implicit in the posture called upanisad. Arapura's essay, though postured as critical, sounds the very depth of traditional understanding, guided as it is in a most stringent way by Sankara, the illustrious commentator. At the same time, the essay also mediates this understanding for Western thought and experience.

Dharma is one of the most pervasive concepts of Hindu spirituality. As a social concept, it refers to the moral code, law, natural and positive, and also, preeminently, to the various duties of individuals. The normative ordering called *dharma* in its legal, moral, social, and political aspects is the subject of exploration in the *Dharmasastra*(s) and the *Arthasastra*(s). The *Ramayana* and the *Mahabbharata*, on the other hand, exemplify an understanding of the spirituality of *dharma* in concrete settings. The epic heroes are idealizations of character representing the different stations of life that Hindu treatises on *dharma* recognize. Not only the seer and the recluse but also the ideal king, ideal wife, brother, friend, the diligent student, the citizen in his vocation are presented in these epics. These encyclopedias of classical Hindu life and wisdom recognized as later Vedic sources by historians are viewed also by tradition as an extended sequel to Vedic spirituality.

In Part 2, entitled "The Spiritual Horizon of Dharma," there are three essays. Kenneth H. Post analyzes the "Spiritual Foundations of Caste," drawing his material from writings called *dharmasūtra*(s). He views them as political in the Western classical sense. The prescription of social order is a type of political thought outlining the best human order. In this highly informative but critical essay, the author draws the conclusion that looking at caste in the light of spiritual texts, one can see caste as a manifestation of a beginningless justice which is sovereign over all things. K. R. Sundararajan, in his essay entitled "The Ideal of the Perfect Life: The *Rāmāyaṇa*," analyzes the epic in terms of the filial and social roles of the chief characters: Rama is the ideal son, husband, king, and friend; and Sita, the ideal wife. Bharata, even more than Rama himself exemplifies an ideal brother. *Dharma* vis-à-vis the mythical universe of gods and animals and forces of nature means cosmic harmony sustained through noninterference by all the inhabitants of the universe. *Dharma* is *human dharma*, a model to be emulated even by nonhumans. Arun Kumar Mookerjee, in his thought-provoking essay entitled "Dharma as the Goal: The *Mahābhārata*," focuses on the spiritual teachings of the epic, extolling *dharma* as both *sakāma*, "with desire," and *niṣkāma*, "without desire." It teaches nonviolence yet does not consider war an evil. The author says that there is no contradiction, since *dharma* is different from rules of morality and the two may or may not go together. *Dharma* and common morality represent a two-level ethics in which the latter is subordinate to the former and exception is given to the latter by this relation. Distinguishing between the *Ramayana* and the *Mahabharata*, the author says in conclusion that in the *Ramayana* God himself had come to set an example of a life of *dharma* through mortal sufferings, whereas in the *Mahabharata* humans set the example. A life of *dharma* bridges earth and heaven, though salvation (*mokṣa*) surpasses even heaven.

The religious quest that is characteristic of the Veda, the *Śmrti* and the *Dharmaśāstra*(s) constitutes the foundation of what may loosely be called the "brahminical" spirituality. Outside of it and along with it is the śrāmaṇic tradition, which represents the extrabrahminical spiritual quest stretching back to a dim past. Jainism and Buddhism are typical of such traditions. Not accepting the spiritual authority of the Veda, they admitted all members of the community into their order without regard to social rank or station. In Part 3, "Srāmaṇic Spirituality," Sagar Mal Jain, a reputed authority on the subject and a practicing member of the Jaina community, gives in his "The Jaina Spirit and Spirituality" a comprehensive account of the concepts and terms that are used in Jaina thought, drawing copiously from the Jaina canonical literature. Liberation is a state of being and not a case of losing one's innate identity. Elucidating further, the author observes that the ultimate goal of the soul is equanimity, "*samatā*." Spiritual discipline is nothing but a sustained practice of equanimity. Simultaneous cultivation of insight knowledge and conduct is the unique feature of Jaina spiritual life. The fourteen stages of spiritual development, which the author lists with clarity and conviction, provide a most impressive account of the spiritual journey.

Yoga is generally taken to be the art and science of reaching down inside oneself and summoning vital resources. It is similar to commando training, where the trainee tackles more and more difficult obstacles until he can cascade down cliffs. Yoga, however, is more than an overcoming of obstacles. The most pervasive feature of the spiritual disciplines alike of brahmanic and śrāmanic religions, yoga is a positive, spiritual pursuit imbued with a quest for freedom and immortal life, harnessing all the three built-in avenues which are open to human beings in their life of endeavor: body, speech, and mind. Part 4, "The Spiritual Quest for Immortality and Freedom," accordingly comprises articles devoted to these three areas of yogic disciplines: the body-behavioral yoga, that is, the yoga of human action—the yoga, in other words, of being-in-the-world represented in the teachings of the *Gitā;* the yoga of Patanjali, *prima facie* a psycho-mental discipline, though inclusive among other things also of physical culture aspects; and the yoga also of speech. The grammarian tradition of Bhartṛhari teaches the yoga based on *sabda,* "the word," as the direct way of realizing the divine.

Ravi Ravindra, writing on "Yoga: The Royal Path to Freedom," begins with the impressive statement that the transformation of the mind which the central yoga of Patañjali entails is not literally through one's effort or practice but indeed is the unfolding of nature's own potential tendency. Yoga merely eliminates the obstacles to the natural unfolding of oneself so that one may realize one's true spiritual nature. *Puruṣa,* the "spirit," simply is. It is independent of all the forces and controls of *prakṛti* or "nature." What is the spirituality of the discipline of yoga? The author observes that "sacrificing" *citta,* the "mind," to *prakṛti* for the sake of *puruṣa,* is what renders the yogic process in effect "spiritual." In a section on the *Gītā* and yoga, the author adverts to the more holistic yoga taught in the *Gītā*—*buddhiyoga* with its emphasis on integrated *buddhi,* "intellect," which can have a vision of the *puruṣa.* The following paper by Arvind Sharma, appropriately, is "Buddhiyoga in the *Bhagavadgita.*" Identifying the different senses in its cosmic and individual connotations, Sharma finally focuses on *sthira-buddhi,* "steadfastness of intellection," which had a key role in controlling the mind. Truly speaking, it is the self-transcendence of *buddhi* leading to integration with ultimate reality. Explaining the contemporary relevance of this idea, the author considers as crucial the distinction that it makes between transcendence and denial. It is crucial for interreligious dialogue and especially for modern life, if only as a corrective to its hyperactive tendencies.

Harold Coward begins his paper entitled "The Reflective Word: Spirituality in the Grammarian Tradition of India" with the remark that for the Hindu grammarians words are reflections of the Divine and at the same time the means by which the Divine may be known. Three aspects of spirituality involved here are isolated: the existential experience of the word involving, among other things, the function of mantra chanting, the study and teaching of the word, and finally the yoga of the word which consists in intuiting word-meaning as the essence of consciousness and, therefore, as prompting all beings toward spiritual activity.

The term Vedanta, as earlier explained, means primarily the Upanisads but secondarily *Brahmasutra*(s) (200 B.C.) and only derivatively Sankara's (ca. A.D. 800) historic commentary on them as well as on the *Bhagavadgita.* A "philosophic discipline," *śāstra,* as well as a scheme of ethical-spiritual practice, *sādhanā,* the Vedanta exemplifies a cognitive and contemplative approach to a realization of spirit. Part 5, entitled "Vedanta as Reflective Spirituality," is central to the volume as it spans in extent and importance the earlier and later spiritual orientations. Even to understand the momentous reconstructions of Vedanta on the lines of *bhakti* which originate from other commentaries on the *Brahmasutra,* it is imperative that one come to terms with the "nondualistic" Vedanta of Sankara. There are at least nine different commentaries, *bhāṣya*(s) (ca. A.D. 900–1800), on the *Brahmasutra*(s), each of which has been the starting point of a tradition within the Tradition, *sampradāya*, bearing the descriptive labels of *Viśiṣṭādvaita*, "nondualism, but qualified as theism," *dvaitavedanta*, "Vedanta that is dualistic," and *dvaitadvaita*, "nondualism that is yet dualistic," and so on. Historically the debate, overt or implicit, has always been as if between Sankara and Rāmānuja, Sankara and Madhva, Sankara and Nimbarka or Vallabha or others.

The essay "Vedanta as Philosophy of Spiritual Life" is by Kalidas Bhattacharyya. The foremost philosopher of his generation, extending from the forties to early eighties of this century, he was second only to his father, the renowned K. C. Bhattacharyya, whose article "Advaitavada and its Spiritual Significance," published some forty years ago, was a classic on the subject. The editor considers himself privileged that Kalidas Bhattacharyya undertook to write especially for this volume, readily entered into the spirit of this enterprise, and very spontaneously wrote out a long essay on a theme of Advaita relevance for spirituality, namely, "The Witness-consciousness (*Saksi-Caitanya*)." In response to the editor's request that he focus on the aspect of Advaita as a spiritual journey, he had in this original and creative piece of writing thought his way through to the heart of the spirituality of Advaita. It is a philosopher's understanding of the spiritual journey in Advaita, and as such epitomizes and emphasizes the strength of the tradition as a living stream flowing without interruption for thousands of years, into which one can enter through the mode of thinking one's way to its central issue.

The editor wished to include it in this volume, although it is not in the same genre as the other articles. The general reader may be deterred by the opacity of technical language, but the editor ventured to include it in any case, hoping that all those who would grasp the core of Hindu spirituality will bring to bear on this essay their forbearance for technicalities and desire to enter into an alien way of thought. In order to facilitate understanding, a short abstract of the main arguments has been added to the essay as the editor's preamble. A careful and patient reading of the essay will make it possible for readers not only to get a glimpse of the methodology of creative thinking within the parameters of an ancient tradition but also, it is hoped, to gain an insight into the spiritual issue of the ground on which we stand as perceived in Advaita. It is also an example of the point made in the part on scholarship, namely, the possibility of appropriation of the original insight in the language of the times, without discarding the spirit of the tradition. Kalidas Bhattacharyya died before the volume appeared in print. It is with deep gratitude for his involvement in this project and as a mark of respect to his memory that we publish in this volume the last major paper of the eminent philosopher.

If Vedanta as Advaita is a tolerant synthesis of all spiritual worship and experience, the immediacy of its "nondual" experience, itself, however, becomes a focus of concern calling for an uncovering of its hidden horizons of spiritual meaning. Of special relevance is the understanding of spirit that the experience entailed: Is it an "impersonal" absolute which is primarily approached in noetic terms as self-revealed, as all positivity but also, equally, all-cancelling negativity? Or is it rather the Godhead that is thus disclosed in terms of its superpersonal depths, a being who can be prayed to, adored, and who is, directly and centrally, revelation, grace, descent (*avatāra*), teacher? Spirit penetrates the seer's consciousness not merely like the light of day but as life, in the light and inspiration of this enlightened experience—the life of devotion (*bhakti*). Part 6, entitled "Vedanta as Devotion," includes three essays on the major traditions of Vedanta interpreted as devotional theism: S. S. Raghavachar's "The Spiritual Vision of Ramanuja," Krishna Sivaraman's "The Sivadvaita of Srikaṇṭha," and K. T. Pandurangi's "Vedanta as God-Realization." The authors are specialists who speak on and out of the respective traditions in a spirit of appropriating the traditions more originally.

Raghavachar shows how Rāmānuja (ca. A.D. 1100) builds his case for a reoriented scheme of spirituality by drawing from continuous streams of living devotion as well as by critiquing the intellectual consistency of the apophantism of Advaita. The substantive essence of spirituality for Rāmānuja is "*jñāna* that has the form of *bhakti*." *Bhakti*, reminds the author, is no mere emotion, but dwelling in reflection on God with love. *Bhakti* implies a sense of the reality of supreme being issuing in passionate devotion. Only such devotion-suffused meditation can mature into true self-surrender, *prapatti*, wherein the seeker chooses, in the place even of devotional means, God himself to function as all his means. God as spirit is the means as well as the end. Vedanta thus comes full circle from being an austere reflective reaching to the Unconditional to a forceful doctrine of Grace.

Krishna Sivaraman outlines the Saiva counterpart of Rāmānuja in his essay on Sivadvaita. The Spirit of Vedanta is viewed not as impersonal absolute but as Godhead discerned by the significant proper name of Siva. Adored as being of the nature of self-substance (*aham-padārtha-rūpa*) in the invocation by Srikaṇṭha, the Saiva commentator of Vedanta, Siva is Brahman possessed of the energy of consciousness (*citsakti*). Distinguishable but not separate from Brahman, *citsakti* is manifest as the inner space or ether within the Heart-Lotus (*cidambaram*), thus representing the innermost being, the real essence, the basic core of self-hood. Appayya Dīkṣita, who glosses on Srikaṇtha, defines the purport of Sivadvaita as consisting not so much in opposing the Unconditional of Vedanta as in providing the corrective to its understanding: the Unconditional is also of the nature of unconditional Grace; through a propitiation of the grace of Siva alone, by meditating on it as the space within the sanctum of one's heart, is inculcated a desire or yearning for the saving truth.

Pandurangi presents the tradition of Dvaita Vedanta. Madhva (ca. A.D. 1300) perceives God (Visnu) as the central theme of Vedanta and as indeed the one that holds together the Vedic, upanisadic, epic, and puranic traditions. It is because God possesses infinite attributes (*pūrṇa*) that He is described as possessing contradictory attributes and as being beyond words and concepts. Madhva, as the eminent advocate of divine duality (*dvaita*), separates the plane of divine presence from the plane of human adoration. God and souls are alike spiritual in their nature, the latter, however, having their very essence in being entirely dependent on God. Dependence is thus seen as the doctrinal thrust of Vedanta.

The Hindu religion has been looked upon by some as excessively spiritual to the point of neglecting the world of nature and culture, of overlooking human reality, vitality, and creativity. This is a misconception. The world, seen as rooted in Spirit, indeed acquires great significance. The world is an increasing unfolding of the values implicit in reality, matter, life, mind, intelligence, and spirit. Values are molded and made possible by a congenial environment, which itself is a reflection of cosmic order. Part 7, "Spirituality and Human Life," is designed to explore the spiritual aspects of human life in relation to nature, art, music, health, and human welfare. Two of these are treated in this volume, and the rest postponed to the next volume. Klaus K. Klostermaier, one of the most insightful Indianists of the Western world, writes on "Spirituality and Nature" and interprets the Hindu spiritual traditions and Samkhya specifically as exemplifying the effort to demonstrate the ways in which nature is working for the good of the spirit. "The Truth which makes free," Klostermaier concludes according to Sankhya as well as modern science, "is not the one set down in doctrines and formulae, nor is it the explanation of events and mechanisms whether through bodies or concepts. Rather it is the one which is encountered in ever new insights into the nature of nature."

S. N. Bhavasar and Gertrud Kiem are the authors of the essay on "Spirituality and Health." Well-being pertains both to physical welfare and to spiritual felicity. Health is not mere absence of disease but positive well-being making for joy in life and in all works spiritual. Drawing from the most authoritative text on *Āyurveda,* the name of Hindu medical science, the authors explain how healing according to Indian medicine could be achieved, but only with some sense of the values which suffuse the Hindu culture. Beginning with the correlation between medicine and the Sankhya school of thought, the *Caraka Samhita* systematically sets forth analyses of health, ill health, pathogenesis, treatment, recurrence of diseases, the condition of natural homeostasis, and physician-patient relationship. The authors, both teachers and practitioners of *Āyurveda,* have given a lucid presentation of the text and its analyses.

One of the distinguishing features of a tradition is its sense of continuity. Those who visited India—the Greek, the Chinese, the Arab, and the European—experienced the sense of a living culture conscious of its continuity and unity in terms of an underlying vision and a way of life. Can the spirit of the Veda and Vedanta in its pristine quality be said to be a living experience today? The final part, "Contemporary Expression of the Classical Spirit," includes two lucidly written essays, one on Ramana and Candraśekharendra by R. Balasubramanian, and the other on Sri Anandamayi Ma by Bithika Mukerji. The choice of the subjects was made by the editor but the contributors had the freedom to develop their essays in the light of their closeness to and involvement with the respective spiritual leaders. The choice could have been any among a host of others who are exemplars of the classical spirit in days since the time of Sri Ramakrishna (who himself is the subject of a paper in the next volume). The editor chose three of the most contemporary of them, two of them living memories and one still a living presence. They typify Hindu spirituality in terms of its very classical conservative form and its meaningfulness today. The three of them in different ways exemplify spirituality mirrored in life as simply lived and also as a reflection from within life.

R. Balasubramanian writes on "Two Contemporary Exemplars of the Hindu Tradition," namely, Bhagavan Ramana (1879–1950) and Candrasekharendra Sarasvati (b. 1894). Both are in the tradition of gurus and are also "knowers of Brahman." Ramana turned the attention of the enquirer to the more urgent and immediate problems of self-inquiry. In the tradition of Vedanta as reflective spirituality, Ramana invokes inquiry as the spiritual means for the elimination of the "I" through discovering the source of "I." Unveiling the self is self-realization. Sri Candrasekharendra Sarasvati, the sixty-eighth Sankaracharya of the Kanci *Kāmakoṭi-pīṭha,* true to his title, the "world-teacher" shows by his life and teachings the relevance of the Hindu scriptures for the generality of humanity and not merely for "Hindus," which name he criticizes as an outsider's account. Sri Sarasvati recalls by his dynamic presence the image of Adi-Sankara, "the immaculate saint who was divine and yet human, whose saving grace was universal in its sweep."

Bithika Mukerji begins her essay on Anandamayi Ma with the disclaimer that the great saint was neither a spiritual teacher nor even a mystic. The author observes that her presence was always overwhelming on every kind of audience through the divine presence permeating the atmosphere. The heart was buoyed on a wave of joyousness unimaginable before, true to the name by which the saint was known. The importance of the world and what it entailed in terms of duties and obligations to family, society, and country are, observes the author, affirmed by the saint in no uncertain terms as the ground from where the quest for self-realization begins. In the pull of the world a sense of duty must prevail; evil must be suppressed and justice upheld. Only this must be counterbalanced by the call to renunciation. In an age where the separation between religion and spirituality begins to color the spirit of India, Sri Anandamayi could still speak meaningfully of the one Reality as the "unity of vision and resonance" revealed as the Vedic spirit. Bithika Mukerji's article forms a fitting finale to this volume in terms of the understanding of spirituality as implying a presence before which is awakened, enkindled, and sustained the longing for the quest for truth and faith in its ultimate fulfillment.

Now it remains for the editor to express his deep debt of gratitude to a host of young scholars who made it possible for this volume to acquire its present form. Kay Koppedreyer went through with great diligence and patience many of the essays in this as well as the second volume, Drs. Margarette Chatterji, Luitgard Soni, Wayne Barody, Anna Kutty, Bettina Baumer, Mark Dyczkowski, and G. Subbiah corrected errors and helped with suggestions for editing some essays. Swami Viravahu of Dharmapuram Mutt was a great encouragement, especially for the working of the introduction. Bettina Baumer also assisted in supplying the photographs for this and the following volume. It is, however, to Bithika Mukerji that the editor wants to acknowledge his particular gratitude. She has a major share in the designing of the volumes as well as in the more arduous task of maintaining communication with contributors in India through personal meetings and correspondence. Lastly, the editor take pleasure in thanking the general editor for his own personal involvement in the issues that are discussed and for his sustaining encouragement toward the completion of this work.

Notes

1. Karl Jaspers, *The Origin and Goal of History*, trans. Michael Bullock (New Haven: Yale University Press, 1953) 1ff.
2. See Ewert Cousins, "Interpretation of Tradition in a Global Context," in *The Annual Publication of the College Theology Society 1983*, Vol. 29 (Chico, CA: Scholars Press, 1984) 95–107.

General Bibliography and Abbreviations

General Bibliography

This bibliography is selective and is confined only to more recent writings which directly or otherwise address the task of thinking of spirituality in relation to Hindu culture, religion, and philosophy.

Anirvan, *Buddhiyoga of the Gita and Other Essays.* New Delhi: Biblia Impex Private, 1983. Especially the essays on "Spiritual Values" and "The Spiritual Quest."

Sri Aurobindo. *The Foundations of Indian Culture.* Pondichery, Vol. 14. Sri Aurobindo Birth Centenary Library, 1971. Especially the five subsections on "Religion and Spirituality," pp. 121–95.

The Bases of Indian Culture, Commemoration Volume of Swami Abhadananda. Ed. Shree Amiya Kumar Mazumdar and Swami Prajnananda. Calcutta: Ramakrishna Vedanta Math, 1971.

Coomaraswamy. *2 Selected Papers Metaphysics.* Ed. Roger Lipsy. Bollingen Series. Princeton: University Press.

Moore, Charles. *The Dance of Siva.* Fourteen essays with an introductory preface by Roman Rolland. Delhi: Munshiram.

——, ed. *The Indian Mind: Essentials of Indian Philosophy and Culture.* An East-West Centre Book. Hawaii, 1978.

The Cultural Heritage of India. 5 vols. Calcutta: Ramakrishna Mission, Institute of Culture.

Vol. 1, *The Early Phases* (introduction by Radhakrishnan, 1937; reprint, 1976)

Vol. 2, *Ithihasa Puranas, Dharma and Other Sources* (introduction by Dr. C. V. Ramaswami Iyer, 1952; reprint, 1969).

Vol. 3, *The Philosophies* (ed. Haridas Bhattacharya; introduction by T. R. V. Murti, 1953; reprint, 1969).

Vol. 4, *The Religions* (ed. Haridas Bhattacharya; introduction by Bhagavan Das, 1956; reprint, 1969).

Vol. 5, *Languages and Literatures* (ed. Suniti K. Chatterjee, 1978). All these volumes have their focus on India, "the Hindu Spirit."

Mahadevan, T. M. P. *Spiritual Perspectives.* Delhi: Arnold Heineman, 1975.

Murthy, K. S. *The Indian Spirit.* Waltair, Andhra: University Press Series, 1965.

Murti, T. R. V. *Studies in Indian Thought: The Collected Papers of Professor T. R. V. Murti.* Ed. Harold G. Coward. New Delhi: Motilal Banarsidas, 1983. Especially the essays on "The Philosophy of Spirit" and "The Concept of Freedom as Redemption."

Prabhavananda Swamy. *The Spiritual Heritage of India.* Garden City, NY: Doubleday, 1963; 2nd ed., Hollywood Vedanta Press, 1969.

Raju, P. T. *Spirit and Self.* New Delhi: South Asian Publishers, 1982. Especially the first two essays, "The Concept of the Spiritual in Indian Thought" and "Comparative Philosophy and Spiritual Values."

———. *Structural Depths of Indian Thought.* New Delhi: South Asian Publishers, 1985.

Radhakrishnan. *Eastern Religion and Western Thought.* New York: Oxford University Press, 1959. Especially chap. 11, "The Supreme Spiritual Ideal: The Hindu View."

Saher, P. J. *Eastern Wisdom and Western Thought.* London: Allen & Unwin, 1969.

Sarkar. *Dynamic Facets of Indian Thought.* Vol. 1, *Vedas to the Auxilliary Scriptures.* Delhi: Manohar Publications, 1980.

Abbreviations

AB	Aitareya Brāhmaṇam
AL	*Ananda Lahari*
Ādi	Ādi Parva
ĀDS	*Āpastamba Dharmasūtra*
AT	*Adhyātma-tattvāloka*
AU	Aitareya Upanisad
AV	Atharvaveda
BĀU	Brahadaranyaka Upanisad
BDS	*Baudhāyana Dharmasūtra*
BG	*Bhagavadgītā*
BhP	*Bhāgavata Purāṇa*
BM	*Brama-mīmāmsā*
BS	*Brahmasūtra*

ChU	Chandogya Upanisad
CR	*The Collected Works of Ramaṇa Maharishi*
Gau	*Gautama Dharmasūtra*
GKP	Gurumaṅdalārcana Karma Paddhati
Iśā U	Īsā Upanisad
Kaivalya U	Kaivalya Upanisad
Kaṭha U	Kaṭha Upanisad
KP	Kaurma Purāṇa
KU	Kena Upanisad
Maitrāyani U	*Maitrāyani Upanisad*
Maitri U	Maitri Upanisad
MĀU	Mandukhya Upanisad
MS	Manu Smṛti
MU	Mundaka Upanisad
NS	*Niyamasāra*
PB	*Pañcaviṃśabrāhmana*
PD	*Pañcadaśī*
PPUP	Paramahaṅsa Parivrājaka Upanisad
RV	*Ṛg Veda*
ŚB	Śatapatha Brāhmaṇam
ŚK	Śabda Kalpadruma
SMD	*Sivarkamani-Dipika*
SN	*Sivadvaita Nirnaya*
SS	*Samayasāra*
SvU	Svestasvatara Upanisad
TA	*Taittirīya Āraṇyaka*
TB	Taittirīya Brāhmaṇam
TR	*The Teachings of Ramana Maharishi*
TS	*Tattvārtha Sūtra*
T Samhita	Taittiriya Samhitā
TU	*Taittirīya Bhāṣya*
TU Bhāṣya	*Taittirīya Upanisad Bhāṣya*
US	*Uttarādhyayana Sūtra*
VājSam	*Vājasaneyisaṁhitā*
VP	*Vākyapadīya*
VS	*Vedantāsutras*
YS	*Yogasutra*
YV	*Yajurveda*

Scheme of Transliteration

Vowels	a ā i ī u ū ṛ ṝ ḷ e ai o au
anusvāra	ṁ
visarga	ḥ
Consonants	
gutturals	k kh g gh n
palatals	c ch j jh ñ
cerebrals	ṭ ṭh ḍ ḍh ṇ
dentals	t th d dh n
labials	p ph b bh m
semivowels	y r l v
sibilants	s as in *sun*
	ś palatal sibilant pronounced like the soft *s* of Russian
	ṣ cerebral sibilant as in *shun.*
aspirate	h
medial	ḻ (in Tamil)

Part One

THE VEDIC SPIRIT

1. There was neither Non-existence nor Existence,
nor was there the Earth or Sky beyond;
What was the covering, whence and at whose shelter
was there the primeval Water with depth unfathomed?

2. Death was not then, nor was there Immortality,
there was no sign of day and night;
That One in breathless space breathed on its own,
apart from that there was just nothing.

3. Darkness at the beginning was covered with darkness,
and this All was indiscriminated chaos;
All was then in the Void contained, only the One
hath emerged with its mighty radiance.

4. Thence arose primal Desire in the beginning,
the first seed of the Mind;
Wise sages searched into the heart of mystery,
and found Existence's kinship in Non-existence.

5. Sideways extended their severing line,
what was above and what below it?
Begetters were there and mighty Potencies there,
sacrificial acts here, fulfilling Energy up yonder.

6. Who indeed knows, who can here declare,
whence and wherewith comes the Creation?
Gods are later than this Creation's origin,
who knows then whence it issued into being?

7. This Creation thus issued forth thence,
But was it founded or not?
The Lord of Creation, who in Transcendence reposed,
indeed knows this, or knows not?

8. With that *puruṣa*, the first of beings,
Consecrated on grass;
The gods sacrificed, the *ṛṣi*(s) of old,
And the *ṛṣi*(s) that followed

9. From that Sacrifice, the cosmic offering,
dripped butter, the gathering life-force;
Therefrom were formed the creatures of air,
of the forest and of home.

10. From that Sacrifice, the cosmic offering,
    issued forth Ṛcas and Sāma-hymns;
From that were born rhythmic metres,
    from that also Yajus came.

11. From that were horses born, and animals
    with two rows of teeth;
Therefrom were kine generated,
    from that came forth goats and sheep.

12. When the *puruṣa* was divided thus,
    how many divisions did they make?
What is it they called his mouth, what his arms,
    what his thighs and feet?

13. The *Brāhmaṇa* was his mouth,
    the *Rājanya* made of his two arms;
His thighs came to be the *Vaiśya,*
    from his two feet was the *Śūdra* born.

14. The Moon arose from his mind,
    and the Sun hath come out of his eye;
From his mouth arose Indra and Agni,
    while his breath gave rise to Vāyu.

15. From his navel was retained Mid-region,
    while Heaven was sustained from his head;
From his feeth the Earth, from ear the directions,[?]
    the worlds were conceived thus.

16. Of this thence were the seven barriers,
    and thrice sevenfold fire was made;
When gods had the Sacrifice prepared,
    with *puruṣa* as the sacrificial beast.

17. With Sacrifice thus the gods sacrificed,
    and thence were revealed first Ordinances [?];
The virtuous attain the highest region,
    wherein dwell gods, the sacrificers of old.

RV 10.129 (trans. Rajendra P. Pandeya)

1

The Vision of the Vedic Seer

RAJENDRA P. PANDEYA

THE SPIRITUAL VISION OF THE VEDA has inspired and set the pattern for much of later Indian theological and philosophical thought. It bespeaks a clear sense of reality, an outlook and a *Weltanschauung* through its most vivid imageries and colorful symbols, covering in its encyclopedic scope every aspect of human existence, the material, mental, and spiritual in a fully integrated way. In this integration, or harmony, indeed, lies its true "spirituality": The Vedas are four in number—*Rg Veda*, *Yajurveda*, *Sāmaveda*, and *Atharvaveda*. The first is the oldest and most important, while the other three are largely constituted by incorporation and elaboration of it. Although the *Atharvaveda* does indeed contain original material of significance, it is, even so, demonstrably grounded in the older Ṛgvedic ideas. Accordingly, we will depend largely on the *Rg Veda* for our source material.

The traditional meaning of "Veda" is "the knowledge of Truth," and those who in their wisdom discover the way of Truth and remain committed to it throughout their life are called *ṛṣi*(s), "seers." What the Vedas mean by "Truth" (*satya*) in human terms is, first, that Truth is the goal of human knowledge, and, second, that it is also the path leading toward it. The first meaning corresponds to that of *satyadharma* (*Taittirīya Samhitā* 3.3.11.9), "the vocation of Truth," or simply *dharma*, which sustains all beings, according to their own nature and in harmony with each other. Thus, the very endeavor to make Truth one's goal is already to establish, or at least endeavor to establish, oneself in harmony with others. In its second sense, Truth is understood as *ṛta*, or *vrata*, the eternal path of divine righteousness for all beings, including humans and gods, which must be followed in thought and action to discover and maintain oneself in Truth (Rg Veda 4.51.7, abbreviated as RV). For the Vedic seer (*ṛṣi*), therefore, no particular part or aspect of human life or nature is spiritually more or less valuable than any other. The whole of human life and nature, it follows, is spiritually significant, and anything that threatens their harmony is to be considered evil (*anṛta*). The Vedic insight into the nature of Truth, accordingly, provides a means to distinguish what is true and right from that which is false and evil, without implying a disrupting of the manifest unity of life and nature.

The Ṛṣi

The *ṛṣi* is the Vedic seer, the sage who directly perceives Truth unfolding through the successive layers of reality. The principle of conscious harmony between humanity and reality is uniformly present, both in the dynamics of being and in the dynamics of nature. It is this principle, singularly important, that we have to keep ever before us in trying to understand the spiritual vision of the Vedic *ṛṣi*(s); for, in the enlightened consciousness of the *ṛṣi*, a cosmic harmony unfolds within his own being and pervades his relationship, as human, with the gods and with nature. Thus, the RV calls the *ṛṣi* a poet, a seer, and a knower of *ṛta*, the eternal cosmic harmony.

In other words, the Vedic *ṛṣi* is the revealer of a universal vision in which the conflicts between thought and action, perception and imagination, inner and outer, body and mind, mundane and divine, the one and the many, light and darkness, life and death, and good and the not-good are seen to yield and converge harmoniously at a deeper level of being and understanding. It is a level of being and understanding repeatedly acclaimed in the Veda as beyond all verbal categories, names, and forms. The Vedic *ṛṣi*(s) functioning at this level of being and understanding seem to lose their own personal identity in the process and rediscover it in an ancestral affinity with the *ṛṣi*(s) of the past and present, as well as with the gods. It is not surprising, therefore, that the *ṛṣi*(s) of certain Vedic hymns often bear the same names as the gods to whom the hymns are addressed or the *ṛṣi*(s) of the past. This identification is one of the reasons why the Vedas are not considered to be of human origin (*apauruṣeya*): they are authorless in the sense that they are not, strictly, the creation or composition of any author, human or even divine.

A more important and fundamental reason for this view of the Veda as eternal revelation and therefore authorless is the Vedic idea of Truth: Truth is eternal and moves by its own force, a force that does not depend on any external agency. The Veda as Truth is therefore not in need of an author to manifest itself. Even sounds, images, and words are not essential for its manifestation. The Vedic *ṛṣi*(s) apprehended it fully formed, through their mind's eye. "Mark the Truth, thou who knowest, do mark that Truth—the eternal Truth that flows in full stream" (RV 5.12.2). In other words, Truth is self-revealing, and it suffers no limitation or distortion from within; therefore, the *ṛṣi*(s) perceive it in a way akin to self-revelation, free of constraints. The Vedas, incorporating this self-revealing and self-revealed Truth are, therefore, said to be eternal. They are transmitted through the *ṛṣi*, who assimilates, collects, and codifies the revealed Truth, thus bringing it into history. It is for this reason that the Vedas are called *saṁhitā*, "collections," and *śruti*, "that which is heard."

The *ṛṣi* is said to be a *kavi*, which means both poet and sage. He is a *kavi* just as the gods are, and, as the *Atharvaveda* (abbreviated AV) says, nature is the eternal poetry of these (12.1.63) gods whose distinctive quality is wisdom. The *ṛṣi*'s poetic vision is his spiritual insight, which marks the awakening within him of Speech (RV 8.9.16). It is the repository of Truth and Wisdom which, as the *Gopatha Brahmana* says (1.2.10), marks the spirit of the Rg Veda.

Speech (*Vāk*)

Speech is called the "queen of the gods" (*rāṣṭrī*, RV 10.125 line 3) and "the ultimate heights on which the gods repose" (ibid., line 7), while elsewhere (1.164.39) it is declared that "one who knows not Speech to be the abode of gods, of what use to him are the Vedic verses; those who know this are restored unto it." However Speech does not reveal herself to everyone:

> One man has ne'er seen *Vāk*, and yet he sees: one man has hearing but has never heard her. But to another has she shown her (bodily) beauty as a fond well-dressed woman to her husband. (10.71.4)
>
> It is only the *ṛṣi* who truly "sees" and hears Speech, while he who is ignorant and dull wanders on in profitless illusion, the speech he hears or sees yielding neither fruit nor blossom. (10.71.3,5)

The Vedas, therefore, identify Speech in its essence as *ṛc*, the luminous speech, and mantra, the meditatively fixed speech. It is this which stirs in the heart and mind of the *ṛṣi* and not the merely spoken word, for the latter has not as yet entered the psycho-physical stream of being. Speech first enters the stream of consciousness in the form of luminous universal symbols which represent its first embodiment and articulation. Next it enters the vital stream of one's being, where it is represented by the functions of the senses, the images of memory, and imagination as well as by the vital urges. At this stage the configuration of Speech is less subtle but more articulate than at the preceding stage without there being, however, any loss in its spontaneity. The final stage is that of entry into the physical stream of a person's being, where it assumes the form of the spoken word.

The two Rgvedic hymns 10.71 and 10.125 describe Speech in its human and divine aspects, extolling both their difference and unity, in terms which although expressly mystical are not beyond comprehension. The first hymn (10.71) is addressed to Knowledge (*jñāna*) and tells of the human effort required to unravel the hidden stages of Speech. It speaks of the origin of Speech in the *ṛṣi*'s mind, where it is pure and intimate. This purity and intimacy inherent in Speech are exhibited in the act of naming, in which the word and its object are manifest in harmonious union. Naming is here characterized as the spiritual activity of the god Bṛhaspati (who is also the *ṛṣi* of the hymn), whose action is the secret and sacred means of making known the hidden treasures of Speech. Naming, as a spiritual act, is in this hymn identified with *yajña*, the Vedic sacrifice: it is not common speaking. *Yajña*, as we will explain later, symbolizes in the Veda the rite of purification whereby the gross gives way to the subtle.

Denotation is the act of using gross speech forms symbolically to signify the vital functions, including those of the senses as well as the images of memory and imagination. The appropriate verbal symbols corresponding to these functions and images in turn correlate with the subtle luminous symbols representing beings and things in their true nature. These luminous form symbols, therefore, are the true names, and the knowing of them is knowledge. Elsewhere the act of naming is described as the method of "measuring speech by Speech" (RV 1.164.24). One who is incapable of using this method is said to have attained Speech in a sinful manner, because it is not in accordance with the purifying spirit of *yajña*, and therefore his use of words as symbols amounts only to the "spinning of words in ignorance."

In hymn 10.125 (see also AV 4.30), Speech successively identifies herself with the various gods and with the essence of all beings. She declares herself to be underlying all the vital functions. Spiritual disposition and wisdom become possible only through her blessings. She is the founder of communities and the great bestower of riches on those who follow her course. Finally, she is the creator of the worlds in her swift dynamism which transcends Heaven and Earth. In this hymn it is creativity, the ontological function of Speech, that is extolled, unlike the earlier hymn, which bears upon knowledge, its epistemic function. Later, when we discuss the Vedic conception of creation, it will be made clear that the two, creativity and knowedge, combine in one's being making the manifold creation possible.

The One

The Rg Veda draws a clear distinction between the *ṛṣi*, who has known the Veda as the revealed Truth directly, and the ordinary human being, who can only have faith and worship this revealed Truth indirectly. At the same time, however, one's indirect belief and worship in fact prepare one eventually to attain Truth for oneself. An important aspect of this preparation is to realize the importance of the principle that "speech measures Speech," which the Vedas themselves apply in the form of a mystical etymology of symbols that offers a means of unraveling their underlying meaning. These verbal symbols, in effect, represent the hierarchy of gods which constitutes the outer, varied form of the One.

The deeper meaning of the Vedic hymns is the revelation of Truth as the One (*ekam*). Hence, the hymns themselves are considered to constitute the eternal transcendent space in which divine beings—the gods—repose, while those men—the *ṛṣi*(s)—who understand the hymns in this way share in their divinity. The Vedic notion of the divine, therefore, unfolds itself in the structured relationship between the One, gods, and humans within the transcendent space found in the deeper meaning of Speech, which takes the form of the Vedic hymns. The unfolding of this structured relation in the Veda follows a long and complex course. The description given here, therefore, is a highly simplified version.

The most direct statement concerning the One occurs in several passages: "To what is One, sages give many a title" (RV 1.164.46), "the sages represent the One in the manner of many" (RV 10.114.5), "the One becomes manifest in all this" (RV 8.58, *khil,* 10:2), "God is indeed the One" (AV 10.8.28), "my salutation to the One Lord of the world" (AV 2.2.1–2), and so on. These passages are remarkable as they identify the One in such a way that what is spoken of and represented as *many,* that is, the world or nature, achieves its expression in and through that One. The One, the Unborn (*aja*), is therefore taken to be the first principle and cause of everything. Except the Unborn One, everything else, including the gods, is said to be born. However, the way the One appears and expands as *many* is admitted in the Veda to be a supreme mystery. Its understanding is considered problematic and paradoxical as may be seen in the following Ṛgvedic lines:

> Who hath beheld him as he sprang to being, seen how the boneless One supports the bony? (1.164.4)
>
> What was that One who in the Unborn's image hath established and fixed firm these worlds' six regions? (1.164.6)

One may wonder about the apparent skepticism of such passages, and pause to consider whether a state of ultimate questioning may not more truly reflect the spiritual mood. How can one be certain that it is the One which is here being treated thematically in an attitude of inquiring introspection ultimately to assume the form of an absolute mystery? In reply it may be seen that the Vedas, especially the Rg Veda, contain many passages, more numerous and frequent than such apparently skeptical ones, which record the Vedic vision directly and spontaneously:

> The One (Indra), and none else, has made all things in due order. (1.52.14)
> The One (Viṣṇu) supports all the worlds. (1.154.4)
> The One (Uṣa) illumines all this. (8.58 (val. 10).2)
> The One Ruler (Indra), the Lord of Strength, is the Sovereign of this world. (8.37.3)

In these passages, the concept of the One has crept in almost silently in adjectival form, that is, as qualifying a particular god; though in each case it performs the very same function of juxtaposing the idea of the One and the Many, noted in the earlier passages. An important consequence of this function is that it reduces the opacity of the paradox and provides an opening into the mystery relating to the human understanding of the One. Of particular significance is the use of the word "one" in the following passage: "The One hath entered both Heaven and Earth each of which is one" (RV 3.7.4). The silent presence of the One is indicated here in the use of the verb form in singular (*āviveśa*), without using "the One" (*ekaḥ*), while the expression "one" is used to qualify each of the pair of Heaven and Earth (*roḍaśi*). This construction suggests that it is in a state of silence that the One enters into "ones," the beings. The transcendence of the One is reconciled with its immanence in the "ones." For this reason the *ṛṣi*(s) did not deny the multitude of gods even as they tirelessly emphasized their essential unity in the One.

The One's absolute, transcendent, yet pervasive expansion, does not admit any categorization, not even in terms of "existence" or "nonexistence," because the sense of oneness disclosed in it goes beyond all distinctions and limitations. Hence, it is transcendence itself, of which it alone is capable. To convey this idea, Vedic formulations of the One tend toward mystical and paradoxical statements which concern the multileveled nature of human understanding. The celebrated *Nāsadīyasūkta* of the RV 10.129, therefore, cannot help being mystical and paradoxical in describing the absolute transcendence:

1. There was neither Non-existence nor Existence,
   Nor was there the Earth or Sky beyond,
   What was the covering, whence, and at whose shelter,
   Was there the primeval Water with depth unfathomed?

2. Death was not then, nor was there Immortality,
   There was no sign of day and night,
   That One in the breathless space breathed on its own,
   Apart from that there was nothing whatever.

Creation

The subject of the hymn 10.129 is creation. The underlying sense of the hymn seems to be that absolute transcendence must transform itself into a pure immanence so that creation may emerge out of it, a point more directly expressed in a number of other hymns (e.g., RV 1.164.6 and 46; and AV 9.5). The *Nāsadīyasūkta,* however, makes additional points regarding creation. In subsequent verses of the *Sūkta* (cited in full at the beginning of the essay) it clearly states that the One, the transcendent, is not directly involved in the creative process. In fact, while the One *is*—that is, simply abides as one—no creation can take place, and as a result, there are none of the oppositions that arise within creation, such as existence and nonexistence, death and immortality, earth and sky, day and night. Creation is the process of the One's expansion into the *all,* which at this stage is contained in the void, of the primeval procreative waters (*āpaḥ*), "the darkness covered with darkness" of the undifferentiated chaos. The One *is* "in the breathless space breathing on its own" (*ānīd avātam svadhayā tad ekam,* literally "that one breathed calmly self-sustained" [Muir]). Here the breathless space symbolizes the universal or comprehensive expansion into the *all* which is not distinct from Oneness and is therefore described as its mighty radiance. The One's mighty radiance, "the fulfilling energy up yonder," gives rise to the first form from within the void of the waters (*āpaḥ*) which is desire (*kāma*).

The primal desire's arising in this manner evinces two very important factors in the creative process: (1) the transformation of the One's absolute transcendence into pure immanence, whereby the primal desire projects itself as psychic energy, that is, as the "first seed of mind"; and (2) the projection of this psychic energy, which has the immediate effect of distinguishing itself from the corresponding matter (potencies) manifest within the void. Thus, with the arising of desire the ground is ready for creative activity in which psychic energy works on matter to create further forms out of it.

Clearly this hymn is concerned with the grounding of creation in the One. The grounding must be understood in a twofold manner as both immanent and transcendent. The Lord of creation is immanent, but the repose of this immanence is absolute transcendence. This state of creation would thus seem to render its secret beyond even the comprehension of the sages. Indeed, the hymn itself says that the secret of creation is realized only in the depth of the heart (*hṛdi*), that is, by means of exclusive devotion.

Hence, the last verse of this hymn indicates the essential limitation of the capacity of comprehension on the part of both the gods and *ṛṣi*(s); it need not be construed as an expression of ultimate skepticism. It describes an ontological situation which suggests that only faith brings one near the realization of the absolute transcendence and pure immanence of the One. As RV 10.151 says, with faith (*śraddhā*) alone can one attain proximity to the Divine and live forever rich and happy, even as the gods in the beginning could attain the right initiative only by reposing their faith in the fulfilling divine energy underlying the primeval waters.

It is, therefore, this faith which forms the real background of Vedic spirituality and religion; it is by it that the prayers, hymns, verbalizing of prayers, and the mind disposed to pray (*iḍā*) alike take their shape. Those oriented in this manner are called twice-born (*dvija*), as the sages—both gods and *ṛṣi*(s)—are said to be (RV 1.60.1; 6.50.2; 10.61.19). The gods and *ṛṣi*(s) are for this reason kin. The notion of being "twice born," therefore, implies the coming to be of both gods and *ṛṣi*(s) at two different levels, namely, the physical (outer, gross) and the psychic (inner, subtle). However, with the gods it is the psychic that comes first, followed by the physical, whereas with the *ṛṣi*(s) the physical represents the first birth, which is then followed by the psychical. (The physical is at one further remove from spirit than the psychical and therefore more opaque or dense, in a manner of speaking, from the side of manifestation.) The gods are accordingly invoked to help man in his attempt to make the transition from a physical birth to a psychic one, for the gods are wise beings (i.e., more open to spirit) from the very beginning, that is, from the moment of their birth—as their name *jātavedas,* "born wise," indicates.

Creation hymns, such as RV 10.81 and 10.82, reveal that creation has a spiritual beginning, not a material one, in the form of a sacrifice, with "the darkness covering the darkness," that is, the unique and opaque grossness of the primeval water, as its first oblation. The sacrificer is the immanent God (Viśvakarman), who activates by his radiant presence the opaque and gross primeval waters thereby setting the creative processes in motion.

The immanent God of creation does not embody the creative process, nor is He active as the energy or the stuff of creation. His mode of involvement in creation is described in the hymns as an all-encompassing pervasion, which is symbolized by saying that His eyes, arms, feet, and mouths are everywhere. As the "first mover," He moves the primeval waters, the movement of which is likened to the motion of wings that carries upward. All that moves in the creative process are the primeval waters, which now become manifest in many forms, the first of which is the duality of Heaven and Earth, representations respectively of matter and desire. The same primeval water irradiated by the immanent God's glory is *Hiraṇyagarbha,* the "Golden Womb," so named because of its pervasive radiance and capacity to generate forms. He is Viśvakarman, who, as "wise in mind" and "mighty in mind," is the *ṛṣi*, wisdom itself incarnate and the repository of all that is divine.

The hymns also suggest that an awareness of the existence of the Lord and the mystery of His creation has essentially to follow the inward course of meditation, for pure immanence yields to human comprehension only when it is interiorized into one's being. The hymns state that Viśvakarman rests in the One, the Unborn, beyond the seven *ṛṣi*(s), who symbolize man's seven openings into the world, namely, the five senses, mind (*manas*) and intellect. The human person desiring to know the creator, therefore, must inwardly transcend these openings into the world. This process reflects the Vedic concept of creation, namely, that the human person serves as the model of the immanent presence of God in the world. Both God and humans are indwellers. The human being, like the Lord of creation, is capable of developing an immanence, an inwardness into his or her own being, a capacity which alone finds the path to wisdom.

The *Pūruṣasūkta* of the RV (10.90) deliberately uses the word "*puruṣa,*" "man" (meaning human person), for the supreme principle to emphasize the indwelling aspect of God and the human. This term also serves to indicate that *yajña,* the sacrifice as pure creative force, is manifest only to the indwelling being capable of illuminated inwardness in respect of a given grossness, to the indwelling God in respect of creation and to the indwelling self of a human person in respect of his or her psycho-physical body.

The first two verses of the *Pūruṣasūkta* describe the pervasive nature of the immanent *puruṣa* in the same allegorical terms as those of the hymn discussed above (10.81), namely, as one who possesses a thousand heads, arms, and feet. From the third verse on, however, creation is elaborated in a new form:

> Mightier than His might is *purusa,*
> One-fourth of whom is all that has come into being,
> While three-fourths of him resides in the region of immortality.
>
> With three-fourths hath *puruṣa* risen up,
> With one-fourth having become again this,
> Thence spreading over what eats and does not eat.
>
> From Him came forth Virāj,
> And from Virāj was born the *puruṣa,*
> Embodied at birth, he strode far and wide.

With *puruṣa* as the oblation gods performed sacrifice,
Spring was its butter, summer the woods,
And Autumn was its invocation.

With that *puruṣa,* the first of beings,
Consecrated on grass, the gods sacrificed,
The *ṛṣi*(s) of old and the *ṛṣi*(s) that followed.

(RV 10.90.3–7)

The might of *puruṣa* the indweller God is expressed in this creation, which by virtue of God's presence abides as a self-renewing and eternal process. But, lest one misunderstand that God thus immanent in the world process is indistinct from it, we are immediately reminded that God, the indwelling *puruṣa,* is greater than His might, in the sense that God essentially transcends the world process. Creation itself is divided into two distinct regions, the region of immortality and that of death. The region of immortality consists of three divisions: the eternal self-creating process (*ṛta*), the gods (including the Golden Womb, *Hiraṇyagarbha*), and the indwelling *puruṣa* (in the mortal frame of a human being). The region of death, on the other hand, is the eater-eaten plenum otherwise called *annam* (food). Now the indwelling *puruṣa* in the form of a human being is embodied in the form of eater-eaten plenum.

The primordial energy, now called *virāj* and earlier identified with the primal desire, achieves the unity between immortality and death in the form of a human person, making of him "the mortal brother of the immortal" (1.164.30, 38). *Virāj* having come into being, having become operative, gives rise to the embodied being called "the primeval man" (*ādipuruṣa*). Man, that is, the human person, is said to hold together death and immortality, truth and falsity (AV 10.12.14).

The *yajña* which is the basis of creation was discovered by the gods, the firstborn beings, to be incorporated into one's being (AV 10.2.14). In the form of the seven sources of knowledge of illumination (the five senses, *manas,* and intellect): "man's head is the abode of gods, which vitality, food and mind defend" (AV 10.2.27). Later in the hymn these same gods are called the *ṛṣi*(s) of old (*sādhyā*) who perform with the "man," that is, the *puruṣa,* the sacrifice of creation. In this symbolic sacrifice, the whole, eternal, self-regenerating process, symbolized by the cycle of spring, summer, and autumn, enters as its ritualistic content, whereas the human, the embodied being, is the sacrificial beast (*paśu*). In other words, the human cognitive functions are directed in specific ways to reveal distinct kinds of beings—objects, animals, birds, the Vedic hymns themselves—in short, all of manifest nature.

The *Pūrusasūkta* verses (RV 10.90.12–16) locate the points of *puruṣa*'s being from whence the manifold creation flows. Thus, the four vital points—mouth, arms, thighs, and feet—symbolize the four social functions—speech or communication, protection, procreation and preservation, and physical action. Again, four social orders—*Brāhmaṇa, Rājanya, Vaiśya,* and *Sūdra*—represent the external ordering of the human being. Then come the four psychic functions, symbolized by the Moon, Sun, Indra and Fire (*Agni*), and Wind (*Vāyu*), namely, the mind, senses, self-luminous and appropriative intellect, and the life-force. These psychic functions, however, are revelatory of some basic cosmic functions. The first two refer to the phenomena of constant change and emergence into being, symbolized respectively by the Moon and Sun. "The Sun and the Moon move in the sea of the sky with self-generated energy, the one seeing all, and the other shaping itself ever anew" (AV 7.81.1).

The other two psychic functions represent at the cosmic level the manifestations of selfness as contrasted with everything else and the fluidity which breaks through its monadic itselfness and establishes the continuity of life between different individual selfnesses. The two relatively subtler cosmic functions are symbolized by Fire (*agni,* and also Indra) and Wind. The Vedas treat the natural phenomenon of fire as the symbol of selfhood in the form of *Vaiśvānara agni,* "cosmic man-fire," and selfhood (*svarāj*), which is the most distinctive feature of Indra, the king of the gods. Similarly, Wind (*Vāyu*) is thought to represent the life-force in the form of vital breath (*prāṇa*). Thus, it can be seen that the structural constitution of the human being discloses the very structure of the world.

Perhaps the human being as the model of creation is more than just an analogy. Apart from establishing the parallel of the indwelling spirit in both humanity and the universe, the analogy is clearly meant to emphasize that the human being is *disclosive* of the world structure and, in that sense, it is also *constitutive* of it. For this reason the disclosiveness that obtains in the human being is called the "sacrifice" (*yajña*), the path of Truth manifesting the first ordinance (*dharma*), following which the *ṛṣi*(s) in all ages are said to attain the highest wisdom and immortality.

The Vedic Gods

The gods, who are a part of the totality of living beings, are set apart from the others, especially humans, as well as from the One. Being many, they are obviously not the same as the One. Again, being many they are, like other beings, born or created. But, unlike other beings, they do not suffer pain or death. The Rg Veda says that they are equally full and great (8.30.1), because they are essentially assembled together in the same divine energy (3.55.11). The Vedic *ṛṣi*(s), desiring to understand the One, the underlying and hidden Reality, have found the oneness of the gods within the realm of beings most assuring. They worshiped the gods both for their [the *ṛṣi*(s)'] own well-being in this world and for the attainment of the highest wisdom; in fact, they found the two closely related. For this point to be clear one must understand the way the Vedas conceived of the gods.

In keeping with the view of beings as a mode of expansion, the Vedic perception of the nature of gods discloses the sense of expansion–either in terms of an exercise of the primordial Divine Energy, whence they are referred to as bulls, steeds, etc. or in terms of the luminous dimension of the primal cosmic desire, which RV (10.121.7) symbolizes as fire, the first product of the primeval waters (*āpaḥ*). Aspects of this luminous dimension of the gods are called sages (*vidvas*), visionary poets (*kavi*), etc. and for the same reason, luminous natural phenomena such as the sun, moon, dawn, sky, or fire, etc., are taken to symbolize the gods. Each is a "child of the light" (*divaḥ-śiśu*) referring to the luminous dimension of the god's nature (RV 9.38.5). Similarly the gods are also called the "sons of divine energy" (*sūnu-sāhasaḥ*). Thus, the Vedic gods represent the basic principles of creation, and, in that respect, they become the guardians of the world and indeed of humanity. It is not surprising, therefore, that they are worshiped in order that they may bestow all kinds of riches, worldly as well as spiritual. They are the holy ones, the gods of all humanity (RV 8.30.2,4).

It is in this light that we should understand such Ṛgvedic passages as the following: "He (Indra) who with might hath extended all that exists" (7.23.1); "Thou (Agni) who hath encompassed Heaven and Earth with splendour and glory" (6.1.11); "He (Agni) the son of energy and the sacred one hath from a distance spread out with light like the sun" (6.12.1); "Thou (Waters) whom the sun with his bright beams hath expanded" (7.47.4).

We find ideas of expansion and luminosity combined here. In fact, these two ideas are so basic to the ontology of the Rg Veda, as well as in the other Vedas, that they underlie the very meaning of the names of the major Vedic gods. Thus, the name "Indra" is derived from the root *in,* meaning "to shine," Varuṇa and Viṣnu from the root *vṛ,* meaning "to encompass" or "to cover." Thus, RV 7.99.1 says of Viṣṇu that "He extends beyond, measuring all with his body"; that is, he is the encompassing being. Again Viṣṇu is characterized as being "invested with rays of light" (*sipiviṣṭaḥ*). The word *mātrā,* also in the same verse, is comparable to the use of the word *māyā,* which occurs frequently in the RV to denote the creative energy which measures or encompasses. When this energy is referred to in relation to the gods, it exhibits an extra quality of luminosity (RV 10.177), but that extra quality

1. Image of Agni with Flames, 10th century.
Mathura Museum.

2. Ṛṣis, early 10th century.
Brahmapurisvara Temple, south wall.

is missing when it is spoken of with respect to the demon *vṛtra* (e.g., in RV 2.11.9) or the *dasyu*(s), who are the men who do not follow the path of Truth (RV 3.34.6–9).

The celebrated dual godheads of the Veda *Dyāvāpṛthviḥ,* Heaven and Earth, symbolized the two primordial forms of encompassing or extension: *Dyaus* (Heaven) comes from the root *dyu,* "to shine," and *Pṛthvi* (Earth) from the root *pṛth,* "to extend." Accordingly, the god Dyaus represents luminous expansion, whereas the goddess Pṛthvi represents sheer extension, with or without the accompanying luminosity. The Earth taken in its own being, therefore, symbolizes matter, and as such it is the source of all material beings, including the embodied beings such as the human person. For this reason the Earth is adored as the mother goddess. On the other hand, the luminous Dyaus (Heaven), being the fountainhead of whatever is spiritual, is revered as the Father (RV 6.70.6; AV 9.10.12, 12.1.12). Again, the pair Heaven and Earth is said to be the parents of all gods (RV 1.106.3). Perhaps this divine pair represents, in the eyes of the Vedic *ṛsi*(s), the primeval productive waters (*āpaḥ*) in the form of the Golden Womb (*Hiraṇyagarbha*). This productive pair is said to encompass all beings, including the gods—just as the gods are said to encompass the material manifestations of Heaven and Earth.

In fact, like this pair, Heaven and Earth, all the gods have both a material and a spiritual manifestation, the two corresponding to the two births mentioned earlier. Since in the case of the gods the spiritual birth is the first, they are not limited by material existence. In the case of the humans, however, the physical birth is the first. Therefore the human psyche remains tied to it so that, unlike the gods, the human has to make an effort in order to attain to the spiritual; this is also the reason for the importance of the human action (*karma*). The human being's constitution is, even so, the same as that of the gods, which makes the human their natural partner both materially and spiritually.

It is important to note that what is here called material is not opposed to the spiritual. The Vedic *ṛṣi*(s) are not averse to the enjoyment of material riches, provided it follows the way of the righteous. They even consider such enjoyment essential for the fulfillment of human life, even as the body is an essential aspect of the person. A contented and enriched earthly life of long duration is therefore considered to be desirable and even conducive to human spiritual well-being. The Vedic gods, the immortal beings, perfectly harmonizing the material and the spiritual, enjoyment and the light of wisdom, are thus constantly invoked by the Vedic (*ṛṣi*(s) who desire a similar gain for themselves as well as for all who follow the path of Truth.

The gods in the Vedas are said to belong to three distinct categories. These categories relate to three distinct forms of luminous expansion, namely, *samrāj, virāj,* and *svarāj,* corresponding to three regions: heaven, earth, and the middle region. These three regions are presided over by Surya or Mitra-Varuṇa, Agni, and Indra or Vāyu, in that order. All the other Vedic gods share in the manifestations of one or more of these gods (RV 10.158.1; cf. *Nirukta* 1.5).

The three expressions, *samrāj, virāj,* and *svarāj,* share the common root element *rāj,* meaning "to shine" or "to rule." The root *rāj,* whether used by itself or in a compound, is often connected with the manifest nature and function of the Vedic gods. In fact, the combination of its two senses, "to shine" and "to rule," is the defining feature of the Vedic gods. The inseparability of these two senses of *rāj* is highlighted in the three expressions *samrāj, virāj,* and *svarāj.* These three terms exhaust every possible way of denoting being as expansion. Thus, (1) *svarāj* denotes self-luminosity (*sva* stands for self-reference), or shining in one's own glory, even as the One transformed into the immanent human being (*puruṣa*) shines throughout the progressive expansion of creation. (2) *Virāj* denotes that which illumines others, or the "shining in reflected glory," that is, the appearance of beings on the world scene. And (3) *samrāj* is the illumination of the universal order (*ṛta*), which holds these two together in cosmic harmony.

The notion of *svarāj* as self-luminosity is expressed in the following Ṛgvedic passages: "Self-luminous Indra, mightiest of all, waxed in his home" (1.61.9) and "I (Indra) become glorious by my own glory" (1.165.8). The expression *svarāj* is often attributed to Indra, the principal god of the Vedas. Indra in his glory is said to surpass the magnitude of the earth, heaven, and middle region. He is everywhere and sees everything. The glory and the glorious acts of Indra arise from his own being but are not *caused.* This glory, although an attribute of Indra, has its own being and is not merely an effect *caused* by certain actions. Hence, the ascription of *svarāj* to Indra. Other similar qualities attributed to Indra are *svabhānu* (self-effulgent), *svayaśas* (self-glorified), *svardṛśam* (looking like the sun) and *svarvit* (bestower of light like the sun). The idea basic to all these attributes is the center or core which, during expansion, holds together what flows out. This center or core when thus characterized with a conscious direction as in the present case signifies selfhood.

Immortality (*aṁṛta*) and pleasure (*priya*) are associated with *svarāj* (RV 5.58.1 and 5.82.2) and are also associated with the Self (ātman). For example, RV 1.73.2 says that Agni, like the Self, is the source of pleasure and the ground of the being of all things. This association is reminiscent of the very first hymn of the RV, where in the opening line Agni is lauded as the god of the sacrifice (*yajña*), its eternal preserver, the sacrificing priest and the one in whom all the gifts of the sacrifice are contained. It is not surprising, therefore, that we find Indra-Agni as important dual gods in the Vedas.

The Self

The significance of *sva* as the Self (Ātman) opens up yet another dimension of *svarāj*. It comes to denote the principle of cosmic selfhood (see, e.g., RV 5.58.1, which speaks of "the *svarāj* of immortality"). The same diffusion of consciousness that discloses the immanent self at the center of that diffusion gives rise in the human person to the awareness of God as that which is immanent in creation. Indra is meant to symbolize this cosmic selfhood: by the exercise of his mystical energy (*māyā*) the great bestower Indra expands himself out into a plurality of forms (RV 3.53.8; 6.47.18). At the physical level this same symbolism is expressed as the sun being the Self of the universe.

With the notion of selfhood (*svarāj*) comes opposition, namely, the *other*, which is the outflowing extension moving away from its center, the Self. The other is expressed by the Vedic notion of *virāj*. Thus, even though Indra represents the cosmic selfhood, he cannot be equated with God, the immanent Lord of creation, because for God the outflowing extendedness of creation never presents itself in the form of an opposition; God pervades creation as its immanent Lord (*Vājasaneyisaṁhitā* [abbreviated as *VājSam*] 40.1), only to reassert His transcendence in the form of the One (*VājSam* 40.5). Indra, however, insofar as he has no association with supreme transcendence has to engage himself in a continuous effort to guide the course of the world. No doubt as a mighty god he succeeds, but without transcendence his sovereignty can never overcome the opposition between the Self and the other posed by the world. In other words, *virāj* can only be in opposition to *svarāj*.

The Otherness of the Human Person

The AV 8.10.1 describes *virāj* as this world in the beginning, as a unique and unarticulated self-subsistence. This description implies the absence of any selfhood in *virāj* as such. However, when understood in the form of an extended world, *virāj* is merely a projection of the human senses and mind, which objectively articulate it so as to discover a fully structured meaning. In the AV 19.6.9, the human person, i.e., the *puruṣa*, by virtue of the exercise of the sense organs, is equated with *virāj*, which now in turn is explained as "that in whose illuminative agency the multitude of things become manifest." In simple words, it means that the process of *virāj* in which the objective world takes shape results from one's capacity to project oneself through speech, which is the denotating or the objectively identifying agency of human subjectivity. In the analysis of the *Pūruṣasūkta* above, we noted the same point. Also we noted that in this process, *puruṣa* is sacrificed. This image of sacrifice now takes on a deeper meaning in the sense that through objective projections, human consciousness turns away from its essential inwardness, the Self, and thus from the immanent Lord of the world.

This account of the human person's severed relationship with God is singularly important, for it explains how and why the human person's journey back to God has to move inevitably, but tenuously, through the multitude of gods which in the Veda are symbolized by natural phenomena (and in later classical Hinduism by iconic forms). The human person's relation with nature is harmonious; this harmony is expressed in the Veda by the notion of *ṛta*, the universal order, which leads one gradually from the given natural order to the spiritual order through the ethical order. Hence, the close relationship between *virāj* and *ṛta*.

Accordingly, for the Vedic *ṛṣi*, the ethical-religious human consciousness is necessarily related to the person's empirical consciousness, which brings about the cherished harmony between humanity and nature. The empirical human consciousness is called "ignorance" (*avidyā*), as it reveals its own limits by associating with the ever-changing character of the world and thus with the nature of death. Thus, one can truly overcome death only by the right understanding of ignorance (*avidyā*) (*VājSam* 40.11.14). The higher stratum of consciousness is called *knowledge* (*vidyā*) as it reveals the *puruṣa* immanent in the world and the *puruṣa* immanent in the human body; this knowledge alone leads one to immortality and infinite bliss, *amṛta* (*Vājsam* 40.11.14). The same idea is conveyed in the Ṛgvedic use of the expression "the ignorant" (*avidvān*), alike for the generality of humans, for "the wise" (*vidvān*), and for the gods (6.15.10; 1.120.2 etc.). For the gods, the worldly or natural is always symbolic, whereas for humans it is real or concrete as an integral part of their being.

The way *virāj* emerges in the form of the extended world, in and through the instrumentality of projecting human consciousness, is understood to follow an eternal pattern. *Ṛta*, in the sense of "the flow of water" or "seasonal cycle" in nature, stands for this pattern. Thus, the RV says that "the whole world shines forth in the light of *ṛta*." Again, the Rg Veda attributes a decisive role to *ṛta* in the creation of the world and significantly conceives its creativity on the model of sacrifice (*yajña*) or austerity (*tapas*), which clearly indicates the affinity that the Vedas find between the natural order, on the one hand, and the ethical-religious on the other.

This perfect harmony between the different orders is *ṛta* in its full sense. It is the cosmic order which holds for all times and which is binding for all —humans, gods, and nature. It operates as a set of self-evident divine ordinances in the form of *samrāj*, the principle of harmonious manifestation. The god to whom it is frequently attributed is Varuṇa, the root of whose name, *vṛ*, means "to choose," "to will-to-do-good," and also "to cover," or "to encompass." In keeping with these basic meanings, Varuṇa is often paired with Mitra (representing cosmic harmony) or with Indra (representing the cosmic identity which alone makes free will possible). Varuṇa is the king of gods and humans, because he is the keeper of the cosmic order, whereas Indra is the first and foremost among gods, because he symbolizes the luminous identity which all gods, and also humans, share. Hence, it is quite natural that for the Vedic person, conscious of selfhood and of the presence of the immanent God in the world, Indra is the most important of all gods. Indra is indeed the chief god, but Varuṇa is no less important because Varuṇa alone opens up the path of virtuous action and thought, which leads one to one's own identity in harmony with one's psycho-physical nature.

The human being occupies a central place in the Vedic conception of existence. He begins his journey in the world as a mortal being, but one who is capable of dispelling the darkness of death by the exercise of his enlightened mind. [He is likewise capable of fulfilling himself as a member of given sociocultural groups as well as of various classes according to his activities.] Most important of all, he has the unique capacity to see the distinction—as well as the relation—between ordinary human existence and the *ṛṣi* existence on the one hand, and between the human-situation and the divine manifestation in nature on the other. The *VājSam* 8.35 alludes to this by saying that whereas the *ṛṣi*(s) take recourse to the hymns in their relation with the Divine, ordinary humans follow the path of worship through sacrifice. The important difference between the two is that hymns record the direct revelation of the Divine, whereas the sacrifices make use of these hymns in the ritual and therefore relate only indirectly to the Divine. Moreover, the sacrifice is performed in the spirit of religious self-denial (*tapas*). Hence, the sacrificer states, "O Indra-Varuṇa, while performing the sacrifice (*yajña*) by means of austerity (*tapas*), I have seen that you gave to the *ṛṣi*'s speech, wisdom and hymns" (RV 8.59 [Khil.11].6).

Thus, the Vedic understanding of the human person's being takes into account two distinct aspects. It recognizes that the human has essentially an earthly existence and so calls the human "made-of-earth" (*kṣitija*). But at the same time it recognizes that as a human being (*manuṣya*), he or she is endowed with an inwardness, in the form of the mind, which enables transcendence of earth-bound nature. As the *Maitrāyaṇī-Saṁhitā* 4.2.1 puts it, "One who knows the essence of man in human beings, becomes indeed endowed with mind." This knowledge opens up for the human the path to *ṛṣi*-hood.

Harmony as Spiritual Bliss

The last hymn (10.191) of the RV is addressed to Agni, the symbol of self-identity at the earthly level. It expresses the idea of harmony of minds most vividly:

> O ye men, assemble, speak together,
> Let your minds be of one accord,
> Partaking like gods of old in harmony,
> Share in the bestowed treasures, etc.

It is harmony of mind which is disclosed in the *ṛṣi*'s prayers and which establishes them near to the gods. Thus, for example, a *ṛṣi* prays in the *Taittirīya Samhitā:* "We meditate on the Lord's harmonious mind to obtain the noble truths (*satyadharma*)" (3.3.11.9; also cf. AV 7.17.2). The RV (1.114.3, 4, and 9) speaks of the harmonious mind of Rudra, the god who removes one's manifold sufferings, as conducive to one's happiness and well-being. Directed by a harmonious mind, the human person's senses develop the capacity to perceive in natural phenomena the manifestation of the divine and thus become a source of happiness (*sukha,* that is, *su-kha* or "openings of happiness"). And since this happiness is an expression of spirituality, it has the effect of spiritualizing the very bodily being of the human, and his or her body becomes the abode of the luminous Self (Brahmapura). The AV declares:

> The one who knows the abode of Brahman thus,
> as surrounded by the immortal (*amṛta*),
>
> . . . .
>
> The one who knows that abode of Brahman,
> Whereof the man is called the indweller (*puruṣa*),
>
> . . . .
>
> With eight wheels and nine doors,
> It is *ayodhyā,* the abode of the gods,
> Hence it is called the golden sheath,
> Covered with Heaven's glorious light.
>
> (10.2.29–32)

The RV 1.103.4:8 calls the same human body the "slave's abode" (*dāsīpura*), symbolized in *vṛtra*-like existence, implying that the endless conflicts the human suffers at the material and vital level of existence confine him as if in a prison. As the abode of Brahman (Brahmapura) it is significantly called *ayodhyā*, meaning "free of conflicts." This *ayodhyā* is the abode of gods, that is, the senses, including the mind (*manas*) located in the body with its nine doors that now reveal the Divine manifest in natural phenomena. The eight wheels of the body are the eight organs of human action: speech, the procreative organ, anus, two hands, two feet, and mouth. They are wheels because they are involved in cyclic activity, in such a way that if the human consciousness fails to go beyond them, spiritual progress is impossible. But when the organs of action are harmonized with the senses through the agency of the enlightened mind, all their actions, done in the spirit of sacrifice, become embedded in the Divine (RV 1.89.8), and therefore the happiness which had only occasionally come their way now surrounds them on all sides and forever. Thus invested with spiritual enlightenment, the embodied being of the human is called the "golden sheath," the abode of the luminous Self, and this golden sheath is said to be contained in three spokes, namely, the three supports in the form of the material body, the senses, and actions, which the enlightened mind holds together in a threefold way, corresponding to three distinct kinds of synthesis obtaining at three levels of one's being as described above.

The enlightened mind, which discovers the immanent Self as the luminous center of the body, prepares one for the supreme spiritual edification of being, namely, the comprehension of God as immanent in the world, a comprehension that becomes possible only with the right unfolding of one's own being. But this comprehension necessarily reaches beyond the gods, the manifest divine symbols, to the One beyond symbols (*VājSam* 32.3). In other words, a human comprehension of the immanent God immediately establishes Him as the transcendent One.

The enlightened mind, which transforms one's very material-vital-psychological outlook that provides a spiritual foundation for society and the world, naturally also seeks out the basis of spirituality itself. This quest is a step toward the understanding that the primordial life-force itself is spiritual, that the mighty Lord enters from above into the human and every other being in the world (RV 4.58.1–3); the one God (*Asura*), meaning here supreme life-force, sustains all the gods (RV 10.121.7). To grasp the root of spirituality, however, one's enlightened mind must undergo a further transformation to assume an attitude of worship (*iḍā*) which is the highest form of human wisdom that has the reverence for God as its core. This sense of reverence arises in the mind when it is in harmony with the heart, where one's innermost thoughts and feelings reside. In the Vedas, this harmony of heart and mind is called *śraddhā,* devout faith, which provides the impetus to reach the final, most spiritual level.

Accordingly, it is through faith (*śraddhā*) that one is said to attain divine riches (RV 10.151.4); it constitutes one's good fortune, luck (*bhaga*). Again, faith is that which sustains an understanding of Truth and sacrifice (RV 10.151.1; AV 10.6.4; *VājSam* 19.30). Nature itself undergoes a fundamental transformation in light of this spiritual vision: what was earlier food (*annam*) and wealth (*rāyi*) now becomes *soma,* the drink offered to the gods in the sacrifice, which symbolizes divine happiness and spiritual purity, for which reason *soma* is called the "purifying one" (*pavamān*) and the "blissful one" (*indu*) (RV 9.113.7–11). The spiritual person has a share in this *soma* insofar as his individual Self breaks through the confining sheath of the empirical and social ego and harmonizes with the universal Self, the immanent God in the world, by virtue of which he comes to comprehend the nature of the Supreme Lord of the universe.

This spiritual insight gives an entirely new meaning to the Vedic ritual. No more can the sacrifice take the form of a mere ritual action. Now the very being of man, moved by a devout mind and absolute faith, assumes the form of the sacrifice. Man himself embodies the sacrifice and offers *soma,* his spiritual happiness, as oblation not only to gods but to God himself. Thus, the RV 5.81.1 says that the sacrifice in which the spiritually awakened mind is harnessed attains to harmony and reaches up to God, in the harmonious synthesis of the world itself, for God is the immanent Lord of the world.

This universal harmony (*ṛta*), which is achieved by the sacrifice, is described in the RV 5.52.10 as fourfold: in respect to embodied beings (*apatha*), the world (*vipatha*), the immanent Self (*antaspatha*) and the universal order (*anupatha*). The all-embracing harmony disclosed in the spiritual state of one's being changes his perception of the world so that it manifests as expansion of spiritual happiness itself.

> The winds blow sweet, the rivers flow sweet,
> For the men on the path of *ṛta,*
> So be the plants sweet for us.
> Sweet be the nights and sweet the dawns,
> May sweet be terrestrial expansion
> Sweet be our Father Heaven to us.
> May the tree bear us sweets,
> May the sun be full of sweets,
> May our cows give sweets to us.
>
> (RV 1.90.6–8)

The tree, sun, and cows figure in the Vedas as symbols of the world, the luminous Self, and the enlightened mind which in their various ways contribute to the creative constitution of manifest beings. These symbols represent the harmony between humanity and nature reached in the state of spiritual happiness. The same harmony between humans and the gods is also reached in a similar way, for, as the next verse of the hymn states,

> May Mitra be the source of happiness to us,
> Varuṇa, Aryamān, bless us with happiness,
> Bless us with happiness, O Indra and Bṛhaspati,
> Viṣṇu of mighty stride, be blissful for us.

For one following the path of *ṛta*, the path of happiness through reverent closeness to God, this verse is as much an entreaty made to the gods as a mark of recognition that they and humans are essentially united in the state of spiritual happiness (*aṁṛta*) disclosed in and through *ṛta*.

The Spirituality of 'Theanthropocosmic' Integration

Thus we find that the Vedic conception of spiritual harmony culminates in a kind of metaphysical unity of being disclosed to the *ṛṣi*, the one pure of mind and heart. Purity of mind helps one rise above the ceaseless conflicts and confusions of the unenlightened existence and reach up to a state of creative unity of opposites, the opposites of *svarāj* and *virāj* harmoniously held together in *samrāj*, which are, as we noted earlier, the basic Vedic ontological principles. The purity of heart gains for the *ṛṣi* a harmony between material-vital existence and psychical-intellectual existence, between action and understanding, which is reflected in the Vedic conception of *yajña* as the path to the knowledge of truth and the everlasting happiness. The two points of harmony thus reached—cosmic harmony due to purity of mind and harmony in the individual life due to purity of heart—are, however, brought further together in the universally unitary and obligatory principle of *ṛta*, whence the interchangeable use of the key Vedic words—*ṛta*, *yajña*, and *satya* (truth). Finally, from this universal principle, *ṛta*, follows the realization of the unity of being, the reality that is cosmic and transcendent. This supreme unity of being, the One, is indivisible and immutable, beyond all possibility of opposites. Hence, the Vedas significantly use a unitary conception of *puruṣa* to express the coordinated aspects of transcendence and immanence. Moveover, a most wonderful spiritual discovery of all times is that the Vedic sages discover this *puruṣa* in the very being of the human self.

One can hardly exaggerate in concluding that the spiritual message of the Vedic *ṛṣi*(s) has the essential ingredients of a universal religion. It has a fairly elaborate and penetrating cosmology, though couched in esoteric symbolisms; it has a system of ethical norms to regulate life here and to prepare a human being for spiritual growth; it has evolved an elaborate religious ritualism (*yajña*) satisfying both to its lay followers and intellectual leaders; and it has an eschatology, though a nebulous one, that explains the phenomenon of death and the possibility of final human destiny. Above all, the most unique and striking characteristic is the unshakable faith it has in the capacity and strength of humans to rise above all odds (natural, supernatural, or psychological) and reach up to the highest spiritual heights.

With manifest exuberance, the *ṛṣi* aspires to ennoble spiritually all humans (RV 9.63.5). It is of little surprise, therefore, that the modern Indian reawakening, following the example of past occasions in the long and continuous history of Indian culture and civilization, eagerly looks back to the Vedas for its spiritual succor and fulfillment.

Bibliography

Sources

Aitareya Brahmana of the Rgveda. Edited, translated, and explained by M. Haug. Allahabad, 1974. Reprint of 1922.

Atharvaveda Samhita. Edited by R. Roth and W. D. Whitney. Berlin, 1955. Translated by W. D. Whitney. Harvard Oriental Series 7, 8. Cambridge, MA: Harvard University Press, 1905.

Atharva-Veda-Saṁhitā (Sauhaka). With Sāyaṇāchārya's commentary. Edited by Visva Bandhu. Hoshiarpur: Vishveshvaranand Vedic Research Institute, 1960. English translation with commentary by R. T. H. Griffith. Chowkhamba Sanskrit Series. Reprint. Varanasi, 1968.

Bṛhad-Devatā (Saunaka). Edited by A. A. Macdonell. Harvard Oriental Series 5, 6. Cambridge, MA: Harvard University Press, 1904.

Macdonell, A. A., and A. B. Keith. *Vedic Index.* Oxford, 1912.

Nirukta of Yaska. Edited by Bhadkamkar. Bombay Sanskrit and Prakrit Series 85. Poona, 1942.

Ṛgveda-Saṁhitā, with Ṛgarthadīpikā of Venkatamadhava. Ed. Laksman Sarup. 6 vols. Lahore: Motilal Banarasi Dass, 1939. English translation with commentary by R. T. H. Griffith. 2 vols. Chowkhamba Sanskrit Series. 5th ed. Varanasi, 1971.

Rgveda Samhita. Edited by Max Muller. 4 vols. 2nd ed. London, 1890–92. Translated by R. T. H. Griffith. Varanasi, 1963. Reprint of 1899.

Sāma-Veda-Saṁhitā. With Sāyaṇāchārya's commentary. Edited by Satyavrata Samasrami. Calcutta: Asiatic Society of Bengal, 1976. English translation with commentary by R. T. H. Griffith. Chowkhamba Sanskrit Series. 4th ed. Varanasi, 1963.

Satapatha Brhamana. Translated by J. Eggeling. Sacred Books of the East. Oxford: Clarendon Press, 1882.

Śukla-Yajurveda-Saṁhitā. With commentaries of Uvata and Mahīdhar. Edited by Pandit Jagdishlal Shastri. Varanasi: Motilal Banarasi Dass, 1971. English translation with commentary by R. T. H. Griffith. Banaras: E. J. Lazarus, 1957.

Taittiriya Brahmana. Poona, 1898.

Taittriya Samhita. Calcutta: Bibliotheca Indica, 1860. Translated by A. B. Keith. Harvard Oriental Series 19. Cambridge, MA: Harvard University Press, 1914.

Yajurveda, Vajasaneyi Samhita. Edited by A. Weber. London, 1852. Texts of the White Yajurveda. Translated by R. T. H. Griffith. Benares, 1889.

Studies

Aguilar, H. *The Sacrifice in the Rgveda*. Delhi: Bhartiya Vidya Prakasham, 1976.

Aurobindo. *On the Veda*. Pondicherry: Shri Aurobindo Ashram, 1964.

Bose, A. C. *The Call of the Vedas*. Bombay: Bhartiya Vidya Bhavan, 1970.

Brown, W. N. "The creation myth of the Rig Veda." *Journal of the American Oriental Society* 62 (1942) 85–98.

Buddha Prakash. "The Meaning of Yajna." S. P., 17th All India Oriental Congress, Ahmedabad, 1953.

Coomaraswamy, A. K. *The Vedas: Essay in translation and exegesis*. Bechenham: Prologos Books, 1976.

Dandekar, R. N. "Universe in Vedic Thought." *India Major*. Leiden: Brill, 1972.

Kramrisch, S. "The Triple structure of creation in the Rgveda." *History of Religion* 2, no. 1 (1962).

Majumdar, R. C., ed. *History and Culture of the Indian People:* Vol. 1, *The Vedic Age*. Bombay: Bhartiya Vidya Bhavan, 1951.

O'Flaherty, W. D. *The Rig Veda: An Anthology*. London: Penguin, 1981.

Panikkar, R. *The Vedic Experience*. London: Darton, Longman & Todd, 1977.

Potdar, K. R. *Sacrifice in the Rgveda*. Bombay: Bhartiya Vidya Bhavan, 1953.

2

The Spirituality of the Vedic Sacrifice

Hriday R. Sharma

The spiritual import of *yajña* has been explained at a great length in the Vedas. According to it, the whole process of creation comprises just two basic elements: one dry and the other moist. The dry element relates to fire and the moist to *soma* (a juice of the *soma* plant) (ŚB 1.6.3.23). They respectively are the eater and the edible and in the body as the element of *prāṇa* or vital energy and food (ŚB 10.6.2.1; 4). The theory of the cosmos as made of and permeated by fire and *soma* is consolidated by these ideas. In the context of the spiritual significance of *yajña*, the sacrificial fire which consumes the oblation and thereby gains in strength to rise skyward is symbolic of the fire of *prāṇa*, which is stimulated by all that it accepts as food to rise upward toward immortality. This cooperative junction of upliftment in the body carried out by *prāṇa*, "vital breath," and *anne*, "food," together is termed *uktha* (TB 2.8.8.1; ŚB 10.6.2.10). These profoundly meaningful aspects of the ritualistic process of *yajña* are brought to light in the following way.

The Vedic sages in the course of their meditation experienced an invisible primal force inherent in all of nature, both animate and inanimate (ŚB 10.3.5.1), which they strove constantly to comprehend. Their spiritual efforts led them ultimately to envisage the reality of One Supreme Being at the root of all phenomena, which, in its diverse forms, manifests Itself in the universe it animates. They realized also that man[1] becomes enlightened to the degree in which he is absorbed in this Power, which permeates creation as its ultimate support (RV 1.164.46; 39). Through the sacrificial rite, man plays out his active and conscious participation in this gradual process of purification and upgrading, thus contributing toward it. The mystic fire on the sacrificial altar is a liberating force (ŚB 7.1.2.21); through its agency man is freed from the impurities accumulated in the pursuit of solely selfish interests and is made capable of feeling the pulsation of the infinite in himself (ŚB 7.1.2.23). Once man realizes his place in the scheme of existence he is obliged to sacrifice in thankful recognition of all that life has offered him. By pouring oblations into the fire, the sacrificer gains access to the world of Light and having thus emptied himself of impurities is refilled with the nectar of life which pours down from heaven and so enjoys good health and, with all his faculties fortified, a full span of life. At the deeper spiritual level a long life symbolizes man's identification with the supreme Self, the undecaying Absolute, attained by renouncing this moral identity through the symbolic act of sacrifice. The sages attained the higher world through the performance of *yajña,* so the sacrificer seeks to develop within himself the power to rise from his earthly abode to the powerful higher world (AV 18.1.61, *VājSam* 8.12).

Although many things are offered in the sacrifice, the principal offering is that of *soma,* which is an inebriating drink produced from a creeper. The preparation and offering of this drink are an important Vedic ritual. Indeed, traditional etymology derives the word for "sacrifice," *yajña,* from *yañja,* which is the activated sacrificial *Soma* (ŚB 3.9.4.23).

When the *soma* is poured onto the sacrificial fire in the daily morning rite, it (the fire) becomes symbolically infused with immortality. The fire, thus transformed, is considered to be the soul of all the gods. The sacrificer, by partaking of the remanants of the *soma* left in its container, similarly absorbs into his own body the same element of immortality and thus is said to be granted a full span of life in the sense that he attains to the state of immortality (ŚB 9.5.1.7; 10; 11).

The vital fire deep in the soul, stimulated by the sanctified oblation, blazes upwards (ŚB 10.6.4.10). Through the performance of sacrifice, the sacrificer is ultimately transformed into the Immortal Man, the Divine Lunar Being in whom all the sixteen lunar digits are fully formed, each digit being a measure of the development of consciousness. Thus, the entire creation comes under three heads: the unconscious, the internally conscious, and the conscious. In the first category are stones and metals; the second category includes plants and trees; and the third is the world of animals including worms and insects at one end of the scale and man at the other. Unconscious objects possess six parts out of the sixteen, those internally conscious possess seven, and man is endowed with eight. The perfect being is he in whom all the sixteen parts of consciousness have fully unfolded—he is called the "one who is of sixteen parts" (*sodaśi*)—the Immortal Man (*VājSam* 32.5).

The sages felt that *yajña* was a perpetual process simultaneous operating in the human body as well as in the universe, through the interaction of two polarized sources of vitality, namely, the sacrificial fire (*agni*) and the *soma* (RV 9.20.6; 9.36.6). The fire symbolizes the principle of energy and *soma* that of water. Fire, this cosmic energy, assumes the nature of the Eater; and *soma*, the water, that of food (RV 1.59.2; TB 2.8; 8.1). Fire and *soma*, thus complementing each other, constitute the universe composed of fire and *soma*. Thus the cosmic *yajña* is continuously and spontaneously performed throughout the universe. The ancient sages sought to channelize the perpetual flow of this cosmic *yajña* through the activity of the vital breath (*prāṇa*) in the embodied soul, by symbolically associating it with the components of the ritual, that is, the sacrificial altar, the sacrificial fire and the *soma*.

The sacrifice has thus three aspects—cosmic, vital, and mundane—and so is conceived to take place at three levels each of which is a triad consisting of a deity, form of Speech, and abode. Speech (*Vāk*)—in the form of the *Ṛg Veda*, the earth and the Fire-god (Agni) form the triad of the first order. Speech as the *Yajurveda*, the middle region (*Antarikṣa*) with Indra or Vāyu as the deity constitute the next set of three, while the third set consists of the *Sāmaveda*, Heavenly Region (*Dyu*) and the sun (*Āditya*) (*Nirukta* 7.2; AB 5.32). In this way, the three Speeches, *Ṛk*, *Yajus*, and *Sāma*, the three abodes, namely, the earth, middle region, and heaven alongwith the three deities, Agni, Indra or Vāyu, and Āditya, act as the media for the circulation of the *yajña* of nature. The earth (*Pṛthvi*) in the first category, represents all the gross elements in the universe; they are expressed through the Speech of the *Ṛg Veda* and have Fire as their divine essence. The middle Region (*Antarikṣa*) of the second category is represented by the orientation and extension in space of every object in the universe from its center to the outer periphery expressed as the Speech of the *Yajurveda* with Vāyu as presiding deity. The outer surrounding periphery is represented by the *Dyurloka:* the heavenly region in the third category, in conjunction with the *Sāmaveda* as Speech and the Sun (Āditya) as the deity. These three are related to one another as are the parts of the light of a lamp: the flame which is visible and gross is of the first order, the extent of its light belongs to the second order, while the region beyond its field of illumination is the third order. In the solar sphere, demarcated by these tripartite categories, the principle symbolized by the *Yajurveda* as Speech in the form of the god of the Wind (Vāyu) situated in the Middle Region is being offered as an oblation into the principle of Speech as the *Ṛg Veda* in the Fire (*Agni*) inherent in the Earth region (*Pṛthvi*) and is thus constantly losing itself in the Speech of the *Sāmaveda* in the Sun of the Heavenly Region (*Dyu*). These three worlds—Earth (*Pṛthvi*), Middle Region (*Antarikṣa*) and Heaven (*Dyu*) figure as symbols in the mundane sacrifice in the same order as they do in the cosmic *yajña.* The earth of the *gārhapatya* fire, placed to the west of the sacrificial altar, symbolizes the Earth; the one to the east of the *gārhapatya* fire, which is located in the middle of the altar, represents the Middle Region, while the sacrificial pit of the *āhvanīya* fire, to the east of the altar, symbolizes the Heavenly region (ŚB 7.1.2.12). The *soma* and oblations are taken from the central altar, then ritually sanctified on the *gārhapatya* fire, and then finally consigned to the *āhvanīya* fire. Thus, it travels from the center to the lower earthly region from whence it goes to Heaven.

When the sacrifice is interiorized, the heart is regarded as the center. The upward moving breath (*prāṇa*) is the fire located in the parts of the body above the heart. This breath is regarded a being full of positive divine powers. The downward moving breath (*apāna*) resides in the organs below the heart and represents water which associated with pollution; it is regarded as being constituted by the negative demonic powers which symbolize death. (Water is here associated with impurity because blown by the wind, it produces foam, mud, and so on [ŚB 6.1.3.2; 3].) In the heart, situated between these divine and demonic poles, the soul, identified with Prajāpati, the Lord of Creatures, resides as the pervasive breath (*nyāna*), which regulates the other two (ŚB 6.1.2.12). Thus, in the internal *yajña,* the vital principle operates constantly in this threefold form (Kaṭha U 2.2.3). (These three vital principles activating the body figure in later scriptures [of *kuṇḍalinī yoga*] as the three *nādis* [vital channels]: *iḍā, Piṅgalā,* and *susumnā*. The breath which normally moves through *iḍā* and *Piṅgalā*, when flowing through *susumnā*, rises upward to the Immortal Self, the Supreme Being, in whom the seeker experiences the total merger of his individuality. In the course of time, this process of "*prāṇayoga*" comes to be known as "the awakening of *kuṇḍalinī*" [BSS pp. 185–86].)

Parallel to these three manifestations of vitality flowing through the body, man undergoes three births. The first is from his parents; the second is brought about by the sacrament which entitles him to perform the Vedic sacrifice; and the third birth takes places through the funeral rites performed on the body after death. Realizing these three births man is fully purified and is assimilated into the third fire, that of the cremation pyre, and becomes permanently established in the Supreme Self (ŚB 11.2.1.1). *Yajña* brings about the second birth, which is the foundationhead of that eternal flow toward the final goal of all three (ŚB 11.9.1.4).

3. Scene of Worship, late 2nd century.
Indian sculpture, Sātāvahana dynasty.

The Form of the Vedic Ritual

As a preliminary to any *yajña,* the sacrificial offerings have to be selected and purified. This is done on the basis of the assumption that there is a subtle principle which pervades all that is edible (for it is food which is being offered to the gods) which is called *medha,* meaning literally "the essence of sacrificial oblation." The more of it that is present in some thing, the worthier it is to be offered as an oblation. The sages credited certain edibles such as rice, barley, ghee, milk, animal flesh (either of a goat or horse), as well as *soma,* with being rich in *medha* and so to be offered in sacrifice (AB 7.1; ŚB 5.1.3.7).

In the *yajña,* it is not these things as such but this underlying principle which, concentrated and activated, is being offered. The process by which *medha* was extracted from the offerings as their essence before they were offered to the sacrificial fire was that by which they were purified.

The inner, spiritual counterpart of this preliminary process of purification concerned the sacrificer himself. It involved the extension of his soul-force (*tejas*), in the course of the preliminary rite, through all of time and space. Thus, he was to extend it through a day, a fortnight, a month, a season, a half a year, and finally, the full year, which symbolizes the totality of the perpetual recurrence of eternal Time (ŚB 1.6.3.36). In the spatial plane, he was to extend it to the individual, family, village, province, country, and beyond. In this way, an identification is sought to be established with the eternal and ubiquitous transcendental Being (ŚB 11.2.1.2).

After this comes the ritual lighting of the fire, the *Agnyādhāna,* which was preferably performed on the new-moon day in the month of *Vaisākha* (April-May), or else it could be done whenever a need was felt to offer a *yajña* (ŚB 2.1.3.9; 11.1.1.7). The fire was lit in the prescribed way by the rubbing together of sticks and placed in the hearths of the three fires. The fire was then stoked while a prescribed set of verses was recited.

In the internalized counterpart of this ritual the inner fire called *Vaiśvānara* is inflamed and led up the body. This led to the establishment of the cosmic soul-force (*tejas*) inherent in fire in the ten forms of the vital breath (*prāṇa*) as well as in the soul (ŚB 11.2.1.2).

After the fire was lit and blazing, the sacrificer, accompanied by his wife, began the fire-offering (*Agnihotra*), which he repeated regularly throughout life by offering milk, rice, curd, etc. to Agni, the god of the fire and Prajāpati, the Lord of the Creatures in the evening, and to Āditya, the Sun-god and Prajāpati in the morning.

The *Agnihotra* symbolized the Sun-god (ŚB 2.3.1.1). The Sun, shining and moving through the sky is in this context identified with Yama, the god of death. This is because those living beings who reside in the region below it are subject to death (ŚB 2.3.3.7; 2.3.3.8), whereas the gods who live above the solar sphere are immortal and free from the fear of death. It is the Sun which, controlling by its rays all that lives on the face of the earth, brings about the death of all living beings. But the man who performs the fire sacrifice every morning and evening ascends to the higher world beyond the Sun when physical death comes to him in due time and, having attained thus to immortality, is freed from the bondage of recurring death (ŚB 2.3.3.9). Thus, the absolute essence of the soul-force (*tejas*) manifests as the Sun-god and the Fire-god. Fire presides over the earth, the abode of mortals, and the Sun presides over the Abode of the Immortals, which a mortal can attain if, by performing fire sacrifice, he lays hold of the flux of cosmic power (*tejas*) released by thus conjoining Sun and Fire (RV 10.88.6,7).

After the performance of the fire sacrifice, which takes a day and a night, the fortnight-long sacrifice of the *Darśapūrṇamāsa* is performed, starting on a full-moon or a new-moon day. It consists of two major parts: the *Pūrṇamāsa* and the *Darśa* each of which consists in turn of a number of principal and secondary sacrificial rites which take place on various lunar days supplementing each other to form a single whole. This *yajña* is performed by the sacrificer accompanied by his wife with the help of four Vedic priests called *adhvaryu, brahmā, hotā* and *agnīdh*.

Pūrṇamāsa and *Darśa* symbolize Mind and Speech respectively (ŚB 11.2.4.7). Thus, wholesome food serves as a sacrificial offering to the body. Transformed into its nutritive essence (*urk*) ("*urk*" is the essence of water, corns, herbs, etc. [*VājSam* 18.54]), it is assimilated into the vital fire of the breath which sustains the mind. This vital fire is Speech (*Vāk*), which through its constant activity covers the mind with layer after layer of its own self-generated tendencies and impressions. This constant building up of the mind by Speech in the form of vital fire is the aim of the *Darśapūrṇamāsa* (AB 2.3.3[15]). This *yajña* elevates the vital breaths in the body and orients them toward the soul that it may attain the perfection of the Supreme Soul (ŚB 11.1.2.3).

Next in the ascending scale of time comes the *yajña* called *Cāturmāsya*, which is performed every four months. Four sacrifices belong to this group, three of which are offered on the full-moon days of the first, fourth, and ninth months of the year, while the fourth is offered on the first day of the waxing moon which marks the beginning of the first month and so is the first day of the lunar year (which falls somewhere between February and March).

At the spiritual level, the performer of the *Cāturmāsya* is empowered to implant within himself the pervasive form of Prajāpati, who is the Supreme Being viewed as Immortality symbolized by the year. Through the first sacrifice of the *Cāturmāsya* the sacrificer incorporates in himself the right arm of Prajāpati. Similarly, the right thigh, the left thigh, and the left arm of Supreme Being are respectively incorporated by the sacrificer through the following three sacrifices. Thus, the sacrificer, through the fourfold assimilation of the vitality of Agni (The Fire), can install within himself the Eternal Being as Prajāpati (ŚB 11.5.2.1; 8).

The cycle of *Cāturmāsya Yajña* being completed, there follows the ceremony of *Paśuyāga,* to be performed twice a year, at intervals of six months. In this *homa,* the heart, marrow, and other extractions from goats, sheep, and other sacrificial animals are consigned to the fire on the principal oblations. Through this performance, the sacrificer absorbs in himself the *medha* or essence of the oblations and thereby sublimates the period of one year into *aṁṛta āyu* or immortal life.

This half-yearly sacrifice is followed by the *Soma yajña,* symbolic of the whole year. It combines all three kinds of *yajña*(s), namely, those in which cereals are offered, those in which animals are sacrificed, and those in which *soma* is offered. Even so, the main offering is that of the *Soma.* This ingredient of *Soma,* which pervades all the three *loka*(s) (regions), namely, *pṛthvi* (earth), *antarikṣa* (atmosphere), and *dyu* (space), is extremely energizing (ŚB 3.9.4.12). On special days, such as the new-moon day, this nectar-life *Soma* is produced in the herb called *aśānā* at particular spots on rocky hills. In some places, it is also known as *dudhāna* or *uśānā* (ŚB 1.6.4.5; 3.4.3.13). By drinking the *Soma* contents obtained from *Somayāga,* the sacrificer establishes in himself the effulgent *amṛtabhāva* or nectarlike quality in the form of the annual cycle, and this very state of incarnating the eternal cycle of the year in oneself is known as being established in the state of *Prajāpati* in the form of *Annāda* (the Eater of food) (ŚB 1.6.3.37; AB 14.4; 5; 6).

When all of the above sacrifices have been performed, one is entitled to offer a *Cayanayāga,* through which the sacrificer is identified with *Vāyu*—the Air immanent in all creation—and so gains the Eye of Knowledge (*jñānacakṣu*) existing in the spatial extension as consciousness (ŚB 6.1.1.5). *Cayanayāga* comes at the end of the *Somayāga.* Symbolizing as it does the annual periodicity of time, it imparts to the performer the faculty of perception. Now, the performer of *Cayanayāga* projects upon himself an identification with the permanence of *Vāyu* and the other material elements which constitute the world.

The *Cayanayāga* requires the construction of five altar piles next to each other, symbolizing the four directions—east, west, north, and south. The upper pile is the fifth created by Prajāpati as a manifestation of himself as the year (ŚB 6.1.2.19). The shape of these five together is like that of a flying hawk the head of which symbolizes the vital principle in the head and corresponds to the *Āhavanīya* fire to the east. In the same way, the eye, the head, the right ear, the left ear, the central vital principle or soul and Speech or mouth of the sacrificer correspond respectively to the head, the right wing, the left wing, the soul, and the tail of the hawk. Again, the five piles are the hair, skin, flesh, bone, and marrow. By performing this *yajña* the sacrificer endows these parts with immortality, the nectar of perfect knowledge, and acquires equality with Prajāpati. This is because it is said that in ancient times, the vital breath in the sacrificer's body assumed this form by performing this *yajña* and was lifted up to the level of Prajāpati to become one with him. Again, in the same hawk form, Prajāpati created the gods while the gods in their turn, in this form, acquired immortality.

Thus, having performed the Vedic *yajña*(s), the performer achieves a configuration of the perennial annual cycle as immortality (*aṁṛta*) within himself, and at last performs the *Puruṣamedha* sacrifice. In this *yajña*, the performer takes the vow to consummate his total identification with the entire universe, with all that it contains, thus becoming one with Prajāpati, the Cosmic Person (*Virāt Puruṣa*) (ŚB 1.3.6.1.1). Since to Prajāpati the Cosmic Person as the Eater, all that the world contains is related as food, the performer of *Puruṣamedha-Yajña* deems all things, all creatures, even human beings of all the four *varṇa*(s), as sacrificial animals. As man is the earthly image of the Cosmic Person, he is honored as the best oblation for this *yajña* and is accepted as food (*medha*) for the *Virāṭ Puruṣa* (ŚB 13.6.2.10). But these human beings offered as sacrificial animals are not killed, but are sent away with great honor after their *Paryāgnikaraṇa-saṃskāra*, that is, the ceremony of carrying fire round them as sacrificial animals.

In this way, having performed *Puruṣamedha Yajña*, the performer attains expansion of his identity to cover the entire universe and by inhalation absorbs the sacrificial fire within himself. After this, he goes, a solitary self, to the forest, leaving the worldly life behind forever. There in seclusion he passes the rest of his life in continual meditation on the Self and at last merges in the Supreme Reality. He may also stay near his village, absorbed in meditation on the Truth of the inner Self (ŚB 13.6.2.20).

The Vedic Origin of Samnyāsa Āśrama

In the Vedas, one comes across the basic principles constituting what later *smrti* writings describe as the fourth *āśrama* (stage of life), namely, *samnyāsa,* which is an essential aspect of the spiritual heritage of India. The term *Brahmabhāva* (the state of Brahman) is often applied in the Vedic literature to indicate *samnyāsa āśrama. Brahmabhāva* implies a state unaffected by morality and immorality, merit and sin, and such other pairs of opposites as results of *Karma,* and an effort to keep unshrouded one's perpetual identity with the Supreme Soul permeating all conscient and inconscient levels of creation. A person thus engaged in practicing *Brahmabhāva* really deserves to be called *Brāhmaṇā* or *Brahmavettā,* a knower of Brahman (ŚB 14.4.2.28).

The Vedic *yajña*(s) one performs as a principal means of attaining to this *Brahmabhāva.* When one's body and mind are cleaned of all impurities by the performance of these *yajña*(s), and one's worldly attachments are nullified, one gives up all worldly possessions by performing the last *yajña, Puruṣamedha,* and retires to the forest. Meditating on the Self, in the seclusion of the forest, as he becomes firmly established in detachment and renunciation, he leaves the company of the retired contemplators as a solitary recluse to pass silently into *Brahmabhāva* (ŚB 13.6.2.20).

Apart from the series of *yajña*(s), there are injunctions in the Vedas for practicing other disciplines, such as *Brahmacarya,* penance, faith, and so on for achieving the same goal (ŚB 14.4.2.25).

In some contexts, *Brahmabhāva* has been signified by the word, *Viraja,* or "the state without impurities" (ŚB 14.4.2.23). The *Taittirīya Āranyaka* expatiates at great length upon the will to cleanse the Self of all kinds of impurity (*mala*) in order to be established in *Brahmabhāva* (TA 10.65.1–5; 66.1–14).

In latter periods, *samnyāsa āśrama* or *Brahmāśrama* was instituted in a developed form by the *Purāṇa*(s) and other *smrti* scriptures, evidently on the basis of this state of *Brahmabhāva* described in the Vedas (ŚK, Kāṅḍa V, p. 252; KP chap. 27). According to *Manu,* it is only after having performed *Prajāpatiyeṣṭi,* a *smārtayajña,* that one is entitled to pass on from *gṛhastha āśrama* to *vānaprastha* or *samnyāsa* (MS 6.38).

Some scholars hold that *Prajāpatiyeṣṭi* is only a modified form of *Puruṣamedha* (ŚB 13.6.2.20; *Harīswāmi Bhāṣya,* n. 3). This is confirmed by the current tradition of *Virajā Homa* performed at the time of initiating an aspirant in *samnyāsa* (PPUP). At this sacrifice, the same mantras of the *Taittirīya Āranyaka,* expounding the state of *Viraja,* are recited (GKP, pp. 130–34).

From the above points, it obviously follows that the state of *Brahmabhāva* described in the Vedas has come to be known as *Brahmabhāva* or *samnyāsa āśrama,* with the passage of time. The characteristics of *samnyāsa āśrama* suggest their being derived from the Vedas.

Note

1. The word "man" and the masculine pronouns used by the author for the agent or performer of the sacrificial act are retained even at the risk of connoting some form of sexism. The Vedas speak of the concealed divinity in man as the "performer of rites" *yajamāna* without expressly denying equality in manifestation (as well as concealment) of the divine in man and woman. It is only the Tantra that declares the divinity of woman in the context of ritual and worship. See the article on Tantra in vol. 7 of World Spirituality. —Ed.

3

Truth, Teaching, and Tradition

WAYNE WHILLIER

THE CORPUS OF VEDA AS *śruti* (the Tradition based on revelation) is the foundation of Hinduism and perhaps the only criterion of Hindu orthodoxy; its transmission from teacher to pupil in unbroken succession (*sampradāya*) is the lifeline of the Tradition. The term "tradition" implies a "handing over" (*sampradāna*) from which arises the necessity to consider the nature of that which is handed over, the teachers and their students to whom this task is entrusted, and the appropriate conditions within which the handing over takes place.

Modern scholars have been critical of the Indian claim that Hinduism rests firmly upon Vedic foundations, pointing to a discontinuity of pantheon, ritual, doctrine, and devotional attitude between the religion of the Vedic Age and what has come to be called Hinduism. Such differences exist, but because Hinduism is inexplicable without reference to Vedism, this consideration of the teacher–student relationship begins with the RV, not to recount the formal aspects of education, which have been covered thoroughly elsewhere,[1] but to explore two striking features of Vedism which govern a particular aspect of the teacher–student relationship that develops from the RV to the *upaniṣad*(s) to dominate the Hindu spiritual tradition: the concern with that which is handed over as esoteric truth and the exclusivism which governs the conditions of handing over.

Although, all things considered, Vedism is the most ancient form of Hinduism, Hinduism, as we know it, came to be between the sixth and the fourth century B.C., when the ritual activity of Vedism came to an end with the loss of the ritual framework. Popular Hinduism flourished after the *upaniṣad*(s), the earliest of which are contemporary with the breakdown of the close association of myth and ritual characteristic of the earlier age. The transition from Vedism to Hinduism represents a triumph of caste ideology, which is central to Hinduism, over the contest ideology of Vedism; the triumph of individual worship over the cult, and of philosophy and the quest for intuitive truth over ritual performance. The triumph of caste ideology brought with it a new understanding of truth as private and personal, and a rigorous ordering of humanity on the basis of one's proximity to that truth. It represents a triumph of the private and esoteric over the public in matters of truth; a triumph for the *brāhman*(s),[2] the highest caste, who emerged as the supreme spiritual authorities of the Tradition, entrusted to guard and preserve the sacred and secret truths of the Vedas.

Myth and Ritual in the Vedas

The religion presented in the RV is a liturgy first and a mythology second.[3] The primary ritual act is the sacrifice (*yajña*), an act of homage consisting of oblation in the sacred fire (Agni), generally as a supplication, accompanied by the recitation of formulas (*yajus*) and the singing of *sāman*(s) (songs) and *stotra*(s) (hymns). Prayers are always associated with the cult. Sacrifices can be vegetable (*iṣṭi*), animal (*paśu*), or, in the most ancient context, human (*puruṣamedha*). Soma, an intoxicating drink, the preparation of which is a complex ritual event in itself, is the most excellent offering. Sacrifices are either domestic (*gṛhya*) or public (*śrauta*) according to the benefits desired and the number of priests and fires employed in the ritual. The patron of the sacrifice, the *yajamāna*, for whom the ritual is performed and to whom the benefit accrues, pays the expenses including the honoraria (*dakṣiṇā*) to the functionaries, and assumes a functionary role in the ritual, perhaps including his wife. Rites are of two types: obligatory (*nitya*) or occasional (*kāmya*, or *naimittika*), both public and private. Every sacrifice must have a purpose or end (*yajñānta*) for the *yajamāna*, which determines the ritual mode, the offering, and when it is to be held.

The sacred fire purifies and, as the intermediary between humans and the gods, carries the oblation to the gods. Sacrifice has great power (*prabhāva*) in this world and others, the purpose of sacrifice being to generate, harness and direct the power to specific ends. The notion that speech in conjunction with the sacrifice generates effective power is central to Vedic ritual. The ritual order sustained the cosmic order; in the ritual context, the fickle powers of the divine order could be supplicated, enticed, or even coerced by the power of sacred ritual speech. The primary officiating priests at the *śrauta* rites, chosen for specific ceremonies and given precise roles, are the *hotṛ* (the pourer of the libation and the chief reciter who recites the RV), the *advaryu* (who recites the *yajus* [ritual formulas of the YV], maintains the fires, and cooks the oblation), the *udgātṛ* (who sings the *sāman*(s) of the SV), and various lesser functionaries.

The great, mysterious power pervading the universe, the *bráhman,* could be manifested and controlled through or by an enigmatic ritual utterance called *bráhman,* verbal ritual manifestations of power. The *brahmán* as ritual priest has a privileged relationship to or access to the *bráhman* as power, instrument of power, or manifestation of power. When the *brahmán* participates in the ritual, it is through the *brahmodya* (the ritual debate on *bráhman;* see below); and, although the *brahmán* may recite *yajus* and sing *sāman*(s) during expiations, he is primarily the silent priest, in which capacity he also has a special relation to the *bráhman* which also implies silence. Originally perhaps one of two participants in the simple early preclassical sacrifice, the role of the *brahmán* was to take over or defeat death by assuming the impurity of the patron through the consumption of ritual food and the acceptance of honoraria.[4] The *brahmán* priest emerged as a central figure in the developed ritual—without a specific functionary role, but because of his knowledge (*Nirukta* 1.3.3), which allowed him to oversee in silence (PB 18.1.13) the specific tasks of the other functionaries. In the classical ritual, the *brahmán* oversees the ritual as the most learned functionary, following it mentally as the *bhiṣaj* (healer), "healing" it when necessary to correct errors in performance of the ritual. The *Prāyaścitta* is a ritual of expiation for error committed in the performance of rituals, a need that would increasingly be met by the *brahmán* functionary toward the close of the Vedic Age, as the focus of the ritual developed from concern with the overcoming of impurity to concern with exactitude in ritual performance.

Although the great Vedic myths, the cosmogonic myths, are not used or implied in the rites,[5] many of the rites incorporate an agonistic component, which seems to be based on a mythological prototype of conflict dramatizing the rivalry of opposing powers that govern the cosmos—order (*ṛta*) and chaos or destruction (*anṛta*). The rituals are a cosmological drama dedicated to the overcoming of impurity and the regeneration of life. The concern with conflict and the precariousness of the relationship between those who know and those who do not know, between the true guardians of the ritual and the revilers of the ritual pervades the RV. Throughout the public rites especially, the rites refer to and contend with enemies, directly or obliquely, who are sometimes historical but sometimes ritual.

The combative model is established in the cosmogonic myth of the exploits of Indra, the great war-god, in his overcoming of the demon Vṛtra; in the ongoing battle between the *deva*(s) (gods) and *asura*(s) (counter-gods), the *asura*(s) are constantly outwitted in sacrificial contests. The combative model was extended and transposed to ritual concerns as in the Indra/Bṛhaspati myth and applied to enemies of the cult such as the Paṇis. Some hymns are adapted directly for ritual purposes. "The Vedic sacrifice is presented as a kind of drama, with its actors, its dialogue, its portions set to music, its interludes and its climaxes."[6] The drama is heightened by contest components such as horse racing, gambling, and mock battles integrated into the ritual format to produce an atmosphere similar to a potlatch, complete with competitive ritual distribution of wealth. The ritualized mock battles reflect a "ceremonial sediment of social rivalry,"[7] and while the fights became ceremonial, they probably retained a component of real violence. Poetic debates, elaborate contests in the *sabhā* (assembly) dedicated to the attainment of power and gifts, were an important type of ritual contest. The poetic contests appear to have maintained the vitality of the battle model in keeping with the RV, wherein the power of sacred speech is portrayed in vivid battle imagery in such accounts as Bṛhaspati's use of the *bráhman* (see below) to slay the enemies of the sacrifice, perhaps indicating that "late in the Rgvedic period the power of the ritual had come to be considered greater than that of the gods whom the priests invoked with the aid of ritual."[8] While races, battles, and gift-giving competitions were the events reserved for patrons, the poetic debates seem to have been exclusive to the priestly poets in addition to their normal task of composing and reciting sacrificial hymns. The poet debater would represent the patron or the patron's party as a functionary, anticipating the purely priestly *brahmodya*(s) (ritual enigmatic question-and-answer exchanges) of later Vedism.

The history of Vedic ritual was governed in part by the progressive transformation and rationalization of the agonistic element of ritual, which was based originally in the instability and insecurity of ongoing conflict in a warring society. With the actual wars over, the conflict motif survives in the developed rites, but with increasing obscurity. The agonism is portrayed in various expressions of the complementary relationship of the forces of *ṛta* and *anṛta*—life and death, the pure and the impure—with both the protagonists and antagonists "participating" in the ritual, as in the PB (5.5.13) in the opposition of the praiser (*abhigara*) and reviler (*apagara*), the task of the former being to drive away the "evil lot" of the latter in the ancient Mahāvrata ritual. In the early rites both parties in the rivalry are often included in the ritual as participants, but in the classical ritual the role of the antagonist has been assimilated; the antagonist has been defeated by the protagonist. While the complexity of the protagonist/antagonist relationship is most clear in the *brahmodya*(s) of the *brāhmaṇa*(s), it exists in simple terms in the relationship of the priest and the patron. In the early ritual the responsibility of the *brahmán* was to assume the burden of death and impurity on behalf of the patron through the taking of food and gifts:

> The two poles of the ritual, death and rebirth, are assumed in the complementary pair patron-brahman. At the acme of the ritual, the moment of birth, when the daksinās are distributed, a reversal takes place: the diksita patron sheds his death impurity and is reborn a pure brahmin. The brahmin on the other hand takes over the burden of death. . . . This pair, through exchange and the reversal of roles, maintains the continuity of the cosmos.[9]

The ritual developed in the attempt to minimize the dangers of pollution and stabilize the spiritually precarious role of the priest. The function of the agonistic components was transformed. Reconciliation of disparate and agonistic components of the ritual, led to the absolute autonomy of the ritual officiant, minimizing the possiblity of pollution through the ritual isolation of the officiant. With the collapse of the contest ideology, death and impurity are ritually assimilated; the instability of the rivalry/reciprocity of the ritual participants in the exchange of evil and impurity is overcome and the ritual becomes the domain of purity alone. The end result of this evolution was the exile of the *yajamāna* to solitude as the *śrotriya brāhman*, whose purity remains intact by virtue of his independence of the necessity of public ritual contact.

The relationship between the *brahmán* and the *yajamāna* is both definite and ancient. In the early ritual, the *yajamāna* was ritually reborn a *brāhman*, whatever his caste, just as the *kṣatriya* was transformed into a *brāhman* in the Rājasūya (royal consecration ritual) indicating that neither *brāhman*(s) nor *kṣatriya*(s) were regarded as closed groups.[10] The role exchange and ritual reciprocity which had prevailed in Vedism came to an end with the triumph of caste ideology over the contest ideology. With the advent of popular Hinduism, the notions of pure and impure become the watchword of Hinduism, and the distinction between private and public, forest and village, became absolute.

The assimilation of death and impurity can be seen in the increasing tendency to reductionism in speculations on the orders of phenomenal dependencies and metrical equivalences in the *brāhmaṇa*(s) and the *upaniṣad*(s). In the SB the explicit concern with death in the ritual context occurs in a *brahmodya* contest between Prajāpati (the progenitor of man, and archetype of the ritual functionary) and Death in the search for the equivalences (*bandhutā*(s)), the understanding of which provides the triumph over Death. The notion of equivalences or correlations (*bandhutā*(s)), or bonds (*nidāna*(s)) between the divine and the ritual world is presupposed in the RV and developed into complex systems of relationships in the *brāhmaṇa*(s) within an understanding of truth as mystery. The parties in the *brahmodya* exchange obscure insights on the bonds between this world, the realm of Death, and the divine world until, finally, Prajāpati conquers Death. Prajāpati is no longer ritually dependent on Death; the necessity of the reciprocal relationship between the ritual protagonist and antagonist is undercut; the exchange between the two, hitherto necessary for overcoming the opponent—evil, pollution, or death—is no longer necessary, as Prajāpati has discovered the links between the ritual world and the divine world—the equivalences to the meter of the ritual chant. Because of the importance of the chant, the art of the chant is necessarily an exacting art, and as demonstrated in the opening chapters of the ChU, learning, performing, and transmitting the art are complex matters governed by rigorous, secret rules regarding both procedures and privileges.

With the defeat of the ritual antagonist Prajāpati is ritually independent. The ritual has been individualized; in effect, the officiant is isolated in the purity and solitude of the ritual realm. As long as purity can be maintained by virtue of independence from the antagonist, the "other," the solitary ritualist will overcome the adversary, death. With the overcoming of the necessity of ritual exchange, the role exchange which had featured in the complementary relationship of the priest/patron, *brahmán/kṣatriya* was no longer necessary, and, with the increasing entrenchment of caste ideology, no longer possible: the *śrotriya brāhman,* fearful of the pollution of public contact and ritually dependent on no one, became a living ritual, the embodiment of purity, in the solitude of the forest. Impurity was relegated to the low castes for whom the doctrine of rebirth presented the only possibility for overcoming their natural pollution. The affairs of the world were left to the *kṣatriya;* a world that neither the pure nor the impure could participate in, but for totally different reasons.

Questions about the meaning of the Veda and the purpose of ritual performance were raised early on in the Tradition. In the RV (7.103), the "Frog hymn" mocks mindless recitation in a satirical account of brahmanical chanting; 10.82.7 describes the *ukthaśa*(s) (reciters) as *asutṛp,* which may mean " 'those who steal with breath' (with reference to the efforts of learned recitations of the other)."[11] The earliest interpretation of the Veda, the *Nirukta* (700–500 B.C.), mentions one by the name of Kautsa, who maintained that the Vedic *mantra*(s) had no meaning, no semantic value. The *mantra*(s) are not intended to convey meaning; what is important is the "accomplishment of the ritual form" (1.15).[12] On the other hand, *Nirukta* 1.18 firmly rejects the position of the *vedapāṭhaka*(s) (those dedicated to ritual recitation without understanding) as inadequate: "He is the bearer of a burden only, the blockhead who, having studied does not understand the meaning of the Veda. But he who knows the meaning obtains all good fortune and, with his sins purged off by knowledge, attains heaven."[13] Such early criticism of the "mindlessness" of the *vedapāṭhaka*(s) within the Tradition provides a basis for the subsequent complex development of Vedic exegeses and philosophies of language. Having established that ritual performance without understanding is fruitless–that knowledge is the key to good fortune–the *Nirukta* legitimates its own task by providing a theological account of why it is necessary to recover the meaning of Veda:

> Seers had direct intuitive insight into duty. They by oral instruction handed down the hymns to later generations who were destitute of the direct intuitive insight. The later generations, declining in (power of) oral communication, compiled this work, the Veda, and the auxiliary Vedic treatises, in order to comprehend their meaning. (1.20)[14]

The intuitive insight of the poet-visionaries (*ṛṣī*(s)) provides the model to which later generations must aspire. Knowledge in its highest form is intuitive and it must be cultivated as it has been lost to the natural capacity of later generations. Because such knowledge is intuitive, it will necessarily be intimate. This model of knowledge, learning, and teaching was actualized in the *upaniṣad*(s), where the necessity of accuracy central to the *vedapāṭhaka* tradition is complemented by the intimacy of the teacher–student relationship committed to the attainment of intuitive insight.

Truth as Enigma: *bráhman* and *brahmodya*

The Tradition has held that the *ṛṣī*(s), the visionary poets of the Veda who possessed intuitive insight (*dhītī*), were unlike ordinary mortals. The poets possessed the extraordinary capacity or spiritual suitability to "catch" a vision (*dhīḥ*) of the divine order; they then applied their linguistic skills to transpose the visions into the rich and complex images of the Vedic hymns. The key to understanding the Veda is found in its poetics,[15] which, in the RV, sets the foundation for the commitment to esoteric knowledge that emerged supreme in the *upaniṣad*(s). The ritually effective word provides power by which the ritual sustains the divine order. The secrets of the divine order are veiled in the poetic imagery as riddles (even as jokes and obscentities), paradoxes, and number puzzles–deliberately enigmatic truths, in keeping with a common practice in the ancient world of employing riddles as a test or ordeal to identify the mentally or ritually unfit.

The *bráhman* is a type of enigma composed of obscure images founded upon the mysterious great power that pervades reality, the *bráhman*, or manifestations of or instruments of that power which is available to one who comprehends the secret of the enigma. The power of the *bráhman* is an instrument for transcendence.[16] The *bráhman* is the gate of consciousness (*brahmaṇe gātum)* (RV 4.4.6a), mysterious in that it employs contradictions from within the empirical realm, not to reconcile those contradictions, but to initiate a higher mode of comprehension that goes beyond the empirical order. RV 1.152.5 distinguishes the *bráhman* from riddles as *acittam brahma,* the "thought-surpassing" mystery.[17] In keeping with the esoteric tradition, that which is true must be kept hidden (*guhā nihita*), for the relationship between the knower and the known is as privileged and intimate as the relationship between a husband and wife, or a father and son. One's proximity to that which is true is equal to the truth of oneself. Accordingly, that which is true is hidden from that which is not of the nature of the self.

RV 10.189 indicates that the *bráhman* was used in the ritual context; and, by extension, throughout the early texts ritual allies such as Brahmaṇaspati use the *bráhman* as a weapon to protect or restore the sacrifice. RV 10.71 provides an account of the symposium, the verbal contest, the context within which poets were set against one another in order to determine those who know from those who claim to know but wander elsewhere (v. 8). The power of words and proximity to that power set humans apart from one another and in opposition to one another, but, on the other hand, a bond is established among those ritually and mentally fit for experience of the power of the *bráhman.* In RV 10.71, the companion (*sakhi*) or fellow of the brotherhood (*sakhya*) shares with his friends an understanding, in varying degrees, by virtue of their common access to a higher form of understanding (*brāhmaṇā ye manīṣiṇaḥ;* 1.164.45). Just as in the later Tradition a teacher or father teaches that which is true, i.e., that of the self, to one who is most like the self, a son or one capable of being defined as a son, and hides and refuses to teach the truth to all who are not of the nature of the self, so also the *sakhi,* the visionary poet of the brotherhood, hides the truth in obscure images and complex meter from those who do not share his higher kind of understanding, the ordinary person (*manuṣya;* RV 1.164.45). The *bráhman,* the powerful word utterance, is that in/by which the truth is hidden; it is the instrument of the hiding, but, like a beautiful woman, it both conceals and reveals.

An *upaniṣad* is a speculation on the *bráhman* utilizing "énergie connective comprimée en énigmes."[18] The development from the simple enigma to *brahmodya* provides an account of the development from the contest ideology of the Vedic Age to the philosophical speculations and doctrine of early Hinduism. "It seems that the Brahmán priest and the Brahmodya (the verbal contest) form a parallel in that both have to be connected with the singular *bráhman* (the object of knowledge and the subject of the debate). . . ."[19] The *brahmodya* is a ritualized, purely priestly extension of the poetic debates, centered on the *bráhman* and consisting of enigmatic question-and-answer responses. Speculative *brahmaodya*(s) on cosmological questions occur in the RV. The question-and-answer riddles are more fully developed in the AV to include didactic stanzas. The *brahmodya* becomes a fixed formal element in some of the rites such as the *Aśvamedha,* but it comes into its own as a teaching device in a more flexible form in the ŚB, wherein it provides the framework for quasi-philosophical exchange between opponents in what is recognized as a teacher–student relationship (cf. 10.1.4.10); also in that text (4.6.9.20), the *brahmodya* is directly associated with dialogue (*vākovākya:* "speech and reply").

The development of the *brahmodya* as a teaching device is significant, as it signals the breakdown of the opposition of the protagonist/antagonist parties in the formal contest situation in that the "other" is acknowledged as both necessary and legitimate; hence, the "degenerate hull"[20] of the *brahmodya* serves as a device for developing and teaching specific doctrines into the speculative philosophy of the *upaniṣad*(s). Originally, the idea of the *brahmodya* was not to arrive at an "answer," but to generate through the tension of opposing formulations the power of the intuition (*dhītī*) of the *bandhu*(s) that unite and sustain the ritual and divine worlds.[21] The objective in the *brahmodya* was to reduce the antagonist to silence, as in the ŚB (11.6.2.4), where Janaka retreats after having been reduced to silence by Yājñavalkya, the great philosopher of the BĀU. To reduce the opponent to silence was to "overpower" the opponent in the literal sense. In the BĀU at 3.1.2 Yājñavalkya challenges his opponents and reduces them to silence except in one instance where the same point is made by subjecting Śākalya to the challenge to retrieve the argument of the opponents (3.9.18). The threat of real physical danger for failure in the debate, a remnant of violence from an earlier age, is mentioned three times—twice as a threat and once when the consequence actually occurs, where Uddālaka Āruṇi threatens that Yājñavalkya's head will fall off, probably be severed, if he does not know the correct answer to the riddle having accepted Uddālaka's challenge (3.7.1.); where Gārgī is threatened with losing her head for overquestioning (3.6); where Śākalya's head is severed because he cannot respond to the challenge (3.9.27). Also, as in the role exchange of the priest/patron, there still exists the possibility of role exchange whereby the victor would assume the identity of the loser, and the loser would become the pupil of the winner. In the famous debate in the court of King Janaka of Videha, Yājñavalkya attends the royal court, calls for disputations (4.1.1), defeats the opposition in debate, and, at 4.4.23, the king offers to become his slave, avoiding death because of his rank. The case of Janaka is particularly interesting, as we know from ŚB 11.6.2.10 that he became a *brāhman* after winning a debate on the meaning of the offerings of the *Agnihotra.* The text, however, provides an indication of the movement away from the possibility of role change and exchange prevalent in the earlier Tradition at 2.1.15 where Ajātaśatru explains to Gargya that it is ". . . contrary to the course of things that a *brāhman* should come to a *kṣatriya,* thinking 'He will tell me Brahma,' before accepting him as a pupil." On matters of doctrine, the roles of the *brāhman* and the *kṣatriya* and the truths and teachings appropriate to those roles are beginning to become ossified, anticipating the rigorous exclusivism of classical caste ideology.

With the development of the *brahmodya* to its use as a pedagogical device, "the solution [to the brahmodya], if given, is placed after the silence in a different context, to wit in a teacher–pupil relationship."[22] This transition is illustrated by comparing the example of Janaka and Yājñavalkya to Uddālaka, also a key figure in both the BĀU, and ChU, who, in the JB (1.296), at the crucial moment of the *brahmodya,* remains silent but gives the answer later to his pupils. He retreats, silent but not in defeat. Silence has come to represent wisdom rather than ignorance.

In the BĀU the debate/teachings take place in a public context but for one notable example worth citing in full as it represents the negation of the public contest ideology, and signals the revolutionary victory of esoteric philosophic doctrine over poetic imagery in the pursuit of truth:

> "Yājñavalkya," said he [the (opponent)/student, Ārthabhāga], "when the voice of this dead man goes into fire, his breath into wind, his eyes into the sun, his mind into the moon, his hearing into the quarters of heaven, his body into the earth, his soul (*ātman*) into space, the hairs of his head into plants, the hairs of his body into trees, and his blood and semen are placed in water, what then becomes of this person (purusa)?" "Ārthabhāga, my dear, take my hand. We two only will know of this. This is not for us [to speak of] in public." The two went away and deliberated. What they said was *karma* (action). What they praised was *karma.* Verily, one becomes good by good action, bad by bad action. Thereupon Jāratkārava Ārthabhāga held his peace. (BĀU 3.2.13)[23]

The protagonist/antagonist have become teacher and student; deliberation has replaced conflict between the parties, but conflict remains in the moral and metaphysical opposition of good and bad, the mystery of which the teacher *shares* with the student to account for why human beings are different.

With this development, the *brahmodya* has evolved from the vitality of an agonistic encounter for the purpose of generating the power of the *bráhman,* of becoming powerful by becoming one with the power of the *bráhman,* to a framework for solving philosophic problems. The "truth" of the *bráhman* is no longer the manifestation of power in the context of a public festival event, but the truth of a secret doctrine to be communicated in private to none but the worthy. The encounter between opposing parties, no longer dynamic, is increasingly characterized as the opposition between those who have legitimate access to truth and those who do not; the dispensation of truth and the disposal of impurity move to becoming mutually exclusive hereditary specialities.

Truth and Hierarchy

In the early Vedic context, *karma* refers to activity within the pure realm of ritual, but in the teaching of Yājñavalkya to Ārthabhāga, the term means any kind of human activity, good and bad, pure and impure. The Vedic ritualist's obsession with the overcoming of death and impurity is paralleled in the development of doctrine from the early doctrine of resurrection, to concern with repeated death (*punarmṛtyu*), to the mechanics of rebirth as taught by Pravāhaṇa in the BĀU and ChU, to liberation from death (*mokṣa*). The concern with death is typically brahmanic. The ritualist's solution to the problem of death had been to reconcile agonistic components of the rite, isolating the functionary in absolute purity: Yājñavalkya's doctrine challenges the ritualist's solution by reestablishing the opposition of good and bad, pure and impure. At BĀU 4.4.22, freedom from death and fear requires transcending both good and evil. Yājñavalkya's doctrine of moral action stands midway in the development from the resurrection doctrine of Vedism and the Hindu doctrine of rebirth; it represents a revolution in thought because it utilizes the *brahmodya* format to expound doctrine, affirms the radical distinction between public and private truth, and sets the stage for the doctrine of rebirth upon which the human hierarchy of classical caste ideology is built.

Apart from a late hymn in the RV (10.90) wherein the four *varṇa*(s) result from the dismemberment of the Cosmic Man, the caste system as a rigid, hierarchical and hereditary ordering of persons is ignored in the Veda.[24] To the contrary, the flexibility of the possibility of role change and exchange distinguishes Vedism from the later situation.

Several notions which develop to become significant in caste ideology occur in the RV in fledgling form: the ideas of *vrata* (vow) and *dharma* (duty) appear, primarily in ritual contexts, in the requirement of humans and gods to properly devote their function in the conflict between order and chaos. While the term *karma* denotes ritual action in Vedism, the ritual transformation of *pāpa* (evil) to *śrī* (good fortune) may indicate a Vedic basis for the general concept of merit transfer. On the other hand, concepts like

4. Dakshināmurti, 11th century.
Brahadīsvara Temple, south wall (detail).

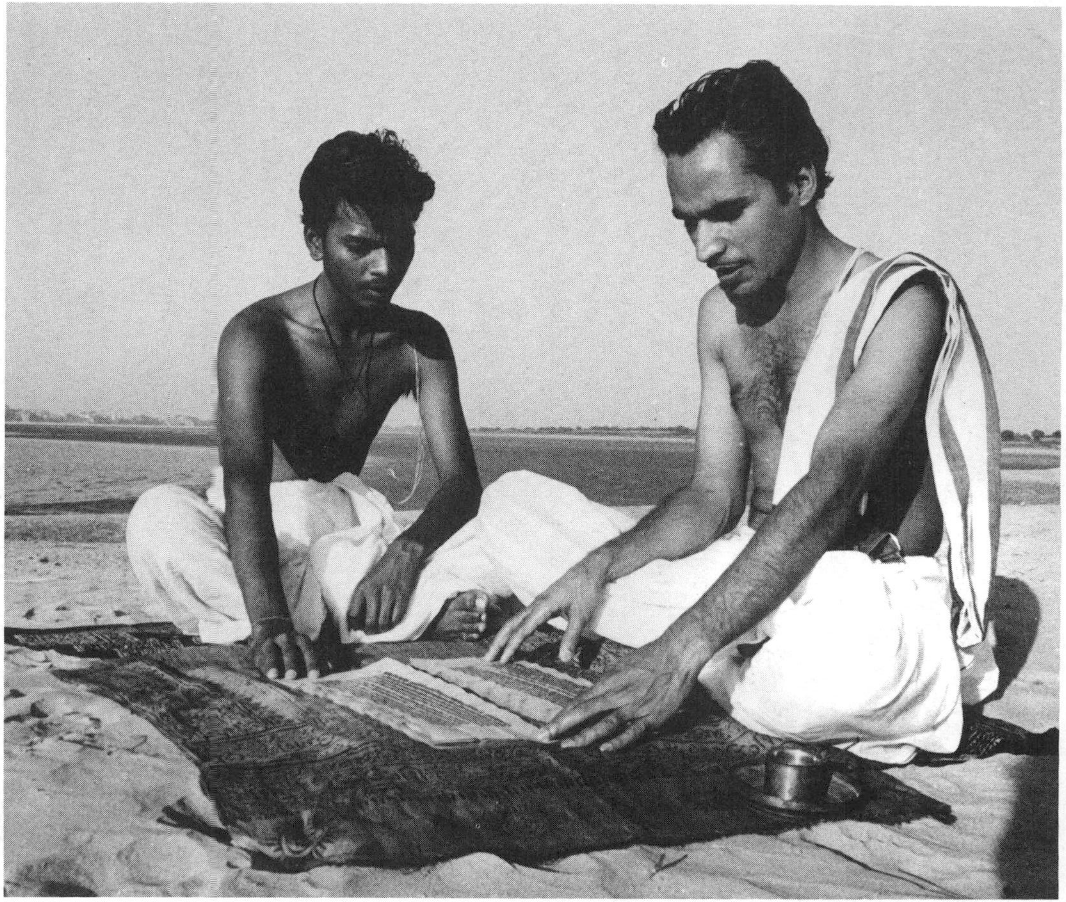

5. Teaching the Holy Scriptures.

vrata(s) (vows), *saṁskāra*(s) (rites of purification), *śāpa*(s) (curses), and *vara-dāna*(s) (boons) and the donation of merit, and expiatory rituals generally, represent a form of merit transfer that contradicts the *karma* doctrine, perhaps indicating that the doctrine is not uncategorically fundamental to Hinduism.

Although *varṇa* (caste) is not an operative principle, the RV does present a general understanding of hierarchy such that those who stand with or close to truth are clearly distinguished from those who do not. Humanity is divided into two broad but unequal categories: those who know, trust, and perform the proper rituals in the proper manner exist in fundamental opposition to those who do not. The visionary poet (*ṛṣi*) is the paradigm of the highest proper human understanding against which other mortals are measured (*Nirukta* 1.20). The *ṛṣi* exemplifies a mode of higher understanding which involves being one with such truth in that truth as *ṛta*, Order or the Law that governs everything, is the truth of sacred speech[25] and the visionary who is one with such speech is one with truth as Law. From the model of the *ṛṣi*, the foundation for an ontology based on knowledge is established in the RV with the distinction between those who know and those who do not know. Those who have the capacities for vision and sacred speech and use them properly are *brāhman*(s) whose consciousness goes beyond normal understanding. RV 1.164.45 sets such persons apart from ordinary humans who are not one with sacred speech. RV 10.71 distinguishes three particular ways of not being one with the truth, apart from the broad general category of the ordinary mortal: (1) there are those (v. 8) who, being simply unequal to the double task of transcendent vision and divine speech, are left behind (*vi jahur*) because of lack of insight in the ritual debate; (2) there are those (v. 9) who are designated evil (*pāpayā*) because, while they claim to be privileged to sacred speech, their speech has not been won in the proper debate or ritual context, and (3) there are those (v. 5) who are in the proper context of the brotherhood (*sakhye*), but do not make it as far as the debate because they are (self-) intoxicated and do not have powerful enough *māyā* (in this instance, perhaps "creative power, ability to manifest" through speech[26] to succeed in the debate).

Language of family and lineage provides images to portray the intimacy of relationship between those who have access to the *bráhman:* sacred speech presents herself like a wife to the visionary (RV 10.71.4). Within the framework of the old resurrection doctrine in the RV and the *brāhmaṇa*(s) the "Fathers" are the founders of the human race; the founders of *brāhman* families; the totality of the dead. The Sanskrit terms for father and son (*pitṛ*, *putra:* 6.9.2; cf. 1.164.22) serve as code words in the debate ideology of the

RV to designate the parties in an exchange on the *bráhman.*[27] The intimate image of the father and son is used to indicate the proper model for important and intimate relationships. In the ritual texts, for example, in a reversible relationship that generates immortality, man is identified with his personal sacred fire as father and son.[28] From the standpoint of the teacher–student relationship and the necessity of the accurate transmission of powerful hereditary secrets, lineage is an important matter, but the matter of lineage raises another problem. In the RV (10.69.11) and the earlier *brāhmaṇa*(s) (AB 7.13.9), the father is said to be reborn in the son. The father gains immortality through the son. In the ChU, however, the knowledge of the secret hereditary teaching takes one beyond fear and death. A contradiction arises because the having of sons, in the act itself and in the continuation of the self in the son, ties one to the world of rebirth (*saṃsāra*).

The contradictory demand for both self-transcendence and self-perpetuation represents a clash on the idea of immortality between Vedism and the emerging Hinduism, between *dharma* (duty) and *mokṣa* (liberation): the physical immortality that is furthered by the procreation of progeny in Vedism is at odds with the spiritual immortality that is furthered by sexual abstinence in Hinduism. However, the conflict between independence and dependence, solitude and the social life, is ingrained in the very basis of Vedism: the attainment of one's personal sacred fire with which one is identified—whereby, therefore, one is immortal—is most frequently mentioned in the context of obtaining the *aupāsana* or homefire through marriage where the fire is received through the in-laws, i.e., through the female, a practice that "sits uncomfortable with the strong brahmanical stress on the patrilineage and, more specifically, with the otherwise emphasized double identification of the householder with his son and with his fire."[29] In the Vedic context one cannot be independent of the "other."

At 1.4.2ff. the BĀU provides an account of cosmogony to explain the basis of the conflict between solitude and dependence. There is no fear when the self is alone: "assuredly it is from a second that fear arises." There is no sexual delight in solitude; therefore, one desires a second: "Oneself is like a half-fragment . . . therefore the space is filled by a wife" (1.4.3).[30] But while a wife brings wholeness and sexual gratification to the incompleteness of solitude, she also brings fear. Dependence on the "other" is again the necessary condition for immortality through procreation and the basis of fear as well.

One resolution of the dilemma is presented at BĀU 1.4.17:

> . . . even today when one is lonely one wishes: "Would that I had a wife, thus I would procreate. Would that I had wealth, then I would offer sacrifice." So far as he does not obtain any one of these, he thinks that he is, assuredly, incomplete. Now his completeness is as follows: his mind truly is his self (*ātman*), his voice his wife . . . his body (*ātman*) is his work [*karma*], for with his body he performs work [*karma*] (1.4.17).[31]

Emancipation from the dependence that binds one to others brings completeness, overcomes fear, and establishes the priority of solitude. But from the standpoint of Tradition a further problem remains, for to renounce the world is to deny the Veda.

BĀU 6.4.4 deals with the question of dependence in the context of the dangers of merit transfer and the necessity of having sons. How is it that mortal men, "*brāhman*(s) by descent," die, impotent and devoid of merit? Loss of merit in the sexual act causes the inability to procreate male progeny, without which the mortal *brāhman*(s) cannot conquer death. Protection against the problem of merit loss is afforded by the knowledge of a powerful mantra, a verbal truth (6.4.4). It is said that he who knows the truth of the mantra gains as much strength as one who performs the Vājapeya (the Vedic "strength libation" [6.4.3]); and if knowing thus he practices sexual intercourse, "he turns the good deeds of women to himself. But he who practices sexual intercourse without knowing this—women turn his good deeds unto themselves" (6.4.3). The secret of the husband's procreative power is the power of the secret mantra. Because the power of his mantra(s), as curse or blessing can cause merit transfer, the *śrotriya* (learned *brāhman*) is superior (BĀU 6.4.12; ŚB 6.1.8).

A clue to the nature of the undisclosed mantra by which the husband avoids merit loss is presented in the Vājapeya, with which the power of the mantra is compared. The Vājapeya in the ŚB (5.1.1.1–5.1.2.18) begins with an account of the establishment of the sacrifice; the mid portion presents several forms of competition appropriate to *either brāhman*(s) or *kṣatriya*(s); the conclusion involves the climbing of the sacrificial pole by the sacrificer and his wife in what appears to be an ancient fertility rite. In the beginning, in a race competition between the *deva*(s) and the *asura*(s), Bṛhaspati, who is intimately related to the *bráhman*, was consecrated by Savitṛ. He won the sacrifice (Prajāpati) and ascended to the upper region (5.11.4). In the end of the ritual, when about to ascend the pole at 5.2.1.0, the sacrificer says, " 'Come wife, ascend we the sky!' [as Bṛhaspati had done] Now as to why he addresses his wife: she, the wife in sooth is one half of his own self; hence as long as he does not obtain her, so long he is not regenerated, for so long is he incomplete." Having ascended the pole, the sacrificer looks down, mutters [again emulating Bṛhaspati]: "Homage be to mother Earth Homage be to mother Earth." The basis for the mantra is then given:

> For when Brhaspati had been consecrated, the Earth was afraid of him, thinking, "Something great surely has he become now that he has been consecrated: I fear lest he may rend me asunder! And Bṛhaspati was also afraid of the Earth, thinking, "I fear that she may shake me off." *Hence by that (formula) he entered into a friendly relation with her; for a mother does not hurt her son, nor does a son hurt his mother.* (ŚB 5.2.1.18)[32]

The overcoming of fear of the "other" occurs with the transformation of the relationship of husband/wife to one of son/wife through the expression of the self as the son. As the ĀDS. puts it, "Now it can be perceived by the sense that the (father) has been reproduced separately (in the son); for the likeness (of a father and a son) is even visible, only (their) bodies are different" (2.9.24.2).[33]

The exchange of merit between husband and wife involves an agonistic situation of the sort found in the archaic ritual format. Copulation is a dangerous act for the male because of the risk of merit loss. As the priest's role was precarious in the exchange with the patron of *śrī* for *pāpa,* so also the male partner's role is precarious because he may lose his good deeds, which are the instruments of both his rebirth and his self perpetuation through a son. The power of the secret mantra and the understanding of the proper links—no longer from ritual to cosmos, but from father to son—overcome the conflict.

The BĀU also makes it clear that one basis of the relationship between father and son is the mandate to teach and learn which binds the two. The dying father says:

> "Bring thus the all [the son], let him assist me from this world" . . . Therefore they call "world-procuring" a son who has been instructed [". . . he is able through the discharge of appointed filial duties, to help the departed spirit of his father to attain a better world than would otherwise be possible"]. Therefore they instruct him. When one who has this knowledge [one thus instructed] departs from this world, he enters into the son with these vital breaths. . . . Whatever wrong has been done by him, his son frees him from it all. . . . By his son a father stands firm in this world. (BĀU 1.5.17)[34]

In the ChU the father/son model of Uddālaka and Śvetaketu is used to exemplify the ideal teacher–student relationship for the accurate perpetuation of the secret truth (*brahmopaniṣadam*) and to make the point that such truth is transmitted within the lineage and only to the eldest son or one who is worthy (3.11.4,5). "Worthiness" is posited as an alternative to the conservatism of transmission by lineage alone. The explicit question of *gotra* and the general question of worthiness appear in the Satyakāma story to establish the legitimacy of his role as a student (4.4.1ff.), where it is concluded that Satyakāma, although apparently illegitimate, must be a *brāhman, by nature* (4.4.5),[35] because he does not lie. He is, therefore, eligible to learn the secret teaching of the *brāhman*(s), despite the fact that his patrilineage is unknown. One who is worthy is taken on as a son. As a student of the Veda he will be reborn as the "son" of the teacher. Only the twice born (*dvi-ja*) may formally partake of the Tradition through the study of Veda, and the initiation sacrament (the *Upanayana*) into formal studentship is regarded as a second birth and in that context the teacher and student are father and son. The AV extolls the student of the Vedas (*brahmacārin*) as one who fills the gods and teacher with fervor (*tapas*) (11.5.1,2) and generates the *bráhman* (11.5.7). The teacher becomes pregnant with the student: "The teacher, taking [him] in charge (*upa-nī*), makes the Vedic student an embryo within; he bears him in his belly three nights; the gods gather unto him to see him when born" (11.5.1–3; cf. ŚB 11.5.4.12).[36] In this way, the Tradition accommodates the abstinence of the *śrotriya* within the mandate to have sons. The BDS says:

> Of two kinds, forsooth, is the virile energy of a famous Brāhmana who is learned in the Vedas, (that which resides) above the navel and the other (that resides) below the navel. Through that which (resides) above the navel, his offspring is produced when he initiates Brāhmanas, when he teaches them . . . when he makes them holy. All these are his children. But through that which resides below the navel the children of his body are produced. Therefore they never say to a Śrotriya who is versed in the Vedas, Thou art destitute of offspring. (1.11.21.13)[37]

Thus, in terms of *sampradāya* the Tradition allows a legitimate alternative to birthright.

The ChU radicalizes the distinction between public and private both in terms of arenas of teaching and the truths appropriate to those arenas. The intimate nature of the truth of the *brāhman* necessitates that the secret truth be taught in an intimate context, while the public or political nature of the truth of the *kṣatriya* allows for the teaching of that truth in the public context of the assembly or the crowd. The distinction between the two realms of truth caused a split between power and authority in the Tradition; the spiritual authority renounced the social life for the solitude of the forest, away from the forces of impurity; the matters of the social world are left to the king, who possesses worldly power but no spiritual authority.[38] The BĀU (6.2.1–16) and ChU (5.3.1–5.10.8) portray different degrees of specialization of function in similar accounts of an encounter between a *brāhman* (Śvetaketu) and a *rājanya* (Pravāhaṇa) on the matter of *karma* and rebirth. The accounts are parallel but for several details that are significant from the standpoint of the relationship of the truths appropriate to each realm. Many of the characteristics of the *brahmodya* are present, but in degenerate form. The remnant of an agonistic encounter takes place in a public assembly; the positing of the enigmatic but systematized questions; the reduction of the incapable (in this case ignorant) opponent to silence. The five questions on rebirth put to the young *brāhman* by Pravāhaṇa are an assimilation of the antagonists of the *brahmodya* contest. The defeated opponent is not threatened with physical harm, but in each account the son, Śvetaketu, transfers responsibility for his loss to his father, Uddālaka, who proceeds to seek the answers to the five questions.

In the BĀU, Uddālaka formally becomes a student of the king, while in the ChU he does not. The reason for the father not knowing the answers and, therefore, not having taught them to his son differs in the two accounts. In both texts, Pravāhaṇa, the *kṣatriya,* proceeds to declare a teaching on rebirth which the *brāhman* did not seem to know previously. In the BĀU the *brāhman* is told that he does not know the truth because his forefathers, his grandfather (6.2.8), did not know the teaching and, therefore, could not teach it to him. In the ChU, however, Uddālaka is told that the reason that he does not know the answers to the five questions on rebirth is that the answers involve a political teaching (*praśāsanam*) (5.3.7). In the context of the ChU it is clear that the reason for the *brāhman*('s) ignorance of the teaching and his apparent unconcern with it is that it is not appropriate to his *gotra.* The *praśāsanam* is a political teaching appropriate to *kṣatriya*(s). In the ChU the *brāhman* does not become the student of the *kṣatriya,* but he does, formally, in the BĀU. At BĀU 6.2.8, Pravāhaṇa states that his knowledge has not dwelt with *brāhman*(s) before, and he voices his concern about the possibility of incurring physical harm for violating the proper lines of transmission in teaching the *brāhman:* "So truly may not you and your grandfathers injure us." But he teaches him anyway, saying, "Who can refuse?" when the student approaches the teacher observing the proprieties of discipleship. The priority of lineage is acknowledged, but, at the same time, the possibility of student-teacher exchange between *brāman*(s) and *kṣatriya*(s) is still held open.

The difference between the *brāhman* and *kṣatriya* on dependence and rebirth can be seen in the role of ritual in the respective teachings. For the *brāhman* ritual knowledge provides the knowledge of dependence and takes one to the threshold of the secret teaching, to that which takes one beyond fear. The doctrine of *karma* is an account of the necessity of the reality of diversity in that coming-to-be. Knowledge of these teachings causes one to possess a pure, virtuous world (*puṇya-loko* [5.10.10]), and such knowledge brings one the best things, that which one desires, in the best worlds, but the secret truth is the truth of independence that takes one beyond rebirth, beyond fear, and beyond the worlds.

The mechanics of rebirth provide an account of human diversity and why human beings behave differently. One is what one knows. Human beings are different because they have different natural capacities to know. Because of this the ruler is presented with a problem on two levels, social and metaphysical: (1) The king must deal with the problem of social evil (5.10.9)—that is, the criminals among his subjects. The king must therefore understand the necessity and the foundation of law. With this knowledge he avoids pollution and obtains a virtuous kingdom. (2) In a kingdom free of criminals, the king's subjects are ordered not by their choices but by their natures, according to their conduct (*ramaṇīya-caraṇāḥ/kapūya-caraṇāḥ* [5.10.7]) in previous lives. Pravāhaṇa's account of rebirth at 5.3.3 to 5.11 is one part of a theological political teaching in that it concerns a problem of rule: how to rule subjects who, by choice, are polluting, without polluting oneself. It is a theological teaching in that the metaphysics of *karma* explain the necessity of the diversity of human behavior. The conclusion of the teaching by Aśvapati, a king, to the five *śrotriya*(s) (5.11.1ff.), also in the form of a degenerate *brahmodya*, concerns how to rule those dependent subjects who are polluting by nature, without becoming polluted (4.24.4).

In the ChU, the king's teaching on rebirth is a political teaching in that the *kṣatriya*'s concern with necessity and dependence is governed by the necessity of the *kṣatriya* to rule. The *brāhman*(s) must know the truth beyond dependence, but the *kṣatriya*(s) must know the truth *of* dependence because within the social-political realm the ruler is that upon whom all beings depend. The image of food is used to make this point: Jānaśruti is great, as many depend on him for food (4.1.1); because of Aśvapati's knowledge he is able to feed a *śūdra* without fear of pollution (5.24.4). Pravāhaṇa's doctrine of rebirth explains the relationship between procreation, food, death, and rebirth. From the standpoint of the *kṣatriya*, the argument explains the existence of the lowly within the political realm; why the yonder world is not filled (5.10.8), why the necessity of the political order persists.

The importance of lineage is twofold from the standpoint of the *brāhman*(s): it accomplishes the handing over (*sampradāna*) of the repository of truth in a guarded way in order to prevent that truth from being defiled by those who are not, by nature—that is, by birth— appropriate to that truth by demanding the most intimate and nonpublic line of transmission, father to son. As the father is reborn in the son (RV 5.4.10; 6.70.3), one teaches the one who is most like the self, the son, who *is* the father (ChU 2.13.2; ŚB 12.4.3.1). For the father, the teaching of the son is an exercise in self-understanding.

Lineage is an important consideration in the teaching accounts of the *brāhman*(s) to establish the legitimacy and authority of the teacher as well as the legitimacy of the pupil. For a son to inherit the truth involves the necessity of learning the Veda as the precondition to the secret teaching (ChU 6.1.1); so-called *brāhman*(s) by association (*brahmabandhu*) are unlearned (*anūcya*) in Veda (6.1.1). The complement to transmission of truth by birthright alone is "worthiness," which, in the cases of Satyakāma and Upakosala, involves the understanding of dependence and the ordering of desire in the right direction—toward "that" upon which all things are dependent, *brahman*. Knowledge of "that" can only be given by a teacher (ChU 4.9.3; 4.15.1). The truth of the teaching is equal to the authority of the teacher. The text declares Uddālaka's authority early on and establishes that the intimacy of the father–son teaching relationship is the ideal setting for the most accurate transmission (*sampradāna*) of the secret truths which are the revealed core of the Tradition.

The sociological expression of the hierarchical distinction between those who may teach and learn the secret truth and those who may not arises from acceptance of this fact:

> The sacrificial ritual is *brahman* . . . [the] prayer that is divine, is *brahman*. . . . The whole ritual was the *brahman;* and hence the ritual literature is the *brahmana*, and the person who achieves the sublime super-human power, by his prayer or mantra, was the *brahmana*.[39]

By virtue of the relationship of "*bráhman*" as "power," "ritual," "powerful prayer and speech," and "participant" at the core of ritual which is the *raison d'être* of Vedism, the preeminence of the *brahmán/brāhman* is implicit in Vedism. On this basis the Tradition has recognized the *ṛṣi*(s) as the progenitors of *brahmán/brāhman* families, legitimizing the sacred duty of the *brāhman*(s) to maintain the revealed Tradition.

Notes

1. See R. K. Mookerji, *Ancient Indian Education;* M. Hara, "Hindu and Sanskrit Concepts of Teacher," in *Sanskrit and Indian Studies: Essays in Honour of Daniel H. H. Ingalls*, 93–118; W. Cenkner, *A Tradition of Teachers: Śaṅkara and the Jagadgurus Today*.

2. Because this work is intended for nonspecialist readers, technical and textual references have been kept to a minimum. Some clarification of the use of particular terms might assist

the reader at this point: the term *brāhmaṇa*(s) refers to the strata of texts between the *saṃhitā*(s) and the *upaniṣad*(s); *brāhman* and *brahmán* have been used to distinguish the priestly class and the priestly functionary, respectively; *bráhman* denotes the mystic power pervading the universe, or the enigmatic utterances founded upon or manifestations of the *bráhman; brahmodya* refers to a ritual priestly debate wherein the *bráhman* (enigma) is employed by the *brahmán* (priest). For the state of scholarly debate on the relationship of these terms and concepts, see H. W. Bodewitz, "The Fourth Priest (The *BRAHMÁN*) in Vedic Ritual," in *Selected Studies on Ritual in Indian Religions,* 33–68. While I agree with Prof. Bodewitz that the poetical aspect of the *brahmán*('s) role should not be overestimated (p. 49), W. L. Johnson's study ("Into a Thousand Similes: Image and Symbol in the Rgvedic Enigmatic Sense of Reality and Some Beginnings of Indian Speculation"), to which Bodewitz does not refer, supports J. Gonda's argument (*Notes on Brahman*) that the *bráhman* is both poem and power, despite Johnson's overemphasis on the poetical.

3. L. Renou, *Religions of Ancient India,* 29.

4. J. C. Heesterman, "Brahmin, Ritual and Renouncer," *Wiener Zeitschrift für die Kunde S.u.O Asiens* 8 (1964) 1–31.

5. Renou, *Ancient India,* 16.

6. Renou, *Vedic India,* 101.

7. F. B. J. Kuiper, "The Ancient Aryan Verbal Contest," *Indo-Iranian Journal* 4 (1969) 217–81.

8. N. W. Brown, *Man in the Universe: Some Cultural Continuities in India,* 27.

9. Heesterman, "Brahmin, Ritual and Renouncer," 4.

10. Ibid., 7–10.

11. L. Renou, *The Destiny of the Veda in India,* 24.

12. L. Sarup, trans., *The Nighaṇṭu and Nirukta of Yāska,* 16.

13. Ibid., 18.

14. Ibid., 20.

15. Renou, *The Destiny of the Veda in India,* 16.

16. See especially, Johnson, "Into a Thousand Similes."

17. ". . . 'la formulation inaccessible à l'intelligence (commune)'. . . ;" L. Renou in collaboration with Lilian Silburn, "Sur la notion de bráhman," *Journal Asiatique* 237 (1949) 12.

18. Ibid., 43.

19. Bodewitz, "The Fourth Priest," 37.

20. J. C. Heesterman, "On the Origin of the Nastika," *Wiener Zeitschrift für die Kunde S.u.O. Asiens* 12–13 (1968–69) 175.

21. Renou, "Sur la notion de bráhman," 13, 18, 43.

22. Heesterman, "Origin of the Nastika," 174.

23. R. E. Hume, trans., *The Thirteen Principal Upanishads* (2nd ed., rev.; London, 1931) 110.

24. L. Dumont, *Homo Hierarchicus.*

25. H. Lüders, *Varuṇa,* 2:420–85.

26. Johnson, "Into a Thousand Similes," 254 n. 28.

27. Ibid., 256 n. 33.

28. J. C. Heesterman, "Other Folk's Fire," in *Agni: The Ritual of the Fire Altar,* 2:77.

29. Ibid., 81.

30. Hume, *Principal Upanishads,* 81.

31. Ibid., 85.

32. *Sacred Books of the East,* ed. F. Max Müller (50 vols.; Delhi, 1966): vol. 41, *Śatapathabrāhmaṇa,* trans. J. Eggeling, p. 34.

33. *Sacred Books of the East,* ed. F. Max Müller (50 vols.; Delhi, 1966): vol. 2, *Sacred Laws of the Aryas: Āpastamba Dharmasūtra,* trans. George Bühler, p. 159.

34. Hume, *Principal Upanishads,* 90.

35. On the phrase "None but a *Brahmana* could thus speak out" (*ChU.* 5.4.5), Śaṅkara comments in his *bhāṣya,* "No one who is not a Brahmana could speak out so openly and straightforwardly; it is *Brāhmaṇas* alone, not others, who are by their very nature straightforward" (*The Chāndogyopaniṣad,* trans. G. Jha [Poona, 1942] 191–92.

36. W. D. Whitney, trans., *Atharvaveda,* 8:636.

37. *Sacred Books of the East,* ed. F. Max Müller (50 vols.; Delhi, 1966): vol. 14, *Baudhāyana Dharmasūtra,* trans. George Bühler, pp. 209–10.

38. See J. C. Heesterman, "Power and Authority in Indian Tradition," in *Tradition and Politics in South Asia.*

39. S. A. Dange, *Pastoral Symbolism from the Ṛgveda,* 106.

Bibliography

Sources

Aufrecht, T., ed. *Die Hymnen Des Rigveda.* Berlin, 1861–63.

Bühler, G., trans. *Āpastamba Dharmasūtra.* Vol. 2 of *Sacred Books of the East.* Edited by F. Max Müller. 50 vols. Delhi, 1966.

——. *Baudhāyana Dharmasūtra.* Vol. 14 of *Sacred Books of the East.* Edited by F. Max Müller. 50 vols. Delhi, 1966.

Caland, W., trans. *Pañcaviṃśabrāhmaṇa.* Bibliotheca Indica 255. Calcutta: Asiatic Society of Bengal, 1931.

Eggeling, T., trans. *Śatapathabrāhmaṇa.* Vols. 12, 26, 41, 43, 44 of *Sacred Books of the East.* Edited by F. Max Müller. 50 vols. Delhi, 1974.

Griffith, R. T. H., trans. *Yajurveda.* Banares, 1957.

Hume, R. E., trans. *Bṛhadāraṇyakopaniṣad.* In *The Thirteen Principal Upanishads.* Oxford, 1931.

Jha, G., trans. *The Chāndogyopaniṣad.* With the commentary of Śaṇkara. Poona Oriental Series 78. Poona: Oriental Book Agency, 1942.

Keith, A. B., trans. *Aitareyabrāhmaṇa.* In *Rigveda Brāhmaṇas.* Harvard Oriental Series 24. Cambridge, MA: Harvard University Press, 1920.

——. *Taittirīyasaṃhitā.* Harvard Oriental Series 18–19. Cambridge, MA: Harvard University Press, 1914.

Sarup, L., trans. *The Nighaṇṭa and Nirukta of Yāska.* Delhi, 1962.

Whitney, W. D., trans. *Atharvaveda.* Harvard Oriental Series 7–8. Cambridge, MA: Harvard University Press, 1905.

Studies

Bodewitz, H. W. "The Fourth Priest (The *BRAHMÁN*) in Vedic Ritual." In *Selected Studies On Ritual in Indian Religions,* 33–68. Edited by R. Kloppenborg. Leiden, 1983.

Brown, N. W. *Man in the Universe: Some Cultural Continuities in India.* Berkeley, 1966.
Cenkner, W. *The Tradition of Teachers: Śaṅkara and the Jagadgurus Today.* Delhi: Motilal Banarsidass, 1983.
Dange, S. A. *Pastoral Symbolism from the Ṛgveda.* Poona, 1970.
Dumont, L. "World Renunciation in Indian Religions." *Contrib. to Ind. Soc.* 4 (1960) 32–62.
——. "Kingship in Ancient India." *Contrib. to Ind. Soc.* 6 (1962) 48–77.
——. *Homo Hierarchicus: An Essay on the Caste System.* Translated by Mark Sainsbury. Chicago, 1970.
Gonda, J. *Notes on Brahman.* Utrecht, 1950.
——. *The Vision of the Vedic Seers.* The Hague, 1963.
——. *Change and Continuity in Indian Religion.* The Hague, 1965.
——. *Ancient Indian Kingship From the Religious Point of View.* Leiden, 1969.
——. *Dual Deities in the Religion of the Veda.* Amsterdam, 1974.
Gonda, J., ed. *A History of Indian Literature:* vol. I,1, *Vedic Literature.* Wiesbaden, 1975.
Hara, M., "Hindu and Sanskrit Concepts of Teacher." In *Sanskrit and Indian Studies: Essays in Honour of Daniel H. H. Ingalls,* 93–118. Edited by M. Nagatome et al. London, 1980.
Hauer, J. W. *Der Vrātya.* Stuttgart, 1927.
Heesterman, J. C. *The Ancient Indian Royal Consecration.* 's-Gravenhage, 1957.
——. "Vrātya and Sacrifice." *Indo-Iranian Journal* 6 (1962) 1–37.
——. "Brahmin, Ritual and Renouncer." *Wiener Zeitschrift für die Kunde S.u.O. Asiens* 8 (1964) 1–31.
——. "The Case of the Severed Head." *Wiener Zeitschrift für die Kunde S.u.O. Asiens* 11 (1967) 22–43.
——. "On the Origin of the Nastika." *Wiener Zeitschrift für die Kunde S.u.O. Asiens* 12–13 (1968–69) 171–85.
——. "Priesthood and the Brahmin." *Contrib. to Ind. Soc.* n.s. 5 (1971) 43–47.
——. "The Conundrum of the King's Authority." In *Kingship and Authority in South Asia.* Edited by J. F. Richards. Madison, 1978.
——. "Veda and Dharma." In *The Concept of Duty in South Asia,* 80–95. Edited by J. D. Derrett and W. D. O'Flaherty. New Delhi, 1978.
——. "Power and Authority in Indian Tradition." In *Tradition and Politics in South Asia,* 61–85. Edited by J. R. Moore. Delhi, 1979.
——. "Other Folk's Fire." In *Agni: The Ritual of the Fire Altar.* Edited by Fritz Staal. 2 vols. Berkeley, 1983.
Johnson, W. L. "Into a Thousand Similes: Image and Symbol in the Rgvedic Enigmatic Sense of Reality and Some Beginnings of Indian Speculation." Ph.D. diss., Wisconsin, 1973.
Kaelberg, W. "Tapas, Birth and Spiritual Rebirth in the Veda." *History of Religions* 15 (1976) 343–86.
Kuiper, F. B. J. "The Ancient Aryan Verbal Contest." *Indo-Iranian Journal* 4 (1969) 217–81.
Lüders, H. *Varuṇa.* 2 vols. Göttingen, 1951.
Mookerji, R. K. *Ancient Indian Education.* Delhi, 1969.

O'Flaherty, W. "Karma and Rebirth in the Vedas and Puranas." In *Karma and Rebirth in Classical Indian Traditions.* Edited by W. O'Flaherty. Berkeley, 1980.
Renou, L., "La valeur du silence dans le culte vedique." *Journal of the American Oriental Society* 69 (1949) 11–18.
——. With Lilian Silburn. "Sur la notion de bráhman." *Journal Asiatique* 237 (1949) 7–46.
——. *Religions of Ancient India.* London, 1953.
——. "Les pouvoirs de la parole dans le Rgveda." In *Études Vediques et Pāṇinéennes,* vol. 1, pp. 1–27. Paris, 1955.
——. *Vedic India.* Calcutta, 1957.
——. "Enigma in the Ancient Literature of India." *Diogenes* No. 29 (1960) 32–41.
——. "Recherches sur le ritual védique: La place du Rig-Veda dans l'ordonnance du culte." *Journal Asiatique* 250 (1962) 161–84.
——. *The Destiny of the Veda in India.* Delhi, 1965.
Staal, F. "Ritual Syntax." In *Sanskrit and Indian Studies: Essays in Honour of Daniel H. H. Ingalls,* 93–118. Edited by M. Nagatome et al. London, 1980.
——, ed. *Agni: The Ritual of the Fire Altar.* 2 vols. Berkeley, 1983.

4

Spirit and Spiritual Knowledge in the Upaniṣads

JOHN G. ARAPURA

THE UPANIṢAD(S), WHICH STAND at the fountainhead of Indian religion's greatest tradition (Vedanta), have a unique conception of the Spirit and spiritual knowledge—and hence of salvation as well. It consists in speaking in identical ways about the supreme Being, that is, as Spirit in the objective sense (Brahman) and as the supreme Self, Spirit in the subjectve sense (Ātman), the latter having its ultimate conceptual base in what we know as our own self. Further, what we know as our own self goes all the way to the point of absolute identity with the supreme Being, or supreme Spirit, resulting in a vision of the human being and its destiny which has no parallel in the world. The purpose of spiritual knowledge is to realize the human being's oneness with the supreme Spirit.

The term "spiritual knowledge" stands for the Sanskrit terms *Brahma-vidyā* and *Ātma-vidyā* (or, *Adhyātma-vidyā*), formed respectively by combining *vidyā*, having both the theoretical and practical senses of knowledge, with the respective terms *Brahman* and *Ātman*. And as their sources are interchangeable, they too are interchangeable: one may switch indifferently from one to the other, as is the accepted custom in the tradition.

In order to be able to understand this wholly extraordinary vision of the Spirit and spiritual knowledge, a correct perception of its source, that is, the *Upaniṣad*(s) is indispensable. It is important to know how the *Upaniṣad*(s) came by it. Is it by means of mere speculation, in the way in which, given the disposition, even now we can possibly think up such things? These questions will make it necessary for us to consider the nature of the *Upaniṣad*(s).

What Are the Upaniṣad(s)?

They are the corpus of utterances about Brahman/Ātman and of the unique kind of spiritual knowledge pertaining to Brahman/Ātman. Everywhere they speak of these subject matters and of everything else only in relation to these, whether it be the world, earth, sky, the elements, food, life-breath, mind, speech, or human and other beings. All talk radiates from them and eventually is led back to them.

The *Upaniṣad*(s)' own understanding of themselves is of great importance in grasping their message. They see themselves as the concluding part of the Vedas, and hence as the manifestation of the eternal Logos (*Vāk*) in human, linguistic form. They consider themselves to be the quintessence (*rasānām rasaḥ*) of the Vedas (ChU 3.5.4). They are the ultimate secret, revealed in an earlier epoch (*vedānte paramaṁ guhyaṁ pūrvakalpe pracoditam*) (SvU 6.22). The great ascetics have properly ascertained the meaning of the Upaniṣadic knowledge (*vedānta-vijñāna suniścitārthāḥ yatayaḥ*) (MU 3.2.6).

They are *Brahma-vidyā/Ātma-vidyā* themselves, in the form of language. Their sole purpose is to show Brahman/Ātman, to show them as that "which is to be seen, as that which is to be heard, as that as that which is to be thought, as that which is to be contemplated" (*ātma vā are draṣṭavyaḥ śrotavyo mantavyo nididhyāsanavyaḥ*) (BĀU 2.4.5). It is added: "Verily, by the seeing of, by the hearing of, by the thinking of, by the understanding of the *Ātman,* all this (the world of variety) is known."

The *Upaniṣad*(s) themselves contain clues to their role as a kind of special agency in gathering and preparing that knowledge of Brahman which is intended for human beings. For instance, ChU 3.5.1,2 likens the *Upaniṣad*(s) to bees that make honey, and Brahman to the flower which provides the sweet juices the bees collect for making honey, and it describes the collecting as a profound and concentrated brooding (*abhi-tapas*) upon Brahman.

There is another significant characteristic of the *Upaniṣad*(s) which must be dwelt upon: that consists in the very word *upaniṣad.* Although, in respect of origin, the word must have come into being entirely accidentally, there were, undoubtedly, some deliberate efforts to put into it meanings that were significant of the subject matter. The word was formed from three particles *upa, ni,* and *sad,* which in their combination mean, translating backward, "sitting devotedly nearby," reflecting the position which the listeners and learners must have assumed in the physical vicinity of the teachers. Gradually, this fact supplied an imagery by which to express an important aspect of the spiritual essence of the teaching, which is to bring about a devoted posture of proximity to Brahman. Such a proximity is an especially challenging idea, because it is not calculated even remotely to suggest that the infinite distance at which Brahman dwells can be abolished or overcome; the distance is reinforced in multifarious statements by the *Upaniṣad*(s) themselves. The word *para,* meaning "beyond," is usually employed in reference to Brahman, either as an adjective or by itself. Likewise, in many places the superlative of that word, *parama,* is also employed, and especially as an adjective for Ātman, partly to differentiate between the supreme Self and the human, individual self. Even the expression *parātpara* (beyond the beyond) is brought into play (MU 3.2.8). No doubt, language simply is found inadequate to indicate this transcendence.

And yet the proximity that is asserted—for which the word *upaniṣad* itself stands—is to that which always remains beyond, beyond-most, or beyond the beyond. Therefore, it is not anything like the standard way of complementing transcendence with immanence. This is clearly the distinctiveness of the *Upaniṣad*(s), that they declare, embody, and, in fact, *are* the devoted posture of proximity to the absolutely transcendent Spirit, in its pure *transcendence.*

In most of the modern writings on the *Upaniṣad*(s) and on Vedanta generally, the self-understanding by the *Upaniṣad*(s) of themselves as what brings into being the actuality of nearness to the absolutely transcendent Spirit finds no place. Instead, there is a great deal of glib talk of idealism, especially inspired by the fact that the word *ātman,* which also means the individual human self (to be written with a small "a" in this case), readily lends itself to the notion of subject-hood. With such talk also goes the belief that the so-called idealistic contents of the *Upaniṣad*(s) are something simply thought up by some gifted ancient thinkers, assisted by deep mystical experiences. This is not doing justice to the *Upaniṣad*(s).

The *Upaniṣad*(s) are not simply the products of thought, but are the self-guaranteed possibility of thinking, viewing, and knowing reality in a certain way, a way that is unparalleled. Likewise, they are not just the outcome of mystical experience, but its ensured possibility. Thus, they go much deeper than speculative thought and mystical experience; rather, they can generate these perpetually and without end. This is the case because the *Upaniṣad*(s) are the Logos (*Vāk*) in its self-manifestation—and the Logos is the assurance of both thought and mystical experience; it is that which makes them possible.

The *Upaniṣad*(s) as postures of proximity to Brahman themselves offer positions from which to see, hear, think, and contemplate Brahman. That is the sense underlying the saying "Āman should be seen, heard, etc." They also furnish positions which we can stake out when we are on the "lookout" for (*speculate* on) ultimate meanings that, paradoxically enough, are already gathered and prepared by the *Upaniṣad*(s), which work like bees to follow their own self imagery.

A few of such positions are worth pondering over. These ones are themselves in a strange and arresting way described as *upaniṣad,* that is, sitting near [Brahman]; that is why they are selected. However, we must think of them not necessarily as being themselves special but as exemplary and representative of the *Upaniṣad*(s) as a whole. In any case, they are deeply instructive. Further, the word "speculate," used by us, is also relevant, inasmuch as it has to do, in the case here, essentially with vantage points from which to "look out" and seize clues to what Brahman, as the ultimate ground of all meanings, is. Thus, the posture of proximity to Brahman is attained in different ways, and each of them has a definite correspondence to the kinds of quests for meaning that we human beings characteristically undertake. Now we will turn to a few of these exemplary positions, which accord with our own typical kinds of quests for meaning.

1. KU 4.6.7:

> That (*tat*), verily, is what is called the dearest of all; the dearest of all is to be meditated on. Whosoever knows it thus is desired by all beings.
>
> [The inquirer:] "Tell me the *upaniṣad*." [The teacher:] "The *upaniṣad* has been spoken; we have told thee the *upaniṣad* pertaining to Brahman."

"The dearest of all" (*tadvanam*) is described as an *upaniṣad* because it is, overtly, a mysterious expression and, inherently, a vantage point from which to look out for, and perceive, the truest essence of "eros," which moves man to the highest, and, provided he grasps that essence, moves all beings to him. It is also significant that the word used for "meditation" [upon it] here, as in many other places in the *Upaniṣad*(s) is *upāsana*, which has other synonyms like *dhyāna*. But this one has a special meaning. Hence, that which should be meditated on is *upāsitavyam*, employed in this place, as in many others. The word *upāsana* comes from two of the particles (*upa* and *sad*), from which *upaniṣad* itself has been formed. As it has an active sense, it has the profound significance of actualizing the posture of proximity to Brahman through some powerful clue or other that is given.

2. BĀU 2.1.20:

> As a spider moves about on its web, as tiny sparks come forth from fire, even so, from this Ātman do come forth all vital breaths, all worlds, all deities, all beings. Its *upaniṣad* is the Truth of truth. Vital breaths are the truth and their Truth is It (Ātman).

3. The mystic chant at the end of the TU:

> I am food, I am food, I am food; I am the eater of food, I am the eater of food, I am the eater of food; I am the [nutrition] synthesizer, I am the synthesizer, I am the synthesizer; I am the firstborn of world-order, prior to the gods, in the navel of immortality. Whoso gives me, he verily saves. I am the food that eats the eater of food. I have overwhelmed the entire universe, [I am] the many-hued light. He (or, for him) who knows this: this is the *upaniṣad*.

This chant, typical of everything else in the *Upaniṣad*(s), is too full of symbolisms to be understood readily. Food, *annam,* is a basic symbol for organic life material. The line "I am the firstborn of world-order" in the original is *aham asmi prathamajā ṛtasya.* The expression *prathamajā ṛtasya* (firstborn of world-order) has been interpreted by the great elucidator of classical Śaṇkara commentaries, Ānandagiri, to mean *Hiraṇyagarbha,* the Golden Germ that produced the cosmos. The expression, however, is from RV 1.64.36, where it more likely stands for the Logos (*Vāk*). But the difference is not such as to destroy the progression indicated in the chant, for the Logos and the Golden Germ too meet—as the essential upward movement is of life to a higher life–light continuum. The Logos, like the self-generative principle of life symbolized by the Golden Germ, moves toward light in this chant, and the Logos itself is a form of light, as evidence in BĀU 4.3.5: "Logos indeed is his light." This chant is a mystic account of the way the growth of organisms opens up into that greatest of all mysteries, that is, the many-hued light (of consciousness), including the transition from perishability through the "navel of immortality," through the Logos (or the self-generative power of Life), and beyond.

In these three typical instances of what have been designated in the contexts themselves as *upaniṣad,* a kind of lookout for, and seizing of, at least three areas of humanity's primary quests take place. The first, "dearest of all," concerns the "eros," or what moves the Spirit, and what man wants to grasp as absolutely worthy of love such that he himself, as a consequence of grasping it, becomes lovable. The second concerns the inherent thrust of the intellect, i.e., that of the intellect which devotes itself to seeing the connections among different levels of truth, and to the Truth that makes true things true—which we can extend under our modern conditions to cover the reliable truths of the sciences and metaphysics, inasmuch as they have also an undeniable spiritual bearing. The third, as already explained, relates to humanity's quest for the organic continuity and wholeness of life, on its way defying mortality, and eventually opening itself up to the light of consciousness, which in its turn reaches down and suffuses all the lower levels, so that we can say "the body thinks," "the body feels," "the body knows," and so on. The importance of the body in spiritual practice, especially in Yoga, needs certainly to be stressed, as also the organism's linkage with the light of consciousness.

Speculation understood in this way, as a function wholly under the control of the Logos, hence opening doors to the sphere of ultimate meanings in the tenor of our quests, as constituting the foundation upon which we can stand and resist the threat of meaninglessness, of non-being, is of undeniable importance in spiritual life. Mystical experience, which by its nature is a step ahead, must only accord with such a foundation of meanings. Hence, mystical experience too, inasmuch as its perpetual possibility is stored in the *Upaniṣad*(s), rests squarely on the Logos. One should never cease to stress the Logos as the essence of the *Upaniṣad*(s). Even the expression *neti neti* (not this, not this), so celebrated a formula of the *Upaniṣad*(s) (BĀU 2.3.6; 3.9.26; 4.2.4; 4.4.22; 4.5.15), is intrinsically of the nature of the Logos and has nothing at all to do with being nonrational, in the manner it is often represented.

Both speculation and mysticism are activities of human beings, and they are possible only because of the Logos, whose complete self-active condition is that full spiritual knowledge (i.e., *Brahma-vidyā/Ātma-vidyā*) of which the *Upaniṣad*(s) are embodiments. This spiritual knowledge is gathered directly from the supreme Spirit (i.e., Brahman/Ātman) and not from even the highest of human activities. It is housed in the *Upaniṣad*(s), inasmuch as they are but the self-active manifestation of the Logos. Accordingly, the human practice of this spiritual knowledge is nothing but participation in the self-active possibility of the Logos by way of the *Upaniṣad*(s). That is the sum and substance of spiritual knowledge as in the *Upaniṣad*(s) called *Brahma-vidyā*, or *Ātma-vidyā*. Nevertheless, the *Upaniṣad*(s) are granted their unique significance because (1) they are the Logos in its self-active condition; (2) they embody stations of proximity to that which is, and remains, beyond, beyond-most, and beyond the beyond, without compromises worked out on the basis of unvanquishable human finitude and ignorance.

The *Upaniṣad*(s) themselves *are* the possibility of the spiritual life housed in them, and that spiritual life is one of gnosis, nonetheless gnosis of Brahman/Ātman. The last clause will show that in the *Upaniṣad*(s), gnosis always goes with Brahman/Ātman, and as such it is the fullness of the spiritual knowledge and the sole condition under which creative thought and mystical experience, on humanity's part, can happen. Here now we have reached the point at which we must consider *vidyā* pertaining to Brahman/Ātman.

Spiritual Knowledge as Brahma-vidyā/Ātma-vidyā

In order to grasp the issue of spiritual knowledge as *Brahma-vidyā (Ātma-vidyā*), we have to have a clear idea of how the *Upaniṣad*(s) use the base terms *Brahman* and *Ātman*. Now, as we have indicated before, these two are used synonymously whenever the knowledge of the selfsame Being preceding the word *vidyā* (or its synonym *jñāna*, cognate with "gnosis") is at issue, which is so, most often, implicitly. There is, however, another use of *Ātman,* where the word stands for the individual human self, which sometimes also occurs in the *Upaniṣad*(s). We must only note this and not necessarily go into it in any detail in our present discussion.

There is, no doubt, a certain difference in the origins of the two terms *Brahman* and *Ātman,* which is already overcome in the *Upaniṣad*(s) under the notion of *vidyā* pertaining to them as a single undifferentiated *vidyā,* although *Brahma-vidyā* should be considered normative, because of the fact that Brahman is in origin the more distinctively religious term, in view of its earlier Vedic association with prayer, power, potency of sacrifices, dynamic self-expansion, and self-growth. *Brahman* came to be a name, the most sacred and mysterious of all, standing for the supreme Spirit. On the other hand, *Ātman* is not a name; it is a word which earlier had other possible connotations like breath, but in the *Upaniṣad*(s) we see it as a word with the closest association with the pronoun "I," indicating the supreme Spirit in accordance with it. It is a word expressing that entity which identifies itself first as "I am" and then only by any other name.

In BĀU 1.4.1–17 we find a fascinating double account of the genesis of all things from Ātman and Brahman side by side:

> In the beginning this [world] was only the Ātman, in the shape of a person. Looking around he saw nothing else. He first said "I am." Thus arose the pronoun "I." Therefore, even now when one is called out he answers "This is I," and then identifies himself by whatever his other name is. (1.4.1).

The word "I" is also designated a posture of proximity, an *upaniṣad*(s), to the mystery of Being, in BĀU 5.5.4: And "in the beginning Brahman indeed was this [world]. It knew itself as 'I am Brahman'. . ." (1.4.10).

These citations show a fundamental truth: Without a name Ātman knows itself only as "I am"; with the name it knows itself as "I am Brahman." We can see that in every respect Brahman and Ātman are the same for the *Upaniṣad*(s), although on the whole there is a greater word-magic in the term Brahman, which evokes associations of power, sacrificial potency, and that which is beyond all that we can reach.

However, the utterly fascinating point is that while the supreme Reality is one and the same, it can be referred to by two terms and described identically by them, and, obversely, while there are two parallel terms and corresponding descriptions, the Reality referred to is one and the same. It is not at all a case of our being able to substitute one of the terms for the other in every given instance of their respective occurrences but of the fundamental fact that the Reality is the same. This is the unique case in the world literature of two notions being distinct without being different. The same is true of *Brahma-vidyā* and *Ātma-vidyā*. There is no doubt at all that, in respect to spiritual knowledge, this phenomenon offers a most fascinating prospect: that we can contemplate the same supreme Spirit and in identical ways, though under the governance of two terms that are distinct but not different in what they refer to—and this not because we have decided in favor of it but because the *Upaniṣad*(s) themselves give us the unmistakable guidance in that regard.

We *contemplate* the supreme Spirit, but we do so by *meditating* on the revelatory statements (*vākya*(s)) which constitute what are called by the word *upaniṣad* and as such are stations of proximity to the supreme Spirit. On the contrary, we do not *meditate* on the supreme Spirit (Being, the Ultimate Reality, or whatever), neither do we *contemplate* the revelatory words. The procedure laid out by the *Upaniṣad*(s) and the tradition taking its rise from them are meticulous in these matters. It is also the case that mere contemplation of the Supreme without the revelatory utterances to meditate on as avenues thereto are not what the *Upaniṣad*(s) and their tradition recommend. That kind of contemplation would be no more than an internal reorganization of what in a different way takes the form of speculation, and in its results it would be no more fruitful or decisive than that.

The spiritual knowledge as *Brahma-vidyā/Ātma-vidyā* would be impossible without recourse to meditation (*upāsana*) on the statements of the Logos which reveal—that is, show—Brahman/Ātman, nevertheless wrapped in language which inevitably conceals—or, rather, paradoxically speaking, reveals—only to the extent that the concealment is itself successful and effective. So the prayer is thrice addressed to the sun-god in the *Upaniṣad*(s) (Iśā U 15; BĀU 5.15.1; Maitri U 6.35.): "The face of Truth is covered with a golden disc; unveil it, O Sun god, so that I who stand established in *dharma* may behold it" (*hiranmayena pātreṇa satyasyāpihitam mukham; tat tvam pūṣan apāvṛṇu satya-dharmāya dṛṣṭaye*). This is the reason why revelation, in the last resort, is what takes place in the understanding that engages itself with the statements of the *Upaniṣad*(s), through *upāsana*, which always has the spirit of the last recited supplication in constant attendance.

The statements of the *Upaniṣad*(s) pertaining to Brahman/Ātman are many and varied, covering the bulk of the large corpus of our *Upaniṣad*(s). They are many and diverse in kind, tone, and form. But they all bring us new knowledge—of the same Reality, no doubt—and hence are called *anadhigata*, or unprecedented. They are also *abādhita*, that is, not falsifiable by anything else that we can call knowledge. Some statements seem to favor the notion that Brahman is possessed of qualities such as would be attributable to a supreme personal God, Creator, Sustainer, Benign Giver, Omnipresent Being, etc. Thus, for example, we have descriptions like: "This shining, immortal person" (BĀU 2.5.1); "Omnipresent God" (SvU 2.16); "rewarder"

(ChU 4.15.3), etc. On the other hand, there are attribute-denying statements, the most famous of that class being *neti neti* (not this, not this). Is there an internal split within the *Upaniṣad*(s) on this matter? Historically, theologians have ranged themselves on the one side or the other of this seemingly great divide. But Śaṇkara, the greatest of all the commentators, underplays this division as he observes: "It is not possible to say that the *Upaniṣad*(s) endorse the view that there is a divergence, in type, of descriptions of Brahman. The difference exists only for the purpose of facilitating different meditations (*upāsana*(s)), and in truth there is no difference—that is the purport" (*ataśca na bhinnākāra-yogo brahmaṇa śāstrīya iti śakyate vaktum. bhedasya upāsanārthatvāt abhede tātparyāt* [*Commentary* on the *Brahmasūtra* 3.2.12]). The solution seems to be this: despite the apparent divergence in the descriptions, in respect of *Brahma-vidyā/Ātma-vidyā,* they are utterly homogenous.

In the *Upaniṣad*(s) and their subsequent tradition, the descriptions of the highest Spirit serve the purpose of ultimate spiritual liberation, that is, *mukti.* They are, however, not placed in the relation of means to end or in any kind of relation that implies their being different, though distinguishable within the condition of our aspiration for knowledge and liberation (*mukti*), that is, insofar as we see them as but discrete states within, rather than as the essence of, Being that already envelops all beings and all states.

That Thou Art

The *Upaniṣad*(s) show that human existence is such that it is governed by the subtlest of spiritual dialectics, according to which we become unaware of what we are and yet, salutarily enough, are able to turn such unawareness itself into a dynamic that enables us to aspire. And the Logos, in the form of the *Upaniṣad*(s), performs its other function of giving us knowledge of what we are, right under the conditions of our very unawareness. Thus comes the Voice both from beyond the beyond and from the ultimate depth of our own self, loaded and weighted as we are by layers upon layers of ignorance. The Voice is such that the two sources from which it comes, the beyond the beyond and the ultimate depth of our own self, are no longer separated as two. It encompasses the deepest mystery of Being, namely, that we are *there,* at that point which is indicated by beyondness in relation to the Beyond itself. That is the Voice which says "that thou art"—*tat tvam asi*—which is the greatest of the Upaniṣadic utterances, that is, if we should grade them at all.

"That thou art" is the climactic wisdom of the *Upaniṣad*(s), given utterance in a dramatic encounter between a father (also teacher) and son (also pupil) recorded in ChU, chapter 6. The son Śvetaketu was taken by the father Uddālaka through a shattering dialectic which prepared him to receive the final instruction "by which the unheard becomes heard, the unthought becomes thought, the un-understood, understood." A lengthy and penetrating discourse on Being (*sat*) takes place at first, from which reflections on various phenomena which have come out of Being prompt the declaration made—altogether nine times—at the end of each reflection: "That which is the subtle essence, in which all this has its self, that is the truth, that is the Ātman, that art thou, O Śvetaketu; so be it." Śaṇkara comments: "This self is known as Being, and it is through the Self (Ātman) that the whole world is imbued wth self-hood" (*etena sadākhayenā 'tmanātmatvāt sarvam idaṁ jagat*).

This great utterance is the heart of the entire tradition of spiritual knowledge stemming from the *Upaniṣad*(s), which has appeared as foolishness to some and been a stumbling block to others. But for the *Upaniṣad*(s) it is the make-or-break truth. According to Śaṇkara, "all teachings of the *Upaniṣad*(s) point to one thing only, i.e., the unity of the individual with the supreme Spirit, expressed by the paradigmatic utterance 'that thou art'" (*itaśca tattvam asi vākyam vastu-parametyāha-sarvopaniṣaditi*) (The *Commentary* on ChU 6.16.3).

In order to understand "that thou art" one has to understand both what is meant by "that" and what is meant by "thou," "thou" being really the "I" obverted, that is, by being spoken to in the utterance of the Logos, and hence what comes to its own, having pushed out the inauthentic meanings such as the ego-sense that prevails in one's consciousness before hearing the utterance. That means that outside of the Logos one does not know the "I." The "I" has to be opened up by being shown that it is identical with "that." It is not something one can reach by mere contemplation that has no Logos-ground; it can only be reached by meditation (*upāsana*) upon what has been heard. But one can also contemplate it, aided by such concrete meditation, though not otherwise, as the utterance of the Logos alone can shatter the ordinary illusions. The contemplative thrust is, no doubt, there and must be accorded the freedom for full play both when we are dealing with the question of what is ultimately out there and when we are dealing with what is ultimately in our own selves. But to identify them is not one of the possibilities of mere contemplation, any more than it is one of the possibilities of mere speculation.

In any case this identity is the truth that resides at the center of the Upaniṣadic approach to the spiritual knowledge. But it is not a bare idea, either to be asserted or to be affirmed as a belief. On the contrary, it is understood as fullness that makes everything full, like the Truth that makes all true things true. It lives through all the worlds, all the vast and intricate structures of subtle and gross levels of Being, all the multifarious worlds of Becoming, not excluding the intricate mechanisms of reincarnation.

In the way the *Upaniṣad*(s) depict it, everything in the world, as seen and directed by the unseen Logos, leads up to "that thou art," while, if we step outside the *Upaniṣad*(s), it is not easy to see how things in the world, principles, relations, systematic arrangement of concepts, processes of inferences, systems of deductions, etc., could lead up to it, although the classical treatises of Indian philosophy have attempted to make it possible. But the last named too were not unaware of the great power as well as the great limitations under which they were working, inasmuch as they knew that they were building canals from the boundless lake of the *Upaniṣad*(s) themselves, nonetheless through terrains of accustomed human thinking and experience.

We do not say that the Logos "spoke" (in the past tense), as though the speaking is finished and done with. Rather, we say it "speaks," in and through the *Upaniṣad*(s); it still speaks, it always speaks as the very life of the language that appropriates what is being said, and so says it also. In this sense, the possibility of the spiritual knowledge, far from being extinguished or even gone into dead letter, dwells blazingly in the language which both keeps on saying and seizes that which is being said. M. Heidegger's description of language as the House of Being, if properly adapted, could have a message for us.[1] We are, however, concerned here only with "being" (what is indicated by *asi* in Sanskrit), not in any general sense but in the Upaniṣadic sense of oneness with the supreme Spirit as expressed by the utterance "that thou art." There can be no more revolutionary way of being than this, inasmuch as it overturns everything conceivable, and yet permits and even warrants the rebuilding of all things from this ground. Rebuilding the world from this ground would be the most creative task that the spiritual knowledge of the oneness of our own self with the supreme Spirit can entrust to us. This would be the continuing reenactment of the event, with the narration of which the AU commences: "The Self (Ātman) verily was this, one only, in the beginning. Nothing else whatsoever winked. He thought 'let me now create the worlds.' He created these worlds, water, light rays, death and the waters. . . . He thought, 'here now are the worlds, let me now create the guardians of the worlds.' From the waters themselves he drew forth the person and gave him shape. . . ."

Under the qualifications that we have to add to it, in view of the character of our kind of spiritual knowledge—and only under those qualifications—the following statement by Heidegger should prove very helpful: "In order to be who we are, we human beings remain committed to and within the

6. Seated Ascetics, 4th century A.D. Indian, Kashmir, Harwan.

being of language, and can never step out of it and look at it from somewhere else. Thus we always see the nature of language only to the extent to which language itself has us in view, has appropriated us to itself."[2]

The special ministration of the *Upaniṣad*(s) as that through which language continues to speak, even taking over as though it were the *Vicar of Being,* the very task of appropriation, is to put us, that is, the whole world, in the place and posture which is their own, namely, that of proximity to Brahman. That is where the possibility of realizing the identity with Brahman begins to translate into *lovable, intelligible, livable* reality, freed from the fog that seems to surround it when viewed from positions other than the postures characterizable by the word *upaniṣad.* These three attributes—lovable. intelligible, and livable—are the outcome of the three typical postures of nearness that we described earlier. It is undoubtedly true that the fog surrounding the idea of identity with Brahman is thick and impenetrable when looked at from ordinary religious and philosophical angles of vision, making the idea scary and uninviting.

The central characteristic of the Upaniṣadic vision of identity with Brahman is that such an identity is already there, timelessly, and yet is something obscured by ignorance (*avidyā*). We need to have an agency—the Logos—that will remove our blindfold of ignorance and enable us to see, to enter the gnosis of identity with Brahman. The ChU itself, in the course of the great teaching on "that thou art," narrates the following moving allegory (ChU 6.14.1–2):

> Just as, my dear, one might lead a person away from the Gāndhāra country, with his eyes blindfolded and leave him in a deserted place, and just as that person would cry out in all directions saying "I have been left here blindfolded, I have been left here blindfolded."
>
> And just as if [a passerby] removed his blindfold and told him "In that direction lies the Gāndhāra country, go in that direction," whereupon being so informed, and able to judge [for himself] he would, by asking [his way] from village to village, reach Gāndhāra. . . ."

The journey depicted here is simply one from ignorance to knowledge. The Logos puts us on the way. Posture means pointing the face in the direction of the identity with Brahman, rather than anything merely stationary. This is where we can see the Logos itself taking on the entirely new character of enacting a directional movement, implicit in the posture, that is, because the posture also means "poised to go forward." At this point we must bring to the surface the *praxis* of the spiritual knowledge which we have been considering. *Brahma-vidyā/Ātma-vidyā.* Therefore, let us turn to that as the final part of our discussion.

The Question of Praxis

This is a very big matter in the *Upaniṣad*(s) and one in which every approach—there are several—penetrates every other approach. We may start with the Logos-language aspect of *praxis*, as befits the major attention we have devoted to that up to now. But we learn that we cannot isolate it from the ritual, the ethical, and what we may single out, perhaps, by the name "yogic," inasmuch as it is well known for its practical character. However, everything else we have mentioned is practical too.

As for Logos-language we have all along been made aware of its role in revealing and speaking and in giving knowledge of things that cannot be known otherwise. But we have also just seen something of its power to enact the directional movement implicit in the posture called *upaniṣad*. But something new is still coming: we see it as a vehicle that can actually carry the aspirant toward identity with Brahman. In that character we meet with it in the form of invocation and chant, and this is most elaborately expressed in the ChU, which may be described, in large part, as a gigantic laying out of the hidden meanings of the most sacred of the sounds, *AUM*, the primordial phoneme, or *akṣara*. That *Upaniṣad* begins thus: "*AUM* is this phoneme (*aum iti etad akṣaram*), meditate on it as the *udgītha* (which is the most potent of the Vedic chants), for one sings the chant with *AUM*." Śaṇkara comments that *AUM* is the addressing name for the supreme Spirit (*aum ityedat akṣaram paramātmo 'bhidhānaṁ nediṣṭam*). In that sense, *AUM* is the declaratory name *Brahman* itself, expressed in an address form. It is also a symbol (*pratīkam*) of the supreme Spirit. Hence, meditate on it (*upāsīta*) as the old sacred chant—*udgītha*—says the *Upaniṣad* itself. In several places in the explanation that follows in that same first section of the first chapter [and further on as well] there are references to "one who knows this" (*ya etad evam vidvān; etad evam veda*). The word for "know" here is from the root *vid*, from which comes *vidyā*, as also *veda* and *vidvān*, both meaning "one who knows," "that which knows." This knowing is extraordinary in its connotation in that it is depicted as a participant in what may be called true doing. It rescues doing (*karma*, or *kriyā*) from the latter's naturally ambivalent equipoise toward what is true and what is untrue. So this section concludes with the statement: "One who knows thus, and one who does not know, both do [it]. But knowledge and ignorance, are divergent. What one does with knowledge (*vidyā*), attentive reverence (*śraddhā*) and *upaniṣad*, that indeed becomes the greater in power. This truly is the explanation of the phoneme [AUM]."

As observed, a good part, the earlier part, of the ChU has to do with chanting for the sake of invoking, that is, "evoking" into the active expression of the Logos, as vehicle and means of fulfillment, the power which is distinctly that of knowledge.

In a strange way, several of the great *Upaniṣad*(s) can be said to take some aspect of *praxis* or other as the approach to spiritual knowledge. If the ChU has chant as the route, then the BĀU may be said to have the sacrificial act (rite) in the same way. It also utters the auspicious sound *AUM* at the commencement, but proceeds immediately to describe the cosmos as the horse that is ritually sacrificed. But as already remarked, interpenetration of chant, rite performance, ethics, and yoga, etc. is ubiquitous. In several of the *Upaniṣad*(s), cosmology is an important element, not for the purposes of theoretical contemplation but for the purposes of practical meditation (*upāsana*), based on some key, verbally expressed symbol or the ultimate phoneme *AUM* itself standing for the self-evoking aspect of Brahman.

The idea of *AUM* itself is used in different *Upaniṣad*(s) in various ways. Thus, as a supreme instance, let us take up the MĀU, which also commences with the same four words that the ChU begins with: "*AUM* is this phoneme" (*aum iti etat akṣaram*). But it goes on to link it with the cosmos, with the words "[it is] all this" (*idam Sarvam*), including within it the three divisions of time; the three natural states (*sthāna*) of consciousness—waking, dreaming, and deep sleep—and the corresponding three cosmic levels, also pointing, in respect of both consciousness states and cosmic levels, to a fourth (*turīya*) that transcends them. Nonetheless, *AUM* here too is the vehicle that gathers up all levels of cosmic and psychic Being and carries them to the point where they are resolved, itself remaining, however, as the Ātman. Therefore, "one who knows this enters the very Ātman with one's *ātman*" (MĀU 12).

AUM is *praxis* itself, as expressed in meditation and utterance. *AUM* is the transcending act, which is well described, likened to the discharge of the arrow, in the MU 2.2.4: "Taking as the bow the great Upaniṣadic weapon, one should place in it the arrow sharpened by meditation. Drawing it with a mind immersed in meditation of that [Brahman], know the imperishable [Brahman] as the target." *Praxis* in the MU has much to do with ascetic discrimination that tends toward a wise combination of renunciation and work (in the ritual sense). "Sporting in the Ātman, rejoicing in the Ātman, doing work, such a one is the greatest among the knowers of Brahman" (3.1.4).

The *Īśā* too has a similar approach to *praxis*, combining the spirit of renunciation with the spirit of dutiful work and service, but controlled by a sense of total and universal divine presence. The first two stanzas of this short *Upaniṣad* contain a call to find joy in renunciation and simultaneously to seek a long life (of a hundred years' duration) devoted to work. The ethical approach to *praxis* is most prominent in this *Upaniṣad*, as in parts of most others, especially the MU.

At the end now, we must deal with the Yoga approach to *praxis*. Of the places in the *Upaniṣads* where this figures largely we must mention Kaṭha U 1.3.12–17; SvU 2.8–13; Maitri U 6.18ff.

In the Kaṭha U the word path (*pathaḥ*) is itself used to indicate yogic *praxis*, where there is a rousing call to wake up. "Arise, awake. . . . Sharp as the edge of a razor, hard to traverse, untreadable is this path, the wise ones declare."

The SvU speaks about crossing the fearsome streams by the raft of Brahman (2.8) and recommends "holding the body in poise . . . enabling the senses and the mind to enter the heart." It furnishes the prescriptions for the control of breath, seating oneself in the right environment for concentration etc., and also describes the first results of yogic progress, such as lightness, healthiness, steadiness, glow of complexion, melodiousness of voice, etc.

The Maitri U gives a list of members (*ṣaḍanga*) of yoga (breath control, withdrawal of the senses, meditation, concentration, reasoning, and absorptive union). [The Yoga system of Patañjali, however, has eight members, commencing with two preliminary moral steps, negative and positive—restraint and commitment, respectively—and body position (*āsana*) added, and reasoning (*tarka*) taken out.] There are also clear prescriptions for remaining void of conceptions and for achieving non-thought (or disengagement from thinking, de-thinking, we might say) (6.20). Further, this *Upaniṣad* discusses meditation on *AUM,* which to it is the sound by which one achieves what is non-sound. [Non-sound is very much the same as *turīya,* or the "fourth," of the MĀU.]

Before we conclude our inquiry into the *praxis* aspect of the Upaniṣadic spiritual knowledge, we have to observe that we have not even scratched the surface of what these great texts have to say on it, just as that would be true of spiritual knowledge *per se*. Yet what we have been able to cover would give a rather useful, preliminary, preview of the matter. At this point, another observation may be made, which concerns the air of tranquillity that completely pervades the entire vision of *Brahma-vidyā/Ātman-vidyā* as well as its *praxis*. It does belong entirely to, is the supreme instance of and the total embodiment of, the tranquillity of the Spirit. All creativity, all making—and all unmaking—all becoming and passing away are under the gnosis which eternally keeps coming to us in the words "that art thou," enabling us to remain in a posture of proximity to what is Ultimately Real.

The Question of Study of the Upaniṣads within Spiritual Praxis

The spiritual *praxis* taught by the *Upaniṣad*(s) definitely includes, and indeed in a preeminent way, something called "study" (*svādhyāya*). It is clear that the subject of study is what is characterizable by the name *upaniṣad*, some no doubt already formed as texts, and some yet to be formed, around subtle indications of certain concrete postures of proximity to Brahman, thanks to the Logos (*Vāk*). The answer to the puzzle of how the *Upaniṣad*(s) could have meant some already existing texts as subject of study becomes quite simple if we but realize that the emergence of the *Upaniṣad*(s) as texts took place during a certain dispensation of grace, within a certain span of time, where each present moment of speaking was a self-conscious junction of the past and the future, of what has already taken place and what still dwelt in the region of anticipation. This defiance of history is the freedom that marks the *Upaniṣad*(s) as the sacred texts that they are.

Earlier on in this essay, we made two remarks which may be recalled here apropos of the place of the *Upaniṣad*(s) within spiritual *praxis:* (1) "The human practice of this spiritual knowledge is nothing but participation in the self-active possibility of the Logos by way of the *Upaniṣad*(s)"; (2) "The *Upaniṣad*(s) themselves *are* the possibility of spiritual life housed in them." Now, "study" (*svādhyāya*) is the human activity of unlocking and releasing such possibility. It is coordinate with other spiritual activities, principally meditation (*upāsanā*), contemplation (*dhyāna, nididhyāsana*), etc., aimed at *Brahman*-realization (*sākṣātkāra*).

What is meant by study is the search of the scriptures, the *Upaniṣad*(s) as a whole, within the frame of reference of what the *Upaniṣad*(s) are, as we have already explained. It is conducted in terms of the inexhaustible plenitude of truths that they reveal, holding the searcher in a state of unending wonder and astonishment. Study, no doubt, has something specifically to do with the life of the mind, inasmuch as it provides our own regenerated thought with the unprecedented knowledge that its real ground is gnosis itself, it especially being newly empowered to review its own previous gropings in search of Ultimate Reality.

This dimension of study is central to the spirituality of the *Upaniṣad*(s). It makes possible, along with meditation and all the rest, a mode of being which reflects and shapes itself in accordance with gnosis. As for gnosis, the *Upaniṣad*(s) do not give us cause to think that it is one path, or way (*mārga*), among several, including such things as devotion (*bhakti*) and action/rite (*karma*). Gnosis, on the other hand, is the whole thing, all-embracing, certainly including devotion but in a special way action/rite also. For it abhors nothing whatsoever that is holy.

This spirituality is, so to say, suspended from above, from the Spirit (Brahman/Ātman) itself, and not something projected by human efforts upward. The so-called way of gnosis is simply a way of describing this gnosis spirituality starting with the Spirit itself. In fact, insofar as it is not a description of something that a human being does, it cannot be spoken of as a "way" (*mārga*) at all. This spirituality is not the characterization of some particular activity or attribute of human beings, discernible within the individual and collective human psyche, even if it were possible to establish such things without being challenged by an opposite point of view, as all views are. Accordingly, even if "a rumor of angels" were to be proved by psycho-social study (particular reference here being to Peter Berger's book by that name), the *Upaniṣad*(s) would be entirely indifferent to it. Furthermore, the spirituality of the *Upaniṣad*(s) would be altogether independent of what may or may not be established as the beginnings of human religious belief, or the end thereof, for that matter. In like manner, it does not also depend on the efficacy and veracity of mysticism, although it is able to render mysticism authentic in a preeminent manner.

However, when one is seized by the independent, authentic spirituality of the *Upaniṣad*(s) through studious engagement with it, one would also realize that it is truly the actualization of what man is capable of doing with himself spiritually (though not *by* himself) provided he is set on the course of knowing the Spirit. What is purely human is this proviso, which, by its essential nature, is subjected to a self-obliterating dialectic, for no one who has been set on the course of knowing the Spirit could seriously think that he had a genuine alternative to the contrary. Hence, in this sense the question of an optional way does not arise within the sphere of gnosis.

Now, as for the clause "the actualization of what man is capable of doing with himself spiritually," there is a catch, despite the proviso that man is set on the course of knowing the Spirit, for, on deeper reflection upon the way of human beings and upon human nature, we will discover that even that proviso, in order to be fulfilled, will have to be taken over by the *Upaniṣad*(s). In this connection we must recall a statement made at an earlier stage with respect to the *Upaniṣad*(s) taking over as the *Vicar of Being*, the very task of appropriating the posture of proximity to Brahman. Yet, as in the case of everything vicarous, man must do his part, which means fulfilling to the best of his Yoga-nurtured ability all spiritual and moral/ritual things he would otherwise be called upon to fulfill, based upon the laws of the heart as well as the laws of religion. And yet, beyond these laws appears the new spiritual dimension of "study" (of the *Upaniṣad*(s)), which has to do solely with gnosis. This dimension, however, does not by any means imply neglect of the obligation to fulfill the preceding laws, though it is independent of them. The following passage (TU 1.9.1) will illustrate the matter well, being the charge given to the newly ordained disciples sent out into the world in these words:

> [Observe] the holy order of the cosmos (*ṛta*) as well as study and teaching (of the *Upaniṣads*); truth as well as study and teaching; penance as well as study and teaching; control of external organs as well as study and teaching; control of internal senses as well as study and teaching; sacrificial fires as well as study and teaching; [specifically] the *Agnihotra* sacrifice [burnt offering] as well as study and teaching; hospitality as well as study and teaching; [care for] the human race as well as study and teaching; [concern for] continuance of the human race as well as study and teaching; [the sacred obligation of] begetting as well as study and teaching.

It would have been noticed that each of these laws, ritual/ethical, is followed by the admonition to study and to teach. To begin with, it must be understood that the holy order of the cosmos (*ṛta*) is here enjoined as something to be performed regularly as a rite and in fact that character is attached to all those things individually mentioned subsequently. As Śaṇkara explains, "these things, *ṛta*, etc., are something to be observed as rites" (*etāni ṛtādīni anuṣṭeyāni iti vākyaśeṣaḥ*).

Ultimately it may be said that man has to approach even moral things through that which makes them moral, through their transcendent element, by reverting to the ritual, in which sense it may be truly said that the ritual is man's authentic approach to the moral realm directly via its concealed upper opening, although in the deluded world it may appear to be divorced from that realm, both to those who do as well as to those who witness or watch.

What is added to the fulfillment of the listed laws of the heart and religion is study and teaching. As has already been called attention to, the word "study" is an insipid translation of *svādhyāya*—and "teaching" an even blander translation of *pravacana*, which may be more literally rendered as "forth-telling," that is, telling with no holds barred, with no prevarication or superimposition or distortion. Śaṇkara gives as equivalents to these *adhyayana* and *adhyāpana*, which mean learning for oneself and causing others to learn respectively, two sides of the same, essentially contiguous spiritual fact. As for the side of causing others to learn, or *pravacana* (*adhyāpana*), we learn that it is not an afterthought or innocent continuation of study, but its true destiny. Śaṇkara interprets it as the *Brahman-sacrifice*, *brahmayajña*, showing that, while following in the wake of other rites, it is the highest rite (or, rather, non-rite), inasmuch as it is the gnosis act focused on Brahman. Now the very existence of the *Upaniṣad*(s) is above all the performance of this rite, and the learner but participates in it by virtue of his study, which is the preparation to undertake meditation (*upāsana*).

What is called *brahmayajña* is the nonspecific *upāsana*, the highest of all, but it is, nonetheless, conducted through specific *upāsana*(s) (steps), as *brahmayajña* itself encourages the use of symbols. And as for *upāsana*, it is not the case that when we begin it we leave the *Upaniṣad*(s) behind and do it on our own. For the *Upaniṣad*(s), insofar as they are the *Vicar of Being*, are already in the business of *upāsana*, and our business is but to participate in what is being done, most of all in their existence.

In order to discover this we do not have far to go, for the very passage we have just quoted is set in the context of the *Upaniṣad*(s) themselves being in the business of *upāsana*, which, again, expressed nonspecfically, is *brahmayajña* as such. The context is the preceding section (TU 1.8). A few pages back we referred to the beginning of the ChU, which is a call to meditate (do *upāsana*) on *AUM* the syllable as the *udgītha*, the most potent of the Vedic chants. We also referred there to Śaṇkara's comment that *AUM* is the addressing name for Brahman, that it is a symbol (*pratīkam*) of Brahman. In the context we are speaking about now (TU 1.8.1) that symbolic identity of *AUM* and *Brahman*, for the sake of *upāsana*, is expressly stated:

> *AUM* is *Brahman*. *AUM* is all. *AUM* is "the doing after" (*anukṛti*) [the rite that follows itself]. On uttering "recite," they recite. With *AUM* they sing the holy canticles (*sāmans*). With *AUM* the *Adhvaryu* priest utters the response. With *AUM* the Brahmān priest recites the introductory praise. With *AUM* one says "even so" or consents (*anujānāti*) to the burnt-offering rite (*agnihotram*). With *AUM* a *Brahman*-knower says "May I obtain Brahman" and he obtains Brahman.

This is one of the passages which express the approach to gnosis in terms of the dialectics of the rites, thereby taking the rites too beyond themselves: such, of course, is the character of what we have come across as *brahmayajña*, or *Brahman-sacrifice*. But here it is conducted by means of the specific *upāsana* on *AUM* as the symbol of Brahman. The *Upaniṣad* itself is the conduct of this *upāsana*, and we but participate in it.

But it is always necessary to remember that the *Upaniṣad*(s) are texts of orthodoxy, which means that no excess, even of the symbolic, is permitted. Every self-exceeding mysticism too is under check. Scrupulous adherence to the operational canons of every level of reality is required. The symbol (*pratīka*) is not in the *Upaniṣad*(s) an accidental, laissez-faire arrival, as might be in the case of poetry, but something deliberately chosen by reason of a prior resolution on the part of the chooser and also by reason of some rationally determinable innate property of the object chosen—and sanctioned by the tradition. In cases especially when the symbol is visual, a further consecration (*abhiṣeka*) is necessary. Then it properly becomes an image (*pratimā*). But in the case of *AUM*, otherwise called *praṇava*, it comes self-consecrated, but still works like an image.

Accordingly, commenting on the Upaniṣadic declaration "*AUM* is Brahman," Śaṇkara writes: "The Logos in the form of *AUM* is Brahman. So it must be up-held [or, be-held] by the mind, meditated on/worshipped" (*aumityetad śabdarūpam brahmeti manasā dhārayedupāsīta*). There is no tendency to attribute properties of consciousness to *AUM:* that would be excessiveness of the symbolic enterprise. And yet *upāsana* on *AUM* is efficacious. For as Śaṇkara's expositor Ānandagiri observes:

> How can *AUM* being a mere sound [or Logos] and as such [inherently] non-sentient, and devoid of knowledge, grant the fruits of meditation? [Answer:] As in the case of adoration offered to an image it is God alone who always grants the fruits, even so is the modality here (*nanu auṁkārasya śabdamātrasya acetanatvād-aham-anena upāsīta iti jñānābhāvāt kaṭham phaladātṛtvam syat . . . pratimādyar-canamiva sarvadhā īśvara eva phaladātā iti bhāva*).

It is also abundantly clear that the fact that the *Upaniṣad*(s) act as the *Vicar of Being* does not entail the slightest tendency to deify them or generate some kind of book-worship. As for *upāsana,* it is what the *Upaniṣad*(s) themselves do—and are—and by virtue of that fact, we do; it is not something done *to* them, or *upon* them. They bear the symbols but are not symbols themselves.

Their position as the manifestation of the Logos and as the *Vicar of Being* is something to be maintained, and no doubt even debated, with the aid of logic. Yet alongside that, they are studied not only for the wonder they constantly open to us, but also so that we may participate in what they themselves are and do, which no human being, however learned, intelligent, or wise, which no philosopher, no scientist, no sage, or, for that matter, no saint, can be or do—or know. They contain many ladders of descent of gnosis—which are also ladders of ascent for us. Because of that the *Upaniṣad*(s) own *upāsana*(s) are a waiting for the *parousia* of gnosis; and our participation too is such waiting. The ChU itself tells us in 3.14.1, *sarvam khalu idam brahma* (All is *Brahman;* translate it as "all is well because all is Brahman"); *tajjalān* (it is that from which everything comes forth, in which everything is preserved and lives); *iti śānta upāsīta* ([therefore] meditatively wait, silently, quietly). Let us add, "for the *parousia*."

Notes

1. M. Heidegger, *The Way to Language* (New York: Harper & Row, 1971) 5, 21, 135.
2. Ibid., 134.

Bibliography

Sources

Gambhirananda, Swami, trans. *Eight Upaniṣads.* Vols. 1 and 2. With the commentary of Śaṇkara. Calcutta: Advaita Ashram, 1973, 1977.

——. *The Chandogyopanisad.* With the commentary of Śaṇkara. Calcutta: Advaita Ashram, 1986

Jha, Sir Ganganatha, trans. *The Chāndogyopaniṣad.* With the commentary of Śaṇkara. Poona Oriental Series 78. Poona: Oriental Book Agency, 1942.

Madhavananda, Swami, trans. *The Brhadaranyaka Upanisad.* With the commentary of Śaṇkara. Mayavati: Almora, 1950.

Nikhilananda, Swami. *The Mandukya Upanisad.* With *Gaudapadakarika* and the commentary of Śaṇkara. Mysore: Ramakrishna Ashram, 1955, 1958, etc.

——. *The Upanisads.* Translation with introduction, notes, and explanations, based on the commentaries of Śaṇkara. New York: Bonanza Books, 1949–59.

Pandit, M. P. *The Upanisads: The Gateway of Knowledge.* Madras: Ganesh, 1966.

Radhakrishnan, S. *The Principal Upanisads.* Edited with introduction; text in roman; translation and notes. London: Allen & Unwin, 1951.

Renou, Louis. *Les Upanisads.* Texte et traduction sous la direction de Louis Renou. Paris: Adrien-Maisonneuve, 1948.

Studies

Arapura, J. G. *Gnosis and the Question of Thought in Vedanta.* Dordrecht, Holland, 1986.

——. *Hermeneutical Essays on Vedantic Topics.* Delhi: Motilal Banarsidass, 1986.

Deussen, Paul. *The Philosophy of the Upanishads.* Translated by A. S. Gedden. New York: Dover, 1966.

Part Two

THE SPIRITUAL HORIZON OF DHARMA

5

Spiritual Foundations of Caste

KENNETH H. POST

CASTE REFERS TO A HIERARCHICAL classification of people in India whereby they are known to themselves and to others. While the living phenomenon of caste is awesomely complex in its distinctions and implications for human activity, it is identified within the texts held sacred by most Hindus as consisting essentially of four main divisions, who are from best to worst *Brāhmin, Kṣatriya, Vaiśya,* and *Śūdra.* The first three of these are called the twice-born castes and are "caste" proper. Chaṇḍālās and the untouchables are sometimes considered to be castes and to be continuous with Śūdras, but in the ChU, for example, they are treated as less than some types of animals. This social division is described and prescribed in a large set of texts, written roughly between the fifth century B.C. and the fifth century A.D., called *dharmasūtra*(s), which have the character of legal codes.

The prescription of social order is a type of political thought. Any thinking and hence writing which has a bearing on the ordering of human society is political thought, and hence all of the writings called *dharmasūtra*(s) together with their commentaries are political thought. But when one asks for the reasons for these particular thoughts and asks, more particularly, what reason we have for thinking that these thoughts outline the best human order, then political philosophy has begun. The fundamental reasons which lead to the conclusion that a particular ordering of human beings is best are the foundations of that order. Insofar as those foundations are seen to rest in or be explained within the teachings of God or revelation, they may be called spiritual foundations or, to use Spinoza's language, "theologico-political" foundations. While *dharmaśāstra* has in it few fundamental reasons or examples of political philosophy, it refers us to other sacred revelations for its foundations. In these revelations and the explanation of their reasons by commentators occur the spiritual foundations of the caste system. By tracing these foundations back through to the *dharma-sūtra*(s), it will be evident that they are in fact the reasons according to the tradition for what is prescribed.

The understanding of caste among recent scholars has for the most part been relegated to those concerned with describing caste as it has existed in India over the last century.[1] Studies concerned with a theoretical account such as those of L. Dumont and É. Senart have tended to rely on original insights into the structuring principles of human society instead of giving an account of indigenous written thoughts on the matter. Thus, a tradition of scholarship about Indian political philosophy has failed to materialize, in spite of some isolated efforts.[2] There are a number of causes for this, not the least of which is the relatively recent tradition in Western political philosophy of separating political thought from religious and cultural conditioning.[3] Another cause is the character of Hindu political thought: its own tradition of political philosophy as we know it is scant, and the tradition most common to modern scholars, that of Vedanta, argues that political philosophy is impossible, as will be discussed below. Finally, the interaction of the lack of scholarly historical interest among sociologists of India, the lack of cross-cultural historical studies among political philosophers, and the absence of political philosophy in recognizable form in Indian literature has supported a widespread tendency among students of Indian philosophy to consider religion and theology separately from political and social order.[4]

All of these reasons notwithstanding, it is a commonplace among students of caste to state at the very least that there is a close relation between religion and caste. More particularly and pertinent to the theme of this article, it is the religious leaders or teachers who determine questions of caste violation and consequent loss of caste.[5] It is, moreover, commonplace among students of classical Indian legal literature to state that the foundation of social and political order is asserted by the indigenous tradition to rest in the Veda.[6] How this foundation is laid has been most often a matter of conjecture or, at best, cataloguing.[7] Theoretical accounts of how this foundation could have been laid within the terms of the tradition are very few. The most outstanding description of how the literary tradition views caste law to be established is in G. Jha, *Hindu Law in Its Sources.* There the foundation of law is said to rest in four primary things:

> From the above we conclude that all authorities are agreed on the following points—(a) The Veda is the first and paramount authority; (b) the Smṛti is authoritative only in so far as it is not repugnant to the Veda, to which it owes its authority; and only on matters on which we have no paramount authority; (c) Practices or Customs are trustworthy guides, only as they are

> current among the "cultured," and then too only those that are not repugnant to Vedic or Smṛti texts; (d) the judgement of the "Assembly" of the learned is to be accepted as authoritative only when it is not repugnant to the Veda, and only when the judgement is "unbiased" by improper feelings. There is not a single text, or "explanation," which favours the opinion that Custom is to override original texts—an opinion that has been upheld by the privy Council, and endorsed by eminent writers on Anglo-Hindu Law. Neither Vijñaneshvara (*Mitāksarā*) nor Jīmūtavāhana (*Dharmaratna*) nor Nīlakaṇṭha (*Mayūkha*) countenances any such view; and these three are regarded by our lawyers as the founders of the principal "Schools of Law."[8]

There can be little question that the Veda, by which is meant the *saṃhitā*(s), *brāhmaṇa*(s), and *upaniṣad*(s) was thought by the *dharmaśāstra* to be the foundation for all social order.[9] But caste is what determines access to Veda. Hopkins points out, for example, that the castes are ordered in part by their degree of access to Veda.[10] The doorway to Veda is in fact to have caste;[11] but without the knowledge of how to behave, which rests in Veda, losing caste is almost inevitable unless, of course, one is correctly instructed by a *Brāhmin.* It follows that the crucial information which Veda must provide is what actions result in the loss of caste. Without this information, law would be cut off from its foundation and human beings would not have access to salvation.

In what follows, the theoretical reasons within the terms of the classical tradition for grounding social order in Veda will be explored and the implications of these reasons for a particular theological view of human spirit will be considered. The centrality of justice and hence political and social order to the classical religious tradition having been seen, we will then examine the legal texts that determine loss of caste or exclusion from the regulated social order. By looking at what causes the loss of caste we will be able to see what the presence of caste represents within the terms of the classical tradition. The presence of caste is central to the possibility of access to the Veda and hence salvation. In examining the *dharmasūtra*(s) in which loss of caste is described, it will become evident that this is in fact one of the rare parts in which Veda is specifically quoted and referred to in detail.

We note that caste is established at the same time in Veda that it is taught that the overcoming of caste is part of salvation. The reason for this paradox is that caste is established by the argument that right human political order cannot be determined by reason alone, while salvation rests in knowledge itself. The absence of political philosophy in India is due to the belief in Hinduism that reason is not capable of discovering right political order. The foundation of social order is in fact human ignorance, coupled with right actions. That is, one's caste is determined by a history of right actions and the absence of that knowledge which is sufficient to cause the end of rebirth. Caste is at once an affirmation of justice and right actions and a reminder of the pervasive existence of wrong and the ignorance of those participating in existence. Caste is a constant reminder of the contingency of political order and the fact that human welfare transcends the political.

The Reasoning of the ChU about Caste and Capital Crime

The most important Vedic text about caste and the loss of caste is ChU 5.3–5.10. The importance of this passage is recognized by the fact that all of *Vedāntasutra*(s) III.1 (also called *Brahmasūtra*(s)) is devoted to discussing this part of the ChU. What caste means to the tradition or what its foundations are by the religion's own account is said in the commentaries on these sutras. The commentary of Śaṇkara on *Vedāntasutra*(s) III.1.8 and III.2.41 states clearly that the conditions of all creatures are due to previous actions for which they are responsible. The foundation of caste is reward or punishment for actions in a previous life.

> Moreover, the different degrees of enjoyment which are implied in the difference of birth on the part of the living beings point, as they cannot be accidental, to the existence of such a remainder of works. For we know from scripture that good fortune as well as misfortune is caused by good and evil works. Sm*ri*ti also teaches that the members of the different castes and âsramas do, in accordance with their works, at first enjoy the fruit of their works and then enter into new existences, in which they are distinguished from each other by locality, caste, family, shape, length of life, knowledge, conduct, property, pleasure, and intelligence; which doctrine implies that they descend with a remainder of their works. (Thibaut, pt. 2; 3, 1, 8, p. 114)

Rāmānuja in his comment on the same passage quotes *Gautama Dharma Sūtra* 2,11,12–13 and *Āpastamba-dharma-sūtra* 2,1,2–3 in support of the same view. "The castes and the stages in life depend on one's own Karman. . . ."[12] That is, all the conditions of all the creatures are just and one of these conditions is caste (*varnā*).

Śaṇkara's comment on *Vedāntasutra*(s) II.1.34 is consistent with this view: ". . . the circumstance of the creation being unequal is due to the merit and demerit of the living creatures created, and is not a fault for which the Lord is to blame" (Thibaut, pt. 1, p. 358). Thus, the Hindu commentators observe that many people exist in terrible conditions and undergo great misfortune. In contemplating these things the question arises, how could a good God permit such things: the starvation of the young, incurable diseases, and the wretched untouchables. The commentators answer that these conditions—

in fact, all differences in condition—are due to the actions[13] of these creatures and entities in previous lives. They were responsible for these actions and therefore the present conditions are just. This argument to preserve the goodness of God and the assurance that God rules with justice leads to the next question. How could there ever have come to be any differences at all? It follows from this, according to Śaṇkara and Rāmānuja, that the differences in the world must be beginningless (*Vedāntasutras* [*VS*] II.1.35). The foundations consisting of justice, a good God, and the beginninglessness of creation are what dictate the existence of caste. Caste, in other words, is implicit to the beginninglessness of creation. It follows for human beings from their responsibility for their own fates that they must learn to do what is right. But how can what it is right to do be determined if the causes of present conditions are locked away in previous births? What is right is in principle unknowable without revelation or Veda.

Śaṇkara offers two other arguments in two places for the necessity of scripture for both knowledge about right action and for release from transmigration. In *VS* II.1.11 he argues from the diversity of human opinions and the difficulty of the subject of political or moral order to the necessity of Veda for certain knowledge about foundational principles. In *VS* III.1.26 he argues from the absence of any ultimate categorical imperatives to the need for scripture to set down rules which are not bound together by any perceptible logical coherency.

> Our knowledge of what is duty and the contrary of duty depends entirely on scripture. The knowledge of one action being right and another wrong is based on scripture only; for it lies out of the cognizance of the senses, and there moreover is, in the case of right and wrong, an entire want of binding rules as to place, time and occasion. What in one place, at one time, on one occasion is performed as a right action, is a wrong action in another place, at another time, on another occasion; none therefore can know, without scripture, what is either right or wrong. (Thibaut, pt. 2, p. 131)

The example that follows is one in which killing, which is prohibited in some circumstances, is required in others.

The impossibility of human reason determining right action and hence right social order thus has at least three causes. (1) Whatever exists now is based on the results of a beginningless series of actions by beginningless entities all of which have a just outcome, but this set of results arises not from the immediate past but from a set of unknowable previous births.[14] (2) What is right or wrong varies with the circumstances so much that right or wrong cannot be deduced or extrapolated from one correct action to the next. Equal justice under the law is not only impossible, but law cannot be regulated by precedents as each case is necessarily unique.[15] (3) Human opinion is so diverse that reason is powerless to reach any accurate assessment of it. Political philosophy under these circumstances is a futile activity. Reason is powerless to explain political order, and consequently the foundation for human beings of political order must be ignorance. Thus it is that only those who know in the ChU can violate caste prohibitions with impunity (ChU 5.10.10 and ChU 5.24.4).

The consequence of loss of access to Veda is uncertainty about right action, and uncertainty about right action means that wrong action is virtually inevitable. Thus, the most important sanction with respect to human behavior becomes the loss of access to Veda. This sanction is what distinguishes twice-born caste from non-twice-born (*VS* I.3.34 and I.2.38). The most important laws about human behavior will then be those describing what must absolutely be avoided in order not to lose caste. These are the laws which then are in fact foundational to political and social order. To put it differently, if all people were to do things leading to loss of caste over a long time, there would not be a caste system because no one would be born into the twice-born castes. Conversely, those born into the twice-born castes know at least that they have not done the most reprehensible things.

Dharmasūtra(s) on Capital Crime and Loss of Caste

The *Gautama Dharma Sūtra* (*Gau*), considered by many to be the earliest of the extant *dharmasūtra*(s), was considered to be especially important by followers of the ChU,[16] and is certainly one of the most clearly organized. This makes it a useful *dharmasūtra* to study for discerning the relation of the different components of *dharmasūtra*(s) in general to themselves and for studying the relation of Veda to law.

The text, broadly speaking, describes how the castes live, how to avoid loss of caste—particularly subsequent to death—and what is most likely to produce loss of caste in the next life. Caste then can be seen as a prescribed way of life which is self-perpetuating and which has certain behavioral limits beyond which caste is lost. Caste is sustained by behaving in accord with caste prescriptions. Negatively, caste is the result of not having done those things which cause loss of caste. One is a caste member by virtue of obedience from all time to the rules of caste. Insofar as one is concerned about caste in general and not specific castes, the foundation of caste is, according to *Gau* XXI, not having ever done those things which cause the irreparable loss of caste. Conversely, as will be discussed later, those without caste will have committed, at some point in their previous lives, one of the crimes causing loss of caste. Assuming that human beings are the products of rebirth, or, in other words, assuming the beginninglessness of creation, the prescriptive foundation of caste is most likely to be found by examining what causes the loss of caste.

Gau XXI sets forth the actions causing loss of caste while *Gau* XXII–XXIV describes possible penances. Thus the institution of caste is described negatively as follows:

> To be an outcaste means to be deprived of the right to follow the lawful occupations of twice-born men, and to be deprived after death of the rewards of meritorious deeds. Some call (this condition) hell. (*Āpastamba* . . . , *Gau* XXI.4–6, p. 277

The basic crimes causing loss of caste are listed in *Gau* XXI.1–3.

> The murderer of a Brahmana,
> he who drinks spiritous liquor,
> the violator of a Guru's bed,
> he who has connexion with the female relatives of his mother and of his father (within six degrees) or with sisters and their female offspring,
> he who steals (the gold of a Brahmana), an atheist,
> he who constantly repeats blamable acts,
> he who does not cast off persons guilty of a crime causing loss of caste, and
> he who forsakes blameless (relatives), become outcasts.
> Likewise those who instigate others to acts causing loss of caste, and he who for a (whole) year associates with outcasts. [*Āpastamba* . . . , pp. 276–77]

The remainder of *Gau* XXI describes this list in more detail. The text states that according to Manu, the first three of the crimes in this list cannot be expiated and therefore the text pays most attention to these three crimes. It offers a series of difficult penances for each crime in contrast to the statement about expiation. This contrast might be resolved by the recognition that the penances are virtually impossible to perform. Thus, *Gau* XXII is concerned with murder; *Gau* XXIII is concerned with drinking and adultery; *Gau* XXIV is about having committed these three types of crimes without having been discovered. Not having been discovered relieves the criminal of both the need for difficult penance and consequently concern about loss of caste. The list of serious crimes (*mahāpātaka*) is revised somewhat in the concluding summary statement of *Gau* XXIV.10, which is very similar to *Manu* XI.55, IX.235 and XI.48–54.

> Or, for the murder of a Brahmana, for drinking spiritous liquor, for stealing (gold), and for the violation of a Guru's bed, he may perform . . . [*Āpastamba* . . . , p. 290)

The text describes different degrees of commission of these crimes. Its discussion of intentional *Brāhmin* murder is instructive. All *dharmasūtra*(s) are in agreement that *Brāhmin* murder is the one crime for which there cannot be expiation. *Gau* XXI.9 describes the loss of caste of a woman as firstly "by procuring abortion," that is, by performing a type of *Brāhmin* murder. *Gau* XXI.20–22 describes acts which come progressively closer to *Brāhmin* murder immediately after which comes *Gau* XXII, penances for *Brāhmin* murder. Following these penances a list of murders in declining order of importance begins with three kinds of *Brāhmin* murder (*Gau* XXII.11–13): (1) a failed attempt in the life of a *Brāhmin;* (2) killing a female *Brāhmin* who is not polluted by menstruation; and (3) killing a *Brāhmin* embryo at any stage of gestation.[17] The list of murders then is ordered from *Kṣatriya*(s) to frogs and all the way down to prostitutes. It is noteworthy that while penances for drinking and stealing are followed by the statements "he will be purified after death," the same statement does not follow after the penances for *Brāhmin* murder (with the possible exception of a vaguer but similar statement at *Gau* XXII.6). This would then lend weight to the statement in *Manu Smṛti* (as opposed to the statement ascribed to Manu in *Gau*) that no atonement for killing a *Brāhmin* is possible.[18] It follows that the twice-born have not committed the crimes mentioned. If they have committed the crimes, they have performed the proper penance where the crime admits of expiation.

Through all these examples of discussions of crimes which cause loss of caste certain consistencies are striking. One consistency is that, while lists of such crimes may vary among texts, each text is likely to list as well four particular crimes: killing a *Brāhmin*, stealing gold, drinking alcohol, and adultery with one's guru's wife. Each of these major types of crime is likely to have a number of ways of being committed. All of the texts, though, are most clear on only one type of ambiguous variation; they all explain that abortion of a *Brāhmin* at any stage of development is a type of *Brāhmin* murder. While atonement is permitted for each of these crimes with the common exception of murder, in practice any of the atonements for the *mahāpātaka*(s) would most likely result in an excruciating death. Only *Āpastamba* allows atonement for *Brāhmin* murder. Thus, the *mahāpātaka*(s) and most particularly *Brāhmin* murder are characterized by causing loss of caste in this life and in future lives and not being atoned for. They are things, in other words, which establish the boundary between caste and absence of caste.

7. Sannyāsi at the Ganges, Varanasi.

ChU and *Dharmaśāstra* on Capital Crime

The centrality of the *mahāpātaka*(s) as boundaries for the entire caste system and hence *dharmaśāstra* would seem to be the reason for the ChU 5.3–5.10 discussing the foundations of the *mahāpātaka*(s). In fact ChU 5.10.9 is a primary link between *dharmaśāstra* and the Veda, because the verse is paraphrased, if not quoted, in the *dharmasūtra*(s); is the object of a large explanation in one of the most important *upaniṣad*(s); and this explanation occupies the thought of a very large part of the *Vedāntasutras* which we have already discussed. The theological and the political come together at this point. The reason is stated most succinctly by Śaṇkara in his introduction to ChU 5.3–5.10:

> For the purpose of creating a feeling of Disgust in the minds of persons seeking for Liberation, it is necessary to describe the process of Births and Deaths relating to the whole world–from Brahma down to the tuft of grass. (trans. Jha, p. 236)

The *mahāpātaka*(s) are described in the ChU as follows:

> The gold thief and liquor drinker,
> the defiler of the guru's bed and brāhmin killer
> these four fall and
> fifth, the associate of them. (ChU 5.10.9)

Manu among all the *dharmasūtra*(s) discussed bears the closest resemblance to this stanza:

> Killing a brāhmin, drinking liquor,
> theft, adultery with a Guru's wife
> they declare the greatest falls
> and associating with those.

In reviewing the *dharmasūtra*(s) we have noted that *Brāhmin* murder is the most serious of the crimes and usually heads the list. Why is it then fourth in the list of the ChU? In the *dharmasūtra*(s) scarcely any attention is paid to atonement suitable for an associate of the first four crimes. How then will the ChU deal with this fifth *mahāpātaka?* We noted as well that *Brāhmin* murder always explicitly includes *Brāhmin* abortion. Will the ChU establish this as well? In short, how true are the *dharmasūtra*(s) to their Vedic precedent, and how thoroughly is this passage in the ChU concerned with the question of loss of caste due to capital crime?

ChU 5.10.7 orders rebirth from the best possible to the worst thus: *Brāhmin, Kṣatriya, Vaiśya,* dog, pig, *Candāla.* ChU 5.10.8 describes an even worse fate for those having committed *mahāpātaka*(s): They become "small, continually returning creatures" without hope of ceasing to be reborn. ChU 6.9.3 and 6.10.2 list eight creatures, four of whom are small and two of whom are closely related to the dog and pig: the wolf and boar. This list is thus also from best to worst: tiger, lion, wolf, boar, worm, fly, gnat, mosquito. The list then of four *mahāpātaka*(s) in ChU 5.10.9, which proceeds from the least serious to the most serious with the crime of association simply added on in the manner of the *dharmasūtra*(s), is ordered in the same way as are the lists of possible resulting births. The ordeal for theft followed by the punishment described in ChU 6.16 is sufficiently terrifying that the other worse crimes and punishments do not need mentioning. However, it would follow that the crime of association, because it is milder than the crime of the person associated with, should be discussed. Thus, ChU 5.10.10 states specifically how associates of criminals, which would include those charged with upholding the law, can be freed from the pollution of their company. They can be freed from such pollution by understanding ChU 5.3–5.10.

ChU 5.3–5.10 or, as the *VS* refer to them, "Questions and Answers" is ordered by explaining five questions which are stated at the beginning of this section (ChU 5.3). The fourth question is answered by describing the loss of caste resulting from the *mahāpātaka*(s). Loss of caste means being condemned as well to continual rebirth and to never being able to go to the world of the gods (i.e., that world, *asau lokah*) either as the food of the gods (*soma*) or as a god. Thus the fourth question, "Do you know how that world never becomes full?" (ChU 5.3.3), is answered; and the text reminds us that it has been answered by saying "By this that world does not become full" (ChU 5.10.8). Knowing about the possible ways in which "that world" could become filled up is the object of the first, second, and third questions. That is, the text leads up to the explanation that loss of caste means the loss of the possibility of either going to heaven, never returning to this life, or never being reborn again. Caste in this sense then means the possibility of salvation, including salvation from existence within caste. The explanation in detail of the process of rebirth, which includes an explanation of how each member of each caste comes to be and what is implicit metaphysically to this process, constitutes the answers to the first three questions: where creatures go when they die, how they are reborn, and what the difference is between those who are reborn on earth and those who are reborn among the gods. Thus, ChU 5.10.7 says simply, "Those whose conduct here has been good will quickly attain a good womb: a brāhmin womb, kṣatriya womb or vaiśya womb." That is, the caste system is founded on the good and proper behavior in previous births of members of those castes.

The belief that all conditions of all creatures are just or that justice is the foundation of all creation is thus a foundation of caste. This means, as discussed earlier, that there can be no beings which are not the object of justice. It means as well that there can be no life which is designated by a caste which is not good, or is not the object of justice, that is to say, was not meant to be as a caste member. This clear development of an argument in the sequence of the first four questions indicates why the fifth question, how water comes to have a human voice in the fifth oblation comes after the fourth question about crime and punishment. The fifth question seeks the reasons for prohibiting abortion; it is not concerned with rebirth *per se,* which would cause it to come logically after the third question.

The fifth question is answered by tracing the origin of human life from "that world" of the gods to which human beings wish to return (ChU 5.4) through *soma,* rain, food and semen (5.8), each of which is given by the gods and each of which is composed of persons being carried through rebirth until they turn into a human being during intercourse. The concern of each *dharmasūtra* to include abortion with *Brāhmin* murder is thus being carefully bolstered by the ChU in its answer to the fifth question, a question which follows the question about the *mahāpātaka*(s). The fifth question follows the question about the results of *Brāhmin* murder because it establishes the reasons for considering abortion to be a specific form of *Brāhmin* murder.

> Woman is . . . fire. . . . In this fire the gods offer semen. From this oblation arises the fetus. Thus indeed in the fifth oblation water comes to have a human voice. This fetus enclosed in the membrane, having lain inside for ten or nine months or more or less, then comes to be born. (ChU 5.8–5.9)

Thus, it is that ChU 5.3–5.10 in the context of ChU 4.10–6.16, arguably the most important theological text in Vedanta, is a carefully argued set of reasons establishing the dividing line between caste and the absence of caste with reference to the five *mahāpātaka*(s) as they are understood, or came to be understood, by the *dharmasūtra*(s), The focus of at least ChU 5.3–6.16 is upon those acts for which loss of caste and with it loss of hope for all eternity is virtually irrevocable. The most serious of such acts is killing a *Brāhmin.* The elaboration in the ChU of what a human life is, so as to leave no doubt and thereby to prohibit equally the murder of a male or female *Brāhmin* from conception until natural death, is reflected by an equally careful explanation of *Brāhmin* murder and the penalties for it in the *dharmasūtra*(s). The ChU focuses the reader's attention in particular on the reasons for including *Brāhmin* abortion as one type of *Brāhmin* murder as it is in the *dharmasūtra*(s), by asking in the fifth question when human life begins.

The person asking these questions is a *Kṣatriya*. The person who is not able to answer them is Śvetaketu. Śvetaketu has just told the *Kṣatriya* that Śvetaketu's father had instructed him. The instruction given to Śvetaketu by his father is the entire sixth chapter of the ChU; that is, the chapter following this one about "Questions and Answers." The famous sixth chapter is filled with those highest spiritual truths of Hinduism upon which Vedanta stands. ChU 6.4.5 is explicit in saying that there is nothing beyond it which can be known. ChU 6.8–6.16 repeats again and again that "the true" has been pointed out. Yet with all of this highest truth understood (6.16), Śvetaketu still knows none of the answers about the knowledge of rule or the foundations of the caste system. He is not able to deduce them from the highest truths, nor has any other *Brāhmin*.

> Wait a while, [the king] commanded him, then he said: "As to what you have told me, O Gautama, this knowledge has never yet come to brāhmins before you; and therefore in all the worlds has the rule belonged to the ksatriya only." (ChU 5.3.7)

Knowing the highest truths, according to the ChU, still does not allow one to know that according to which rule is possible. The literary premise in the ChU of the foundational account of caste in 5.3–5.10 is that in fact political philosophy is not possible even for the most wise. To know what is true is still to not know what is true about political order. It is this which Śaṇkara makes evident, as we have noted at the beginning of the essay. But Śaṇkara describes there the truths of ChU 6.1–6.8 as the premises which can be shown to be logically bound to ChU 5.3–5.10. That is, he points out that beginninglessness, which is argued for in ChU 6.1–6.8, is foundational to the account of a creation which is in accord with justice, as is argued in ChU 5.3–5.10.

The spiritual foundation of caste is therefore this beginninglessness which implies that it is impossible to deduce from nature just or right action but at the same time affirms that all things are ruled by justice. That justice—or crimes and punishments—is described in the ChU and is also described in very similar terms in the *dharmasūtra*(s). The primary distinction which follows from these crimes is between caste and non-caste. Thus, caste, according to the spiritual texts, is a manifestation of a beginningless justice which is sovereign over all things and which treats certain particular crimes as of paramount significance.

Notes

1. Pauline Kolenda, *Caste in Contemporary India: Beyond Organic Solidarity* (Menlo Park, CA: Benjamin/Cummings, 1978) 39–42. See, for example: Marriott and Inden. Perhaps the

most widely respected contemporary work on caste is L. Dumont, *Homo Hierarchicus.* This book's bibliography and text are a good example of modern study of caste as a living phenomenon. The work is marred by a lack of many important non-French authors. Thus, although Rousseau is discussed, Kant, Hobbes, and Locke are not. Among scholars of Indian political order, G. Jha and J. D. M. Derrett are not mentioned. The works of these two authors and those of P. V. Kane are the major works about classical treatises on caste.

2. Ludo Rocher, "Droit Hindou Ancien," in *Introduction Bibliographique à L'Histoire du Droit et à L'Éthnologie Juridique,* no. 6, ed. by John Gilissen (Brussels, 1965). This and the bibliography of Dandekar (see below) are notable for the absence of more than a handful of attempts to understand political order in India as having coherent reasons. R. N. Dandekar, *Vedic Bibliography,* vol. 3 (Poona: Bhandarkar Oriental Research Institute, 1973), section 66 Varna: Caste, pp. 657–69 and section 71 Polity, pp. 688–700. Two examples of such attempts are V. P. Varma, *Studies in Hindu Political Thought,* and A. E. Combs and K. H. Post, *The Foundations of Political Order in Genesis and the Chāndogya Upaniṣad* (Lewiston and Queenston: Edwin Mellen, 1987).

3. Leo Strauss, *Spinoza's Critique of Religion* (the main body of this book was first published in 1930; New York: Schocken Books, 1965). For a discussion of political philosophy, see Leo Strauss, *What is Political Philosophy?* (New York: Free Press, 1959). The principal editor of Hobbes's *Leviathan* takes this so much for granted that he does not even mention that more than half the *Leviathan* is engaged in the discussion of religion and in delimiting its relation with political order. See Thomas Hobbes, *Leviathan* (edited with an introduction by C. B. MacPherson; first published 1651; New York: Penguin Books, 1980). Dumont (p. 29) in noting this separation draws attention to A. de Tocqueville's observation about the mutual reinforcement of religion and democracy in the United States. Dumont (p. 42) also observes that contemporary Hindu apologists in order to appeal to the West have attempted to argue that there is no relation between caste and religion.

De Tocqueville himself observed as follows: ". . . I found that they [Catholic priests in the United States] all agreed with each other except about details; all thought that the main reason for the quiet sway of religion over their country was the complete separation of church and state. I have no hesitation in stating that throughout my stay in America I met nobody, lay or cleric, who did not agree about that" (*Democracy in America,* trans. G. Lawrence; ed. J. P. Mayer [Garden City, NY: Doubleday, 1969]) 295.

4. Thus, while *Pūrva Mīmāmsā* and *Nyāya* are considered to be among the "Six Systems" of Indian philosophy and yet are also important to the legal tradition, one searches in vain among many accounts for even an acknowledgment of this fact. On this importance, see Ganganatha Jha, *Hindu Law in Its Sources,* 2:iv–v; idem, trans., *The Vivādachintāmaṇi of Vāchaspati Mishra* (Baroda: Oriental Institute, 1942). On *Nyāya* contribution to law, see J. D. M. Derrett, "An Indian Contribution to the Study of Property," in *Essays in Classical and Modern Hindu Law* (Leiden: Brill, 1976) 1:333–57. For some of the discussion in Pūrva Mīmāmsā on caste, see Kumārila Bhaṭṭa, *Tantravārttika,* trans. G. Jha (2 vols.; Calcutta: Asiatic Society of Bengal, 1924), in particular 1:104–216 on I.III.1–I.III.5; and G. Jha, trans., *Śābara-Bhāṣya,* Vol. 1, no. 66 in *Gaekwad's Oriental Series* (first published 1933; Baroda: Oriental Institute, 1973) 87–102 on I.III.1–I.III.5.

5. Bernard Barber, "Social Mobility in Hindu India" and Burton Stein, "Social Mobility and Medieval South Indian Hindu Sects," in *Social Mobility in the Caste System in India: An Interdisciplinary Symposium,* ed. J. Silverberg (The Hague: Mouton, 1968). For an exemplary case of the role of religion and loss of caste, see Robert Hayden, "Excommunication as Everyday Event and Ultimate Sanction: The Nature of Suspension from an Indian Caste," *Journal*

of Asian Studies 42/2 (1983) 291–307. Also on loss of caste, see J. A. Dubois, *Hindu Manners,* 38. For further support on examining a possible qualification of the relation between religion and caste due to Islam in India, see Daniel M. Neuman, review of "Caste and Social Stratification among Muslims in India" by Imtiaz Ahmed. *Journal of Asian Studies* 40 (1981) 400–402. A classic observation of this relation between religion and political order as well as caste and Islam was articulated by Alberuni. Edward Sachau, trans., *Alberuni's India,* ed. A. T. Embree (New York: Norton, 1971) 89ff. More recently a similar observation was made by the Abbé Dubois (*Hindu Manners,* 30). For a view of this relation, which saw it as so tightly bound that it is necessary to destroy one in order to destroy the other, see B. R. Ambedkar, *Annihilation of Caste.* For a scholarly disagreement with Ambedkar that Buddhism provides an alternative to caste while still arguing for the relation between caste and religion, see R. Lingat, "The Buddhist Manu or the Propagation of Hindu Law in Hinayanist Indochina," *Annals of the Bhandarkar Oriental Research Institute* (1949) 30:284–97. For the most famous modern observation of this relation which saw it as merely contingent, see Gandhi, *The Essential Gandhi: His Life, Work, and Ideas,* ed. Louis Fischer (New York: Vintage Books, 1962) 134–35.

6. See Jha, *Hindu Law.* R. Lingat, *The Classical Law of India,* trans. J. D. M. Derrett (Berkeley: University of California Press, 1973) 7–9. P. V. Kane, *History of Dharmaśāstra,* vol. 1, pt. 1 (first published 1930; revised; Poona: Bhandarkar Oriental Research Institute, 1968) 6–9. On "Caste" see vol. 2, pt. 1 (1941). On "Penances," see vol. 4 (first published 1953; 2nd ed. 1973); J. D. M. Derrett, "Dharmaśāstra and Juridical Literature," 17–18. But this commonplace is critically qualified without dismissing it elsewhere by Derrett (p. 21); see also idem, "Religion and the Making of the Hindu Law," in *Religion, Law and the State of India* (London: Faber & Faber, 1968) 97–121.

7. For conjectures, see Derrett and Lingat; for catalogues see Albrecht Weber, "Collectanea über die Kastenverhältnisse in den Brâhmana und Sûtra. Vom Herausgeber," *Indische Studien* (1868) V.10:1–160; J. Muir, *Original Sanskrit Texts on the Origin and History of the People of India, Their Religion and Institutions,* vol. 1 (first published 1872; Amsterdam: Oriental Press, 1967).

8. Ganganatha Jha, *Hindu Law,* 1:48. See also Kane, *History,* vol. 1, pt. 1 (2nd ed. 1968) 6ff.

9. "The Veda is the source of the sacred law" (*Gautama-Sūtra,* I.1, p. 173). And "the authority (for these duties) is the agreement of those who know the law, (and the authorities for the latter are) the Vedas alone" (*Āpastamba-dharma-sūtra,* I,1,1,1–2, p. 1). See also Manu II,6,12 in *The Laws of Manu,* trans. G. Bühler.

10. The *Śūdra* "may not study nor hear the Vedas recited but he may be present at the small family sacrifices and religious ceremonies" (E. Hopkins, *Mutual Relations,* 103). The *Vaiśya* "reads Veda" (p. 104). The *Kṣatriya* "may at times teach the holy law, he is at all times to study" (p. 105). Unlike the other castes, the *Brāhmin*(s) are to study and teach Veda and arrange sacrifices (pp. 3, 15, 19 and 26).

11. See Śaṇkara's favorable discussion of the prohibition in Manu against *Śūdra*(s)' hearing the Veda, in Thibaut, trans., *The Vedānta Sūtras of Bādarāyana* I,3,39, pt. 1, pp. 228–29.

12. R. D. Karmarkar, ed. and trans., *Śrībhāṣya of Rāmānuja,* pt. 3, vol. 1 in *University of Poona Sanskrit and Prakrit Series* (Poona: B.O.R.I., 1964) 785.

13. J. A. B. Van Buitenen, trans., *Rāmānuja's Vedārthasaṃgraha* (Poona: Deccan College, 1956) #90, p. 247.

14. Sureśvara in his *Naiṣkarmya-siddhi* (#81) draws the ultimate conclusion from this about

how truly unknowable these causes are by pointing out that since *saṃsāra* is beginningless karmic energy amassed by everyone is limitless in extent. Therefore, as well, to overcome this through a few actions is hopeless.

15. Derrett, "The Concept of Law According to Medhatithi, A Pre-Islamic Indian Jurist," in *Essays in Classical and Modern Hindu Law,* 1:178, 196 (see n. 4 above).

16. Kane, *History,* vol. 1, pt. 1, pp. 22ff. *Āpastamba . . . ,* pp. xlix–lvii (this is the most thorough account of these two points).

17. "This verse is quoted in *Mitaksara* (3.251), according to which 'avijnate garbha' indicates the stage of pregnancy before the sex of the child has been determined;—it adds that though the fact of the child in the womb belonging to the Brahmana-caste would make the offender liable to the expiation for Brahmana-slaying,—yet, in as much as the possibility of the child being female might lead one to think that the guilt of killing a female would be a 'minor sin' and hence involve a lighter expiation,—it becomes necessary to emphasize the necessity of performing the heavier expiation" (G. Jha, *Manu-Smriti: Notes,* pt. 2, Explanatory (Calcutta: University of Calcutta, 1924) p. 813, verse LXXXVII. On abortion in Manu, see also Manu V.66–90.

18. See Jha, *Manu-Smriti: Notes,* pt. 2, p. 814, for discussion of atonement for *Brāhmin* murder. Not all authorities agree that this verse of Manu means no atonement is possible, e.g., *Mitaksara* (3.226). It might be noted that the *mahāpātaka*(s) appear, through what some believe to be an interpolation, in *Kauṭilīya Arthaśāstra* (4.8.27). For Kane's discussion of the *mahāpātaka*(s) see *History,* 4:10–32.

Bibliography

Sources

Āpastamba-dharma-sūtra Gautama-sūtra (*The Sacred Laws of the Âryas as Taught in the Schools of Âpastamba, Gautama, Vâsishtha, and Baudhâyana*). Translated by G. Bühler. Pt. 1, vol. 2 of *Sacred Books of the East.* Oxford: Clarendon Press, 1879.

Gautama-Dharmasutra with Maskari Bhashya. Edited by L. Srinivasacharya. Bibliotheca Sanskrita No. 50 in Government Oriental Library Series. Mysore: Government Branch Press, 1917.

Jha, Ganganatha. *Hindu Law in Its Sources.* 2 Vols. Allahabad: The Indian Press, 1930, 1933.

——, trans. *The Chāndogyopaniṣad.* With the commentary of Śaṇkara. Poona Oriental Series 78. Poona: Oriental Book Agency, 1942.

Kangle, P., ed. and trans. *The Kautiliya Arthasastra.* 3 Parts. 2nd ed. University of Bombay Studies Sanskrit, Prakrit and Pali 1. Bombay: University of Bombay, 1969.

Mānava Dharma Sūtra (*The Laws of Manu*). Translated by G. Bühler. Vol. 25 of *Sacred Books of the East.* Delhi: Motilal Banarsidass, 1975.

Thibaut, George, trans. *The Vedānta Sūtras of Bādarāyana.* 2 Parts. Part 1, first published, 1890. Part 2, first published, 1896. New York: Dover, 1962.

Studies

Ambedkar, B. R. *Annihilation of Caste.* Jullundur City, Punjab: Bheem Patrika Publications, 1971.

Derrett, J. Duncan M. "Dharmaśāstra and Juridical Literature." In *A History of Indian Literature.* Edited by Jan Gonda. Wiesbaden: Harrassowitz, 1973. V.IV: 1–75.

Dubois, J. A. *Hindu Manners, Customs, and Ceremonies.* Edited and translated by H. K. Beauchamp. First published 1816. Delhi: Oxford University Press, 1972.

Dumont, Louis. *Homo Hierarchicus: An Essay on the Caste System.* Translated by Mark Sainsbury. Chicago: University of Chicago Press, 1970.

Dutt, N. K. *Origin and Growth of Caste in India.* Vol. 1. Calcutta: Firma K. L. Mukhopadhyay, 1968.

Ghurye, G. S. *Caste and Race in India.* First published 1932. Bombay: Popular Prakashan, 1969.

Hayden, Robert. "Excommunication as Everyday Event and Ultimate Sanction: The Nature of Suspension from an Indian Caste." *Journal of Asian Studies* 42/2 (1983) 291–307.

Hopkins, Edward. *The Mutual Relations of the Four Castes According to the Mānavadharmaçāstram.* Leipzig: Breitkopf & Härtel, 1881.

Kane, P. V. *History of Dharmaśāstra.* 5 vols. Poona: Bhandarkar Oriental Research Institute, 1930–74.

Marriott, McKim, and R. B. Inden. "Caste Systems." In *The New Encyclopaedia Britannica,* Macropaedia, 3:982ff. 15th ed. Chicago: Encyclopaedia Britannica, 1978.

Senart, Émile. *Caste in India: The Facts and the System.* Translated by E. D. Ross. London: Methuen, 1930.

Varma, V. P. *Studies in Hindu Political Thought and Its Metaphysical Foundations.* First published 1954. Delhi: Motilal Banarsidass, 1974.

Weber, Max. *The Religion of India: The Sociology of Hinduism and Buddhism.* Edited and translated by H. Gerth and D. Martindale. New York: Free Press, 1968.

6

The Ideal of the Perfect Life: *The Rāmāyaṇa*

K. R. SUNDARARAJAN

THE RĀMĀYAṆA IS ONE OF THE popular stories of India known to most Hindus, often told to children at home by the parents and grandparents. It is the story of a hero called Rāma, who was the son of Dasaratha, ruler of the kingdom of Ayodhya in the ancient past. The story tells us about the life of Rāma, his childhood, the trials and tribulations that he faced when he assumed the responsibility of his family and of kingship in succession to his father. The epic is so popular in India that we have many regional renderings in various languages and dialects written at different periods of time. Of these renderings, the *Rāmāyaṇam* of Kamban in Tamil (eleventh and twelfth centuries) and *Rāmacaritamānas* by Tulsidas in Hindi (sixteenth century) are especially important. These regional versions reflect in a significant sense the regional cultural differences of India, and they are different from what may be considered the story's original version in Sanskrit by Vālmīki known as the *Vālmīki Rāmayaṇa,* possibly written during the fourth century B.C. Though Vālmīki gives a literary shape to the story of Rāma, it can be said that it was popular even long before he rendered it in poetry form. Perhaps Vālmīki had access to many of the traditional recitations of the story when he began his literary task. In the course of time the story of Rāma went beyond the boundaries of India, to Śri Lanka, Malaysia, Indonesia, Philippines, Nepal, Laos, and Tibet and became an integral part of their epic literature.

In its popular version the *Rāmāyaṇa* has seven sections, and these are called respectively, *Bāla kānda, Ayodhya kānda, Āraṇya kānda, Kiṣkinda kānda, Sundara kānda, Yuddha kānda, and Uttara kānda.* Of the seven books, the seventh one, *Uttara kānda,* is considered by scholars to be a larger addition to the original story of Vālmīki, possibly added during the third century A.D. Many scholars also believe that there are interpolations in the first book, especially those passages which depict Rāma as a human manifestation of the god Viṣṇu, which could be assigned to the first century A.D. It is generally held that Rāma in the "original" Vālmīki epic was depicted only as a human hero and that those passages, mainly in *Bāla kānda*, where his divine roots are traced and his links wth Viṣṇu emphasized, are to be considered later additions to the story. However, these interpolations, which were made shortly after the period of Vālmīki, show us something significant about the Hindu perception of Rāma. Rāma is no ordinary hero; rather, he is superhuman and his story, the *Rāmāyaṇa*, is a sacred story.

The birth stories of Rāma show him to be a divine being in human form. As a manifestation (*avatāra*) of Viṣṇu, Rāma is entrusted with the task of defeating the disruptive and evil forces of Rāvaṇa, a powerful demon king. However, the story is developed in such a way that in fulfilling this task, Rāma comes to function as an exemplary model of social and familial behavior. Divine concern for the well-being of all living things is the heartening theme a Hindu finds in the story of Rāma a theme most relevant to his day-to-day living. Piety is the value exemplified by Rāma and many others in the story. Accordingly, I intend to analyze the *Rāmāyaṇa* in terms of the filial and social roles of its chief characters and thus elucidate its spirituality.

The Story of the Rāmāyaṇa

Let us first look briefly into the story of Rāma as presented in the six books of Vālmīki. Dasaratha, the king of Kosala, having no son to succeed him, decided to perform a special type of sacrifice in order to be blessed by the other gods with a son. Pressed by gods and celestial beings, Viṣṇu, one of the important gods in the Hindu pantheon, decides to manifest himself in human form as the son of Dasaratha in order to destroy Rāvaṇa, the king of demons, who has been making life miserable for everyone in the universe by his evil deeds. Viṣṇu appears to Dasaratha in the midst of the sacrifice and hands a magic potion to him with the instruction that it should be divided into four portions and given to his three wives, who would then give birth to four sons. The eldest son born to Dasaratha is named Rāma, and his brothers are named Bharata, Lakṣmaṇa, and Satrughna. In the course of time Rāma attends the court of Janaka, king of Videha, and wins the hand of his daughter Sītā by winning an archery contest. Rāma and Sītā are married and they live happily at the court of Dasaratha.

As Dasaratha grows old, he names his eldest son Rāma as his heir to the throne. But the second wife of Dasaratha, Kaikeyi, at the promptings of her maidservant wants to install her own son, Bharata, on the throne. She reminds Dasaratha of a boon that he promised her a long time ago for saving his life on the battlefield and demands its fulfillment in the designation of her own son, Bharata, as the heir to the throne and in the banishment of Rāma from the kingdom for a period of thirteen years. Dasaratha, having no choice, gives in to the demands of Kaikeyi. Rāma willingly accepts his banishment and goes away with his brother, Lakṣmaṇa, and his wife, Sītā. Meanwhile, heartbroken at the turn of events, the old king Dasaratha dies. At the same time messengers are sent from Ayodhya to recall Bharata from his grandparents' home and assume the kingship of Kosala. Bharata at first refuses but finally agrees to rule only as the regent of the exiled Rāma, for the duration of his exile.

Meanwhile, Rāma, Sītā, and Lakṣmaṇa dwell as hermits in the forest of Daṇḍaka, where Rāma destroys many demons who were harassing the hermits and ascetics in the forest. Rāvaṇa, the demon king of Laṅka, decides to kidnap Sītā to take revenge on Rāma for killing many of his demon subjects and kinsmen. While Rāma and Lakṣmaṇa go off in pursuit of a magical deer, he takes Sītā away by force and keeps her captive near his palace in Laṅka. Rāma and Lakṣmaṇa search for Sītā far and wide and in the process enlist the support of Sugrīva, one of the leaders of the monkey kingdom, and his minister, Hanumān. In this episode Rāma kills Vāli, the brother of Sugrīva who was ruling the monkeys, and installs Sugrīva as the king of the monkeys.

Instructed by Sugrīva, Hanumān goes in search of Sītā, and, leaping over a sea with his extraordinary powers, he locates her, captive of Rāvaṇa on the island of Laṅka. With the aid of a great army of monkeys and bears, Rāma builds a causeway of stones across the sea to Laṅka. After a fierce battle, Rāma, Lakṣmaṇa, and their allies slay Rāvaṇa and his hosts, and rescue Sītā. However, as Sītā has dwelt under the roof of another person, Rāma at first refuses to rake her back as his wife. In order to prove her innocence and fidelity to Rāma even in captivity, Sītā seeks testimony of the fire-god, Agni, by throwing herself into a fire. But the fire does not burn her, and the god of fire, Agni, emerges to testify in favor of Sītā. After this proof of innocence she is reunited with Rāma, and the two return to Ayodhya. Bharata returns the kingdom to Rāma and Rāma rules Ayodhya justly for a long time.

Mythical Universe of Rāmāyaṇa

As in many traditional stories, the *Rāmāyaṇa* presents a hero, a villain, the struggle between the two and the ultimate triumph of the hero. The story operates within the context of a mythical universe peopled by gods, demons, humans, animals, and birds. There are also personified powers that control the different facets of nature, such as the king of the ocean. This mythical universe is both hierarchical and pluralistic in structure. At the top of the hierarchy are the gods, followed by the demons, humans, animals, and nature in descending order. The structure is pluralistic in the sense that below the level of the gods, groups function almost independently of one another. Ideally, the demons lead their life in their own realm, humans in their realm, and so also the animals. The demons should not interfere with the humans, and the humans in turn should not interfere with the animals or with the normal functioning of nature. The structure, however, tolerates some degree of marginal interference. The demons may harass the humans in the forests, and the humans may hunt a few animals for food. Demons, humans, and animals enjoy equality in terms of having direct access to the gods. Gods could bless demons, humans, and also the animals. For instance, Hanumān is considered superior in his wisdom to any human. Again, another monkey by name Nāla, blessed by the gods, is considered a very skillful civil engineer, especially in the construction of bridges.

Rāvaṇa's role as the prime villain in the *Rāmāyaṇa* has to be seen in the context of this mythical universe. In the story he gains his status as a villain for two reasons. One is obvious: this demon king abducts the wife of our hero. The other, though less obvious, is perhaps most important: he creates cosmic imbalance by his many actions directed against the gods themselves, against human beings, and even against the forces of nature. He oversteps his boundaries and interferes directly in the life of other beings in the universe, thus causing a great deal of suffering and grief for the nondemon inhabitants of the universe. While requesting Viṣṇu to manifest himself as Dasaratha's son, the gods describe Rāvaṇa's actions:

> Rāvaṇa perpetually troubles us . . . and we are helpless and forced to endure his fearful oppression. The lord of the *rākṣasa*(s) has inspired terror in the three worlds. . . . Provoking the sages, the *yakṣa*(s) *gandharva*(s), brahmins and other beings, he tramples them under foot. . . . In his presence the sun ceases to shine, the wind fails to blow, and before him the oceans, garlanded with waters, are still.

The first unconventional thing that Rāvaṇa has done is to become more powerful than the gods themselves. Because he undertook severe penances, Rāvaṇa is blessed by God Brahmā so that he will not meet his death either by the hands of the gods or the demons. Strengthened by this favor, Rāvaṇa begins to persecute the gods themselves. He does not stop there; he extends his powers to other regions. He persecutes the humans (sages and *Brāhmins*) and he terrorizes nature (sun, wind, and ocean). The ultimate superiority of the gods and the principle of noninterference have been clearly violated by the actions of Rāvaṇa, thus creating a kind of cosmic confusion and chaos.

Rāvaṇa's abduction of Sītā could be seen merely as a conflict between two individuals. However, the successful resolution of this conflict in the *Rāmāyaṇa* is not brought about by a direct one-to-one combat between Rāma and Rāvaṇa. It becomes a kind of cosmic struggle as Rāma and other beings oppressed by Rāvaṇa join hands. Rāma fights Rāvaṇa supported by an army of monkeys and bears. The king of the sea promises to support a bridge to move Rāma's army to Laṅka. In an earlier instance there is a vulture by the name of Jaṭāyu, who tries to prevent the abduction of Sītā from her forest hermitage and gives up his life in that process. Jaṭāyu's brother, an old vulture by the name of Sampāthi, tells Hanumān about the location of Laṅka, so that Hanumān could search for Sītā and find her. From these instances we see that the support Rāma gains is not simply for the recovery of Sītā but also for the restoration of balance and harmony in the universe. When Rāvaṇa is killed, these two goals are accomplished. Rāma asserts his personal and family honor; he also fulfills the purpose of his divine incarnation by restoring cosmic harmony and balance.

Rāma as Ideal Man

Let us now look into the characterization of Rāma, and examine his conduct and exemplary nature. Rāma is the ideal man in the story, and his ideal nature is shown by the different roles that he plays in the family and in society as a son, husband, friend, and as a king. He also has a minor role as a brother in the epic. First let us look at his role as the ideal son. This role is characterized by Rāma's strict observance of filial piety in obeying the commands of his parents and respecting their wishes. Heeding the commands of his stepmother Kaikeyi, Rāma is ready to go into exile. He tells Kaikeyi that if it is her wish that he should go into exile he would do so; she need not consult his father Dasaratha in this regard: "Assuredly, O Kaikeyi, thou regardest me to be without virtue, since thou has deemed it necessary to consult the king in this matter, thou being in authority over me, one word from thee would have sufficed" (*Ayodhya kānda,* 19f.). He shows respect for his stepmother in attempting to explain away her conduct in terms of destiny by calling Kaikeyi an instrument in the hands of destiny:

> It is destiny one should recognize in my banishment. . . . How should Kaikeyi wish to inflict pain on me, were it not inspired by destiny? I am convinced that the cruel words she uttered to prevent my being enthroned and to exact my banishment were due to destiny and nothing else. How otherwise could a princess of so noble a nature and so virtuous ill-treat me like a common shrew in the presence of her consort?

For Rāma, the commands of parents are binding upon children even if these commands were given at some moment of anger. Rāma gives this response to Lakṣmaṇa when he argues that Dasaratha has lost his sense of balance and reasoning because of old age and that his words at this stage of life need not be obeyed. The words of a teacher and father are binding, whatever be the circumstances, Rāma tells Lakṣmaṇa (*Ayodhya kānda,* 21). In another context, Rāma points out that loyalty to one's promise is the essence of all virtues and that one is bound by whatever promises he has made, even though the person to whom he has made the promise may not be alive anymore. Though Dasaratha dies, Rāma's commitment to his exile does not change. As a son, he is under an obligation to fulfill the promises he has made to his father. Therefore, filial piety for Rāma consists in total and unconditional obedience.

While Rāma, by accepting his banishment without a question, presents a picture of a most obedient son, his brothers, Lakṣmaṇa and Bharata, show youthful anger and a spirit of rebellion against their parents. Lakṣmaṇa is highly critical of his father Dasaratha; he feels Dasaratha is no longer fit as a king since now he rules by his passions rather than by reason and wisdom. Dasaratha has no right to hand over the reign of the kingdom to Kaikeyi, Lakṣmaṇa tells Rāma, because the kingdom is the birthright of Rāma, the eldest son of Dasaratha. Lakṣmaṇa even offers to kill Dasaratha and place Rāma on the throne (*Ayodhya kānda,* 21). Bharata, likewise, does not always treat his mother with the respect due to a parent. He condemns Kaikeyi in very strong language when he learns that she plotted to send Rāma away in exile so that he (Bharata) could be crowned as the king of Kosala. Bharata tells his brother Satrughṇa in language not fit for any son, "I would myself have put the wicked Kaikeyi to death for her heinous conduct, did I not fear that the virtuous Rāma would reproach me for the death of my mother."

Thus, the epic seems to highlight the ideal behavior of Rāma as a son against the backdrop of the somewhat less virtuous characterization of his brothers in the same role. One wonders whether they are indeed his alter ego who take the burden of giving expression to fallible human responses and emotions arising out of the child–parent relationship. They seem to free Rāma for a fuller, model presentation as a son whose words and actions are clearly based on the virtue of filial piety. After all, the four sons of Dasaratha are manifestations of one and the same Viṣṇu.

Interestingly enough, the *Rāmāyaṇa* also presents a situation where the commands of the father and mother are at odds with each other. When Rāma takes the news of his banishment to his mother Kausalya, she is stunned and orders Rāma not to leave Ayodhya. She also reminds Rāma that her words as his mother are as binding as the words of his father exiling him for thirteen years. She even cites the example of the sage Kasyapa who gained heaven by "obeying his mother and living at home while undergoing excellent penance . . ." (*Ayodhya kānda,* 25). To these statements of Kausalya, Rāma responds by simply reaffirming his determination to leave Ayodhya, "since he cannot disregard the commands of his father."

There are possibly two ways in which we could understand the position that Rāma takes here. Though we find him saying that he who receives a command from his father or mother cannot disregard it (*Ayodhya kānda,* 21), when their wishes are in conflict, he chooses to abide by the words of his father, rather than those of his mother. From one perspective, the words of one's father are more binding for a son than the words of a mother. The other way to understand Rāma's decision here would be to stress the point that the commands he received from his father preceded those of his mother. Since he has already promised his father that he would go away in exile—and loyalty to one's word is the essence of all virtues—he is unable to fulfill the wishes of his mother.

This situation is "doubly advantageous" from an ethical point of view. Here Rāma is able to uphold both filial piety (though partially!) and the virtue of loyalty to one's words. Had he chosen to follow his mother, he would have broken his promises to his father and fulfilled his filial piety only partially, that is, on the mother's side. In this situation Rāma as an ideal son chose to fulfill two important moral codes rather than fulfilling the conditions of only one. Unfortunately, *Rāmāyaṇa* does not provide us a clear-cut means for the resolution of the conflict situation within the sphere of filial piety.

Related to the theme of filial piety, Rāma's words and actions show a clear concern for "family honor." This concern comes out dramatically when Rāma kills Rāvaṇa and then meets Sītā face to face. He tells Sītā that all his actions leading to her rescue from Rāvaṇa should not be understood as done exclusively for her sake:

> What a man should do in order to wipe out an insult, I have done by slaying Rāvaṇa for I guard mine honor jealously. . . . I was careful to wipe out the affront paid to me completely and to avenge the insult offered to my illustrious house. (*Yuddha kānda,* 117)

He refuses at first to have Sītā back with him in her rightful place as his wife, saying that no man of honor would "permit himself to take back a woman who has dwelt in the house of another" and "how can I reclaim you, I who boast of belonging to an illustrious house?" Here Rāma seems to express two major concerns: first, that the abduction of Sītā is an affront to the honor of his royal family; second, that it is an affront to his role as a husband, whose duty, first and foremost, is to protect his wife. However, there is a third factor which is very present in Rāma's search for Sītā and his eventual recovery of her: this is Rāma's love for Sītā. The epic provides us with a considerable description of Rāma's pain and suffering at the abduction of Sītā and his longing to be reunited with her.

Behaving "heroically" Rāma suppresses this fact when he meets Sītā and claims that his actions against Rāvaṇa are motivated primarily by concerns for personal and family honor. Rāma's action here could be understood as a reflection of Indian culture, where larger and wider family concerns often claim a priority over one's personal relationship, as in the case of a husband with his wife. From a man's perspective, his affection and love of his wife ought to be subordinated to the interests of the family as a whole. His familial responsibilities, which include care of his parents and responsibilities toward brothers and sisters sometimes claim priority over his relationship with his wife—though one should not overstate the case.

In this role as husband, Rāma is, by and large, portrayed as "ideal." In terms of his personal relationship wth his wife, he is caring and concerned about her welfare. It is out of concern for Sītā's welfare that Rāma tells her to stay in Ayodhya during the time of his exile. He points out the dangers of life in the forest:

> I speak in your own interest; I do not know of any who is happy in the forest. . . . Fearful roaring from lions inhabiting the caverns, mingled with the thunder of cataracts, may be heard and render the forest a source of danger. Wild beasts wander at will in these solitudes, and beholding man, attack him with fury, O Sītā; therefore life in the forest is full of dangers. (*Ayodhya kānda,* 28)

However, when he finds Sītā very firm in her decision to accompany him to the forest, he agrees to take her.

"Though capable of protecting you in the forest," Rāma tells Sītā, "yet I did not fully know your mind in the matter and therefore declined to take you to share my exile." Here Rāma stresses the fact that he is capable of protecting her even in the dreadful forest. A husband should be able to protect his wife, and it is indeed his foremost duty. The protection that a husband offers is a part of caring for his wife. This duty is as integral and important to the role of husband as filial piety is to the role of a son. As Rāma tells Sītā when he finds her determined to follow him in exile: "Seeing that you are determined to remain with me . . . I cannot abandon you, as a son cannot withdraw his love from his parents" (*Ayodhya kānda,* 30).

The theme of Rāma as the ideal prince/king is perhaps one of the most powerful that we find in *Rāmāyaṇa*. The story of the *Rāmāyaṇa* centers on life in one of the royal houses, the house of Ikṣvākus, and, therefore, the focus on the role of a prince or king is only natural. As to what the duties and obligations of a king are and how a king should behave, there is a long discourse on this in the first book of *Rāmāyaṇa*. The context is the effort of Bharata to change the mind of Rāma, so that he would end his exile and return to Ayodhya and assume the burden of kingship. Rāma refuses on the ground that it would violate the solemn promise he had made to his father, and he begins to advise Bharata about how he should rule the kingdom of Ayodhya. Rāma gives his advice in the form of a series of questions that he poses to Bharata:

> Has the kingdom suffered from your youthful inexperiences? Have you in service, for the tending of sacred fires, a brahmin who is versed in the traditions intelligent and just? Have you overcome sleep? In the second half of the night do you reflect on the means to ensure success in your enterprise? Have you got counselors who are prudent, brave, skillful and perspicacious? Are your ministers incorruptible? Are the leaders of your army brave? Do the men and women live happily in your kingdom? Have you as a king eschewed the fourteen failings: atheism, dissimulation, inattention, anger, procrastination, lack of discrimination in companionship, gratification of senses, disregard of counsel, consultation with those who advocate what is ill advised, failure to carry out what has been decided, disclosure of counsel received, omission of sacred practice in the early morning and desire to enter into combat with all thy foes at the same time?

Rāmāyaṇa depicts the kingdom ruled by Dasaratha as a model society. In his kingdom everyone practiced his *varṇadharma* (the caste duty), the men and women of Ayodhya were of righteous conduct and were self-controlled (*Bāla kānda,* 6). The implication here is that if the king rules properly, the subjects will also behave properly and fulfill their duties and responsibilities. Hence, the primary responsibility of maintaining the proper functioning of society rests with the king and the royal house. A king has to maintain the highest standards of personal morality. He has to protect his subjects, and this duty requires vigilance on his part against the forces of evil and the forces of disruption both within his kingdom and outside it.

The need for a king or a prince to fight against the forces of evil creates interesting situations when Rāma goes into exile. Rāma, though dressed as a mendicant, carries his weapons with him, unlike a mendicant, to signify that he is indeed a prince in exile. Again, unlike a mendicant, he resorts to violence and kills demons not only for self-protection or the protection of Sītā but also for the protection of the sages in the forest who are being harassed by them. Here Rāma sees himself essentially as a prince in exile who has the responsibility of protecting the life and property of his

8. Viṣnu Standing, 11th century. Lucknow Museum.

subjects. The sages who welcome Rāma into the Daṇḍaka forest also remind him of his "royal role": "O Raghava, we being under thy dominion, should be protected by you, whether living in the capital or the forest. . . ."

For Rāma there is no apparent conflict between his role as a prince in exile and the ascetic life he must lead during his exile. Sītā, however, finds tension and conflict in Rāma's two roles and advises him to take the life of a mendicant seriously, by giving up his weapons and refraining from killing anyone. She tells Rāma: "The bearing of arms and retirement to the forest, practice of war and the exercise of asceticism are opposed to each other; let us therefore honour the moral code that pertains to peace" (*Āraṇya kānda*, 19f.). In response to Sītā, Rāma reaffirms his role as a warrior and points out that coming from a royal family, he cannot be deaf to the cry for help coming from sages at Daṇḍaka forest: ". . . I promised my protection to the sages of Dandaka forest. . . . As long as I live, therefore, I cannot violate the promise given to the ascetics."

It is also in his role as a prince in exile that Rāma justifies his act of killing the monkey king, Vāli, and crowning Vāli's younger brother, Sugrīva, as his successor to the monkey kingdom. Rāma accuses Vāli of gross moral violation and points out that Vāli has flouted the moral code when he forcibly took away the wife of Sugrīva and made her one of his queens after exiling Sugrīva. The punishment for such moral violations, Rāma points out, is death. "Being a warrior of an illustrious race, I am unable to brook your villany. . . . Though Bharata is the Supreme monarch, we carry out his behests. How can you, who has broken the law, escape punishment?" (*Kiṣkinda kānda*, 18). For Rāma, the Kiṣkinda area is under the domain of Bharata, and, therefore, as king's representative, he has not only the power but also the duty to punish the evildoers in the domain of his king.

However, Rāma fails to respond adequately to the point raised by Vāli that after all they are monkeys and the humans have no right to interfere in their conflict. Furthermore, Vāli appears to suggest that human standards of morality should not be used in judging the behavior and actions of animals. A monkey should be judged by the standards of "monkey dharma" and not by the standards of "human dharma." Vāli's contention seems to be consistent with the *Weltanschauung* of the *Rāmāyaṇa*, which, as we have shown above, permits a plurality of life-styles and moral codes and establishes the principle of noninterference as the source of social and universal harmony.

It is difficult to assess Rāma's conduct here, since the justification or the condemnation of his action partly rests upon his role as a prince in exile. It is possible that Rāma saw the life of an ascetic to be one of material deprivation and physical discomfort, rather than one in which strict adherence to the principles of nonviolence is required. Unlike many ascetics, Rāma has the burden of protecting Sītā even during his exile. Furthermore, Rāma as a prince in exile and as *kṣatriya* (warrior) wearing ascetic garments felt that the protection of the subject is the foremost duty of a prince/king, which should be fulfilled under all circumstances.

In looking at Rāma's role as a friend, what strikes us is his attitude of indulgence toward his friends. While Rāma punishes Vāli on the grounds of human morality, Rāma is basically tolerant to Sugrīva. Even when he gets angry with Sugrīva for not acting on his promise to search for Sītā, Rāma complains wearily to Lakṣmaṇa that this monkey "is not a civilized being." Instead of rushing to punish Sugrīva for his inaction, he sends Lakṣmaṇa with a warning message to get busy, reminding him of his earlier promise to Rāma. Rāma is also greatly attached to his friends, and this is shown in Rāma's friendship with Jaṭāyu, a vulture, who tries to prevent Rāvaṇa from abducting Sītā and gets killed in the process. Mourning over the death of Jaṭāyu, Rāma tells Lakṣmaṇa: "I hold the king of birds in the same veneration as I did the illustrious and fortunate monarch Dasaratha, Lakṣmaṇa, do thou bring fuel that I may ignite the pyre of that king of vultures who dies for me" (*Aranya kānda,* 65). He also tells Lakṣmaṇa that his grief for Jaṭāyu, who has died for his sake, is greater than his grief at the loss of Sītā. Rāma holds Jaṭāyu in veneration, and he regards him as a father for whom he must, as a son, perform funeral rites. Jaṭāyu is an "older friend" known to Dasaratha, and age undoubtedly demands respect. While "respectful love" characterizes Rāma's relationship with Jaṭāyu, his friendship with Vibhīṣaṇa shows another feature which is the very basis of long-lasting friendship—namely, trust.

Vibhīṣaṇa is the younger brother of Rāvaṇa, who advises the demon king that he should return Sītā immediately and make friends with Rāma. Rāvaṇa, being proud of his own powers, considers Vibhīṣaṇa's advice as unwise and beneath him as a king of valor and glory. Therefore, Rāvaṇa, in anger, exiles his brother, who in his turn decides to join hands with Rāma. He goes to the shore where Rāma's army is gathered and seeks Rāma's friendship and protection. All the counselors of Rāma, except Hanumān, the minister of Sugrīva, warn Rāma about the dangers involved in taking Rāvaṇa's own brother into their fold as an ally. They suspect, with justification, of course, that Vibhīṣaṇa is a spy sent by Rāvaṇa himself. Hanumān, however, points out the advantages of having someone who has been with the enemy and who could provide Rāma and his army with important information regarding enemy strength and deployment. Hanumān feels that the rift between Vibhīṣaṇa and Rāvaṇa is genuine and therefore Vibhīṣaṇa should be gladly accepted as their ally.

Rāma, however, rejects all these arguments when he accepts Vibhīṣaṇa as a friend; for Rāma the primary basis of friendship is trust, and all other practical considerations are only secondary in importance: "I shall never refuse to receive one who presents himself as a friend," Rāma says, "even if I was mistaken; no honest man could reproach me for it" (*Yuddha kānda,* 18,18f.). A friend should be accepted as a friend without any reservations and the question as to what he could do to benefit one materially should be of no consequence. Such a welcome with open hands, Rāma points out, is also consistent with his status as a prince. He tells Sugrīva: "Any being who has sought refuge with me, saying–'I am thine,' is assured of my protection. I swear it. Bring this stranger to me, O monkey, whether he be Vibhīṣaṇa or Rāvaṇa himself." It is one of the prime duties of *kṣatriya* to offer protection unreservedly to one who seeks it.

Rāma in his role as brother in *Rāmāyaṇa* can also be seen in many respects as an "ideal brother." He is concerned with the welfare of his brothers, and as their eldest he is kind to them. The story, however, does not elaborate very much on this role, and what we have are only fragments of descriptions scattered here and there. Rāma shows no bitterness when Kaikeyi informs him that his brother will rule Ayodhya in his place. He tells Sītā later that Bharata and Satrughṇa are as dear to him as his life breaths (*Ayodhya kānda,* 26). When Bharata comes in search of him in the Daṇḍaka forest he quells the suspicions of Lakṣmaṇa regarding any ulterior motives by reminding him that Bharata is as dear to him as his own life: "Hearing of my exile and that I was wearing matted locks and antelope skin . . . in his devotion to me and the distress that troubles his mind, Bharata has come to see me; his arrival has no other purpose" (*Ayodhya kānda,* 97).

While this is Rāma's "ideal perception" of Bharata, *Rāmāyaṇa* also gives us some indication that Rāma was not always as comfortable with Bharata as he was with his other brother, Lakṣmaṇa. While Lakṣmaṇa calls Bharata wretched, perverse, and proud (*Ayodhya kānda,* 31), Rāma refrains from using such harsh expressions concerning Bharata. Yet he does not always seem to hold Bharata in high esteem. This aloofness is apparent in the advice Rāma gives to Sītā as to how she should conduct herself in Ayodhya during his absence:

> Do not speak in praise of me in Bharata's presence, he advises Sītā; in times of prosperity men do not suffer the praise of their rivals gladly, therefore do not extol my virtues before him. Have a care never even to utter my name so that it may prove possible for you to live in peace with him. (*Ayodhya kānda,* 27)

In another place Rāma expresses his own fear that Bharata may not treat his mother, Kausalya, properly during his absence. He tells Lakṣmaṇa before leaving for exile: "Kaikeyi, having obtained the kingdom, will not bring happiness to her companions. She will not regard the needs of Kausalya and Sumitra, nor will Bharata when he has ascended the throne and is subject to Kaikeyi's jurisdiction" (*Ayodhya kānda,* 31).

It is interesting to see that in spite of these secret misgivings of Rāma about Bharata, Bharata seems to emerge as a better character than Rāma in his role as a brother. Although his mother offers the throne of Ayodhya, Bharata refuses to accept it. This action of Kaikeyi enrages Bharata instead of pleasing him, and he accuses her of having brought disgrace to him personally and to the family (*Ayodhya kānda,* 74). Bharata strongly condemns the action of his mother since he feels that what she has done is contrary to the long-established tradition of royal succession:

> Amongst the princes it is always the eldest who is crowned; this is the established law of royalty and especially with Iksvākus. Today thou has set those strict observers of law at naught, they who are distinguished by their ancestral practices and noble traditions. (*Ayodhya kānda,* 73)

Again Bharata tells Kaikeyi that he has no ambition for the throne and that the burden of the throne, if placed on him, is too heavy for him to carry: "How could a calf sustain the weight borne by a bull?" he asks Kaikeyi (*Ayodhya kānda,* 73). "Dost thou not know that the chief support of our family is Rāma, the eldest son, the equal of his father, born of Kausalya . . . ?" (*Ayodhya kānda,* 74). Bharata treats his eldest brother reverentially and as equal to his father, Dasaratha, and the absence of Rāma from Ayodhya at a critical time when Dasaratha is dead is a situation of desperation rather than of rejoicing. He feels strongly that Rāma does not deserve banishment, since a prince could be banished only for serious moral violations.

> What reason didst thou advance for sending away that illustrious hero, master of himself, who was always a stranger to suffering, into exile, wearing robes of bark? I deem thou wert unaware of my devotion to Raghava Rāma, and therefore, desiring the kingdom, thou didst let loose this calamity. (*Ayodhya kānda,* 73)

Bharata's determination to bring Rāma back and crown him as the king and take upon himself the period of exile in exchange is a very clear indication of his greatness and nobility. While Rāma seems to have some doubts about the nobility of Bharata, Bharata has nothing but devotion and profound admiration for his brother Rāma. Possibly he is, even more than

Rāma, a model for brotherliness. Guha, the king of Niṣada, whom Bharata meets while searching for his brother Rāma in the Daṇḍaka forest seems to express this perception of Bharata, when he says:

> What a great man you are! I shall not meet your equal on earth. Without any effort on your part you got a great kingdom you could take with all honour. Nobody will blame you if you did it and yet you renounce it in pursuit of what you consider it to be great duty. You are so great that I cannot see your equal anywhere. (*Ayodhya kānda,* 85)

Sītā as the Ideal Woman

Having emphasized the model image of Rāma, let us now turn our attention to some of the women characters in the *Rāmāyaṇa*. There are three important women in the story: Sītā, wife of Rāma, Kausalya, eldest wife of Dasaratha, and Kaikeyi, the second wife of Dasaratha. Of these three characters Sītā is important to us in terms of understanding the role of an ideal wife; Kausalya and Kaikeyi tell us something significant about the role of women as mothers.

Let us first look at the description of Sītā. If the role of husband is depicted as providing protection for his wife, the role of a wife in the *Rāmāyaṇa* is presented as one of fidelity to her husband. This fidelity is seen in two ways: first, in service rendered by the wife to her husband, and, second, in total faithfulness to her husband. These two roles are emphasized by Rāma when he advises his mother, Kausalya, against leaving her husband, Dasaratha, in Ayodhya and following her son to the forest: "As long as she lives, a woman's God and master is her husband. Even a pious woman given over to fasting and spiritual practices . . . is treading on an evil path if she be not attentive to her lord" (*Ayodhya kānda,* 25). It is the same argument that Sītā advances in her attempt to convince Rāma to take her with him on his exile:

> For a woman it is not her father, son, nor her mother, friends, nor her own self, but the husband, who in this world and the next is ever her sole means of salvation. . . . In truth whether it be in palaces, in chariots, or in heaven, wherever the shadow of the feet of her consort falls, it must be followed. (*Ayodhya kānda,* 27)

Though Rāma commands her to stay in Ayodhya out of concern for the hardship she is likely to face in the forest, she feels it is her prime duty as a wife to follow him and share his hardship and suffering. Sītā tells Rāma that she should be permitted to accompany him and serve him wherever he goes.

The loyalty of the wife is also demonstrated by Sītā's faithfulness to Rāma during the time of her forced confinement by Rāvaṇa. When Rāma frees her after killing Rāvaṇa, he raises the question about her integrity and character at the time of captivity. "A suspicion has arisen with regard to your conduct," Rāma tells Sītā, "How could Rāvaṇa, beholding your ravishing and celestial beauty, have respected your person during the time you lived in his abode?" (*Yuddha kānda,* 117f.).

To this Sītā, wiping her tears and in gentle and faltering voice, responds, "That which is under my control, my heart, has remained faithful to you; my body was at the mercy of another; not being mistress of the situation, what could I do?"

Certainly Hanumān would have attested to her faithfulness, if he was called upon to do so, since he saw her in captivity when he came to Laṅka in search of her. In the story, however, her faithfulness is attested to by the god of fire, when Sītā appeals to him to testify to her purity. "Neither by word, feeling or glance has thy lovely consort shown herself unworthy of thy noble qualities," says the god of fire to Rāma, "Maithili [Sītā] never gave place in her heart to a single thought for the titan [Rāvaṇa] and was solely absorbed in you" (*Yuddha kānda,* 120).

Sītā's loyalty to Rāma is based on love. Even in captivity Sītā is totally absorbed in the thought of Rāma. It is this absorption that enabled her to overcome the pain of her physical separation from her husband. Unlike a husband's love for his wife, which is restricted by considerations of personal and family honor and by family loyalty, the wife's love for her husband apparently has no such limiting factors. He is indeed her sole refuge and "means of salvation."

Interestingly enough, as we turn to the consideration of a woman's role as mother, we find certain limiting conditions emerging in a woman's expression of love for her husband. In *Rāmāyaṇa*, Sītā's role is primarily that of a wife. The *Rāmāyaṇa* does not tell us much about her role as daughter of King Janaka, nor as a mother. In order to study the role and responsibilities of a mother we should look into the characters of Kaikeyi and Kausalya. Kaikeyi does not shine well in the role of the wife of Dasaratha. Kausalya describes her as a venomous serpent (*Ayodhya kānda,* 43); even Dasaratha feels disenchanted with this young and beautiful wife of his after she demands two boons, and he disowns her after Rāma goes into exile.

However, if we look at Kaikeyi in the role of a mother, she emerges in a somewhat better light. It is not difficult to see that Kaikeyi's demand that Rāma should be exiled comes out of her apprehension for the welfare of her son, Bharata. Though Bharata himself does not see dangers to his life at the hands of Rāma, Kaikeyi, influenced by the clever arguments of Mantharā, the maidservant, comes to see dangers for Bharata in the coronation of Rāma. In the Mantharā–Kaikeyi episode we see a process of change from a Kaikeyi who feels delighted at the news of Rāma's oncoming coronation to a Kaikeyi who perceives a threat to her son's life in Rāma's coronation.

Let us now look at some of the arguments advanced by Mantharā to understand the change in Kaikeyi's feelings. The first argument advanced by Mantharā stresses the possibility that with the coronation of Rāma, Kausalya, Rāma's mother, would become more influential in the court of Dasaratha than Kaikeyi herself. Mantharā cautions:

> O illustrious princess, thy destruction is at hand; King Dasaratha is about to proclaim Rāma regent of the kingdom! I am plunged into a bottomless pit of fear, I am overwhelmed with grief, I am as if consumed by fire on thy account and have hastened to seek thee out. (*Ayodhya kānda,* 7)

Playing on the rivalry between Kaikeyi and Kausalya, Mantharā complains that Dasaratha has proved himself to be cunning in declaring Rāma to be his successor: "While with thee, he [Dasaratha] overwhelms thee with caresses, but to-day he is manifesting his real concern for Kausalya" (*Ayodhya kānda,* 7). Kaikeyi at this point refuses to be moved by the arguments of Mantharā and declares her happiness at the coronation of Rāma: "I see no difference between Rāma and Bharata, I rejoice that Rāma should become the regent of the empire."

Not able to change the mind of Kaikeyi on the ground of her rivalry with Kausalya, Mantharā begins to argue that the coronation of Rāma would have serious consequences for the safety of Bharata. She identifies Rāma as Bharata's enemy and points out that Rāma would see Bharata as a direct threat to his power and position and therefore, "ascending the throne without hindrance, Rāma will either banish Bharata or have him put to death" (*Ayodhya kānda,* 8).

Then Mantharā reminds Kaikeyi that as a mother it is her duty to protect Bharata from the oppression of Rāma. Mantharā also shows Kaikeyi that she has the means to do so. "Demand the two boons that Dasaratha has given to you," Mantharā tells Kaikeyi. "Exile Rāma and crown Bharata as the king of Ayodhya."

It is because of this appeal to her motherly instinct and motherly responsibilities that Kaikeyi fails in her duties as a wife, and undoubtedly she holds the responsibility for the untimely death of her husband, Dasaratha. Dasaratha dies heartbroken at the departure of his beloved son Rāma, who has been exiled by the demands of Kaikeyi. Still firm in her role as a mother she tells Bharata, who returns to Ayodhya after Rāma's departure and the subsequent death of Dasaratha:

> It is I, my son, learning that he [Rāma] was to be enthroned, who demanded the crown for thee and the exile of Rāma from thy sire. . . . This very day, O my virtuous son, take possession of the crown; I have done all these things for thy sake. (*Ayodhya kānda*, 72)

In the *Rāmāyaṇa*, we find that mothers are generally very attached to their sons. While Kaikeyi's love for her son forces her to demand the boons from Dasaratha exiling Rāma, it is the love of Rāma that makes Kausalya, mother of Rāma, declare that she would follow her son into exile. In both instances we find that considerations of their wifely duties have been overridden. It appears that the role of mother would create conflict with the role of wife. Interestingly enough, as soon as a wife assumes the role of a mother, her loyalties tend to shift from her husband to her children. In the cases of Kaikeyi and Kausalya, the conflict is resolved in favor of their sons. Only with great difficulty does Rāma succeed in changing the mind of his mother, who finally agrees to stay in Ayodhya and serve her husband Dasaratha in his old age. *Rāmāyaṇa* does not give us a clear-cut solution to the conflict in these two roles of women. The reason is that the ideal woman in this story, Sītā, plays only one role—that of a wife. Had she also played the role of mother and responded in "tensional situations" such as those faced by Kausalya and Kaikeyi, an "ideal solution" may have been posited.

Dharma—Ideal Life

Having surveyed some of the important characters of the story, let us summarize our findings about the religious life portrayed in the *Rāmāyaṇa*. The notion of *dharma* is central. *Dharma*, coming from the root word meaning "to sustain," has wide ranges of application in the *Rāmāyaṇa*. In the mythical universe peopled by the gods, demons, humans, animals, and forces of nature, it means cosmic harmony sustained through the observance of the principle of noninterference by all the inhabitants of the universe. Within each realm, *dharma* stands for the sustaining principle of social harmony: proper behavior determined by the intrinsic nature of inhabitants themselves. The *Rāmāyaṇa* teaches the proper action of a man through its hero, Rāma, who plays the roles of ideal son, husband, king, and friend in the epic. Sītā tells us about the ideal wife, while Bharata, more than Rāma, exemplifies the role of an ideal brother. We discern the possible roles of a mother by looking at the characters of Kausalya and Kaikeyi.

The conflict between Rāvaṇa and Rāma is a confrontation between forces that create cosmic and social disharmony and forces that maintain cosmic and social harmony. Cosmic harmony is maintained by the gods, who assume a superior status as guardians of a universe comprised of demons, humans, animals, and forces of nature. While cosmic harmony is established by the gods, social harmony is maintained by kings, who rule in exemplary fashion and maintain conditions necessary for the fulfillment of duties and obligations by their subjects. Rāvaṇa's actions have first undermined the status of the gods; instead of being the guardians and guarantors of cosmic harmony, the gods have become helpless victims of Rāvaṇa's tyranny. Second, Rāvaṇa has acted in such a way that life among humans has also been affected; even nature appears to have been terrorized by Rāvaṇa. The struggle of Rāma against Rāvaṇa under these circumstances becomes a cosmic struggle where every kind of life affected by the tyrannical actions of Rāvaṇa comes forth to help Rāma. The god Viṣṇu manifests himself personally as Rāma, and monkeys, vultures, etc., join in the struggle. It is through the success of Rāma's mission that cosmic harmony is reestablished and the inhabitants of the world return to their dharmic obligations in their own territory.

It should be pointed out in conclusion that in spite of the *Rāmāyaṇa*'s advocacy of a pluralistic world with diverse, but appropriate, codes of moral behavior for the different inhabitants of the world, the *Rāmāyaṇa* also holds that human morality is superior to that of demons and animals. One explanation for the superiority of a monkey like Hanumān is that he is able to meet the standards of human *dharma.* For instance, Rāma comments on the wisdom of Hanumān after their first meeting at Kiṣkinda forest: "Only one versed in *Ṛg Veda,* one who is conversant with *Yajur* and *Sāmaveda* would speak thus. He has studied grammar thoroughly; though he has spoken at length, it has been void of error" (*Kiṣkinda kānda,* 3). Hanumān is not simply glorified for his physical strength, which he is supposed to have gained as the son of the god of wind, but also for his profound wisdom and faultless behavior. The *Rāmāyaṇa* tells us that even among the *rākṣasa*(s) there are superior ones, like Vibhīṣaṇa, the brother of Rāvaṇa, who adhere to a higher standard of morality. Though Rāvaṇa has physical powers far excelling that of human beings, he is not considered a superior being in the epic, but a villain who exercises his power without proper moral control. But Vibhīṣaṇa is described even by Surpanakha, his own sister, as "virtuous" and hence a "stranger" to the *rākṣasa* way of life! (*Āraṇya kānda,* 17).

In this way, the outstanding or exceptional nature of a few animals and demons is attributed to the ability of these select beings to rise above their own standards of morality and conform to a universal *dharma,* which is indeed human *dharma.* Human *dharma* is a model to be followed even by nonhumans. There is some kind of expectation in the *Rāmāyaṇa* that at least the rulers among the demons and animals should conform to this "higher standard of morality." For instance Jaṭāyu, the vulture king, reminds Rāvaṇa, who is about to abduct Sītā, that it is indeed the duty of a king to protect women: "A noble person will ever eschew that which may bring reproach to him and protects another's wife as if she were his own" (*Āraṇya kānda,* 50).

Similarly in the encounter between Rāma and Vāli we find Rāma imposing human standards of morality and judging Vāli in the light of it, ignoring Vāli's claim that his conduct as a monkey has to be judged only in terms of monkey-*dharma.* Likewise, when Lakṣmaṇa rebukes Sugrīva by saying that for one who is guilty of ingratitude no expiation is possible (*Kiṣkinda kānda,* 34), he is using human standards of morality to judge Sugrīva, in spite of Tārā's plea that Sugrīva is, after all, a monkey (*Kiṣkinda kānda,* 33). These examples could be seen as situations where a pluralistic view of morality conflicts with one based on the notion of a universal *dharma.* The difficulty one experiences in passing a final judgment on the conduct of Rāma, especially with Vāli, is due to these two differing views of moral behavior in the *Rāmāyaṇa.*

Probably the way that the *Rāmāyaṇa* resolves the tension between a pluralistic view of moral behavior and the idea of a universal morality could be stated as follows: while cosmic and social harmony are achieved by each group of inhabitants functioning within its own realm, such harmony can be sustained only by exceptional leadership in each group. The exceptional quality stems from the ability of the leaders to conform not only to their group *dharma* but also to the demands of universal *dharma.* Rule by such "enlightened, exceptional leaders" alone guarantees social and cosmic harmony. Such leaders would respect the territorial rights of other groups in the world and would not violate others' borders.

This emphasis on leadership seems only natural in the setting of the *Rāmāyaṇa*, since the story is not about common people but about a royal family in India. In some sense, conformity to a universal code is expected only of the leaders of various groups in the *Rāmāyaṇa.* While a common monkey could behave in a "monkey fashion" following "monkey-*dharma,*" the leader of the monkeys has to conform to a higher standard of morality. Again, while a common *rākṣasa* (demon) could follow the "*rākṣasa* way of life," the leader among the *rākṣasa*(s) has to conform to the standards of a higher code of moral behavior. The story of Rāma is thus a story where unwise rulers are unseated and wise persons are placed on the throne. If Rāma rules the human world, Vibhīṣaṇa rules the *rākṣasa* (demon) kingdom; and Sugrīva, guided by the wise Hanumān, rules the monkey kingdom. Thus, these "superior beings" are a source of order. Their presence promoted by the intervention of the incarnate Lord creates a world where "*dharma* is restored and *adharma* is destroyed." A glimpse of this world emerges as the final picture of the *Rāmāyaṇa*.

Bibliography

Sources

Dutt, M. N. *The Ramayana.* Translated into English prose from the original Sanskrit of Valmiki. 3 vols. Calcutta, 1892–94.
Griffith, R. T. H. *The Ramayana of Valmiki.* Benaras, 1915.
Khan, Benjamin. *The Concept of Dharma in Valmiki Ramayana.* Delhi, 1965.
Sen, M. L. *The Ramayana.* Translated from the original of Valmiki. A modernized version in English prose. 3 vols. Calcutta, 1927.

Studies

Raghavan, V., ed. *The Ramayana Tradition in Asia.* Delhi, 1980.
Sastri, K. S. Ramaswami. *Studies in Ramayana.* Baroda, 1944.
Sastri, V. S. S. *Lectures on Ramayana.* Reprint, Madras, 1952.
Vaidya, C. V. *The Riddle of Ramayana.* Rev. ed. Delhi, 1972.
Wurm, Alois. *Character Portrayals in the Ramayana of Valmiki, A Systematic Presentation.* Delhi, 1976.

7

Dharma as the Goal: The Mahābhārata

Arun Kumar Mookerjee

The Mahābhārata is a *jayagrantha,* as is said in the *mangalācaraṇa* (salutation to God before undertaking any task) as well as in the *Ādi Parva* (*Ādi* 75.20). *Jaya* is a technical term for the whole of the eighteen *Purāṇa*(s), *Rāmāyaṇa, Viṣṇudharmaśāstra*(s), *Śivadharmaśāstra*(s), and the *Mahābhārata* (the "fifth Veda") composed by Vedavyasa Kṛṣṇadvaipāyana. Vaiśampāyana, a disciple of Vedavyāsa, recited the one hundred thousand verses of the *Mahābhārata* at Takṣasīlā (now Taxila in Rawalpindi district, Pakistan) in the presence of King Janmejaya, great grandson of Arjuna. Without the episodic and didactic diversions, the story of the *Mahābhārata* extends to twenty-four thousand verses. A shortened form comprising one hundred and fifty verses was also written (*Ādi* 160.63–65). Sauti Ugraśravā, a bard by profession, retold it in Naimiṣāraṇya (now Nimsar in Sitapur district of Uttar Pradesh) before the ascetics there who wanted to hear this "great history and great *śāstra*" in one book (*Ādi* 1.17–21). Vedavyāsa says that the *Mahābhārata* "principally" records the rise of the Kuru dynasty, Gāndhārī's righteousness, Vidura's wisdom, and Kuntī's patience, Kṛṣṇa's glory, the Pāṇḍava(s)' adherence to Truth, and Duryodhana and his companions' ill treatment toward them (*Ādi* 1.61–62). It was composed around an epic war that destroyed the Kuru dynasty.

The Kuru dynasty was so named after King Kuru. In the *Ṛg Veda* the dynasty was known as Puru, also Bharata. As is said in the *Ādi Parva,* chap. 90, King Kuru was the thirty-eighth and King Vicitravīrya the forty-sixth in the line of descent from Nārāyaṇa. Pāṇḍu and Dhṛtarāṣṭra were legally sons of King Vicitravīrya, although the sage Vedavyāsa actually fathered them. Vidura was another son of Vedavyāsa, though not by a queen of King Vicitravīrya. Pāṇḍu had five sons: Yudhiṣṭhira, Bhīma, and Arjuna, by Queen Kuntī, and Nakula and Sahadeva by Queen Mādrī. They again were not actually fathered by the king. The custom of the time allowed that such sons be counted as legal heirs, of course, with the consent of the wife. Bhīṣma was the elder brother of King Vicitravīrya, who abdicated the throne in favor of his younger brother and took a vow not to marry, even though to marry and set up a household was regarded as a matter of *dharma.* He did this for the sake of his father, King Śāntanu. The king was infatuated with Satyavatī, an exquisitely beautiful girl belonging to the Dāsa race. Her father was willing to give her in marriage to the king on condition that her son would be the king and the descendants inherit the throne. King Śāntanu did not agree to this, but Bhīṣma agreed and brought the marriage about. Even today Hindus perform *tarpaṇa* (the religious rite in which water is offered to ancestor) to this wise man. Hindus believe that the forefathers expect this gift of water from their sons. Not to offer this ritual water is to commit the sin of *pratyavāya;* that is to say, the ritual performance is a matter of simple duty which earns no merit for the performer while negligence brings punishment. The younger son Pāṇḍu became king after the death of King Vicitravīrya, because Dhṛtarāṣṭra was blind. (There was an injunction that a king must not have any physical deformity.) Dhṛtarāṣṭra had a hundred sons by Princess Gāndhārī, Duryodhana being the eldest of them.

The feud that led ultimately to the great war arose over the question of succession to the throne. It was legally due to Yudhiṣṭhira, the eldest son of King Pāṇḍu, who was also the oldest of all the Kaurava brothers. Duryodhana tried to eliminate his rivals in the meanest possible ways but did not succeed. Once they were sent to live in a beautiful house at Vāraṇāvata, which was made of highly flammable material. Forewarned by Vidura of Duryodhana's intention to set the house ablaze, they escaped by a secret tunnel and lived for some time hiding in the forests. They managed to reach Pāncāla, the powerful kingdom lying between the Ganges and the Yamunā, and here the *svayamvara-sabhā* (assembly of suitors called for the bride to choose her groom) of Princess Draupadī was taking place. The Pāṇḍava(s) were given the wedding garland by her. This news reached Hastnāpura. Persuaded by Vidura, Dhṛtarāṣṭra brought them back and gave them Khāṇḍavaprastha as a share of the kingdom. The Pāṇḍava(s) established their royal seat at Indraprastha (now part of Delhi). King Yudhiṣṭira performed the *rājasūya* sacrifice with great pomp and splendor and brought under his sovereignty many kings including the powerful king Jarāsandha of Magadha (which is today Patna in Bihar). The king was killed in a duel with Bhīmasena and his son Sahadeva was put on the throne.

But the spectacular rise of the Pāṇḍava(s) under the benign rule of the pious and dutiful Yudhiṣṭhira only attracted jealousy and enmity from Duryodhana and his friends. Dhṛtaraṣṭra was persuaded with little difficulty to invite Yudhiṣṭhira to a game of dice with high stakes. It was a custom of the time that one could not refuse such an invitation; rather, as in other traditions one could not refuse a challenge in a duel. Śakuni, the Gāndhāra prince and brother of Gāndhārī, played for Duryodhana. He was a trickster at this game. Moreover, the bet was a very strange one. Yudhiṣṭhira lost his kingdom and the freedom of his brothers and Draupadī.

The insult meted out publicly to the queen of the Pāṇḍava(s) by Duryodhana, Duḥśāsana and Karṇa in the court of Hastināpura was never forgotten by the Pāṇḍava(s). Bhīmasena took a vow of revenge that he would kill and drink the blood of Duḥśāsana and smash the thigh of Duryodhana with his mace in battle. However, thanks to Vidura's advice, Dhṛtarāṣṭra sent the Pāṇḍava(s) back with honor to their kingdom, to the utter dismay and anger of Duryodhana and his friends. Along with Śakuni and Karṇa Duryodhana again persuaded Dhṛtarāṣṭra to invite Yudhiṣṭhira to a game of dice, in spite of Gāndhārī's strong disapproval. Pious Gāndhārī never concealed her displeasure about Karṇa and Śakuni and said after the war, and even before, that Duryodhana, Duḥśāsana, Śakuni, and Karṇa were all responsible for the destruction of the Kuru dynasty. The devoted wife did not even spare the blind king Dhṛtarāṣṭra for his affection for an undeserving son, an infatuation that prevailed against his sense of truth and justice. Droṇa, the Brahmin warrior and teacher of the princes of the Kuru house (in the art and science of war and weapons); Bhīṣma; Aśvatthāmā, the son of Droṇa; Vikarṇa, the man of piety among Duryodhana's brothers; Somadatta, the Kaurava king of Baḥlīk (probably the country between the Ravi and the Sutlej); Bhuriśravā, the son of Somadatta, and many others urged upon the blind prince not to accede to Duryodhana's pleadings. No heed was paid to these great heroes who were destined to die at the hands of the Pāṇḍava(s) at Kurukṣetra.

Responding to the invitation, Yudhiṣṭhira came again to the court of Hastināpura. Again the trickster defeated the honest man. By the terms of the stake, the Pāṇḍava(s) were sent in exile to the forest for twelve years plus one year of living incognito. (If detected during the thirteenth year another twelve years of forest life would follow.) Khāṇḍavaprastha was thus misappropriated by Duryodhana to the kingdom of Hastināpura.

The *Vana Parva,* depicting the life of exile in the forests, is rich in episodic and didactic material. It is the lengthiest part after the *Śānti Parva.* Toward the end of the twelfth year of life in the forest the god of *dharma* (the god who dispenses justice in accordance with *dharma*) in the guise of a *yakṣa* (demigod) came to test Yudhiṣṭhira's steadfastness in the path of *dharma.* His wise answers to a number of tricky questions pleased the god. To one of these questions Yudhiṣṭhira replied that the best way the common man should follow is that of the pious and honest, because it is difficult to decide an issue by appeal to the great *Vedas,* to so many canonical books (*smṛtiśāstra*), and the differing opinions of sage-scholars (*muni*). To another he replied that one's mother is greater than the earth and one's father was higher than the sky. The last question concerned who could be considered the wealthiest man? Yudhiṣṭhira replied: The one who can get above personal likes and dislikes, who remains unperturbed in pleasure and pain, is not disturbed by thoughts of past sufferings and apprehensions about the future.

At the end of the thirteenth year the Pāṇḍava(s) returned to claim the throne. In the meantime they found another strong ally in the king of Matsya (in Rājasthan, probably the Jaipur of today) with whom they had lived incognito in the thirteenth year of exile. Princess Uttarā of Matsya was betrothed to Abhimanyu, Arjuna's son by Subhadrā and one of the great heroes of the epic war. The claim of the Pāṇḍava(s) was now supported by the strong alliance of Pāñcāla, Matsya, and the Yādava confederacy of Bhoja-Vṛṣṇi-Andhaka. As war seemed more and more imminent Kṛṣṇa was sent to Hastināpura by Yudhiṣṭhira for a last effort to keep the peace. Duryodhana paid no heed to any good counsel and even refused to concede five villages to the Pāṇḍava(s). He would not concede even an inch of ground without a war.

So the war broke out. On the tenth day Bhīṣma fell wounded by Arjuna as he turned his back and refused to fight with prince Śikhaṇḍī of Pāñcāla before him. The prince was believed to be not a complete man. Bhīṣma remained alive on a bed of arrows for fifty-eight days before death came. Droṇa was killed in a dubious way by prince Dhṛṣṭadyumna of Pāñcāla after waging a fearful battle for five days. On the seventeenth day Karṇa the great warrior fell. Yudhiṣṭhira said that after the long thirteen years he would enjoy a sleep. Duryodhana was then wailing for Karṇa like a child. King Śalya, brother of Queen Mādrī, died the next day at the hands of Sahadeva. Śakuni also died. Wounded and exhausted, Duryodhana left the battlefield and went into hiding in a lake. But he was hunted out and goaded into a duel with Bhīmasena. He fell grievously wounded with both his thighs broken by a mace. The same night Aśvatthāmā raided the sleeping camp of the Pāṇḍava(s) along with Kṛpa and Kṛtavarma. Before dawn Duryodhana died satisfied that Aśvatthāmā had avenged the death of his own father but also distressed by the killing of Dhṛṣṭadyumna and Draupadī's five sons (in mistake for the five Pāṇḍava(s)) with the rest of the Pāñcāla and Matsya warriors. The Pāṇḍava brothers, Kṛṣṇa, and Sātyaki, were not in the camp. Thus ended the eighteen-day war.

The last rites for the dead were performed. Kuntī asked Yudhiṣṭhira to do the rites for Karṇa. She revealed his identity for the first time. Karṇa was the eldest son born to her before marriage and he had been abandoned to conceal her shame. But he was received and brought up by a *sūta* (literally, a carrier, might be carrier of tales, i.e., bards, or builder and driver of chariots). Karṇa grew up as a great hero but found no place among the *Kṣatriya*(s) (the class of warriors). No one except Kuntī and Kṛṣṇa knew his identity. Duryodhana made him a king and earned his friendship. Meanness and greatness lived side by side in Karṇa's character. Just before the war Kṛṣṇa, without the knowledge of anybody else, offered him the throne as the eldest Pāṇḍava. Karṇa refused to leave his *sūta* wife and children, and to betray the gratitude he owed to Duryodhana. Kuntī also tried and failed. But he vowed to his mother that her five sons would remain alive and that he would not fight and harm any of them except Arjuna. Karṇa kept his vow as a matter of *dharma.* Yudhiṣṭhira and his brothers broke down at the shocking revelation that they had killed their own brother. Karṇa was not only known for his valor but also for his charity, hospitality, and fidelity.

The last rites to Bhīṣma waiting for his auspicious hour of death were the responsibility of Yudhiṣṭhira and others. Bhīṣma consoled grief-stricken Yudhiṣṭhira and gave him sermons on *dharma* for salvation and *dharma* as *trivarga.* This is the *Śānti Parva* of *Mahābhārata* followed by the *Anusāsana Parva.*

After a reign of thirty-six years Yudhiṣṭhira placed Parikṣit, posthumous son of Abhimanyu, on the throne of Hastināpura. Vajra, grandson of Kṛṣṇa, was made king at Indraprastha. Yuyutsu, the righteous son of Dhṛtarāṣṭra by an attendant maid, was charged with the responsibility that once Bhīṣma and Dhṛtaraṣṭra after him had held. Yudhiṣṭhira then asked Subhadrā to look after both the houses of Kuru and Yadu and make them adhere to *dharma.* The Yadāvas had already done themselves to death. Kṛṣṇa and Balarāma left their mortal existence. All obligations fulfilled, Yudhiṣṭhira set foot on the journey to eternity with his brothers and Draupadī. The god of *dharma* followed the *Dharmarāja* to the gates of heaven in the guise of a faithful dog.

The Significance of the Epic

Scholars agree that the *Mahābhārata* war did take place in the distant past. However, opinions differ widely over the date. In *Ādi Parva* 2.13 it is said that in Samanta Pañcaka (land of five lakes, Kurukṣetra) the Kuru-Pāṇḍava war was fought at the end of the Dvāpara era and the beginning of the Kali era. M. M. Haridas Siddhāntavāgīsa and C. V. Vaidya reckon from this that it took place in 3101 B.C. Vaidya has also pointed to the writings of Greek historians quoting from the work of Megasthenes on India in support of his contention. The European indologists, however, suggest various dates between 1500 B.C. and 900 B.C. There is also a difference of opinion about the date of the composition of the *Mahābhārata.* Tradition says that it was composed after the death of King Parikṣit and before the serpent sacrifice at Takṣasīlā and puts it at 3041 B.C. European scholars mostly think that an original composition of the fourth or fifth century B.C. later grew in bulk from additions by unknown writers and bards up till the early Christian era. Hopkins was in search of a "core-*Mahābhārata*." Winternitz and others presented a theory that an original composition on Kuru-Pāñcāla war wherein Kauravas (meaning sons of Dhṛtarāṣṭra) were the heroes, was later modified into the present form. They have also suggested motives for such a conversion.

Even without agreeing with these ingenious theories it can be said that there have been interpolations by unknown writers, detectable now not so much by the style and language of composition as by the variations in the different texts available. In the critical edition published from the Bhandarkar Research Institute, Poona, under the guidance of V. S. Sukthankar, different manuscripts available at Poona (Government Manuscript Collection), London (Indian Office Library), Baroda (Central Library), Mysore (Oriental Library), Tanjore (Palace Library), Cochin (State Library), and many other places, were collated. Reconstructing the text has given highest position to Kasmir manuscripts, which mostly conform with the Southern Tanjore manuscripts. He also was careful to record what is common between the two and the Viśvabhārati manuscripts. In collating different texts Sukthankar has pointed to the influence of Bhārgava Brāhmins who contributed to the *Mahābhārata* by their ethical ideas. In Bengal M. M. Haridas Siddhāntavāgīsa published a version of the *Mahābhārata* by collating Nīlakaṇṭha's text (dubbed as the vulgate edition by Sukthankar) with a handwritten manuscript constructing the text by his grandfather, the Bangabasi edition by Pandit Kālibar Vedāntavāgīsa, the Burdwan Raj edition, and the Kumbhakōṇam edition of the Southern recension. The text edited by the Mahāmahopādhyāya does not differ much from Sukthankar's critical edition.

Whatever has come to us by way of different texts and by way of different editions points to the undeniable fact that the *Mahābhārata* is a document of the life and ideas of the people of India up to the turn of an epoch.

It gives us the picture of a highly complex society compared to that of the Vedas and *Rāmāyaṇa*. Undoubtedly the *Mahābhārata* is guided by the *Manu Smṛti* (canonical laws laid down by Manu), by the common and particular duties of the four *varṇa*(s) (Brahmin, Kṣatriya, Vaiśya, and Śūdra) prescribed by it. Yet the society of the *Mahābhārata* appears to be very liberal. Droṇa and Aśvatthāmā were Brahmins turned Kṣatriya(s). Yudhiṣṭhira tells his curse-stricken forefather Nahuṣa that it has become difficult to decide the *varṇa* because of cross-marriages. A Brahmin must be truthful, benevolent, forgiving, honest, amiable, strictly religious, and kind. One who lacks these qualities is not a Brahmin. A Śūdra having these qualities is a Brahmin (*Ādi* 151.21, 25–26). Vidura was born of a Śūdra mother and neither in marriage nor in *varṇa* was ever given the status of Brahmin or Kṣatriya or Vaiśya; and Dharmavyādha the hunter was born of Śūdra parents and yet was engaged in his traditional profession. Yet Vidura was not only a most pious man, an unstained character in the gallery of characters in the *Mahābhārata*, but he was held in high esteem by all—except, of course, Duryodhana, and was believed to be the God Dharma born as a man, on account of a curse given by an ascetic. And Kauśika the Brahmin took lessons in *dharma* from Dharmavyādha (*Vana Parva*).

Performing the duties of the station of life one belongs to by *trivarga* (*dharma, artha, kāma*) and ultimately attaining worthiness by *niṣkāma-karma* (duty for the sake of duty) or by *saṁnyāsa* (renunciation) man could attain *paramagati*, that is, salvation. It was by this faith and philosophy that the culture and society of the *Mahābhārata* flourished. Through all the vicissitudes of historical events the *Mahābhārata* carried this message of the good life, a life of duty as prescribed in the sacred books, and expressed a faith in human capability to achieve the greatest value in life. For over and above the differences in *varṇa*, profession, social placement, etc., it is the ethical being of man that stands supreme. The *Mahābhārata* is not a tragic record of the futility of man's life and purpose, a record of the holocaust of a fratricidal war. At the passing of the Vedic age, it liberalized the Brahmanic religion, disciplined life and society by laying down prescriptions in the form of *rājadharma*, that is, a king's duties as well as the duties of a common householder, *mokṣadharma*, etc. The novelty of *Mahābhārata* is that all these duties of particular stations of life have not been made ends in themselves but subordinate to a concept of *dharma*. While the Vedas became the prerogative of the Brahmins and were thus closed to the larger section of the people, the *Mahābhārata* came as the fifth Veda surpassing the *Upaniṣad*(s) and four Vedas in scope and size (*Ādi* 2.230, 234) and encompassing all their teachings (*Ādi* 1.17–21). Bringing together for the people both the archaic and the historical material, it has given every Indian his cultural and historical identity. As *dharmaśāstra* it has revealed to man his duties and purpose in life. The epic war that it depicts may be regarded as a saga. In ferocity, suffering, and heroism, it was unrivaled. Only ten persons, seven on the Pāṇḍava side and three on the Kaurava side survived. Magnificent heroes fought and fell on both sides. But what made all the difference was neither fate nor heroism but adherence to *dharma*. Gāndhārī said before the war that irrespective of advantages and disadvantages the balance of *dharma* was in favor of the Pāṇḍava(s). The *Mahābhārata* is much more than a narration of an epic war. Throughout the ages it has taught a philosophy of life and practice. It has been a source of innumerable poetic creations in all ages, (*Abhijñāna Śākuntalam* of Kālīdāsa is only one example).

An Eschatological Myth or a Dharma Śāstra?

Much has been written on the *Mahābhārata* by way of commentary by many Western and Indian scholars of the recent past. Much is being written even now. Of recent interest are the writings of cultural anthropologists like Georges Dumezil. Such scholars are in search of an Indo-European matrix of thought. They regard the tales within tales in the *Mahābhārata* as archaic myths transformed into legends. It is true that the *Mahābhārata* in its episodic material goes beyond the Vedic ages and tells a prehistory. Searching these tales, scholars claim to have discovered beneath them a primitive eschatological myth transposed into an epic of a great battle. The Scandinavian myth of the Ragnarök, and the *Mahābhārata* battle are instances of what they call Indo-European parallels. Dumezil suggests that Abhimanyu's death is a point in instance. It is comparable to the death of Baldur in the battle of Ragnarök, where the gods brought in the Doom. Abhimanyu was celestially the son of Soma (moon). And, of the six great warriors who killed him, many were divine incarnations: Bṛhaspati (Droṇa); Surya (Karṇa), the Marutas (Kṛtavarma), the Rudras (Kṛpa). Thus, Dumezil explains how both good and bad men could be on both sides contributing to the Doom awaiting spiritually distressed mankind. The epic drama is supposedly played around Demon, Destiny, Aryamān, and Mitra, who are transposed in one version of the *Mahābhārata* into Duryodhana, Dhṛtarāṣṭra, Vidura, and Yudhiṣṭhira, together with the ancient ideas of Renaissance or Resurrection after the Doom. In their study of the *Mahābhārata* they were trying to locate religious symbols and analyze their meanings and relevance for an underlying universal structure of human thought and culture. Spirituality is man's response to his own inadequacies and external evils. Against skepticism man has, through the ages, systematized his faith and commitment in a good, moral life here and a happy life hereafter. The ethos in man has looked to the hope for a new beginning whenever there was distress due to a fall from cherished norms of life and society.

The search of some scholars for a primitive eschatological myth and Indo-European parallels in the *Mahābhārata* is a commendable attempt at understanding this encyclopedic composition. Fortunately for us, they are not inspired restorers of a so-called epic nucleus nor objectors to the episodic matter in it. None of them has yet been struck by that too-ingenious theory that the present *Mahābhārata* is really an inverted version of an original one in which Kṛṣṇa had no role. Also they have not bothered themselves about such indological ingenuities as that Gāndhārī was deceitfully betrothed to the blind prince Dhṛtarāṣtra and wore a bandage over her eyes by day and night to give her family and her husband a guilty feeling in retaliation; that Draupadī was an arrogant, opinionated, selfish, untrustworthy young woman and an inveterate troublemaker throughout her life; or that Kṛṣṇa, reciter of the *Bhagavadgītā* and God incarnate, was a Machiavellian schemer aiding the Pāṇḍava(s) with shrewd counsel often of dubious moral worth.

The *Mahābhārata* is primarily a *dharmaśāstra* collected in a historical time, and the eschatological myth in it is less than a secondary theme. *Dharma,* unlike religious symbols, is not an artifact, a point that the cultural anthropologists seem to have missed. In one version of the *Mahābhārata* there is mention of a mythological social contract (*Śānti* 67) which is instructive. In ancient times, when there was no king and force reigned supreme, some men of morals collected and framed certain rules of law (*dharma*) that anyone cruel in speech, aggressive in nature, lascivious, or robber of others' properties should be excommunicated. These men thereafter went to Brahmā, the Creator, and prayed for a king, whereby Manu became the first king on earth morally bound to look after the good of the subjects in return for obedience. Thus, the sense of adherence to *dharma* has no beginning even in mythology. A culture is a repertory of its own experience to help codify the moral sense into prescriptions. This is what we call *dharma.*

The Spiritual Teaching of the Epic

In a general way *dharma* means prescriptions, the observance of which keeps human beings from falling from the station of life or from their own true selves. This is what Kṛṣṇa says in the *Mahābhārata* (*Karṇa* 70). Adherence to *dharma* protects men from evils created by men. This Sanskrit word, *dharma,* can be derived from the root *ṛ* with *dhana* and *mak* as prefix and suffix respectively. It also is derived from the root *dhṛ* with *man* as suffix. In the *Mahābhārata* it has been used in both the senses. By the first, *dharma* is a means to attain *dhana,* that is, value, both material and spiritual. By the second derivation it means that which preserves creation and protects it from harm and bestows good. In a very important sense *dharma* is the law of both human and nonhuman existence, the *ṛta* in the *Ṛg Veda.* The prescriptions define *dharma* in the human situation, for man's material and spiritual good. *Dharma* has two ways, one prescribes actions leading to the achievement of *artha* (the economic good) and *kāma* (the hedonistic good). It is *sakāmadharma,* that is, observance of *dharma* with desire for *artha* and *kāma. Dharma* with *artha* and *kāma* is called the *trivarga* and is prescribed for a householder. By *artha* is meant riches, might, skill, family, health, fame, and enjoyable objects. *Kāma* is enjoyment itself; it is desire for pleasure. To achieve *artha* and *kāma* by means other than the prescribed *dharma* is to commit a wrong—that is, sin. To acquire them in the prescribed way is good—that is, merit. *Dharma* in its other way is *niṣkāma,* that is, without a desire of anything for one's own. *Sakāmadharma* earns the performer merit to enjoy earthly and heavenly pleasures as long as the merit lasts. *Niṣkāma dharma* brings the performer salvation and breaks the chain of life and death (*Śānti* 227). Thus it is said in the Vedas that we shall perform sacrifices (*yajña*) and drink *soma* to enjoy heaven; this is the practice of *sakāmadharma.* The heavenly pleasures will wear out in time for one to reenter the cycle of life and death.

Regarding the relative merit of *dharma, artha, kāma,* and *mokṣa,* there is a dialogue among Vidura and five Pāṇḍava(s) (*Śānti* 167). Yudhiṣṭhira opened the dialogue by saying that with *dharma, artha,* and *kāma* is carried out our daily life. Of these three, which is superior to which? To this Vidura said that learning, asceticism and meditation (*tapasyā*), forgiveness, simplicity, kindness, truthfulness, and restraint are the elements of *dharma.* Taken severally, *dharma* is the highest value. *Artha* is subservient to *dharma. Kāma,* taken by itself, is inferior to the other two. Then Arjuna said that *artha* is the principal value because it is the aid to *karma,* pursuits of life like farming, trade, dairy, industry, etc. With *artha* one can achieve enjoyable objects in life, can perform the prescriptions of *dharma* in a better way. Also the motivation to acquire *artha* is very strong in man. Nakula and Sahadeva said that *dharma* and *artha* should go together. Man must adhere to *dharma* and earn *artha* without transgressing *dharma.* It will then be like nectar mixed with honey. With *dharma-artha* one should go for enjoyments of life. Bhīmasena's answer was a notable one. He said *kāma* or desire is the driving force of life. It is by desire for the pleasures of heaven that great sages are motivated and are engaged in religious performances, austerity, etc. It is by desire that the trader, the farmer, artists, and artisans are engaged in their respective professions. *Kāma* is the essence even in all our prescribed behaviors and our efforts at earning riches, fame, etc. *Dharma* and *artha,* that is, prescripts and riches, are useless without *kāma.* But it is best to pursue the *trivarga,* the "triple" value, that is, *dharma-artha-kāma.* To pursue only one of them is worst, two only better. Thus, Bhīmasena is advocating *sakāmadharma,* though taken severally *kāma* is the best of the three values. An intriguing point in this discourse is that he is looking for a driving principle in our behavior of all kinds. This principle, he says, is *kāma,* desire or love for happiness and enjoyment, but at the same time he does not want to override *dharma,* that is, prescription.

Yudhiṣṭhira spoke last. *Mokṣa* is the highest value, he said. One should do the duties of his station of life without any self-seeking. This is practicing *dharma* with indifference to sin or merit, riches or poverty, pleasure or pain.

9. A view of an ascetic, ca. 715. Detail from a panel of Arjuna's penance.

10. Visnu's Nṛsimha, 17th/18th century. Prince of Wales Museum.

Such is *niṣkāma dharma,* which alone can break the cycle of life and death, supersede merit and sin, and lead to salvation in the absolute (*mokṣa, brahmaprāpti*). Bhīṣma also told them that *mokṣa* is the highest value for man (*parama puruṣārtha*) (*Śānti* 174–80). Quoting ancient tales, he told them that both pain and pleasure are transitory, one following the other in a causal cycle driven by persisting desire. Of the two—happiness gained by effort driven by desire and happiness gained by forsaking desire—the latter is preferable because it frees man from the cycle of pleasure and pain. Bhīṣma said that once King Yayāti, one of the great forefathers of the Kurus, asked the sage Bodhya how he acquired the wisdom that gave him a quietude such that nothing could disturb him. Sage Bodhya replied that he learned from the tale of Pingalā the prostitute that hopes of desire brought pain and frustration; from the tale of the heron that killing for one's own pleasure invited antagonism from others; from the snake that there was no compulsion about building a home and that a mendicant should live without one: from the bee that an ascetic need not bother about food for living and that he could collect alms from the householders; from the tale of the arrow maker that if he did his job with necessary attention and devotion nothing could distract him, not even the presence of a king; from the tale of the maiden who threw away the extra bracelets because they were resounding too much that if one wanted to avoid disturbance one could get away from it by leaving the company (*Śānti* 178). The teaching is that one can take to the *niṣkāma dharma* of *saṁnyāsa* (renunciation) and practice *yoga,* or one may take to the *niṣkāma dharma* of a *gṛhī* (householder, family man) that Vidura practiced. For others, it should be *trivarga, dharma-artha-kāma.* Bhīṣma's instructions to Yudhiṣthira and others covered both.

The supreme teaching of the *Mahābhārata* is *dharma* in the sense of both *sakāma* and *niṣkāma dharma.* It taught King Yudhiṣthira how to become an ideal ruler. The fundamental point in these instructions was that a king was bound by law (*dharma,* prescriptions), and his commands were only rules of law. As a matter of *dharma,* a king must look to the welfare of his subjects, secure the kingdom from external attack, keep men to their stations of duty, decide carefully on war and peace, maintain a well-trained army and efficient police and intelligence services. If necessary, the king shall take to a scorched-earth policy in the face of an enemy attack. So long as one remains a king he should follow the *trivarga* guided by *dharma,* not by *kāma* as Bhīmasena had said, like an ideal householder (*Śānti* 69). Then Bhīṣma talked about the personal qualities that a king should have, like earning riches without cruelty, being brave without being a braggart, etc., and the qualities that a king must not have, such as showing charity to the greedy, trusting a man of ill will, indulgence in sex, etc. (*Śānti* 70). The king shall also be a shrewd ruler and shall put up a show as is necessary like actors. Pretension of friendship with a strong enemy and at the same time preparing secretly for war at an opportune moment against him was a valuable piece of advice that Bhīṣma gave Yudhiṣthira as a matter of *dharma* (*Śānti* 140). Bhīṣma also gave such advice as abjuration of anger, adherence to truth, proper distribution of wealth and earning, forgiveness, having children by one's own wife, purity of thought and action, nonviolence, simplicity, and care for the dependents—the ninefold *dharma*. During the war Kṛṣṇa told Arjuna that nonviolence (not to injure others) is a great *dharma* and that telling a lie is preferable to violence. In the same place he says that there is nothing greater than truth (*Karṇa* 70). In this context, Kṛṣṇa's reply to Sanjaya, Dhṛtarāṣṭra's envoy to Yudhiṣthira just before the war broke out, is quite interesting.

Sanjaya, tryng to dissuade Yudhiṣthira from war in the name of *dharma*, said that one who takes *dharma* as superior to *kāma* and *artha* is great. Desire for *artha* binds one to sorrow. Therefore, Yudhiṣthira, the champion of *dharma*, had better live by begging than killing such men as Droṇa, Aśvatthāmā, Kṛpa, Salya, Vikarṇa, Duryodhana, Karṇa. War is evil, desire is a blemish on the pious soul. That war has no necessary connection with virtue or vice, but that war is unmitigated evil is evident from the fact that a senseless fellow or a sinner may win wealth by war while the sensible and virtuous may lose. Why should, therefore, Yudhiṣthira wage a war and leave the path of *dharma*? He must not be led by ill-advising ministers. They are really his detractors in his journey to *mokṣa*, the highest *dharma*. To this Kṛṣṇa replied that no one could abandon his station of duty. One must act, and act according to the injunctions, prescriptions of *dharma*. Knowledge for the sake of knowledge is really empty; it must guide action. The whole universe is in activity without respite, nothing is at rest. Indra is the king of gods because he is untiring in his care and concern for them and sticks to truth and *dharma*, looking to others before looking into his own happiness. Bṛhaspati is the supreme guru because he practices perfect reticence and rectitude. Yudhiṣthira is a Kṣatriya and had his duties already prescribed. Along with study of scriptures and performances of religious rites he was engaged even more with arms. A Kṣatriya living a good life of a householder would attain the merit of heaven if he fell in battle. Yudhiṣthira, called by the duty of his station in life, was going to war. He must get back his kingdom. As for *mokṣa*, he would attain it ultimately by pursuit of *niṣkāma dharma* and learning the scriptures and thereby living a holy life. No one could therefore accuse him of any deviation (*Udyoga* 27).

On his return Sanjaya told Dhṛtarāṣṭra that Yudhiṣthira, a perfect follower of *dharma* and well versed in scriptures and generous as a man, only wanted to get back the part of the kingdom that Dhṛtarāṣṭra had given him (although the entire Kuru kingdom legitimately belonged to him). To escape from one's station, that is, to neglect the duties that define a station of life in this creation, is a fall from one's true being. Arjuna was goaded to pick up arms again and fight by the Lord Kṛṣṇa when the warrior became stricken by the thought of the Doom looming large and the thought of killing the near and dear ones. After the war Yudhiṣṭhira, in a melancholy mood, wanted to abandon his kingdom and take to a forest life. Bhīṣma, Vyāsa, Kṛṣṇa, and others consoling him in his sorrow nevertheless reminded him of his duties as a king. Kṛṣṇa even told him that he, the *Dharmarāja* (Yudhiṣṭhira) was becoming too occupied with his personal sorrow and bereavements. (It reminds one of Rāma's deciding to abandon his beloved queen Sītā. Rāmachandra could very well abdicate the throne and live with Sītā like a common man, but Rāmachandra the king could not leave his place of duty on account of personal love and sorrow.) Only by fulfilling the obligations of his immediate station in life can man take the next step to his journey to salvation. Till the realization of *mokṣadharma*, man has to act and enjoy or suffer the fruits of his own acts. Charity, religious devotion, knowledge of the Vedas, composure, compassion, nonviolence, etc., help life flourish in *dharma* and help preserve the creation. Action negates action and thus man ultimately goes beyond pleasure and sorrow, friendship and enmity, sense of loss and gain, etc., and becomes indifferent to the vicissitudes of life, leading to self-realization and *mokṣa*. In this context one may remember what Yudhiṣṭhira himself had once told Draupadī during their hard days in the forest—that he did his duties without any expectation of return, observed charity, and performed religious rites because he should and that he did the duties of a householder by the prescriptions and by the ways shown by the virtuous (*Vana* 27.2–4). This he said when Draupadī complained, like an unbeliever in a moment of sorrow and distress, that *dharma* was not protecting one who would rather forsake her along with the brothers than deviate from the path of *dharma*. Then he told Draupadī that he himself caused the sorrow to them by his own acts. He had very well detected the fraud of Śakuni but lost his composure and was led to irrational acts by his anger, something that he should not have done.

The Transmoral Dimension of Dharma

It may appear paradoxical that the concept of *dharma* in the *Mahābhārata* teaches nonviolence yet does not consider war an evil, teaches truth along with deception, and so on. Critics of the ethics of the *Mahābhārata* have called it dubious and its great character Machiavellian. For did not Sanatsujāta, one of the twelve great teachers of *dharma*, say that an act of sin is a necessity where one must commit it for the sake of *dharma* itself? (*Udyoga*

42.23). Does it not appear then that *dharma* and sin might go together? Instances can be multiplied. The incident of Droṇa's killing is often pointedly referred to. After the fall of Bhīṣma, Droṇa was made the supreme commander and threatened to destroy the Pāṇḍava army. To contain or rather eliminate him, a course of deception was devised and adopted at the insistence of Kṛṣṇa. It was known beforehand that Droṇa could be killed only if he would involuntarily give up his arms at the loss of one dearest to him. Next to Arjuna, the dearest to this great guru was his son Aśvatthāmā. Bhīmasena, simple-minded as he was, killed the giant elephant of the same name which King Bhagadatta rode and started shouting that Aśvartthāmā was dead. Droṇa did not believe him, for he knew that his son was an invincible warrior like Arjuna. He asked Yudhiṣṭhira, the *Dharmarājā*, the champion of *dharma*, if it were true. Yudhiṣṭhira would not tell a lie, but Kṛṣṇa pleaded with him. Reluctantly, Yudhiṣṭhira told the lie that Aśvatthāmā was dead. In grief Droṇa left arms and armor and sat down with a will to die (*prāyopavesana*) a ritual suicide. Being thus vulnerable, he was killed.

One may also point to the four accusations made by Gāndhāri. It may be recalled that each day of the eighteen-day war when Duryodhana came to ask for the blessings of his mother he was told that victory would be on the side of *dharma*. Before the war broke out she gave her last warning that, other things being equal, the balance of *dharma* was on the side of the Pāṇḍava(s) (*Udyoga* 120.52). Therefore her accusations bore weight. She said that Bhīmasena, encouraged by Kṛṣṇa, hit Duryodhana below the belt to kill him and win; that Arjuna without any warning cut off the right arm of King Bhurisravā engaged in fighting Sātyaki (the great Yadu warrior); that Sātyaki killed the incapacitated Bhurisravā when the latter had abandoned arms and sat down with a will to die; and that Kṛṣṇa was indifferent to the fate of the Kuru dynasty (Pāṇḍava(s) and sons of Dhṛtarāṣtra are all Kurus) in this self-annihilating war, even though he and he alone could stop it, if necessary, by force. Gāndhārī cursed him that he would be instrumental in a similar destruction of his own people, the Yadus. Incidentally, the same accusation was made against Kṛṣṇa by sage Uttanka (Aśvamedha 53). Yet the epic war of *Mahābhārata* was said to be a war for the sake of *dharma*, and the Pāṇḍava(s) deservedly won it. How can we explain that in spite of her grief over the death of her sons and the massive destruction on both sides and the four very legitimate accusations, Gāndhārī had no doubt that the Pāṇḍava(s) had won a war of *dharma?*

This great concept of *dharma* delineated in the *Mahābhārata* deserves indeed more careful attention than a passing remark. *Dharma* and rules of morality are different, and they may or may not go together. Violation of a moral rule does not necessarily imply a deviation from *dharma*, though there is a necessity the other way. *Dharma* commands absolute obligation, whereas the rules of morality are contingent on their situation of application. In a case where violation of rule is also a violation of *dharma* and calls for punishment, it is retributive in nature: the suffering clears the guilt to bring back the person to the path of *dharma*. When it is said that truth is the locus of *dharma*, this Truth does not mean the same thing as truth-telling. Bhīṣma tells Yudhiṣṭhira (*Śānti* 162) that Truth is the highest *dharma*, and it has thirteen elements—impartiality, control of the senses, absence of avarice, forgiveness, modesty, endurance, freedom from envy, generosity, contemplation, simplicity, patience, kindness, and nonviolence. Upon these rests *dharma*. Moral rules are related to merit and sin, *dharma* with *mokṣa*, that is, salvation. Some of the moral rules are, in fact, rules of *dharma*. As specific laws they replace the general ones in specific cases.

Kṛṣṇa says that the Vedic prescriptions are the main source of *dharma*. But one may have to decide about *dharma* in a given case not covered by the Vedic injunctions. Here one must decide starting from the premise that *dharma* makes possible the rise and prosperity of the people, ameliorates sufferings, and ultimately leads to *mokṣa* (*Karṇa* 70). Bhīṣma says (*Śānti* 259) that the injunctions of the Vedas, the *smṛti* (canonical scriptures), and ways of the pious men (*śiṣṭācāra*) show the path of *dharma*. In case of doubt, these three again shall be the means of right decision. For the common people, of course, the ways of the pious and virtuous men are the best. The hunter's sermon to Kauśika the Brahmin, retold to Yudhiṣṭhira by Mārkaṇḍeya (*Vana* 175.59–66) elucidates the meaning of *śiṣṭācāra* (way of the pious men). Performance of religious rites (*yajña*), charity, meditation, reading scriptures, and behavior in accordance with truth are the marks of piety. The pious abjures pleasure, anger, deceit, greed, crookedness and remain contented in the way of *dharma*. The essence of the Vedas is the element of truth; the essence of truth is control of the senses; the essence of the control of sense is the sacrifice of self-interest. All these three are eminently characteristic of pious men.

So Yudhiṣṭhira went to war in pursuance of the specific *dharma* prescribed for a Kṣatriya king. When Kṛṣṇa was returning empty-handed from Duryodhana's court in his last bid for peace, he met Kuntī residing at Vidura's house. Kuntī told Kṛṣṇa that her sons must go to war, whatever be the cost. Death in battle was preferable to abdication of the station of duty. She told the ancient tale of Vidulā and her defeated and demoralized son, and hoped that like Vidulā she would be able to send her sons to fight heroically the great battle like true Kṣatriyas (*Udyoga* 123–128.24). Therefore, the general prescription of nonviolence is here limited or superseded by a specific prescription of *rājadharma*, the warriors' and kings' *dharma*. Only by right observance of *rājadharma* first could Yudhiṣṭhira move to *mokṣadharma*.

Yudhiṣṭhira was punished for telling a lie that Aśvatthāmā was dead. He knew that he was committing a punishable wrong because, directly or indirectly, his own interest was involved in the war. But he accepted personal suffering for something greater than his own interest. On the other hand, Kauśika the Brahmin fell into hell for telling a truth. Some innocent men chased by bandits concealed themselves in the woods. The truthful Brahmin, when asked about their whereabouts, told the truth. As a result those men lost their lives (*Karṇa* 70). Here a lie was preferable to truth, as shown by the result. The logic of the situation here decides the morality, sin or merit and hell or heaven, consequent upon actions. Here *dharma* was not involved directly, but the result of the action went against the *dharma* as nonviolence, that is, noninjury to innocent persons. The Brahmin failed to judge the situation of his action, failed to appreciate the fact that in the human situation a general rule of morality without exceptions cannot be formulated. Here the result with reference to *dharma* decided the right or wrong of a particular action.

Arjuna and Sātyaki were rightly accused by Gāndhārī for their acts of violence against the king Bhurisravā. It was condemned as wrong then and there by friends and foes alike. It was against a Kṣatriya's code of conduct in war. It was a sin against a specific *dharma*. So was Bhimasena's act of hitting Duryodhana on his thigh. Bhīmasena's plea that he was bound by a vow to break by mace Duryodhana's thigh and fell him in battle because of the immodesty shown to Draupadī was not accepted in the *Mahābhārata*. The vow itself was wrong and the act following it was a sin against a specific *dharma*. Kṛṣṇa also silently accepted the accusation of aiding and abetting in the sin. He reasonably apprehended that Bhīmasena would not be able to defeat the skill of Duryodhana. He was in no doubt that Yudhiṣṭhira again had committed a mistake by inviting Duryodhana to a duel and giving him the choice of arms and opponent. Kṛṣṇa covered this human failure and accepted the blame from his elder brother Balarāma and Gāndhārī. Contrast with this the tale of Balāka the hunter told to Arjuna by Kṛṣṇa himself during the incident of Arjuna's vow (*Karṇa* 70). He killed a blind animal while it was drinking water. But this earned him merit instead of sin because he destroyed the fearful killer that the animal was.

Should it be that one taking a vow could break it, that there is nothing such as personal and social morality? Is the entire common-life moral structure that contingent? If so, it would not be possible to carry on our everyday life, for this would destroy the mutual confidence people have regarding promise-keeping. The answer is provided in the incident involving Arjuna and Yudhiṣṭhira (*Karṇa* 70). Arjuna had taken a vow that should anyone dare tell him to surrender his Gāndīva (the sacred and fearful bow of Arjuna given him by God) to someone else he would kill him. Wounded and disgraced in defeat, Yudhiṣṭhira was beaten back by Karṇa, who was mercilessly destroying the Pāṇḍava army. He very much wanted Arjuna to face Karṇa and kill him before the Pāṇḍava(s) were destroyed. But Arjuna was engaged in fighting elsewhere in the battlefield. When Yudhiṣṭhira found Arjuna, he reproached him angrily and told him that he was unworthy of the Gāndīva and had better give it to someone else and retire. Arjuna took out his sword. Kṛṣṇa intervened. Hearing of his vow, he reproached him that taking such a vow was an act of foolishness leading to another foolish act against *dharma*, against the truth of nonviolence. True, Yudhiṣṭhira's reproaches would not matter much had there not been such a thoughtless vow. Now this was one aspect of the incident. Kṛṣṇa then asked Arjuna to keep his vow by severely insulting Yudhiṣṭhira, the most respected character in the *Mahābhārata* after Bhīṣma. His brothers and Draupadī and Kṛṣṇa himself were obedient and respectful toward him. He was called *Dharmarāja*, "the king of *dharma*, by all. Therefore, to insult such a revered person was like killing him. Arjuna did that but broke down in remorse for doing so and was about to kill himself. Kṛṣṇa again stopped him. Self-killing is a greater sin than what Arjuna did to Yudhiṣṭhira. Let Arjuna speak loud and boast about himself; for that would be annihilating his own self, a punishment. Arjuna did so and then fell at the feet of his revered elder brother. Evidently, in the *Mahābhārata* both the personal and public aspects of morality were neither overlooked nor degraded. Only they are contingent on and subordinate to *dharma*, the supreme teaching not only of the *Mahābhārata* but of Indian culture and society as a whole, since Vedic times. *Dharma* and common morality may be called a two-level ethics, provided that one keeps in mind this relation of subordination of the latter to the former and the rule of exception given to the latter by this relation. A vow or obligation ceases to be sacrosanct if it goes against the elements of truth upon which *dharma* rests, the *vidhi* (positive injunctions) and *niṣedha* (negative injunctions) prescribed in the scriptures, restated and elaborated in the *Mahābhārata*.

Gāndhārī's curse to Kṛṣṇa may be treated as an epilogue to this essay. Kṛṣṇa smiled and said to Gāndhārī that she only uttered now what he had decided long before. These words suggest the turn of the epoch. After the massive destruction of life at the Kurukṣetra war only the Yadus remained, Kṛṣṇa's own people. To the same allegation as Gāndhārī's, Kṛṣṇa told sage Uttanka that the infatuation and haughtiness of the house of Dhṛtarāṣṭra had baffled all his efforts at peace. The war of destruction was unavoidable; the Doom was inevitable. However, Duryodhana and others earned the merit of heaven as good Kṣatriyas, and the surviving Pāṇḍava(s) were protecting *dharma*. This pacified the sage Uttanka and he saw in Kṛṣṇa the Being brighter than a thousand suns, the destroyer of the sinners and preserver of *dharma*. Now the time came for the Yadus who had lost their footing in *dharma*. The time for the Pāṇḍava(s) was also over. It was well indicated when Arjuna failed with his Gāndīva to protect the womenfolk and treasures of Kṛṣṇa's house from the attack of the *dasyū*(s). Kṛṣṇa had already resurrected the stillborn son of Uttarā, Abhimanyu's wife. The Pāṇḍava(s) placed Parikṣit on the throne and embarked on their "last journey."

This concept of doom and resurrection or renaissance read into the *Mahābhārata* by Dumezil and others following him is interesting no doubt. An epoch ended with the Doom brought about by men and gods together. The epic war came inexorably upon a fallen people with death and destruction. Nobody, however little responsible for tampering with the ethical foundations of human existence, was spared. Everybody had his share of punishment.

Another epoch began with hope of a *dharmarājya* (rule of *dharma*) resting on a young unblemished king born of the fire of the Doom. But Gāndhārī's accusations had a positive message which has been overlooked. She did not accuse Yudhiṣṭhira of any breach of *dharma*, specific or general. As a king he observed *niṣkāma dharma*, an advancement upon *trivarga*. It prepared him, made him worthy of salvation. No wonder that *dharma* itself laid the bridge between morality and immorality for the *Dharmarāja*. One by one his beloved wife and brothers fell on the way for even trifling faults that they had failed to overcome in mortal life: Draupadī's partiality to Arjuna, Sahadeva's pride for his wisdom, very handsome Nakula's pride for his physical beauty, Arjuna's proud boast that he would kill all his enemies in a day of battle, Bhīmasena's pride for his physical prowess. As they fell, the *Dharmarāja* did not look back but left them to the inexorable law of *karma*, of action bringing its own result. Indra, the god of heaven, came to receive him, but Yudhiṣṭhira would not leave the faithful dog which had followed him all the way, even to the gates of paradise. He could leave his wife and brothers because he could not prevail against death, but it was different with the dog, who was alive and devoted to him. At this the god of *dharma* appeared and blessed him so that he could enter heaven in his mortal frame because of his steadfastness to *dharma*, wisdom, and kindness to all. Yudhiṣṭhira then wanted to meet his brothers and Draupadī and was led to hell. He decided to live there among his dear ones, as heaven had no special charm for him. The god of *dharma* came to him again and told him that a king has to suffer hell at least once as a punishment, because in performing his duties even a good king might be under compulsion of violating a moral rule, though not necessarily the law of *dharma*. Yudhiṣṭhira deserved to be punished for telling a lie to Droṇa that Aśvatthāmā had died in battle. The punishment retributively cleansed Yudhiṣṭhira of the sin against truth-telling. The god of *dharma* told him that this was the third time that he had tested Yudhiṣṭhira regarding his adherence to *dharma* and was pleased that he was pure in thought and deed. Along with his near and dear ones he entered heaven and thus the mortal became physically related to the realm of immortality. In the *Rāmāyaṇa* God himself had come to set an example of a life of *dharma* through mortal sufferings. In the *Mahābhārata* it was man that set the example. The life of King Yudhiṣṭhira, the central figure of the epic, is the tale of a pilgrim's progress. The message of the *Mahābhārata* is that there is no discontinuity between earth and heaven, that a life of *dharma* bridges them and that heaven is surpassed in *mokṣa*, salvation, the *paramagati*, which is the ultimate.

Bibliography

Sources

Texts

Mahābhārata. Royal Asiatic Society edition. Calcutta, 1834–1839. This is the first printed text of *Mahābhārata*.

Mahābhārata. Edited by Protap Chandra Roy. Calcutta, 1883–1896. A critical edition based on the Asiatic Society edition and the Burdwan-Raj edition. The latter itself is a critical edition collated from eighteen manuscripts found in different parts of India. Southern recension texts also were used.

Mahābhārata. Edited by Gopal Narayan. Bombay, 1913. Based on Nīlakaṇṭha's text.

Mahābhārata. Edited by P. P. S. Śāstri. Madras, 1931. A critical edition based on the Southern recension manuscripts.

Mahābhārata.. Edited, with commentary by M. M. Haridas Siddhāntavāgīsa. Calcutta, 1931.

Mahābhārata. Edited by V. S. Sukthankar. Bhandarkar Oriental Research Institute. Pune, 1933–1966. This critical edition, widely used now for reference, does not differ significantly from the Siddhāntavāgīsa's text.

Translations

Arnold, Channing, trans. *Mahābhārata.* Longman's Indian Classics Series. Calcutta: Longmans, 1920.

Iyer, Balasubramania, trans. *Mahābhārata: yakṣa prasna.* Bombay: Bharatiya Vidya Bhawan, 1963. Questions put to Yudhiṣṭhira by the God of *Dharma* in the guise of a demi-god. It is a part of *Vana Parva,* variously called *Aranyaka Parva.*

Lal, P., trans. *Mahābhārata of Vyāsa.* Condensed from Sanskrit Text. New Delhi: Vikas Publishing House, 1980.

Roy, Protap Chandra, trans. *Mahābhārata of Krishna Dwaipāyana Vyāsa.* Edited by Haralal Haldar. 12 vols. 2nd ed. Calcutta: Oriental Publishing Co. 1st ed., 1925. A critical edition.

Van Buitenen, J. A. B., trans. and ed. *Mahābhārata.* 2 vols. Chicago: University of Chicago Press, 1975.

Studies

Acosta, Josephine Nacorda. *The Sublime in the Mahābhārata.* Santo Tomas, 1976.

Agarwala, G. C., ed. *Age of Bharata War.* Delhi: Motilal Banarasidas, 1979.

Banerjee, S. C. *Indian Society in the Mahābhārata: Based on Smriti Material in the Mahābhārata.* Varanasi, 1976.

Dumezil, Georges. *The Destiny of a King.* Translated by Alf Hiltebeitel. Chicago: University of Chicago Press, 1971. This is a part of the book *Mythe et epopée,* not yet translated in to English.

Edwards, P. Rice. *Mahābhārata–An Analysis.* Bombay, 1934.

Gandy, Wallace. *The Pāndava Princes.* London, 1918.

Ghose, Aurobindo. *Vyāsa and Vālmiki.* Pondicherry Aurobindo Asram, 1956.

Gupta, S. P., and K. S. Ramachandra, eds. *Mahābhārata: Myth and Reality.* Delhi: Agamprakasan, 1976.

Held, G. D. *The Mahābhārata–An Ethnological Study.* London, 1935.

Hiltebeitel, Alf. *The Ritual of Battle: Krishna in the Mahābhārata.* Ithaca, NY: Cornell University Press, 1976.

Sarkar, D. C. *Bharata War and Puranik Genealogies.* Calcutta: University of Calcutta, 1969.

Sukthankar, V. S. *Critical Studies in the Mahābhārata.* Memorial Edition. Pune, 1944.

——. *On the Meaning of the Mahābhārata.* Bombay: Asiatic Society of Bombay, 1957.

Vaidya, C. V. *Mahābhārata–A Criticism.* Bombay, 1905. 2nd ed. New Delhi: Cosmo Publications, 1983.

Part Three

THE SRAMANIC SPIRITUALITY

8

The Jaina Spirit and Spirituality

Sagar Mal Jain

Indian religions can be classified as belonging to two principal groups, namely, Brāhmanic and Śramaṇic. Jainism along with Buddhism belongs to the Śramaṇic group. There were some other Śramaṇic religions also, but either they disappeared in the course of time, as Ājīvaka(s), or they became part and parcel of the great Hindu religion like Sāṁkhya-yoga and other ascetic systems.

The Śramaṇic tradition as a whole emphasizes the renunciation of worldly belongings and pleasures in the quest to achieve emancipation from worldly existence and the cycle of birth and death. Emancipation (*mukti, nirvāṇa, kaivalya*) and renunciation (*tyāga, saṁnyāsa, vairāgya*) are the two themes addressed principally. Early Vedic religion stresses instead the material welfare of the individual and does not generally favor asceticism. The Śramaṇic tradition cultivated a different set of ideas, which included austerity, renunciation of the world, escape from the cycle of rebirth, the supremacy of man, right ethical conduct, the equality of all beings along with a strong opposition to the supremacy of Brāhmanical orthodoxy.

Jainism, A Specifically Indian Religion

Mahāvīra, although traditionally reckoned to be the twenty-fourth of a series of enlightened Jain teachers—literally, "ford-makers" (*Tīrthaṅkara*)—is (after Pārśva, the twenty-third) the first known historical figure to have systematically expounded in present form the tenets of Jainism. He was a contemporary of Gautama, the Buddha. Both flourished in the sixth century B.C. at a time when the caste-laden and ritualistic Vedic religion had touched its lowest ebb. They both challenged the infallibility of the Vedas and the hitherto barely disputed superiority of the Brahmin. Both were "atheists" who championed man's supremacy, for they believed that man himself is the maker of his own destiny, who through his moral life and spiritual practices, can attain, unaided, the highest goals.

Although their perspective was similar as partaking of a "Śramaṇic" tradition, Buddhism managed to establish itself as a world religion while Jainism never found a firm foothold on foreign soil. On the other hand, Buddhism was totally uprooted from its place of origin, whereas Jainism persisted and proliferated but was, nevertheless, confined in the land of its birth throughout the period of Indian history. Why did these two religions suffer such diametrically opposed fates? There are many reasons for this: Buddhism found royal patrons like Aśoka (third century B.C.) and Kaniṣka (first century A.D.), who were fired with a missionary zeal to spread it outside India and to the territories in their empires across the Indian borders. Although Jainism also benefited from the royal patronage of great Indian emperors such as Candragupta Maurya (beginning of the fourth century B.C.) and Khāravela (second century B.C.) and Kumārapāla (twelfth century A.D.), they did not try to have proselytes or converts for Jainism outside India. Jaina monks themselves would not agree to travel abroad for this purpose because it would have been very difficult for them to observe their strict code of conduct outside their country nor were they willing to modify it.

The Buddha, on the contrary, recommended, as it is well known, moderation, which avoids extremes, and he maintained a certain flexibility in the moral code prescribed for the monks and nuns. But although the ideal of finding a "middle way" permitted adaptation to alien norms and the spread of Buddhism, it also entailed the eventual eradication of Buddhism in India because moderation was used as an excuse for laxity, while adaptability permitted its gradual absorption into Hinduism. Jainism, on the other hand, has throughout been extremist and has adhered strictly to its original code of conduct. It remained a closed group little understood by those who were not its adherents—so much so that even Hinduism with its unusually powerful capacity for absorption of alien religious traditions could not assimilate it.

The main objective of Jainism is to emancipate man from suffering. It tries to track down suffering to its very root, which according to *Uttarādhyayana Sūtra* (abbreviated as *US*) 32.19, is the craving for pleasure present in all worlds including the gods. Although it is true that materialism seeks to eliminate suffering, it aims to do so by fulfillment of desire and so cannot erradicate the primal cause from which the stream of suffering wells up. As the same text cited above says in another context (9, 48), if an infinite number of gold and silver mountains could be conjured up they could still not extinguish desire, because desires are each as infinite as space. If mankind is to be freed from selfishness, violence, exploitation, corruption, and the affliction stemming from them, it is necessary to outgrow a materialistic outlook on life and to develop a higher, spiritual attitude. To quote the same text again:

> The self is both the agent and the enjoyer of happiness and misery. It is its own friend when acting righteously and foe when it acts otherwise. The unconquered self is its own enemy along with the unvanquished passions and senses, O monk I having conquered them behave correctly. (20.37)

In another Jaina text, the *Āurapaccakkhānam*, it is said:

> Only the soul endowed with knowledge and insight is permanently mine, all other objects are alien to me and are merely of the nature of external adjuncts. All the great miseries suffered by the self are born of "my-ness," that is attachment toward these alien associations and so it is imperative to abandon completely (this) notion of external objects as being mine. (26.27)

Abandonment of "my-ness" or attachment is the only means to self-realization, because as long as man is attached, his attention is fixed not on the self—that is, the self in its idealized perfection—but on the non-self—that is, material objects. Materialism thrives on this object-oriented attitude or indulgence in the "non-self." The right standpoint regards the self as of supreme value and aims at the realization of its quiddity—that is, ideal, unconditioned state as the pure knower free from attachment and passions. The *Samayasāra* (209) says: "The self endowed with right insight realises the pure soul as that whose nature is knowledge." The right view, then, is one which regards the self as the pure cognizing subject (*śuddha dṛṣṭṛ*) distinct from non-self.

The very name of one of the oldest of the Jaina sects, the *Nigganthadhamma*, implies these notions. A *niggantha* is one who untied the "knot of the heart," that is, the complex of "my-ness," he is, in other words, one who has eradicated his passions (*vāsanā*). The word "Jaina" also conveys the same meaning: a true Jaina is one who has "conquered" his passions. According to Lord Mahāvīra, "to remain attached to sensuous objects is to remain in the whirl" (*Ācārāṅga* 1.1.5). The attachment for sensuous objects is the root of our worldly existence (1.2.1). Further, it is said in the *US* (1.3.1) only he who knows the nature of sensuous objects possesses the self, knowledge, scripture, law (*dharma*) and Truth (*baṁbha*). The five senses together with anger, pride, delusion, and desire are different to conquer, but when the self is conquered so are all these (9.16).

Just as the female crane is produced from its egg and the egg from the crane, in the same way desire is produced by delusion and delusion by desire (32.6). Attachment and hatred are the seeds of karma, which have delusion as their source, while karma is the root of birth and death. The cycle of birth and death is the soul cause of misery. "Misery ceases for a man who is not deluded while delusion ceases for one who has no desire, desire ceases for one who has no greed, while greed ceases for one who has no attachment" (32.7–8). According to *Tattvārtha Sūtra* (abbreviated as *TS*), a famous Jaina text, false insight, nonabstinence, spiritual inertia, passion, and action are the five conditions of bondage (8.1). False insight, false understanding, and false conduct are also responsible for worldly existence and bondage. False understanding and conduct depend on false insight. Thus, false insight is one of the most important factors which make for bondage; indeed, nonabstinence, spiritual inertia, and passion are due to it. Although the activities of the mind, body, and speech are considered to be the cause of bondage, they can be so only when under the direction of false insight and passion. They are merely the cause of the influx of karmic matter (see below), not bondage. These two, namely, false insight and passion, are mutually dependent, like egg and hen or seed and tree. Passion is due to false insight and which in its turn is due to passion.

Bondage and Liberation

According to Jaina philosophy every activity of the body, speech, and mind is attended by an influx of subtle atoms of karmic matter of a specific kind and quantity with a specific duration and intensity of mild or intense power of fruition. Karma in Jainism is bondage. It binds the soul to the body and is responsible for worldly existence. Karma veils the soul's innate faculties of infinite knowledge, perception, bliss and power. It is also responsible for pleasant and unpleasant experiences. According to Vidyānandi there are two functions of karma, namely, the obscuration and corruption of the natural faculties of the soul.

Karma is of eight types, namely, those which obscure knowledge, obscure insight, generate sensation, and delude insight and conduct; and those which determine age, personality, social status and obstruct the soul's infinite energy. The first two, the fourth, and the eighth types are considered to be "destructive" (*ghāti*) karma, because they obscure the natural faculties of infinite knowledge, perception, bliss, and power respectively. The rest are "nondestructive" (*aghāti*) karma, because they are only responsible for bodily existence in the present life. It is only due to "deluding" karma (*mohanīya* karma) that the cycle of birth and death continues because it is responsible for false insight and passions.

The *US* says that, just as a tree with its root dried up does not grow even though it is watered, similarly actions do not bear fruit when delusion (*moha* or *avidyā*) is destroyed (28,30). One who is devoid of right insight (*darśana*) cannot attain right knowledge (*jñāna*), in the absence of which there can be no rectitude of the will (*caraṇa guṇa*), and so cannot attain final emancipation (32.9).

The attainment of liberation is the pivot on which all the ethical-religious philosophies of India revolve. Jainism maintains that liberation is the state of the perfect and purified soul; it does not entail the losing of personal identity. Thus, in the *Niyamasāra* (abbreviated as *NS*) "being" (*astitva*) is considered one of the qualities of a liberated soul (181).

In the state of liberation there is neither pain nor pleasure, nor any obstruction, annoyance, delusion, or anxiety. By shedding all the karmic particles of the four destructive karmas, the soul attains *Arhat*-hood, a state of perfect dispassion (*vītarāgadaśā*). As long as the lower nondestructive karmas are not exhausted, the liberated soul remains in a highly refined physical body and preaches the truth to the world. When these four karmas —personality-determining, status-determining, sensation-determining and age-determining—are exhausted by shedding the physical and karmic body, the soul of the Arhat goes up to the highest region of the universe (*siddhaśilā*) and remains there eternally enjoying perfect knowledge, perfect perception and perfect bliss and perfect power (*NS* 181, 182). Thus, emanicipation, according to Jainism, is nothing but the realization of one's own real nature.

The Nature of the Self

Defining the nature of the self, the *Ācārāṅga* says: "The Self is the Knower and the Knower is the Self" (1.5.5). As long as the self manifests itself as enjoyer and an agent, it is not in its ideal state as the pure Knower who is not swayed by alternative feelings and desires toward the objects which come to him. He enjoys them indifferently and is therefore not subjected to attachment or bondage. "Just as quartz is by nature pure and white and does not really become colored in the presence of colored objects but appears to be so by reflecting their color, similarly the pure Knower is not modified by attachment, etc." (*Samayasāra* 300) (abbreviated *SS*). "It is due to attachment and other defects that it appears to be altered. Love, hatred and other mental activities are not the soul's personal modifications. They are due to karmic matter. In reality the soul is the pure Knower" (*SS* 301).

The Prākrit term *samāiya* or *samabhāva* has different meanings in various contexts. Sometimes it means a balanced state of mind which is undisturbed by any kind of sorrow or excitement, pleasure or pain, and achievement or disappointment. It also denotes a feeling of equality with fellow beings, thus conveying the meaning of social equality and integration. Ethically, it denotes rectitude. Thus, the term *samabhāva* indicates a balanced mental state as well as well-regulated social relatedness. It is also indicative of the true essence of self or selfhood.

In a Jaina text known as the *Bhagavatīsūtra,* a conversation takes place between Lord Mahāvīra and Gautama. Gautama asks Mahāvīra, "What is the nature of the soul?" To which Mahāvīra answers, "The nature of the soul is equanimity." Gautama again asks, "What is the ultimate goal of the soul?" and Mahāvīra replies, "The ultimate goal of the soul is also equanimity" (1.9).

This fundamental doctrine is also supported by Ācārya Kundakunda in his famous work the *SS,* in which Jaina spirituality reaches its high-water mark. He is the only person who used the term *samaya* or *samayasāra* for the soul (*ātman*). The Ācārya, it seems, has purposely used this word for Ātman. No commentator of *SS* seems to have raised the question: Why has Kundakunda used the word *samaya* for Jiva or soul? The term *samaya* appears to be the Prākrit form of the Sanskrit words *samaḥ+yaḥ,* meaning one who has the quality of equanimity, i.e., *samatva;* one who has *samatva* as his essential nature is called *samayasāra.* Thus, according to Kundakunda, the real nature as well as the ultimate goal of the soul is equanimity.

Furthermore, according to Jain ethics, the way through which this ultimate end can be achieved is also *samatā* (*samāhi* or *samāi* in Prākrit). Thus, the three basic elements of Jain ethics—the nature of moral agent, the ultimate goal, and the path through which it can be achieved—are all equanimity. According to the Jaina view, equanimity is our true potential nature, and spiritual discipline is nothing but the practice of equanimity. The threefold path of Right Insight, Right Knowledge, and Right Conduct depends solely on it. The threefold path is only an application of equanimity in the three aspects of our conscious life—knowing, feeling, and willing.

What is the justification for saying that our essential nature or our aim of life is equanimity or that equanimity should be the directive principle of our life? Whenever a living organism fails to maintain its physiological equilibrium and to adjust itself to its environment, it tends toward death. Death is nothing but a failure of equilibrium. Thus, we can say that where there is life, there are efforts to avoid imbalance and to maintain equilibrium.

Life is a continuous process of adjustment; and at the mental level, adjustment is nothing but a process of restoring mental peace, harmony, and integration. In this way we can say that the Jaina concept of equanimity as the real nature of the soul has a sound basis for its justification both in our organic and psychological nature. Second, a profound sense of the equality of all living beings can give us a true basis for living harmoniously with our fellow creatures. The famous Jain philosopher Umāsvāti in his *TS* maintains that the nature of individual souls is to serve one another (*Paraśparopagrāho jīvānām* 5.15). Again in the *Ācārāṅga* (1.8.3.2) equanimity has been referred to as the very essence of religion (*dharma*). *Dharma* is nothing but the fundamental nature of any existent (*vatthu sahāvo dhammo*), and equanimity or balanced state of mind reflects the real nature of the self.

The *Adhyātma-tattvāloka* (abbreviated as *AT*) says that the self is both the binding network of the phenomenal universe (*saṃsāra*) and salvation from it. It remains in bondage as long as it is conditioned by the karmas and under the domination of the senses and passions, but when it has full control over them, it is emancipated (*AT* 417). In his commentary on the *SS*, the commentator says, "emancipation (*mukti*) consists of the elimination of alien (karmic) matter (*para-dravya*) and the realization of one's own real nature" (*SS Ātmakhyātiṭīka* 305). Ācārya Hemacandrasūri also maintains in his famous work the *Yogaśāstra* that "the Self, conditioned and overwhelmed by the senses is in bondage while the one that regains control over them, is said by the enlightened one to be free" (415). The self yoked to desire is bound, but when it sheds its desires, it emerges in its pristine purity, and is liberated.

For the Jainas the spiritual goal is within oneself, not outside. That which is realized by spiritual discipline is not an external object but the full manifestation of one's own inner potentialities; the inner potential of the self remains the same at the beginning and right to the end of the quest: the difference lies only in its realization or actualization of the potentials. Just as a seed is capable of developing into a tree and actualizes this capacity by becoming a tree, so does the soul (*ātman*), which is potentially the supreme Soul (*paramātmā*). Realization of the self through the self expresses the spirit of Jaina religious quest. The godhood which is already present in the self has to be made manifest, and the soul has to be hatched into the pure soul (*śuddhātmā*).

The Spiritual Path

As is the case with the goal, so also with the path to liberation. The path is not different from the self. The path of emanicipation is also the soul stuff:

> Right knowledge, Right Insight, renunciation, discipline and yoga are the means to realize the real nature of the self. The Self itself is knowledge, insight, renunciation, discipline and Yoga. What appears as knowledge, insight and conduct is no other than the Self. From a practical point of view they are said to be different from the Self, but from ultimate standpoint they

> are the same. Right faith, knowledge and conduct should always be pursued by a saint, but he must know that all these three are in reality the Self Itself. (*SS* 18, 19)

In the *TS* (1.1) Right Insight, Right Knowledge, and Right Conduct have been said to constitute the path. In the *US* (28.2) and in the works of Kundakunda (*Sīlapāhuda* 10), Right Penance is added to these three, although later Jaina thinkers consider Right Penance under Right Conduct and so generally recognize a threefold path to liberation.

Some Indian thinkers believe that the cultivation of only one is sufficient for an aspirant to attain this goal, but the Jainas do not agree. According to them only a cultivation of all the three—insight, knowledge, and conduct—can lead to release. The absence of any one of these constituents makes emancipation impossible. "Knowledge is impossible without right insight and without right knowledge right conduct is not possible while without right conduct liberation is unattainable. Thus all three are required for the attainment of emancipation" (*US* 28.30).

Right Insight

For some Jaina thinkers *darśana* means "intuition" (*prajñā*) as distinct from knowledge acquired by means of the senses or inference. For others it also denotes self-realization. In Jain scriptures the word *darśana* or *daṁsaṇa* sometimes means simply "philosophy" in the sense of a view of ultimate reality, the world, and the self. Genuine Right Insight is a firm belief in the true and pure nature of the soul. In the *US* and the *TS* it means "faith" or "belief" in the seven principles, namely, self, not-self, influx, bondage, etc. In later Jaina literature *darśana* is an attitude of devotion to the *Tīrthaṅkara* ("ford-makers" or enlightened teachers of the past), the preceptor (guru), and religion (*dharma*). Thus, in the Jaina tradition, Right Insight has a wide range of meanings including self-realization, intuition, view, faith, and devotion.

Although faith and devotion thus have a place in Jainism, the notion of divine grace has no place. The soul itself is the architect of its own destiny. The Jainas believe that true devotion to the *Tīrthaṅkara*(s) yields fruitful results yet the *Tīrthaṅkara*(s) themselves do not literally help in any way. The aspirant contemplates their nature and thereby realizes his or her own as the two natures are inherently the same, A Gujarāti Jaina poet has expressed this idea in the following way:

> Just as a lion cub brought up in a herd of sheep realizes his real nature to be that of a lion after seeing one, so too the aspirant realizes his own true nature to be that of an Arhat by worshiping the Arhat.

Right Insight operates in three domains. The first consists in a firm belief and, ultimately, in a direct awareness that an eternal soul exists as the agent of actions to which it is subject and that it can attain liberation from them. The second comprises a balanced state of mind, the realization of the blissful nature of the self and a yearning for truth, detachment, compassion, and an awareness of the distinction between virtue and vice. Lastly, Right Insight comprises firm belief in the Jaina doctrine free of doubts, and its cultivation, freedom from desire for worldly pleasures, an attitude of dispassion which does not cling to the pleasant or beautiful and shuns the painful, the ugly, or the tedious, a correct understanding of genuine Jaina spirituality, the cultivation of one's own spiritual qualities, selfless love for fellow beings and the propagation of Right Insight to others through good works and by setting an example of austerity.

The Right Knowledge

Right Knowledge is a correct knowledge of seven fundamental categories, namely, the nature of the individual soul, insentient matter, the influx of karmic matter, stoppage of this influx, bondage, the shedding of accumulated karmic matter, and liberation. In short, it is the knowledge both of ultimate reality and the factors that make for bondage and release. It comprises the knowledge of all things in all their infinite facets. The Jainas maintain that one-sided knowledge or a biased standpoint is false, because it ignores the infinite aspects of things; as long as it persists, Right Knowledge is not possible.

At the same time Jainism maintains that Right Knowledge consists in the discrimation between the self and the non-self. The self, the Knower, cannot be made the object of knowledge: it is not possible to know the self on the basis of a knower–known relationship. The Knower can never become an object of knowledge. This makes the knowledge of the self unique and quite different from the knowledge of the non-self, which arises through the knower–known relationship. Thus, no object of knowledge can be the self, but only non-self. But even though Right Knowledge is the knowledge of the self in itself, it can only be known with reference to the non-self. Knowing the nature of non-self and differentiating it from self constitute discrimination, which itself, therefore, ultimately is Right Knowledge. The *SS* makes an exhaustive study of the nature of "discrimination" (*bheda vijñāna*); indeed, this is the guiding theme of the work:

> Anger etc. are the consequences of the power to bear fruit of karmic matter and thus they are not the real nature of the Self. The Self is merely the

> Knower. The Jinas teach that the various kinds of fruits and the operation of the karmas are not the real nature of the Self. The Self is the pure Knower. (207, 210)
>
> He who is emancipated (*siddha*) has become so by discriminating the Self from the Non-self while he who is in bondage has failed to do so. (Commentary on *SS*, 132)

Right Knowledge, therefore, is the knowledge of our own inherent nature; it is not a mere academic knowledge of scripture or doctrine but the inner experience of our own self and its inherent godliness. It is the awakened state of our pure consciousness (*apramattadaśā*), that of the pure witness (*sākṣībhāva*) who is omniscient but does not act.

The Jaina maintains that there are five basic types of knowledge, indirect or direct. The first two types are the indirect knowledge that we gain of reality through the operation of the senses and mind as well as through language or scripture. The third is the direct knowledge born of the sensory perception of the external world. The fourth one is telepathy or knowledge of other minds, which is acquired through the practice of penance or Yoga. The fifth one is that form of direct knowledge which is had in the liberated state. This is perfect knowledge (*kevala-jñāna*), which intuits all that exists in all its modes in the past, present, and future. When the veil of the four destructive karmas is completely removed, omniscience dawns. Kundakunda adds that the liberated soul (*kevalin*) is not only omniscient in this sense but has a perfect knowledge of his own self (*NS* 158). Indeed, this is the highest level of Right Knowledge which is to be attained. In Jainism (Right) Knowledge is that which helps (man) to understand the nature of reality, controls the mind, and purifies the soul. It is through (Right) Knowledge that the ties of attachment are severed, interest in the ultimate good is developed, and the feelings of universal friendship strengthened (*Mūlācāra* 5.70.71).

Right Conduct

Right Conduct is explained on two different levels. First, at the highest level Right Conduct is a state in which the soul is completely free from passions and perversity; it is one of self-awareness and self-absorption. In this state the self enjoys its own nature and abides undisturbed, free of external motivations. Kundakunda in the *Pravacanasāra* says: "Conduct is Dharma, Dharma is equanimity and equanimity is that state in which the Self is free from delusion and mental tension" (1.7). At the lower level of practical

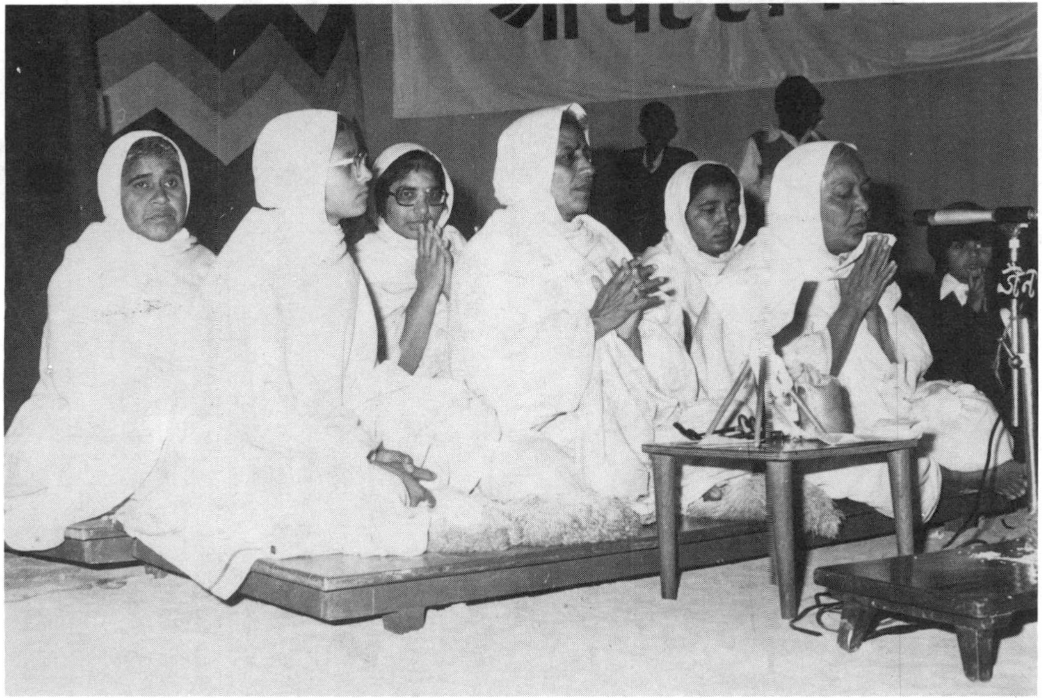

11. A scene of praying the tīrthankaras by the nuns of the Svetambara Jaina sect.

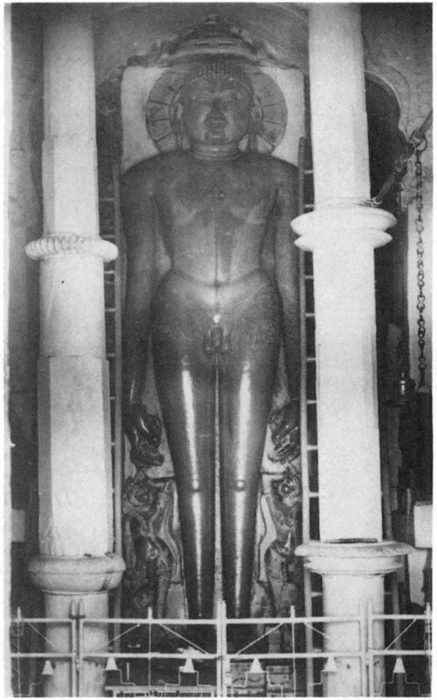

12. Digambar, Jina image, 11th century. Khajuraho.

concerns, Right Conduct is to adopt the rules of discipline prescribed in the Jaina *Āgama*(s).

Every human action has two aspects–extrinsic (*dravya*) and intrinsic (*bhāva*). The extrinsic merit of an action is assessed by others and depends on its outer social results. Its intrinsic merit depends on the intention or motive of him who acts. It is the purity of intention or motive, not the external results, that makes an action intrinsically good or bad. Kundakunda says:

> A person behaving carelessly with his mind full of passion incurs the sin of causing injury, whether actual injury results or not; conversely one who is free of passion and firm in the observance of mindfulness (*samiti*), is not bound by sin even if injury results by his conduct. (3.17)

A contemporary historian of Indian philosophy sums up the Jaina view in very clear terms:

> Jaina ethics emphasizes purity of motive as distinguished from consequences of actions. It considers an action to be right if it is actuated by good intention (*abhisandhi*), though it leads to the unhappiness of others. It considers an action to be wrong if it is actuated by a bad intention though it leads to the happiness of others. An intention is pure when it is devoid of attachment, aversion, delusion and passions. It is impure when it is distressing and aggressive.[1]

Jainism, however, does give due consideration to the consequences of an action from a practical point of view. The external aspect of moral conduct should not be neglected. Thus, according to Jaina philosophers purity of thought should be followed by right action, and so a code of conduct for both householders and monks is prescribed.

Jaina texts prescribe detailed rules regulating the conduct of Jaina householders, monks, and nuns. The eating of meat, drinking of alcohol, sexual license, dishonesty, and violence are strongly condemned. The ideal Jaina householder should be honest in all his dealings and take care to marry his sons and daughters into respectable Jaina families. He should select a decent residence, neither too secluded nor too central, and should keep the company of pious folk. Living within his means he should be charitable to the poor and to mendicant monks, listen to their religious discourse, and treat them with respect and reverence. He must be regular in his diet and be alert not to indulge the senses, disciplining himself all the time in order to overcome his evil tendencies and passions. He should observe the twelve vows of noninjury, refraining from falsehood, theft, sexual promiscuity; limiting one's possessions; limiting enjoyment of consumable and subconsumable items; vowing not to commit purposeless acts; practicing equanimity;

refraining from worldly activities for fixed periods of time; observing weekly fasts and certain essential daily duties such as the worship of the enlightened Arhats, devotion to the spiritual preceptor, the study of scripture along with a moderate practice of penance and meditation. Stress is also laid on his duty to work for the benefit of society and to give what he can to the needy and to the community of monks.

The code of conduct for a Jaina monk or nun lays great stress on the practice of nonviolence (*ahiṁsā*), and the other four great vows, truth, nonstealing, celibacy, and nonpossession, along with self-restraint, meditation, and abstinence. According to the Jaina, a monk is bound to observe a number of rules from which the householder is exempt. Thus, for example, although neither the monk nor the householder is allowed to eat after sunset, the monk must not eat more than once during the day. Monks and nuns, as one would expect, should abstain from all sexual activity; moreover, they should avoid all contact with members of the opposite sex. All personal possessions, except those essential for spiritual discipline, should be given up. Monks and nuns should eat only what is given to them. When moving about they should take care not to injure any living being, and so they are admonished to scrutinize the ground before them as they walk and not to go out at night. They should take care not to talk excessively or speak badly of others. Reverence for their superiors, preceptors, and the perfected coupled with the practice of austerity (particularly fasting), meditation, and detachment from worldly concerns should be their constant occupation.

Jaina thinkers all agree on the order of these three constituents of the path to liberation. The priority of Right Insight is generally accepted. Jaina scripture points out that Right Conduct and Right Knowledge are impossible in the absence of Right Insight. Kundakunda says

> Those who are devoid of Right Insight will never attain Right Knowledge, even if they practice severe penance for thousands of millions of years.
>
> Those who have fallen from Right Insight are depraved. There is no liberation for one devoid of Right Insight. Even those who have fallen from Right Conduct may attain liberation but not those who have fallen from Right Insight. (*Darśanaprābhṛta* 5, 6)

Bhadrabāhu also voices the same view in his gloss on *Ācārāṅga*. He says that penance, knowledge, and action bear good fruits only through Right Insight (221). Even so, in order to cultivate Right Insight, the suppression or elimination of the more extreme passions is essential. Thus Right Conduct proceeds from Right Insight and Right Insight from Right Conduct. Mahāvīra prescribed a course of discipline in which the coordination of action with knowledge along with insight is indispensable. Again, although the priority of Right Knowledge over Right Conduct is generally accepted, even so it cannot lead to liberation unless it is followed by Right Conduct. The *Sūtrakṛtāṅga* says that "whether a man is a Brahmin, or a *bhikṣu,* ("monk") or a knower of many scriptures, he will suffer on account of his actions, if they are not good" (2.1.3). It is also said in the *US* that knowledge of various languages and many scriptures does not, in itself, elevate a person. Those who are addicted to vice and regard themselves as learned are really ignorant. They offer only verbal satisfaction to their souls (6.11). In his gloss on *Āvaśyaka Sūtra* Bhadrabāhu says: "Even the knower of many scriptures cannot cross the ocean of transmigration (*saṃsāra*) if his actions are not good" (9). He adds: "Just as a chariot on one wheel cannot move and a blind or a lame man cannot reach his destination by himself, in the same way knowledge or action alone cannot lead one to liberation" (10–11). Thus the Jaina path seeks to combine both aspects and to develop a person's inherent spiritual qualities in every respect so that he or she may attain the ultimate goal.

Jaina Festivals

Jaina festivals do not aim at entertainment; they are meant for the spiritual development of the self through the practice of austerities. Among the festivals of the Jainas, the best known is *Paryuṣaṇa,* which means literally "a period of worship." It is celebrated in the lunar month of Bhādrapada (August-September) by all Jains. When the festival starts, the lay followers of Jainism observe a fast and spend their time mostly in worshiping jina icons, listening to religious discourses and reading religious books. Throughout this period the pious Jaina takes care to examine his conscience daily in the morning and evening. On the last day Śvetāṁbara Jainas observe a fast, attend religious discourses, confess their moral lapses and sins committed during the year, and undertake penances alone for them. On that day they ask forgiveness from all irrespective of whether they are friends or foes and declare: "I forgive all living beings and pray that they all will forgive me. I am friendly to all living beings and bear nobody ill-will" (*Āvaśyaka Sūtra* and *Mūlācāra,* 2,8).

During these feast days, the observance of nonviolence is considered to be a primary duty. Indeed, in ancient times Jaina preceptors exercised their influence to get rulers to ordain that these be days of nonviolence. In addition to this main festival, *Navapadoli, Aṣṭāhnika Parva, Akṣayatṛtīyā, śrutapañcamī*, and the days of conception, birth, initiation, enlightenment, and emancipation (*nirvāṇa*) of the *Tīrthaṅkara*(s) are also observed as festive occasions. The days on which Lord Mahāvīra was born and attained enlightenment are also observed with great enthusiasm by the entire Jaina community.

Spirituality and Altruism

Although Jainism unambiguously asserts that a chaste, secluded way of life is the best possible, at the same time it teaches that personal spiritual development achieved through penance should be for the benefit of the community. Mahāvīra's own life bears testimony to this. After spending twelve years alone performing austerities, he went back to society to establish a social order of monks, nuns, laymen, and laywomen and guided it up to the last moment of his life. Jainism thus proceeds from individual betterment inevitably to that of the society. The individual is the primary unit of society; hence, as long as individuals remain under the grip of passion there is no question of social amelioration. As long as a moral and spiritual consciousness is not developed in one's own individual life, order and peace cannot be established in one's social life. The institutions that are formed for the fulfillment of selfish motives are of no lasting benefit to society. The teaching of Mahāvīra is that abstention in individual life can be the source of positive social welfare. It is said in the *Praśnavyākaraṇa-sūtra:* "The preaching of the Lord is for the welfare of all the beings of the world." The fivefold discipline of nonviolence, truth, honesty, sexual purity, and indifference to material gain is not for personal edification alone but also aims at the social good (2.1.1; 2.1.4). That Jaina philosophers have always given priority to the good of others over one's own is reflected in the graded ideals of the "ford-maker" (*Tīrthaṅkara*), "enlightened group teacher" (*gaṇadhara*), and liberated soul (*sāmānya kevalin*), who are all equally enlightened beings working respectively for the universal, communal, and individual good, the *Tīrthaṅkara*(s) having the highest place.

Spirituality and Life-negation

The recognition of spiritual values does not mean that physical and material values should be completely rejected. Material values need not be a hindrance to spiritual development; in fact, they should be made subservient to it. It is said in the *Niśīthabhāṣya* that "knowledge leads to salvation, the body is the means to knowledge and food the means to (nourish the) body." The body is the vessel which ferries a person to the other shore of eternal bliss. From this point of view, the fulfillment of bodily needs has both value and importance. The body is a means to liberation and therefore deserves care (4159; see also *Oghaniryukti* 47 and *Bṛhadkalpa bhāṣya* 931). Even so, our attention should be fixed not on the vessel—the means—but on the shore—the end to which it leads. As the vessel, the body is a means and not an end. Here we have a criterion that brings into relief the difference between spirituality and materialism. The profane materialist believes that the fulfillment of bodily needs is an end in itself, whereas a person of spirit directs it as the means to higher spiritual values. The essential point is not the fulfillment or rejection of bodily needs but the establishment of tranquillity and peace in the life of both the individual and society. Hence, the fulfillment of bodily needs is welcomed to the extent to which it furthers this cause; but when it does not, it ought to be rejected.

> When the senses come in contact with their objects, then the concomitant experience of pleasure or pain also arises. It is not possible in actual life to effectively alienate the senses from the sensations of their objects and thus to eradicate the experience of pleasure and pain. Hence what we must renounce are not sensory experiences but the attraction or repulsion they evoke in the mind. Attraction and repulsion are the effects of the involvement of the Self in either pleasant or unpleasant sense-objects—they cannot arise in one who is detached and indifferent. (*Ācārāṅga* book 11, chap. 15; *US* 32.100–107)

Thus, the essential teaching of Jainism is the avoidance of attachment, not the negation of life.

The Specific Features of Spirituality

Jaina spirituality, by cutting itself free from the concept of an Almighty God, vindicates the virtues of autonomy and self-sufficiency. Religion, which preaches reliance on God or on other supernatural forces, espouses heteronomy and leaves living beings to the mercy of some unknown force. Jainism declares that neither God nor any other power determines one's destiny. One is oneself the builder of one's own destiny through his or her good and bad actions. There is no God as the controller of the universe. Divinity is inherent in oneself; one can attain the level of the supreme (*Paramātman*) through one's own efforts alone. It is said that the soul itself is God. Instead of looking up for the grace of any power, one must look within to realize the supreme state through self-exertion.

Jainism denies all such misconceptions as the caste system entails, which stratify human communities and discriminate between human beings. According to Jainism all humans are equal. One is not high or low because one is born into some particular caste or class because of one's power or property, but by virtue of one's conduct. The *US* severely criticizes caste hierarchies and the assumed superiority of Brahmins, asserting instead that a real Brahmin is one who is completely unattached, talented, and of good conduct. It is not the caste but moral and spiritual upliftment that truly counts.

Although Jainism condemns the fire sacrifice, the making of offerings to the ancestors, and a ritual ablution, along with all the other rituals which play such a prominent role in Hinduism as a whole, it does so with the intention of assigning a deeper spiritual significance to them. Thus, the *US* states that penance is the sacrificial fire; the individual soul the fireplace; the propensities of mind, speech, and body the ladles; the body is the dried cow dung; Karma the fuel; while self-control and right exertion are the recitations of mantras and that only as such is the fire sacrifice recommended by the sages. Again, the pond is religious law; celibacy is the holy bathing place; and tranquillity the bath. It is only by bathing in this way that the soul is made pure and freed from karmic dirt (12.43–41).

In the same vein Jainism asserts that self-restraint and self-purification are superior to the giving of alms and the performance of rituals. Thus, Jainism lends a spiritual perspective to ritual to free religion from ritualism and concentrate on the essential, which is the purification and realization of the auto-motivated self.

Nonviolence, in the sense of regard for life, is accepted as an ideal by almost all the religions of the world, but none pursues it as meticulously as Jainism, which prohibits not only the killing of human beings and animals but even of plants. To hurt plants is also considered to be an act of violence or *hiṁsā*. Respect or regard for life should be total as well as unconditional. Life, in whatever form it may be, should be respected; we have no right to deprive a living being of its life. The *Daśavaikālika* says: "Every living being wants to live and not to die; this is the reason why the sages prohibit violence" (6.10). Although Jainism sets as its goal the ideal of total nonviolence, external as well as internal, yet the realization of this ideal in practice is by no means easy. Nonviolence is a spiritual ideal fully realizable only on the spiritual plane. A human being, however, is not just a spiritual but also a physical being and so cannot avoid all possible forms of injury either to himself or herself or his or her fellow creatures. Man can only strive toward a fully nonviolent life, and only to the extent that he succeeds can he rise above the physical level. However, violence that is intentional can be avoided. A deliberate violence relates to our mental proclivities. A human is master of his or her thoughts, and so it is obligatory for all to be nonviolent in this sphere. Other forms of violence are inevitable—namely, that violence necessary for self-defense and the execution of daily tasks—because a human, despite his or her inherently spiritual nature, lives also on the physical level.

Jainas consider nonviolence to be the essence of religion; it is its eternal and purest form. To be religious and to observe nonviolence are one and the same. Nonviolence is the sole criterion of a truly moral life. Indeed, it is only through nonviolence and regard for life that we can establish peace in the world.

Jainism believes that the views, ideologies, and faiths of others should be respected. In the *Sūtrakṛtāṅga* Mahāvīra says: "Those who praise their own faith or ideology and blame that of their opponents and thus distort the truth, will be kept confined in the cycle of birth and death" (1.1.2.23).

The Jaina doctrine of *anekānta* ("manifoldness") allows that all things are many-sided and can be viewed from various angles. The view of our opponent may also be true in certain respects, and if it is so, then we have no right to condemn it and declare it to be totally false. Jainism proposes an integral approach for the understanding of the nature of reality, teaches religious tolerance, and advocates a democratic accommodation of viewpoints.

The Stages of Spiritual Development (*Guṇasthāna*)

There are fourteen stages of spiritual development, from the lowest level of false insight to the highest level of Godhood taught in the *Prajñāpana*, *Ṣaṭkhaṇḍāgama* and in the works of Kundakunda as well as other Jaina thinkers. These fourteen stages are technically called *guṇasthāna*, meaning literally "stages or stations of excellence." They are adapted to the level, nature, and quality of the aspirant's knowledge, insight, and conduct, which are consonant with the degree to which his karma is operational.

1. The first stage is called "false insights" (*mithyādṛṣṭi*). This is the lowest stage, and it is from here that the efforts for the spiritual development and attainment of Right Insights are made. However, the soul in the grip of extreme passions—anger, pride, deceit, and greed—never evolves beyond this stage. If he is a type of soul incapable of attaining liberation (*abhavya*), literally "nondevout," he will remain at this stage for an indefinite period, while those souls capable of enlightenment (*bhavya*), literally "devout," reside here for only a limited span of time.

False insights are of five kinds: the acceptance of a one-sided or extremist view (*ekānta*); the acceptance of a view that runs counter to facts or reality (*viparīta*); a veneration of false creeds (*vinaya*); doubt or instability of faith (*saṁśaya*); ignorance of the real nature of things (*ajñāna*).

2. The second stage is called "a foretaste of Right Insight" (*sāsvādana-samyag dṛṣṭi*). This is an intermediate stage when the soul falls from the level of Right Views to that of False View but has not quite fallen. This stage is so called because the soul has had a taste of Right view, wherefore there is hesitation before accepting false ones.

3. The third stage is technically known as "the combination of Right and False Views" (*saṁyagmithyā dṛṣṭi*). This is a mixed state of right and false insight like the taste of curd mixed with sugar, which is neither sweet nor sour. It is a state of doubt. At this stage the soul accepts neither false nor right view. In the opinion of a contemporary scholar this stage is one of confusion:

> After getting insight into the right attitude for the first time it is possible that a man may at the same time begin to feel that what is right may not be right and he may cling to false ideologies also. . . . This stage is that of an active struggle between right and wrong. Right and wrong both present themselves before the mind each claiming to be superior while the mind is capable of choosing between them.[2]

4. The fourth stage is called "Right Insight but without self-control" (*āvirata saṁyagdṛṣṭi*). In reality this is the first stage in the upward journey of the soul toward its spiritual goal. It is here that the soul gets its first glimpse of truth. The soul can now distinguish between right and wrong but because of its spiritual weakness cannot quit the path of immorality. In other words, at this stage the soul has insight but lacks self-control. Those who have a firm faith in the doctrines yet feel unable to follow their moral code are at this stage.

5. The fifth stage is known as "Right Insight but with partial self-control" (*deśaviratasaṁyagdṛṣṭi*). This is a stage of Right Views in which the soul does partially observe the moral code. A householder who possesses the Right Insight and observes the vows of a householder comes in this category. At this stage the soul knows what is right and also tries to practice it but cannot have a full control over its passions because of self-control being only partially effective. After attaining the fourth stage, if it develops spiritual strength and has control over the less extreme passions, it attains this stage.

6. The sixth stage is called "complete self-control but with spiritual inertia" (*pramattasamyatā*). It is the stage in which the soul observes Right Conduct as becomes the monk. Even so, attachment to the body lingers because of a degree of spiritual inertia which persists. Although the soul observes Right Conduct, there is still a lack of self-awareness and so it must continue to overcome the subtler passions and inertia to climb further.

7. The seventh stage is that of "self-control with freedom from spiritual

inertia" (*apramatta-samyatā*). At this stage the soul has full control over its passions and observes the moral code without any negligence and feels no attachment for the body. From this stage on there are two ways open: one is to climb up through the suppression of the passions (*upaśamaśreṇī*), and the other is through their total eradication (*kṣapakaśreṇī*). The person who climbs the ladder of spiritual progress by merely suppressing his passions is bound to fall, but he who ascends through the annihilation of his passions ultimately attains liberation (*nirvāṇa*) through their extinction.

8. The eighth stage of spiritual development is called "unprecedented activity" (*apūrvakaraṇa*). At this stage the soul acquires extraordinary purity and spiritual strength, and thus becomes capable of diminishing the duration and the intensity of the previously binding karmas. The soul performs the four acts of destroying the duration and intensity of karma, transforming the quality of karmic matter, and controlling of an unprecedented kind of duration. (This total process is technically known as "unprecedented activity.") At this stage the soul for the first time experiences genuine spiritual bliss and tranquillity.

9. The ninth stage is called "non-ceasing operation" (*anivṛttikaraṇa*). There is still an occasional possibility of the soul being affected by gross passions (*bādara-samparāya*), although it has a power to control them. The subtle sexual passions subside, yet others remain along with subtle greed; so the fear of the possible onset of gross passions persists. At the end of this stage the struggle for spiritual progress comes to an end and the soul spontaneously ascends to the tenth rung of the ladder.

10. This stage is named "subtle attachment" (*sūkṣmasamparāya*) because at this stage only a subtle form of greed remains. This greed amounts to a subtle unconscious attachment to the body. When this subtle attachment subsides, the soul ascends to the next stage. The soul that has progressed spiritually following the way of repression (*upaśamaśreṇī*) ascends to the eleventh stage, but the soul that has followed the path of the eradication of passion (*kṣapakaśreṇī*) proceeds directly to the twelfth stage.

11. This stage is known as "the subdual of the deluding" (*upaśānta mohanīya*) because in this stage the remains of deluding karma persist albeit in a subdued form. It is the highest stage for those who ascend along the ladder of repression. But ultimately repressed passions are bound to surface again and ruffle the tranquillity of mind leading invariably to a fall from this stage. Clearly Jainism does not advocate the repression of the passions as a means to spiritual progress.

12. The twelfth stage in the spiritual development of the soul is called "destruction of delusion" (*kṣīṇamoha*). The soul that ascends through the

ladder of the annihilation of passion (*kṣapakaśreṇī*) attains this stage directly. Here deluding karma, which is the main obstacle to spiritual progress, is completely destroyed, and the soul ascends to the thirteenth stage.

13. This stage is known as "karma united omniscient" (*sayogī-kevalī*). Here the soul attains the four infinities, namely, infinite knowledge, perception, bliss, and power, and thus becomes omniscient. It is the highest stage of spiritual development—that of one who is liberated in this life in which only those nonbinding karmas that determine the persistence of the body continue to operate.

14. The last stage is called "karma-liberated omniscient" (*ayogi-kevalī*). In this state the omniscient soul has complete control of the activities of its body, speech, and mind and prepares itself for final emancipation. The remaining karmas cease to operate, and the soul, leaving the body, proceeds to its heavenly abode.

Underlying the theory of fourteen stages of spiritual development lies a typology of souls set on the spiritual journey. Kundakunda, Karttikeya, Yogīndu, Haribhadra, Ānandaghana, and Yaśovijaya describe three broad levels of spiritual development which answer to three types of souls comprehending the aforementioned fourteen stages.

The Extroverted Soul (*bahirātman*) is gripped by false insight and so fails to distinguish between itself and the body. It regards external things as its own and takes keen interest in worldly pleasures. Those souls in the station of the first three kinds described above belong to this category.

The Introverted Soul (*antarātman*), on the other hand, possesses Right Insight and therefore clearly distinguishes itself from the body and its external belongings. An introverted soul does not take interest in worldly pleasures but meditates on its own real nature. This introverted soul is of three levels. The one that possesses Right Insight but does not observe Right Conduct is considered to be the lowest. Next comes the one that possesses Right Insight and also observes Right Conduct to a certain extent. The highest type of introverted soul is the one that possesses perfect Right Insight and also observes the Right Conduct. The lowest types belong to the fourth stage of spiritual development, the middling to fifth and sixth stages, while those ranging from the seventh to the twelfth stages are the highest types of introverted souls.

The Supreme Soul (*paramātmā*) is the soul that realizes its potentialities of infinite knowledge, perception, bliss, and power and has completely annihilated karmic impurity to become thus perfect and pure. This is the soul that is truly free from attachment and aversion (*vītarāga*) and has finally conquered all the passions and senses. The souls belonging to the thirteenth and fourteenth stages belong to this category and are, accordingly, of two kinds

—*arhat* and *siddha*. The former is one who has attained omniscience but continues to live in the body, while the *siddha* is one who has destroyed every last trace of karma and has attained final and eternal release, free forever of the body.

Notes

1. J. N. Sinha, *Indian Philosophy* (Calcutta: Sinha Publishing House, 1970) 2:261.
2. T. G. Kalghatagi, *Some Problems of Jain Psychology*, 156.

Bibliography

Sources

Ācārāṅga. Translated by Hermann Jacobi. Vol. 22 of *Sacred Books of the East.* Reprinted. Delhi: Motilal Banarasidas, 1964.

Daśavaikālika. Translated by K. C. Lalawani. Delhi: Motilal Banarasidas, 1973.

Gomattasāra—Nemichandra. Translated by J. L. Jaini. Lucknow: Central Jaina Publishing House, 1927.

Nigranthpravacan. Comp. Muni Chawth Malji. Translated by K. V. Abhyankar. Ratlam: Sri Jainodaya Pustak Prakashak Samiti, 1936.

Niyamasāra—Kundakunda. Translated by Uggar Sain. Lucknow: Central Jain Publishing House, 1931.

Puruṣārthasiddhyupāya—Amritacandra. Translated by Ajit Prasad. Lucknow: Central Jain Publishing House.

Samansuttam. Comp. Jinendra Varni. Varanasi: Sarva Seva Samgha, 1975.

Samayasāra—Kundakunda. Translated by J. L. Jaini. Lucknow: Central Jain Publishing House, 1931.

Tattvārtha Sūtra—Umāswāti. Ahemadabad: L. D. Institute of Indology.

Uttarādhyāyana and *Sūtrakṛtaṅga.* Translated by Hermann Jacobi. Vol 45 of *Sacred Books of The East.* Reprinted. Delhi: Motilal Banarasidas, 1964.

Studies

Bhattacharya, Hari Satya. *Real in Jaina Metaphysics.* Bombay: Seth Santidas Khetsi Trust, 1966.

———. *Jain Moral Doctrine.* Bombay: Jain Sahitya Vikas Mandal, 1956.

Bhargav, Dayanand. *Jaina Ethics.* Delhi: Motilal Banarasidas, 1968.

Desai, S. M. *Haribhadra's Yoga Works and Psychosynthesis.* Ahmedabad: L. D. Institute of Indology, 1983.

Jain, S. C. *Structure and Function of Soul in Jainism.* Delhi: Bhāratīya Jñānapīṭh, 1978.

Jaini, J. L. *Outlines of Jainism.* Indore: J. L. Jaini Trust, 1979.

Jaini, Padmanabhas. *The Jaina Path of Purification.* Delhi: Motilal Banarasidas, 1981.

Joshi, L. M. *Facets of Jaina Religiousness in Comparative Light.* Ahmedabad: L. D. Institute of Indology, 1981.

Kalghatagi, T. G. *Some Problems of Jain Psychology.* Dharwar: Karnatak University, 1961.

Mehta, M. L. *Jaina Philosophy.* Varanasi: P. Research Institute.

Mukherjee, Satakari. *The Jaina Philsophy of Non-Absolutism.* Calcutta: The Bhārati Mahāvidyālaya, 1944.

Padmaraja, Y. *Jain Theories of Realities and Knowledge.* Bombay: Jain Sahitya Vikas Mandal.

Sogani, K. C. *Ethical Doctrines of Jainas.* Solapur: Lalchand Hirachand Dosi Jain Saṅskriti Saṁrakṣaka Saṁgh, 1967.

Stevenson, Sinclair. *The Heart of Jainism.* New Delhi: Munshiram Monoharlal.

Tatia, N. M. *Studies in Jaina Philosophy.* Varanasi: Jain Cultural Research Society.

Williams, R. *The Jaina Yoga.* London: Oxford University Press, 1962.

Part Four

THE SPIRITUAL QUEST FOR IMMORTALITY AND FREEDOM

9

Yoga: The Royal Path to Freedom

Ravi Ravindra

According to Patañjali's *Yogasutra,* the classical text on Yoga, the purpose of Yoga is to lead to the silence of the mind (1.2). This silence is the prerequisite condition for the mind to be able to reflect accurately the objective reality without introducing its own subjective distortions. Yoga does not create this reality, which is above the mind, but only prepares the mind to apprehend it, by assisting in the transformation of the mind—from an ordinary mind full of noise, like a whole army of frenzied and drunken monkeys—to a still mind.

Even this transformation is not literally brought about by any effort or practice, as the *Yogasutra* (4.2–3) reminds us, but is an unfolding of nature's own potential tendency. The practice and discipline are necessary only for removing the obstacles to this unfolding, just as a gardener removes the weeds for the sake of a healthy crop. Yoga attempts to eliminate the obstacles to the natural unfolding and development of the human being so that his or her true and real nature may be realized. This real nature is independent of the contingent conditioning of space-time, thought-feeling, fear-pleasure and form-species. In other words, the real inner being, called *puruṣa,* is independent of all the forces and controls of *prakṛti,* that is, causal nature, both subtle and gross. The real is above and behind the actual. The sole purpose not only of a given human incarnation but of the whole *prakṛti,* as the *Yogasutra* (2.21) tells us, is this ralization. In this realization alone is enlightenment and freedom.

Yoga is one of the six classical *darśana*(s) (perspectives, visions) aiming at the attainment of the ultimate reality. Out of these six schools of Indian philosophy, the school of *Sāṁkhya* is often associated with Yoga, and the two are frequently coupled together. There does not seem to be much basis for this association, for Yoga and *Sāṁkhya* for a very long time have represented two distinct approaches, even though there are some similarities in their underlying cosmologies. On the other hand, all the schools of thought in India, even the ones opposed to Yoga in its metaphysical doctrines, such as the school of Vedanta, have recognized the great value of the practical aspects of Yoga. In practical terms, Yoga can be said to constitute the very essence of the spirituality of India. Dating from a period prior to the ascendancy of the Aryans in India, it has had an enormous influence on all forms of Indian spirituality, including the Buddhist and Jain, and later the Sufi and the Christian.

The word *yoga* is derived from the root *yuj,* which means to unite or to join together, much like the etymological meaning of the word "religion." Yoga aims at the union of the human and the divine—all within oneself. It is a way to one's wholeness, an integration of all aspects and levels of oneself. One must not imagine that Yoga is only a collection of certain practices devoid of a metaphysical basis. In fact, Yoga is a perfectly structured and integrated world view aiming at the transformation of a human being from his actual and unrefined form to a perfected form. The *prākṛta* (literally, "natural," "common," "vulgar," "unrefined") state is one in which a person compulsively repeats his actions, in reaction to the forces of *prakṛti,* which are active both outside him and inside. Through Yoga he can become *samskrita* (literally, "well made," "well put together") and thus no longer be wholly at the mercy of natural forces and inclinations. It can be said that Yoga aims at freedom from nature, including the freedom from human nature; its flight is to the transcendence of humanity and the cosmos, into pure being.

Yoga is religion, science, and art, since it is concerned with being (*sat*), knowing (*jñana*), and doing (*karma*). The aim of Yoga, however, is beyond these three and beyond any opposites they imply. Mythologically, sometimes Yoga is personified as the son of *dharma* and *kriyā: dharma* is essentially the order that is the support of the cosmos, and *kriyā*, as action and performance, is a *sakti* (energy, power) of Viṣṇu in one of his incarnations. The importance of Yoga in the Indian tradition is obvious: a name or an epithet of Siva is *Yoganātha,* of Viṣṇu *Yogapati,* and of Kṛṣṇa *Yogeśvara,* in each case meaning essentially "the master or lord of Yoga." Without the mastery of Yoga, indeed, nothing can be accomplished rightly. As the *Yogasikhā Upanisad* (1.67) says: "Verily there is no merit higher than Yoga, no good higher than Yoga, no subtlety higher than Yoga; there is nothing that is higher than Yoga."

The Central Yoga

Although there are many kinds of *yoga*(s), some of which will be briefly discussed later on in this paper, such as *karmayoga* (the Yoga of works), *bhaktiyoga* (the Yoga of love), etc., the Indian tradition has in general maintained that there is only one Yoga, with varying emphasis on different aspects and methods employed in various schools of Yoga. The most authoritative, "revealed," text of classical Yoga is the *Yogasutra* (*Aphorisms of Yoga;* abbreviated as YS), the compilation of which is attributed to Patañjali. Nothing very much is known about Patañjali, not even when he lived. It is possible that the *Yogasutra* text was compiled sometime between the second century B.C. and the fourth century A.D. In any case, there is no question that most of the ideas and practices mentioned in the *Yogasutra* were already familiar to the guru(s) (teachers) of Indian spirituality, and they passed them on to their disciples with appropriate instructions and initiations. As is the mark of the *sūtra* (literally, "thread") literature, the *Yogasutra* presents the ideas in an extremely terse manner, leaving it to the individual teacher to expound the ideas more fully in his own circle of disciples; no doubt, in the process, each teacher emphasized the aspects that he himself found most useful.

The aim of Yoga is set out in the beginning of *Yogasutra,* in its most celebrated and most debated aphorism (1.2), namely, *yogah cittavrtti nirodhah* ("Yoga is the removal of the fluctuations of consciousness"). One practices Yoga for steadying attention, which is constantly undergoing fluctuations (*vrtti*(s)). These fluctuations may be pleasant or unpleasant but are, in any case, distractions from the point of view of the steady attention of a quiet mind. These *vrtti*(s) are grouped under five different headings by Patañjali, corresponding to the activities of the ordinary mind, namely, *pramāṇa* (judging, comparing, discursive activity), *viparyaya* (misjudging, misperception), *vikalpa* (verbal association, imagination), *nidrā* (dreaming, sleeping), and *smrti* (memory, clinging to the past experience). According to an underlying assumption of Yoga, the mind, which is confined to the above modes, is limited in scope and cannot know the objective truth about anything. The mind is not the true knower: it can infer or quote authority or make hypotheses or speculate about the nature of reality, but it cannot see the objects directly, from the inside, as it were, as they really are in themselves. In order to allow the direct seeing to take place, the mind, which by its very nature attempts to mediate between the object and the subject, has to be quietened. When the mind is totally silent and totally alert, both the real subject (*puruṣa*) and the real object (*prakṛti*) are simultaneously present to it: the seer is there; what is to be seen is there; and the seeing takes place without distortion. Then there is no comparing or judging, no misunderstanding, no fantasizing, no dozing off in heedlessness, nor any clinging to past knowledge. There is simply the seeing. That state is called *kaivalya* (literally, "aloneness"). It is not the aloneness of the seer, separated from the seen, as is unfortunately far too often maintained as a goal of Yoga, but the aloneness of *seeing* in its purity, without any distortions introduced by the organs of perception, namely, the mind, the heart, and the senses. The aim of Yoga is clear seeing, which is the sole power of the seer and only of the seer (*puruṣa*), not of the mind.

It is of utmost importance, from the point of view of Yoga, to distinguish between the mind (*citta*) and the real seer (*puruṣa*). *Citta* pretends to know, but it is of the nature of the known and the seen—that is, an *object* rather than the pure *subject.* This misidentification between the seer (subject) and the seen (object)—which is the mistaking of the *citta* with its fluctuations and its sorrows for the *puruṣa,* which is without sorrow and without alterations—is the fundamental error from which all other problems and suffering arise (YS 3–17). This basic ignorance is what gives rise to *asmitā* (I-am-this-ness, egoism). This is a limitation by particularization: *puruṣa* says "I am"; *asmitā* says "I am *this*" or "I am *that.*" From this egoism comes the strong desire to perpetuate this specialization of itself and the resulting separation from all else, manifesting itself as a wish to continue living (*abhiniveśa*) as this separate entity. This wish is maintained by indulging in "I-like-this" (*rāga,* attraction) or "I-do-not-like-this" (*dveṣa,* aversion). The means for freedom from the fundamental ignorance, leading to all sorrow, is an unceasing vision of discernment (*viveka-khyāti*). This vision of discernment alone can permit transcendental insight (*prajñā*) to arise. Nothing can force the appearance of this insight; all one can do is to prepare the ground for it. Since it is said that the whole purpose for the existence of the mind as well as the rest of *prakṛti* is to serve *puruṣa,* it is only natural that if the ground is properly prepared, the transcendental insight will arise.

The ground to be prepared is the entire psychosomatic organism, *śarīra,* for it is through that and in that whole organism that *puruṣa* sees and *prajñā* arises, not the mind alone nor the heart nor the physical body by itself. One with dulled senses has as little chance of coming to *prajñā* as the one with a stupid mind or with an unfeeling heart. Agitation in any part of the entire organism causes a fluctuation of attention. And every act—including mental acts like thoughts, volitions, intentions—leaves an impression (*saṁskāra*) on the psyche, which in turn lodges itself in the various tensions, postures, and gestures of the physical body. These impressions in turn create tendencies (*vāsanā*) which dispose one toward certain sorts of actions. The really deep tendencies cut across the boundaries of what we ordinarily call life and death—that is, the life and death of the physical body. This, in short, is the law of *karma* (action, act, work): as one acts, so one is, and as one is, so one acts. It is less to say that one reaps what one sows; it is more in accordance with the ideas of Yoga that every act makes a person a little different from before, and this different person now naturally acts according to what he is. Within the realm of *prakṛti* and *karma,* he is not anything except his actions, thoughts, feelings—all the conditioning of the past. A person is an expression of the working out of the law of *karma.* One repeats oneself helplessly, at the same level, neurotically, precisely because one does not know what one does and why. But just as there is a cosmic tendency for this mechanical repetition (*pravṛtti*), there is also a cosmic tendency for waking up to one's real situation (*nivṛtti*) so that one may alter it with effort.

The effort required, with the ultimate aim of coming to the vision of discernment (*viveka-khāyti*), which alone may lead to true insight (*prajñā*), is enormously difficult for the simple reason that a total cleansing of the deepest recesses of one's entire consciousness is required. Otherwise, subtle impressions and tendencies will reassert themselves, leading one into a repetitious circle. What is needed is a counterflow (*pratiprasava*) to the ordinary tendencies of *prakṛti,* a turning around (in Greek *metanoia,* usually translated as "repentance" in the New Testament). It is only by the reversal of the usual tendencies of the mind that its agitations can be quietened and it can know its right and proper place with respect to the *puruṣa:* that of the *known* rather than the *knower* (YS 2.10; 4.18–22). However pure and refined the mind is, in the terminology of the YS, even if the mind is constituted of pure *sattva* (luminosity, purity), it is distinct from the *puruṣa* and is radically inferior to it in its power of seeing.

The Limbs of Yoga

The counterflow of the usual tendencies of the mind is attained through the eight limbs of Yoga by steady practice (*abhyāsa*) and increasing inwardness (*vairāgya*). Elsewhere, in YS 2.1–2, a different scheme is indicated: austerity, self-study, and devotion to the Lord constitute *kriyā-yoga,* which has as its purpose the lessening of the causes-of-sorrow (*kleśa*) and the cultivation of *samādhi* (settled intelligence, silence). Here we shall follow the much more elaborated scheme (YS 2.28–55; 3.1–8) of the eight limbs: *yama, niyama, āsana, prāṇāyāma, pratyāhāra, dhāraṇā, dhyāna,* and *samādhi.* The first one, *yama,* refers to the various self-restraints comprising abstention from violence, falsehood, theft, incontinence, and aquisitiveness. The second limb, *niyama,* consists in the observances of purity, contentment, austerity, self-study, and devotion to the Lord. (The last three observances are the same that were said earlier to constitute *kriyā-yoga.*) The third and fourth limbs, *āsana* and *prāṇāyāma,* are concerned with the rght posture, which makes one both relaxed and alert, and the proper regulation of breathing for steadying the attention. These two limbs by themselves are often elaborated in terms of numerous postures and breathing exercises in schools of *haṭha-yoga,* Yoga of force, dealing mainly with the physical culture aspect of Yoga. Sometimes one encounters great displays of ascetic prowess which have nothing whatever to do with Yoga proper. The fifth limb, *pratyāhāra,* is the inward turning of the senses so that they can be freed of the external impressions in order to obey the mind.

These five limbs constitute the outer group out of the eight limbs of Yoga, the other three being the more inner limbs. *Dhāraṇā* is concentration in which the consciousness is bound to a single spot; *dhyāna* is contemplation or meditative absorption in which there is an uninterrupted flow of attention from the observer to the observed. So far the observer has acted as the center of consciousness which sees. When that center is removed–that is to say, when the observing is done by *puruṣa,* through the mind emptied of itself–that state is called *samādhi,* a state of silence, settled intelligence, and emptied mind, in which the mind becomes the object and reflects it truly, as it is. As an inversion of the usual mode of knowing, in which the mind receives the impressions about the object from the senses and imposes its own fluctuations (*vṛtti*(s)) upon the object, in *samādhi* the mind acts as the arena in which there is no subjective or personal center of consciousness which can introduce any distortion of the object; there is only the pure seeing. No agency or organ mediates between the object and the seeing. Thus, the insight obtained in the state of *samādhi* is neither sensual nor mental, nor is it to do with feelings. It is not personal knowledge, nor is it subjective. It refers wholly and exclusively to the object; it is completely objective insight–of the object as it is and as it chooses to reveal itself, without any violation or forcing from the observer, for, at the moment of pure seeing, the observer as a separated center of consciousness does not exist. As the YS says (1.48–49; 2.15; 3.54), the insight in the state of *samādhi* is truth bearing (*ṛtambharā*). The scope of this insight is different from the scope of the knowledge gained from tradition or inference. Unlike the latter knowledge, the insight of *prajñā* reveals the unique particularity, rather than an abstract generality, of the object. (For this reason, the mystical insight is often considered closer to a sense perception rather than discursive knowledge; it is clear, however, that in *prajñā* the senses are extremely refined and turned inward and do not mediate between the seer and the object.) Unlike the mental knowledge, in which there is an opposition between the object

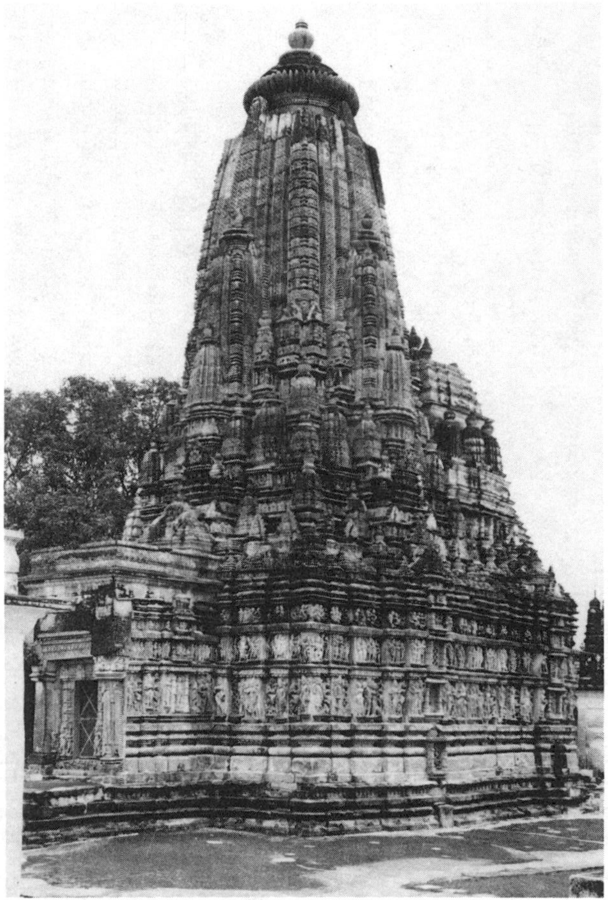

13. Jaina Temple of Pārsvanātha,
11th century. Khajuraho.

14. Chovisi of Rṣabhanātha, 9th century.
Museum and Picture Gallery, Baroda.

and the modalities of the mind, an opposition that inevitably leads to sorrow, the insight of *prajñā*, born of sustained vision of discernment, is said to be the "deliverer"; it can pertain to any object—large or small, far or near—and any time—past, present or future—for it is without time sequence, present everywhere at once.

It may be remarked that the various steps of Yoga are ordered yet are not sequentially linear in the sense that the completion of one step is required before the next one can be undertaken. Some of the apparent linearity arises from the analytical and linguistic nature of the exposition. Earlier steps are preparatory to the later ones, but they are not absolutely necessary. Nor are they completely sufficient in determining the later steps. A right physical posture or moral conduct may aid internal development but does not guarantee it. More often, the external behavior reflects the internal development. As an example, a person does not necessarily become wise by breathing or thinking in a particular way; he breathes and thinks in that way because he is wise.

The three inner limbs of Yoga, namely, *dhāraṇā, dhyāna,* and *samādhi,* together constitute what is called *saṁyama* (discipline, constraint). It is the application of *saṁyama* to any object which leads to the direct perception (*sākṣātkāra*) of it because in the state of quietude in which the *vṛtti*(s) are removed the *citta* is like a transparent jewel taking on the true color of the object which fuses (*samāpatti*) with it (YS 1.41). The special attention which prevails in the state of *saṁyama* can be brought to bear on any aspect of *prakṛti,* which, as was said earlier, encompasses all that can be an object of perception, however subtle.

Here, therefore, is the basic research method of the yogic natural science: to bring a completely quiet mind and to wait without agitation or projection, letting the object reveal itself in its own true nature, by coloring the transparent mind with its own color. This science is further extended by the principles of analogy and isomorphism between the macrocosmos and the microcosmos which is the human organism. A particularly striking example of this isomorphism is to be found in the *Yoga darsana Upanisad* (4.48–53), where the eternal *tirtha* (sacred ford, holy water, place of pilgrimage) is considered inferior to the *tirtha* in the body, and external mountains and other places are identified with the various parts of the organism:

> The Mount Meru is in the head
> and Kedāra in your brow;
> between your eyebrows, near your nose,
> know, dear disciple, that Vāraṇasī stands;
> in your heart is the confluence
> of the Ganges and the Yamunā;

lastly, Kamalālaya
is to be found in the *mulādhāra,*

To prefer "real" *tirtha*(s)
to those concealed in your body,
is to prefer common potsherds
to diamonds laid in your hands.

Your sins will be washed away,
whether you have made love with your wife
or even with your own daughter,
if you carry out the pilgrimages
within your own body from one *tirtha* to another.

True yogis who worship the *ātman* in themslves
have no need of water *tirtha*(s)
or of gods of wood and clay.

The *tirtha*(s) of your body
infinitely surpass those of the world,
and the *tirtha*-of-the-soul is the greatest of them:
the others are nothing beside it.

Yoga and Power

A large number of aphorisms in the YS 3.16–53 describe the knowledge and the powers gained by attending to various objects in the state of *samyama.* For example, we are told that through *samyama* on the sun, one gains insight into the solar system, and by *samyama* on the moon, knowledge of the arrangement of the stars (YS 3.26–27). Similarly, many occult or extraordinary powers, *siddhi*(s), accrue to the *yogi* by bringing the state of *samyama* to bear on the various aspects of oneself: for example, by *samyama* on the relation between the ear and ether, one acquires the divine ear by which one can hear at a distance or hear extremely subtle and unusually inaudible sounds. Many other powers are mentioned by Patañjali; however, none of them is his main concern. These powers may be present from birth or may be acquired by other means such as drugs or mantras (literally, "mind-instrument"; special sounds usually given by a teacher to a disciple for recitation) or physical austerities (YS 4.1). There is no suggestion that there is anything wrong with these powers, or more than the suggestion that there is anything wrong with the mind as it is. The point is more that the mind as it is is an inadequate instrument for true knowledge; similarly, these powers, however vast, are inadequate as the goal of true knowledge. The *yogi*(s) who get preocuppied with them are likely to get sidetracked from the true path of Yoga. Therefore, these powers are seen as temptations and, along with heightened sensory experiences, are regarded as obstacles to sustained *samādhi* (YS 3.36–37).

The Spirituality of Yoga Discipline

So far there is an object which is being seen, without a personal center of consciousness acting as the seer. The real seer is *puruṣa,* which is not personally mine or yours; it is the pure power of seeing. In a continuation of the Vedic sacrifice (*yajña*), in Yoga one sacrifices the limiting mind for the sake of the unlimited power to see, a sacrifice of one's separated self–with all of one's fears and hopes, likes and dislikes, sorrows and pleasures, failures and ambitions–for the sake of the Only One who truly sees. Then follows the sacrifice of the seen for the sake of the Only One who truly is. This comes about in *nirbīja samādhi* (seedless silence), when there is no separated object but the *puruṣa,* there is no separated subject but the *puruṣa,* there is no knowing except the *puruṣa.* The seer, the seen, and the seeing are all One; there is no other. This is the state of *kaivalya*–of aloneness, not because there is an opposition or a separation but simply because there is no "other." With respect to this state of *samādhi,* the previously labeled "inner" limbs of Yoga are also outer. This *samādhi* is also called *dharma-megha-samādhi* (silence in the cloud of right order). Thence follows the ending of all the causes of sorrow, of all the blemishes and imperfections; little remains to be known, for the insight in this state is infinite; the purpose of the human incarnation is fulfilled and the *yogi* is completely free and established in the pure awareness of *puruṣa* (YS 4.29–34).

In this movement from one's personal self to the Self, from the identification with *citta* to the identification with *puruṣa,* one is placing oneself in the right internal order. The sacrificing (Latin *sacre facere,* "to make sacred") of *citta* and *prakṛti* for the sake of *puruṣa* is precisely what renders them sacred and gives them significance. In this process of transformation, many stages are described in the YS, as are the corresponding many levels of silence (*samādhi*). As a whole, the process of Yoga involves the liberating of *puruṣa* from within the psychosomatic organism, much like a sculptor releases a figure from the stone by chiseling and discarding. The organism and *prakṛti* in general are no more impediments to *puruṣa* than the stone is to the sculpture. Nor is *prakṛti* considered unreal or a mental projection. "She" is very real, and though "she" can overwhelm the mind with her dynamism and charms and veil the truth from it, yet in "her" proper place and function "she" exists in order to serve *puruṣa.* Thus, the discipline of Yoga is against the ordinary current. All the eight limbs of Yoga place constraints on the usual activity of our desires, inclinations, bodies, breath, senses, mind attention, and ego, so that they may be brought under control of something higher. The more controlled and quietened these various aspects of ourselves are, the greater is the development of the vision of discernment. This, in its turn, leads to the removal of ignorance about our true identity. Then we realize that we have been identifying ourselves only with our mental-physical self which is of the nature of the object rather than the real seer. When this misidentification is broken and we no longer rely on the mind for true insight, the natural conflict between the whole and the part—that is, between what is and the projections of the mind—is dissolved. That leads to the removal of sorrow and its underlying causes, and to the cultivation of deeper and deeper silence, and finally to the aloneness of the pure awareness.

Other Yogas

What we have described so far is the classical Yoga, the central Yoga, sometimes called the *rāja yoga* (the royal yoga). Already we have mentioned *kriyā-yoga,* noted in the YS (2.1–2), consisting of austerity, self-study, and devotion to the Lord; and *haṭha-yoga,* which focuses on the physical culture aspect of Yoga and concentrates on the *āsana*(s) and *prāṇāyāma.* Many other different forms of Yoga have arisen owing to different emphases or exaggerations of one aspect or another. For example, Patañjali mentions (YS 1.29–40) that inwardness can be cultivated and the distractions of the mind attenuated by the practice of concentration on a single principle, or by the projection of friendliness, compassion, and equanimity toward others, or by the appropriate retention and expulsion of breath, or by dwelling on those who have conquered attachment, or by attending to inner sensations, etc. Corresponding to each one of these possible techniques, whole schools have arisen which cultivate one or the other method, which can be called by a specific *yoga.* Over time, *yoga* has thus come to stand for any spiritual path, method, or technique—although, in general, the goal of all these *yoga*(s) is the same as that of the central Yoga, even when expressed in terms of the particular metaphysics and metaphors of their own schools.

It is in the very nature of the multifarious uses to which the word *yoga* can be and has been put that no exhaustive list of all the *yoga*(s) can be given. Among the well-known varieties are *mantra-yoga,* which makes use of the recitation of special sounds usually given by a teacher to a disciple; *laya-yoga,* in which one makes use of the inner sound for merging the mind into the infinite; *kuṇḍalinī yoga,* which describes the whole process of Yoga in terms of the wakening and rising through the various centers in the subtle body (*cakras*) of the cosmic energy usually lying dormant coiled up at the base of the spine; and the various *yoga*(s) mentioned and elaborated in the *Bhagavadgītā*. The theory and the practice of *kuṇḍalinī yoga* have been much developed in the Tantric literature describing in detail the movements and transformations of the energies (*sakti*) in the body. (See entry on *Tantra* in Vol. 7 of World Spirituality.)

Yoga and the Bhagavadgītā

The *Bhagavadgītā* expands the use of the word *yoga* enormously. In addition to the well-known *yoga*(s) called *karmayoga* (yoga of action), *bhakti-yoga* (yoga of love and devotion), *jñana yoga* (yoga of knowledge), every chapter in the BG ends with a colophon labeling it a *yoga.* For example, the first chapter of the BG ends with the colophon (not perhaps found in the earliest texts) calling it "The Yoga of Arjuna's Confusion," and the eleventh chapter is called "The Yoga of the Vision of Cosmic Form," and so on. Anything that can be made use of in the quest for the Absolute and be harmonized with the general principles of Yoga can be called a specific sort of *yoga.*

Three further remarks can be parenthetically made here about the BG, since they are relevant to a discussion of Yoga. First, the BG is absolutely essential for an understanding of Yoga; in addition to the YS it is a test *par excellence* on Yoga. Second, the BG extends the range and understanding of Yoga at least in two different ways. By forging a link between the classical Yoga and other metaphysical systems and metaphors, it enlarges our vision of the scope of Yoga. By the whole setting of the battlefield, insistence on action in this world of *prakṛti,* and the presence of Kṛṣṇa himself as a model *yogi,* one is reminded that not only is there no conflict between *prakṛti* and *puruṣa* but that rightly seen *prakṛti* can and does serve the purposes of *puruṣa.* Furthermore, a free *puruṣa,* such as is exemplified by the instance of Kṛṣṇa, acts in *prakṛti* not from compulsion but from freedom and compassion—as and when he sees the need for it.

Third, it does not seem to have been noticed by various commentators that the central yoga that Kṛṣṇa teaches in the BG is *buddhiyoga* (*yoga* of integrated intelligence and discernment) of which the various aspects are *yoga*(s) like *karmayoga, bhakti-yoga* and *jñana yoga,* etc. The place of *buddhi* in the *Bhagavadgītā* is central. Kṛṣṇa advises Arjuna to "seek refuge in *buddhi*" (BG 2.49). "To them who are constantly integrated worshiping me with love, I give that *buddhiyoga* by which they may draw near to me" (BG 10.10). Later, during the process of summing up his entire teaching, Kṛṣṇa says again, "Renouncing mentally all actions to me, making me your goal, relying on *buddhiyoga,* become constantly mindful of me. Mindful of me, you will overcome all obstacles by my grace. But if because of selfcenteredness you will not listen, you will perish" (BG 18.57–58).[1] It is only the integrated *buddhi* which can have a vision of the *puruṣa* and follow his dictates. *Buddhi* is what gives a focus to an integral *yoga*, for example, of the sort elaborated by Sri Aurobindo in the twentieth century, very much under the influence of the BG. (For entry on Sri Aurobindo, see Vol. 7 of World Spirituality.) This is what corresponds precisely to the *viveka-khyāti* (vision of discernment) in the YS by which alone the root ignorance can be removed.

Yoga and Psychotherapy

It is certainly true that a certain psychic healing takes place in Yoga; however, that is not its aim. Rather, Yoga proper assumes psychic health, as it does physical health. It has been repeatedly said by all teachers of Yoga that Yoga is not for those who are not physically, mentally, and emotionally healthy.[2] Yoga is no more psychotherapy than it is physiotherapy, particularly when one keeps in mind that in all schools of Indian thought—and especially in the YS—body and mind (both included in the word *sarīra*) are of a piece: they are both material, although their materiality may be at different levels of subtlety. As we have seen above, the most significant aspect of Yoga, and the one which distinguishes it from the physio-psychotherapy, is the transcendence of its aim. That which a *yogi* seeks does not serve his own purposes. In fact, as long as he has his own purposes, he cannot really be open to higher and sacred purposes. The whole meaning of Yoga can be understood as progressive freedom from the hindrances that impede one's availability to the purposes of the suprapersonal intelligence. The major hindrance is what we usually call our ego or self; as long as it serves its own ends, it cannot serve the ends of the real Self.

Yoga physiology and psychology take their direction and significance from the reality which is beyond the body or the psyche. This is what renders the physio-psychology of Yoga sacred, because they have been sacrificed. The cultivation of the body or the mind for its own sake is not Yoga. The psychic healing of Yoga has its center above the psyche; here the wholeness aspired to is that of holiness. Normal physical and psychological functioning is necessary but not sufficient; without the movement along the vertical spiritual axis, any adjustment in the psyche constitutes only a horizontal arrangement of subtle matter. What Yoga aims at is right internal order, which is primarily vertical. It is the stillness of the psyche that is required so that the *puruṣa* may be heard and may hear. Patañjali had defined Yoga, in terms of its procedure, as the controlling of the fluctuations of consciousness (*citta*); Vyāsa, in his commentary on the YS (*Yoga Bhāṣya* 1.1) defines Yoga in terms of its aim as silence (*samādhi*). Then the *puruṣa* abides in its own true form.

Notes

1. For a further discussion, see the first part of A. H. Armstrong and R. Ravindra, "The Dimensions of the Self: *Buddhi* in the *Bhagavad Gītā* and *Psyche* in Plotinus," *Religious Studies* 15 (1979) 327–42.

2. For a fuller discussion of the relationship between psychotherapy and Yoga, see H. Jacobs, *Western Psychotherapy and Hindu-Sādhanā;* and R. Ravindra, "Is Religion Psychotherapy?–An Indian View," *Religious Studies* 14 (1978) 389–97.

Bibliography

The reference material of the whole subject of Yoga is extremely vast and of variable quality. There is a particularly glaring lack, however, of both accurate and readable translation of Patañjali's *Yogasutra;* the popular translations are often inaccurate or tendentious, and the scholarly translations, in general, tend to be excessively literal and pedantic, and without experiential insight. What follows is a very selected bibliography; additional references can be found in these works.

Sources

Deshpande, P. Y. *The Authentic Yoga: A fresh look at Patañjali's Yoga Sutras with a new translation, notes and comments.* London: Rider, 1978.

Feuerstein, Georg. *The Yoga-Sūtra of Patañjali: A new translation and commentary.* Folestone: Wm. Dawson & Sons, Ltd., 1979.

Studies

Armstrong, A. Hilary, and R. Ravindra. "The Dimensions of the Self: *Buddhi* in the *Bhagavad Gītā* and *Psyche* in Plotinus." *Religious Studies* 15 (1979) 327–42. Reprinted in *Neoplatonism and Indian Thought.* Edited by R. Baine Harris. Albany: State University of New York Press, 1982.

Coward, Harold G. "Psychology and Karma." In *Philosophy East and West.* Vol. 33, no. 1. 1983. Reprinted in *The American Theosophist* 71/10 (1983).

Eliade, Mircea. *Patañjali and Yoga.* Translated by Charles Lam Markmann. New York: Schocken Books, 1975.

——. *Yoga: Immortality and Freedom.* Translated by Willard R. Trask. Princeton: University Press, 1969.

Feuerstein, George. *The Philosophy of Classical Yoga.* Manchester: University Press, 1982.

Jacobs, Hans. *Western Psychotherapy and Hindu-Sādhanā.* London: Allen & Unwin, 1961.

Melasecchi, Beniamino. "Introductory Notes to the Epistemology of Patañjali." *East and West* n.s. 30 (1980) 147–56.

Ravindra, Ravi. "Is Religion Psychotherapy?—An Indian View." *Religious Studies* 14 (1978) 389–97.

Varenne, Jean. *Yoga and the Hindu Tradition.* Translated by Derek Coltman. Chicago: University of Chicago Press, 1976.

10

Buddhiyoga in the *Bhagavadgītā*

Arvind Sharma

The *Bhagavadgītā* (henceforth referred to as the *Gītā*) can be looked upon in several ways. One such possibility is to look upon it as a guide to God-realization.[1] The *Gītā* can also be seen as essentially espousing either several or one of several *yoga*(s).[2] One such *yoga* included in the *Gītā* is *buddhiyoga* (2.49; 10.10; 17.57). This paper will examine the role of *buddhiyoga* as developed in the *Gītā* as a mode of God-realization. Before this task is undertaken, however, a few preliminary remarks on the word *buddhi* would be in order.

The Concept of buddhi

The root *budh* and its derivatives appear in the Vedas in the sense of "kindling" or "awakening" and are, as Anirvan shows, sometimes applied to Agni.[3] The word *buddhi* as such seems to appear for the first time in the *Sāmkhyāyana Brahmana*. Other words more or less synonymous with *buddhi* which appear in the Vedas "are *dhi* with its derivative *dhiti* and its cognate *didhiti*," as well as *manīsā*.[4]

It is in the Upaniṣads, however, that the word acquires a decidedly philosophical semantic ambience. That this should be the case with its occurrence in the *Kaṭha Upaniṣad* (1.3.3) is particularly significant in view of the similarites between this Upaniṣad and the *Gītā*.[5] It occurs there in the context of the famous metaphor of the chariot. It is a point worth remarking that the *Gītā* itself represents a dialogue between Kṛṣṇa and Arjuna on a chariot, though one would hesitate to press the point too far.

Subsequently, in "epic philosophy, which stands midway between the

Sāṁkhya-yoga of the Upaniṣads and the classical Sāṁkhya, *buddhi* is both a cosmological and a psychological principle."[6] In the *Mahābhārata*, *buddhi* is described as the trunk, the first evolute from the seed of *avyakta*.

On the basis of such a survey of the word *buddhi*, which also encompasses Buddhism and the philosophical systems, Anirvan draws the following three conclusions:

> (1) It has been universally admitted that *buddhi*, whether as a spiritual stage or an instrumentation, is something above the mental plane; (2) it has both a *psychological* and a *cosmic* aspect, the relation between the two in spiritual realization being that between a means and an end; (3) its intrinsic character is in the nature of an illumination granted by divine grace, so aptly expressed by Shri Ramakrishna; when remonstrating against an intellectual speculation about spiritual experiences, he cried: "No, not that way! He makes you see in a blaze-up, you know!"[7]

One must now turn to examination of the term *buddhi* in the *Gītā* itself, wherein it "has not been pinned down to any precise definition, but has been left as a plastic word suggestive of many . . . meanings. . . ."[8]

The Role of buddhi in *Gītā*

In order to understand fully this role one must begin by reviewing the general concept of human personality as understood in the *Gītā*, especially in the context of *buddhi*. Such a profile is presented in *Gītā* (3.42.43):

> They say the senses are high,
> Yet the mind is higher than the senses.
> The power of concentration transcends the mind.
> Still, there he is who is beyond that power.
>
> Thus understanding him who is beyond concentration,
> You yourself, gaining strength by yourself,
> You, Warrior, must slay
> the formidable enemy in the form of desire.[9]

The substance of the verse may be presented schematically in the following manner:

ātman	(Self)
buddhi	(intellect)
manas	(mind)
indrīya(s)	(senses)

This is an ascending hierarchy of elements which compose the human being, and of these *buddhi* is the penultimate one. On the realization of the Self (*ātman*), self-realization is achieved. It is easy to see how *buddhi*, as the penultimate constituent of the human being, is likely to be of key significance in the scheme. After this point, however, the situation begins to get complicated. For the word *buddhi* also occurs in the elaboration not merely of the human psyche but also of the cosmos. Such a picture is presented in *Gītā* 13.5, 6:

> This sums up the field with its changes:
> the gross elements; self-awareness;
> The Great Principle and the unmanifest;
> the ten senses of action and perception;
>
> With these, thought; the five ranges of the senses;
> desire, hate, pleasantness, unpleasantness;
> The aggregate of sense and matter;
> Consciousness; mental steadiness.[10]

In this verse the material constituents of the universe and the senses as constituents of the human personality are spoken of in the same breath. A question thus naturally arises: How are these two pictures of the universal or cosmic, and the individual or psychic, to be integrated so as to yield a comprehensive picture in the light of which the role of *buddhi* as a technique of spiritual realization could be elaborated?

No such integration, it seems, has been attempted in the *Gītā* itself. But a parallel situation as it is found in the *Sāṁkhya-yoga* school of Hindu philosophy may be of some interest here. In *Sāṁkhya-yoga* the twenty-five constituent elements of the system are elaborated thus:

(1) *puruṣa*		(2) *prakṛti* (3) *mahat* ("intellect") (4) *ahaṁkāra* ("egoism")	
			(16–20) subtle elements
(5) *manas*	(6–10) sensory organs	(11–15) motor organs	
			(21–25) gross elements

It will at once be noticed (*Gītā* 3.42) that out of the organs (*indrīya*(s)), the mind (*manas*), the *buddhi* (under the name of *mahat*) and He—the self under the name of *puruṣa*—appear in this chart. So also from 13.5, 6 the gross elements (*mahābhūta*(s)), *ahaṁkāra* ("egoism"), *avyakta* (under the name of *prakṛti*) the mind (as the eleventh) and the ten senses (*indrīya*(s)). The verse includes the fields of senses as well (*indriyagocaras*).

This combination, if not conflation, of the cosmic and the psychic may baffle the reader. It has been a puzzle for students of *Sāṁkhya-yoga*. For terms such as *buddhi* ("intellect") or *ahaṁkāra* ("egoism") *prima facie* make little sense at the cosmic level, while they are obviously meaningful in terms of the context of the individual psyche. Nature (*prakṛti*) as such makes little sense at the psychic level (as understood in the system) but obviously does so at the cosmic level. M. Hiriyanna speculates that this discrepant terminology may indicate a "forced separation" between *puruṣa* and *prakṛti*—to achieve the dualistic stance of *Sāṁkhya* and *yoga*. After citing an Upaniṣadic passage in which God is described as "hidden in his own *gunas*," Hiriyanna remarks:

> This integral view of ultimate reality found in the Upanishads, we must take it, has been meddled with here as a result of dualistic bias; and spirit has been separated from nature, rendering the whole doctrine unintelligible. Its failure to account satisfactorily for the co-operation between Puruṣa and Prakṛti is the natural consequence of this forced separation of the two. Such an explanation also throws light on the names given to some of the evolutes of Prakṛti like "intellect" (*mahat*), "egoism" (*ahaṁkāra*), etc. As cosmic entities, they would then represent the psychic organs of the *universal* self which is immanent in Prakṛti as a whole. But as the notion of such a self was dropped when the doctrine emerged from the Upanishadic teaching, their designations naturally came to be quite arbitrary and perplexing. The other explanation is to suppose that the system was originally purely naturalistic and that the notion of Puruṣa or spirit, for which there is really no need by the side of self-evolving and self-regulating Prakṛti, was imported into it on the analogy of other doctrines.[12]

Now in *Sāṁkhya-yoga*, *buddhi* by itself is used as both a cosmic and a psychic entity. The relation between the two aspects is thus understood in *Sāṁkhya yoga*.

> The most important concept in the Yoga system is that of *citta*, loosely rendered as "mind." *Citta* is the same as the Sāṅkhya *mahat* or *buddhi*. It is the first product of *prakrti;* and in it is the *purusa* reflected. Receiving the reflection of *purusa*, the *citta* becomes conscious, and functions in various ways. By itself the *citta* is all-pervading, and is called the *kārana-citta* (the cause-mind). But, when it is in association with a body, it contracts or expands as the case may be, and is called *kārya-citta* (the effect mind). The

object of yoga is to make the *citta* assume its original, pure unmodified status, and thus release the *puruṣa* from its travail.[13]

If we now relate this discussion to the *Gītā*, confining our interest to *buddhi* in the whole picture, it can be clearly seen that the word *buddhi* is used both in a cosmic and a psychic sense in the text. This is the first important point to bear in mind concerning the spirituality imparted by the word *buddhi* as used in the *Gītā*. The second is that this double usage possesses spiritual significance, for it is by transcending the individual *buddhi* and gaining access to the *cosmic buddhi* that one proceeds toward realization. However, the two senses of the word are rarely, if ever, used simultaneously or in the same context, so that the relationship between the two is implicit rather than explicit.

Further reflection also discloses the fact that even in their different cosmic and individual usages the word *buddhi* could possess different layers of meaning, and unless these are correctly identified, the exact spiritual path involved in the concept of *buddhi-yoga* will be difficult to chart. The different senses in which the word *buddhi* has been employed in its cosmic and individual connotations now need to be identified.

The word *buddhi* is used in its cosmic sense in 7.4 as a part of the eightfold *aparā prakṛti* and as one of the constituents of the *kṣetra* in 13.5. In both of these contexts Kṛṣṇa's superiority over *prakṛti* and *kṣetra* is clearly established. The use here seems to be fairly consistent. It is in the use of the word *buddhi* in an a-cosmic sense that one encounters variation.

At one level in the *Gītā* the word *buddhi* is not used in the sense of a form of *yoga* but for discriminative and determinative intelligence in general. In these contexts it merely has the general signification of wisdom and indeed is used in the context of the distinction between *sāṁkhya* and *yoga* and not itself as a *yoga*. This is the first semantic level of *buddhi* which may be identified in the *Gītā*. This seems to be the case with *Gītā* 2.39–44:

> This is the Wisdom of the Sāṁkhya to thee, O Pārtha (Arjuna). Listen now to the wisdom of the Yoga. If Your intelligence accepts it, thou shalt cast away the bondage of works.
>
> In this path, no effort is ever lost and no obstacle prevails; even a little of this righteousness (*dharma*) saves from great fear.
>
> The undiscerning who rejoice in the letter of the Veda, who contend that there is nothing else, whose nature is desire and who are intent on heaven, proclaim these flowery words that result in rebirth as the fruit of actions and (lay down) various specialized rites for the attainment of enjoyment and power.[14]

The second semantic level in the use of the word *buddhi* emerges when the *Gītā* clearly starts extolling *karmayoga,* beginning with 2.47. In the use of *buddhi* at the first level the sense of wisdom was too general to possess any special spiritual significance. But its use in the context of *karmayoga* imparts to *buddhi* an added dimension and significance, for the following claims are now made on behalf of *buddhi*: (1) *buddhi* is superior to *karma* (2.49). What seems to be meant is that "work without desire for fruit" (*buddhi*) is superior to "work with desire for fruit" (*karma*).[15] (2) One endowed with *buddhi* gives up both good and evil deeds. This follows from the earlier point, for good and evil acts acquire a character by their intentionality. Such a person "acts, but his actions do not stand in the way of release," and it is on this account that *yoga* is called skill in action—that is, it "is the art of working without desire."[16] (3) Those endowed with *buddhi* eschew all actions (2.51). (4) When *buddhi* is no longer confused by conflicting scriptural injunctions (2.52–53) it will attain to *yoga.*

It is worth noting that while the sense of *buddhi* has been spiritually upgraded once it is made ancillary to *karmayoga,* it is not yet a *yoga* in its own right. In this context in the *Gītā,* the word *buddhi* is still a floater which can be set to any use. In 3.1, 2, the word is used in what we have identified as its second-level usage in the first verse and its first-level usage in the second.

> If thou deemest that (the path of) understanding is more excellent than (the path of) action, O Janārdana (Kṛṣṇa), when then dost thou urge me to do this savage deed, O Keśava (Kṛṣṇa)?
>
> With an apparently confused utterance thou seemest to bewilder my intelligence. Tell (me) then decisively the one thing by which I can attain to the highest good.[17]

The first-level usage of intelligence in general is clearly the sense in 3.26, as also in 5.2.17, 28.

Toward the end of the second chapter, however, a third and higher sense of the word *buddhi* is beginning to crystallize. This happens in the context of description of the *sthitaprajna,* where the word *prajña* often has the sense of *buddhi* and indeed in 2.62–67 the key role of *buddhi* in controlling the mind is emphasized. In 5.20 one actually encounters the word one has been waiting for—*sthirabuddhi.*

The description is identical to that of the *sthitaprajna* (2.53) and includes the point that just as the *sthitaprajna* attains to Brahman, so does the *sthirabuddhi.*[18]

The Path of buddhiyoga

Now that the usages of the word have been clarified, the path of *buddhiyoga* can be charted with greater confidence.

How does one attain the *summum bonum* by practicing *buddhiyoga?*

One first recognizes the existence of *buddhi* as one of the constituents of one's personality along with the senses, mind, etc. This sense is clearly established by the use of the word *buddhi* in 5.11; 6.43; 18.30–33; etc.

The second step consists in the recognition that the *buddhi* could be used to control these other elements of personality to take one further along the spiritual goal. In this respect two aspects of the regulative power of *buddhi* are emphasized: (1) singlemindedness and steadfastness (2.41, 66; 6.25; etc.) and (2) equipoise and equanimity (6.9; etc.). These help to advance the aspirant along the spiritual path.

Once the second step has been accomplished, the spiritual aspirant is ready for the third. Such a *buddhi* can serve as an ancillum to any of the three major *yoga*(s) usually identified as propounded in the *Gītā*.[19] Thus, in the context of *karmayoga* it is said (2.49):

> For action is far inferior
> To discipline of mental attitude, Dhanamjaya.
> In the mental attitude seek they (religious) refuge;
> Wretched are those whose motive is the fruit (of action).[20]

In the context of *bhakti-yoga* it is similarly stated (10.10):

> To them, constantly disciplined,
> Revering Me with love,
> I give that discipline of mind,
> Whereby they go unto Me.[21]

Again, in the last chapter of the *Gītā* a similar sentiment is expressed, though in more Pelagian than Augustinian terms this time (18.57):

> With thy thoughts all actions
> Casting upon Me, devoted to Me,
> Turning to discipline of mentality
> Keep thy mind ever fixed on Me.[22]

The connection of *buddhi* with *jñana yoga* remains to be established. This can be clearly seen in 6.18–23:

. Wandering monks with staff and watering-bowl near the Ganges.

When the thought, controlled,
  Settles on the self alone,
The man free from longing for all desires
  Is then called disciplined.

As a lamp stationed in a windless place
  Flickers not, this image is recorded
of the disciplined man controlled in thought,
  Practising discipline of the self.

When the thought comes to rest,
  Checked by the practice of discipline,
And when, the self by the self
  Contemplating, he finds satisfaction in the self;

That supernal bliss which
  Is to be grasped by the consciousness and is
beyond the senses,
  When he knows this, and not in the least
    Swerves from the truth, abiding fixed (in it);

And which having gained, other gain
  He counts none higher than it;
In which establishd, by no misery,
  However grievous, is he moved;

This (state), let him know—is known as discipline;
With determination must be practised this
  Discipline, with heart undismayed.[23]

The crucial verse is 8.21, wherein the transcendental bliss is described as *buddhigrāhya.* Radhakrishnan comments:

> While the Supreme is beyond perception by the senses, it is seizable by reason, not by the reason which deals with sense data and frames concepts on their basis but reason which works in its own right. When it does so, it becomes aware of things not indirectly, through the medium of the senses or the relations based on them, but by becoming one with them. All true knowledge is knowledge by identity. Our knowledge through physical contact or mental symbiosis is indirect and approximate. Religion is contemplative realization of God.[24]

At this point a question naturally arises. The expression *buddhiyoga* itself occurs in the *Gītā* thrice (as noted earlier). Why then must it be treated as ancillary to the other major *yoga*(s) and not a *yoga* in its own right?

The answer, it could be argued, is to be found in the schematic limitation imposed on *buddhi* as being penultimate to the *ātman.* R. C. Zaehner's observations on this point are pertinent (though his treatment of *buddhiyoga* in general has been criticized):[25]

> *Buddhi* is the highest faculty in man's material nature, for in the Gītā as in Marxism man's psychological faculties, even the highest of them, are rooted in the matter. Yet there is something ambivalent about *buddhi* in the Gītā: it seems to stand on the brink between the world of pure spirit (the self) and man's physical and psychic nature. According to the Gītā's own definition *buddhi* corresponds more or less exactly to what we in the West call "soul," since it is not only intellect but also will. . . .
>
> The soul, then, as the organ of integration, is that which brings the whole human personality into subjection to the self: its true function is to spiritualize matter, for it is ideally the bridge between spirit and matter rather like the sacrificial fire, the mouth of Brahman, which is the bridge between Brahman understood as the sacrifice and Brahman understood as timeless being.[26]

Zaehner's position, however, ties the interpretation of *buddhi* too closely to the *Sāṁkhya-Yoga* scheme. It can have other connotations in the *Gītā* which serve to raise its status. This seems to be confirmed by Sankara's gloss on *Bhagavadgītā* 2.51, wherein he suggests that if in the context *buddhi* signifies the supreme end (*paramārthadarśanalakṣaṇa*), then liberation is directly involved. He writes:

> For, men of Wisdom, possessing evenness of mind, cast of the fruit of works i.e., escape from good and bad births. They then attain knowledge. While still alive, they are released from the bond of birth, and attain the supreme abode of Vishnu—the state of *moksha* or liberation—which is free from all turmoils.
>
> Or, the Wisdom (*buddhi*) referred to in the three verses (II.49–51) may be the Sāṅkhya (not the Yoga) Wisdom, the knowledge of the Absolute Reality, (corresponding to the wide-spread expanse of water), which arises when the mind is purified by Karma-Yoga; for, it is said in II.50 that wisdom directly brings about the destruction of good and bad deeds.[27]

Sankara's optional interpretation is the only one offered by Madhva on 2.49. He glosses *buddhiyogāt* as *jñānalakṣaṇāt.*[28] On the other hand, Abhinavagupta gives the verse a rather idiosyncratic interpretation,[29] and Jñāneśvara almost reverses the apparent sense of the verse.[30]

> O Arjuna, the evenly balanced mind is the essence of Yoga; wherein the mind and pure intelligence are united. When we consider this Yoga of pure intelligence, the Yoga of action with attachment appears in many ways to be inferior, O Partha.
>
> But this Yoga of pure intelligence only becomes attainable when the Yoga of action is practised; for action that remains after desire for its fruit is renounced naturally leads to evenness of mind.

> The Yoga of pure intelligence, therefore, is steady, O Arjuna. Concentrate on it and relinquish any desire for the fruit of action.
>
> Those who have practised this Yoga have reached the other shore and have freed themselves from the bondage of sin and merit.

Yet Hanuman's *Paiśācabhāṣya* and Nīlakaṇṭha's *Bhāvadīpīkā* make out a stronger case for *buddhiyoga* in its own right and Ānandagiri supports Sankara strongly.[31]

Thus, two answers can be given to the question of whether *buddhiyoga* can be a *yoga* in its own right. On the basis of the standard presentation of the *yoga*(s) in the *Gītā* the answer would tend to be no; but on the basis of the commentarial literature and on the basis of *Gītā*'s own flexibility in its treatment of the *yoga*(s) a qualified yes is possible.

The Integrality of buddhiyoga

Indeed, A. H. Armstrong and R. Ravindra have plausibly argued the case for *buddhiyoga* as an independent *yoga* within the *Gītā*. According to them, "the path of action or *karma yoga*, the path of love or *bhakti yoga*, the path of meditation or *dhyāna yoga* and the path of knowledge or *jñāna yoga* constitute the four limbs of the *buddhiyoga* of the *Bhagavadgītā* which integrates them into an organic whole."[32]

When *buddhiyoga* is treated as an independent *yoga* in its own right and not as ancillary to *jñāna yoga*, *bhakti-yoga*, and *karmayoga*, then the following steps on the spiritual path are involved: (1) integration of the *buddhi*; (2) integration by the *buddhi*; (3) self-transcendence of *buddhi*,[33] leading to integration with the ultimate reality. These may be referred to as the first, second, and third integrations.

The initial integration is lucidly and succinctly summarized by Armstrong and Ravindra. The points are so closely interwoven that the steps involved in the first integration are best presented in their own words:

> The initial integration, according to the Gītā, consists in the unification of *buddhi*. For this purpose, essentially three renunciations are recommended. First is the renunciation of inaction, for Kṛṣṇa; himself, although he needs to do nothing, is constantly engaged in action; if he were to stop working, all the worlds would perish. The second renunciation is that of anxiety about and attachment to the fruits of action. One must do what needs to be done for sustaining the world, understanding the principle of reciprocal maintenance between gods and men, as sacrifice and worship (*yajña*), casting all actions on Kṛṣṇa (BG 3.11–12, 19–25).

> The third renunciation has already been mentioned, namely the renunciation of *saṁkalpa* which is imagination and desire-will. "The wise men consider it to be renunciation: to give up works dictated by desire" (BG 18.2).
>
> Corresponding to these three renunciations, three definitions of *yoga* are given in the *Gītā*, indicating different instructions for and stages of transformation of man (It hardly needs mentioning that these stages are in no sense linear or mutually exclusive). *Yoga* is skill in action, it is equanimity in failure and success, and it is the disconnecting of the connection with *duhkha* (suffering), the connection that is forged by desire and imagination. (BG 2.48, 50; 6.23–24).[34]

Such a *buddhi* is able to bring about "a harmonious functioning of the whole of one's psychosomatic organism, effecting the second integration of *buddhiyoga*."[35] This second integration by *buddhiyoga* is best illustrated by an example not given in the *Gītā* but implicit in it. This example is provided by the famous chariot metaphor of the *Kaṭha Upaniṣad*, an Upaniṣad on which the *Gītā* at times draws literally[36] and whose metaphor coincides with the situation in which the *Gītā* is revealed, namely, on a chariot.[37] The relevant passage from the *Kaṭha Upaniṣad* runs as follows (1.3.3–11):

The Parable of the Chariot

> Know the Self as the lord of the chariot and the body as, verily, the chariot, know the intellect as the charioteer and the mind as, verily, the reins.
>
> The senses, they say, are the horses; the objects of sense the paths (they range over); (the self) associated with the body, the senses and the mind—wise men declare—is the enjoyer.
>
> He who has no understanding, whose mind is always unrestrained, his senses are out of control, as wicked horses are for a charioteer.
>
> He, however, who has understanding, whose mind is always restrained, his senses are under control, as good horses are for a charioteer.
>
> He, however, who has no understanding, who has no control over his mind (and is) ever impure, reaches not that goal but comes back into mundane life.
>
> He, however, who has understanding, who has control over his mind and (is) ever pure, reaches that goal from which he is not born again.
>
> He who has the understanding of the driver of the chariot and controls the rein of his mind, he reaches the end of the journey, that supreme abode of the all-pervading.[38]

Buddhi is called *sārathi* or charioteer toward the beginning and again as *vijñāna* at the end in 1.3.3 and 1.3.9. The metaphor is fully in keeping with the spirit of the *Gītā* and illustrates the second integration.

The third integration follows a slightly diferent course. Two points are important in this context. The first is that "although *buddhi* itself is a part of lower nature, it is only through purified *buddhi* that one can go beyond *prakṛti*."[39] At this point it may reasonably be asked whether the knowledge of what is beyond *buddhi* is attainable through *buddhi*.

> Whether such knowledge is at all attainable, so long as its means continues to be the internal organ, which is a product of *prakṛti* and therefore consists not merely of *sattva* but also of *rajas* and *tamas*. In answering this question, it is necessary to remember that it is not the internal organ as such that limits our view of the world in the manner described above. For, in its intrinsic nature, it is essentially *sāttvic* and is therefore specially fitted to be the means of revealing correctly all that is. Actually, however, *rajas* or *tamas* predominates in it as a result of the past history of the person to whom it belongs; and it is the relative predominance of either which accounts for whatever limitations it may possess as an organ of knowledge. By subduing these impediments to clear perception through proper self-discipline and restoring the internal organ to its natural purity, man may completely transform his outlook upon life and the world.[40]

The second point follows from the above. "From the level of purified *buddhi*, the movement" which leads to Reality "is in a wholly different direction"[41] and leads to salvation by leading the aspirant to *ātman* or *brāhman* or Kṛṣṇa.

Contemporary Relevance of buddhiyoga

In this last section one may endeavor to place the *buddhiyoga* of the *Gītā* in the broader context of (a) the dialogue of world religions and (b) the leading of a spiritual life in the modern world.

As is well known, the scheme of the various *yoga*(s) of Hinduism can provide one basis for ecumenical dialogue. *Bhakti-yoga* provides a good example of this point. Huston Smith observes, for example, that "all the basic principles of *bhakti yoga* are richly exemplified in Christianity. Indeed from the Hindu point of view Christianity is one great brilliantly lit *bhakti* highway toward God. . . ."[42] *Buddhiyoga* can also similarly serve as a basis for dialogue. In fact, because it lacks the specificity of the three main *yoga*(s)—*jñāna*, *bhakti*, and *karma*, and because it can be connected with all three of them generally, it may even serve as more of a bridge across religious traditions than any of the other three *yoga*(s). For if *buddhiyoga* implies a spirituality which transcends the level of ordinary mental activity and partakes of something supermental, then it could well constitute the high ground toward which the various distinct religious traditions converge.

This brings one to a consideration of *buddhiyoga* in the context of modern life. If *buddhiyoga* implies the transcendence rather than the denial of ordinary rationality, and if the temper of modern times is suffused with rationality, then the modern rational culture might still retain its rational character and yet make contact with genuine spirituality through the practice of *buddhiyoga* as espoused in the *Gītā*. This principle can be seen as operating in two ways. Modern life is characterized by activity. In such a context "the call to *buddhi* as a means of probing the depths of the inner being and discovering the true nature of the universal individual"[43] can be a useful corrective of the cult of hyperactivity. But more generally:

> [*Buddhiyoga*] provides us with that rational procedure of self exceeding which forms the keynote of all human aspirations, whether they point to above or to below. Its rationale is to be found in the logical scheme of Sāṅkhyan principles, where *buddhi* which forms the core of man's Nature occupies a peculiar position which marks the farthest limit to which the concept of an upward march of evolutionary Nature can rise. . . . Below him are the world of concrete and abstract objective reals of materialized entities . . . characteristically in him are the principles of Mind and Ego, imperfectly illumined by the principle of Intelligence (*buddhi*) . . . and above him, overtopping the highest flights of his Pure Intelligence are the infinitudes of the Unmanifest and the Ineffable. What he can hope and attain to by a comprehensively rational manipulation of the forces of his being is to be poised in that Illumination which forms a connecting link between his worlds of the Real and the Ideal.[44]

Thus, the relevance of *buddhiyoga* to both the dialogue of world religions and life in the modern world arises out of its universal and universalizing potential.[45]

To conclude: The spirituality of *buddhiyoga* in the *Gītā* can be viewed in three concentric circles, each larger than the other: (1) in the context of *Sāṁkhya-yoga*, (2) in the context of the triple *yoga*(s) of *jñāna*, *bhakti*, and *karma*, and (3) as a *yoga* in its own right. With each such contextual shift the spiritual center of *buddhiyoga* is strengthened, its circumference enlarged, and its relevance to interreligious dialogue and modern life enhanced.

Notes

1. S. Radhakrishnan, *The Bhagavadgītā*, 11ff.
2. Arvind Sharma, *Thresholds in Hindu-Buddhist Studies*, 112–33.
3. See Anirvan, *Buddhiyoga of the Gītā and Other Essays*, 2.
4. Ibid., 3.
5. See S. C. Roy, *The Bhagavadgītā and Modern Scholarship* (London: Luzac, 1941) 142–43.

6. Anirvan, *Buddhiyoga,* 5.
7. Ibid., 7 (emphasis added).
8. Ibid.
9. Kees W. Bolle, *The Bhagavadgītā: A New Translation,* 48, 49.
10. Ibid., 152–53. The *Gītā* does not connect the cosmic *buddhi* as *mahat* with the individual *buddhi*, so much so that some writers allude only to cosmic *buddhi* in their discussions (Franklin Edgerton, *The Bhagavadgītā,* 141). Commentators on the *Gītā* such as Rāmānuja also keep the two senses of the word *buddhi* quite distinct (J. A. B. Van Buitenen, *Rāmānuja on the Bhagavadgita,* 100, 142).
11. M. Hiriyanna, *The Essentials of Indian Philosophy,* 111.
12. Ibid., 127–28.
13. T. M. P. Mahadevan, *Outlines of Hinduism* (Bombay: Chetana Limited, 1970) 125. For the use of *buddhi* as associated with the body, see J. A. B. Van Buitenen, *Rāmānuja,* 102, 122, 134.
14. S. Radhakrishnan, *Bhagavadgītā,* 114, 116, 117, 118, for translation. Rāmānuja's gloss here is of particular relevance (see Van Buitenen, *Rāmānuja,* 59–60): "The text discriminates between two kinds of *buddhi*: (a) a *buddhi* marked by decision; (b) a *buddhi* not marked by decision.

(a) The *buddhi* that is marked by decision is concerned with those acts which an aspirant should perform to attain release. It is marked by decision because it presupposes decisive knowledge of the proper form of the *ātman.* With all various acts it remains essentially the same because it concerns these acts in so far as they lead to the same result, release. The purpose of the *śāstras* is always this same result; so the *buddhi* concerned with all various acts prescribed by the *śāstra* is always the same.

(b) The *buddhi* that is not marked by decision is concerned with desiderative acts. When acts are performed in order to materialize certain desires, then no more is required than the knowledge that the *ātman* as an entity differs from the *prakṛti.* The decisive knowledge of the proper form of the *ātman* is not needed for that, for the desire for a certain result—e.g. heaven—the execution of the means leading to that result, and the enjoyment of that result are perfectly possible and not all incompatible without such a decisive knowledge. *Buddhis* concerned with desiderative acts are numberless. Besides, various acts, even if ordered to obtain a single result, have many branches, because the same acts may have a number of adventitious results."

15. W. Douglas P. Hill, *The Bhagavadgītā,* 91 nn. 1, 2.
16. Ibid., n. 4. Despite his penchant for identifying Buddhist connotations of the words used in the *Gītā*, R. C. Zaehner seems to miss the cue here (*The Bhagavadgītā,* 147). Buddhist teaching distinguishes between *pāpa* and *puṇya* or bad and good actions which produce such results and skillful (*Kuśala*) actions which produce no such results.
17. See Zaehner, *Bhagavadgītā,* 131, for translation.
18. Bolle, *Bhagavadgītā,* 66, 67.
19. See Hill, *Bhagavadgītā,* 561ff.; Radhakrishnan, *Bhagavadgītā,* 50–75, etc.
20. See Franklin Edgerton, trans., *The Bhagavadgītā,* Part 1, 24, 25.
21. Ibid., 98, 99.
22. Ibid., 174, 175.
23. Ibid., 64, 65.
24. Radhakrishnan, *Bhagavadgītā,* 201.
25. Puruṣottama Bilimoria, "R.C. Zaehner's treatment of the Bhagavadgita," *The Journal of Studies in the Bhagavadgītā* 3 (1983) 89–97.

26. Zaehner, *Bhagavadgītā*, 22, 23.
27. Alladi Mahadeva Sastry, trans., *The Bhagavadgītā*.
28. Viśveśatīrtha, et al., eds., *Gītābhāṣya of Śrī Madhwāchārya with Prameya Deepika of Śrī Jayatīrtha*, 85.
29. Arvind Sharma, trans., *Abinavagupta Gītārthasaṅgraha*, 113.
30. H. M. Lambert, ed., *Jñāneshvari*, 1:70.
31. G. S. Sadhale, ed., *The Bhagavadgītā with Eleven Commentaries*, 1:198, 199, 205.
32. A. H. Armstrong and R. Ravindra, "The Dimensions of the Self: *Buddhi* in the *Bhagavad Gītā* and *Psyche* in Plotinus," *Religious Studies* 15 (1979) 333.
33. Ibid., 329.
34. Ibid., 330.
35. Ibid.
36. M. Hiriyanna, *Outlines of Indian Philosophy*, 130.
37. Armstrong and Ravindra, "Dimensions of the Self," 333–34.
38. S. Radhakrishnan, *The Principal Upaniṣads* (London: Allen & Unwin, 1953) 623–24.
39. Armstrong and Ravindra, "Dimensions of the Self," 332.
40. M. Hiriyanna, *Essentials of Indian Philosophy*, 118. By internal organ or *aṅtaḥkaraṇa* is meant *manas, ahaṁkāra,* and *buddhi* (ibid., 112), *buddhi* being primary. Also see Surendranath Dasgupta, *A History of Indian Philosophy*, 1:472 n. 1.
41. Armstrong and Ravindra, "Dimensions of the Self," 332.
42. Huston Smith, *The Religions of Man*, 40. See also pp. 43–44.
43. Anirvan, *Buddhiyoga*, 62.
44. Ibid., 75.
45. This centrality of *buddhi* in the context of God-realization and how it can be an element in the dialogue of religions were recognized centuries ago by the Muslim savant Alberuni. See Edward C. Sachau, trans. and ed., *Alberuni's India*, 49, 85.

Bibliography

Sources

Edgerton, Franklin. *The Bhagavadgītā*, Part I. Cambridge, MA: Harvard University Press, 1948.

——. *The Bhagavadgītā*. Cambridge, MA: Harvard University Press, 1972.

Hill, W. Douglas P. *The Bhagavadgītā*. 2nd ed. Oxford: Oxford University Press, 1966.

Radhakrishnan, S. *The Bhagavadgītā*. London: Allen & Unwin, 1949.

Sadhale, G. S., ed. *The Bhagavadgītā with Eleven Commentaries*, Vol. 1. Bombay: The Gujarati Printing Press, 1935.

Sastry, Alladi Mahadeva, trans. *The Bhagavadgītā with the Commentary of Sri Śankarāchārya*. Madras: Samata Books, 1979.

Sharma, Arvind, trans. *Abhinavagupta Gītārthasaṅgraha*. Leiden: Brill, 1983.

Viśveśatīrtha et al., eds. *Gītābhāṣya of Śrī Madhwāchārya with Prameya Deepikā of Śrī Jayatīrtha*. Bangalore: Poorṇaprajña Vidyapeeṭha, 1981.

Studies

Anirvan. *Buddhiyoga of the Gītā and Other Essays.* New Delhi: Biblio Impex Privat, 1981.

Armstrong, A. H., and R. Ravindra. "The Dimensions of the Self: *Buddhi* in the *Bhagavad Gītā* and *Psyche* in Plotinus." *Religious Studies* 15 (1979) 327–42.

Bhattacharya, Haridas, ed. *The Cultural Heritage of India.* Vol. 2. Calcutta: The Ramakrishna Mission Institute of Culture, 1962.

Bilimoria, Puruṣottama. "R.C. Zaehner's Treatment of the Bhagavadgita." *The Journal of Studies in the Bhagavadgītā* 3 (1983) 87–111.

Bolle, Kees W. *The Bhagavadgītā: A New Translation.* Berkeley: University of California Press, 1979.

Dasgupta, Surendranath. *A History of Indian Philosophy,* Vol. 2. Delhi: Motilal Banarsidass, 1975.

Hiriyanna, M. *The Essentials of Indian Philosophy.* London: Allen & Unwin, 1964.

——. *Outlines of Indian Philosophy.* London: Allen & Unwin, 1964.

Lambert, H. M., ed. *Jñāneshvari,* Vol 1. London: Allen & Unwin, 1967.

Roy, S. C. *The Bhagavadgītā and Modern Scholarship.* London: Luzac, 1941.

Sharma, Arvind. *Thresholds in Hindu-Buddhist Studies.* Calcutta: Minerva Associates, 1979.

Sachau, Edward C., trans. and ed. *Alberuni's India.* Delhi: S. Chand, 1964. First Indian reprint.

Smith, Huston. *The Religions of Man.* New York: Harper & Row, 1965.

Van Buitenen, J. A. B. *Rāmānuja on the Bhagavadgītā.* Delhi: Motilal Banarsidass, 1968.

Zaehner, R. C. *The Bhagavadgītā.* Oxford: Oxford University Press, 1966.

Zimmer, Heinrich. *Philosophies of India.* Edited by Joseph Campbell. New York: Meridian Books, 1964.

11

The Reflective Word: Spirituality in the Grammarian Tradition of India

HAROLD G. COWARD

In the beginning was the Word,
And the Word was with God,
And the Word was God.
The Gospel according to John 1:1

Many who look do not see language,
Many who listen do not hear it.
It reveals itself like a loving
And well adorned wife to her husband.
Ṛg Veda 10.71.4

THE GOAL OF PHILOSOPHY IN INDIA does not stop with rational analysis but pushes on to spiritual realization. Indian philosophy "found its consummation in an enriched life, in the fulness of spiritual outlook, the highest perfection that ethical and intellectual discipline could aspire after. It always aimed at the inwardization of the truth discovered and no philosophy which failed to end in this glorious expansion of spiritual life was deemed to be worthy of human allegiance."[1] Like other philosophic traditions of India (e.g., *Sāṁkhya-yoga* and Vedānta), the Grammarians emphasized spiritual realization as the ultimate objective of their discipline. Knowledge and correct use of words brings about both spiritual merit (*dharma*) which leads to heaven (*svarga*) and complete spiritual realization (*mokṣa*).[2] For the Hindu Grammarians words are reflections of the Divine and at the same time the means by which the Divine may be known. Words are looked upon as spiritualized sound—as the music of the soul. For the Grammarian it is not the outward sound that constitutes the real word. The spoken syllables serve only to evoke the inner spiritual word—as the ever-vibrating sphere of divine consciousness.[3] Thus, the Grammarians teach Yoga upon words (*Sabdapurvayoga*) as the most direct way of realizing the Divine. Like a mirror, words reflect and reveal the Divine.[4] Meditation upon words maximizes the impact of this reflection and induces a sympathetic vibration within one's own consciousness. Consequently, Mādhava, the great medieval Hindu scholar, concludes that the study of words "is the straight royal road of the travellers to emancipation."[5]

In analyzing the way in which the Hindu Grammarians understand the religious function of language, the following three aspects of spirituality will be examined: (1) the existential experience of the word, (2) the formulation of teaching about the word, and (3) the Yoga of the word. Throughout, the aim will be to present the Hindu Grammarians in their context.

The Existential Experience of the Word

The Grammarian tradition, arising from the Veda, takes language as of Divine origin (*Daivī Vāk*), as Spirit descending and embodying itself in phenomena, assuming various guises and disclosing its real nature to the sensitive soul.[6] For the Grammarians, the Vedic seer or *ṛṣi* was taken as the sensitive soul *par excellence.* The approach of the *ṛṣi* to the Divine Word is characterized not by logical reasoning but by intuitive inspiration. The consciousness of the *ṛṣi* was so purified that the Divine Word was clearly reflected in it, just as the sun is reflected in a clear still pond. Thus, the *ṛṣi* was not the composer of the word, but the seer of an eternal impersonal truth. Such a vision comes to the mind in a flash of intuition (*dhī*), which is beyond all purely sensuous perception.[7] The *ṛṣi* is thought of as having been emptied of himself and filled with the Divine. Therefore the words that he spoke were not his own words, but the Divine Word reflected through his purified consciousness. This suprahuman origin lent such words a healing and saving power. It is this existential experience of the Divine Word as being at once inherently powerful and inherently teleological that is so difficult for modern minds to comprehend. Yet these are the very characteristics that underlie Indian cultic ritual and chant, and the reflective spirituality of the Grammarians. From this viewpoint, purely formulated and properly pronounced words are bearers of spiritual power. Such mantras are judged to be linguistic expressions of ultimate reality, revealed by *dhī* or supersensuous vision and recited as a rite to actualize their inherent power affecting both the worshiper and the whole of the cosmos.[8]

The earliest mantras were given by the *ṛṣi*(s) in poetic form. The poetic expression of the vision left it open to various levels of experience and interpretation by those who heard it from the *ṛṣi*. On a lower level many of the Vedic hymns might be taken to represent a naturalistic or polytheistic perception of reality. But, on a higher level, it can also be held that the visions of the *ṛṣi*(s) evidence a monistic approach in which the various Vedic gods are simply descriptive names representing various manifestations of the one Divine Word (*Śabdabrahman*). Similarly, the different branches of the Veda (*Ṛg, Sāma, Yajur, Atharva*) and the divisons into different forms (e.g., *saṃhitā, brāhmaṇa*(s), *upaniṣad*(s)) are given for the convenience of study and so as to make contact with people at different levels of mental purification (V.P. 1.5). For example, on a lower level, the sacrificial ritual, which had been present to some degree in the Vedic hymns, was given greater development and importance in the *brāhmaṇa*(s). This meant that the *ṛṣi* of the Vedic hymns, the inspired singer of truth, now tends to become the possessor of a revealed scripture and the repeater of a magical formula. But while the majority of Brāhmins during the period of the *brāhmaṇa*(s) may have concentrated on establishing an authoritative systematization of the ritual sacrificial aspects of the Vedic hymns, there were always some inspired teachers who resisted rigid formalizing and focused on the subjective spirituality of the Vedic word. Because of their efforts, evidence may be found in the *brāhmaṇa*(s) of early struggles toward the formulation of the philosophic statements of the Upaniṣadic Seers.[9] In the view of the Grammarians, these different outward forms are taken by the once Divine Word so as to engage each individual at his or her own level of spiritual development. But through it all it is the ideal of the *ṛṣi* that dominates. It is the *ṛṣi* who first "hears" or "sees" the Veda and speaks it aloud for the benefit of all others. And it is to the *ṛṣi* that all others must approximate in their spiritual quest. This ideal experience of the Word by the *ṛṣi* has been well described by the contemporary Hindu poet Śrī Aurobindo:

> The language of the Veda itself is *śruti*, a rhythm not composed by the intellect but heard, a divine word that came vibrating out of the Infinite to the inner audience of the man who had previously made himself fit for the impersonal knowledge.[10]

Aurobindo emphasizes that the approach of the *ṛṣi* is not aimed at rational speculation or aesthetic originality, but rather at the practical achievement of the spiritual goal—the supersensuous vision in which the Divine Word is clearly reflected for his benefit and for the benefit of others around him.

Stress on the oral or spoken form is an important aspect of the Grammarian view of the Word. Thinking is seen as internal speaking to which not enough *prāṇa* or breath energy has been added to make it overt. Writing is merely a coded recording which can never perfectly represent all the nuances of the spoken word, and is therefore always secondary. With regard to the relationship between written and spoken language, the Grammarian approach is opposite to that taken in modern Western scholarship. In modern biblical studies, for example, the aim of the scholar is to get back to the earliest available written manuscript and then to use that as a criterion against which to check the text that is in use today. Because of human failings, errors such as mistakes in copying may have crept in over the years. These errors would not be present in the earlier manuscript. In addition, the modern school of form criticism has argued that before many of the scriptures (e.g., the Gospels) were written down there was a period of oral transmission during which time the text (e.g., the original teachings of Jesus) was modified by the needs of the people and the particular conditions under which they lived. Thus, the period of oral transmission is judged to have been unreliable because of its inability to carry forward the original sayings in a pure and unchanged form.[11]

The Grammarian practice is the exact opposite of this. When India achieved independence in 1947, one of the first acts of the new government was to establish a commission of senior scholars to go from place to place and listen to the assembled Brāhmins reciting the Vedas. They would listen for errors in meter, accent, *sandhi,* and for any loss or change in words. They had mastered the pure presentation of the Vedas through many years of careful oral practice and checking with their teachers. And the teachers of the present senior scholars had got it not from books but from oral practice with the best teachers of the generation before them, and so on in an unbroken oral tradition back to the Vedas. It is not the dead or entombed manuscript but the correct and clear speaking of the word in the here and now that makes for a living language and scripture. Large numbers of copies of *The Living Bible* stacked in bookstores or reverently placed on personal bookshelves are not true language or living scripture according to Grammarians. Only when a passage is so well learned that it is with one wherever one goes is the Word really known. In such a state the Word becomes part of, or even more exactly is, one's consciousness. Books and all written forms are not knowledge in this sense of the Word, and represent, for the Grammarian, a lower, inferior, second order of language suitable only for the dull or the uneducated.

The Spiritual Function of Mantra Chanting

Although most of what has been said above is accepted by other orthodox schools of classical Hinduism, there is one tenet that is specific to the

Grammarians and which at the same time provides the foundation for the widespread Hindu practice of mantra chanting (*japa*). The Grammarians teach that there is a direct, eternal relationship between the uttered word and its meaning or referent (VP 1.123–25).[12] The oral repetition of a word or phrase (*mantra*) thus automatically evokes the referent of the word, and whatever spiritual power may be attached thereto. With this tenet in mind the mantra chanting which dominates both traditional and contemporary Hindu spiritual discipline can be understood.[13] In line with Grammarian teaching, such devotional mantras are not thought of as products of discursive thought, human wisdom, or poetic fantasy, but as "flashlights of the eternal truth, seen by those eminent men who have come into supersensuous contact with the Unseen."[14] The Grammarians understand their special role within Hinduism (and the world) as the controlling and purifying of the use of mantra so that its spiritual powers will not be wasted or misused (VP 1.11–12).

Proper grammatical usage, correct pronunciation, etc. are crucial not only for the success of Vedic mantras and rituals but also for all other branches of knowledge. Whether it be the communication of meaning within the human sciences or the identification of ritual action with the divine, it is *mantra śakti* (power) which enables it all to happen. In both Vedic and Tantric ritual, mantra is the catalyst that allows the sacred potential of the ritual setting to become a reality. Especially important in this connection is the Grammarian's contention, "It is with the meanings conveyed by words that actions are connected" (VP 1.62). Were it not for the reflective power of words, no connection would be made between the ritual action and the divine, and then both Veda and Tantra would be powerless.

The Study and Teaching of the Word

Ancient Indian thought was sensitive to language both in its phenomenal and metaphysical aspects. It is remarkable that in the ancient hymns of the *Ṛg Veda* a semitechnical vocabulary was already developed to deal with such linguistic matters as language composition, poetic creation, inspiration, illumination, vision, and so on.[15] But even though there was careful concern for the phenomena or outer aspects of language, the Grammarians always paid equal attention to the inner or metaphysical aspects of language. They seem to have successfully avoided the two reductionistic mistakes of modern Western language speculation. They did not reduce language to being a merely human convention having only scientific or factual referents; nor did they fall into the error of metaphysical reductionism which so devalues the meanings of human words that language ends up as obscure mysticism. Grammarians like Paṇīnī and Patañjali, and etymologists like Yāska were clearly concerned with human speech in the everyday empirical world; but they also made room for metaphysical study. Similarly the great Hindu philosopher of language Bhartṛhari begins his *Vākyapadīya* with a metaphysical inquiry into the nature and origin of language in relation to Brahman, but then goes on in chapters 2 and 3 to explore technical grammatical points involved in the everyday use of language. In classical Hindu thought on language, the study of a given phenomenon and the contemplation of it as a metaphysical mystery do not preclude each other.

The ability of language to deal with ordinary human things and yet at the same time to be metaphysically grounded is further evidenced in the distinctive Indian notion of creativity. Here again the Indian approach shows itself to be more encompassing and insightful than the bifurcated and too narrow view of the modern West. Whereas modern persons think of creativity in terms of a writer creating something "original" or "new," the classical Indian conception is quite different. As Klaus Klostermaier points out: "The great creative geniuses of India, men like Gautama the Buddha or Śaṅkara, take care to explain their thought not as *creation* but as a retracing of forgotten eternal truth. They compare their activity to the clearing of an overgrown ancient path in the jungle, not to the making of a new path."[16] The creative effort of the *ṛṣi*—the composer or "seer" of the word—is not to manufacture something new out of his own imagination, but rather to relate ordinary things to their forgotten eternal truth. In this perspective both the technical study of grammar and the philosophical analysis of language are seen as intellectual "brush-clearing" activities which together open the way for a rediscovery of the eternal truth as reflected in everyday objects and events. Sanskrit grammar was an attempt to discipline and explain the behavior of a spoken language, so that the inner meaning could shine forth unobstructed.

It was this latter aspect, the perceiving of the intended meaning, that commanded the attention of the Indian philosophers of language among whom Bhartṛhari (A.D. 480) consistently ranks as the most important.[17] In Bhartṛhari's major work, the *Vākyapadīya*, the ways in which Indian philosophy conceives the outer word form to be united with its inner meaning are discussed. Bhartṛhari's own position has come to be known as the Sphoṭa Theory after the Sanskrit term *sphuṭ*, which means "to burst forth" or, when applied to language, "a bursting forth of illumination or insight." V. S. Apte in his Sanskrit-English Dictionary defines *sphoṭa* as the idea that bursts out or flashes on the mind when a sound is uttered.

Bhartṛhari's Sphoṭa Theory of Language

The original conception of *sphoṭa* seems to come from early in the Vedic period of Hindu thought. *Vāk* or speech was taken as a manifestation of the all-pervading Brahman. The mantra *AUM* was regarded as the primordial speech sound from which all forms of *Vāk* are thought to have evolved. This sacred syllable is said to have flashed forth into the heart of Brahman while he was absorbed in deep meditation and to have given birth to the Vedas containing all knowledge. At the very beginning of the *Vākyapadīya,* Bhartṛhari restates these very teachings as the foundation for his own thinking (VP 1.5–10). Just as the original unitary Veda has been handed down in many ways by the *ṛṣi* for the sake of communication, so also the unitary *sphoṭa* is manifested as a series of uttered sounds for the purposes of expression and communication. Although the various manifestations of the one Veda may vary in form and style of expression (*dhvani*) from poet to poet and from region to region, it is the same divine truth (*dharma*) that is being expressed throughout.

Bhartṛhari makes clear that it is the word-meaning which, as the essence of consciousness, urges all beings toward purposeful spiritual activity. If the word were absent, everything would be insentient like a piece of wood (VP 1.26): hence Bhartṛhari's description of the Absolute as *Śabdabrahman* (Word-consciousness). When everything is merged in *Śabdabrahman,* no expression of words takes place—no meaning is available through mantras (VP 1.123). But when the Absolute is awakened and meanings are reflected through work, then the knowledge and spiritual power which are intertwined with consciousness can be clearly perceived and known. Because consciousness is of the nature of word-meaning, the consciousnss of any sentient being cannot go beyond or lack word-meaning (VP 1.126). When no meaning is understood, it is not due to a lack of word-meaning in consciousness but rather due to ignorance or absent-mindedness obscuring the reflection of the word-meaning.

The reason for the speaking of mantras is traced to the nature of word-consciousness by Bhartṛhari. *Vākyapadīya* 1.51 states that word-consciousness itself contains an inner energy (*kratu*) which seeks to burst forth into expression. In the experience of the *ṛṣi,* this inner *kratu* is the cause of the one Veda being reflected in many mantras (VP 1.5). The *ṛṣi* see the Veda as a unitary truth, but for the purpose of manifesting that truth to others allow the word to be reflected in the forms of the various mantras. On a simple level this *kratu* is experienced when, at the moment of having an insight, we feel ourselves impelled to express it—to share it by putting it into words.

Bhartṛhari develops his theory of language by maintaining that the *sphoṭa*, the meaning-whole, is something over and above the uttered or written letters. The individual letter sounds (*dhvani*) vary with the speaker (accent, speed of delivery, etc.); but this does not matter, since they are uttered only for the purpose of reflecting the changeless *sphoṭa* which exists within the speaker and is potentially present within the consciousness of every hearer. The *dhvani*(s), the apparent external differences, are simply various external reflections of the one internal *sphoṭa*. The process of ordinary communication is explained as follows. At first the word exists in the mind of the speaker as a unitary gestalt or *sphoṭa*. When he utters it, he produces a sequence of different sounds so that it appears to have differentiation. The listener, although first hearing a series of sounds, ultimately perceives the utterance as a unity–"the light bulb coming on" image of the cartoon. This "Ah ha!" experience of the listener is his mental perception of the same *sphoṭa* with which the speaker began, and it is then that the meaning of the word first seen by the speaker is also known by the hearer. Contrary to most theories of communication Bhartṛhari's view is that meaning is not conveyed from the speaker to the hearer; rather, the spoken words serve only as the stimulus to reveal or uncover the meaning which was already present in the mind of the hearer (VP 1.44–46).

Returning to the experience of the *ṛṣi*, the central or essential idea of the Vedic poem is a given that is inherently present in the poet's consciousness —and in the consciousness of everyone else. At the first moment of its revelation, the *ṛṣi* is completely caught up into this unitary idea, gestalt or *sphoṭa*. But when he starts to examine the idea with an eye to its communication, he has withdrawn himself from the first intimate unity with the idea or inspiration itself and now experiences it as a twofold reflection. On the one hand, there is the objective meaning (*artha*), which he is seeking to communicate, and, on the other, there are the words and phrases (*dhvani*(s)) he will utter. For Bhartṛhari these two aspects of word-sound (*dhvani*) and word meaning (*artha*), differentiated in the mind and yet integrated like two sides of the same coin, constitute the *sphoṭa*. Bhartṛhari emphasizes the meaning-bearing or revelatory function of this two-sided gestalt, the *sphoṭa*, which he maintains is eternal, divine, and inherent in consciousness (VP 1.23–26).

When a child is learning a word or an adult is trying to grasp an idea, the first cognition is often erroneous. Having failed to grasp the whole *sphoṭa*, the listener asks, "What did you say?" As the speaker repeats the same words, or perhaps uses different words in attempting to communicate the same idea, there arises a progressively clearer cognition of the *sphoṭa*. Finally there is a completely clear cognition of the whole *sphoṭa* and its two-sided reflection. This Bhartṛhari describes as a case of special perception or intuition (*pratibhā*) (VP 1.83–84). In a more philosophic sense, *sphoṭa* may be described as the transcendent ground in which the spoken syllables and the reflected meaning find themselves united.

Maṇḍana Miśra illustrates Bhartṛhari's theory with the analogy of a jeweler who assesses the genuineness of a precious stone but with increasing clarity. Each cognition leaves its *saṁskāra* or common memory trace. The last cognition, helped by the *saṁskāra* of the previous one, fully perceives the genuineness of the stone. But for the *saṁskāra*(s) of the intervening cognitions, there would be no difference between the last one and the first one. An important point is that the jeweler is described as "expert," meaning that before beginning the examination he already had the image of a precious stone ingrained in his subconscious, and it was this image (like the inhering *sphoṭa*) that was revealed to the jeweler's mind by his series of partial (and, since partial, also erroneous) perceptions.[18]

In these examples there is a necessary perception of the parts prior to the perception of the whole. This aspect is brought out clearly by Bhartṛhari, who describes the painter as going through three stages when he paints a picture: "When a painter wishes to paint a figure having parts like that of a man, he first sees it gradually in a sequence, then as the object of a single cognition, and then paints it on cloth or on a wall in sequence" (VP 1.52). So also the hearer of a word perceives the word in a sequence of letters which manifest in him the whole word as the object of a single cognition. As a speaker, however, he utters the whole word in its differentiated appearance as a sequence of letters. It is in this context that the perception of the many letters, before the final perception of the unitary *sphoṭa*, is described as error, illusion, or appearance. But it is a unique kind of error in that it has a fixed sequence and form. It ultimately leads to the perception of the truth and is thus regarded as a universal error. The chief cause of this universal error is described as *avidyā* or the limitaton of the individual self-consciousness. A characteristic of this *avidyā* is that it provides no other means for cognizing the *sphoṭa*, except the letters. That is why all individual selves universally experience the same error with regard to speech, but it is an error that ultimately leads to cognition of truth. It is only through this error or appearance of differentiation that the divine *Śabdabrahman* comes within the range of worldly experience so that we ordinary mortals have a way of comprehending it (VP 1.85).

Bhartṛhari focuses on the *vākya-sphoṭa* or sentence-meaning as the true form of reflection of the divine. Although he sometimes speaks about letter-sounds (*varṇa*) or individual words (*pada*) as meaning-bearing units (*sphoṭa*), it is clear that for Bhartṛhari the true reflection of the *sphoṭa* is found in the sentence.[19] This has important implications for single-word mantras. Since the fundamental unit of meaning is a complete thought (*vākya-sphoṭa*), single words must be single-word sentences with the missing words being understood. For example, when the young child says "mama," it is clear that whole ideas are being expressed, for example, "I want mama!" Even when a word is used merely in the form of a substantive noun (e.g., "tree"), the verb "to be" is always understood so that what is indicated is really a complete thought (e.g., "this is a tree") (VP 1.24–26). In this fashion Bhartṛhari provides a way to understand single-word mantras meaningfully. A devotee chanting "Siva" may well be evoking the meaning "Come, Siva" or "Siva, possess me" with each repetition (VP 1.326).

In Vedic ritual, mantra is experienced on various levels from the loud chanting of the *hotṛ* to silently rehearsed knowledge of the most esoteric *bandhu*(s). Much of the argument over the meaningfulness of mantras arises from a lack of awareness of the different levels of language. On one level there is *pratibhā* or the intuitive flashlike understanding of the sentence-meaning of the mantra as a whole. At this level the fullness of intuited meaning is experienced in the "seen" unity of *artha* and *dhvani* in *sphoṭa*. This is the direct supersensuous perception of the truth of the mantra which occurs at the mystical level of language—when "mystical" is understood in its classical sense as a special kind of perception marked by greater clarity than ordinary sense perception. Bhartṛhari calls this level of mantra experience *pasyanti* (the seeing one) (VP 1.142)—the full meaning of the mantra, the reality it has reflected, stands revealed. This is the *ṛṣi*'s direct "seeing" of truth, and the Tantric devotee's visionary experience of the deity. Yet, for the uninitiated, for the one who has not yet had the experience, it is precisely this level of mantra that will appear to be nonexistent and meaningless. If, because of one's ignorance, the *pasyanti* reflection is obscured from "sight," then the uttering of the mantra will indeed seem to be an empty exercise.

Bhartṛhari calls the level of the uttered words of the sentence *vaikharī vāk*. At the *vaikharī* level every sound is inherently meaningful in that each sound attempts to reveal the *sphoṭa*. Repetition of the uttered souuds of the mantra, especially if spoken clearly and correctly, will each time reflect afresh the *sphoṭa* until finally the obscuring ignorance is purged and the meaning-whole of the mantra is seen (*pratibhā*). Between these two levels of uttering (*vaikharī*) and supersensuous seeing (*pasyanti*), there is a middle or *madhyamā vāk* corresponding to the *vākya-sphoṭa* in its mental separation into sentence-meaning and a sequence of manifesting sounds, none of which

16. Brāhmaṇi, 9th century A.D.

has yet been uttered (VP 1:142). For Bhartṛhari the silent practice of mantra is accounted for by *madhyamā* and is, of course, both real and meaningful.

When all three levels of language are taken into account, as they are by Bhartṛhari, it would seem that all Vedic and Tantric types of mantra practice can be analyzed and shown to be meaningful. In cases where the *avidyā* of the speaker or the hearer obstructs the evocative power of the mantra, it may indeed be experienced as meaningless. But even then the mantra is still inherently meaningful as is shown when through repeated practice the *sphoṭa* is finally revealed and by the fact that the purified person, not afflicted by *avidyā*, hears and understands the meaning even though the person uttering the mantra does not. The argument, of course, is circular; and, if it were merely a theoretical argument, then Bhartṛhari's explanation would have no power and would have been discarded long ago. The *Vākyapadīya* appeals not to argument but to empirical evidence—the direct perception of the meaning-whole (*sphoṭa*) of the mantra. As long as such direct perception is reflected in the experience of people, Bhartṛhari's explanation of the meaningfulness of mantras will remain viable.

The logic of Bhartṛhari's philosophy of language is that the whole is prior to the parts. This results in an ascending hierarchy of speech levels. Just as the phonemes are only unreal abstractions of the word, so also words are unreal abstractions of the sentence and sentences unreal abstractions of the paragraph. Even the paragraph is not the ultimate unity, since it is only an unreal division of the chapter of the book. At the top of this language hierarchy there is only one indivisible reality within our literary self (*Śabdabrahman*), which, because of our human ignorance, limitation, or *avidyā* can only manifest itself in such partial reflections as the book, the chapter, the paragraph, the sentence, and the word.

T. R. V. Murti has concisely summed up Bhartṛhari's analysis of language:

> Language is not an accidental, dispensable garb which could be put on and put off. It grows with thought or rather thought grows with it. In the ultimate analysis they may be identical. Bhartrhari in his *Vākyapadīya* (I:124) asserts this basic truth: "There is no cognition without the operation of the word; shot through and through is cognition by the word, as it were. All knowledge is illumined by the word." It is not that we have a thought, well-formed and complete, and then seek a word to express it; or that we have a lonely word which we seek to connect with a thought. Word and thought develop together, or rather they are the expressions of one deep spiritual impulse to know and to communicate.[20]

This is a very different understanding of language from most modern linguistic theories. The contention of the Sphoṭa Theory of the Hindu

Grammarians is that the overt word sounds simply reflect or reveal, but do not create, the idea. The idea or *sphoṭa* is a given which is present in all consciousness. This resonates with our ordinary experience. In talking over coffee, in writing an essay, in singing a hymn or saying a prayer, one starts with an idea which, when clear in our mind, creates an impulse for expression. Then there is the mental struggle to break down the idea or *sphoṭa* and press it out into words or sentences. But no matter how hard one tries, the whole of the original idea can never be fully reflected in words. Something always remains leftover and unsaid. If meaning were communicated by conveying or passing the actual meaning or revelation from one to another, then meaning would constantly be lost and eventually words would cease to communicate. However, Bhartṛhari and the Grammarians maintain that communication is possible only because language and its meaning are grounded in a common consciousness which is Divine in nature. It is this divine basis in consciousness which allows language to function as a Yoga—a means of spiritual realization.

The Yoga of the Word

For the Hindu the ultimate goal of spirituality is union with the Divine (*mokṣa*). Before Bhartṛhari, Patañjali in his *Mahābhāṣya* included in the aims of the study of Grammar (*Vyākaraṇa*) the attainment of heaven (*svarga*) through the correct use of words, and union with the great God (*mokṣa*).[21] Bhartṛhari emphasizes the aim of Grammar as leading both to *svarga* and *mokṣa* not only in the *Vākyapadīya* but also in his commentary on Patañjali's *Mahābhāṣya.*[22] At the beginning of the *Vākyapadīya* Bhartṛhari says Grammar (*Vyākaraṇa*) is the door leading to liberation (1.14); it is the straight royal road for those who desire salvation (1.16); and by means of it one attains the supreme Brahman (1.22). At the end of the first chapter Bhartṛhari returns to the topic and states that "the purificaton of the word is the means to the attainment of the Supreme Self. One who knows the essence of its activity attains the immortal Brahman" (VP 1.131). The Yoga of the Word, then, has the power to take one from the ordinary experience of the word all the way to union with the Divine.

The first and prerequisite step is the purging of corrupt forms from one's everyday language. While Bhartṛhari allows that corrupt forms of words can convey meaning, spiritual merit can be attained only by the knowledge and use of the correct forms of words. This is the spiritual role of grammar. As Bhartṛhari puts it in the *Vṛtti* on 1.131: When speech is purified by the adoption of the grammatically correct forms and all obstruction in the shape of incorrect forms is removed, there results a spiritual merit which brings the experience of well-being (*abhyudaya*). This *abhyudaya* is also translated into English as "moral power" of the sort that begins to move us in the direction of identifying ourselves with the Divine.[23] This is the first step in the Yoga of the Word—the repeated use of grammatically correct language which generates more and more *abhyudaya* until the way is prepared through the lower levels of language (*vaikharī* and *madhyamā vāk*) for the dawning of the mystical vision (*paśyanti*).

For the modern mind it is hard to imagine just how the grammatically correct use of words could be understood as generating moral power, spiritual well-being, and the dawning of the mystical vision. Incorrect usage results from attempts by humans to change the sequencing of language to suit themselves, without regard for the Divine Word. Such ego-centered word-use leaves behind memory traces (*saṁskāra*(s)) which serve to conflict and obscure the proper sequencing of *Śabdabrahman*. Without the aid of grammar and its purifying rules such a confused mental state is the usual result. The truth of the Vedic teaching and glimpses of *Śabdabrahman* are obscured within consciousness by the layers of *saṁskāra*(s) from incorrect word-use. Strict adherence to grammar and its teaching of correct word-use gradually results in removal of these obscuring *saṁskāra*(s) from consciousness. As the proper, non–ego-centered sequencing of language is established, the truth of the Vedic teaching can be seen and responded to. Then increased moral power and the first glimpses of the Divine Word are experienced. This is the truly creative function of the Word—not the making of something new by human ego-centered activity (the modern Western notion of creativity) but the revelation of the real nature of things through the reflective power of language. Only when the rules of grammar are followed is word-use crystalline enough to let the Divine show through. Repeated practice of proper word-use restores to language its mirrorlike quality enabling a reflection of the transcendent Word to take place. Such a polishing and purification of the mind and its constituent word structures is the goal of the first stage in the Yoga of the Word.

The second stage occurs when the purified reflective power of the word is focused upon until union with *Śabdabrahman* is realized. Bhartṛhari describes the process in the *Vṛtti* on *Vākyapadīya* 1.31.

> After taking his stand on the word which lies beyond the activity of breath, after having taken rest in oneself by the union resulting in the suppression of sequence.
>
> After having purified speech and after having rested it on the mind, after having broken its bonds and made it bond-free.
>
> After having reached the inner light, he with his knots cut, becomes united with the Supreme Light.

The middle passage should be taken first. Speech has been purified (stage 1) until the mind is functioning using only correct grammatical structures. This is what the phrase "resting it on the mind" implies. The purging of ego-attachment is essential in such a purification and must be carried even further in stage 2. The "breaking of bonds" refers to the *saṁskāra*(s)or memory traces and their tainted motivations left by egocentric activity—in either spoken words (*vaikharī vāk*) or inner thoughts (*madhyamā vāk*). These ego-bonds are removed by meditating on the Divine Word (*Śabda-brahman*), so the purified forms of language are being clearly reflected. The amount of such meditation required will be equal to the strength needed to negate the egocentric *saṁskarā*(s) stored up within the mind.

The first passage emphasizes the need for "suppression of sequence." The sequencing of the Divine Word into thoughts and uttered sounds must now be suppressed. While such sequencing of language is essential in ordinary day-to-day activities, as well as in the understanding of the Vedic teaching, there comes a time when all that must be left behind. Immersion in worldly life as a student or householder, while necessary and good in itself, is not the ultimate goal. Study of the Vedic texts, while necessary, is not to be clung to as if it were the final end. Attachment to language use in either of these areas is only indicative of a failure to go beyond ego. Especially damaging is ego attachment to the Vedic words themselves—a textual literalism or fundamentalism which reminds one of a line from T. S. Eliot's play *Murder in the Cathedral:* "To do the right deed for the wrong reason is the greatest sin."[24] Spiritual pride is always tragic, and spiritual pride attached to the Divine Word is especially so. The Grammarian practice of *Sabdapurvayoga* guards against such a result by insisting that the sequenced word of scripture be allowed to carry one beyond itself to union with the Divine. This will undoubtedly be the most difficult obstacle for the Grammarian *yogi* to overcome. After having honed his grammatical style and knowledge of scripture to a fine edge, it will be difficult to let go of that laboriously won achievement. But that is exactly what Bhartṛhari requires, otherwise the *saṁskāra* of ego attachment to the uttered word will block out the reflection of the Divine in it.

Giving up attachment to sequenced language, purified though it may be, implies moving from spoken words (*vaikharī*) and inner thoughts (*madhyamā*) to the direct mystical vision (*pasyanti*, *pratibhā*, or *sphoṭa*). As the first passage indicates, the function of breath here is important. In *vaikharī* breath is very active in producing the sequence of uttered sounds. At the level of inner thought (*madhyamā*) breath is still active though in a more subtle way in fashioning sequences of thought. *Pasyanti* lies beyond the activity of breath and sequence (VP 1.142). The mind is quiet and focused, allowing the *pratibhā* perception of *Śabdabraham.* Thus, through *Sabdapurvayoga* or the Yoga of the Word, we are to pass on from the gross sequence to subtle sequence and finally to that stage where sequence is entirely eliminated. Like a perfectly still pond, consciousness, when stilled from its sequencing activity, clearly reflects the reality before it. For Bhartṛhari, it is the Divine Word (*Śabdabrahman*), the essence of consciousness, which stands revealed at the center of the stilled mind.

Passage three reflects just such an experience:

> After having reached the inner light, he, with his knots cut, becomes united with the Supreme Light.

Although the "cutting of the knots" is not defined by Bhartṛhari, Vṛṣabha describes it as a cutting of the bonds and knots of "ego-sense." Going beyond the ego-sense of "I" and "mine" is obviously a major challenge in *Sabdapurvayoga.* It is repeatedly mentioned by Bhartṛhari. For example, in the *Vṛtti* on VP 1.130 he says that those who know the Yoga of the Word break the knots of ego-sense and are merged with the Divine Word. If ego attachment in any form remains, the *pasyanti* stage will not be fully realized. In the *Vṛtti* on 1.142 *pasyanti* seems to be endowed with a number of phases (of increasingly pure reflection). In the lowest it seems to be still echoing some of the faint sequencing activty of *madhyamā*. At a higher level it assumes a quality in which all word-forms are submerged beyond recognition. At the highest level it completely transcends all associations with word-forms. Hence, *pasyanti* can reflect worldly word-forms and can also totally transcend them. Even though it may come into contact with the sequenced and often egocentric word-forms of *vakharī* and *madhyamā*, it remains pure, untouched, and spiritual in nature. To those who are trapped in ego-knots and impure word-usage, *pasyanti* may appear to be mixed up and contaminated. But in reality it is not. As one adopts correct word-forms, through a rigorous and reverent study of grammar, one's consciousness is purified and the true inner vision of *pasyanti* revealed. The word-forms are seen for what they are, namely, partial manifestations of the one Divine Word which in *pasyanti* stands clearly revealed. *Sabdapurvayoga* is the meditational exercise in which the mind is concentrated on the unity of the Divine Word and turned away from the diversity of thoughts and sounds that manifest it (VP 1.14). Gaurinath Sastri suggests that the whole meditational process with its culmination in the vision of the Divine Word and final reunion with it is poetically described in the *Ṛg Veda* stanza *Mahādevo martyam āviveśa.*

> The spiritual aspirant reaches the Essence of Speech—the pure luminous Eternal Verbum, which lies beyond the vital plane (*prāṇavṛttim atibhrānte*) by withdrawing his mind from external nature (*ātmānaṁ saṁhṛtya*) and fixing it up on his inner nature (*ātmani*). This entails the dissolution of temporal sequence of thought activity (*krama-samhara-yogena*). The purification of the Verbum results from this and the aspirant enters into it having severed all his ties with the material objective plane. This leads him to the attainment of the internal light and he becomes identical with the undying and undecaying Spirit, the Word Absolute.[25]

Bhartṛhari claims that in the spirituality attained through the practice of *Sabdapurvayoga* a greater measure of Divine Light shines through: "Those persons in whom correct speech exists in a greater measure, in them also resides, in a greater measure, the holy form of the Creator" (VP 1.120, *Vṛtti*). As long as a Grammarian in the state of spirituality is alive, the Divine Light of the Word resides in him as in a covered vessel. When such a one dies, this holy luster merges into *Śabdabrahman*, its source (VP 1.120, *Vṛtti*).

Sabdapurvayoga demonstrates that the meaningfulness of words is not merely intellectual; it is meaningfulness which has spiritual power. With the proper *yoga*, words have the power to remove ignorance (*avidyā*), reveal truth (*dharma*), and release (*mokṣa*). *Vākyapadīya* 1.5 *Vṛtti* states it clearly: "Just as making gifts, performing austerities and practising continence are means of attaining heaven, it has been said: When, by practising the Vedas, the vast darkness is removed, that supreme, bright, imperishable light comes into being in this very birth" (VP 1.137). It is not only this lofty goal of final release that is claimed for the spiritual power of words, but also the very availability of human reasoning. Without the fixed power of words to convey meaning, inference through words could not take place (VP 1.137). Because of the power inherent in mantras for both human inference and divine truth, great care must be given to the *yoga* of words.

In Hindu *yoga*, the repeated chanting of mantras is an instrument of power. The more difficulties (*saṁskāra*(s)) there are to be overcome, the more repetitions are needed. *Vākyapadīya* 1.14 makes clear that repeated use of correct mantras removes all impurities, purifies all knowledge, and leads to release. The psychological mechanism is described by Bhartṛhari as a holding of the *sphoṭa* in place by continued chanting. Just as from a distance, or in semidarkness, it takes repeated cognition of an object before one sees it correctly, so also repeated chanting of the mantra results in *sphoṭa* being perceived in all its fullness. Maṇḍana Miśra describes it as a series of progressively clearer impressions until a clear and correct apprehension takes place in the end.[26] To begin with, such mantra chanting will be mainly at the *vaikharī* or outer-word level. But as spiritual improvement is made the chant will be more and more internalized on the *madhyamā* or inner-word level. Eventually all sequenced chanting activity will submerge into the still steady mantra *samādhi* of *pasyanti*, and the final goal of *Sabdapurvayoga* will have been realized.

For the Hindu Grammarian our outer words and inner thoughts are but reflections, more or less perfect, of the one Divine Word. The great *ṛṣi*(s) or seers recognized this and made themselves empty channels through which the Divine Word could reverberate with little distortion. The great Grammarian teachers, basing themselves on the utterances of the *ṛṣi*(s), formulated this wisdom into a teaching informing all of life, and even into a pathway to final liberation.

Although not all may agree with the spiritual vision of the Hindu Grammarians, it must be conceded that we do find here a view of language which makes sense of poetry, revealed scripture, science, the mystical chanting of mantras, and which, in addition, strongly resonates with our ordinary everyday experience of coffee-cup chat. It is a way of seeing language which effectively explains why it is that sometimes when we listen we do not hear. It also teaches how to remove the obstructions in one's consciousness so that real hearing becomes possible and suggests in a different way the ultimate wisdom of the observation, "In the beginning was the Word, and the Word was with God, and the Word was God."

Notes

1. Gaurinath Sastri, *A Study in the Dialectics of Sphoṭa* (Delhi: Motilal Banarsidass, 1980) 80.
2. K. A. Subramania Iyer, *Bhartṛhari*, 58.
3. P. K. Chakravarti, *The Linguistic Speculations of the Hindus*, 52.
4. *The Vākyapadīya of Bhartṛhari with the Vṛtti* (hereafter abbreviated as VP), 1:20.
5. *The Sarva-Darśana-Saṁgraha of Madhava*, trans. by E. B. Cowell (Varanasi: Chowkhamba Sanskrit Series Office, 1978 reprinting) 220.
6. T. R. V. Murti, "The Philosophy of Language in the Indian Context," in *Studies in Indian Thought*, ed. Harold Coward (Delhi: Motilal Banarsidass, 1983) 361.
7. J. Gonda, *The Vision of the Vedic Poets* (The Hague: Mouton, 1963) 17.
8. Harold Coward, "The Meaning and Power of *Mantras* in Bhartṛhari's Vākyapadīya," *Studies in Religion* 11 (1982) 367–75.
9. S. Radhakrishnan, *Indian Philosophy* (London: Allen & Unwin, 1962) 1:125–36.
10. Aurobindo Ghose, *On the Veda* (Pondichery: Sri Aurobindo Ashram Press, 1956) 6.
11. See, for example, Harvey McArthur, *In Search of the Historical Jews* (New York: Scribner, 1969) 6–7.
12. See also the discussion of K. Kunjunni Raja, *Indian Theories of Meaning*, 142ff.

13. Practices included here range from the ancient mantras chanted as part of the Vedic rituals to such modern American phenomena as the chanting of the Lord's name by the Hare Krishna movement and the initiation to mantra meditation by TM (transcendental meditation).

14. J. Gonda, "The Indian Mantra," *Oriens* 16 (1964) 247.

15. F. Staal, "The Concept of Metalanguage and Its Indian Background," *The Journal of Indian Philosophy* 3 (1975) 319.

16. Klaus Klostermaier, "The Creative Function of the Word," in *Language in Indian Philosophy and Religion,* ed. Harold Coward (Waterloo: Wilfrid Laurier University Press, 1978) 6.

17. See Coward, *Bhartṛhari.*

18. *The Sphoṭasiddhi of Maṇḍana Miśra,* trans. K. A. Subramania Iyer (Poona: Deccan College, 1966) *kārikā* 18ff.

19. See especially the *Second Khāṇḍa* of the *Vākyapadīya,* in which he establishes the *vākya-sphoṭa* over against the view of the *mīmāmsakas.*

20. T. R. V. Murti, "The Philosophy of Language in the Indian Context," in *Studies in Indian Thought,* ed. Harold Coward (Delhi: Motilal Banarsidass, 1983) 358.

21. See K. A. Subramania Iyer, "Bhartṛhari as a Means of Attaining Mokṣa," *The Adyar Library Bulletin* 28 (1964) 112–13.

22. K. A. Subramania Iyer, *Bhartṛhari,* 58.

23. Gaurinath Sastri, *A Study in the Dialectics of Sphoṭa* (Delhi: Motilal Banarsidass, 1980) 82.

24. T. S. Eliot, *Murder in the Cathedral* (London: Faber & Faber, 1955) 44.

25. Gaurinath Sastri, *A Study in the Dialectics of Sphoṭa* (Delhi: Motilal Banarsidass 1980) 85.

26. *The Sphoṭasiddhi of Maṇḍana Miśra,* trans. K. A. Subramania Iyer (Poona: Deccan College, 1966) *kārikā* 19–20.

Bibliography

Sources

The Vākyapadīya of Bhartṛhari with the Vṛtti. Translated by K. A. Subramania Iyer. Poona: Deccan College, 1965 (chap. 1), 1971 (chap. 2, part 1).

The Sphotasiddhi of Mandana Misra. Translated by K. A. Subramania Iyer. Poona: Deccan College, 1966.

Studies

Chakrabarti, T. *Indian Aesthetics and Science of Language.* Calcutta: Sanskrit Pustak Bhandar, 1971.

Chakravarti, P. K. *The Linguistic Speculations of the Hindus.* Calcutta: Unversity of Calcutta, 1933.

Coward, Harold G. *Bhartṛhari.* Boston: Twayne Pub1ishers, 1976.

——. *Sphota Theory of Language.* Columbia, MO: South Asia Books, 1980.

Iyer, K. A. Subramania. *Bhartrhari: A Study of the Vakyapadiya in the Light of the Ancient Commentaries.* Poona: Deccan College, 1969.

Kaviraj, Gopinath. "The Doctrine of Pratibha in Indian Philosophy." *Annals of the Bhandarakar Oriental Research Institute* (1924) 1–18 and 113–32.

Murti, T. R. V. "Some Thoughts on the Indian Philosophy of Language." Presidential Address to the 37th Indian Philosophical Congress, 1963.

Raja, K. Kunjunni. *Indian Theories of Meaning.* Adyar: Adyar Library, 1963.

Sastri, Gaurinath. *The Philosophy of Word and Meaning.* Calcutta: Sanskrit College, 1959.

Part Five

VEDANTA AS REFLECTIVE SPIRITUALITY

12

Vedanta as Philosophy of Spiritual Life

Kalidas Bhattacharyya

Editor's Abstract

In addition to my treatment of this article in the Introduction, it seems reasonable to provide a readable overview of its contents. The résumé that is presented here highlights the central theme of the author's article as well as of the elaborate sequel that the author wrote to that article but which, alas, could not be included in this volume.

The term "Vedanta" as the label of a characteristic form of reflective spirituality refers to a philosophic vision of the "transcendent" reality variously described as Being, Consciousness, or Spirit. Two ideas are significantly combined: the Transcendent is directly experienced, though at a level removed from the normal sensory or intellectual kind; and, second, it is experienced as the culmination of a cognitive, evaluative inquiry. The dynamism of the knowing act is the clue here. Knowing as contrasted with other mental states like emotion and will has the distinction of being intuited as a transcendent act—that is to say, as *not* a natural phenomenon at all. Anything that may be described as dynamic is ever trans-natural though it behaves in and through nature. The expression "transcendental" as used here, incidentally, may be understood not in the Kantian sense as asserting or entailing the dependence of the world of experience on the activities of reason. It is used as characteristic of reflective activity emphasizing what is both intuitively—that is, immediately—experienced and at the same time perceived as not of the order of nature but of spirit.

Knowing act is transcendent in the sense that one identical knowing act runs through all cognitive episodes and, indeed, even colligates all the episodic cognitions of all persons. The latter aspect, to be sure, is not directly experienced in all its clarity in normal, ordinary life, but one is not without intimations of it even here. There are different levels of experiencing this transcendent knowing act, the lower of each of them being more engrossed in Nature than the one just above it. Philosophy as appositional to spiritual life is a reflective consideration of what is implied in the very fact of experiencing something, and there is always the demand for actual or possible experience of whatever is disclosed. Spiritual journey for Vedanta as, preeminently, a cognitive discipline, consists of a step-by-step progress in attaining higher and higher experience. As experience does not go on of itself unfolding that way, there arises the need for a journey at least for the less gifted. One has first to be convinced intellectually of the theoretical character of that experience as a step in the direction of evoking it in oneself through a progressive self-correction by means of sustained reflection. Intellectual maneuver is necessary and inescapable for the human being as distinctly a thinking being, but is not sufficient, as what is aimed at is direct, unmediated experience. In the final analysis, Vedanta, true to its name, relies on the testimony of scripture as the criterion of transcendent experiences. The central scriptural "affirmations" of an unaffirmable identity between oneself and the transcendent mediate between uncovered consciousness and the self-correcting experience.

One of the ways of understanding the "transcendental" character of the knowing act is in terms of distinguishing "noticing" from becoming reflectively aware of something. A mental state is noticed unreflectively on a par with the mental state itself, whereas the awareness of a knowing act is of its very nature reflective. Episodic cognitions quite as much as other noticeable subjectivities like emotions, wish, and similar other states of mind are not intrinsically conscious. If they are noticed as they occur it is because they can by virtue of their constitution reflect or absorb pure consciousness. The psychic states are made of the stuff of nonconscious matter at high degrees of attenuation being manifestations of the brighter phase of Nature which brings it closer and closer to consciousness. A systematic culture of self-training, then, consists of a stepwise dissociation from Nature through purification, that is, a freeing of the "bright" from its entanglement with the gross, namely, the "active" and "inert" aspects of Nature. What is generally called introspection in psychology Vedanta comprehends under consciousness, showing itself and also showing the modes of the mind that absorb or reflect it. It is like light revealing itself and revealing things, simultaneously and in their succession. Such is what is technically termed witness-consciousness in Vedanta.

The act of knowing at any of the stages of its progressively increased reflectivity relates to the object known, not through the mode of referring but through withdrawal, paradoxical as it may sound. In bringing itself into greater and greater focus, reflection as a form of self-consciousness does not mean consciousness experiencing itself as object but, rather, as having a better and freer relation to the original object itself. Experience as reflective—that is, as self-consciously withdrawing into itself—continues as in itself while also behaving naturalistically as episodic knowledge of this object or that event. It is like light and its self-illumination, vis-à-vis its refractions in and through the things that are lighted.

Another name of this withdrawal is freedom. Pure consciousness is the ultimate reached through a continuously graded withdrawal from whatever is "object." Alternately stated, it is freedom into itself through freedom from objects. The more I face myself—that is, I stand at a distance, as it were—the better and in a truer perspective I view the erstwhile object. I view things as they ought to be viewed *sui generis,* by consciousness. This is spiritual experience, experience as much of withdrawal from Nature as of itself in its purity and self-containedness.

Withdrawal, to continue the analysis further, at every step from Nature is also the direct experience at every such second step that Nature had been at the earlier stages covered by darkness or, more correctly, that Nature itself was darkness. One feels that once experienced in true perspective Nature is totally "naught." Total disappearance is the ultimate truth of "darkness," though darkness is characterizable neither as "is there" nor as "is not there." Nature through continuous self-purification in the form of progressive dissociation ceases increasingly to becloud consciousness, but this is possible according to Vedanta because transcendental consciousness had throughout been peering through that Nature. Consciousness has been peering since the state of Nature as life; and higher up below the specifically human stage, it peers in forms of life, instinct, subconsciousness; and, higher still, at the stage of cognitive intellect which uniquely defines the human level, consciousness starts peering through its thinning form like the rays of the sun from behind the cloud. The states of "freedom while alive," of "abiding in the state of pure witness" represent the last link with cognitive mind or Intellect which disappears either with physical decease or automatically in course of time like rays of the sun disappearing automatically with the morning sun showing itself. Nature, technically called in Vedanta *māyā*, with its paraphernalia, is explained only as these paraphernalia disapper one after another as one advances on the spiritual journey, finally dragging *māyā* itself along with them. This, incidentally, is a species of direct experience, a retrospective and nonetheless immediate, experience.

Māyā at the point of disappearance with consciousness as always before peering is what has been called "witness-consciousness." It truly belongs to consciousness proper though only vicariously through the intermediation of the beclouding of Nature in its last traces. Reflection as a function of the latter—that is, of the intellect—is not consciousness itself but its nonsubstantial duplicate or foil. It is, one may say, consciousness itself but misplaced or deflected by *māyā*, as the reflection of my face in a mirror is not another but my face itself though not where it ought to have been. At higher and higher stages of intellection, consciousness is a better and better duplicate, as is the case with reflection of the moon first on a lake with waves, then on one with ripples, and then on a calm, absolutely unruffled sheet of water. Consciousness, Vedanta asserts against all dualist accounts, is bodily there though fused with *māyā* as fire remains identified with an iron ball, the ball glowing more and more with fire there manifesting more and more. The term "seer Nature" is aptest meaning that Nature at its highest stage of manifestation perceives pure consciousness through itself as the medium.

Pure consciousness need not, as by itself, be a disinterested onlooker though it can also be that in the context of *māyā* without any loss of its purity. Illusions, hallucinations, and dreams are directly experienced by consciousness as modifications of *māyā*, as also in the case of other modifications of mind or intellect brought through fusion. There is, indeed, no substantial distinction between the two types, as objects in normal cases as only "intended" by mind are not different from illusions where there are no objects in Nature corresponding to the modifications.

The passage in the spiritual journey beyond the self-purification of Intellect to the resplendent presence of consciousness in complete uncoveredness is effected, preeminently, in Vedanta through hearing of the revealed "word." The scripture will have to speak out through the Master the central truth in order that the gap between the seeker and the truth may vanish. As Spirit, the ultimate transcendent reality, is nonpersonal (which is not less personal), any intelligible attitude to it would have to be a serene cognitive, direct experience. Direct experience keeps on associated with the emotive attitude of devotion and the active one of performing action, but knowledge holds the field throughout. To be sure, the Absolute reality is approached differently through the various degrees of dominance of knowledge, emotion, and will throughout the journey in all transcendentalisms, but Vedanta will insist that the Absolute as such is none of them but only pure consciousness in the literal sense of the term.

BEFORE ADDRESSING THE CENTRAL QUESTION of Vedanta as typically a "philosophic" orientation of spirituality, one may reflect on the general sense of "philosophy" itself as the name of a viable intellectual pursuit similar to and yet significantly different from other theoretical approaches. Philosophy is a second-order—that is, reflective—study of experience. Indeed, in an important sense every study is reflective, that is, second-order. What then distinguishes "philosophy" from other second-order studies is that it is as much second-order as also a first-order of a sort. It is a first-order experience somehow carried over bodily to the second order and suffusing all thought, reason, logic operative there, or possibly a new direct first-order experience somehow supervening at that second level and dominating all thought processes operative there. Philosophy is a knowing-how or why as well as a knowing-that and is in that sense a spiritual experience or realization.

It is this feature in a manner that seems unique to the reflective spirituality of Vedanta that stands underscored as the demand behind the conceptualization of philosophy as a self-avowed "philosophic vision" (*darśana*).[1] Vedanta as a *darśana* becomes defined and refined as a philosophically debatable issue in the writings of Gauḍapāda (seventh century), Sankara (eighth century) and the post-Sankara Vedantins (ninth to seventeenth century).[2] Philosophy, as the name of a self-conscious evaluative inquiry (*yukti*, *manana*, *vicāra*, *upapatti*) cultivated by them self-consciously and unapologetically in a polemical setting, is a species of "thinking" in the service of and also itself constitutive of some direct experience, though at a level removed from one that we normally have in our daily life. Let us call the normal kind "experience" (*anubhava*, "cognition derived from personal observation," *parokṣa*, "mediate cognition within the range of observation") and the one removed from that level but which becomes realized through a special cognitive process as "Experience" with "E" capitalized (as translation of *anubhava* or *anubhūti*,[3] *jñāna* or *jñapti*, "understanding" or insight, *aparokṣa*, literally, "not beyond observation," i.e., direct, immediate, unobjectified, cognitive experience, *samyagdarśana*, "perfect intuition").

Our normal first-level direct experience is either (1) sensuous, that is, visual, auditory, tactual, etc.—each singly or several such in combination—

always apprising us of reals out there in space and time, or (2) psychological, meaning that the contents are experienced as events, static or dynamic, in our mind, occupying moments or stretches of time.[4] Every such first-level experience is an affair in Nature, Nature comprising not only whatever is in space and time but also whatever is causally determined (and determining), and perhaps more important than that, whatever is always an *object* (*viṣaya, dṛśya, jñeya*) either just to take note of or study, that is, describe correctly and explain. Object, understood in this sense, necessarily presupposes what stands "subjective" (*visayin, dṛk, jñāna*) in relation to the object that either takes note, describes, and explains or is itself the noting, describing, and explaining.

Could this *subject* be, in its turn, itself an object, it too would well belong to the same Nature as a constituent. But the whole difficulty lies precisely there. Were it an object, there must have been some other *subject* taking note of, describing, and/or explaining it; and in that case either that *subject* would fall outside Nature or, if it too could in its turn be an object to another subject, one would have either to stop at this second subject arbitrarily or get entangled in a vicious indefinite regress.

But one may find this refusal to proceed further backward arbitrary. Do we not often find in Nature one and the same thing chasing another thing and being itself also chased? If *as chasing* it could somehow be debarred from belonging to Nature, it *as chased* does certainly belong there and is, that way, an *object* of chase. One and the same knowledge, likewise, may, on one occasion or from one point of view, be *knowing* as subject (*kartṛ*, "nominative") and yet, on another occasion or from another point of view, be *known* as object (*karma*, "accusative"). If, now, the same knowledge (i.e., an episodic knowledge) can also be known as an object, there is no point in trying to keep it outside Nature.

Further, should an indefinite regress be necessarily vicious? Most of the causal series, for example, are indefinite, the search for cause, cause of cause, cause of that further cause, etc., being continuable unendingly, and yet nobody finds fault with that inquiry. All the causes are in their turn effects too and all equally belong to Nature.

The reply to these questions (to anticipate the response of Vedanta) is as follows: The alleged simplicity of all these situations is due to a concealed equivocation. When, for example, a ball B strikes another, say A, this A can be understood as either simple A or "A as struck"; and, correspondingly, B is either simple B or "B as striking." So far as the simple A and the simple B are concerned apart from their struckness and strikingness, there is nothing wrong about there being B behind A, C behind B, D behind C, and so on. But as soon as the features "struck" and "striking" are taken into consideration the regress stops. For if there is a C behind B, that B is no "B as striking" but first simple B and then, if one likes to consider it so, "B as struck," never "striking B." So too is the case with "chasing B": when B is chased it is either simple B or "chased B," not "chasing B" (except, of course, when the entire chasing-chased drama is a topic for reflective meta-study).

What thus applies to the instances of striking-and-struck and chasing-and-chased applies all the more demonstrably to the case on hand, namely, knowing-and-known (*karma-kartṛ*). B that has known A may well, in its turn, be known by C and so is also the case with that C, and so on; but this does not mean that what C now knows is B-as-*knowing*—B either as a knower or literally as a process of knowing—and similarly with that C, and so on. Thus, the knower as knower—and, what practically means the same thing, knowing as act—cannot be directly known as an object. *Vijñātāram āre kena vijānīyāt?* "By what could one know that (by) which (one) knows?" (BĀU 4.5.15). It may be spoken of as an object retrospectively, and there may well be a systematic meta-study of this act, but there is no direct awareness of it quite simply as "object."[5]

This is the reason why since the earliest days of philosophy and mathematics there has been so much controversy around the concept of motion; and this ambiguity pertains as much to translatory molar motion as to motion that is vibratory or of any other form passing under the names "power" or "disposition," provided, of course, these are not mere colligatory terms standing for some series of facts. They are, in each case, indicative of some comprehensive unity; and this unity, obviously because it does not stand in the same footing with the facts of the series concerned, must have transcended them. But though it thus belongs to a higher level, it is directly known nonetheless, and this distinguishes its position from the "second-level" or "meta-level" of science. Whereas at the meta-level of science nothing is directly experienced—intuited, perceived, one may say—at the second level in the present context—that is, of "transcendental" philosophy like Vedanta—it is directly experienced (*anubhava*). This is what distinguishes the transcendent from (scientific=intellectual) theories which too are said to belong to a sort of second level. The transcendent that belongs to the second level is yet directly intuited (*anubhūti, jñapti*); it is Experience itself. It is no mere word, no concept or hypothesis (theory). The series of momentary facts—better, those facts as forming the series—all belong to Nature, but the dynamic unity we are speaking of is overnatural, a second-level *fact;* and the relation between the two is never like that between any two natural facts.[6]

The Dynamism of the Knowing Act

The dynamism of the *knowing act* provides the point of entry into Vedanta. Knowing as an act is the dynamic principle that comprehends so many mental states like sensations (*nirvikalpa*), naturalistic mental connecting of such sensations—one with another discretely (*savikalpa*)—images (*vikalpa*), as different types of maturation of unconscious and subconscious traces, and empirical conceptions that connect different mental unities just already formed. When we say that knowing act, as dynamic, comprehends sensations and the said "connecting" conceptions, images, and others, we do not mean by "connection" any act or any form of dynamism. These connecting principles are themselves, in their turn, and therefore as naturalistically understood, all static—each a static bit, and the result too equally static, though more extensive. No natural mental phenomenon—not even what is called unconscious trace or disposition—is dynamic in the proper sense of the term. It is dynamic only in the loose sense of being an intermediate static link, absolutely at the same level with what it is the link between; and the resulting total too, even where this total is understood as something additional to the constituents among which the link too is one, is on the same level. If unconscious dispositions are ordinarily understood as dynamic, this is all as a matter of theory and, so far, only a retrospective, distant, intellectual account, not what is directly apprehended as dynamic.

In contradistinction to the above stands knowing as a transcendent act. It may be formulated as the single underlying thesis of the *way of knowledge*, which has the patent of Vedanta. The thesis is this: No case of knowledge is ever intuited as both a natural phenomenon and an act. It is this distinction which distinguishes cognition from emotion and volition. Episodic knowledge is always noticed either as a natural incident occurring over there or as a particular finite-spanned series of such incidents—in either case no act; and in case such condition is dispositional, it is only some unconscious trace or a body of such traces left by some conscious cognition(s), and remains as trace, somehow concealed in the mind, and in some extreme cases, as a kind of unearned stock built unnoticed by some retrospectively specifiable physical, physiological, hereditary and/or social antecedents, and—whichever way it is generated—affecting our conscious life. Such unconscious makeup is not only never perceived as act; it is not perceived at all. From the beginning to the end, as we have noted, it is a hypothesis, a conceptual construct, though it may be wholly justified as any good scientific hypothesis is. If, again, it is said to *affect* our conscious life, this does not mean any *activity* exercised. It means nothing more than the fact that it is a *cause* of what it is said to generate. Is not a cause static in itself but still said to generate the effect as though the cause is exercising itself, as though it is "acting," as a matter of linguistic device? It describes nothing factual and, if somehow still justified, is still only a matter of theory, nothing that is perceived immediately. The underlying thesis of great relevance for the understanding of Spirit in Vedanta is this: Dynamism is ever trans-natural, though in some forms it behaves in and through Nature and thus only *appears* to be natural in order, as it were, ultimately to turn our (wholly) natural attitude toward trans-naturality.[7]

Before we close this topic of so-called natural dynamism let us consider for a while another kind of dynamism (alleged to be found in Nature) which is not so much a process as some power, some potentiality, some living capability of assuming under appropriate circumstances newer and newer forms. What we like, however, to emphasize in this connection is that process and power are not really two distinct affairs. A process, we have seen, taken as one unitary dynamism, is, over and above being a series of successive units, a trans-natural reality too. Power is nothing but this trans-natural side of process.

This is as much true of physical potentialities like tension, elasticity, and other forces as of emotional moods and sentiments and, in our volitional life, wishes and desires, the common characteristic of these potentialities being that, by themselves, none of them are manifest enough to claim full actuality and yet are sufficiently evident as the guiding principle from within. The mental ones of these potentialities constitute what is generally called the subconscious, and these potentialities, physical as well as mental,[8] openly defy all positivistic interpretation. They are not wholly reducible to a series of discretes that may be only, as a matter of theory, treated as forming some sort of unity.

Our task in referring to these phenomena of Nature which point beyond themselves is to show the following: what is directly experienced as colligating in the form of process and/or power cognitive episodes that form particular series (whether these be the series of episodic cognitions, with or without substantial time gaps, of one and the same object in Nature or the series of all such episodes in one's whole life and, therefore, about diverse objects at different times, or even whether they comprise all such series of lifetime cognitions), what is so directly experienced as colligating and, therefore, as power is what is called "knowing" as *act*. The act-character is, of course, unquestionably experienced—and, of course, experienced directly—in the first of the three cases just mentioned. But we shall show in the sections that follow that with some studied effort we can, however indistinctly, also experience one identical knowing act running through all the cognitive episodes in the life history of each one of us. I experience mine, you yours, and so on. The one knowing act that colligates all the episodic cognitions of all persons, if there be one—and Vedanta spirituality in its generality anchors on a faith in its reality—is indeed least experienced. But one cannot say therefore that it is not experienced. It requires a good deal of meditative-reflective practice on the part of one seeking to capture it. There are thus different levels of experiencing this transcendent knowing act, the lower of each of them being more engrossed in Nature than the one just above it.

If transcendent knowing gets engrossed in—that is, operates through—different levels, these levels may be viewed as levels of Nature but also equally as levels of transcendence. In the former case Nature, in a manner of speaking, has clearer and clearer experience of transcendence. In the latter case it is the transcendent which, in the opposite direction, as it were, gets more and more involved in Nature. And this is true not merely of knowing-act as transcendent vis-à-vis Nature; it is true equally of all types of transcendence we have listed till now. The subconscious, for example, is experienced at the lowest level as just peering; at the next higher level as more in itself, that is, as generating such and such mental events, affecting in such and such ways our lowest level mental affairs; and at the next higher level as nearer cognitive act proper. The same happens, though that requires much greater perspicuity, with physical potentialities like tension and elasticity. Physical and mental (all natural phenomena) potentialities, in other words, themselves symbolize a sense of or a nisus toward transcendence. They are suggestive of transcendence but as dimly discerned because of the circumstance of its expressing itself in and through natural settings. Knowing-as-act, on the contrary, shows itself as fully and genuinely transcendent, though at the same time operating in and through and in the form of natural mental episodes called knowledge-events.

Philosophy as "Spiritual Discipline"

Whoever, thus, in saying "A causes B," understands no activity on A's part, and nothing also as the potentiality of B in A, understands causality, activity, potentiality, power, process, and similar other notions intellectually—that is to say, as it were, from a distance and as a matter of theory, not as directly experienced. One may, if one likes, build systematic theories of these paradoxical phenomena, and parallel *theorists*, namely, those who do and do not admit transcendence as only a matter of theory, may go on arguing with one another, and, quite conceivably, there may or may not be a final intellectual court of appeal. And this is, after all, the situation that philosophy understood on the model of science as a second-order theoretic quest reflects throughout its history. But, for a philosophy which could be called metaphysics in the sense of a quest for or consideration of what is implied in the very fact of experiencing something—a sense which makes "philosophy" appositional to spiritual life—the central problem is how far, and how much, these evanescents are (immediately) experienced and, if one likes to add, how much what is missed at one stage can be recovered at the next and so on, whether unending or not.

Another question equally important for philosophy, thus understood, is: Given the predisposition to experience spiritual freedom, how to nourish and cultivate this immediate experience—actual though partly, at one stage, and, from the point of view of that stage, only possible (and that too partly) for the next stage, and so on. The question, for philosophy in this specific sense, is never all intellectual: there is always the demand for actual or possible experience of whatever is disclosed. Obviously, too, as the things said exhibit, as it were, a vector toward the transcendent—that is, as involving *demands,* to use a more expressive term covering all the things we are speaking of, from process, through motion, force, tension, subconsciousness, to knowing act—the experience is not merely one that is immediately had but also one which, unless there is an absolute experience to be reached, is ever *to be,* ever in future. Here, in philosophy, therefore, the approach is necessarily progressive, proceeding from one step or level to another, till the final step, if there is any, is attained in the immediacy of experience or realization. Such step-by-step progress in attaining higher and higher experience is called *sādhana* in the specific Vedantic sense, a species, one may say, of transcendental reflection, keeping in mind that reflection is constitutive of a self-conscious immediate experience. More specifically, it is inner *praxis* (*antaranga sādhanā*).

Not that it is therefore all mystical experience, impervious to a rational intellectual approach. Only it is no *mere* theory, no *mere* intellectual construction, not even anything that being constitutionally unamenable to direct experience is *only* inferred. It may well also be logically constructed or inferred; but it is something that demands *pari passu* that it be directly experienced—not merely obtained intellectually as so experienceable but refusing to stop short of actual direct experience. A theory as such, as an intellectual construction, is indeed in no need of experiential grasp, but what should we do if the theory contemplated is about experience itself, about what some *experience* is or is-to-be? The answer implied lies in nothing short of attaining or realizing that experience *directly* and precisely in the form that was constructed for it in theory. Should we not, in other words, try to experience the full content of the theory?

Gifted enough, one could, of course, through continuing experiential self-correction and self-improvement, through *experience* correcting and improving itself stage by stage, reach or at least approach its correctest form as depicted in the theory, though without any prior intellectual knowledge of that theory. The only test, so far, of the reliability of that experience is its successful immediate removal of all doubts about it. Indeed, for these gifted few, there is no need for this kind of intellectual maneuvering. But obviously there is no harm either except that it would be useless distraction for him or her to intellectualize the experience.

What is thus gratuitous for them is, however, a necessity for others for whom, because of various predispositions, (direct) experience does not go on unfolding itself that way. Such less gifted persons have first to be convinced intellectually of the theoretical character of that experience, and only then is it possible for them even to evoke in themselves that experience, through progressive self-correction, in its theoretically stipulated form. Yet, however, for them, this intellectual maneuvering—even when it is in its best logical form—is no more than a much-needed strong catalytic—at worst, a means to draw their attention and persuade them. Intellect only introduces the seeker to this task and, to an extent, keeps one steadfast on the track of fingerposting the right direction. The task may be compared to a teacher's imparting lessons to a student. The lessons, as intellectually formulated, first seek to interest the student and then prompt him to have the ideas by and for himself and, not only that, to guide him at every crucial turn. The main thing, however—namely, to *have* the ideas—the student needs to do for himself.

Intellectual superstructure, we may note, has yet another important use. Every such superstructure is not only an aid and a guide to having the desired experience; it being an *intellectual* superstructure tends necessarily to guard that experience from all actual and possible onslaughts of other rival superstructures that may have centered on some other stipulated experience or been themselves sheer theories never purporting to mature into an experience. This safeguarding function proceeds generally in two opposite directions, one positive and the other negative, often conjointly, as supplementing each other. The negative procedure consists in intellectually demolishing competing theories and the positive one builds, in addition, a systematic intellectual bulwark around the desired experience.

So far we have been concerned with the relation between an *experience* to be had, that is, realized, and the corresponding intellectual superstructure. What, however, would be the relation, one might ask, if it is not some *experience* but something nonsubjective that is to be come by or at least encountered (supposing that it could be encountered exactly in the form in which it is intellectually worked out)? There is an answer to this. If there is any such nonsubjective content, it is to be contacted either empirically (i.e., through our senses) or conceivably in the way that is called in Indian transcendentalism, *paramārthika dṛṣṭi*, "transcendental insight," which may be described as pure (nonsensuous) intuition. If, now, that content is only to be empirically had, the problem would only be to actualize the stipulated conditions under which the content could be perceived; the feasibility of such actualization is so easily, almost instinctively, taken for granted that it poses no problem for anyone. Even if it be extremely difficult to actualize those conditions, like—what was almost inconceivable till the other day—going over to a distant planet, its feasibility being granted, there remains no further hurdle.

However, as soon as the content to be had is stipulated as nonsensuous, the problem becomes complicated. In such cases we meet with at least three different possibilities. Either it is left there as a mere theory, only a theoretical construction, nothing demanding to be actually encountered as over there, or one understands it even as a theory, but somehow in terms of what are sensuously perceivable or at least relevantly in the context, however remote, of such perceivable contents, or again, in case it defies even that interpretation and yet refuses to be left as a mere theoretical construction, it may be understood as something overnatural (transcendental) which yet is undeniable and accessible through (overnatural) supersensuous pure intuition. There is nothing absurd about this third possibility. Once we have granted that some experience can be understood as to be had, that is, to be acceded somehow, there should be no difficulty about a *content* to be so approached, for the procedure is the same in either case: through transcendental reflection, through suprasensuous pure intuition, it is intelligible that we can contact contents as well as have the experience itself. And such contents are not all otiose, not all inflictions through bad use of language. We have already come across instances of "contents" of similar nature: tension, elasticity, subconsciousness, etc., and—underlying all these forms of potentialities—an ultimate genuine transcendence, not very far, as we have seen, from the knowing act.

It is this relation between intellectual maneuver and direct realization which as the pivotal point of Vedantic methodology was first developed by the Vedantists of different schools—and most elaborately by Sankara and those who followed him in exegeting *Brahmasūtras* (2.1.11, *tarkāpratiṣṭhānāt*, "because reasoning is ill founded"). The only point that Sankara added in this connection was that bare intellectual logomachy led nowhere, that aggressive intellectualists quarrel with one another endlessly. This additional Advaita contention, however, is not to be construed as a cheap

17. Dancing Ganes, 10/11 century A.D.

castigation of (intellectual) "science" that changes its theories too often. Had it been that sort of castigation the Advaitins would be open to a ready rebuff: in matters natural (empirical), which are in the last resort given to our senses and systematically connected with one another by the principles of logic, no one can expect finality, because, first, the data presented to sense are always contingent and again the application of logical principles themselves, necessary though, may well go wrong on various empirical grounds. It is for these reasons that scientists consider it proper not to commit themselves finally to a theory and, yet, not also to doubt every such theory consciously from the beginning. Their attitude is, "we accept it as a correct theory till it is proved wrong."

No Vedantist–indeed, no Indian thinker–thoroughgoing skeptic of the past, who questioned the viability of induction, can have anything against this normal healthy attitude. Though the theory may in the future prove inadequate in the light of unfolding empirical knowledge, it has not failed up till now. This is the underlying assumption of accepting the scope of inference within its range, a perfectly innocuous position. What the Advaitins have claimed is only that it is useless to quarrel intellectually over a thing which, as far as the points the quarrel is about are concerned, stands directly experienced[9] (provided, of course, on some other specific ground that immediate experience is not suspected, which, however, is not to the point here). This is true as much when that direct experience is pure intuition as when it is sensuous perception.

Transcendence, Reality, and Knowledge

So, pure immediate experience, another name of which is knowing-act, and equally any content that is so experienced, is overnatural, that is, transcendent. If it is an act, it, however transcendent, is, of its own nature, directed to some content which just insofar as that pure act is directed toward it, is itself equally pure; and it will be shown later that this pure content (with all its varieties) is as much independent of it (the knowing act) as also not. *Natural* contents which are sensuously perceived (or perceivable) are perceived clearly as what are independent of that empirical perception and independent, so far, of whatever pure knowing act too is involved in that perception. If some empirical idealists have tried to understand such contents to be dependent on (in extreme cases, nothing but) the corresponding empirical perceptions, this they could do only by ultimately highlighting their dependence on the *pure* knowing act.

Transcendence, then, is a theoretical, that is, cognitive, act amounting to "knowing." It is a theoretical act that is experienced immediately as directed to a content which is as much other than the act as also identical with it in the sense that it is somehow constructed *sui generis.* The content even as content, that is, as other than the act, is apprehended in the very same experience as yet coming out of the act, the act, in other words, taking shape that way.

What is distinctive of Vedanta transcendentalism in thus analyzing theoretic consciousness (cognitive act) is that it does not assume that Nature alone is the reality principle. There is not the tacit acceptance that whatever can be sense-perceived is alone, definitionally, real. The unquestioned ultimate criterion of reality is *just* givenness, not necessarily givenness *to the senses.* If transcendent contents are given to pure intuition there is no reason why they should not be called real.

The crucial point is that all theoretic contents, whether sense given or intuited purely, are *given,* the very defining mark of theoreticality, that is, of cognition being the givenness, in any manner, of the content. Therefore, every theoretic experience, Vedanta would assert, marks a grade of knowledge. Neither would Vedanta scout employing the religious language of the transcendent as graciously showing itself or exercising itself through the empirical. But it would equally admit the possiblity of its showing itself too in isolation, that is, as *not* the empirical at worst in some relation of subordination or coordination with other so-called transcendents. The truly transcendent is pure freedom. To state the same differently: Because even as itself it is real, indeed the very principle of reality, one could aspire after it and legitimately seek to experience it, to have it by itself as well as also, quite conceivably, find that it is the throbbing dynamism of the empirical world itself, which means encountering this world, Nature, in a new spiritual perspective.

In the latter case, to use a different language but still in terms of experience, the transcendent is experienced as livingly liquifying itself and running through—and that way permeating every bit of this empirical world. Here too one may experience it either in that dynamic form only as some unspecifiable, unpinpointable, life principle of the world or, alternatively, as the "in-itself" and, therefore, the very much pinpointable transcendent constantly running through every detail of the world. The Mahāyāna Buddhists, particularly the Mādhyamikas, and some extreme Sākta Tāntrika(s) would come under the first category and all other Indian transcendentalists under the second. This second one, again, to pursue the division still further, may be said to have two subtypes, according as emphasis is laid on the in-itself transcendent or on the transcendent-as-working. The former is the view of the Advaita-Vedantins who, though provisionally they recognize the functional side, would seek ultimately to get away from it, leaving it so much to the limbo of nothingness that as once experienced it appears in retrospect to have been a wholly inexplicable magic show. The latter subtype is the view of integral transcendentalists like orthodox Saiva(s) and the Vaiṣṇava(s). [For entries relating to Rāmānuja and Madhva schools of Vaisnavism, as also on the Saiva school of Sivadvaita, see below, chapters 13 and 14, and for those on Tantra, Bengal Vaisnavism and Saivasiddhanta, see Vol. 7 of World Spirituality.]

So transcendence is (directly) experienced, and this Experience is knowledge. Transcendence, in other words, is no mere concept in the service of intellectually constructed theories, though such theories, heard from others, can prompt one, to whatever extent, to uncover that Experience. But only "can": there is no must about it, no necessity that one who understands the intellectual account shall have that direct experience. It all depends on whether the hearer has already *some* inkling of the experience of transcendence, in the form of a nascent disposition to spiritual freedom (*mumukṣutva*), and whether an appropriate speaker (guru) has succeeded in invoking in him some modicum of that experience not only through those intellectual presentations but, more importantly, through other suggestions, persuasions, and training, the latter being nothing necessarily occult.

In other words, the master speaker, over and above the mode of ratiocination—sometimes even without any such ratiocination—converts the already predisposed hearer more decisively, baptizes him, and brings him totally over to his (speaker's) side, exactly as an able, good school teacher does for students. This is the truth behind what the Indian philosophers have often so much relied on, namely, revelation or testimony (*sabda-pramāṇa*), and when the transcendent experiences thus had, and to be had, are considered either as already deposited in the cultural bank for ages unknown or, more intelligibly, as eternal pristine experiences best spoken out by messiahs, prophets, and *ṛṣi*(s), "seers," the total fund of these truths and their statements is called scripture.

The Self-validity of Knowledge

That some statements of scripture may conflict with our experience and, therefore, seem not evident or true is no argument against *sabda-pramāṇa*, "the evidence of scripture." Our ordinary perceptions may also turn out similarly "false," and so also even theories; but, even then, we have no other way but to turn to some perception after all, that is, to some immediate experience or, in the case of theories, to some theory again. What we mean by this is (1) that mere theoretical possiblity of some statement (whether of immediate experience or of some theory) turning out false is not its weakness (2) that it is only when some *actual* error is found that we turn to correcting it, and (3) that till such correction is accomplished we either stick to it despite all its weakness or from now on alert ourselves and proceed more circumspectly.

The modern distinction, worked out in Western philosophy, between knowledge and belief is largely inappropriate in this context. If the distinction is at all valid, it is so at most in case (3); but even there the case is not that belief in A gets strengthened or transformed into knowledge of A, but, rather, that knowledge of A had thinned into belief in A. So far as getting strengthened is concerned, belief in A gets strengthened, after correction, into knowledge of B. The modern Western distinction between belief and knowledge is meant only to idolize science, that is, theoretical construction, over immediate experience—over sense perception or pure spiritual intuition. But we have already seen that science is not, that way, superior in status, that is, entitled to greater credence than immediate experience and its systematic description.

Indian thinkers do, indeed, often distinguish between knowledge and valid knowledge in their discussion of the "validity" (*prāmāṇya*) of knowledge (*pramā*) or "means to attaining that knowledge" (*pramāṇa*). But that is quite another problem and should not be confounded with the Western distinction between belief and knowledge. With the Indians the question is whether—and, if yes, how far—to have knowledge is or is not different from having it as valid. (Having knowledge of A as valid means here both "valid knowledge" as such and being somehow aware too that the knowledge is valid.) From this standpoint, "valid" means what is fully useful in life (*samarthapravṛttijanaka* or *arthakriyākārī*), the test of validity consisting in the fact or assurance that it is so useful.

The only difference between some schools of thought and Vedanta here is that while others hold that this validity is something additional (*parataḥ*) to a cognition *qua* cognition, for Vedanta it is in an important sense "intrinsic" (*svataḥ*).[10] But even then the difference is not fundamental enough. Both hold that every knowledge, as it occurs, is initially *taken* or used as valid; but while for the other schools it may yet well be *actually* invalid, that is, unusable, for the Vedantins it is *actually* also valid, for while having it we do not ever, they contend, question its validity. Though this much is admitted by other thinkers too, for they also do not question it as long as no contrary case or some defect is actually pointed out, the Vedantins argue that their difference with others centers on what exactly happens when the cognition turns out—that is to say, is experienced as invalid. This invalidation, according to them, is definitely a big jolt, so much so that we feel sure we were not on the lookout for it. Before that jolt occurs the situation remains peaceful, and, with the jolt, it is perforce driven out, which means that knowledge *per se* is (*utpattau*), and is experienced as (*jñaptau*), valid. So far as direct experience is concerned, this is undeniable.

Knowing-act as Revelatory and Creative

The most serious question Vedanta faces is this: Is the knowing act something experienced—that is to say, some *object* of experience—or is it experience itself? If it is experience itself, has it, or has it not, any object other than itself? Is the experience conceivably somehow its own object?

The problem can be answered in more ways than one (finding echoes of support in the different lines of development of Vedanta).[11] One is the idealistic solution: So far as broad general features of empirical objects are concerned, objects are but self-concretizations and self-projections of the knowing-act at different levels of transcendence. That being the case, it follows that the experience of these contents is automatically that experience experiencing itself, self-consciously constructing those contents and projecting them over against itself. As self-consciously creative, it is consciousness, in that very act, as much of the creations as of itself.

The standard objection to "idealism" is well known: the objects that are said to be created by consciousness, however nonempirical they may be paraded to be, are or have to be, in the first place, existent by themselves. If they are thus self-subsistent, their constructedness is perhaps only the way in which they are apprehended, now only adjectivally hanging on to them. The reply of Vedanta to this objection brings out the noetic bias of its spirituality. The very question whether the content is self-subsistent or not can be asked only when the content is understood in the context of knowledge. The in-itself content is, nevertheless, the content *known* as in itself, *known* as other than knowledge—in the language of Advaita Vedanta, known as (hitherto) unknown.[12] We add "necessarily" in every such case, our thesis being that the otherness, the unknownness, of the content—in effect, its in-itself-ness—is necessarily *known* that way—that is to say, necessarily in the context of knowledge. In other words all independence of the content—not merely the content but even its alleged independence—necessarily depends on knowledge, is knowledge-centric. To be (or have been) independent of knowledge is itself a basic category of knowledge. It is knowledge finding itself to have been absent.

Even at the original perceiving stage of knowledge one may distinguish between two aspects of the object perceived. One of these is the "thing" itself (*padārtha, vastu*), and the second, the thing as perceived which may be called "object" (*viṣaya, jñeya*). Not that at the original perceiving stage they (the aspects) stand obviously distinguished, far less separate from one another. But first, unless they were somehow distinguished, even at that stage there could be no explanation of perceptual illusion. Correction of perceptual illusion, rather the reflective awareness of what the illusory "object" was during the period of illusion, testifies, phenomenologically speaking, to a nascent awareness of such distinction: the illusory content–say, the "snake"–was not actually there in itself but was yet verily that real itself as presented. It is perceived as "object"–that is, as *this*–and not as a "thing." It should be noted here that such awareness is not a matter of theory or post-factum intellectual construction but a species of direct, though retrospective, awareness.

If at the stage of perception the *object* as *the thing-as-perceived* serves all our purposes–cognitive as well as noncognitive–we may well remain content with it and feel no urgency (except a useless scholastic one) in prying into the nature of the thing as it is which, so far, is no more than just a dark background–some thing that may well be–one may even say "has to be"–admitted but to no special gain, neither cognitive nor noncognitive. In the Advaita-Vedantic language, this gratuitous "thing" is precisely the *ajñana* ("nescience"). The essence of the "thing" is its claim to be independent epistemologically, as "out there" in its own right. Such a claim is false and ought to be dispensed with, but what it does instead is to obscure by such claim the "purity" of the knowing-act. It becomes the dominant factor in a knowledge-situation. The knowing-act itself is eclipsed, at best reduced to another event, an item of nature, or at worst some epiphenomenon hanging onto some bodily state, more neuro-behavioristically, to some subtle neural state of affairs. The mere forward-lookingness in its objective pole is called *māyā* (the term *ajñana*, "nescience," is also used, though as yet without its vicious declaration of independence). Speaking from the subjective pole the same is only the disinterested viewer (*sākṣin*) or, better, disinterested viewing or viewership (*sākṣitā*), in respect of the very forms it assumes at different stages of the forward-lookingness (and even, one may say, of its vicarious declaration of independence). One may feel hesitant to go the whole length with Advaita-Vedantin in reducing the independent thing to a species of "nescience," a reification, as it were, of the demonic claim to exist "out there" independently. But nothing, equally, is gained by admitting it as unknown and unknowable, as bracketed or as a dark background.

Knowing-act and Reflective Awareness

Whatever is subjective–mental or transcendental–is somehow *noticed*, even though unreflectively. This noticing, so far, is absolutely the same thing as the subjective state said to be noticed, and nobody finds any problem there. Every subjective state is, almost by definition, a noticed state. Should one, however, on this analogy, plead that the (transcendental) knowing-act too is noticed that way, he would miss a substantial difference between the two cases. *Noticing* a mental state is no reflective awareness, no form of self-consciousness; but the awareness of knowing-act, the awareness that there is the knowing-act, is, of its very nature, reflective, even though this awareness and the knowing-act are the same in just the way "noticing" and the subjective state noticed are the same. Until the difference between the two cases is substantially smoothed there is no such easy passage from one to the other. All Vedantins—indeed, all transcendentalists—have smoothed the passage, and it is because they have first done this that they could apply the analogy of the "noticed" self-identity to the awareness of knowing-act.

The standard Western understanding of the issue is well known: cognitions, feelings, emotions, wish, will, etc. are all (different) modes of *consciousness*, though it is not necessarily meant thereby that through them runs a self-identical, numerically single, consciousness much as there is no such numerically one, self-identical color running through the different specifiable colors. Many in the West have admitted such single self-identical consciousness, but many equally have not.

Vedantic transcendentalists steer a middle course. For them, episodic cognitions, quite as much as other episodic *notice*able subjectivities, are none of them *intrinsically* conscious, that is, no original conscious mode; and if they are still all equally noticeable as they occur, this is because, on account of their peculiar constitution, they can absorb or reflect pure consciousness. Self, according to them, either is itself or consists of consciousness, which consciousness, therefore, is so far pure and numerically one for each individual person. All psychic states as capable of absorbing or reflecting this pure consciousness are made, so far, of nonconscious matter at high degrees of attenuation or thinness and transparency. The thinner and more transparent it is, the more it absorbs or reflects that pure consciousness, thinness (*laghutva*) and transparency (negatively, *anāvaraṇakatva*, "non-veiledness," and positively, *prakāśakatva*, "manifestness,") being two manifestations of the best phase—(one may call it "constituent") of matter, called *sattva*—the phase which brings it closer and closer to consciousness according as the phase shows itself better and better, that is, as thinner and thinner and more and more transparent.

Those of the transcendentalists who hold that the thinner and more transparent episodic subjectivities (*aṅtaḥkaraṇa vṛtti*(s)) absorb pure consciousness more and more as it were, defining or determining it, are known in such circles as "determination-theorists" (*avacchedavādin*(s)) and those who theorize that these subjectivities reflect (or, alternatively, hold the reflections of) pure consciousness are known as "reflection-theorists" (*pratibimbavādin*(s)). For both, the thinner and the more transparent the (mental) "modifications" (*vrtti*(s)) the closer they partake of pure consciousness so that at their thinnest and transparentest stage they either coalesce with that pure consciousness or, eliminating themselves altogether, leave the entire room for it. The *vrtti*(s) are of various kinds: some, as identified with pure consciousness in the way stated above, as either absorbing or reflecting it, reveal—that is to say, *refer to*—things (maybe to themselves too in cases of introspection) as objects and are, on that account, called knowledge-events (*vrittijñāna*); some again, identified in the same way with pure consciousness, stand merely as noticed—we mean, those which are called feelings, emotions, wishes, wills—and all these (the knowledge-events as well as those which are noncognitive) stand there with only borrowed consciousness, not as themselves modes of consciousness.

The account we have given so far of Vedantic trancendentalism involves a good deal of theorizing but is not in any part a mere theory. Every part of it strives for an exact description of what is recovered in direct experience. It is a description of what adepts have experienced, step by step, and what they expect others to experience through systematic culture, called self-training (*sādhana*). The description is of the systematic culture of stepwise dissociation from Nature, through systematic purification (freeing of *sattva*, i.e., the bright from its entanglement with *rajas*, the active, and *tamas*, the inert) of the mind. Mind is as much an item of Nature as any other. It starts at the lowest, with dissocation of the body from the outside world and then through step-by-step dissociation, first from this body, then from the lower stages of the mind, then again step by step from higher and still higher stages of the mind, which dissociate stages (beginning from the dissociation of the body from the rest of Nature right up to the most dissociate mental stage), though all still belonging to Nature, are yet progressively getting freed of their dense grossness. Intellectual understanding may, as we have seen, aid, or even quicken, this progressive realization; but as a theoretical activity it is only a distant aid. Nearer aids are performance of prescribed duties, observance of prescribed rituals and yogic exercises. All these, however, are still extrinsic aids (*vahiranga sādhana*): none of them *constitutes* the desired experience at any of its stages.

Vedantism—indeed, transcendentalism—of all types have insisted on the scrupulous performance of all these extrinsic and intrinsic *sādhana*(s) arranged in prior-posterior order, each prior leading to the immediate posterior and then given up like discarding the ladder after climbing. Not that this order and all the steps are enjoined on everybody; some deserving few are exempted from passing through this or that stage and some, in extreme cases, from quite many of these. But whatever that may be, every such stage is a stage of *experience,* running through these stages, parallel to and at least as detailed and systematic as all theory-constructions of *intellectual* transcendentalism.

Knowing-act and Consciousness

Pure consciousness as manifest in *vrtti*(s), even as identified with them, whether as absorbed in or as reflected by them, is the *vrtti*(s) themselves definitely rendered conscious. *Vrtti,* it may be recalled, is a state of the mind not itself consciousness or its mode but a state entailing noticing, showing itself in this respect as distinct from the state of mind of, say, an animal. The mind at the higher, specifically human stage is called *buddhi* or *citta.* Before that, at any lower stage of the mind where this consciousness was not manifest because the mind was not relatively more of *sattva*-constitution, say, for example, at the merely animal stage, no mental state could be *conscious* that way; it was at best *noticed* (though even that is doubtful—at least, even as so noticed, it was not distinguished from another such stage), nothing further supervening. Here, on the other hand, it gets related to (pure) consciousness that somehow supervenes—the consciousness which, though absorbed or reflected, shows not only itself but also that which absorbs or reflects it. One may say (à la Wittgenstein's remark about the function of language) that it not only "shows" without "saying" itself, it equally "shows" (without so far "saying") the relevant *vrtti* too. What, except at any intellectual meta level, is "said" is what *vrtti* is about, that is, the object of this *vrtti.* And there could be no *vrtti* about that *vrtti* itself, no *vrtti* could be an object of another *vrtti.*[13] What is ordinarily called introspection in Western psychology is here, in Vedantic terms, not only consciousness getting identified with that *vrtti,* by way of being absorbed or reflected, but in addition, having that *vrtti* as *object* too.

This, in Indian transcendental philosophy, particularly of the Vedantic type, is called *sākṣi* or witness-awareness or *sākṣitā,* "the state of being witness." This, of course, is a form of reflective awareness, but so also is the case with the pure consciousness "showing" not only itself but the *vrtti* in question too, as is evident wherever something luminous is absorbed or reflected by something which, because of its peculiar constitution (in cases of *vrtti*(s), because of the excess of *sattva*), is capable of absorbing or reflecting it. In the case of a red-hot iron ball, for example, the red-hot fire only shows the ball; it does not have the ball for its object,[14] that is, as other than it. And so is the case with light reflected immediately from a piece of crystal or glass. Reflective experience (otherwise called self-consciousness) need not have itself as over against itself, as its *object.*[15]

It follows, too, that this pure consciousness is singular numerically—at least proximately for every individual person. This is not so merely as a matter of theory, supported on the ground of parsimony. It is also what is immediately experienced. For, first, if the self is constituted of consciousness, then, since each such self is numerically one, so must also be that consciousness. Second, if one maintains that consciousness, at least as cognition, is not numerically one but many cognitive events, then there will be no adequate account of introspection. Introspection is another cognitive event having the earlier cognitive event as its object; but then inevitably there would be the question: Can this introspection be experienced as object by another introspection a step removed? If "yes," then there would be no end to the process of introspection behind introspection, and this indefinite regress would be as explained earlier, positively vicious. There would be no guarantee that there was at all the first unreflective knowledge we started with. The only guarantee that there was this first knowledge is that it came to be introspected, but if even this second introspection is to be guaranteed by another introspection, the required guarantee that any knowledge-event occurred at all would never be forthcoming.

One may here argue that though the primary knowledge-event is known as an object by introspection this introspection, in its turn, is not, and indeed, need not be, so known by a third-level introspection. But then we ask: On what ground do you say this? If this is what you experience directly, then we say we likewise experience another thing also, namely, that this introspection as not distinct, as an event, from a third-level introspection is, equally, nondistinct from any so-called "other" introspection even at that second level. True, at that second level, these "other" introspections have different primary knowledge-events as their objects. But that speaks nothing for their own numerical difference from one another: one and the same light may reveal many things as much successively as simultaneously. So, while each person has numerically one (better, non-many) introspection in direct experience, this singleness is also theoretically justified on the ground of parsimony.

And if it is one for each person, it can also be realized in direct experience as (numerically) one and the same for all persons (*Aitreya Upaniṣad* 5.3). True, the latter is not so directly realized in all its clarity in our normal ordinary life. But even in ordinary everydayness do we not often feel, though vaguely, our identity with one another? Had there been nothing identical running through us we could not have feelings for one another, and the ideal that such love and fellow-feeling inevitably point to is that we are "one"–in whatever diverse ways this oneness is sought to be understood in different religious paths and systems of morality. There is a negative agreement between such divergent ways: the "one" implies non-otherness. Even similarity does not approximate to it. At best, similarity accounts for our similar behavior to something outside us, even to other persons. But that is not love or fellow-feeling which points straight to a glimpsed identity of all consciousness, at least as an ideal. This is the underlying faith of Vedanta. If, again, there is thus ultimately "one" consciousness, and if consciousness is of the very stuff of self, it follows, of necessity, that ultimately there is "one" Self, somehow comprehending the individual selves. Vedanta understands by self pure consciousness itself which is non-dual Experience.

Notes

[The following notes have been prepared by the Editor to elucidate, by reference to the texts of the tradition and secondary writings, some of the terms and concepts that the author uses.]

1 Of the many conceptualizations of "philosophy" in Indian thought *darśana*, from the root *drś*, "to see," is used almost like a proper name (as in the case of *philosophia*) to name the enterprise of systematic thinking. The difference is that the name strictly appropriate for the "end" or goal sought, namely, "vision" is used as the name for the means employed to bring about that end (*karaṇārtha*): discursive thinking *by means of which* is accomplished vision or direct realization, *drsyate anena*. The use of the term is as old as *Mahābhārata* (Sānti Parva 10.45) and the *Vaiśeṣika Sutra* (9.2.13) which uses it in the sense of the vision of the perfected (*ārṣam siddha darsanāccha dharmebhyah*, "cognition by advanced sages as also *the vision of the perfected . . . ones* result from dharma or merits"). The BS uses the term in its nominal and verbal forms to mean scripture (e.g., *darśayati cātho api smaryate* [3.2.17], "the scripture shows or makes known and thus it is also remembered" [i.e., stated in smrti]; *darśanāc ca* [3.2.21], "because of scriptural showing"). It is important to note that the author of the essay uses the term *darśana* in its root sense as entailing and even eventuating in vision or direct experience (*anubhūti*) and not simply as a mental view of the vision, a *theory* of reality.

2 The expression "post-Sankara Vedantins" includes (1) contemporaries of Sankara whom, tradition claims, Sankara "converted" to Advaita persuasion: Maṇḍana Miśra, the author of *Brahma Siddhi*, who is identified, again, by tradition (but disputed by modern scholarship), with Sureśvara, the author of, among other works, *Naiṣkarmya Siddhi;* and (2) a direct disciple of Sankara, Padmapāda, the author of *Pancapādika*, who may be said to inaugurate the Advaita right-wing which includes Prakāsātman, the author of *Pancapādika Vivarana;* Vidyāraṇya, the author of, among other works, *Vivaraṇa Prameya Saṁgraha* (both fourteenth century); Akhandananda, the author of *Tattva Dīpana* (A.D. 1350); Nrsimhasrama, who wrote *Pancapādika vivaraṇa prakāśikā* (sixteenth century); and Ramananda, who

continued the *vivaraṇa* line in his *Vivaraṇopanyāsa* (seventeenth century); (3) another line of Advaita started by Vacaspati Misra (ninth century), the author of, among other works, *Bhāmati* commentary on Sankara's commentary; and his followers, Amalananda, the author of *Vedānta Kalpataru* (thirteenth century); Appayya Dīkṣita, the author of, among several other works, *Kalpataru parimala* (sixteenth century); and Laksminrsimha, the author of *Ābhoga* (seventeenth century); (4) Advaita dialecticians like Sriharsa, the author of *Khaṇḍana-Khaṇḍa-Khādya* (twelfth century); Citsukha, who wrote *Tattvapradīpikā* (thirteenth century); and Madhusudhana, the author of *Advaita Siddhi* (fifteenth century); and (5) figures like Prakāsānanda, the author of *Vedānta Siddhanta Muktāvalī* (sixteenth century), who systematized from the statements of Gauḍapāda, Maṇḍana, Vacaspati, and Sankara himself a logically irrefutable doctrine of *drṣti-srṣti-vāda*, "theory of seeing is creation," giving an idealistic and even a solipsistic turn to Vedanta.

For details about some of the texts and secondary writings, see Bibliography.

[3] *Anubhava* and *anubhuti* mean the same, except that the latter term is feminine in grammatical gender and is used in Vedanta literature in a reified sense ("experience" with a capital "E") and becomes interchangeable with the content experienced. Cf. the opening verse of *Iṣta Siddhi: yānubhūtirajāmeyānantātmā . . . namāmi tām,* "I bow to that Experience which is unborn, unknowable, infinite, is self (itself). . . ." Elucidating its ontological sense as what stands unobjectifiably evident (*svata-siddha*) the commentator says: *anubhūter anubhāvyatve ghaṭādivat ananubhūtitva prasanga iti,* "If experience can be experienced (as the accusative of an act) one will be in the predicament of admitting that experience is non-experience (i.e., an object) like pot and other things." See also *Tattva Pradīpikā* of Citsukha, p. 21 (ed. Nīrṇayasagar).

[4] The general assumption of the Indian philosophers, *pace* the Buddhists, is that static mental events are still *occurrents* occupying three moments—the moment of origination, that of stay, and that of cessation. Dynamic mental affairs (except "dispositions," *samaskāra*(s)) are either not admitted at all or when admitted as in the Mimamsa and in Buddhism are *occurrents* nonetheless, occupying stretches of time, howsoever infinitesimally as in Buddhism. Transcendental affairs (*paramārthika*), being *ex hypothesi* beyond the world of space and time, are for the generality of Indian philosophy non-occurrents.

[5] The Advaita terminology for the subject–object or knower-known polarity is *drk* and *drśya,* what reveals and what is revealed. The subject or knower is already a complex of *drk* and *drśya,* as one may see it clearly in the admission like "I know myself," where "myself" refers to some perception, thought, feeling, or other. The latter, being observable, come under the rubric of *drśya,* thus pointing to a noetic center beyond (or behind) them, which is here labeled *drk. Drk qua* representing a state of the subject is a structure which includes within it the "inner sense" in one of its shifting modes. The general principle on which the Advaitic argument that the "knower as knower, or what is the same, knowing as an act, cannot be known as an object" is stated by Sankara in the form of a logical or semantic rule, *karma-kartr virodha,* "the contradictoriness of the nominative and the accusative" (e.g., commentary on BS 3.3.54; TU 2.1.1). In post-Sankara writings (e.g., *Advaita Siddhi,* p. 268) *drśyatvāt* "because it is of the nature of what is confronted as 'this,' i.e., revealed as object" is used as the "reason" (*hetu*) for demonstrating the nonultimate nature of the presented world based on the aforementioned "epistemological" principle that what is presented as object cannot be identical with the transcendent subject which grounds such presentation, that the *drśya* cannot be *drk.* The implied argument here is not of the type of inferring the presence of fire from observing smoke, a *pramāṇa* in the strict sense of the term but a species of analogical reasoning entailing use and extension of a principle holding good in the empirical

sphere—"experience" as noncapitalized—to one beyond it which yet is not outside the ken of experiential depth—what the author terms "Experience" with a capital "E." For more discussion of *samanyato-drstānumāna,* see "The Place of Reason in Advaita," in M. Hiriyanna, *Indian Philosophical Studies* (Mysore: Kavyalaya Publishers, 1957) 45f.

[6] The relation between two "natural facts" (*drśye*) is one of mere difference (*bheda*) characterized by "mutual negation," while the relation between *drk* ("overnatural") and *drśya,* cannot conceivably be one of difference: *dudrṣṭayor iva parasparāpekṣayā bhedadrṣṭissambhavati natu drṣṭādrṣṭayoh adrṣṭayor vā,* "perceiving of difference is possible between two perceived (facts)" by reciprocal reference but not between the perceived and the unperceived or between two unperceived (facts)" (*Iṣṭa Siddhi,* p. 3, first line). The "second-level fact" is not perceived but is transcendentally apperceived.

[7] What the author means to say here was clarified by him in personal communication thus: "All dynamic situations that are natural only seem to be unitarily dynamic. The dynamism has somehow been smuggled in somewhere, often in the very definition of continuity. Dynamism is only *sought to be understood,* as a natural phenomenon as though immediately perceived like the static units and their series. These are cases where genuine, i.e., trans-natural dynamism pertaining to consciousness) beckons us ever, through Nature, to what is beyond Nature—the transcendent that behaves in and through Nature, though only heuristically. Not merely dynamism, but many other paradoxical phenomena in Nature behave exactly in the same way. They are immediately understood as natural phenomena but, on careful analysis, perceived to be trans-natural, only behaving heuristically as natural, i.e., ever beckoning us from beyond. They are phenomena like Illusion, dream, awareness of Nature as a whole." The above is a positive and spiritually meaningful interpretation by the writer of the Advaitin's recourse to negation to resolve the paradox that while truth is immediacy, reflective awareness of it involves distancing: *adhyaropāpavādābhyām niṣprapancam brahma prapadyate,* "by conscious imputation and (subsequent) recession of all elaboration and expression one alights on the ultimate." Cf. Sankara's *Gītā-bhāsya* 18.66; Sureśvara's *Naiṣkarmya Siddhi* 3.104.

[8] The *Nyāya-Vaiśeṣika* finds a place for these in its scheme. Cf. *Bhāṣā Paricceda* (158) for an account of the varieties of "potentialities" (*vega*) physical and nonphysical and also the commentary *Siddhānta-muktāvalī* on the verses.

[9] Sankara's castigation of mere "reasoning" (*tarka*) in this celebrated section referred to by the author is on grounds of its antinomical character and a consequent lack of finality and stability without the aid of (direct experience of Truth entailed in) the Āgama: *utprekṣāyā nirānkuśatvāt,* "as it will be (only) unbridled imagination." With respect to what is directly experienced as in the analogous instance of perceptual knowledge that "fire is hot," says Sankara, "it would not be reasonably sustainable to understand that men can have differences about it." To quote him again: "*Samyag jñāna* [Experience with a capital 'E,' in the terminology of the author of the essay] which (definitionally speaking) is reality-dependent (*vastu tantram*), is of uniform or unitary essence. What exists 'uniformly' (*eka rūpam*) such is the ultimate (*paramārtham*). . . . How then can what is both arrived at on the strength merely of reasoning (*tarka prabhavam*) and also (consequently) not of one uniform, non-varying content (*ekarūpa anavasthita viṣayam*), lay claim to (the title of) *samyag jñānam*?" What remains essentially and interminably problematic from the point of view of demonstrable knowledge—what Sankara calls *tarka*—is directly and with finality "known" in Experience as the sensation that "fire is hot." The uninterpreted immediacy of the latter is only an analogy for the immediacy of Experience which is higher and not lower than mediate reflective knowledge carrying as it does the element of certainty. The scripture

which alone provides infallible and certain insight into the real is, for the author of the essay, another name for "eternal pristine experience" (see p. 246).

[10] See above, Introduction, p. xxix, about the implied methodology of the principle of autonomy of verbal signs. It is in answer to a possible objection whether verbal knowledge (and therefore the scripture as a source of valid knowledge) does not require to be corroborated by and conform to other experiences, the Mimamsa-Vedanta tradition advocates acceptance of cognition, any cognition, as "self-valid" (*svatah pramāṇa*). Every cognition is self-valid, constitutively, that is, in terms of its coming to be as well as epistemically as experienced, unless contradicted by other factors (*Vedanta Paribhāṣā*, chap. 6, last three paragraphs). For a meticulous discussion of the logical and the epistemological issues involved, against the setting of Indian philosophy, see Jitendra Mohanty, *Gangesa's Theory of Truth*, Introduction, Santiniketan: Visva Bharati, 1966.

[11] For a discussion of these various schools and particularly for the grounds on which idealism (*dṛṣṭi śṛṣti vāda*) is refuted as well as defended, see S. S. Suryanarayana Sastri, trans., *Siddhantalesasamgrah* (Madras: University of Madras, 1935) 2, 32f.; 3, 710ff.

[12] *sarvam vastu jnātatayā vā ajnatatayā vā sākṣī caitanyasya viṣaya eva*, "Everything known or (hitherto) unknown, indeed, remains (revealed as) object to witness consciousness" (*Pancapadikāvivaram*, pp. 83, 84, 85 [Madras: Government Oriental Series, 1958]).

[13] *Vedanta Paribhāṣā*, ibid., 1, 51.

[14] *ayah pindasya dagdhrtvābhāvo'pi dagdhrtvāśraya vahni tādātmya adhyāsād yathā ayodahati iti vyavaharah*, ibid., 1, 7.

[15] For a comprehensive survey of the nuances of meaning of *sākṣi* in Advaita literature, see A. K. Chatterjee and R. R. Dravid, *The Concept of Saksi in Advaita Vedanta* (Varanasi: Banaras Hindu University, 1979).

Bibliography

Sources

Alston, A. J., trans. *The Naiskarmya Siddhi of Sri Suresvara.* London: Shantisadan, 1959.

Devanji, Prahlad Chandrashekha, trans. *Siddhāntabindu by Madhusūdanasarasvati: A Commentary on the Dasasloki of Saṁkarācārya.* Gaekwad's Oriental Series 64. Baroda: Oriental Institute, 1933.

Jagadananda Swami, trans. *Upadeshasahasrī of Sri Sankarāchārya (A Thousand Teachings).* Mylapore, Madras: Sri Ramakrishna Math, 1961.

Jha, Ganganatha, trans. *Advaitasiddhi of Madhusūdana Sarasvati in Indian Thought.* Vol. 6 (1914)–Vol. 10 (1917).

Mahadevan, T. M. P., ed. and trans. *The Sambandha-Vartika of Suresvaracarya.* Madras: University of Madras, 1958.

Sastri, S. S. Suryanarayana, and C. Kunhan Raja, eds. and trans. *The Bhamati of Vacaspati: On Sankara's Brahmasutrabhasya (Catussutri).* Adyar, Madras: Theosophical Publishing House, 1933.

Sastri, S. S. Suryanarayana, trans. *Siddhanta-lesa-sangraha by Appaya Diksita.* Madras: University of Madras, 1935.

——, ed. and trans. *Vedāntaparibhāṣā by Dharmarāja Adhvarin.* Adyar: The Adyar Library, 1942.

Sastri, S. S. Suryanarayana, and Saileswar Sen, trans. *Vivaraṇa-prameya-saṅgraha of Vidyāraṇya.* Madras: Sri Vidya Press, 1941.

Sundaram, P. K. *Istasiddhi of Vimuktātman.* English translation. Madras: Swadharma Swaaryya Sangha, 1980.

Thibaut, George, trans. *The Vedanta Sutras with the commentary of Sankarācārya.* Vols. 34, 38 of *The Sacred Books of the East.* Edited by Max Muller. Oxford: Clarendon Press, 1890, 1896. Reprinted, Delhi: Motilal Banarsidass, 1958.

Venis, Arthur, trans. *The Vedānta Siddhāntamuktāvalī of Prakāsānanda* in *The Pandit.* Benares: E. L. Lazaras, 1890.

Venkataramiah, D., trans. *The Pancapadika of Padmapada.* Gaekwad's Oriental Series 107. Baroda: Oriental Institute, 1948.

Studies

Bhattacharyya, K. C. *Studies in Vedāntism.* Calcutta: University of Calcutta, 1909.

Chaudhuri, Amil Kumar Ray. *Self and Falsity in Advaita Vedānta.* Calcutta: Progressive Publishers, 1955.

Datta, Dhirendra Mohan. *The Six Ways of Knowing: A Critical Study of the Vedānta Theory of Knowledge.* 2nd rev. ed. Calcutta: University of Calcutta, 1960.

Debabrata Sinha. *Metaphysic of Experience in Advaita Vedānta (A Phenomenological Approach).* Delhi: Motilal Banarsidass, 1983.

Deutsch, Eliot. *Advaita Vedānta: A Philosophical Reconstruction.* Honolulu: East-West Center Press, 1969.

Devaraja, N. K. *An Introduction to Saṅkara's Theory of Knowledge.* Delhi: Motilal Banarsidass, 1962.

Hacker, Paul. *Vivarta: Studien zur Geschichte der illusionistischen Kosmologie und Erkenntnistheorie der Inder.* Wiesbaden: Akademie der Wissenschaften und der Literatur in Mainz, 1953.

Malkani, G. R. *Vedantic Epistemology.* Amalner: Indian Institute of Philosophy, 1953.

Sengupta, B. K. *A Critique on the Vivarana School.* Published by the author, 1959.

Part Six

VEDANTA AS DEVOTION

13

The Spiritual Vision of Rāmānuja

S. S. Raghavachar

To be spiritual is to pursue a way of life to achieve a spiritual objective. A purely naturalistic or materialistic view of existence in its totality rules out the possibility of realizing such an objective. A spiritual pursuit naturally carries the idea of an inward direction toward life and not the squandering of energies in the pursuit of external goods. It is a personal and spirit-oriented organization of life. External values only function instrumentally while the primary objective is to make the spirit the central concern of life.

A philosophical perspective accepting the *de facto* plurality of individual spirits will contemplate a pursuit of the spiritual goal as consisting in the effort on each individual's part to recover his or her own spiritual essence in its purity, withdrawing it from materialistic contaminations and distractions. This is roughly the position in the schools of Jainism and Sāṁkhya. Even the Yoga and Nyāya-Vaiśeṣika goals of higher life involve a spiritual journey on the part of individual spirits. There is, however, another perspective: a supreme and all-commanding spirit is the reality of realities and the individual's fulfillment and perfection consist in recovering that infinite center.

In respect of the latter again, two alternative conceptions of spirit seem possible. It may be maintained that the individual as such, the "I" and "thou" of common sense, is just a phenomenal misconstruction of the ultimate spirit; thus, spiritual attainment—namely, realizing of self—would lie in the nullification of the phenomenal encrustation of plurality and individuality and in the realization of the total oneness of the "seeking" finite spirit with the "sought," the absolute Spirit. Spirituality, according to this view, consists in what pertains to the recovery of this basic and ontologically ultimate identity, obscured and missed in mundane consciousness, but regained through a process of inward self-discovery. The attainment of this is not an event in time but just a transmutation of perspective. Such, in broad outline, is the standpoint of Advaita Vedanta.

Rāmānuja's *Viśiṣṭādvaita,*—literally, Advaita *par excellence* or Advaita qualified (as theism), *viśiṣta advaita*—is Vedantic in the sense that it accepts the ultimate reality of a single, supreme Self, Brahman, and its attainment constitutes the supreme goal for the finite individual. However, the individuality of the finite self is no fiction to be dispelled by Vedantic enlightenment but is a final metaphysical fact. The position is theistic in that it recognizes God or the divine Self and also the individual seeking self-perfection. The attainment of Brahman in this view does not mean the dissolution of "individuality," but a perfection of it in and through communion with the Supreme. Neither God nor the individual self is dissolved in the final integration of the two. The individual attains therein his fullness of being as an individual and is engulfed in the rapture of union with, or vision of, God. Further, one does not encounter the Divine from the outside, as it were, but cognizes oneself as an integral factor, or organ, of the supreme object of experience. There is unity between the seeker and the sought, not by way of merger or identification but by the inclusion of the subject in the infinite and immanent object of communion and adoration.

The aforementioned points of view in contrast to the materialistic one have a common link: human perfection lies through attainment of the real, describable as spiritual realization. The Vedantic schools maintain that the ultimate and absolute reality is Brahman and argue that human imperfection, arising from one's straying away from Brahman, is to be overcome by one's integration with it. This integration, according to Advaita, lies in the recognition of the basic identity of the individual and the Absolute. But according to *Viśiṣṭādvaita* of Rāmānuja, neither the uniqueness and transcendent supremacy of the Divine nor the individual identity of the self is abrogated. The individual seeks and finds God in all His glory, without preempting or losing one's individual self-identity but rather developing it to its full extent, thus, finding one's own true self as lodged in the supreme expanse of Godhead. The integration involves infinite addition: no subtraction from either the individual or the Divine takes place. The conception of spiritual life in the school takes shape in accordance with this basic position, which is God-oriented and non-abrogational and integrative. Salvation is union with God wherein the seeker reaches his or her own self-perfection in and through God's self-enriching substantiality.

Sources of Rāmānuja's Vision

The sources for our reconstruction of Rāmānuja's vision of spirituality have a long history and are manifold. As is to be expected, we have to start with Vedic hymns such as the *Puruṣasūkta* and the passages that speak of a single source of the universe and identify it with the supreme deity (see chap. 1). The tendency crystallizes in the Upaniṣads with the concept of a central supreme reality comprehending all and sustaining the totality of the universe. We are not left in doubt as to the nature of humanity's highest goal and the ascent to this reality through philosophical intuition (*jñana*). This ascent is both rendered possible and promoted by a life of righteousness in action and disposition and a progressive attunement to the grand destiny. The cardinal virtues *dāna* (charity), *dama* (restraint), and *dayā* (compassion), the dispositions such as *sama* (equanimity), *uparati* (withdrawal), *titikṣā* (forbearance), and the cultivation of the meditative spirit are inculcated again and again (*Brahmasutra*(s) 3.4.27; BĀU 4.4.23). With that preparation one must listen to and inquire into the spiritual testimony, examine the contents through philosophical criticism, and give oneself to contemplation. This is the pathway of *śravaṇa* (hearing), *manana* (reflection), and *nididhyāsana* (meditation). This ladder culminates in the liberating insight into the final truth. The teachings of the Upaniṣads on the inward journey to Godhead received a magnificent formulation in the *Bhagavadgītā*, the greatest literary presentation of the Vedantic pathway to the Divine. The *Brahmasūtra* of Bādarayaṇa clarifies and justifies this spiritual tradition in terms of a logically coherent, synoptic interpretation. In fact, the whole of the third chapter of the *Brahmasūtra* is devoted to the formulation of the Vedantic doctrine of spiritual advancement. The core of the earliest and most authoritative stand of Vedanta is contained in this threefold textual legacy of the Upaniṣad, the *Gītā*, and the *Brahmasūtra.*

All the religious literature in Sanskrit that follows this legacy amplifies and vividly portrays this direction of teaching. The great epics, the *Rāmāyaṇa* and the vast narrative *Mahābhārata,* and the select *Purāṇa*(s) function as elucidations, elaborations, and embellishments of this weighty direction of spiritual advancement. This bulk of religious Sanskrit literature is a major source of Rāmānuja's conception of spirituality.

In addition, he subscribes to the supplementary source of *Āgama*(s), particularly the *Pāñcarātra-Āgama*(s). The heritage of the *Āgama*(s) was the Vedic piety maturing in the monism of the Upaniṣads presenting the ultimate spiritual reality as Brahman and the way to realizing as portrayed in the *Gītā* and in the ethical and Purāṇic religion as involving the total exercise of oneself toward that end, by way of action, contemplation, and devotion with all its richness of dimension. The *Gītā* in particular contributes the definitive concept of *bhakti* (devotion), including and surpassing the ethical and contemplative processes. Brahman and *bhakti* are the focal points of this rich foundation. The *Pāñcarātra-Āgama* adds the necessary supplement by way of analyzing the aspects of Godhead and the practical prescription for concrete daily living.

Added to these classical Sanskritic streams of inspiration and direction, Rāmānuja inherits a rich collection of devotional poetry in Tamil, carrying the spirit of devotion to a lofty level, composed, or rather sung, by a number of saints lost in the absorbing love of God. It is called *Divya Prabandham,* and the saints are named *Āḻvar*(s), literally meaning the souls submerged in the love of God. The burden of their songs is the varied phases of God-hunger and the exaltation of attainment. This priceless testimony of personal devotion forms an additional source of authority for Rāmānuja and his tradition. [For entries on *Pancarātra* and *Āḻvar*(s) (Nammāḻvār), see Vol. 7 of World Spirituality.]

Scheme of Spirituality

Rāmānuja builds his scheme of spirituality on the strength of these varied and continuous streams of living devotion. His manner of reaction to the inheritance is singular in that it is consciously "philosophical" and often polemical as he has to make his case by questioning the plausibility of the Advaita scheme. He gathers the tradition and shapes it into a philosophical system in his commentary on the Upaniṣads, (focused in *Vedārtha Samgraha*) the *Brahmasūtra,* and the *Gītā.* He invests the tradition with a definitive philosophical identity furnishing guidance for a planned spiritual life. He was followed by a galaxy of commentators. One school simply elucidates his writings, expounding and presenting the full teaching of the master. Another school takes up the compositions of the *Ālvar*(s) and elucidates their import in the light of the philosophical principles of Rāmānuja; yet another school works out the pathway to God flowing from this twofold elucidation. These are usually named *rahasya*(s), "central secrets." Thus, the philosophical-religious literature built up by the followers of Rāmānuja is vast and many-sided in its output. Any account of the spirituality that flows from Rāmānuja's teachings must be based on this immense heritage. We shall outline the march of the spirit as Rāmānuja envisaged it by paying close attention to his own writings.

The substantive essence of spirituality for Rāmānuja is *bhakti. Bhakti* is dwelling in thought on God with love; *bhakti,* alternately expressed, is love generated and sustained by knowledge of God. It is a fusion of understanding and attachment directed to the Divine. To put it in other words, it is the contemplation of God, ripened into an ardent attachment thereto (*Śrībhāṣya* 1.1.1 § 13, 14). *Bhakti* is no mere emotion, if such a psychological fiction were possible. There are lower forms of it in the utilitarian practice of religion or in a quest just for the supramundane. But *bhakti* proper is an assured conviction in the reality of the supreme Being issuing forth in passionate adoration. Its intellectual root grows into the total offering of the thrilled heart. Such an intense ardor toward God is itself the outcome of a deep self-understanding, the understanding for which the individual is real and wins fulfillment of being in apprehending God. Such a self-understanding is no normal or ordinary achievement, but is a result of the elimination of the impediments to understanding. Thus, *bhakti* is the fruition of a steady growth.

We may name the state of the growth in the ascending order as *karma-yoga, jñāna yoga,* and *bhakti-yoga.* Yoga is what may be broadly designated as a spiritual pathway. This three-level ascent constitutes the warp and woof of spirituality. Prior to this way of progression, there should be a basic discerning of the essential philosophical truth concerning the ultimate reality of God as the foundation and goal of finite life, the nature of the cosmos as finite reality set up and animated by Him, and the reality of the finite self as the pilgrim on the way toward the final destiny of life in God. This basic knowledge is to be acquired through a devout study of scriptures and a critical assimilation of their content. Thus, the full scheme of spiritual life consists of the preparatory knowledge, the way of *karma,* the way of self-knowledge, and the consummation of the entire process of *bhakti.* (See, e.g., Yāmuna's *Gītārthasaṁgrahā.*)

Karmayoga

Karmayoga is the progression to God through action. This action is not to be construed as ritualistic action or simply what is described normally as ethical action. It comprises the entire range of human activity. Activity becomes a *yoga,* a spiritual pathway toward God, when suitably sublimated. Rāmānuja, in explicating the grand guidance of the *Gītā,* specifies the manner in which action has to be molded to become a *yoga* (Rāmānuja's commentary on the *Gītā,* chap. 4). It should be God-centered. The center of activity should be God. The agent should so put himself under God's supreme control that he regards Him as the paramount agent and makes himself a tool under the divine management. He should regard action not as something belonging to himself, as a part of his own life, but as forming a part of God's range of activity, as belonging to Him, manifesting divine purpose and expression. Further, whatever is accomplished through action should be surrendered to God, as His own, as a fruition in the service of His glory. This threefold divinization of action is the fundamental character of *karmayoga.*

The human being in his unregenerate condition is subject to a psychological conditioning by the law of *karma.* Under its influence he identifies himself with the body and seeks ends that are contrary to his inward nature as spirit. He does not cognize himself as spirit. His contemplative essence stands obscured, and he is perverted to seek external and material goods. This outward manner of life is itself harnessed in *karmayoga* toward a divine end. The consequence is that the law of *karma* is gradually set aside, and the inward nature as spirit, with knowledge as its basic power, becomes liberated. In this rediscovered intrinsic nature by *karmayoga,* one gives oneself to an understanding of one's own essential nature (*Gītā,* chaps. 4, 18). In this new era of his life he realizes that he transcends the physical system in which he was held captive so long because of the binding action of his past *karma;* he finds that his essential nature consists of *jñāna,* the power to know, and he begins to develop himself through an appropriate utilization of that nature. As he proceeds in that direction, he discovers that the total satiation of his power to know lies in his knowing of God, the reality of realities.

Jñāna Yoga

Thus, *jñāna yoga* is ushered in (*Gītā,* chaps. 2, 4, 5, 6, and 13). It lies in the knowledge of the self as other than the material system, as one whose nature and destiny are knowledge. The gift and propensity of such knowing can find true fulfillment only in the knowledge of God. The procedure and progress here are mainly contemplative. They lie in recognizing the human self as a center of knowing by the exercise of that very knowing itself and by developing that potency to its fullness of actualization through the knowing of God. The way is the knowing of the discovered essence, and the fruition of that essence lies in the knowing of God. Hence, the justness of the description as *jñāna yoga.*

This stage in spiritual progress is posited after *karmayoga* but prior to *bhakti-yoga. Bhakti-yoga* is a total self-abnegation in the love of God. Such an absolute devotion cannot spring except through a clear understanding of the self. The self must be so understood that it cannot reach peace and self-realization except in the vision of God. This precondition cannot arise directly from *karmayoga.* The *karmayogin* practices putting God in the center of his activity, but has not yet come by the certainty that his nature is such that its complete satiation cannot be attained except in God. He is still under the perverting pressure of his past actions, which inhibit his understanding his authentic self; as such he cannot visualize that which could fill him with the final blessedness of self-completion. *Bhakti* in its ideal form requires this self-realization and the consequent recognition of what could effectuate the self's fullness of being. Hence, this link between *karma-yoga* and *bhakti-yoga* is utterly necessary.

Bhakti-Yoga

The Upaniṣads repeatedly proclaim that human emancipation is to be attained by knowledge. They further hold, and the *Brahmasūtra*(s) clarify, that the knowledge in question is not merely a case of intellectual judgment putting an end to error and uncertainty, but a deliberate and willed process of contemplation or meditation. There is the further clarification that this meditation should take on the character of love for the supreme reality, Brahman. The point is brought out in passages of the Upaniṣads that the final good is *conferred* by Brahman in answer to the choice of the devotee to this effect. Thus, it is stated that God "chooses him" for self-revelation, who has chosen Him (MU 3.2.3). The "choice" is a matter of love on the part of the seeker; knowledge passing into meditation in turn passes into love of the nature of "choice." By such consideration Rāmānuja arrives at the conclusion (*Śrībhāṣya* 1.1.1 § 16) that *bhakti*, of the nature of meditation ascending to the level of decisive love, is the supreme and final way or *yoga* of God-attainment.

Rāmānuja quotes an ancient authority, the *vākyakāra*, which has laid down seven steps for this to happen. They are *viveka*, *vimoka*, *abhyāsa*, *kriyā*, *kalyāṇa*, *anavasāda*, and *anuddharṣa*. *Viveka* means the manner of living involving purity of the means of subsistence. *Vimoka* means freedom from hankering after lower pleasures. *Abhyāsa* signifies meditativeness or the inward habit of dwelling on God, so that deliberate and decisive meditation on God may be rendered easy and not contrary to habitual mental processes. *Kriyā* means the performance of righteous deeds. *Kalyāṇa* signifies dispositions such as truthfulness, sincerity, compassion, noninjury to other creatures, freedom from spiritually debilitating broodings. *Anavasāda* is freedom from hopeless depression of spirit. *Anuddharsa* is freedom from foolish exultation of spirit (*Śrībhāṣya* 1.1.1 § 16).

Love of God should thus be evolved through the preparatory disciplines of *karma* and *jñāna*, in the specific ways elucidated above. The *Brahmasūtra* takes care to mention righteous action and ethical virtues such as *sama* (control of mind) and *dama* (control of senses) as discipline preparatory to *bhakti* (*Śrībhāṣya* 111.4.27).

Next, an adequate idea of *bhakti* has to be attained. It is love of God founded on knowledge. It is not any kind of religious interest. It is specially distinguished by the *Gītā* from utilitarian religiosity and explorative interest (7.16). It is fully formed devotion on the part of a *jñāni,* to whom the object of devotion is all in all. This much seems to be clear enough. The practitioner of *bhakti* may have faults and deficiencies. But if real *bhakti* is there, the defects will soon be eliminated. *Bhakti* is self-rectifying. Rāmānuja maintains that it increases through practice (*aharaharabhyāsādheyātiśaya*). It is self-nourishing and grows through practice. It does not remain long as devotion to a remote or unknown object. The *Gītā* is clear on the point that the Divinity "loved" becomes soon an immediate and self-revealing presence to the "lover," using the fine expression *pratyakṣāvagamam* (*Gītā* 9.2), which is understood by Rāmānuja as God becoming an object of perception to the devotee. Devotion is a matter of immediate joy, *susukham* (ibid.), meaning that the lover of God experiences the joy of union. The element of joy in devotion is such that it becomes an end in itself, so much so that salvation is to be counted as a blissful state by virtue of its being a continuation and an increase of the bliss of *bhakti.* Even as Brahman is the reality of realities, *bhakti* is the supreme joy, the joy of joys.

Highest devotion prior to the perceptual awareness of God is called *parā-bhakti.* The resulting vision of God, immediate and direct, is called *para-jñāna,* as distinguished from śāstric or intellectual knowledge. The love generated by the vision is called *paramā-bhakti.* This is the terminology in Rāmānuja's prose prayers named the *Gadyatraya.* There is a further constituent of *bhakti.* It is not a passive state of quiet contentment, but one of active and dynamic life of activity in worship and service. Prompted by the very abundance of love, the devotee goes out of himself, as it were, to serve his beloved object of love or at least place himself in eager readiness to serve. This is called *kaiṅkarya.* The full substance of *bhakti* thus consists of the direct experience of God, the love generated by that experience, and the volitional self-surrender in consequence of active service. It is cognitive, emotional, and conative all combined into an integral flame of adoration. Rāmānuja names the elements as *anubhava* (experience), *prīti* (love), and *kaiṅkarya* (service) in his devotional composition.

One remarkable thought of Rāmānuja in connection with the potency of *bhakti* deserves to be noted, especially as it pertains to the universal availability of *bhakti* to all aspirants. Commenting on *Gītā* 9.29, he says that *bhakti* is the only criterion for divine grace whatever may be other extrinsic considerations such as caste, knowledge, form, and so on. Its presence draws

18. Silent conversation between Viṣṇu and Arjuna, 615. Detail from Nara-Nārāyaṇa panel, Dasāvatāra Temple.

19. Viṣṇu, 10th century. Tanjore Art Gallery.

grace irrespective of other socially disapproved deficiencies of the individual and without it the other grounds of acceptability from the world's point of view are worthless. This spiritual equalization has been a great asset in the *bhakti* tradition in general, and Rāmānuja's inspirers and preceptors in particular included many a saintly non-Brahmin, just as some of his devoted disciples belonged to the so-called lower castes. The inherent tendency of *bhakti* is to universalize and democratize; and it stands well illustrated in the tradition. The *Brahmasūtra* is rather narrowly conservative in its *Apaśūdrādhikśaraṇa* (1.3.9)—"section on unfitness of śūdra"—but the *Gītā* here and elsewhere definitely rises beyond it. That Rāmānuja opts here for the wider perspective one can infer from his commentary on the *Gītā* (9.29–31).

The account of spirituality in the tradition does not terminate here. *Bhakti,* as set down, is an immense and grand process, presupposing heavy preparation and constituting (or reconstituting) all sides of human nature into a single stream of aspiration and effort. Sublime as it is, its full accomplishment, however, is rare and difficult. It thrills enormously, but it presumes enormous competence on the part of the pursuant. Therefore, a lesser way—not lesser from the standpoint of efficacy and fruitfulness, but from that of the demands on humanity, the seeker after God—is set forth. In the course of evolution, it practically turns out to be the principal pathway to God. It is named *prapatti* (self-surrender), or *saraṇāgati* (seeking refuge) or *bhara-samarpaṇa* (burden-transfer).

Prapatti-Yoga

Prapatti is the refuge for the refugeless. If the seeker is capable of reaching God through the instrumentality of his *bhakti, bhakti-marga* (the path of love) is the way for him. If, on the other hand, he is convinced utterly that he cannot master the *sādhana* (discipline), namely, *bhakti,* on account of the feebleness of his knowledge and strength, his impatience for realization, and his failure to fulfill the *śāstra* (scriptural law), *prapatti* is the way for him. God is his goal as in *bhakti,* but in the place of that established means, which he is required to follow, he chooses God himself to function as all his means, his role being merely one of resorting to Him for that purpose. This supplication to God to work as the means for his attaining Him is the fundamental meaning of *prapatti.* It is suitably named *bhara-samarpaṇa,* meaning the humble transfer or offering of the burden and responsibility on the part of humanity to God for bringing about God-attainment. It is called *saraṇāgati,* literally, seeking refuge under the feet. In general, "burden-transfer" signifies the surrendering of responsibility to God for bringing about the good sought after. It may be resorted to for achieving ends other than the highest. It may be for securing the much-valued *bhakti* itself. But in the present context, it is resorting to the act of attaining the supreme end, God-attainment itself, the *summum bonum.* The doctrine of *prapatti* we are considering is of this kind, and it is sought as all-efficient for the purpose. When it is sought for the sake of *bhakti,* it is just the accessory to it, while *bhakti* itself is the principal means adopted for the highest good. *Prapatti* is a universal necessity, although it may be practiced as the sole and adequate means of God-attainment.

We have seen that *bhakti* grows by continuous or repeated practice, while *prapatti* is just giving up of one's responsibility to God once for all. Such a "giving up" should be final and absolute, and as such it cannot be repeated. Otherwise every subsequent giving up would imply that the previous *prapatti* has been withdrawn or canceled, so that it may be worked out again. *Prapatti* is once for all and final. Hence, it cannot be a continuous or repeatable process. There can be only one *prapatti* for *mokṣa.* If renunciation of effort into the custody of God is accomplished, the concern of man in relation to the bringing about of the end ceases absolutely.

Rāmānuja's tradition lists some accessory factors that should go into the complete performance of *prapatti.* First comes *the resolve to be in* conformity to God's will (*ānukūlyasya saṅkalpa*). This carries the implication explicitly drawn by the relevant texts that the devotee should be favorable and good to all creation, as it is the outcome of God's creative love. Then follows the rejection of all that is contrary to the Divine purpose (*prātikūlyasya varjana*). The two together testify to the devotee's conscious assimilation of himself into the sovereign purposes of God as a tool thereof. *Akiñcanya* or *kārpaṇya* signifies a total poverty or nothingness of himself in relation to what he aspires after. In contrast, he has to develop and maintain supreme and unshakable faith in the power and goodness of God. This is *mahāviśvāsa; goptṛtva-varaṇa* or *prārthanā* means prayer for being saved. The principal and central factor is the offering of himself, his surrender and supplication to be accepted and saved. This is alternatively spoken of as *nyāsa, arpaṇa,* or *nikṣepa.* Vedanta Deśika (a fourteenth-century follower of Rāmānuja) in a brief verse sums up the whole process:

> *nyasyāmi akincanaḥ śrīmannanukūlo 'nyavarjitaḥ viśvāsa-prārthanā-pūrvam ātmarakṣābharaṁ tvayi.*
>
> (*Nyāsadaśaka* 2)

> Lord, I, who am nothing, conform to your will and desist being contrary to it, and with faith and prayer, submit to you the burden of saving my soul.

The last and principal item needs a little more clarification. The consciousness of belonging to God and the surrender of the fruits of spiritual endeavor to God are common to all pathways and particularly to *bhakti*. The unique point here is the surrender of spiritual burden and responsibility to God. That is the specific difference of *prapatti*. In other traditions the agent, the devotee, usually bears the weight of responsibility himself for his self-elevation to the supreme attainment. Here, however, even that is surrendered to God.

In the Rāmānujite tradition the surrender is solemnized by the utterance and inward meditation focused on three sacred texts or formulas (mantras). The first one is a simple but comprehensive one. Its first unit is *AUM*. It is interpreted as indicating the supreme Being and the individual self and that the latter lives, moves, and has his being as related to the former as a subsidiary entity. The middle expression, *namaḥ*, is said to signify "self-nullification" or surrender in every possible way, particularly in the matter of attaining the highest good. The last constituent, *Nārāyaṇāya*, names the supreme Being and indicates that the perfection attained through surrender is for purposes of dedication to and service of *Nārāyaṇa*. This is the most important formula by which the devotee is expected to live in his inmost life. This (*AUM, namaḥ Nārāyaṇāya*) is called the *mūla-mantra*, the root formula for meditation.

The second consists of two "self-offering" sentences. One signifies self-surrender on the part of the aspirant. The other means that the resultant good is for offering service to God. This is called *dvaya mantra*, the "twin-formula." The third formula consists of the "last" verse of Śrī Kriṣṇa's instruction to Arjuna in the *Gītā* (18.66). It is appropriately named *carama-śloka* (the ultimate verse). It exhorts Arjuna to discard all other *dharma*(s) or pathways to God-realization and to take refuge in Him, Him alone. It also contains the promise or assurance that the Lord will cleanse him of all sins and that he "should not grieve" (*mā śucaḥ*). The entire philosophy of *prapatti* is elaborately expounded in the elucidation of these three formulas. The greatest writers on them are Parāśara Bhaṭṭa, Piḷḷai Lokācārya, and Vedanta Deśika. Later Rāmānuja tradition sees its ultimate secret. The heart of its message is the pregnant import of these three sacred condensations. They are called the three *rahasya*(s), "secrets" or "mysteries," connoting their centrality, condensation, and preciousness of which the entire philosophical movement and spiritual tradition are looked upon as unfoldments. When one is initiated to the higher life, they are solemnly imparted to the novice. Their acquisition is said to mark his entry into spirituality.

Post-Prapatti Spirituality

We have briefly traversed the course of spirituality designed for the achievement of liberation whose central meaning is the attainment of God. We have concluded with the treatment of *prapatti,* in which a single and complete act is enough to secure freedom from anxiety with regard to the final end of spiritual effort. Since this act is not to be repeated or built up throughout the rest of one's life, how is one to conduct oneself after its right performance during the rest of one's life? This is a highly practical question and it brings in a spirituality not geared to the attainment of the goal of *mokṣa.*

It appears that as Rāmānuja's earthly life was coming to a close, his disciples who were so passionately attached to him gave themselves to deep sorrow and desperate agony. Seeing their plight with his natural compassion, he is said to have delivered a parting message. This message seems to have been accurately recorded (*Rahasyatrayasāra* of Vedanta Deśika, chap. 17):

> If a man has become a *prapanna,* the salvation of his soul is the responsibility of *Bhagavān,* and he himself has nothing to do with it. If he thinks he has anything to do with it, his surrender of responsibility must have been false or insincere. The maintenance of the body depends upon his past *karma* and he should not feel anxious about it. If he feels anxious about it, he is a materialist not believing in the law of *karma.* Therefore neither in regard to his spiritual welfare nor in regard to his bodily welfare, has he anything more to do.

To the question whether one has the license to do as one pleases with oneself, with one's body, mind, and speech, the answer that is given is that to do as one pleases will not be authentic, will not be in keeping with the essential nature (*svarupa*) of oneself:

> It is true that he has nothing more to do with regard to the *upāya* or means, but he should direct these three—mind, body and speech—to the rendering of service which is the goal of his existence. There are five kinds of service which he can render for the rest of his life. (1) To study the *Srībhāṣya* (Rāmānuja's Commentary) and to spread the knowledge obtained therefrom; (2) if the person is not qualified for it, to study the works of the *Āḷvar*(s) and spread their knowledge; (3) if he is not competent to do it, to serve in holy temples through the several modes of service necessary therein; (4) if not competent to do so, to meditate on the meaning of *dvaya;* (5) if not competent to do so, to seek the good will of some Śrīvaiṣṇava who is well disposed towards him and look upon himself as his follower and spend his life with him.

Bibliography

Sources

Bhagavad Gītā Bhāṣya. Translated by M. R. Sampatkumaran. Madras: Prof. M. Rangacharya Memorial Trust, 1969.

Bhāṣyārtha Darpaṇa of Uttamur Viraraghavacharya (Modern Sanskrit Commentary on Ramanuja's *Śribhāṣya*). Madras, 1963 (vol. 1), 1964 (vol. 2).

Saraṇāgati Gadyam, with the commentary of Śruta Prākāśikā. Translated by K. Bhasyam. Madras, 1970.

Srimad Rahasyatrayasāra, Vedanta Desika. Translated with introduction by M. R. Rajagopala Aiyangar. Kumbakonam, 1956.

Śri Bhagavad Rāmānuja Granthamalā: Complete Works in Sanskrit. Edited by P. B. Annangaracharya Swamy. Kanchipuram, 1956.

Śribhāṣya of Rāmānuja. Parts 1–3. Edited by R. D. Karmarkar. University of Poona Sanskrit series. Poona, 1962. (Paragraphs and sections of *Śribhāṣya* are numbered and are utilized in the present chapter.)

Vedānta Sāra of Bhagavad Rāmānuja. Edited by V. Krishnamacharya. Translated by M. B. Narasimha Ayyangar. Madras, 1953.

Vedārtha-Saṃgraha of Rāmānuja. Text and translation by S. S. Raghavachar. Mysore, 1956.

Studies

Carman, John B. *The Theology of Rāmānuja: An Essay in Interreligious Understanding.* New Haven and London: Yale University Press, 1974.

Lacombe, Oliver. *L'Absolu Selon le Vedanta: Les Notions de Brahman et d'Atman dans les systemes de Cankara et Ramanoudja.* Paris: Geuthner.

Lott, Eric J. *God and the Universe in the Vedanta Theology of Ramanuja.* Madras: Ramanuja Research Society, 1976.

Raghavachar, S. S. *Introduction to the Vedārtha Saṃgraha.* Mangalore: Mangalore Trading Assn., 1957.

——. *Śri Rāmānuja on the Gīta.* Mangalore: Sri Ramakrishna Ashrama, 1969.

——. *Śri Rāmānuja on the Upaniṣads.* Madras, 1972.

Ramakrishnananda, Swamy. *Life of Rāmānuja.* Madras: Sri Ramakrishna Math, 1959.

Yamunacharya, M. *Rāmānuja's Teachings in His own Words.* Bhavan's Book University 3. Bombay, 1963.

14

The Sivadvaita of Srikanṭha: Spirit as the Inner Space within the Heart

KRISHNA SIVARAMAN

In the space within the heart lies the controller (*vaśī*,[1] literally, one that draws near or causes to follow along after) of all (beings), the lord (*īśāna*, literally owning master) of all, the ruler (*adhipati*, literally, sovereign or king) of everything.

BĀU 4.4.22

Here in this city of Brahman (the microcosm) is an abode, a delicate (*dahara*, literally, heart-cavity) lotus; within it is an ethereal space (*ākāśa*, literally, sky, vacuity). What thus lies (hidden as the) "within" (*antara*) should indeed be the goal or consummation of one's spiritual quest (*anveṣṭavyam*, "ought to be searched after"). For that, assuredly, should be the object of realization (*vijnāsitavyam*, "ought to be grasped by understanding").

ChU 8.1.1

[Life eternal (*amrtatvam*)], higher than the high, indeed, shines here in the cave of the heart. Those striving for it realize it (*viśanti*). Ascertaining well the import of Vedanta wisdom (*vedānta vijñāna suniścitārthāh*) and striving through the yoga of renunciation, those whose nature is thus rendered transparent come to dwell in the worlds of Brahma and, at the end of time, become supremely immortal (*parāmrtah*), become all liberated.

Kaivalya U 3.4

> Not above, not across, not in the middle, nor has one quite grasped ("Spirit that alone abides," *śivaeva kevalah*). No image (*pratimā*) thereof (literally) bearing likeness unto Him, whose name (proper) is great glory. . . . Those who through heart and mind realize Him as abiding in the Heart (*hrdistham*) become indeed immortal (*amrtās te bhavanti*).[2]
>
> SvU 4–19.20

SRIKANṬHA, IN HIS CELEBRATED commentary on the *Bramasūtra* (BS) explains the Vedanta doctrine along similar lines in significant ways to the commentary of Rāmānuja except that his explanation is Śaiva in content. Theism is the voice of religion whether of Śaiva or Vaiṣṇava kinds, and its doctrine of *theion* entails similar admissions with regard to the world and the individual—the ordered nature of the world which even divine omnipotence respects, the relative freedom of the human will, free at least to the extent of being willfully indifferent to the order of the good and, more importantly, the ontic reality of the world and its evolution and of the individual with its structure of being-in-the-world. These are commonplace features in any doctrine of God, to be sure of great significance specially for considerations of morality and religion.

But the theism or theo-philosophy articulated in the visions of Srikanṭha and Rāmānuja has the additional distinction of being integral to the context of a quest which aims at the goal of spiritual realization. Vedanta is, preeminently, a contemplative-meditative approach to the realization of spirit. The actual progression toward the goal and its symbolic formulation are what make up the great enterprise of "discovering of the spirit" (*adhyātma vidyā*) extolled in the upaniṣads as a true grounding of all conceivable religious endeavors (*sarva vidyā pratiṣṭhā*).

The category of the spiritual is the ultimate comprehensive category of which the "religious" is a, and perhaps not the only, manifestation. *Adhyātman* is the essence of which *vidyā*, the system and cult of religion, is one of several alternative forms. In its highest form in which the spiritual expresses itself, it can only be described as super-religious. Such is Vedanta in its generality, whether it be the reflective or the devotional kind. Super-religious activity in which willing is absolutely disinterested transcends all activity conceived of as religious, for its final objective is an absolute transcendence described as "freedom of spirit" (*mokṣa*). All activity—the ceremonial, ethical, and indeed every kind of human action—to the extent that it becomes a species of "action in inaction" (BG 4.18) will be super-religious or spiritual. Self-knowledge or gnosis of Vedanta, which eschews action as such, is a super-religious good. But so are *bhakti* or devotion in

Rāmānuja's version of Vedanta and the Yoga that transcends *āśrama* restrictions (*atyāśrama yoga*),[3] which finds favor with Srikanṭha. The latter thus spiritualizes even worship as a mode of journey to the inner shrine.

Srikanṭha's exposition or *Exegesis of Brahman* (*Brahma-mīmāmsā*) (BM) (the label under which the Mysore editor of his commentary on BS presents it) bears no proper name as found, for example, in the case of Rāmānuja (*Śribhāṣya*). But it is Śaiva in its clear overtone sharing this distinction with the only other commentary of a later date, all other commentaries on BS after his times being Vaiṣṇava, equating Brahman with Viṣṇu. To Srikanṭha, Śivam is the Godhead, the conceptual and even semantic equivalent of Brahman. Śivam for him is not a sectarian deity, not even the highest of the three gods presiding over the three respective functions of creation, preservation, and dissolution, but the Deitas itself, the God above God, the nameless principle which is also a person who can be "named," but only as the Absolute God (*parmeśvara*) and by other similar descriptions. Descriptive names also function as proper names in the sense that they exclude applicability to others like the world-soul, and Nārāyaṇa, "God confronted by the object."

Srikanṭha's picture of Vedanta one may even deem as also an authoritative exposition of Śaiva philosophy. The Vedas and also preeminently their later developments, the upaniṣads, are compatible with the theism of the foundational texts of Saivism. The conception of the Godhead elaborated therein and adopted by the upaniṣads like the *Svetāsvatara* and the *Atharvasikhā* (perhaps under their influence) was also, according to Srikanṭha, acceptable to the main body of the upaniṣadic teaching as embodied in the BS. It is acceptable both in respect of its "that" and the "what," namely, as the Transcendent (*turīya*) and the Blissful or Benign (*śivam*). The description of MĀU about the "fourth" (*caturtha*) is well known: it is unspeakable (*avyavahārya*), unto which the world stands resolved (*prapancopasamam*), peaceful (*sāntam*), benign (*śivam*), and non-dual (*advaitam*). The "fourth" in a series, characteristically, comprehends complements, supersedes, and cancels the preceding three. Śivam is the "fourth" in this precise sense understood metaphysically in relation to time and its segments of past, present, and the future or the three "states" of consciousness, wakeful dream, and sleep and also, says Srikanṭha, cosmo-theologically in respect of the three functions and functionaries of creation, preservation, and dissolution.

The Śaiva orientation thus renders Srikanṭha's articulation of his vision dissimilar in tone to the theology of Rāmānuja. There is no radical condemnation of the understanding of Vedanta as Absolutism or pure Nondualism, at least so far as it concerns the teaching about Brahman. Thc rejection of the world *qua* the sphere of plurality and difference as "appearance" due to *avidyā* (nescience), the negative side of the teaching, of course, is not acceptable. In line with the general teaching of all schools of Saivism, Srikanṭha reorients *māyavāda*, the doctrine of the phenomenality of the world, into a doctrine of the "power" of Being (*saktivāda*) and replaces Pure Identity with the mystical notion of divine "bi-unity." There is real dynamics in Brahman, though in the nature of the case it cannot be conceptualized in terms of differentiation, either external or internal. There is, consequently, no systematic or sustained critiquing of the concept of *avidyā* like what we have distinctively in Rāmānuja and no vindication, through a dialectical refutation of identity, of an ontology of particulars reciprocally "different" (*bheda*) which has its patent in the writings of Madhva and his school.

The Age and Antecedents of Srikanṭha

Very little is known about the place and period of Srikanṭha or of his antecedents. The *Sankara Digvijayam* of Mādhava refers to him as Srikanta Sivacarya and as the head of a *maṭha* in Gokarnam on the west coast and as the contemporary of Sankara (eighth century) to whom he owned himself defeated in a theological debate (15–70, 71, 72). The work is notoriously unreliable in respect of chronology even as its recounting of the dispute is partisan and trivial. The supercommentary on Srikanṭha's *Bhāṣya* is called *Sivarkamani-Dipika* (SMD) and is written by Appayya Dīkṣita, the celebrated authority in the field of Advaita, as well as Saiva doctrine and ritual (sixteenth century). Appayya also devotes two other independent works in response, as it were, to the challenge that Srikanṭha posed, the spiritual meaning of Srikanṭha's Sivadvaita, *Sivadvaita Nirnaya* (SN) and *Ananda Lahari* (AL). Appayya suggests that Srikanṭha came after Sankara and that Rāmānuja came after Srikanṭha, basing himself on the estimation that Rāmānuja's commentary follows in the wake of Srikanṭha's (*tad anukriti saraṇī*). Srikanṭha's theological position is midway between Sankara and Rāmānuja, marking a transition from an uncompromising apophatic orientation espousing pure, unutterable identity or immediacy as the essence of Brahman-realization to its opposite, equally radical and uncompromising. The latter is the kataphatic ("affirmative") approach, which asserts that Brahman as God is knowable and experienceable. Rāmānuja's reassertion of Vedanta involves the rejection of the very notions of indeterminateness and impersonality as viable locutions for a description of Brahman as consciousness. There is nothing in sensory or rational experience to attest to such experience. Pure identity is a notion philosophically inept even as it is spiritually sterile as descriptive of an experience of immediacy.

Srikanṭha's own position, to be sure, is that Brahman, conceivably and spiritually, is "with attributes" (*saguṇa).*[4] Without any equivocation he speaks of the attributes and acts or activities intrinsic to Brahman, whom he addresses in his invocatory verse as of the form of *sat cit* and *ānanda* but also as Siva and as the form of the word-sense of "I" (*aham padārtha rūpāya*).[5] The latter suggests that Brahman is Godhead who also lends a foothold to a sense of "I" in relation to you and me. Again, significantly later, while discoursing about the spiritual journey and its goal, he says, "Brahman's essence, *qua* the goal sought and attained by the released (*mukta prāpyam*), is *with attribute only*" (BM 3.3.40). But Appayya's point is that the concept of *saguṇa* is used here as elsewhere as the defining characteristic of Brahman only in order to refute the naturalist who identifies Brahman with Nature (*pradhāna*) or those identifying it with the individual self (*jīva*) and thus establish the unambiguous reference to Brahman as pure Spirit. That is why even *mokṣa* entails (SMD 11, p. 357) attainment of parity with *saguṇa* Brahman only. The latter is "consciousness that perceives the manifold" (*vipaścit*), representing the experience of "identity-in-difference." The assertion that a "knower of Brahman becomes Brahman alone" (*brahma vid brahmaiva bhavati* [MU 3.2.10]) does not contradict the sense of release as one of attainment of equality with Brahman because "alone" (*eva*) may be taken to be also "like" (*iva*) as a possible way of splitting the compound (SMD 11, p. 358). Appayya's point, however, is that this leaves the door open for Brahman as pure identity, as indeterminate consciousness experienceable as immediacy and attainable, theologically stated, at the fullness of time marking the final release of all (*sarvamukti*) (SN, p. 75ff.).[6] This distinction, says Appayya, is implied by Srikanṭha at least negatively, but we are precluded from a similar reconstruction in the case of Rāmānuja, whose rejection of the very concept of pure identity renders his position both unequivocal and terminal in this regard. In addition, as we shall advert to it later, Srikanṭha provides also many positive indications in respect of it.

To come back to the question of the period of Srikanṭha. Appayya's argument about Srikanṭha as being closer to Sankara as a kindred spirit may be convincing, but it is doubtful if it can also be chronologically sustained. The only view for which there is some evidence is that the upper limit of the period of Srikanṭha could not be earlier than the first half of the tenth century, at which time lived the Kashmir writer Utpala, the author of the *Īsvara Pratyabhijña Kārikā*. From the latter, Srikanṭha cites a famous verse (*Bhāskarī*, vol. 1, p. 266) more than once in his commentary (BM 1.2.9; 2.1.18; 2.2.38). The verse is to the effect that God of the essence of consciousness or spirit manifests without, the manifold of objects like a yogin materializing objects by sheer will without a material cause. Srikanṭha does not interpret the verse as Abhinavagupta does (in his *Vimaiśinī*) as exemplifying a counterprinciple to cause–effect relation, implying that effect can arise from what is not its assigned cause. "Being without material cause" (*nirupādānam*) means for Srikanṭha being without a material cause *that is external to God.* This distinction aside, Utpala's point of difference from that of Buddhist idealism, which is refuted here—namely, that the external world is affirmable as existent though as reflected in consciousness—is also the point of view of Srikanṭha's Sivadvaita. The monism or non-dualism of Utpala and Abhinavagupta and the doctrine of the identity of power and its possessor and the general understanding of the category of relation as involving both identity and difference are all, also, clearly reflected in Sivadvaita, showing their family resemblance. Srikanṭha's description of consciousness structurally as apperceptive of the manifold of things (*vividam vastu jātam . . . vimrśanti* [BM 3.2.16]) to which reference was made earlier, is reminiscent of the language of Kashmir Saivism and attests to the posteriority of Sivadvaita to it. Srikanṭha's date, in other words, could not be earlier than that of Rāmānuja, but would be about the same time or later. Either of the two could have preceded and even influenced the other in language and also perhaps in thought—and influenced not only in the positive sense but also, in crucial respects, negatively. That too should be considered influence which helped provide a fresh stimulus to reaffirm the respective doctrines.

The fact of the case is that *Śiva viśiṣṭādvaita,* the label that Srikanṭha uses to indicate his view of Brahman (Śiva) as Non-dual in the sense of being "qualified by the world, sentient and non-sentient" (*cidacit prapañca viśiṣṭa*), itself has long antecedents in respect alike of the Śaiva and the *viśiṣṭādvaita* concepts and traditions. The vogue of a particular usage at a particular time is not the issue here. Neither Rāmānuja, in whom the central idea of his doctrine as bequeathed to his tradition clearly bears the name *viśiṣṭādvaita,* nor Srikanṭha, in whose case the same name is used appositionally with Siva but does not quite label a tradition, professes to write an independent commentary and inaugurate something new. Rāmānuja claims to follow in the wake of an allegedly comprehensive exegetical gloss *vrtti,* by one Bodhayana, which is a commentary, within a single folder so to speak, on the *Mīmāmsa Sūtra* of Jaimini as well as on BS of Bādarayaṇa. Bodhāyana's alleged work reflected the assumption that neither contemplative knowledge nor works (rites and duties) can by themselves bring about spiritual freedom but only a combination of the two. Sankara also, perhaps, refers to him in his commentary on BS (1.1.11–19) though the perspective that the latter reportedly represents meets with stern disapproval. (See also his commentary BG 2.11.)

It is quite conceivable that Srikanṭha too drew from it both his terms of "qualified non-dualism" and the holistic vision which he shares with Rāmānuja, namely, that Mīmāṁsā science is one integral whole of which the latter part (*Uttara-Mīmāṁsā*) is Vedanta. ("The sciences of karma-enquiry and Brahman-enquiry expository, in respective order, of worship [*ārādhana*] and the object worshiped [*ārādhya*] are, indeed, one science" BM 1.1.1.) Srikanṭha does not, of course, acknowledge that he follows any previous *vrtti.* In his introductory colophon he pays obeissance to his spiritual teacher (*kalyāṇa guru*) mentioning him as of the name of Sveta, and a "propounder (of the teaching) of the multitudes of scriptures" (*nānāgama vidhāyin*). Appayya interprets the phrase in either of two ways: Sveta was the great contributor (*vidhātr*) of an evaluative exegesis of the scriptures, namely, the upaniṣadic texts (Vedanta) which indeed are the Agama that calls for a hermeneutical discernment with their heterogeneous and *de facto* self-discrepant teachings (*nānāprakāra . . . paraspara viruddhārtatvena avabhāsamāna*). Sveta through his insight into and inculcation of their non-discrepant—that is, unified—sense (*aviruddhārta upadeśa*) clarified their hidden intent, originating thus a theology of the Śaivāgama duly supported by the upaniṣads. The second sense is a more straightforward one: Sveta set the canon (*nirmātr*) of the various Śaivāgama(s), Pāsupata and others. The first sense to which Appayya seems inclined amounts to the admission that Srikanṭha inherited the task that he avowedly addresses in his commentary.[7] (For an entry relating to the Śaivāgama, see Vol. 7 of World Spirituality.)

Another verse of the colophon of Srikanṭha also throws some light on the question of his antecedents:

> This Aphorism of Vyasa (BS) is, verily, the eyes for the wise helping envision (without blur or blemish) Brahman (*Brahma darśine*). What was muddied (*kaluṣitam*) by the previous preceptors (*pūrvācāryaih*) (interpreting it), that has (here) been (clarified and) fulfilled (*prasadyate*) by Srikanṭha.

Srikanṭha's own role in relation to BS is here avowed in a low key. His is not the program of an independent system of ideas to which the aphorisms of Bādarayaṇa may be demonstrated through elaborate exegesis to provide consent. In the picturesque image of SMD, his task is like providing a salve that may be applied to the optical sense to enable it to see clearly. The task of an exegesis should be to render that which it exegetes more accessible than before. SMD also cites (pp. 9, 10) illustrations of such obfuscations by "previous preceptors" which render opaque (in effect though not by intent) the original, in this case BS. The illustrations are from *Sribhāṣya.* SMD is, however, quick to indicate that the preceptors impugned here are the ancestors in the tradition of the "other commentary" from which citations were given. What seems to be implied is that Srikanṭha was aware of the writings from which, presumably, Rāmānuja drew his ideas.

Identity-in-difference, Identity and Pan-organismal Identity

The basis or requirement that underlies the formulation of *viśiṣṭa advaita* stripped of all the refinements that are introduced to distinguish what is thus labeled from other doctrines is a concrete ontological conformity for holding together distinction and unity. It is a fact of experience that the two, namely, distinction and its opposite, coexist and are indeed even in intimate relation with each other. Spirit as the integrating principle of existence is attested by experience—but in relation to the two poles of identity and manifoldness. Understanding of spiritual reality as somehow encompassing both poles is the basic insight of Vedanta, coextensive with its entire history in its earlier emergence as well as in its later sophistications, as when it enters the Schools.

Even Sankara, one may say, subscribes to it when he describes such relation in terms that bring out both its inner incongruity and its inescapability as constitutive of existence itself. The relation between the two spheres is for him a case of intimate copulation between the real and the phenomenal which fakes the real (*satyānrta mithunī krtyam*) like between light and darkness in a twilight zone. The analogy of darkness is precisely in respect of its paradoxical relation to light: it is what is at once revealed and destroyed by light. The analogy could mislead one into thinking of "distinction" (*bheda*) as the negative. While not merely negative, it is nevertheless parasitic upon unity, which it helps to realize. Unity, however, is not similarly parasitic on distinction while at the same time it requires it. Unity requires difference epistemically, that is, in the order of one's apprehending but not constitutively. It is by introducing this distinction between the constitutive and nonconstitutive definition of spirit that Sankara radicalizes the teaching of Vedanta. Identity-in-difference as entailing union of contradictories is denied not of existence, which is the sphere of the effect and is a whole of parts, but only of the "simple" eternal object, namely, spirit (*nitya niravayava viṣayam hi viruddhatvam avocāma dvaitādvaitasya na kārya viṣaya sāvayave,* Sankara's com. BĀU 5.1). Identity and difference as coordinates, in other words, entail distinction of levels of reality.

Earlier Vedanta, however, was holistic in holding fast to an understanding of the spirit itself as at once of the essence of identity and difference. Upholding the sole reality of spirit against an alleged dualism of spirit and nature, Vedanta as reflected in BS (without exegetical reorientation) accepted "modification" (*pariṇāma*) in respect of spirit (BS 1.4.27). The early exponents of Vedanta defended the position of transformation of Brahman or Spirit. Spirit continually changes and yet maintains its identity throughout. Even parts are ascribed to Spirit: the individual and the world are real "parts" (*amśa*) of Spirit. Spirit is one as the whole and many with regard to its aspects. Difference in kind or genre as between spiritual and material was denied, but internal diversity and even individual distinctions were admitted. Does such a view of Spirit accord with the teaching of the upaniṣads? Earlier Vedanta says yes. The upaniṣads emphasize the unity of Being but also sometimes distinguish Spirit from the individual self on the one hand and from the physical universe on the other. Assigning equal validity to the two teachings, which results in the conceptualization of "identity and difference" (*bhedābheda*),[8] may seem simplistic as a way of resolving the discrepancy. But it may also reflect a discernment in depth of the nature of spirit *qua* non-object as simple, too simple for understanding in terms of the categories that we employ when determining the nature of an object. Spirit eludes understanding either as bare unity or as mere plurality because it discloses itself in one's experience as rather a coincidence of the ground and of emanation, of self-sufficiency and self-communication. In Srikaṇṭha's terminology, as it shall presently be seen, Spirit combines within itself the inaccessible depth (*śivam*) as well as the element of cognitive accessibility (*śakti*) or the aspect of self-giving, without which it would not be possible to approach it through reason or revelation, much less experience it as non-dual reality.

One other aspect of earlier Vedanta which again Srikaṇṭha mirrors is its eclectic spirit on the practical side. The vision of "identity in difference" means in terms of practice according an important and even equal status to devotional contemplation (*upāsanā*) and to works (*karma*). The two paths are vitally related and glued together into a single spiritual orientation. The cutting edge of karma, as is well known, is desire or self-interest, even karma in the sense of rite. When, however, karma is transfigured into a spiritual endeavor, it becomes an essential element of self-knowledge. Jaimini, the author of the *Mīmāmsa Sūtra*(s) (and his commentator Upavarṣa even more) concedes that karma is the science of the ideal in conduct alike significant for attaining Heaven (*svarga*) as well as spiritual release (*apavarga*). Earlier Vedanta thus had closest affinity with the Pūrva Mīmāmsā, its own enquiry being viewed as a sequel to it. Doctrinally, again, it did not advocate complete identity between the individual and Spirit in Release (*mokṣa*) but only attaining parity or similarity.

Srikaṇṭha's formulation of *visistadvaita* itself, while thus standing in straight line with *bhedābheda* both as doctrine and practice, seems, however, to be in response to the need to distinguish his position of "unity with difference" from the common thesis of a simple union of contradictories to describe the reality of Spirit. There is identity between Brahman and the created order, but it is neither absolute nor literal. Brahman as spirit is equated with the all in the sense of being identical with the universal essence, the substance of everything, rather than with everything. The Veda (RV 10.90.3) uses the symbolism of quantity: only a quarter of God's abundance suffices to fill up the worlds. What remains exceeds the whole of that which suffices to fill up all that there is. From a consideration of numerous texts which speak of the individual and Brahman as different, it follows that Spirit is one with everything and yet "exceeds" (*adhikam* [BS 2.1.22]) it: "He who having entered within controls individuals" (*Taittirīya Āraṇyaka* 3.2.21); "eternal among the eternal, intelligent among the intelligent" is the description of Spirit given in Kaṭha U (5.13); "two Brahmans are to be known, the higher and the lower" (*Maitrāyani U* 6.22); "the one Lord rules over the perishable (*kṣara*) and the self (*ātman*)" (SvU 1.10).

But alongside these and similar other texts there are also those like the well-known "That Thou art," which affirm identity as the true state of affairs when it comes to Spirit. To be sure, the identity that is here declared is not to be taken literally. The difference between the individual and Brahman is taught not only by the texts like those cited above but also by texts which speak of the states of sleep and departure. In neither of these states which occur and recur in the life of an individual has the latter any knowledge of what is within or without, despite being said to be embraced by the knowing self (*prājña*) (BM 1.3.42). Thus, difference is taught between the two selves as persisting even in sleep and departure. The identity, nevertheless, has to be worked up through meditation contemplating Godhead (*parameśvara*) as identical with oneself. Release cannot be obtained from the state of bondage save through meditation on identity in the form "I am Thou, Thou art I."

The question that most naturally arises then is: Do these passages of the scripture taken as a whole inculcate "difference and non-difference"? Srikaṇṭha faces this question and replies at some length defining his point of view as the resolution of the impasse:

> We are not the advocates who maintain absolute difference (*atyanta bhedavāda*) between Brahman and the world as between, say, a jug and a piece of cloth, that being opposed to the texts which declare their non-distinctness; and we are not advocates of an absolute identity (*atyanta abhedavāda*) and (even less so) of the illusoriness of one of them as in the case of silver and mother-of-pearl; this is equally opposed to the texts which declare difference in the inherent attributes of Brahman and the world. Nor do we hold to the position of (a simultaneous affirmation of) "difference and non-difference"

> (*bhedābheda vāda*), opposed (as such assertion is) to the nature of things (*vastu virodhāt*). We are, however, of those maintaining a "non-dualism of the distinct" (*viśiṣṭādvaita vādinah*) as exemplified (in the relation) between body and the embodied or between a quality and the qualified. (BM 2.1.22)

In further elucidation of the nature of the identity that is imported by the expression "non-dualism of the distinct," Srikanṭha continues:

> By unity of Brahman and the universe we mean their inseparability like that of clay and the jug (made of clay) as cause and effect or like that of the substance and its attribute. A jug, indeed, is not seen apart from clay, nor is a blue-lotus found apart from the blue color. Similarly the "power" (*śakti*), namely, the universe, can never exist without Brahman; while Brahman too is never known to be without his power (*śakti vyatirekeṇa na kadācidapi brahma vijñeyate*) as fire is not seen apart from its heat. Whatever is not known apart from something else, the former is indeed *qualified* by the latter. The second thing in essence *is* the first thing.

Srikanṭha's effort to interpret Spirit is clearly not a battle for "difference." "Differencc," observes Srikanṭha, is "natural" (*bhedasca svābhāvikah*), as body is different from its soul. The "transcendence" (*adhikam*) of the soul in relation to its body, once the two are distinguished, is intelligible. But what needs to be explained is rather the sense of their unity, how the distincts are and function as "one." The world and the selves as bodily parts or "attributes" may be said to be identical with Brahman as they are one with him in their substance, one with His "power" as the clay is "one" with a clay jug. Even in the efforts of early Vedantins to accord equal validity to the principle of distinction or difference, the predilection for unity is significant: Brahman is the matrix and, therefore, the primary real from which everything else is derived.

Two important points in Srikanṭha's understanding of Spirit as "pan-organismal unity" deserve to be underlined: First, he affirms, against the *bhedābheda* view, a less paradoxical position, one that does not look blatantly self-contradictory, underscoring the unchanging character of Brahman which nevertheless is the source, by virtue of its "power," of all change in the modal or adjectival reality that the order of existence represents. In the place of "simultaneous distinction and non-distinction" as description of Spirit is offered, a view of "non-dualism" involving a revision of the concept of non-distinction and, therefore, also of its relation to distinction.

The second point is that Srikanṭha's version of unity is at the same time to be distinguished from pure or absolute identity of Sankara. It is interesting that Srikanṭha refers to the case of the illusory perception of mother-of-pearl as silver as illustration of "absolute identity"; the alleged absoluteness consists in the understanding of idcntity as the truth and the difference as illusory. Even the negation of the difference through which the identity becomes known and affirmed is illusory; otherwise the absolute becomes compromised.

The notion of identity-in-difference is, as observed earlier, indirectly affirmed in Advaita Vedanta though explicitly discountenanced as self-contradictory. When the "silver" that is perceived in a perceptual illusion is corrected and the mother-of-pearl in its real nature known, can one describe the content, which is thus at once the object of illusory perception and later contradiction, as a case of identity-in-difference? Is the presented something sometimes silver and sometimes the mother-of-pearl? The answer is no. The contradicting perception (*bādha*) not merely corrects the illusion but also denies the truth of the "silver." It is not a case of real silver subsequently ceasing to be or appear but of the illusory silver coming to be recognized as illusory. The negation in the contradicting perception of the form "this is *not* silver" negates the silver not only "now," that is, at the time of the occurrence of correction, but also retroactively, at the time of its appearance. The negation exposes its phenomenal character, that is, its intrinsic non-reality, despite its appearance as real. The union of contradictories as "identity-in-difference" is uncritically accepted first only to be rejected when known as contradictory and its truth as pure identity recognized.

The coordinateness of identity and difference, true, presents itself in every act of knowledge but only to give way to a reflection quickened by discrimination, to a relation of identity which is nothing but the identical thing itself. The dualism of identity and difference, in other words, is the dualism not of two reals, say, like Nature and Spirit, but of the real and what appears with a claim to reality—of Brahman and māyā.

The theory of absolute identity of Sankara outlined above, thus, rests on the basis of understanding of negation, by discriminatory knowledge, of illusion. The former, that is, knowledge, typifies Brahman the underlying identity and the latter, namely, illusion, nescience or māyā, to which belongs the sphere of difference. The philosophical perspective underlying Srikaṇṭha's point of view will entail the rejection of this understanding of negation. The negation or sublation of the erroneous is rather a case of control by the larger whole and bringing the part or the partial under it and transforming it into the substance of the whole. The coexistence or coordinateness of identity and difference is not simultaneousness of two reals but of whole and part. The implied understanding of non-distinction or identity is that it is a whole of parts, of substance and attributes, of power and its owner.

Srikaṇṭha does not himself join issues against the māyā doctrine and its logic of negation but clearly defines his version of Advaita as steering clear of it. His "objections" are hermeneutical. The understanding of Spirit as

20. Sādhu engrossed in reading the Sacred Scripture in front of a four-faced Linga and Yoni, symbol of Siva and Sakti.

what fictitiously appears as the individual (as mother-of-pearl fictitiously appears as silver) flies in the face of texts which refer to Brahman as "entering" (*anupraviṣta*) the individual and as standing within it controlling it from inside and a host of other ways indicative of distinction. Passages which declare identity in no unmistakable terms, on which the pure-identity theorist rests his case, teach the relation of pervasion, the self being pervaded by Brahman. It is in this sense, says Srikanṭha (BM 2.3.42), that Brahman is said to be "one" with fishermen, slaves, and gamblers; the latter, like everything else, are pervaded by Brahman. Though the faggot burning is called "fire," the difference between the two is not negated in favor of an underlying identity.

Srikanṭha also urges the following (BM 2.3.49–52) as objections from a spiritual perspective to the position of pure identity: if the individual is "one" with Brahman, as "silver" is one with the mother-of-pearl (even at the time of its appearance, let alone later after being subject to negation), confusion of individual experiences will result. Each individual will be identical with every other. It is futile to invoke the "limitations" of space, time, and personhood to distinguish them, for since Brahman is the only reality, the limitations too belong to Him. Every act and every consequence that mold the being and the future of the individual, every desire and wish that determine action, in short everything that avails to distinguish one individual from another and to keep their experiences separate—things which are extremely significant from a perspective of life as itself embodying a spiritual journey—will be Brahman and their distinctions obliterated.

Srikanṭha's vision of unity as oneness in a "pan-organismal" sense, that is, as exemplified in the embodiedness of a living organism, does justice to the claim of BS that it is a text of the Exegesis of Embodiedness (*sārīraka mimāmsā*). In the Sivadvaita version of Srikanṭha, it is reoriented in the Saiva language of power or energy (*śakti*) and its source, the energizer (*śiva*). The Brahman of Vedanta is neither the energizer nor the energy alone but the one as qualified by the latter. Spirit is thus, distinctively, the material and efficient cause of the universe,[9] immanent in creation and yet transcendent. Spirit takes all forms and effects multiple functions and yet does not become affected. Spirit thus is an identity-in-difference, a non-duality of the distinct, a personality that knows no limitation, a self that is its own other, a grade of Bliss continuous, and yet discontinuous with all finite joys.

The self-identity of Spirit here is not an abstract identity arrived at through a rejection of something for which it is mistaken. Its self-identity is compatible with its diffusion into different determinations. It is an identity with the freedom of differentiation, a unity with the freedom of "othering" into and as the manifold. It is Spirit as "bi-unal," distinguishable as knowledge and will, consciousness and freedom, form and function, being and dynamics. (A German indologist coins the expression *zweieinigkeit* on the model of *Dreieinigkeit,* meaning Trinity.)[10] Spirit is like an indivisible point devoid of the dimensions of length, breadth, and thickness; the latter are potentially there in the point as the power to become. Srikanṭha cites a verse to the effect that *śakti* is built into the very word *sat,* which denotes Being (BM 1.1.5): Śakti and Śiva are (indicated) by the expression *sat* as (respectively) its root and suffix. The manifold world of creation, thus, is the epiphany of Brahman, a manifest expression of the glory of its power. But for this "power" neither attributes nor names nor functions would be predictable of Brahman. It is what in other words makes it at once the Deitas and the deity.

Spiritual Life as Means and the End

The individual, though subject to multiple bonds and a trail of evil, sorrow, and unfreedom, can rise above them because in essence the individual is "one" with Brahman, its "part" (*amśa*) pervaded by it. All the "parts" are not uniform but are subject to different sets of oughts (*dharma*) insofar as they are connected with different corporeal forms though there is a similarity of experience in terms of identities assumed, as "I am tall"; "I am short"; "I am a brahmin." This similarity of finite experience, structured along the divisions of caste, sex, status, and condition, stands distinguished from the experience of those who have risen above finitude and have attained to the state of the Highest Self, whose knowledge and experience are infinite, eternal, and unsurpassable (BM 2.3.45).

The condition of release or spiritual realization can be brought about by meditation preceded by knowledge, that is, a correct knowledge of what is to be meditated on. This is strictly on the basis of the maxim of the upaniṣad (ChU 3.14.1) that the meditator becomes of the essence of what he meditates on (*tat kratu nyāya*). Release comes about not through contemplation of lower ends but through contemplation of him who is eternally free from bonds, "the consort of umā, the highest Lord, the ruler who is the three-eyed, the dark-throated, the peaceful and meditating on whom the sage reaches the source of beings, the witness of all, who is beyond all darkness" (Kaivalya U 7).

The SvU (6.20) employs the language of contra-factual stating the same: When one could roll up the sky like hide then indeed can one hope to reach the end of sorrow without knowing Śivam. If one elects to remain ignorant of Śivam there is no spiritual realization for him. How does one come to know Śivam? By knowledge in the form of contemplation (*samrādhana*) (BM 3.2.23). There is here, to be sure, a circularity: meditation is to be preceded by knowledge and knowledge arises through meditation. But this is only reflective of the continuity and identity characteristic of spiritual life as means and as end. Underlying the theory of contemplation is the doctrine of divine grace that God is knowable through his own self-revelation to the one whom He chooses (Kaṭha U 1.2.23). To one who "worships" by meditation, to such a one the self as spirit reveals its true nature.

In accordance with the aforementioned maxim that underlies contemplation, non-difference from Brahman is the outcome of meditating on Brahman. Those meditating on Brahman acquire his essential and distinctive attributes. Identifying himself with the Lord in yoga, Krishna manifests to Arjuna the powers and the form of the highest Lord (*paramam rūpam aiśvaram*) (BM 3.2.24). Vāmadeva speaks of himself as having become Manu and the Sun and others. Meditation in this sense as fruitful of results may be seen in the instance of contemplation of identity with Garuda (the chief of the feathered race and the implacable enemy of the snake species). By incantation of the Garuda mantra one acquires the virtue of Garuda in nullifying the effect of snakebite.

When meditation has for its object the attainment of a novel and limited result, different results may be aimed at, and in order to secure them different meditations may be combined. But, says Srikaṇṭha, not in the case of meditating on the highest Brahman. Various modes of contemplating him, to be sure, are enumerated (BS 3.3, third quarter) each aiming at the realization of Brahman. The results of each being the same, there is no need to combine the various modes. Likewise, even when contemplation of parts seems to be recommended by the indication of special results, contemplation of the whole is always superior, as the outcome is also of superior value. It is thus said that meditation on *vaisvānara,* "Man universal," as if different, that is, limited, yields the fruit of "eating food." Meditation on him as a whole with limbs contemplated as identical with the heavenly world and so on down to the earth results in "eating food in all worlds, in all beings in all selves" (ChU 5.11–18), which is the experience of Brahman-hood (BM 3.3.55).

Meditation as a spiritual act must be distinguished from the performance of prescribed rites like sacrifice. The latter are not different from any karmic act. Neither of them leads perceptibly to their results; their fruit accrues unseen (*adṛṣṭa*). Not so in meditation, which should be practiced unintermittently and constantly. It should be a continuous representation and not a sporadic act of thought and may thus be seen to bring about its result, namely, Brahman-intuition. The highest Brahman with his divine attributes like omniscience should be thought of constantly in order to realize his nature.

As the author of SMD states in the opening of his commentary, Srikaṇṭha's own attraction seems to be to the meditation on the Lord as the Ether inside the heart-lotus (*cidambaram*). This is evident from his discussion of the multiple references to the Meditation on the Small (*dahara vidyā*) in different upaniṣads and the issue of their identity (BM 3.3.38). Srikaṇṭha's preference for this particular form is that in it is established, unequivocally, the proper object of contemplation, namely, Śiva. The small "ether within the heart" (ChU 8.1.1) is Brahman. It is that "Brahman-world" to which creatures return from day to day and yet know not. It is what is "free from sin, sorrow, old age, and death" (ChU 8.1.5), and such qualifications are applicable only to Brahman, not to the limited self (*jīva*) and not certainly to material nature. Though sometimes reference is made to what is "within" the ether as the ruler and controller (BĀU 4.4.22), meditation is not to be focused on what is within as the dweller. The description of it as free from sin, etc., indicates that the ethereal Space (*ākāśa*) itself is to be contemplated. Srikaṇṭha's point is that a relation of non-difference has to be understood as between the two, that of substance and attribute (BM 1.3.13–16). The "subtle ether of the heart" is but the "radiant expanse of consciousness" (*cidambaram*) which is the attribute of Brahman.[11]

A close review of the *daharavidyā* as expounded in the Mahopanisad (the name by which Srikaṇṭha labels the *Mahānārayaṇa* section of the TU) will reveal, says Srikaṇṭha, that the Absolute God (*Parameśvara*) alone is the object of contemplation throughout (BM 1.2.8). First comes the description that the Lord is minuter than the atom and that he resides inside the cave of the hearts of all creatures; his glory is perceived by him whose sorrows have ceased thanks to Lord's grace. Then it is said that from him proceed the seven *prāṇa*(s) (biomotor force) establishing that he is the immanent material cause of the world. Then is said that Rudra the "great sage" saw *Hiranyagarbha* being born, which attests to his omniscience and world transcendence and as such the efficient cause. The Being of the Supreme ether can be realized by those who having ascertained the sense of Vedanta contemplate Brahman as residing in the lotus of the heart. This Being is *Maheśvara*, that is, Siva. The text, Srikaṇṭha points out, that comes immediately after the *Nārāyaṇa Anuvāka* about Being—that it is Righteousness and Truth, that it is partly dark and partly fair (*krishna pingalam*), and so on—bears it out. The sense of the entire text is one and continuous and vindicates that Parmesvara alone is worthy of contemplation.

One final aspect of meditation as the means of spiritual realization that is unique to Sivadvaita is that the Lord is to be meditated on as identical with self, not as different in any conceivable sense therefrom. The object of meditation is release from the state of bondage. One has, therefore, to meditate on oneself as free from trammels and as identical with the blissful Siva. The Jābāla Śruti, quoted earlier, represents the "performatory utterance" of one in contemplation: "I am Thou, Thou art I." Srikanṭha here parts company with Rāmānuja, who also quotes this verse but understands it to say that the Lord is to be contemplated as the self of selves in the relation of the embodied to the body. As Appayya shows (SN 3.153), if the finite self is the attribute of the Lord, his body, the Lord may be said to be the finite self but not vice versa. The relation being asymmetrical, the two terms cannot be interchanged. Srikanṭha is cautious to observe that if the contemplator looks upon Brahman as identical with himself as doer and enjoyer, he would never be able to intuit the infinite (BM 3.3.51). In contemplation such characteristics of finitude are suppressed, and the qualities of freedom from sin and so on alone are contemplated. The contemplator himself not becoming disembodied still contemplates the identity of Brahman with his own self as free from the defects of bondage and its trail of embodiment.

One that thus attains an intuition of Brahman and becomes equal to Brahman views the world not in its finitude and imperfection but as harmonized with Brahman. He sees, hears, and knows nothing else but Brahman (BM 1.3.8), who as Supreme Bliss possesses the form of this world. With his faculties of mind, speech, and sight under self-rule (TU 1.6), he becomes Brahman whose body is "ether." Not the elemental ether but the effulgent expanse of consciousness (*cidambara prakāśa sarīram*).[12]

Sivadvaita and Vedanta[13]

The great service of Srikanṭha is to uncover the religious form of spiritual consciousness that Vedanta represents. Vedanta is the name for the more comprehensive discipline of a philosophy of the spirit to which investigation of religious consciousness is integral. Vedanta is, indifferently, also a religion of gnosis and/or of devotion, and/or of contemplation. In a philosophy of spirit including, preeminently, that of its expression in the religious form, there is an "enjoying" experience of the overpersonal reality. The overpersonal self or reality is understood enjoyingly, that is, in a nonobjectivistic attitude. Any content that is experienced in explicit references to the subject *I*, even when the reference takes the paradoxical form of self-abnegation, may be said to be experienced in the mode of enjoying. But there is also in a philosophy of spirit the consciousness of a content that is neither objective nor even subjective. The concept "spiritual" points beyond itself. The philosophy of spirit in which there is a necessary reference to the subject culminates in the philosophy of truth. This is the region of the absolute, of transcendental consciousness, where even the *I* as the symbol of reality is negated. In the experience of self-abnegation of religious consciousness, there is no theoretic denial of the subject *I*. In the perspective of the absolute, there is no enjoying experience, as there is of the overpersonal reality in religion. The positive character of the absolute is expressible only by the negation of the *I*, as what I am *not*. The subject or the individual self is unreal, for the absolute alone *is*. When we say the absolute is, we mean by it not reality but truth.[14] Reality is enjoyed but truth is not. The consciousness of truth as what is not understood even in the subjective attitude, let alone not as object, is transcendental consciousness.

There is, thus, a dialectical tension between experience of reality and "experience" of truth, between enjoying consciousness and a transcendental consciousness, between an awareness which is ecstatic in the sense of standing out while at the same time also standing in and an awareness which merely witnesses without reference to an I that witnesses, and, indeed, even not constituted by the duality between witnessing and the witnessed. The polarity and complementariness between Brahman as impersonal Being (*nirguṇa*) and the same as Personal God (*saguṇa*) is an exemplification of the above tension characteristic of experience describable as spiritual.

The great merit of Sivadvaita is, at least according to the estimation of its supercommentator (than whom one cannot be more alive to the tension), that it signifies a mode of reconciliation between the irreconcilables. Whether Srikaṇtha himself intended it that way as Appayya wants to believe is a question for scholarship. What is significant in Sivadvaita is the demonstration of the supreme relevance of Brahman as saguṇa even to establish the doctrine of Nirguna Brahman. The religious form of spiritual consciousness underscores the need for a mediation between the absolute understood as truth beyond the distinction and duality of subject and object and the reality experienced in the interaction between subject and object. The two will otherwise fall apart. There cannot even be a basis for asserting their distinction. The Absolute being truth itself does not include the revelatory function. Truth does not have to be declared in order for it to be true. It does not also suffer by being declared and taught. Hence is felt the need for understanding the Absolute to include also the sense of God to make it accessible to experience. The BS allows for both kinds of interpretation, one nirguṇa and the other saguṇa. Even Sankara accepts that BS has a secondary saguṇa sense, and in his own doctrine of pure Advaita he intends a secondary saguṇa doctrine. There is, however, need for a fresh reopening of the question, as Sankara does not develop systematically what is for him only a secondary doctrine. Secondary though the doctrine be, Sankara is fully alive to the reality of Vedanta as also religion. What Srikanṭha attempts and achieves is to show that the Absolute God (*parameśvara*) alone is the Brahman combining within him the inaccessible depth as Truth and also its self-revelation to make it immanent as the reality of one's experience. Appayya's statement in his introductory verse to his commentary on Srikanṭha is a classical quote:

> All the vast scriptures and Āgamas as well as all the Purānas, Smrtis, Mahābhārata and the rest advocate non-duality; and the Brahama-sutras, causing confusion even to the discerning, is taken to be propounding the theory of non-dualism by ancient teachers like Sankara and others. Nevertheless (the truth of the matter is) through the grace of Siva alone can these arise in one (even) the inkling for the non-dual Truth. Not otherwise.

Notes

[1] The other place where the expression *vaśī* occurs in the upaniṣadic literature is Kaṭha U 2.2.12, which speaks of the "One that draws near" (*eko vaśī*) as, among other things, "abiding in the self" (*ātmastham*). Appayya etymologically derives Śiva from the root *vas*, meaning "to desire or will" and cites the *Mahābhārata* text *śivam iccham manusyānām tasmād devah śivah smrtah* in support. The root *vas* with the suffix *i* added and the resulting word subject to transposition of letters *varṇa vyatyaya* yields the expression śīva. Examples of such transposition of letters are: himsa=simha, paśyaka=kaśyapa. A second etymology that is also proposed is from the root *śiva*, meaning the benign or good *subham, kalyāṇam*, one that causes the good to prevail (by the addition of the suffix *pasatyac*) SMD 1, p. 2. The etymologies, somewhat fanciful (S. N. Dasgupta, *History of Indian Philosophy*, vol. 5 [Cambridge: University Press, 1955] 69), nevertheless make out a plausible case for Śiva as the God of love. Srikanṭha quotes as the text of MU (BM 4.1.16) a statement amounting to the admission that one that utters the hallowed word *śivam*, be he even of the kind of an untouchable outcaste, becomes worthy of close fellowship, which means living with, conversing with, and dining with everyone. This reflects the sense of love which cuts across all barriers, as intrinsic to "sivam." The latter, as word-meaning and sentiment, is corroborated by the vast śaiva religious literature in Tamil, which centers on the equation of divine essence and love.

[2] All the descriptive names, e.g., *pati, īśa, īśvara, maheśvara, parameśvara, amrta*, are contemplated in the light of their meaning as "significant proper" (*yogarūḍi*) names for the Godhead specific to the understanding of Saiva theology. The expression *amrta*, particularly as Srikanṭha demonstrates (BM 1.1.22; 1.2.19; 4.3.13) as naming both the Being that defies death and the state of attainment of deathlessness, preeminently, is interchangeable with Śivam. To the question By reciting what may one gain immortality (*amrtatvam*)? Yajnavalkhya replies (reads the text of the *Jābāla Upanisad*, 3), "by reciting *satarudrīya* 'the hundred names of Rudra' " and adds "these are, verily, the names of *amrta*" (BM 1.1.22). For gaining

a proper perspective on Srikanṭha's comments, both negative and positive, on divine names, it is useful to keep in mind that for him, as it is for Appayya, the names are predicates rather than names of subjects. The issue is one of their relative adequacy and inclusiveness, specially in respect of denoting the soteriological function. They thus provide the ultimate foundation of ontological courage in the face of the anxiety of mortality.

[3] BM 3.4–48.49: *Pāsupatavrta*–"those practising it attain the fruit of the meditation on Rudra, namely, release consisting in the severance of the fetter." It is *atyāśrama* (super-*āśrama*) in the sense of a separate "āśrama" leading to the attainment of Paramasiva. All the virtues of the different stations of life, like those of the student and the ascetic, enter into it. Appayya refers to the *Kāurma Purāṇa* text which equates *pāsupata yoga* with *atyāśrama yoga: evam pāsupatam yogam yogaiśvaryamanuttaman atyāsramamidam jneyam muktaye kena labyate* (1.31). The *Kāurma Purāṇa* speaks of three contemplative yoga(s), *Baudika, Sānkhya,* and *Atyāśrama,* and Appayya grades them as each leading to the next, being respectively the contemplations of *Viṣnu, Sakti, and Śiva, viṣnuśakti śivabhāvanānān uttarot kṛṣṭatvam uktam* (AL verse 1 commentary).

[4] *tadidam brahmasūtrāṇam tātparyam saguṇe śive prakaṭīkartum ācāryyāh praṇīnye bhāṣyam uttamam* (SMD 1, p. 2): "The import of this BS is (indeed) in respect of Śiva (who is) with attributes. To publicise it (without equivocation) the preceptor (Srikanṭha) composed his great commentary."

[5] Srikanṭha himself interprets the sense of *I* (*aham*) later (BM 4.4.19) thus: *ahamiti śakti śivādvayam brahmocyate,* "*I* refers to Spirit *qua* the unity of Energy and Energiser."

[6] According to the doctrine of "universal salvation" (*sarva mukti*), release is attaining the nature of Brahman "with attributes," to begin with, until final Release comes about for all. And then there is merger in Brahman "without attributes," answering to the experience of Pure Immediacy. Appayya reads this as implicit in the various statements made by Sankara throughout his commentary on BS 1.4.16; 2.3.43; 3.2.3; 4.4.7) and thus as compatible with Srikanṭha's idea of release as one of attainment of *Īsvaratva* by meditation on Brahman "with attributes" (SN 3, 2851f.). Appayya explains the doctrine in his encyclopedic work on Advaita, *Siddhanta-lesa-samgrah* (University of Madras) Vol. 2, Sanskrit, p. 450f.): The individual selves being "reflections" of God, when one of them is released that reflection becomes one with the prototype. Until all nescience is destroyed there will continue to be the prototype, but when all of it is destroyed there is no further possibility of reflection and there is merger in Brahman. Radhakrishnan expounds the spirituality of the doctrine and its ramifications in his Hibbert Lectures (*An Idealist View of Life* [London: Allen & Unwin, 1929] 303) and also in a paper entitled *Sarvamukti* in the *Proceedings of the Eighth Session of Indian Philosophical Congress* (Waltair, 1933).

[7] The affinities between Sivadvaita and Saiva Siddhanta, the Tamil tradition that goes by the name and the lineage of Meykantar, are not treated here; they will be included in the next volume. Saiva Siddhanta like Kashmir Saivism typifies the spirituality of Hinduism *in extension* while Srikanṭha's Sivadvaita, in terms of self-understanding, is Vedanta proper. Meykanta's *Civananapotham*, the Tamil Saiva Siddhanta canon, as well as the Sanskritic version of *Sivajnanabodham* (the originality of which was uncritically accepted by the tradition but is disputed by modern scholarship) address *inter alia* the task of clarifying "the unified teaching" (*aviruddhārta upadeśa*) of Vedanta of which Appayya speaks as part of "the determination of the precise import of the Saiva faith" (*śaivārtha nirṇayam*). It is quite conceivable that the spiritual teacher of the name Sveta whom Srikanṭha hails refers to Meykantar, whose proper name, according to the colophon of *Civananapotham,* is Svetavanan. The identity is chronologically sustainable, and even doctrinally Saivasiddhanta admits

to a greater degree of closeness or proximity between its position and that of Sivadvaita than with any other internal school of Saivism. For a discussion of the issue, see S. Suryanarayana Sastri, *The Sivadvaita of Srikanṭha*, 17f.

[8] There is no systematic exploration of the general signifiance of *bhedabheda* for Vedanta in the secondary writings on the subject. The exception is *The Philosophy of Bhedabheda* by P. N. Srinivasachari (Madras: The Adyar Library, 1950). The present writer's participation in the seminars on the subject of Franciscan and Bhakti spirituality organized at St. Bonaventure University in 1986 and 1987 by Ewert Cousins, the general editor of the World Spirituality Series, helped to clarify his ideas vis-à-vis Bonaventure, St. Francis, and Meister Eckhart. *Bhedabheda* and its varieties bear similarities to the types of the "coincidence of opposites" of medieval Christian thought. In any such comparison it is useful to keep in mind the two ways in which the compound *bhedabheda* is split, namely, as coordinative (*dvandva*), according to which the "and" conjoining difference and identity will be an *enumerative* "and" (*bhedasca abhedasca*), and, second, as determinative (*tatpurusa*), in which case the "and" should be a conjunctive "and" (*bhedaviśiṣṭah abhedah*). According to the latter, there is consubstantiality (*tādātmya*) between difference and identity; the distinction between the created order (*cidacit prapanca*) and the Creator (brahman) is, to Srikanṭha, for example, an aspect of the bipolarity within the Creator as power and its source. According to the first way of understanding the compound, it is a case of the coincidence of two things belonging to dissimilar and even opposite classes, a point of view often discredited as contradictory but defended with equal vigor as exemplifying opposites *coinciding* and thus ceasing to be opposed, a position that admittedly defies "thinking" it (*a-cintya*).

[9] A purely theistic doctrine of the externality of the world to God, namely, that God is "efficient cause only," finds its great critic in BS, which points out the incoherencies inherent in such a position (2.2.35–38). Srikanṭha's point is that the criticism of the section is to be understood not as directed against the Śaivāgama but against the Yoga system and its promulgation in the *Hiranyagarbha* Āgama. The latter, like the Naiyayika(s) and some Pāśupata Śaiva(s) hold the view that God is only the efficient cause of the universe, one among other causal factors, which view is unacceptable to the generality of Vedanta. Vedanta rejects the doctrine as opposed to scripture with its thesis of Brahman as the ground of being, the ground material of all that exists (BS 1.4.23–27). It is also opposed to reason: the potter example, Srikanṭha observes, is not convincing because "only as embodied (that is to say, as becoming determinate through the limitation of a body) are agents like the potter seen to relate as cause to materials like clay" (BM 2.2.34). The important thing is that Srikanṭha considers this critique as not applicable to any Śaivāgama properly understood. True, the Saivagama(s) like the *Kāmika, Kārana,* speak of the Lord as the efficient, and not the material, cause, but what they mean thereby to assert, says Appayya, is that the Lord as spirit remains unaffected by change (SMD 1, pp. 560–63). Between the Vedas and the Śaivāgama, Srikanṭha perceives no difference either in purpose or authority or in authorship. The two are equal and, indeed, "identical" (*vede'pi saivāgama iti vyavahāro yuktah*). The distinction between them is pedagogical: the Vedanta as *Brahmavidyā* (a study expounded in the upaniṣads) is limited to the three castes to whom alone are open the ritual initiation necessary for reciting of the Veda. The Āgama is open to study by members of all castes, the limitation to accept here being drawn not on lines of caste, rank, or station in life but strictly in terms of spiritual maturity. Even though Srikanṭha does not develop the implications of the admission and instead subscribes to the Brahminical stipulations regarding eligibility to Vedanta study (BM 1.3.33), it is significant that he perceives the Śaivāgama and its openness to all but the spiritually unripe as implicitly one with that of Vedanta.

[10] H. W. Schomerus, *Arunanti's Sivajnanasiddhiyar,* Band 1 (Wiesbaden: Franz Steiner, 1981) 113.

[11] Srikaṇṭha uses the word *cidambaram* in many places in his commentary to denote the expanse of Spirit as Light, which is not without the suggestion of reference to the shrine and the worship at the sacred temple of Cidambaram in South India. The temple is itself according to *Koil Puranam* (fourteenth century) a symbolism for *daharopasanā,* the township itself where we have the shrine being called by that name and signifying the heart-cavity (*dahara*) of the Cosmic Man (*virāt puruṣa*). *Daharopāsanā,* the worship of the Inner Shrine, is interpreted both macrocosmically, that is, with reference to the worlds that span the thirty-six stadia of the cosmos stretching from the earth to the uppermost principle of Śiva, and also microcosmically, that is, in relation to organic life, spoken of in the upaniṣads as the "city of Brahman." The notion of ethereal space or vacuity itself, again, is a symbol. It indicates Brahman as vast and yet as amenable to personal adoration and devotion. Space, in itself infinitely vast and therefore identifiable not as a thing alongside of other things in it, becomes through the limits of pitcher and other such objects accessible and identified (BM 1.2.7). The above-mentioned *Purānam* lists a host of names as synonyms of *cidambaram,* like *hiranmayakośa,* the "golden sheath," *puṇdarīkam,* "lotus," *guhā,* "cave," *sabhā,* "hall," *paramavyomam,* the "superspace," *satyamāyatanam,* the "abode of truth," and others (*Koil Puranam* 57), all of which are terms used in the upaniṣads to describe spirit.

[12] See n. 11.

[13] In this section some of the ideas and even the terms that are employed are freely drawn from "The Concept of Philosophy" of K. C. Bhattacharyya, written in the thirties and reprinted in *Studies in Philosophy,* ed. Gopinath Bhattacharyya (Calcutta: Progressive Publishers, 1958) vol. 2, chap. 2.

[14] Ibid., 116. The great insight of the author lies in demonstrating that transcendental consciousness lends itself to be elaborated as prototype of the three subjective functions of knowing, willing, and feeling, the "triple" absolute of truth, freedom, and value. The three are assertible as, *alternatively,* the absolute, each elaborated as primary in reference to the other absolutes. The reason for referring to this interesting concept is to indicate the viability from a spiritual perspective, to reverse the relation of *Saguna* and *Nirguna* vidyas as interpreted by Appayya. According to Saiva Siddhanta, which considers itself the fulfillment of Vedanta, the progress of the spiritual journey (as signified by its schemes of thirty-six tattvas, six adhvas, three kinds of *jnāna* and Ten Acts) lies in ascending from the reality as "seen" (*drśya*) to that of the seer (*drk*) but again, proceeding in the ascent to what is beyond the correlation of seeing and the seen, namely, to the Revealer (*darśayita*) who both comprehends and transcends the correlatives. The text of *Sivajnanabodham* (11) is: *drśo darśayitāca ātmā tad darśayitā śivah,* "the self is the knower and revealer but the revealer thereof (who reveals by Himself also knowing) is Śiva." Nirguna vidya itself, which is an admirable focus on the experience of pure identity and immediacy, typifies only an intermediary station marking the sphere of *Puruṣa,* and not the *terminus.* The *terminus* of the journey indicated by Siva tattva consists rather of a realization of freedom in respect of relation, personality, and function. For a fuller discussion of the subject, see K. Sivaraman, *Saivism in Philosophical Perspective* (Varanasi: Motilal Banarsidas, 1973) chap. 9. To this orientation of spirituality, admittedly extra-Vedantic, the distinction between Vedanta and Siddhanta is as between the general and a special doctrine. The latter, far from contradicting the former, is its "hermeneutic," that is, "a way of bringing to light," a supplement providing a greater spiritual access to that which it supplements.

Note: Throughout the chapter spirit (lower case) and Spirit (upper case) occur. The difference in capitalization is intended to distinguish *ātmen, adhyātman*—what is adjective of or appositional to "freedom," in short, the functional side of God in its overlap in respect to the individual self—from Brahman, Śivam, Godhead considered without reference to the cosmic or soteriological functions.

Bibliography

Sources:

Brahma Sūtra Bhāṣya of Srikaṇthacharya with the commentary Sivarkamani Dipika. Edited by R. Halasyanatha Sastri. 2 vols. Bombay: Nirnayasagar Press, 1908, 1918.

Saiva Upanisads. Translated by T. R. Srinivasa Ayyangar. Madras: The Adyar Library, 1953.

Sivadvaita Nirnaya of Appayya Diksita. Text and translation by S. S. Suryanvayana Sastri. Madras: University of Madras, 1930.

Srikaṇtha Bhasya or Commentary of Srikaṇtha on the Brahma Sutras. Translated by Roma Chaudhuri. Calcutta: Prachyavani Series, 1959.

The Vedanta Sutras with Srikaṇtha Bhasya. Translated by A. Mahadeva Sastri. Published in Siddhanta Deepika, Vols. I, IV, V. Madras, 1897, 1899, 1900.

Studies:

Dasgupta, S. N. *History of Indian Philosophy,* Vol. V. Cambridge: University Press, 1955.

Kanti Chandra Pandey. *Bhaskari,* vol. 3. English translation. Lucknow: The Princess of Wales Saraswati Bhawana Texts, 1954.

Radhakrishnan, S., trans. *The Brahma Sutra: The Philosophy of Spiritual Life.* London: Allen & Unwin, 1960.

Roma Chaudhuri. *Doctrine of Srikaṇtha,* Vol. 1. Calcutta: Prachyavani Series, 1962.

——. *Ten Schools of Vedanta,* Part III. Calcutta: Rabindra Bharati University, 1980.

Sivaraman, K. *Saivism in Philosophical Perspective.* Varanasi: Motilal Banarsidas, 1973.

Suryanarayana Sastri, S. S. *The Sivadvaita of Srikaṇtha.* Reprint. Madras: University of Madras, 1972.

15

Vedanta as God-Realization (Madhva)

K. T. PANDURANGI

THE GREATEST MYSTERY OF SPIRITUAL LIFE pertains no doubt to the infinite ways of its manifestations. The richness of the Vedic tradition was enhanced time and again by eminent teachers, who out of the depth of their own inner experiences gave new orientations to its meaning. If Rāmānuja can be said to have concretized the image of Nārāyaṇa the Supreme Deity out of the limitless panoramic vision of the Brahman of Sankara, then Madhva can be said to have given his due place to the human soul also as eternally yearning for the grace of Nārāyaṇa. In Madhva's philosophy man comes into his own, in all his fallenness, finitude, and humility and yet as the creature who is born with the mark of greatness on him because he is akin to God and destined for ultimate liberation.

Madhva was born in A.D. 1238 near a small town called Udipi in the southwest region of India (south of Bombay). After a full life of study, *sādhana,* teaching and the writing of definitive treatises, he departed this world in A.D. 1317. Madhva accepted in his writings the authority of the Vedas as well as the *Pāñcarātra-Āgama,* together with the two great epics and a few of the major *Purāṇa*(s). His knowledge of the religious literature of the country was encyclopedic, and he imbibed from it the quintessence of spirituality. Thus he evolved a synthesis between the Vedic and the Vaiṣṇava traditions. Madhva wrote (before Sayana) a commentary on the first forty hymns of the *Ṛg Veda,* bringing out their spiritual import. He wrote digests of the *Mahābhārata* and the *Rāmāyaṇa.* Madhva believed that all authoritative texts may be interpreted in two ways: the first is to understand it in the ordinary language—that is, in *darśanabhāṣā* (scholastic discourse); the second, more important, way is to understand the *samādhi-bhāṣā* (enstatic discourse) of the texts—that is, the esoteric language of meditation. This is the inner meaning of texts which could be brought out by careful exegeses. His thirty-seven works systematically seek to bring out the *samādhi-bhāṣā* of the Vedas, *Upaniṣad*(s) the *Gītā*, the Epics, and also the *Vaiṣnava-Āgama*(s). He wrote a special work entitled *Tantrsāra* on worship and spiritual symbolism.

Concept of God

The worship of God in all his glory and splendor, surrounded by His divine companions and holding eternal court (*sabhā*) for the enraptured vision of His devotees, marks the advent of the Vaiṣṇava tradition on the spiritual scene. The quality-less and the form-less Brahman of Vedanta here is transformed into God with infinite qualities and innumerable manifestation forms. The supreme deity is Viṣṇu in the Madhva tradition. Viṣṇu is another name for Nārāyaṇa of the earlier tradition of Viśiṣtādvaita. Madhva saw clearly that Viṣṇu as God could hold together the Vedic, Upaniṣadic, Epic, and Purāṇic traditions.

Viṣṇu is the central theme of the entire body of religious literature because He is praised in the Vedas, *Rāmāyaṇa*, *Purāṇa*(s), *Mahābhārata*, in the beginning, in the middle, and at the end (*Harivaṃśa*).

Madhva's concept of God as Viṣṇu is more spiritual than theological. Viṣṇu, the supreme God, is the highest spiritual entity or the Brahman of the *Upaniṣad*(s). Viṣṇu is not only of the nature of *sat*, *cit*, and *ānanda* (being, consciousness, and bliss) but to Him belong all other possible attributes. He in fact possesses an infinite number of attributes (*anantaguṇa paripūrṇa*, or simply *pūrṇa*). He is not limited or conditioned by space, time, etc. or any limiting factors. He is entirely spiritual in nature (*cetanā*). His attributes are also spiritual, nonmaterial (*aprākṛta*). His various forms and manifestations are also spiritual. He is omniscient and omnipotent. He knows, wills, and acts. There is no difference between His attributes and Himself, His powers and Himself, His different forms and manifestations and Himself. He is beyond ordinary perception and human ratiocinations. Then how may He be known? The answer is: Only by His own Grace. He reveals Himself to the deserving, but as He is infinite none may know Him completely. This is brought home by describing Him as possessing contradictory attributes such as being the minutest as well as the biggest, as present in specific places and also everywhere, as formless and as with forms and so on. He has no *prākṛtā* or material form but He does have an *aprākṛta* form. Moreover, He is conveyed by all words, because all words convey some or other attributes and all attributes belong to Him.

He is the only independent principle. All other entities, namely, souls and matter, are entirely dependent on Him. This dependence is in respect of their very essential nature, their functions, and their knowledge (*svarūpa, pravṛtti,* and *pramiti*). Thus, according to Madhva reality has two categories, namely, independence and dependence (*svatantramasvatantram ca prameyaṃ dvividam matam* [*Tattvaviveka,* 1]). Brahman or Viṣṇu is independent, and souls and matter are dependent entities. In this concept of dependence lies the point of departure from earlier Vedantic thought. Madhva emphatically separates the plane of divine presence from the plane of human adoration. At no stage can these merge into each other or one of them be eliminated as unreal. The differences among God, soul, and matter are permanent. This insistence on difference is the basis for the *Dvaitavāda,* "dualistic theory," of Madhva.

God is pure spirit, and matter is entirely dependent on Him even for its very existence. He can manipulate it in any way He likes, and that is how he causes creation, sustenance, dissolution, etc. of the material world. The souls are also spiritual in their original nature (*cetanā*); but they are encased in subtle material bodies (*sūkṣma sarīra*). This togetherness is beginningless in time and cannot be said to be caused. The souls with their subtle bodies go on transmigrating into gross bodies until they discover their true spiritual nature and are liberated from these gross as well as subtle bodies. In their true nature they are akin to God insofar as they are also constituted of *sat, cit,* and *ānanda.* The relation between God and souls is that of reflection. God is the archetype and souls are prototypes (*bimba* and *pratibimba*). Two characteristics mark this relationship: just as a reflection is similar to the entity reflected and is entirely dependent on it, so are souls similar to God and entirely dependent on Him. This metaphor (*bimba-pratibimbabhāva*) of reflection or shadow is utilized only to bring out the two characteristics, namely, similarity and dependence. It should not be stretched to cover other aspects of a reflection, namely, its unreality. Briefly, God and the souls are spiritual in their nature; souls are akin to God in respect of their spiritual nature, and their very essence lies in being entirely dependent upon God.

Divine Involvement in Creation

God is spirit or pure consciousness, as against a material substance which exists at His mercy and under His control. He is not only responsible for creation, sustenance, and dissolution of the material world but also its regulation, providing knowledge to the souls functioning in it, withdrawing such knowledge, involving them in bondage, and releasing them from the bondage. In fact, nothing can happen in the world or to the souls without His will and initiative. As stated earlier, His attributes, actions, etc. are inseparable from Him. His various manifestations are also inseparable from Him. He is immanent in all yet He is transcendent. He is the source of all powers. He enters into the primordial matter and causes its evolution into different stages. At all stages of evolution He is present. Matter is not a modification of spirit. It is not even caused by spirit but it is controlled by spirit. Its evolution is manipulated by spirit. Matter consists in being existent (*sat*) but not in being conscious (*cit*) or of the nature of bliss (*ānanda*). In respect of being existent (*sat*), matter is a reflection (*pratibimba*) of God. That is to say it is dependent on God and is controlled by God. This tradition does not agree with the view that matter is the modification of Brahman, either directly or through *māyā*. Madhva holds the view that Brahman or God is only an efficient cause, an agent who manipulates the evolution of the primordial matter into different stages of the actual world. He is not the material cause by Himself either directly or through *māyā*. Matter is different from spirit and under its control; it is not a modification of spirit. Matter, no doubt, functions as a hindrance against spiritual progress of the soul but it does not and cannot offer any hindrance or resistance to God. Its very existence depends upon God's will.

Spiritual Hierarchy

God's involvement in helping the soul in its spiritual progress is stratified in a hierarchy of deities. Madhva recognizes a scheme of intermediary deities who assist the devotee in his spiritual quest. On the lowest level is Puṣkara, going on to Brahmā the four-faced god, then the goddess Lakṣmī, the divine spouse of Viṣṇu, and lastly, Viṣṇu Himself. These gods are mediators who form the links between the soul and God. In other words, every soul in himself is face to face with God at all stages of his spiritual progress. Here we find a blending of a theological scheme within the framework of spiritual practices. The important concept is the encounter of the soul with God envisioned in a hierarchical stratification at every stage of which the two are linked by spiritual mediators.

The infinite is no doubt present at all stages and manipulates all stages, but it is also pleased to allow the intermediary deities to assist the seeker, the finite soul. The presence of God or the infinite spirit in senses and different parts of the body in different forms such as Aniruddha, Saṅkarṣaṇa, Vasudeva, Nārāyaṇa, etc. is also worked out in some detail. Here again we see a blending of theology and spirituality. What we are concerned with here is the idea of the envelopment of every aspect of the finite spirit by the infinite spirit. It pervades spirit and enters into the material bodies with which it functions during transmigration. The soul, the finite spirit, cannot be away from the infinite spirit. It is never away. It is only a question of being aware of it or not and having rapport with it or not. The position of not being aware and not having rapport is transmigration, and being aware of it and having rapport with it is liberation. It is to attain this state of rapport with the infinite spirit that all efforts of the souls, the finite spirits, have to be directed. Such an endeavor on the part of the soul is called spirituality or efforts for spiritual progress. The meaning and the purpose of such efforts could be fully understood if we keep in mind the nature of both God and the souls, the fact of their being akin to each other in their basic spiritual content, and that they are intimately related as *bimba-pratibimba.* To discover or realize this relationship constitutes spirituality in this tradition.

The Nature of the Soul

In accordance with this tradition the soul's existence is intuitively known through one's own experience of joy and sorrow. Its existence as an agent is also likewise experience and cannot be disputed. Such an experiencer cannot be identified with the body. He is something more than the body and functions through it. He is a finite spiritual entity as against God, who is an infinite spiritual entity. However, the soul, though finite, is a permanent entity. He has no beginning in time nor an end. He has only the states of being dormant, being in transmigration, and being liberated. Before being introduced into transmigration by God he is in a dormant state. Then, on entering the stream of transmigration he functions through his subtle and gross bodies. He goes on changing his gross bodies and is born into different species of living beings. His subtle body continues to be the same. This subtle body is cast away at the time of liberation. Both subtle and gross bodies are material. Casting away all material adjuncts itself is liberation.

God in His mercy introduces the soul into the stream of transmigration to provide him with an opportunity for discovering his true spiritual nature. The soul by resorting to appropriate means of spiritual progress may realize the futility of material life and succeed in casting away his material adjuncts. He has been imprisoned by these material adjuncts all along, and these have been obstructing him from realizing his spiritual nature. He is akin to God in his nature and is intimately linked with God by way of the *bimba-pratibimba* relation. It is to discover this that the way of transmigration is provided as a stepping-stone. The soul is neither God descended to earth, nor is he deluded as a soul. He is a prototype of God, who is an archetype for all souls. Spiritual enlightenment comes to the soul when he knows himself to be totally dependent on God.

Thus, souls are different both from God and matter. These souls are many and are different from each other. Each soul intuitively knows himself. He has an inbuilt capacity to know himself, his joys and sorrows, to discriminate between right and wrong, and certain entities like time and space that cannot be known through any other means. This inbuilt intuitive faculty is termed the witness capacity (*sākṣī* [*Anuvyākhyāna* p. 49]). The capacity to witness is part and parcel of the very essential nature of the soul (*svarupendriya*). It is by this power (*sākṣī*) that the soul discovers the truth of knowledge.

No one can claim to know others as directly as one knows oneself. Since these intuitively realized joys and sorrows differ from person to person, and since this intuitive self-knowledge is private to each one, Madhva accepts the doctrine of the plurality of souls. Sāṁkhya, Nyaya, and Mīmāṁsā also accept this doctrine. Even in Advaita, plurality of souls is not disputed so far as the stage of transmigration is concerned. The more crucial question is whether the liberated soul retains his identity and enjoys the fruits of his spiritual efforts or is only led into a "blissful state" of total self-annihilation. The tradition of Madhva believes in the retention of the identity of each soul even after liberation and in his being in complete harmony with God. Disharmony with God's will is bondage, and complete harmony with His will is liberation. The merger of the souls with God or the elimination of the souls as illusory manifestations is not acceptable to Madhva. Souls are many both during transmigration and after liberation, and each soul enjoys the fruits of his spiritual efforts and endures endlessly in blissful contemplation of God's glory and majesty in the divine *loka* (realm) of Viṣṇu.

Avidyā and Other Factors of Bondage

The Dvaita tradition accepts the concept of a primordial nescience or *avidyā* that eclipses the soul's true nature and also conceals God from his vision. It is not, however, a delusion of an illusory type. It is real ignorance regarding one's own true nature. The soul is dependent on God, but this nescience causes the notion that the soul is independent. The soul is not an independent agent, independent enjoyer, independent owner of his body or senses. He has no independent control over the means or the ends. It is nescience or *avidyā* that makes him believe in his independent agency, independent enjoyership, independent ownership of body, senses, means, ends, etc. Thus, he arrogates to himself an independence that is not true. He thus is in friction with the infinite spirit or God instead of being in harmony with Him. His struggles consist in flouting the will of God instead of being in tune with it. Consequently without realizing his true nature or God's true nature and the kinship between the two he goes on transmigrating into the endless cycle of births and deaths.

Thus, *avidyā* or nescience is the major factor for creating bondage. This is also called *ajñāna.* The concept of *avidyā* or nescience is found in almost all systems of Indian philosophy in one form or other. It is particularly to be found in the Advaita school of Vedanta propounded by Sankara. But there is a vital difference between the Dvaita concept of *avidyā* and the Advaita concept. According to Advaita, this *avidyā* is illusory and it withdraws as soon as the true nature of the soul as identical with Brahman is discovered. But according to Dvaita this *avidyā* is real. It is destroyed as soon as the true nature of God is realized. It is something like a curtain between God and the soul, and it conceals the nature of God from the soul. It also conceals the true spiritual nature of the soul until the soul removes it with spiritual efforts. It offers a double hindrance—namely, concealing the true nature of God and concealing the true nature of the soul. Such ignorance is not a mere illusion, but it is real nescience. The obstruction does not drop by itself but has to be removed by spiritual efforts. To distinguish this concept of *avidyā* from that of Advaita, it is designated *svabhāvajñāna* or natural nescience.

Next to *avidyā* the factor that is responsible for bondage is association with matter or *prakrtisambandha.* Every soul is associated with matter in the form of his subtle body and gross body. In addition, he is attracted toward external matter through the senses. The senses are so made that they naturally look outward and are attracted toward the material world. The soul forgets his own quality of innate bliss and begins to consider the sensous pleasures to be valuable in themselves. Naturally, then, he is affected by losses and gains in the world and suffers and enjoys accordingly. In order to seek sensuous pleasure he indulges in motivated activities or *kāmya-karma*(s) that bind him further. These motivated activities lead to morally good or bad results and build a store of sin or merit that leads to births and rebirths. There will be no end to this vicious circle unless and until the very root of it—namely, association with matter—is destroyed. This needs spiritual efforts.

Freedom of Will

While discussing the question of undertaking spiritual efforts—or, for that matter, any other effort by the soul—a moot point as to whether he has freedom of will at all has to be settled. This question arises because the soul is said to be entirely dependent on God. This is, in fact, a problem for all theistic thinkers, particularly for those who accept absolute supremacy of God. If God wills, then He will initiate the soul into the way of spiritual efforts. The soul's progress in it is also due to God's mercy; otherwise he would fail. The soul will attain liberation and reach the goal if God wills. In fact, it is God's will that is responsible both for bondage and for liberation. The other factors like *avidyā* or nescience, *prakrtisambandha* or the association with matter, *kāmyakarma* or motivated activities, etc. are merely the mechanics of the state of bondage. The real and ultimate ground is God's will. This would seem to leave the soul helpless both in respect of bondage and liberation. Hence, all talk of undertaking spiritual efforts could only be meaningless. Thus, the question of the freedom of will, its scope as well as its limitations, acquires some importance in this tradition.

It is true that the soul is entirely dependent on God in respect of the soul's very existence, functions, and knowledge (*svarūpa, pravṛtti, pramiti*). Without the directions of the indwelling God the soul cannot move. It is completely at His mercy in all respects. But God's scheme of things is well ordered and of the nature of grace itself. Each soul has its own innate inclinations according to its own innate nature. Souls are broadly of three natures. These are *sattvika* or of noble inclination, *rājasa* or of mixed inclination, and *tamasā* or of ignoble inclination. Being thus diversely inclined answers to the inherent natures of these souls and cannot be changed. Changing the very basic nature of these souls would amount to their destruction. Souls, however, are eternal; God does not desire to destroy or change them. He allows them to function as they are. Consequently, since the *rājasa* and *tamasā* souls are not inclined to attain any spiritual progress, they are left to themselves. Even in their worldly functions they move in wrong and ignoble directions, and they are allowed to function according to their basic inclinations. No doubt because of environmental influences sometimes they may move in better directions, but they cannot totally come out of their inherent inclinations. Similarly, *sāttvika* souls, in accordance with their innate nature and inherent inclinations, move toward noble directions. The innate nature is designated *yogyatā*, while the inherent inclination is called *vāsanā*. In tune with these two there takes place activity the beginning of which cannot be traced.

All souls and their activities are eternal. This is designated *anādikarma.*

21. Seṣasāye Viṣnu, The Cosmic Sleep, 615. Dasāvatāra Temple.

This chain of actions determines future actions. In order that souls may shape their own futures a certain amount of freedom of will is granted them by God. This is called *dattasvātantrya* or delegated freedom of will. Within the framework of God's overall will, the fact of innate nature and inherent inclinations, the timeless chain of activities and their moral consequences in terms of sin and merit, the soul has a certain amount of freedom of will to move in the right or wrong directions. If he undertakes moral and spiritual efforts to move toward nobility and spirituality his natural resources in terms of his *sāttvika* nature come to his help. Otherwise he has to rotate in transmigrations. Thus, though there is no absolute freedom of will for the souls in this tradition, Madhva grants a certain amount of delegated freedom of will to allow for the urge for moral and spiritual undertakings. This delegated freedom is without prejudice to the supremacy of God and His overall will guiding all activities of all beings. Within the framework of His overall supervision, variations are found in the behavior of different souls in different ways because of the difference in their innate nature and the use or misuse of the limited freedom given to them.

Spiritual Discipline

Eligibility

Who is eligible for spiritual emancipation? To say that only *sāttvika* souls are eligible is merely a doctrinal position, since nobody can know whether he is a *sāttvika* or not before he discovers his true nature. Therefore, everyone is *prima facie* eligible for undertaking efforts for spiritual progress. There are no social or intellectual restrictions for such eligibility. Whether one belongs to the upper social strata or the lower levels of social strata one is not debarred from eligibility. In fact, simpler methods are prescribed for those who are not learned.

Thus we see that in this tradition the right to worship God personally is made widely available to the devotee, irrespective of his caste and state of learning. The basic requirements for the seeker are three—knowledge, moral and temperamental refinement, and devotion (*adhyayana, sama, dama,* etc. and *bhakti*). In respect of the first—knowledge—the learned have to acquire knowledge through the Vedas or scripture, the men of middle level through the Epics and *Purāṇa*(s), and the men of the lower level, so-called, through the recitation of the name of God. These are termed *vedādhikāra, tantrādhikāra,* and *nāmādhikāra* respectively. All the same, there is no discrimination in the result. It is stated that irrespective of the fact whether one acquires knowledge of God through the Veda or the Epics or by the mere recitation of the name of God one will attain the same state provided he is sincere in his efforts. One result of this relaxation in respect of scriptural study was a vast amount of devotional literature in the native language of the region, that is, Kannaḍa. People of very humble social background attained spiritual progress and wrote inspiringly about their experiences. This literature is known as Haridāsa literature. Purandradāsa was the leader of this literary movement.

The second basic requirement of eligibility—moral and temperamental refinement (*sama, dama,* etc.)—is equally important. Unless one is morally good, one is not eligible for any spiritual undertaking. Any effort in the direction of spiritual progress necessarily presupposes a quality of detachment from sensuous pleasures and material life. Lapses in moral behavior presuppose too much involvement with material ends only; therefore, the two are incongruous. Similarly, anger, greed, hatred, etc. are also incompatible with spiritual life. Hence, cultivation of right temper and maintenance of moral discipline—*sama, dama,* and others—are laid down as one of the basic requirements of eligibility for spiritual effort.

The third requirement, devotion (*bhakti*), the love of God, is most important. Devotion is not conceived of merely as a kind of emotional attachment or mere love in the usual sense. It has a metaphysical and spiritual implication. God and soul are akin to each other in their spiritual content. Like magnetic attraction they have a natural tendency to pull toward each other. This is prevented by *avidyā*. But as the soul goes on practicing *bhakti* or devotion, this obstruction of *avidyā* is slowly weakened and ultimately removed. Therefore, *bhakti* is a necessary requirement for eligibility. Knowledge is intellectual; moral and temperamental refinement is ethical and psychological; and *bhakti* is spiritual, though initially it is also psychological. Thus, the eligibility for spiritual undertakings requires some amount of initial capacity in these three areas. These have to be fully developed in due course.

Means of Spiritual Emancipation

Among the means to be adopted for spiritual progress, detachment (*vairāgya*) is crucial. This is not a negative concept of rejecting worldly things and worldly life, developing a kind of disgust for them. It is an attitude toward valuing each thing according to its worth. It is a value-oriented attitude. Normally one is more attached to his body, his kin, property, and a host of worldly things appropriated as "his," ignoring his own immediate worth as a spiritual entity to the neglect of the possibility of finding joy in himself. This makes him have a disproportionate love and admiration for worldly things, and he feels let down when he is not able to secure these. This leads to disgust and dejection in life. Overcoming this by correctly evaluating the worth of things is *vairāgya.* To be excessively attached is *rāga,* whereas to relate without clinging is *vairāgya.* One has to realize that spiritual joy is higher than material sensuous pleasure. God is the highest repository of spiritual joy. The more the soul is in tune with God the more he realizes his own innate bliss. Therefore, to realize that God is the highest object of love and none else is *vairāgya.* It is a necessary corollary and an aid to *bhakti.*

Karmacaturaṅga or the Fourfold Scheme of Karma

This raises the question of what is the role of *karma* or activity. If the things of this world and the life here is of an inferior nature, is it not better to run away from these activities and this life? Here, again, it is not a question of either continuing with worldly activities or rejecting them, because activities are inescapable. It is a question of having a proper perspective on one's activities. The activities duly incumbent on a person have to be carried out. One does not have a choice of engaging in activity or remaining idle, but one may certainly discard self-centered motives and the arrogance of thinking oneself to be the sole master of one's destiny. Activity with narrow motives is *sakāma-karma* and a hindrance to spiritual progress. Activity without narrow motives is *niṣkāma-karma* and a help to spiritual progress. The Madhva tradition has put forward a unique concept of *karmayoga.* Mere performance of prescribed duties is not *karmayoga.* It has to have a foundation of right knowledge. That is, the knowledge that God is the sole director of all activities. This awareness alone can eliminate all selfish desires motivating engagements in the world and can give an ethical and spiritual content to one's activities. Moreover, the results obtained through these activities loosen the hold of the personal element so that they can be dedicated to God. Thus, the *karmayoga* in this tradition has four important aspects: (1) knowledge or the awareness that the foundation of all activities is divine (*jñāna*); (2) selflessness in motivations (*saṁnyāsa* or *saṃkalpa sannyāsa*); (3) performance of prescribed duties (*vihita karma anusṭhāna*); (4) dedication (*tyāga* or offering of results at the feet of God). This fourfold scheme is known as *karmacaturaṅga.* Madhva has formulated the *karmayoga* of the *Bhagavadgītā* in this way in his commentaries on the *Gītā.* This *karmayoga* is not totally divorced from *jñāna yoga,* nor is it opposed to it. Performance of one's prescribed duties in this way actually helps spiritual progress. Thus, active life is not opposed to spiritual life, provided one maintains the right perspective on it.

Worship and Meditation

The next step in the spiritual efforts of a seeker is *upāsana* or worship and meditation. Worship consists of various *vidyā*(s) such as *prāṇavidyā, Vaisvānara-vidyā, dahara vidyā, madhuvidyā, pancāgnīvidyā, Puruṣa vidyā,* etc. These have esoteric significance and provide knowledge of the Divine Person in different ways. In the tradition of Madhva, these are not considered to be lower levels of worship. They are part and parcel of the process of spiritual experiences and ultimately lead to spiritual emancipation.

The worship of various images and symbols is also recognized by Madhva, as, for example, the important symbolic syllable, *AUM.* In fact, this symbol represents the entire collection of Vedic hymns and all the auspicious attributes of God. The name Brahman is also a symbol of worship, and so are many other names. Mind, sun, ether, etc. are also symbols, but the important point to be borne in mind is that they are not to be substituted for God. *Upaniṣad*(s) list various symbols to be adopted in different contexts, such as stone and bronze images (*pratimā, sālagrama,* etc.). It may be said that whatever evokes the remembrance of God in the devotee may be used as a symbol of worship. Such of the symbols that are being hallowed by the authority of scriptures are naturally conducive to the awakening of religious fervor. Madhva, by lending his authority to the worship of images, widened the scope of devotional worship for every individual. On this one thread were strung the many flowers of the Veda(s), *Upaniṣad*(s), Epics, and *Purāṇa*(s). He solidified the tradition of devotional worship by bringing the entire sweep under the same rubric. The devotional worship of God may be viewed from three aspects: One may meditate on God (1) as if present within the seeker's heart, (2) as if present in front of the devotee, and (3) as if present everywhere (*aṅtaḥ, bahiḥ, sarvagatatvena*). Further, those who are engaged in sacrifices worship God through fire; those who are engaged in yogic practices worship at heart; those who are still in initial stages worship through images; and those who are awakened worship Him everywhere. These three aspects are not mutually exclusive. Those who are engaged in Vedic sacrifices worship God as Fire and may also see Him everywhere. Those who are engaged in yogic practices worship Him in their heart, but they may also be engaged in the worship of images. The enlightened seeker knows that God is everywhere and in everything.

This tradition does not favor *nirguṇopāsanā*, "worship of and meditation on God as devoid of all attributes." On the contrary, it insists on the meditation on God as possessing an infinite number of auspicious attributes. A seeker may not hope to encompass even a few of the qualities of God, let alone an infinity of attributes; therefore, one may choose for oneself one or more attributes especially suited for one's own meditation. According to this scheme those who are capable of meditating on only one attribute are advised to select the attribute *ātma*, which suggests *svāmitva*, "overlordship." The seeker would continuously meditate on God as his overlord. This enables him to realize his own dependence on God and his intimate relationship with God. It indicates his true nature. It slowly weakens the influence of ignorance, and the whole process of spiritual progress can set in.

Those who are a little more advanced may meditate on four attributes suggested by the terms *sat*, *cit*, *ānanda*, and *ātma*. This would be to approach a little closer to the realization of the true nature of God. The spiritual content of both God and the soul is constituted of these qualities, namely, *sat*, *cit*, and *ānanda*. By the concentrated meditation on these, the soul will gradually acquire the knowledge of the akinness of his own nature and Divine nature. The gradual withdrawal of *avidyā* permits the seeker to select further attributes for meditation. He thus encompasses in his knowledge as many attributes of the infinite number as he is capable of bringing within his spiritual vision. The human soul must stop short of the full knowledge of God. It is only Brahmā the four-faced god, also a seeker in this tradition, who is entitled to the meditation on all attributes of Viṣṇu or Nārāyaṇa, the supreme God.

The Concept of Bhakti

Bhakti has already been mentioned as an essential requirement of eligibility for spiritual pursuits. This has to be intensified step by step. It was also mentioned above that *bhakti* is not merely an emotional formulation. It is not mere love of God. It is love of God based on the understanding of the greatness of God. The more one knows God the more one loves Him. The more one loves God the more one knows Him. Thus, knowledge and love are interwoven in the concept of *bhakti*. They are inseparable. The knowledge of God arises in two stages, *parokṣa* (mediate) and *aparokṣa* (immediate). Knowledge obtained through scriptures, through reasoning, etc. is mediate, whereas knowledge directly obtained without the intervention of senses and other means is immediate. According to this tradition the soul has an inbuilt capacity to know certain things directly. This is known as *svarupendriya*, the very self, the knower, who is also the instrument of knowledge. The mediate knowledge of God through the scriptures etc. arises at the initial stages of *bhakti*. This knowledge enhances *bhakti*, which in turn increases knowledge. At each stage it is the grace of God that brings about the consolidations that intensify the seeker's *bhakti* and raises him to a higher plane of knowledge.

The stages of *bhakti* are termed *bhakti, pakvabhakti, paripakvabhakti,* and *atiparipakva bhakti* (devotion, ripened devotion, mature devotion, and fully mature devotion). It is after the third stage of *bhakti* that the seeker is ready for immediate knowledge (*aparokṣa jñāna*) of God. The fourth stage enables him to attain liberation by obtaining the grace of God.

It has already been pointed out that God–the infinite spirit–and the soul–the finite spirit–are related as *bimba-pratibimba,* that is, as archetype and prototype. Both have the same spiritual content of *sat, cit,* and *ānanda.* They are akin to each other and are intimately related, as the soul is *entirely dependent on God in respect of its very essential nature.* But the two are kept away from each other by *avidyā* during transmigration. The soul is unaware of its akinness to God. This state of alienation has to be changed. *Bhakti* being a kind of magnetic drive on the part of the soul toward God, it helps the soul to reach God, enables him to receive the grace of God and to realize His true nature and to know himself as totally subservient to God. This magnetic contact between God and soul continues even after liberation, because *bhakti* at this stage is no longer a mere means. It is an end in itself. Love of God on the part of a liberated soul is an end and not a means. Therefore, now it is called *sādhya bhakti, bhakti* as the terminus of the spiritual journey.

Guru–The Preceptor

In the Indian tradition, guidance from an appropriate preceptor is most important for progress in spiritual life. Madhva has particularly emphasized the role of the preceptor. He himself is believed to be an incarnation of the wind-god Vāyu, who is held to be the chief preceptor for all in this tradition. Vāyu is more specifically known as *prāṇa* (breath of life) or mukhya-prāṇa, the chief sustainer of life. So a life of spiritual endeavor is replete with a galaxy, as it were, of preceptors. All are teachers (*aniyata guru*) who impart knowledge to the seeker in some way or other, but his special preceptor, the "invariable" one (*niyataguru*), also appears to him at the appointed time.

Ordinarily, in our day-to-day efforts we come in contact with many preceptors who impart initial instructions and create a thirst for spiritual knowledge. But in the course of time, when one's thirst is intensified, one reaches or rather recognizes the appointed preceptor and gets his guidance. By appointed preceptors are meant those who will know the spiritual strength of the seeker and will impart instructions in those forms of worship and meditation which can be carried out by that particular seeker. The Madhva tradition has drawn up a scheme of the hierarchy of souls on the basis of their spiritual capacity. Those who are at a higher level may act as preceptors for the beginners, *Vāyu* (mukhyaprāṇa) being the supreme preceptor for all.

Direct Knowledge of God

By practicing the spiritual exercises detailed above, the seeker attains *aparokṣa jñāna,* the immediate knowledge of God. He will have a vision of that form of God which is *bimba* or the archetype for him. Though God is nonmaterial and, therefore, formless in the material sense of the term, he can assume forms with his miraculous power (*acintyaśakti*) and reveal Himself to the seeker. This *aparokṣa jñāna* or the direct vision of God is not to be identified with the mental image adopted by the seeker during meditation. This is accompanied by a kind of brilliance unique to itself. The magnitude of this brilliance goes on increasing according to the receptive capacity of each seeker. Starting from the magnitude of ten lamps it goes beyond the magnitude of a hundred suns. It is against the background of this flood of light that God reveals himself to the seeker. Sometimes the devotee may see only the feet, sometimes the arms with the emblems *sankha* (conch), *cakra* (disk), etc., and sometimes the smiling face. God in His mercy chooses thus to disclose His majestic form in glimpses, as it were, so that the seeker may not be overwhelmed. This *aparokṣa jñāna* (or the direct vision) is not continuous, because the soul cannot bear the full impact of it; but after liberation it is uninterrupted and the soul is forever in the presence of God.

Sravaṇa (hearing), *manana* (contemplation), *nididhyāsana* (meditation) are generally accepted as the three steps that lead to this direct vision of God. In this tradition *sravaṇa* is not mere listening. It is the knowledge of the glory of God acquired through the scriptures and from the preceptor. *Manana* is rational analysis of the knowledge thus obtained. *Nididhyāsana* is meditation leading to *aparokṣa jñāna* or direct vision of God. It is this direct vision brought about by *bhakti* which, coupled with the grace of God (*prasāda*), leads to liberation or spiritual emancipation.

Spiritual Emancipation

The Madhva tradition recognizes four steps in the process of liberation: *karmakṣaya,* discontinuation of the chain of activity; *utkrānti,* the soul coming out of the body; *mārga,* travel to the higher world; and *bhoga,* enjoying the bliss. A vision of God withers away all past deeds. They are no longer effective as causes for any more births and deaths. This is known as the stage of *karmakṣaya,* whereupon the soul is ready to leave the body. The next step is therefore *utkrānti* or the process of being liberated from the material body. The soul not separated from God even in death and with the breath of life (*prāṇa*) leaves the body through the *brahmarandhra*, a point at the center of the head. The liberated soul emerges amid waves of light.

After *utkrānti*, or coming out of the body, the soul has to travel from this mortal world to a higher plane or Brahmaloka. This is called *mārga*. According to Indian tradition, the soul traverses a number of subtle worlds of elements arranged in a hierarchy. It commences from *arci*, the realm of pure light. Then intervenes a world of wind or atmosphere called *ātivāhika*. This is followed by a series of worlds of light bearing the names of days, half of the month, half of the year, year, etc., thereby indicating the level of their light year. The worlds of the sun and moon are also on this path. The world of *dhruva* (pole star) is also mentioned. Ultimately the soul to be liberated reaches Brahmaloka and waits for the appointed time of liberation. This journey of the soul is common to all traditions. Usually three ways are mentioned: *devayāna*, *pitṛyāna*, and *brahmayāna*. The path described above is *devayāna*, meant for those who are to be liberated. *Pitṛyāna* is the path for such departed souls that are to return to this mortal world again for rebirth. This is also known as the *dhūmādi mārga* or the smoky path. *Devayāna* is also known as *arcirādimārga* or the path of light. The third, *brahmayāna*, is not really a route, but it is a state of directly reaching the realm of the supreme God.

Realization of Spiritual Joy

The fourth and the final stage of spiritual emancipation is *bhoga* or enjoying spiritual bliss. The soul is of the nature of bliss itself. Bliss is innate to it and inherent in it. It was eclipsed by *avidyā* and the effects of matter in the form of subtle and gross bodies. Now the soul, being freed both from the body and *avidyā*, is capable of enjoying his own innate nature of bliss. The soul is now completely in harmony with God's will and sees himself in the relation of *bimba-pratibimba* to God. The bliss of the soul is but a reflection of the bliss of God. It is made enjoyable by his devotion to God. Each soul enjoys its bliss to its fullest capacity. Thus, the concept of liberation in Madhva tradition is positive. It does not subscribe to nihilism. God and the liberated soul are eternally in each other's presence. God Himself enjoins upon the souls His will to engage them in His activity. To some He grants the state of *sālokya*, that is, those who remain in one or the other world in order to help other seekers. We know them as great saints. Second, some are given the state of *sāmīpya*, that is, proximity to God, and they attend upon Him. Third, some attain *sārūpya*; that is, they assume forms similar to Him. Finally, some attain *sāyujya*, that is, those who are united with Him and enjoy spiritual bliss. These categories are common to other schools of Vedanta also and are slightly differently interpreted here.

The most important category that emerges out of this tradition of devotion is the concept of dependence on God. The human soul sojourning in this world is called upon to awaken himself and look upon the beauteous and majestic form of God, who is forever awaiting the return of His creature to His own presence to experience forever the bliss of liberation.

Devotional Literature in Kannaḍa

The devotional songs of Purandradāsa in Kannaḍa, the native language, popularized a whole new trend of religious literature and are a special feature of this tradition. This came to be known as Haridāsa literature. Purandradāsa was supported by Kanakadāsa, another great devotee and poet. The songs of Vijayadāsa and Jagannāthadāsa are also very popular. Haridāsa literature is still a living tradition in Karnātaka. Jagannāthadāsa's *Harīkathāmṛtasāra* (eighteenth century) is still read and recited by a large section of the populace. The spring of devotion for God tapped by Madhva became a broad flowing river in the Dāsa literature of this tradition.

Bibliography

Sources

Madhva. *Brahmasutrabhasya* with TP and Marathi translation. Edited by Raddi Rangacharya. Poona, 1926.

——. *Brhadaranyaka Upanisad Bhasya.* Sarvamula Edition. Belgaum.

——. *Chandogya Upanisad Bhasya.* Sarvamula Edition. Belgaum.

——. *Gitabhasya.* Sarvamula Edition. Belgaum.

——. *Gitatatparyanirnaya.* Sarvamula Edition. Belgaum.

——. *Nyayavivaranam.* Sarvamula Edition. Belgaum.

——. *Tattvasamkhyana.* Sarvamula Edition. Belgaum.

Subbarao, S. *Translation of Madhva's Brahmasūtra Bhāṣya.* Madras, 1904.

Studies

Dasgupta, S. N. *A History of Indian Philosophy,* Vol. 4. Cambridge, 1961.

Sharma, B. N. K. *The Brahmasutras and Their Principal Commentaries.* 3 vols. Bombay: Bharatiya Vidya Bhavan, 1971, 1973, 1979.

——. *History of Dvaita School of Vedanta and Its Literature.* 2 vols. Bombay, 1960–61.

——. *Madhva's Teachings in His Own Words.* 2nd ed. Bombay: Bharatiya Vidya Bhavan, 1970.

——. *Philosophy of Sri Madhvacharya.* Bombay: Bharatiya Vidya Bhavan, 1962.

Part Seven

SPIRITUALITY AND HUMAN LIFE

16

Spirituality and Nature

Klaus K. Klostermaier

Generous nature brings about by
manifold means the good of the spirit.
Īśvarakṛṣṇa, *Sāṁkhyakārika* 60

In both the East and the West, traditional religion has been identified with institutional authority and revealed scripture, with sacred ritual and defined doctrine. At the same time in both cultures attempts have persistently been made to reach the transcendent through introspection and through an investigation of the depth dimension of nature. It is with such attempts that the present essay is concerned. Apart from demonstrating that the investigation of nature has been a major concern in Indian tradition, our concern is to describe a "spiritual science" which could be revitalized and which might be appealing to those who find themselves unable to follow the paths of traditional religions.

Nature as Spiritual Guide and Teacher

Anyone familiar with the epic and dramatic literature of India will recall numerous vivid and loving descriptions of nature offered therein. The beauty of the forest through which Rāmā and Sītā proceeded, the peace and tranquillity of the famous hermitages visited by the Pāṇḍava(s), the greatness of the Himalayas, and the awesomeness of the Vindhyas are immortalized in beautifully articulated language. Students of comparative literature have remarked on the richness of the vocabulary employed in these descriptions of nature, the astonishingly great number of species of fauna and flora identified by name and described in detail. Surely, Indian writers have not been unaware of the beauty and greatness of nature—a nature so luxuriant in many parts of the country as to be almost without comparison. This variegated nature serves as the background of human drama and as scaffolding for divine intervention in history.

Over and against this, the way in which nature is seen as a spiritual guide to humanity, as related in an episode in the *Bhāgavata Purāṇa* (11.7.9) (abbreviated as BhP), appears intriguing. A young ascetic, identified in another passage as Dattātreya (BhP 2.7.4), relates how he had adopted nature as guide to wisdom and liberating knowledge. The account of the teachings of the "twenty-four guru(s)" is prefaced by words put into the mouth of the Lord: The investigators of the true nature of the world are uplifted by their own efforts in this world. The self is the infallible guide of the self: through direct perception and through analogy one can work out one's salvation.[1] It is suggested that "true knowledge of nature" leads to "true knowledge of self and God." The twenty-four guru(s) from nature, which Dattātreya has chosen to follow, induce him to adopt practices and rules for his life which reaffirm his ideal of *saṁnyāsa* and through it contribute to his liberation. Nature acts precisely as the human guru does: proposing through words and by example a path leading to insight and realization. A sampling from the lengthy text will suffice to make the point.

The *earth* has taught Dattātreya steadfastness and the wisdom to realize that all things, while pursuing their own activities, do nothing but follow the divine laws which are universally established. Furthermore, the earth has taught him that existence in a body is a being-for-others (*parārtha*) to be lived out in humility and forbearance. *Fire*, too, is an excellent teacher and an example for the ascetic, being "full of splendour and made brighter by the glow of *tapas* . . . not sullied by what is consumed . . . sometimes hidden, sometimes visible, assuming the shape of the fuel which it consumes, burning up past and future sin . . ." (BhP 11.9.27ff.). The *honeybee* teaches the student to go out and collect the essence from all scriptures. It also provides a negative lesson: Do not hoard any food. To substantiate this part of the bee's teachings, the text recounts a popular story about a bee who perished together with its stored-up supply of food.

Finally, Dattātreya learns the most decisive lesson from his *own body:* "This body, subject to birth and death and constantly and ultimately a source of affliction, is my guru as it prompts me to renunciation and discrimination. Though it helps me to contemplate, it really belongs to others. Realizing this I am going forth, renouncing all."

Thus, through physics, biology, anthropology, and psychology, Dattātreya has reached a stage of wisdom which makes him aware of "the true nature of things" and delivers him from any need to transform nature into consumer goods.

In all of this, there is no diminishing of the stature of the human being and no denying the person's very special destiny. The Creator, we are told in the beginning, was not satisfied after having created a great variety of beings. "He rejoiced only when he had created the human body endowed with reason and capable of realizing the Supreme Deity. Having, after many births in this world, acquired the rare human body, however frail, which is still the means of attaining the object of life, a wise man should speedily strive to attain liberation, before this body, constantly subjected to annihilation, is detroyed. The enjoyment of sense pleasures can be had in all species."

Nature as Helpmate of the Spirit

Sāṁkhya stands out among the classical *darśana*(s) (systems of philosophy) as the one most concerned with nature and the evolution of matter. By many it is considered to be the oldest system. It does not refer to scriptural authority; however, many of its basic tenets have been assimilated into mainstream Hindu philosophy and religion: Sāṁkhya has supplied the terminology of *puruṣa* (spirit) and *prakṛti* (matter, nature), of the three *guṇa*(s) (constituents, qualities), the classification of elements and senses. Its overriding concern, as it declares quite explicitly, is the liberation of the spirit.

The fact that it did not include Vedic (or Vedantic) texts and did not offer interpretations of such may have been responsible for its lack of appeal to an age when the word of scripture was declared the only and supreme authority in matters of the spirit.[2] This in turn may be one of the attractive features of the system for us today. It has been noted by all scholars who have worked on Sāṁkhya that on the one hand we have abundant references to Sāṁkhya (and Yoga) in the *Mahābhārata* and in the major *Purāṇa*(s), where quite often Sāṁkhya is used as a generic name for speculative wisdom and systematic thought, and where Kapila appears as *the* teacher of salvation, while on the other hand the classical texts (mainly the *Sāṁkhyasutra*(s) and the *Sāṁkhyakārika*(s) with their commentaries) offer disappointingly little evidence for the greatness of this *darśana.*[3] Especially in the crucial area of linking the liberation effort with detailed analysis of nature, they exhaust themselves in a few general cryptic remarks. Also Yoga, as expounded by Patañjali, does not give us much of a clue. The widespread opinion that Yoga offers the practice based on Sāṁkhya theory is mistaken: although Yoga has adopted, as have most Indian *darśana*(s), a certain amount of technical terminology from Sāṁkhya, the Sāṁkhya as represented in the classical texts could *not* possibly have been its theoretical basis.[4] Moreover, the epic and Purāṇic texts make it quite clear that Sāṁkhya by itself was a path to the liberation of the spirit and not just in conjunction with Yoga.[5]

Thus, in the following essay an attempt has been made to utilize Sāṁkhya passages from the *Mahābhārata* and the *Bhāgavata Purāṇa* to supply details that are not found in the existing *kārikā*(s) and *sūtra*(s).

The *Sāṁkhyakārikā*(s) are fairly cryptic in their account of how a knowledge of nature can become the way to the liberation of the spirit. They contain the remark that "the evolution from *mahat* down to specific elements . . . is for the sake of the liberation of each mind . . . in spite of its apparently being for the sake of nature herself" (*Kārika* 59). Thus, a certain self-transcendence is assumed to be built into nature—the subjectivity of nature linking up with the subjectivity in humanity in constituting the purpose of the evolution of the universe. The subjectivity of nature ceases to play a role for humanity if and when it has fulfilled its purpose.

The *Bhāgavata Purāṇa* has a more detailed and more interesting version of this process, presenting it as a double reflection which leads the spirit back into its own interiority—nature being the medium in which the reflection of the spirit is broken:

> Just as a reflection of the sun in water is discovered with the help of a reflection of that reflection on the wall of the house, and the sun in the heavens can be seen with the help of its own reflection in water, even so the threefold ego is revealed through its reflections on the body, the senses and the mind; and through the ego which contains a reflection of the Spirit is seen God, who is possessed of true wisdom, is absolutely free from egotism and keeps awake even when the subtle elements get merged in the Unmanifest on account of sleep. (BhP 3.27.2ff.)

In reply to the question of how the mind, which is inexorably intertwined with nature, could ever become free from the dominance of the *guṇa*(s), the text replies that as consequence of spiritual practice "*prakṛti* which binds the soul gradually withdraws even as a stick, used to kindle fire, is consumed by the very fire which it produces. . . ."

Sāṁkhya, which devotes so much space to the inquiry into the nature of nature, does not aim at appropriating nature through the senses, or their extension in technology, and it does not cultivate instrumental reason, the tool of such appropriation. The proper attitude for this science of nature is, the texts suggest, detachment from the sense appetites, so as to let the subjectivity of nature appear as it is, before it has been distorted by human interference. This science aims at a knowledge of nature, not at its use.

In its most generic sense, "nature," understood as "*prakṛti*," is not seen as "substance" to which certain qualities are added; rather, it is defined as an "equilibrium of three *guṇa*(s)" without particular name or form. The very choice of the "qualities" universally identified with nature and their applicability to human nature seem to be further proof that Sāṁkhya deals with the subjectivity of nature rather than its objectivity.

The similarity between Sāṁkhya and Pythagorean teachings has been noted before. Out of the Pythagorean fascination with numbers, regular geometric figures, proportions, and correspondences, and via Plato and the Neoplatonists, there grew our mathematics-based modern natural science. The most obvious parallelism between Sāṁkhya and Pythagoras is seen in the centrality of the number five. While the thoroughgoing fascination with numbers (as G. Larson has well shown)[6] in general probably has something to do with the effort to accommodate a variety of phenomena in a grid composed of five-times-five principles, it also hints at a preoccupation (very obvious in Pythagoras) with the Golden Section, so crucial and central in nature.[7] Mathematics provides us with an instrument to envision unity behind the diversity of the phenomena. The liberation of the spirit does come from the contemplation of nature as a whole as Oneness: that is the point of "system," of a "theory" which has to be intuited as a whole and not merely studied piece by piece.

Sāṁkhya aims at the liberation of the spirit by leading it to experience the subjectivity of nature, by actualizing nature's own "better side," its *sattva* quality, and not by interfering with it.

Nature as Mirror Image of the Spirit

What distinguishes the modern scientific inquiry into the nature of nature from Vedanta is a very different orientation in thinking, a different interest. Whereas Vedanta is interested in finding out about what nature *is* in relation to consciousness, modern science wants to find out how it works. It was as clear to the medieval Indian Vedantins as it is to modern Western scientists that "to perform activities the world need not be thought real" (*Pañcadaśī* IX.89). The Vedantic tradition, at whose core is *viveka* (differentiation, reflective contemplation) and which at the same time insists on the oneness of reality, represents a path of liberation through nature, a fulfillment of the human person's own destiny worked out not over and against the exploration of nature but through it.

The experiments which Śvetaketu is asked to perform by his father Uddālaka Aruṇī, dividing a fig, dividing the seeds, mixing salt and water, tasting the mix, quite clearly combine instrumental and reflective analysis of nature. From the question What do you see? the questioner leads to the problem of Where does it come from? and What is it? From an examination of what appears to be part of the external world the question leads to an investigation of the self.[8]

Meanwhile, we have learned to see a great deal inside the seed of the fig; where Śvetaketu could see nothing at all, we see the fine material structure of the cell, the cygotes, the molecules of the amazingly numerous substances, etc. And what Uddālaka Āruṇi considered the atom, has become the subject of big-science research, which finds ever smaller subatomic particles.

Could we still make the transition from physics to meta-physics which the *Upaniṣad*(s) suggest? The readiness to explain the no-longer visible as the source of the visible, to identify the invisible with the all and this with the Self, is no longer there. The theory preceding the actual research evidently determines the results. Where Śvetaketu finds fulfillment and meaning, transcending the object of investigation, the sophisticated contemporary finds meaninglessness and inner emptiness.

Obviously the original experiment is too naïve and too questionable; classical Advaita Vedanta developed a more sophisticated path of liberation through nature. Vidyāraṇya has laid it out in his *Pañcadaśī*[9] in an intriguing manner.

He connects with the Upaniṣadic "experiments" and provides additional support for the transcendence, counteracting a thoroughly worked out anti-metaphysical position.[10] This naturalistic ("scientific") position falls short of a total explanation of the world in terms of causality operating on physical realities. Vidyāraṇya would probably find fairly wide agreement with his observation, "Even if all the learned people of the world try to determine the nature of the world they will find themselves confronted at some stage or other by ignorance" (PD 6.134). While we have an immense body of scientific knowledge concerning details of the working of organisms, we do not have a satisfactory answer to Vidyāraṇya's question, "Tell us, if you can, how the body and the senses came out of the seed, or how consciousness was born in the fetus?" (PD 6.144). The fourteenth-century Indian naturalist's answer—"It is the nature of the seed to evolve into a body with its sense-organs and so forth"—an answer which Vidyāraṇya found unsatisfactory, has not been essentially improved on, and Vidyāraṇya's rejoinder is still valid: "What is the basis of your belief? . . . In the end you will have to say: 'I do not know!' "

At this point Vidyāraṇya begins with his "ultimate" explanation. He employs the term *indrajāla*, "Indra's net," as descriptive of the nature of the physical world.[11] What can be more magical (*indrajālamaparam*) than the fact that the seed in the uterus becomes a conscious individual, that it develops a head, hands, feet, and other organs, that it passes through the states of childhood, youth, and old age, and that it perceives, eats, smells, hears, comes, and goes? (PD 6.147).

Among those who believed that they had all the answers were the medieval Indian logicians. Vidyāraṇya says that although they themselves may be satisfied with their logical explanations, he is not. The nature of the world is not accessible to the rational mind: being so (*acintya*), it cannot fall under the canons of logic. Logic, he says elsewhere, is secondary with regard to experience; logic can at best examine the description of an experience, it cannot create or replace experience as the basic mode of (intellectual) awareness (PD 5.30).

The "seed" (*bīja*) of the world which is thus found to be neither accessible to natural science nor to logic (*acintya*) is termed *māyā*. This *māyā* (a term that is used already in some later Upaniṣadic texts)[12] is circumscribed by Vidyāraṇya on the basis of a depth insight: the apparently contradictory statements that are being made preempt the notion that *māyā* could ever be used either for a naturalistic or a logical explanation of the world.

In deep sleep (*suṣupti*), he claims, we are experiencing *māyābīja*. Deep sleep is the "implicate" form of waking and dreaming, as the seed is the "implicate" form of the tree.[13]

Māyā contains the *vāsanā*(s) ("impressions," potential developments, natural laws?) of the entire universe (PD 6.152). Consciousness reflects (actively) in these states (namely, waking and dreaming) the mental imprints (*buddhi-vāsana*). That seed in association with this reflection emerges in the form of intellect (*dhī*). In the mind (*buddhau*), the consciousness reflection (*cidābhāsa*) is unclearly reflected. This view of things, nature being grounded and contained in an entity neither scientifically nor logically ascertainable and manageable, should not create the impression that we are talking about an "illusion" in the everyday world. Vidyāraṇya is as aware as any of us that "nobody has the power to alter the world of waking and dream states" (PD 6.160). Individual persons as well as the Lord (God) himself are "reflections (*ābhāsa*) in *māyā* of *ātman*." Its reality obviously is accessible only through a third path, a sensibility not employed in science or logic. Between *Īśvara* and *Māyā* there is a kind of mutuality (both being ultimately *acintya*!): *Īśvara* is the *māyā*-reflection of consciousness and at the same time its inner ruler (*antaryāmin*), omniscient (*sarvajña*), and womb of the world (*jagadyoni*).[14]

The Lord, as the "bliss-sheath," is the carrier of all *vāsanā*(s) (information, potentials) of all living beings (PD 6.161): that is his "omniscience." As all-pervading, he is also "all-supporting" (*sarvopādāna,* material cause of the universe) (PD 6.165). He is detectable as "Inner Ruler" through an analysis of the fine structure of the universe: "Where the progress from the subtle to the subtler stops, there do we confront the Inner Ruler" (PD 6.166). "Being minuter than the minute of the second and third degree, the inmost being is not subject to perception; but by deduction and *śruti* his existence is ascertained."

This Lord is the source of the universe (*jagadyoni*), insofar as to him are due the "manifestation" (*āvirbhāva*) and "demanifestation" (*tirobhāva*) of the world. "The world (*jagat*) remains 'implicate' in the Lord. He creates it according to the *karma*(s) of living beings" (PD 6.183). As waking and sleeping complement each other, cancel each other out, but presuppose (each in different ways) someone who is awake or asleep, so also creation and destruction of the universe are complementary and related to an overarching ground.

Obviously Vidyāraṇya is not interested in *māyā* for the sake of *māyā*. *Mukti,* liberation, is the theme and "liberation can only be reached through knowledge of *brahmatattva* (reality of brahman). One's dreaming does not come to an end without one's waking up." This juxtaposition is quite crucial: one cannot dream a dream to its end. Awaking, the only possible end of a dream, is a different condition of being. The dream metaphor is expanded when we are told that "this entire world, *Īśvara* (God), *jīva*(s) (souls), animate and inanimate objects, is a dream in the non-dual *brahma*-reality" (PD 6.211). In a further specification, the whole world is described as a projection of *Māyā* brought forth by *Īśvara* (*ānandamaya*) and Jīva (*vijñānamaya*), and then reprojected on *māyā*. The range of *Īśvara* projection reaches from the desire to create, up to the entering into his own creation; the range of the *jīva* projection spans from waking to release. The obvious paradox is probably intended: the seeming contradiction of externalizing oneself in a visible effect and interiorizing the effect by "entering" it as it were from outside.

Vidyāraṇya (with the sound Advaita tradition behind him) is not declaring that the insight into the utimate nonduality of nature translates into a transcending of the natural laws as far as the body is concerned. He also does not suggest that one has to reverse one's entire thinking: both duality and non-duality are partially known (PD 6.243), and we experience daily that the nature of the world is mysterious (*acintya*) (PD 6.252). While consciousness (the goal) is *acintya* too, it is eternal (*nitya*) over against the momentary character of *māyā*. Also, ontologically the experience of non-duality precedes duality.

The instrument to liberation/enlightenment is *viveka* (discerning vision), a kind of "rationality" which the materialists and the logicians are lacking. It is a "metaphysical sensibility" which cuts, as it were, at a right angle into

22. Lady offering worship to the Pipal Tree.

the infinite plane of *māyā*-derived "reality." It is, finally, nature which, as mirror image of *brahman*, provides all the crucial insights; it is, for instance, through the discovery of the *acintya* aspect of *māyā* that a person realizes the insufficiency of linear logic and a materialistic explanation of reality. It is the realization of the ultimate oneness of *māyā* which directs human awareness to the crucial insight that Reality is One and Undivided. It is the perception of different levels in the phenomenal world which leads the mind to the decisive understanding of degrees of consciousness. It is, finally, the mirror-image quality of nature which in a dialectic makes the spirit find its own reality in itself.

This is not the place to reexamine the vast Advaita Vedanta polemics against Sāṁkhya.[15] A doubt may be raised, however, whether Sāṁkhya is as unqualifiedly dualistic as Advaita contends and whether Advaita is really unqualifiedly monistic. The terminology of the *tattva*(s) (in plural), the reference to irreducibles in the form of *prakṛti* and *puruṣa* and similar matters, makes it quite clear that Sāṁkhya does not fit the Advaita maxim of *brahman satyam jagat mithyā* (brahman is real, the world is false). But this prejudices the issue in favor of a certain terminology. After all, there is a link between *prakṛti* and *puruṣa* without which they could not interact: the "quality" of matter-nature which corresponds to the quality of spirit-nature, the *sattva*, "goodness," in which the spirit discovers itself. It is the "goodness of nature" which helps the spirit attain its own liberation.

On the other hand, does not the (necessary) assumption in Advaita, of two tiers of reality and truth, the *vyavahārika* and the *paramārthika* realms, introduce a dualism far more trenchant and irrevocable than any Sāṁkhya *puruṣa-prakṛti* dualism ever did? Sāṁkhya has a bridge to connect its two "ultimates"; Advaita has none and can maintain its monism only by denying reality to one side of the world.

The opinion, expressed before, that the decline of Sāṁkhya as religion was due to a (fifth-century?) identification of religion with scriptural truth is confirmed by the treatment which Sankara accords to Sāṁkhya in his *Śarīrakabhāṣya:* the first and major objection to the Sāṁkhya conception of *pradhāna* is that it is not "scriptural."[16] Rāmānuja, although taking over much more Sāṁkhya theory than Sankara, agrees on this point.[17]

Nature as Body of God

The *Ṛg Veda*, the most ancient document of Hindu religion, refers to *puruṣa*, the primeval cosmic being, as the source and origin not only of the physical universe but also of religion and the social order. Quite clearly everything in this world was perceived as bodily related to the divine source, the body of God. "The moon was born from his spirit, from his eye was born the sun . . . from his navel arose the sky and from his head originated the heaven . . ." (10.90.13–14).

So evident must have been this conception of the universe as the body of God that, based on it, a convincing case could be made for the overriding importance of the institutional sacrifice and the division of society into the four *varṇa*(s).

The *Brahmaṇa*(s) elaborated this vision and invested it with rich symbolism; the sacrifice as the symbolic reenactment of the creation of the world reflects the body of God in its varied detail. The *Upaniṣad*(s) greatly exploited this idea and developed the parallelism of the macrocosm–microcosm into a path of ultimate liberation.

The *Bhagavadgītā* restates and summarizes a great deal of the Upaniṣadic teaching. It presumes the idea that the Deity dwells in the universe as the soul dwells in the body. Over and above the expression of this by now traditional insight, it offers in its famous eleventh chapter the grandiose vision of the *visvarūpa* of Kṛṣṇa-Viṣṇu. Arjuna has received the oral intruction of Kṛṣṇa concerning his immanence-*cum*-transcendence and he has mentally understood it. What he now desires is to *see* with his own eyes the divine form of the Cosmos-Creator. Kṛṣṇa promises that he would "see here today the whole universe summed up in His body."

Seeing the divine form and, by implication, seeing the world as God's body, requires a "supernatural eye." The "ordinary" eye cannot truly see reality; it grasps only the surface. With this "supernatural vision," a gift of the very same Deity whom he beholds, Arjuna can see the supreme and divine form of God exhibiting itself as "the whole universe, with its manifold divisions gathered together in one, in the body of the God of Gods" (11.7).

In a powerful hymn Arjuna describes the body of God which evokes feelings of awe and of terror in him. Like the splendor of a thousand suns He shines forth. He, who is time, world-destroying. Arjuna praises him as ". . . the one who pervades the entire universe. . . ." Arjuna is shaking with fear; he cannot stand to see the true nature of the God whose body is the universe. And for his sake Kṛṣṇa assumes again the guise of the human being.

This haunting vision of Viṣṇu's *visvarūpa* has influenced a great deal of Hindu theology through the ages. It is a statement about the nature of the world as much as about the nature of God; it explains the importance of worshiping the physical image of God through a variety of physical substances, and it lays out nature and history as ways to God.

Visions of the Deity must have stood at the very beginning of Vaiṣṇavism; to obtain *sākṣātkāra*, a true vision of the Lord has remained the goal of Vaiṣṇava piety. Many an ecstatic and detailed description of God's body has flowed from such experiences. In our own time there are many who claim to have had visions of Kṛṣṇa.

Hindu theologians, while commenting on passages like the one from the *Bhagavadgītā* referred to above, have developed a systematic philosophy of the body of God. Thus Rāmānuja writes in his commentary on the *Bhagavadgītā:* "God has two *prakṛti*(s): a lower and a higher one. The former is constituted by the physical world, the latter by the souls of living beings. All spiritual and non-spiritual things, whether effects or causes, constitute God's body and depend on God who is their soul (*Gītābhāṣya* 7.4ff. [trans. van Buitenen]). Rāmānuja is fond of the Upaniṣadic image where the creation of the world is compared to the activity of the spider, who emits from his body the thread he uses to build his net and then reabsorbs it. The universe, then, is God's body in the sense that it owes its existence—materially as well as causally—entirely to Him. Rāmānuja wishes to make it clear that the analogy between the relationship of the human body and the human soul cannot be pushed too far without distorting the meaning of the world as body of God: "The relation of God to his body is not the same as that of the individual souls to their bodies. With the latter, the bodies, though depending on the souls, serve some purpose for the sustenance of the souls within them. To God his body serves no purpose at all; it serves to nothing but his sport" (*Gītābhāṣya* 7.12).

In addition to this twofold nature, which forms the body of God, God himself has his own supernatural body, constituted by "auspicious qualities peculiar to Him." Only those persons who have the true knowledge of God can perceive the world as God's body, ensouled by *brahman;* all others perceive the world as a multitude of independent objects in a fragmented and fragmentary vision.

Rāmānuja is not propounding a new doctrine; he rearticulates age-old, popular beliefs. He builds up his case with reference to Vedas, *smṛti*(s), *śāstra*(s), and *Purāṇa*(s). His frequent reference to Purāṇic literature demonstrates his conscious linking up with tradition and his affirmation of it. The *Viṣṇu Purāṇa*, accepted by Rāmānuja as well as by most other Vaiṣṇava as revealed scripture, contains a beautiful hymn incorporating the very same ideas (50.19.64ff.). The *Bhāgavata Purāṇa*, again accepted as scripture by a great many Hindus and today one of the most widely read *Purāṇa*(s), contains an account of the creation of the universe which links, limb by limb, the body of God with the material universe. This description is utilized to explain a form of Yoga in which the devotee enters, quite literally, into the body of God and thus comes to a direct experience of the deity (11.1.23ff.). The purpose of this Yoga is to see God in all and all in God, to realize that there is nothing but God in this universe. Apparently the God-universe theme was so important that shortly afterward, in a description of the process of creation, it is repeated. In the second, evolutionary-dynamic account, the same comparisons or identifications of aspects of the universe with God's body are made as in the first, cosmographic-static version. The universe is creatively related to Him, the various entities derive their properties from the various parts of God's body from which they emanate. The mountains derive their hardness from God's bones, the rivers their structure from God's arteries. This second account, too, concludes with the statement, which provides the rationale for such meditations, that "there is nothing in this creation, whether existing as a cause or an effect, which is other than the Lord" (*Bhāgavata Purāṇa* 11.5.6).

While the Vaiṣṇavas have made the idea of the body of God the central truth of their faith, it is not absent from the thought of the Advaitins, who adhere to the idea that ultimately Brahman is formless and as such bodiless. Since it is a central Upaniṣadic idea, Avaitins could not ignore it. Thus, Vidyāraṇya explains in his *Pañcadaśī:* (5.164ff.):

> *Śruti* (revealed scripture) says that the Lord abides in the intellect and has the intellect as his body; but the intellect does not know him, it is itself controlled by him. As threads pervade a piece of cloth and constitute its fabric (*upādāna*), so the Inner Ruler, pervading the whole universe, is the material cause of the universe. Just as the threads are subtler than the cloth, and the fibres of the threads are subtler than the threads themselves, even so, where this progress from the subtle to the subtler stops there do we meet the Inner Ruler.
>
> Being minuter than the minute, the inmost being is not subject to perception; but by reason and by *śruti* his existence is ascertained. . . . As a piece of cloth is said to be the body of the threads which become the cloth, so when the Lord has become the universe it is described as His body.

The Pañcarātra tradition as adopted by Śrīvaiṣṇavism speaks of five different levels of God's bodily presence: in his highest form as *parabrahman* he is all but unknowable by humans and inaccessible to them directly. In his four *vyūha*(s) he creates vehicles of meditation, further particularized and concretized in the *vibhava*(s) commonly known as *avatāra*(s), "descents" of the Deity into an organism of either animal or man. The Deity descends even further, into the heart of each human being as its *antaryāmin* or Inner Ruler, and eventually into a material image as the *arcāvatāra.* This progressive self-diffusion of the divine essence takes place for the sake of returning all things unto the Godhead.

Conclusions

The issue that has been dealt with in this paper has two aspects. One concerns the broad and perennial theme of a "spiritual science," a path to transcendence through an investigation of nature, through a religiosity that does not depend on authoritative pronouncement and revealed scriptural statements. The second concerns the development of Indian religion, the controversies between the followers of Sāṁkhya and of Vedanta, the opposition between "monism" and "dualism." Since the second issue is more likely to lead to definite conclusions and in some way provides the background for the first one, we will first deal with the historical question.

It has been noted before that there is a good deal of similarity between certain ideas expressed in the *Upaniṣad*(s) and in Sāṁkhya sources and that antecedents for both can be traced back to some Ṛgvedic *sūktas*. The Hinduism that emerged after the Gupta restoration, after overcoming Buddhism and Jainism, was not a continuation of pre-Buddhist and pre-Jain religiosity but an institutionalized religion, which strove to outdo Buddhists and Jains in their own areas. Thus, over and against the authority of the omniscient and fully enlightened Buddha, it placed the authority of the infallible eternal Veda; over and against the monistic, idealist Mādhyamaka position based on rational dialectics and logical analysis, it developed the scripture-based monistic idealism of Advaita Vedanta; and typically it fought the ascetical *sangha*-based organization of Gautama and Mahāvīra with the monastic institution of the *Dasanāmi*(s). The popular devotional Buddhist practices were supplanted by even more splendid and elaborate devotional practices centered on Viṣṇu (and to a lesser degree on Siva and Devī). The elements which did not figure in the controversies were neglected. Thus the very interesting "spiritual science" of Sāṁkhya (since it was not based on scripture and authority and did not contribute to a strengthening of the features of casteism and sectarianism which became the hallmark of the new religion) was neglected. With scripture, and one particular brahmanical interpretation of it, becoming the standard of truth, a nature- and not scripture-based kind of truth had no chance.

In Advaita Vedanta the method of realization was no longer a transition from the visible to the invisible, as in the *Upaniṣad*(s), but an appropriation of the verbalized result of the "experiment" of *tat tvam asi.*

Rāmānuja, who claimed to represent the Vedantic tradition better than Sankara, kept more Sāṁkhya in his theology, without giving up the scriptural principle. Since for him the *Viṣṇu Purāṇa* was of the stature of scripture, he accommodated much more of the pre-Advaitic religion than Sankara and his followers.

Pātañjala Yoga, which continued to enjoy popularity, has preserved most of the teaching of one particular form of Sāṁkhya. It derives its truths from a process of introspection into the nature of nature, not unlike that of Sāṁkhya. If one considers that the root *yuj*, from which both the noun *yoga* and the adjective *yujya* are derived, implies not only "yoking" but also "fitting," we can establish an interesting association: Yoga as the search for the "fitting"—fitting into the universe, finding one's fitting place, expressions that are widely used in contemporary biological sciences in order to connote scientific "truth" and applicability of certain techniques. The *Bhagavadgītā* (2.48) describes Yoga as "harmony" (*samatvam yoga ucyate*). The true yogi is a person who "fits" into the whole and thus is at peace with himself and the world. The relentless "discipline" which leads the yogi from one level of the world to the next till he has gone through all of them, and the identification of the freedom of the spirit with the completion of the journey through the universe makes it a veritable "spiritual science."

And this leads us to the first and broader issue, the development of a religion based on "the book of nature." It goes without saying that our culture (which includes our traditions, religious as well as secular) will always color our perception of nature, but there is a marked difference between the acceptance of a world view based on the pronouncements of an ecclesiastical magisterium and a world view based on the consensus of those who are engaged in a search into the principles of nature.

Consequently, one begins to wonder whether those of our Western scientists who have shown a sympathetic interest in Indian thought, and who have found convergences between the new physics and Advaita Vedanta specifically, are, in fact, not closer to Sāṁkhya than to Advaita.[18] By maintaining the objective reality of the physical world and the laws operating in it and by insisting on the meaningfulness of continued research in the natural sciences, they would not be in agreement with Advaita, as shown above, but with (an updated) Sāṁkhya.[19] An Advaitin cannot be a naturalist. He positively discourages any attempt to explore nature; the general properties of nature as ascertained ages ago by the sages are fully sufficient for Advaitic liberation. Sāṁkhya would have much more use for further scientific inquiry.

A surprisingly large number of leading contemporary scientists are suggesting that modern science is a path to rediscover old truths.[20] This discovery apparently depends on ever-renewed inquiries into the nature of nature, on attempts to attune our subjectivity to nature's subjectivity, to discover the structures of reality by reflecting on that which we encounter in nature. While individual scientists sound convincing enough when they speak about their getting a "glimpse of the central order of things" while doing physics, about their need for a "dose of metaphysics," there is as yet no systematic and comprehensive effort to demonstrate the ways in which nature is working for the good of the spirit.

Impressionistic attempts aside, we do not have a modern parallel to classical Sāṁkhya as yet. While basically convinced that natural science can be "a path with a heart,"[21] we have not yet worked out the epistemological presuppositions to connect the interiority of the observer with the interiority of the observed. The solution of the dilemma obviously does not lie in a "subjective natural science" or an "objective history." We are becoming aware again of "wholeness" as a quality of reality comprising objective as well as subjective features and transcending them both. As the physicist-philosopher C. F. V. Weizsäcker expressed it: "If we try to think the whole universe as quantum-theoretical object, the universe 'is' not the multiplicity of objects in it, but it divides into the multiplicity for the multiplying-objectivating views."[22] Even closer to the position advocated here, there comes, in my opinion, the statement of the eminent physicist David Bohm:

> We are led to propose . . . that the more comprehensive deeper and more inward actuality is neither mind nor body but rather a yet higher-dimensional actuality which is their common ground and which is of a nature beyond both. Each of these is then only a relatively independent subtotality and it is implied that this relative independence derives from the higher-dimensional ground in which mind and body are ultimately one (rather as we find that the relative independence of the manifest order derives from the ground of the implicate order). . . .[23]

The "physics" of Sāṁkhya is, in many ways, quite plausible if considered from the standpoint of today's theoretical physics. While it is "atomistic" (algebraic) on the level of a certain complexity, it is nonatomistic (geometric, field-theory-like) on the most fundamental level of *prakṛti* and the *guṇa*(s) before the formation of "beings."

Since Sāṁkhya includes organisms (biology) and sensations as well as consciousness (psychology) in its evolutionary scheme of things, it may offer a basic groundwork for a unified science. It has the added advantage of suggesting a transcendence of matter in the direction of spirit, the identification of the "ghost in the machine," and the correlation of humanity and nature.

It was an unfortunate development both in the East and in the West which suggested that a spiritual person did not have to know anything about nature (and could rely wholly and exclusively on literature, i.e., culture) while a naturalist had to have no regard for the notion of spirit and the reality it stood for. Happily, there were "unorthodox" people in both camps who refused to abide by this artificial dichotomy and who, through their own experiences, were led to the conviction that "generous nature brings about by manifold means the good of the spirit."

Many great scientists, from Kepler to Oppenheimer in the modern West, have recorded their moments of awe and the feeling of receiving a revelation which accompanied great scientific breakthroughs. And many great teachers of spirituality like Plato and Plotinus in the ancient West, or Kapila and Patañjali in the East (not to forget Lao-tze and the compiler of the *I-Ching*) have conceptualized insights into physical nature which guided scientists to fruitful discoveries. "The truth which makes free" is not the one set down in doctrines and formulas. Nor is it the explanation of events and mechanisms, be it through bodies or through concepts. Rather, it is the one which is encountered in ever new insights into the nature of nature.

Notes

1. BhP 11.7.19f.
prāyeṇa manujā loke lokātattvāvicakṣanāḥ/
samuddharanti hyātmānamātmanavaiśubhāsayāt//
ātmano gururatmaiva puruṣasya viśeṣataḥ/
yat pratyakṣānumānabhyām śreyo sāvanuvindate//

2. By equating "the scriptural means of terminating misery" with the perceptible, in which "there is no certainty or finality," it sets itself up against the "new religion" of post-Gupta Hinduism.

3. The question has been extensively addressed by E. Frauwallner in the first volume of his *Geschichte der Indischen Philosophie* (Salzburg, 1953) 228f. and 472ff.

4. On this, see G. Feuerstein, *The Philosophy of Classical Yoga* (Manchester: University Press, 1982) chap. 7, "Patañjala Yoga and Classical Sāṁkhya."

5. Cf. *Bhagavadgītā* 5.6; 13.29ff.

6. G. J. Larson, "The format of technical philosophical writing in ancient India: Inadequacies of conventional translation," in *Philosophy East and West* 36/3 (July 1980) 375–80.

7. Cf. György Doczi, *The Power of Limits.*

8. *Chāṇdogya Upaniṣad* 6.13.3:
sa ya eṣo'aṇimā aitad ātmyam idam sarvaṁ
tat satyaṁ sa ātma tat tvam asi śvetaketo

9. *The Pañcadaśī of Vidyāraṇya Muni with the Vyākhya by Rāmakṛṣṇa,* ed. by Nārāyana Rāmā Ācārya (Bombay, 1949); abbreviated PD; English translation (*Pañcadaśī* only) by Swāmi Swahananda (Madras, 1967).

10. Cf. M. Hiriyanna, "Svabhāva-vāda or Indian Naturalism," in *Indian Philosophical Studies* (Mysore, 1957) 71–78.

11. In the light of this, the following remark by J. A. Wheeler, a leading contemporary astrophysicist, is interesting: "The golden trail of science is surely not to end in nothingness . . . not machinery, but magic may be the better description of the treasure that is waiting" ("From Relativity to Mutability," in *The Physicists' Conception of Nature,* ed. J. Mehra [Dordrecht: Reidel, 1973] 203).

12. Cf. Swāmi Prajñānanda, "Indefinable Māyā in Advaita Vedanta," in *The Bases of Indian Culture* (Calcutta, 1973) 139–60.

13. I am using the words "implicate" and "explicate" so as to evoke an association with the way in which the physicist David Bohm (*Wholeness and the Implicate Order*) uses them, recalling Nicholas of Cusa's example.

14. Cf. Dr. Satya Deva Mitra, "The Advaitic Concept of Abhāsa" in *V. Raghavan Felicitation Volume: Sanskrit and Indological Studies* (Delhi, 1975) 267–89.

15. This polemic permeates all Advaita literature, from Sankara's *Brahmasūtrabhāṣya* through Vidyaraṇya's *Sarvadarśanasaṁgraha* to contemporary Advaita writings. See G. J. Larson, *Classical Sāṁkhya* (Delhi, 1981) 209–35; "Epilogue: Saṅkara's Critique of Classical Sāṁkhya."

16. Sankara (BSB 1.1.5): "It is impossible to find room in the Vedanta texts for the non-intelligent *pradhāna*, the fiction of the Sāṁkhya because it is not founded on Scripture."

17. Rāmānuja (BSB 1.1.5): ". . . those texts can in no way refer to the *pradhāna* and similar entities which rest on inference only. . . ."

18. Thus C. F. v. Weizsäcker ("Who is the Knower in Physics?" in *Spiritual Perspectives*, ed. T. M. P. Mahadevan [Madras, 1971] 148–61), who ends his summary of quantum theory by stating: "This does not seem far from what the Advaita doctrine calls *māyā*." Or even more explicitly Queen Frederica of the Hellenes ("To Advaita through Nuclear Physics" in the same volume [pp. 162–70]), who categorically asserts: "Advaita Vedānta . . . when wedded to theoretical nuclear physics will give us at long last a holistic view of life. The nuclear scientist is moving closer and closer to an Advaitic understanding of the universe."

19. Thus C. F. v. Weizsäcker ("Who is the Knower") insists: ". . . the ascent is not necessarily promoted by leaving the questions of physics aside but rather by unswervingly pursuing them." Or Queen Frederica ("To Advaita"): ". . . the help of the theoretical nuclear physicist is needed, by destroyng the notion of duality he helps to destroy ignorance. . . ."

20. The examples referred to here are found in the works of W. Heisenberg, A. Einstein, and M. Planck. They could easily be amplified. It is surprising how many quotes from religious writings (East and West) are encountered in the works of contemporary scientists like K. Malville (*A Feather for Daedalus*), R. Oppenheimer (*Science and the Common Understanding*), F. Capra (*The Tao of Physics*), V. Nalimov (*Faces of Science, Realms of the Unconscious*) and many others.

21. A central notion of Capra's *Tao of Physics*, taken over from Castaneda's *Teachings of Don Juan*.

22. C. F. v. Weizsäcker-Gopi Krishna, *Biologische Basis religiöser Erfahrung* (Weilheim, 1971) 42.

23. D. Bohm, *Wholeness and the Implicate Order*, 209, 211.

Bibliography

Bohm, D. *Wholeness and the Implicate Order.* London: Routledge & Kegan Paul, 1980.

Buckley, B., and J. Peat, eds. *A Question of Physics.* Toronto: University of Toronto Press, 1979.

Capra, F. *The Tao of Physics.* Shambhala Books, 1975.

Doczi, G. *The Power of Limits.* Shambhala Books, 1981.

Eddington, A. *The Nature of the Physical World.* Ann Arbor: University of Michigan, 1958.
Heimann, B. *Facets of Indian Thought.* London: Routledge & Kegan Paul, 1964.
Heisenberg, W. *Physics and Beyond.* New York: Harper & Row, 1977.
Jones, R. S. *Physics as Metaphor.* Meridian Books, 1982.
Mookerjee, A., and M. Khanna. *The Tantric Way: Art-Science-Ritual.* London: Thames & Hudson, 1977.
Needleman, J. *A Sense of the Cosmos: The Encounter of Modern Science and Ancient Truth.* Garden City, NY: Doubleday, 1975.
Prigogine, I., and I. Stengers. *Order Out of Chaos: Man's New Dialogue with Nature.* New York: Bantam Books, 1984.
Ranganathananda, Swami. *Vedānta and Science.* Calcutta: Ramakrishna Institute of Culture, 1964.
Riepe, D. *The Naturalistic Tradition in Indian Philosophy.* Seattle: University of Washington Press, 1961.
Seal, B. N. *The Positive Sciences of the Ancient Hindus.* Reprint. Delhi: Motilal Banarsidass, 1958.
Siu, G. H. *The Tao of Science.* Cambridge, MA: MIT Press, 1974.
Zukav, G. *The Dancing Wu Li Masters.* New York: Bantam Books, 1979.

17

Spirituality and Health (Āyurveda)

S. N. Bhavasar and Gertrud Kiem

In the Indian system of medicine the well-being of human beings pertains both to their physical welfare and their spiritual felicity. Spirit and matter are commonly understood to symbolize two extreme states of existence, generally opposite to each other. A middle term is conceived which symbolizes life. These three planes of existence generally are covered under three terms—body, mind, and spirit. They stand also for three respective perspectives on life and existence as a whole—physical (matter), biophysical (or psychosomatic life), and metaphysical (spirit). In actual practice, however, each one has to accommodate or account for the other two. The human represents life, the middle plane, wherein both the physical and metaphysical planes unite, by getting duly modified in terms of biophysical equivalence. The human being thus occupies a central position, in which we find both extremes simultaneously exhibiting their own properties, somewhat mollifying, somewhat overpowering, somewhat supporting, or somewhat following each other.

Spirituality, then, signifies here the upper limit, the upper hemisphere of the state of existence, covered under the terms "consciousness," "awareness" (*cit, caitanyam*), as against the lower limit, the lower hemisphere of the state of existence covered under the term "unconsciousness" (*jadam, acit*). This philosophical position is translated in an ethical-religious context as a way of life, based on and governed by higher ideals. Spirituality thus represents an "inner" view of life, that is, a view from the upper to what is "below." In short, spirituality is the life within, expressing and governing the life without. It is the subjective within meeting and accommodating the objective without. It accepts the existence of the soul, as the source and center that balances the extremes, which is designated as *samatva, samya, samyoga,* and others (*sūtra* 7.41 of *Caraka Samhita*).

The Caraka Samhita

The *Caraka Samhita* (*Collections of Caraka*) is considered to be the most authoritative text on *Āyurveda*, inasmuch as it represents an authentic thesaurus of the various aspects of this science, with reference to the fundamental principles of medicine. The term *Āyurveda* consists of two words—*āyus* and *veda*—which in their conjunction mean "knowledge of Life." According to Caraka, it is an *upaveda* or an ancillary branch of the *Atharvaveda* (*sūtra* 30.21). Brahmā himself is considered to be the original propounder of *Āyurveda*. The order of transmission of the knowledge of this science, as set forth in the *Caraka Samhita* is as follows:

> Brahmā, Dakṣa, Prajāpati, the Aśvinī twins, Bharadvāja, Ātreya (a sage mentioned in *Ṛg Veda* and *Atharvaveda*), and his six disciples Agniveśa, Bhela, Jātūkarṇa, Parāśara, Harita, and Kṣārapāṇi are all known as authors of Ayurvedic Treatises in their respective names.

According to the colophon, Agniveśa, on the advice of his preceptor, compiled this work, which was subsequently redacted by Caraka and Dṛḍhabala (who wrote only the last forty-one chapters of the *Caraka Samhita*).

The original work of Agniveśa, written most probably around 1000 B.C., is not available now. There is a great divergence of opinion about the identity and time of Caraka. It is likely that Caraka flourished in the seventh/eighth century B.C. The reason for ascribing this date is that the work seems free of Buddhistic influence. It maintains a Brahmanic style, and the entire nature of the exposition is indicative of the culture of the times. The *Atharvaveda*, while describing the creation of man, mentions several parts of the skeleton which are carefully enumerated; it has a great similarity with the one available in the *Caraka Samhita*. Furthermore, the names of Agniveśa and Caraka are mentioned in the *Aṣṭadhyāyī* of Paṇīnī (sixth century B.C.) and by Patañjali (second century B.C.), which indicates that Caraka and his master were anterior to them.

The term *caraka* is derived from the root *car*, meaning "to move about." There are many legends about the personality of Caraka. One of them says that he was an incarnation of the serpent-god Śesa, who, seeing the miserable state of health of human beings, took birth in the family of a learned sage in Vārāṇasī, redacted Agniveśa's work and propagated Ayurveda among humanity, moving from place to place.

A number of commentaries have been written on the *Caraka Samhita*, in Sanskrit and in the regional languages of India. The most authoritative commentator on Caraka is Cakrapānī (eleventh century A.D.). The entire commentary, except a few verses, is available today (*Āyurveda Dīpikā*).

The popularity of the *Caraka Samhita* had spread beyond the frontiers of India. At the beginning of eighth century A.D. it was translated into Arabic. Caraka's name, as *Sharaka Indianus*, appears in the Latin translation of Avicena, Razes, and Serapion. There is a mention of its translation from Sanskrit into Persian and from Persian into Arabic in Fihrest (A.D. 980). The work is also mentioned by Alberuni, and most probably it was his chief source of the knowledge of medicine. *Āyurveda* is very deeply rooted in Indian culture, but it deals with the fundamental principles of human life, and as such it may be considered to have worldwide validity.

Indian Culture and the Caraka Samhita

It will be useful to give the broad outlines of the philosophical framework which is used by this system of Indian medicine. We shall consider the three most outstanding principles of Indian thought which were current in the time of Caraka: (1) *bheda-abheda* (unity in diversity), (2) *piṇḍa-brahmāṇḍa* (microcosm–macrocosm), (3) *satkāryavāda* (law of self-becoming). These may be briefly explained. One must not forget here that healing according to Indian medicine is not accomplished without some connection being made to the sense of values which suffused Indian culture.

Indian philosophy, as one may see in the above formulations, speaks of reality in two terms, absolute and relative. The former is unmanifest, non-material, without phases, without qualities, without sequence, as against the latter, which is manifest, material, with phases, with qualities, with sequence, etc. In short, the absolute is beyond time-space, while the relative is within time-space. The former is termed *parātpara* (transcendental); it is the source, the origin of creation as a whole and as such beyond ordinary expression or perception (*sūtra* 1.17; 1.28). The method of apprehending the Absolute envisaged and adopted by the ancient seers is that of self-realization through Yoga, which is regarded as direct perception or rather a direct experience of Truth. This state is sometimes described as *samādhi* ("enstasis"), which is characterized by divine bliss (*ānanda*), consciousness (*cit*) and reality (*sat*). To achieve the state of *saccidānanda* is the goal (*sādhya*), and Yoga is the means (*sādhana*). It has been, therefore, rightly said that by the knowledge of the self Indian seers arrived at the knowledge of the universe.

This highest aim has been brought down to a level of practicality and translated into four kinds of pursuits or ends of human life, called *puruṣārtha*—*dharma*, *artha*, *kāma*, and *mokṣa* (*Cikitsa* 1.4.57–58). *Saccidānanda*, mentioned above, is the eternal foundation on which rests this fourfold scheme of life; and both of these serve as a unifying force behind the multifold aspects of Indian culture. By adopting this scheme, it has been possible to frame and shape the various branches of knowledge like the arts, humanities, and literature. All human aspirations—as, for example, *prāneṣaṇa* (desire for life), *vitteṣaṇa* (desire for wealth, amenities, and facilities), and *paralokeṣaṇa* (desire for happiness in life after death)—have to be guided by these four ends (*sūtra* 11.3). *Dharma* and *mokṣa* support and guide all human activities (*sūtra* 5.104) related to *artha* and *kāma*. This also is, as one may see, the injunction of the *Gītā*.

The concept of *mokṣa* is the central issue of all Indian systems of philosophies whether they are monistic, dualistic, or pluralistic. Spirituality, therefore, is a way of life, and as a perspective it has to account for all these categories. All schools are believed to have originated from enlightened seers. There are also some schools which do not possess a written documentary tradition. In general, the following ideas are part of the general philosophical tradition: *svabhāva* (innate nature), *īśvara* (Supreme Godhead), *kāla* (time), *niyati* (determinism, providence, fate, etc.), *yadrccha* (indeterminism, whim, desire, etc.), *bhūta*(s) (inert elements—material factors). All schools utilize these concepts to explain the relationship of the One and Many.

Caraka advises the Ayurvedic student not to get involved in any philosophical school as such, nor even to dawdle unnecessarily over such issues, because all of them have meaning and also a certain part to play in life (*sūtra* 15.20; also *suśruta sarīra* 1.11). Any activity is actually a product, a joint venture of many factors (*samudaya*) (*vimāna* 1.11; *sarīra* 1.47; 3.11). He therefore advises one to follow always a middle path, that is, to adopt a policy of *samatva* (equality), *samya* (equilibrium), and *madhyamāvṛtti* (middle way).

Diversity is a further extension of this very theory of unity in the concept of *piṇḍa-brahmāṇḍa*, the microcosm and macrocosm, which are two modes of creation. It has been elucidated and employed by *Āyurveda* in great detail. The macrocosm is all-pervasive (*vyāpaka*), while the microcosm is the pervaded (*vyāpya*). They are conjoined by a whole and a part relationship. They are one by the principle of unity and are different by the principle of diversity, actually a union of both (*pravṛttih ubhayasya tu*). A common thread exists between them which allows a kind of measurement. The expression "*lokoyam puruṣa sammitaḥ*," when literally translated would mean, "This Cosmic Man has a corresponding, symmetrical equivalence or identity (*sammita*, from *sam+mā*, "to measure equally") with man." Caraka further states that whatever factors are present in man are present also in the Cosmic Man (*śarīra* 4.13; 5.3–5). *Āyurveda* makes use of this concept on all planes. Here too we find subjectivity reflected objectively. The most outstanding feature of this theory is thus stated:

> Just as by release (*visarga*), reception (*ādāna*) and scattering (*vikṣepa*) respectively, the *soma* (moon), the *sūrya* (sun) and *anala* (the fire) uphold the cosmos, the *kapha* (phlegm), *pitta* (bile) and *vāta* or *anīla* (wind) with respective energies uphold the body.

Actually, all the three phases of energy are of the sun alone, but on a lower level they are assigned to the three cosmic gods. This is in harmony with the Ṛgvedic statement, "The Sun is the soul of all things mobile and immobile" (*Ṛg Veda* 1.115.1). It is on this that the theories of southern and northern solstices of the sun have been based and further employed in relation to cosmic health and individual health.

This concept further displays the identity of the sun and time (*kāla*). The sun is said to be the creator of time, and this theory as a whole forms the base for another Ayurvedic concept, namely, *kāla-samprāpti* (temporal precipitation or temporal transformation—*kāla-vipāka*), which in turn is the base for an individual theory of transformation of food in successive body constituents after food is consumed and is digested in the stomach (*śarīra* 1.110). Moreover, the concept of temporal precipitation has been incorporated in pathogenesis (production of disease) and its reversal, that is, treatment, which follow the principle of opposition for the cause and effect phenomena of disease. This concept of time is also the base for the seasonal, monthly, and diurnal concepts of time and the corresponding individual code of conduct. In short, the concept of *piṇḍa-brahmāṇḍa* is responsible for the formulation of the other theories, of *pathya-apathya* (proper and improper) and *sadvṛtta* (individual code of conduct) in relation to *āhāra* (food), *vihāra* (life activities including exercise), and *auṣadha* (medicine). Of course it is needless to point out that all this is stated without violating the overarching ideals of *dharma* and *mokṣa*, as described earlier.

The third extension and derivation of the theories stated above is that of causation. It anticipates other related theories like transformation of cause into effect, modification or illusion theory of cause, and even the theory of nonexistence of the relation of cause and effect. Caraka, however, accepts the *satkāryavāda* (i.e., effect exists in cause), without losing sight of the implications of the other theories, especially from the Ayurvedic point of view. The concepts of *anuvṛtti* (follow-up) and *samtati* (continuity and succession) in relation to life clearly show his attitude (*sūtra* 30–32; *śarīra* 2.42).

The main consideration behind this concept is an identity of cause and effect. What makes them different practically is time and space, and they form the base for deciphering *hetū* (cause), *liṅga* (symptom), and *auṣadha* (treatment). The function of the physician is practically to establish the cause-and-effect relation and resort to it in treatment. *Satkāryavāda* has two

23. Frieze of Musicians and Dancer, ca. 973. India, Pratihara Dynasty.

implications: to infer the cause from the effect, and then, from the cause, to expect the appropriate result. This double approach is described as positive and negative methods of confirmation. On the basis of such reasoning Caraka states that one should attempt to achieve "a reasonable conclusion based upon a necessary causal relationship" rather than work on the presumption of caprice (*yadrccha*), which being bereft of cause-and-effect relationship cannot yield an expected conclusion (*śūtra* 1.135; 20.21).

The three fundamental principles outlined above are accepted and incorporated in *Āyurveda*. Owing to their universality they are called "axioms common to all disciplines." The particular disciplines derive and employ secondary theories from them along with their subsequent extensions, called "specific treatises" and "extended conclusions."

Thus we see that fundamentals are an outcome of the Vedic tradition, and *Āyurveda* is an ancillary to the Veda. Therefore we can cite some of the well-known examples which serve as the base for all Ayurvedic theories.

> Of the One that exists, the learned speak as Many. (RV 1.164.46)
>
> Of one that exists, (the learned) conceive in many ways. (RV 10.114.5).
>
> Indra with his māyās (from *mā*, "to measure," i.e., the creative female principles, creatrix) becomes multi-formed. (RV 6.47.18).
>
> This All, indeed, is brahman. (ChU 3.14.1)
>
> All things made of clay become known, the modification (*vikāra*) being only a name arising from speech—the truth is that it is just clay. (ChU 6.1.4)
>
> My dear! Having seen *ātman*, having heard *ātman*, having pondered over *ātman*, and having reflected on *ātman*, indeed, all becomes known. (BĀU 4.5.6).

The last two citations speak of the method of self-realization, the main road as well as the goal of spirituality. It is also the confirmation of the validity of knowledge. Self-realization is to know, is to become, by way of *ātmajñāna*, of the very nature of knowledge itself.

Caraka very vividly describes this in his very famous verse:

> *loke vitatam ātmānam lokam cātmani paśyatah /*
> *parāvaradṛśaḥ śāntir jñānamūlā na naśyati //*
>
> (*śarīra* 5.20)
>
> He who sees himself extended in the world and sees the world reflected in himself, of such a person, who has seen the highest and the lowest, the *śānti* (peace) which is deeply rooted in him, does not become nonexistent.

This concept is employed by Caraka in the context of treatment:

Jñānabuddhi–pradīpena yo na viśati yogavit /
āturasyāntarātmānaṁ na sa rogān cikitsati //
(*vimāna* 5.22)

By means of a lamp in the form of knowledge and reason, the philosopher physician who does not enter the inner self of the patient will not be able to treat the diseases.

In short, Caraka advises even the patient to be *dhārmika,* "one who follows *dharma* as a discipline," and better still to be a *dharmātma,* "one who has made *dharma* his very soul" (*sūtra* 2–16; 11.17)

Fundamentals of Āyurveda

In the light of the previous spiritual background, it is possible for us to understand and appreciate the practical side of *Āyurveda* and its main concepts.

Caraka accepts human beings as the center of living beings and perceives them from different angles. The human being is a product of *puruṣa* and *prakṛti,* the male and female principles, symbolizing the dichotomy in the whole of creation. They are the primeval parents, opposite to each other, yet complementary to each other. They enter into each other and also follow each other (*paraspara anugatau, paraspara anupraviṣṭau*).

Caraka adopts here the Sāṁkhya philosophy according to which *puruṣa* is a constant immobile factor, indescribable by any properties, and is an abode of knowledge yet seems to be the creator, the seed, while *prakṛti* is the soil, the mutable, variable factor, capable of undergoing any modification in the course of manifestations in terms of creation. *Prakṛti,* endowed with three innate properties, *sattva, rajas, tamas,* when disturbed to a stage of disproportion or imbalance issues forth the creative principles necessary for gross manifestation, leading successively to the lowest stage, that is, matter. The extension of *prakṛti* from its original status to matter comprises twenty-four principles, divided into two categories, major and minor. The former group is of eight principles called *prakṛti* in relation to the other group of sixteen principles called *vikṛti,* that is, modifications (*sūtra* 1.63). The immutable *puruṣa,* when seemingly engaged in creation, is called *rāśi-puruṣa. Puruṣa* is the dweller, and *prakṛti* is the house with nine gates (*śarīra* 1.17).

It is here that Caraka correlates medicine with metaphysics. He states that *puruṣa,* or the self, is in reality the transcendent witness, eternal, without birth and death. Although he is *aja* (unborn), he chooses sometimes to be guided by *prakṛti* and is led into creation. This tendency is called *moha* (captiveness). *Moha* induces action, which has two effects opposite to each other—*icchā* and *dveṣa,* desire or attraction and repulsion (literally, love and hatred) (*śarīra* 1.53; 1.59). This makes the *aja* (the one beyond birth) the *hetuja* (subject to birth with purpose) (*śarīra* 1.53; 1.59). In this lies the beginning of the cyclic pattern of birth and death, held together by the law of succession (*samtati*). This being, therefore, is the abode of happiness and unhappiness, health and ill health, birth and death. Caraka in this context speaks of two bodies of man, the gross and the subtle. He states that the subtle body consists of the soul, mind, ego, consciousness, and the five subtle principles (*tanmātra*(s)). This subtle body can go out of the gross body. Its entry is life and its exit is death; and it forms the link between two lives. However, he states that the succession or continuity is due to the association of body and mind, whether of the gross or of the subtle body.

The *puruṣa* is independent of all dualities which are inherent in the world as a system of energy; that is, the world is composed of heat and cold, the sun and the moon (*suśruta sarīra* 3.4). The duality which refers to all such pairs, day and night, *pitta-kapha* (bile/phlegm), *prāṇa-apāna* (in-break/out-break), *anatarpaṇa-saṃtarpaṇa* (emaciation/overnutrition) does not affect the Cosmic Self; the *puruṣa* is beyond such dualities.

On a still lower level the human person is conceived of as the gross body, senses, mind, and the indwelling soul. The senses play a double role for the human. On the one hand they establish contact with the outside world, while on the other they establish the link between body and mind.

On the material plane, the entire world is created out of and sustained by the five inert gross elements: ether, air, fire, water, and earth. The living body is created out of these five elements and serves as a dwelling place for the *puruṣa.* The human person, as a living being, is called the person with six constituents.

In the human, the essentially nonmaterialistic *ātman* seems, as it were, caught inside a material sheath. The human is *de facto* limited and practically exhibits material properties, like emergence or being created and dissolution, and seems almost identified with matter. Caraka also recognizes the influence of time-space-directions in the order of creation. In Nyaya philosophy they have been treated as substances, which is accepted by Caraka, and they have been assigned meanings and significances—e.g., normal and abnormal (*prākṛta-vikṛta*). As such they are reflected especially in prognosis of death by various methods (*śarīra* 1.16; 1.32). In *indrīyasthāna,* which is one of the most complex, esoteric, and therefore least understood sections of *Āyurveda,* Caraka speaks of signs and symptoms of death, based on the principle of opposition, apposition, symmetry, asymmetry, on physical, biophysical, and metaphysical levels, in relation to the patient. It is here that the seemingly mystic ideas regarding time-space-rotation-direction-sequence (*kāla-deśa-gati-dik-karma*) have been employed. Such profound ideas and their practical application could be possible in the Indian context only through the highest type of meditation, a result of rigorous spiritual discipline.

Over and above all this, Caraka presents a unique spiritual perspective on humanity. He says that if consciousness is accepted as the base from which matter evolves then, as some authorities say, *iti eke,* i.e., *cetanā,* is the only constituent of which humanity is made (*śarīra* 1.16; 1.32). It means that it is consciousness that decides and confirms the existence or nonexistence of life in living beings; and therefore it is the mainstay, or rather the only constituent, of humanity through which and upon which every thing depends. The gross body is the material manifestation of the same and is accepted as the material sheath of the self. This is a very remarkable and startling attitude of perceiving the body itself as adhering to the principle of unity. This interpretation also facilitates and explains the role of an otherwise nonmaterial mode of treatment in the form of mantra, grace, blessing, touch—that is, a form of yogic treatment of the highest order or a spiritual healing.

The perspectives stated above, strictly speaking, are not medical. The medical perspective on the living being, both floral and faunal, is that it is made of *doṣa* (disorder), *dhātu* (bodily juice), *mala* (refuse). *Doṣa*(*s*) are three, *dhātu*(*s*) are seven/eight along with sub-*dhātu*(*s*), and *mala*(*s*) of all types are produced in the process of digestion and conversion from lower to higher *dhātu*(*s*). Even the nonliving substances, like minerals and others, have been perceived in the same manner depending on their effects in the living beings, when used as medicines.

To summarize: The concepts of cause (*hetū*), symptom (*liṅga*), and medicine (*auṣadha*) (*sūtra* 1.24) depend on the aforesaid perspectives. Since the ideas of disorder and disease depend on this, it would be proper first to put forth the idea of health and happiness.

Health in Caraka Samhita

A descriptive definition of health given by Caraka is as follows:

> Disease (*vikāra*) is a loss of equilibrium (*vaisamya*) of body constituents, while health (*prakrti*) is their equilibrium (*samya*). Health (*ārogya*) is called happiness (*sukha*), and ill-health (*vikāra*) is decidedly unhappiness (*duḥkha*).

The property of having more than one nomenclature of health and ill-health (health and ill-health, equilibrium and disequilibrium, happincss and unhappiness) lies in the very idea of multiple levels and dimensions of the same. The term health–ill-health (*prakṛti-vikṛti*) in reality belongs to the level of philosophy especially associated with the Sāṁkhya school, and it is thus a philosophical definition of health. Equilibrium and its loss belong on the one hand again to the Sāṁkhya concept of *prakṛti* and her properties, and on the other hand to medicine proper with respect both to quality and quantity of *doṣa-dhātu-mala.* Happiness and unhappiness indicate the plane of sensibility or sensation, that is, psychology, which is the field proper of the mind. The favorable sensation is happiness; the other one is a sign of unhappiness. Thus, this description correlates the metaphysical, psychological, and medical (biophysical) planes of living beings and recognizes an interpretation of the three regarding health and happiness as well as ill-health and unhappiness.

The most common term for health used in *Āyurveda* is *svāsthya* (health), and for the state of the healthy person, *svastha. Svastha* is a compound formation of *sva+stha,* wherein the former means self and the latter is the verbal derivative from the root *sthā,* "to stand," "to establish," "to maintain." It means, therefore, he who is established, in one's self, the soul. This is the spiritual or the subjective definition of health. Curiously, this is also the yogic description of *samādhi* as it is found in *Yogasutra* of Patañjali. Yoga is defined by Patañjali in his opening aphorism as mastery over the respective patterns of consciousness. The culminating effect of this state is expressed as *tadādrasṭuḥ svarūpe avasthānam,* "then the observer (of spiritual practice) gets established in his own nature." Here too *sva* is *svarūpa,* and *stha* is *avasthānam;* indeed, it is a description of *svastha* in *Āyurveda.* The implication of this definition is that to be established in one's own self is ideal health. This is envisaged by *Āyurveda* and is also the goal of Yoga.

Field of Medicine

Having defined health and ill-health, Caraka goes ahead and states that of *ātman,* mind, and body, the last two are the pedestals for disease and disorder or health and ill-health. *Ātman,* in principle, is the witness, and his office is to grant or withdraw permission to the lower faculties, to impel them or repel from them the stimulants. His highest office is to know, whereas ignorance is his negative aspect. It is in this context that the truism of the hedonistic assumption is acknowledged by Caraka:

> All the activities and tendencies of all living creatures are aimed at achieving happiness; however, the tendency to choose and follow the proper path or the improper path depends upon aspiration for knowledge or for ignorance respectively. (*sūtra* 28.35)

Having clarified the position of the *ātman,* Caraka concentrates on body and mind in detail. He says that the body is subject to three kinds of disorderliness or malfunctioning (*doṣa*) because of the irregularity of the movements of *kapha* (phlegm), *pitta* (bile), and *vāta* (wind). The mind is likewise subject to the *doṣa*(*s*) of the qualities of *tamas* (inertness/darkness) and *rajas* (activity/vibrancy). The third of the triple qualities, namely, *sattva* (light/lucidity, the opposite of inertness as well as darkness) is not a *doṣa.* Diseases also are classified on this basis as physical and mental. This is, however, a general classification, because body and mind are not strictly separable in living beings. They are mutually dependent: "The body is made to follow the mind, the mind is made to follow the body," Caraka states in the same context (*sūtra* 28.35). This means that there is no disease that is purely physical or purely mental; as such each shares the credit of curative power as well as the discredit of causing disease. Labeling a disease indicates simply dominance of one of the two. In short, a disease is psychosomatic or biophysical, though on a practical level this division does hold validity and importance.

Āyurveda and Pathogenesis

Caraka states that knowledge about a disease which would help in making a diagnosis could be acquired through five factors: *nidāna* (cause), *pūrvarūpa* (prodromal symptoms), *rupa* (symptoms proper), *upaśaya* or *anupaśaya* (what causes relief or aggravation), and *samprāpti* (precipitation, i.e., manifestation).

Disease is an effect, a creation, a phenomenon, and that is why it follows the biological process, which requires name and form for its identification and recognition. This in turn is necessary for its treatment and management. Name-and-form (*nāma-rūpa*) is a technical term, which is inherited from the Vedic tradition. The disease with name and form is a gross manifestation, an individualization, personification (*vyakti*), while its cause is its genus (*jāti*). *Āyurveda* believes in uprooting the very cause, the seed of the continuity of disease. Moreover, in practice *nāma-rūpa* helps to differentiate, distinguish, and describe a person as well as a disease.

The other side of this identification is to establish the law of causation, indicating in turn the identity of cause and effect, though they are not synchronous. The disease preeminently is concrete, gross, while the cause is abstract, subtle; therefore, its knowledge can be gained through inference only, substantiated by other means listed above. These five factors, in a sense, form a continuous process of pathogenesis, from its inception to its final manifestation. The last term, *samprāpti,* for practical purposes actually represents all the five. The word *samprāpti* means precipitation (and *jāti* and *ajāti*, the terms used in explication of it, signify birth, genus, emergence, or augmentation). Thus, identification of cause is very important for the treatment of a disease, and this is the reason why Caraka has devoted so much thought to the philosophical theory of causation.

Totality of Disease

From the Ayurvedic point of view, any work is the result of many factors acting together. So also it is the case with the body and the disease. Excepting *ātman*, the witness, the living body consists of three planes—body, senses, and mind—which range from lower to higher, gross to subtle. They also represent the three aspects associated with the three biophysical states related to cause: *prajñā* (mental faculty), *indrīyārthasamyoga* (sensory plane), and *parināma* (material plane)—wherein the effect, the disease, is observed. The mental plane is abstract, subtle; the sensory is both, somewhat abstract, somewhat concrete, somewhat subtle, somewhat gross. The third plane, *parināma*, has two salient features: on the one hand it represents the conversion and transformation of food into the seven (or eight, if *oja*, the vital force, is included) body tissues: *rasa* (lymph), *rakta* (blood), *māṁsa* (muscles), *meda* (fat), *asthi* (bones), *majjā* (bone marrow), and *śukra* (semen). On the other hand, on this material plane the temporal (seasonal) physiological aggravation and subsequent pacification of the *doṣa*(*s*) and eventually the precipitation of a disease take place. These three factors (mind, psyche, and body) pervaded by *vāta*, *pitta*, and *kapha* are always in contact with the external world trying to maintain internal equilibrium among themselves. If that is disturbed, it marks the beginning of disease, which, if nourished, subsequently appears as the disease proper.

Emergence of Disease

Caraka perceives disease as a result rather of a punishment inflicted upon oneself because of offense against the highest office of one's own person, namely, the *prajñā* (discernment). Disease, therefore, is technically called *prajñaparādha* (offense against *prajñā*). It disturbs the smooth working of the living being, giving rise to an opposite cyclic pattern which, if not duly discerned and checked, becomes successively powerful, culminating in an overall downfall of the person as a whole. Offense against a healthy pattern of living may consist in inhibiting or provoking the natural cells that are in motion, curbing those that are already irritated, resorting to unnatural physical feats; excessive indulgences in sex, taking part in those experiences

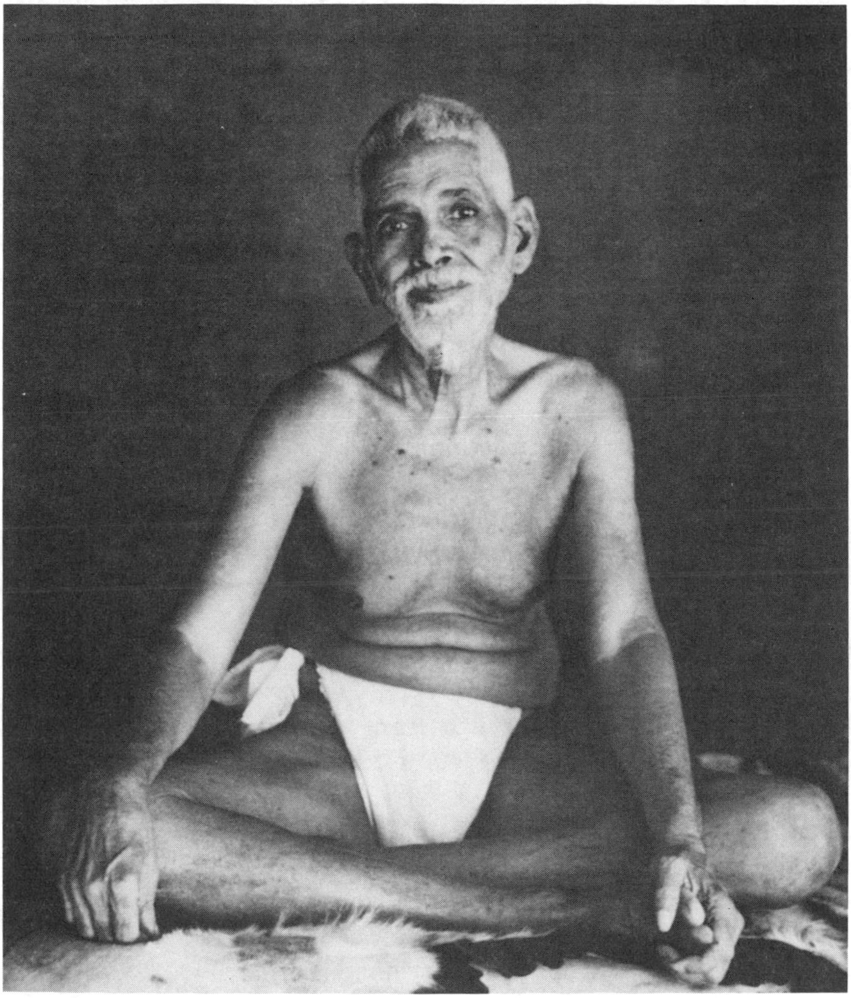

24. Sri Ramaṇa Maharṣi.

which cause excessive excitement, excess regarding work and leisure, unwholesome undertakings, lack of moral conduct and modesty, insulting those worthy of respect, resorting to known unrighteous acts and objects, deliberately traveling in improper regions at improper times, seeking friendship with those whose deeds or undertakings are impure and complicated, abandoning wholesome regimes, resorting to envy, pride, fear, anger, greed, infatuation, intoxication; indulging in actions done through *rajas* and *tamas* (the *doṣa*(*s*) of the mind) etc. All these cause an offense against *prajñā*. *Prajñaparādha* thus pertains to incorrect knowledge which may be grasped by the mind only (*śarīra* 1.102–9).

On the material plane, food is considered to be the main causative factor leading to health or disease. Wholesome food is necessary for health, and unwholesome food leads to diseases. The very factors which in a balanced state prove to be conducive for health, in their unbalanced state give rise to diseases. Nature, therefore, is ultimately the cause of health as well as disease. On the higher plane disease and disorder turn out to be suffering and pain, unhappiness and disharmony. Here etiology changes into ontology because disease is identified as *prajñaparādha*. It is inward, so the cause of suffering must be looked for within oneself. The roots of diseases lie on a higher plane although their manifestations are visible on a lower plane of existence.

Treatment

Though treatment has been viewed from many angles and levels, Caraka speaks of it from a universal standpoint. He defines it as follows: "By whatsoever procedure, the constituents of the body become even, that is called treatment of the disease (*nidāna* 7.19)."

It is clear that the base of treatment is *samatva* or equilibrium. From this perspective Caraka's synonyms for treatment are found to be very significant: *pathya* (literally, that which keeps one on the proper path), *sādhana* (means), *auṣadha* (drug), *prāyaścitta* (expiation), *prakṛti-sādhana* (restoring the constitution to its normalcy), *prati-karma* (counteraction), and *prasamana* (palliation).

In relation to pathogenesis the treatment can be either opposite, that is, a reversal counteracting the causative factors, or apposite, supplying that which has been eliminated or diminished. To give a few examples: for diseases caused by aggravation of *pitta* (bile), such as gastritis, piles, burning hemorrhage, etc., sweet, bitter, astringent, and cold therapeutic measures are advised, whereas for *kapha* (phlegm) disorders such as bronchitis, edema, adiposis, etc., pungent, astringent, bitter, sharp, and hot measures are adopted. For diseases caused by *vāta* (wind), such as arthritis, pain, *anorexia meteorismus*, etc., sweet, sour, salted, unctuous, and warm therapeutic measures are to be applied, which are opposite to the qualities of the increased *doṣa* (body element).

Treatment includes *āhāra* (food) as well as *vihāra* (place of sojourn, exercise, etc.) together with *auṣadhi* (drugs). Medicines are to be prescribed taking into account the patient's constitution, the season, and also the place of residence. For example, in winter or in snowy regions, cold therapy is not to be advised. The physician must also learn to recognize irremediable diseases. Caraka states:

> There are no major actions (performed in the previous life) which do not lead to the corresponding results. Diseases arising out of such actions are not amenable to any therapeutic measures. They are cured only after the results of actions are exhausted, i.e., fully enjoyed.

Diseases arising out of temporal factors such as old age and ultimately death are in a way natural events, and natural manifestations are irremediable.

Mental Disorders

The term *atattvābhiniveśa* (neurotic clinging) describes the final diagnosis for physical as well as mental diseases. In the case of physical diseases we do not require this overall diagnosis, but it becomes most conspicuous in the case of mental disorders. Caraka distinguishes mental disorders caused by external agencies such as evil spirits, demons, demigods, being cursed by offended respectable persons, as well as certain places and times of ill-omen; and psychic reasons such as nonfulfillment of desires, confrontation with that which is undesired, etc. For such psychic diseases, Caraka recommends treatment comprising scriptural readings, telling of sacred beads (rosary), mantra, expiations, fasts, going to temples, etc. By including such nonmedical means of treatment, Caraka has widened the scope. By giving sanction to the supernatural plane of existence he acknowledges the complexities of life and indicates the limits of the material aspect of medicine. Caraka, however, does not lose sight of the subjective nature of diseases. He therefore declares:

> Neither the gods, nor celestial beings, nor evil spirits, nor demons or others by themselves afflict them who themselves remain undisturbed. If (actually) the disease is created out of one's own self as the result of an offense to *prajñā*, one should not blame the gods, the manes, the demons. One should rather regard oneself as the creator of happiness or unhappiness and should therefore follow the beneficial path and not get perturbed. (*nidāna* 7.19–20).

Enumeration of Diseases

Diseases have been classified and categorized in *Āyurveda* from various points of view. Yet the principle of unity in diversity, or one and many, has been the base. The disease is one because it causes pain, suffering (*ruja, pīḍā*). If exogenous (i.e., originating externally) it is preceded by pain and followed by disequilibrium of *vāta, pitta,* and *kapha;* if endogenous (i.e., originating internally), pain is produced afterward. From the standpoint of effect, two types of diseases are distinguished, hot and cold (*āgneya* and *saumya*). Hot are those diseases produced by aggravated *pitta* and *vāta;* and cold, those produced by *kapha* and *vāta.* One and the same disease can be hot and cold depending on its cause (as, for example, fever). Also the location of diseases is twofold: mind and body; and even their etiology can be either exogenous or endogenous. Four types of diseases have to be distinguished regarding their causative factors: extrinsic, *vāta, pitta,* and *kapha;* and regarding prognosis: easily curable, difficult to cure, palliative cure, or incurable. Lastly it has to be said that disorders are innumerable because of innumerable variations in constitution, location, symptoms, etiology, and proportion of causative factors (*sūtra* St. 20.3).

Recurrence of Diseases

"That headache again"; "that fever is back"; "that severe cough has recurred." Such popular statements indicate the recurrence of past disorders and denote their frequency. Some disorders occur at regular intervals or particular seasons. When a physician applies a remedy to avert such recurrence, it is called alleviation of *past* sufferings, keeping free from ailments in the *present,* and avoiding diseases of the *future.* From the preventive and prophylactic point of view medicine shows two broad features: that which creates energy or vigor and that which counteracts the disease. The former is the positive aspect, the latter the negative one (*sūtra* 11.63). To emphasize the importance of prevention of disease, Caraka gives the example of a farmer, who constructs a dam in the field, recalling his past experiences and considering the present and the future, to avoid the episode of crops beings destroyed by floods. By this he is able to break the cycle of loss, unhappiness, and suffering of the past and the future; he gets rid of them and is able to sow the seeds of happiness so as to enjoy the fruits of the same (*śarīra* St. 1.86–89). In this way the body constituents, which are in equilibrium, are not disturbed. When disturbed they regain equilibrium as before. Such type of treatment by the physician is called *naiṣṭhiki-cikitsā* (perpetual treatment), which then applied procures a state wherein there is complete cessation of disease. The very cessation of disease and suffering the treatment needed are *sattvavijaya* (mastery over mind), because ordinarily the fundamental cause of suffering cannot be visualized since it is rooted in the very recurrence of the life cycle itself. It could be known through a divine vision (*divyadarśana*) only. This ability to penetrate to the ultimate cause can be had only through Yoga and *samādhi*, obtained by means of the highest *dhī-dhrti-smṛti* (understanding-seizing-remembering). Thus, if this is at all to be called a treatment, it is truly *naiṣṭhiki-cikitsā*.

Svabhāva (Natural Homeostasis)

In this chapter Caraka states that the diseased *dhātu*(*s*) (body tissues) come to normalcy automatically irrespective of any medical treatment. It is only a question of time. As there is a causative factor for the manifestation (creation) of beings but not for their annihilation, so also a disease needs a causative factor for its arising but none for its cessation. After the removal of the causative factors, the disease will subside on its own. Caraka states here the example of a flame of a lamp which will burn only as long as there is oil; when this is finished, it will by itself be extinguished. Everything which is produced perishes after some time; so also the disease. Here the question arises: Why should we need in this case any treatment at all? According to Caraka, treatment is of the nature of aid to nature. With the help of medicines and therapeutic measures we help the body in eliminating the diseased *doṣa*(*s*) and create the best possible circumstances for the reestablishment of the equilibrium. The medical treatment should always work hand in hand with *svabhāva* without creating more disturbance or suppression of the disease. In this way the body gets a chance to regain its health in the shortest possible time.

Death

In the section on the signs of life and death (*indriyāsthānam*), Caraka deals very minutely with death. Basically he distinguishes timely death—death at the end of one's own life span—from untimely death, which is due to accident or disease before the end of the life span. The latter can be avoided by leading a healthy life based on the three pillars—sleep, food, and celibacy—and consulting a physician in illness. Timely death cannot be avoided as it is a natural phenomenon. Not even the best physician can save a patient whose life span is approaching the end. A good physician first finds out from certain given symptoms the prognosis of the disease. If symptoms of incurability and imminent death are present, such as sudden change in the patient's complexion, voice, smell, taste, shadow, certain dreams, unauspicious signs, etc., the physician should give the patient proper guidance and direct his mind toward the other world. He, however, should not tell the patient about his approaching end but advise him regarding prayers and worship inducing calmness of spirit. It is not required that he should give any medical treatment:

> The physician should not announce the imminence of death without specially being requested, even if he is aware of the onset of such bad prognostic signs. Even if requested specially, he should not say anything about approaching death if such announcement is likely to result in the collapse of the patient or distress his family. On the other hand, if later he comes across auspicious signs of recovery of the patient he should make this announcement positively. Only the physician who is well acquainted with the signs of death is also a knower of the signs of life.

Caraka seems to imply here that recovery, even from death's door (i.e., untimely death), as it were, is always possible. The physician must be discriminating and wise.

Physician–Patient Relationship

A physician who is endowed with good conduct, wisdom, and rationality, who is thrice born, well versed in scriptures, and master of the science of life, should be honored as a preceptor by the people. After completing his training in medicine the physician is considered to be thrice born because Brahma-psyche enters into him (*Cikitsā,* 1.51). Before treating a patient the physician should purify his mind so that he may perceive all the symptoms and enter into the patient's mind. Only those physicians who are accomplished in the administration of therapies, insight, and knowledge of therapeutics, who are endowed with infallible success and bring happiness to the patients, are *prāṇābhisara*(s) (saviors of life) (*sūtra* St. 10.18). The patient, on his part, should not malign or reproach and harm his doctor, and he should fulfill his duty by paying him or offering some gifts to him after the treatment. On the other hand, the physician should consider all his patients as his own sons, protect them sincerely from all troubles, and have compassion on all beings. "*Āyurveda*" as the same text continues, "is given to man by Brahmā for his welfare and not for commercialization or enjoyment. Those physicians who take up the profession only for earning their livelihood are devoted to a heap of dust leaving aside the store of gold."

He who provides life to those being "dragged to the abode of death by severe diseases by cutting the death-net cannot be compared with any other donor in virtue and wealth because there is no charity better than the giving of life." With these words Caraka lays emphasis on the high calling of a doctor and relates the science to the truth stated in the *Taittirīya Upaniṣad* (2, 2–3): "The same life-principle runs through fire, water, the whole cosmos, permeates medical plants vines and trees. This life-breath is the symbol for ultimate truth and thus we worship it.

Bibliography

Sources

Agnivesa's Caraka Saṁhita. Edited by Yadavaji Tikamji. Bombay: Nirnaya Sagar Press, 1941.

Agnivesa's Caraka Saṁhita. Text with English translation by R. K. Sharma. Chowkhamba Sanskrit Series. 2 parts. Varanasi: Chowkhamba, 1976, 1977.

Studies

Filliozat, J. *The Classical Doctrine of Indian Medicine: Its Origins and Its Greek Parallels.* Delhi, 1964.

Larson, Gerald. "Ayurveda and the Hindu Philosophical Systems," *Journal of Philosophy, East and West* 37 (July 1987) 245–59.

Leslie, Charles. *Asian Medicinal Systems: A Comparative Study.* Berkeley: University of California Press, 1976.

Rosu, Arion. *Les conceptions psychologiques dans les textes medicaux indien.* Paris: Institut de civilisation indienne, 1978.

Sharma, P. U. *Indian Medicine in the Classical Age.* Chowkhamba Sanskrit Series 85. Varanasi: Chowkhamba, 1972.

———. *Scientific History of Ayurveda* (in Hindi). Varanasi: Chowkhamba, 1975.

Zimmer, Heinrich R. *Hindu Medicine.* Baltimore: Johns Hopkins University Press, 1948.

Part Eight

CONTEMPORARY EXPRESSIONS OF THE CLASSICAL SPIRIT

18

Two Contemporary Exemplars of the Hindu Tradition: Ramaṇa Maharṣi and Śri Candraśekharendra Sarasvati

R. Balasubramanian

The beliefs and practices of a tradition are transmitted from one generation to another through a galaxy of spiritual masters who not only expound them for the benefit of others but also exemplify them in their lives as a visible affirmation of the way and the truth of the tradition. The Hindu tradition speaks of these spiritual masters as guru(s), who alone are capable of imparting the saving knowledge which is helpful to people, like a boat to cross a river. The *Mahābhārata* (12.313.23) characterizes a guru as a "pilot," and the knowledge which he conveys as a "raft." The characteristics of a guru who is the knower of Brahman (*brahma-vid*) are mentioned by Sankara, the celebrated teacher of Advaita: "One who knows Brahman has his senses tranquilized, wears a smiling face, is free from anxiety and is of fulfilled purpose" (Commentary on the ChU 4.9.2). Both Ramaṇa Maharṣi, the sage of Tiruvannamalai (1879–1950) and Śrī Candraśekharendra Sarasvati, the sage of Kāñcī (1894–), the two great exemplars of Advaita tradition in contemporary India, fully answer the description of the "knower of Brahman" who is also the guru, as pictured by Sankara. Only a person who knows and "remains as" Brahman is free even while remaining in body, and he alone is a guru in the true sense of the term.

The two masters themselves as renewers of the tradition have described the nature of a guru. According to Ramaṇa Maharṣi, "steady abidance in the Self, looking at all with an equal eye, unshakable courage at all times, in all places and circumstances" are the marks of a real *guru.*[1] Only by the grace of a *guru* and by no other accomplishment is it possible to know oneself, which is liberation. By his instruction (*upadesa*), the guru is able to take the disciple near the place of the Self or to make the disciple realize that Brahman, which is thought of as distant and different from himself, is near and not different from himself (*CR,* 49). According to Śrī Candraśekharendra Sarasvati, a guru who knows the truth and is free from bondage helps others to attain the saving knowledge through scriptural study and practices of the tradition.

The Advent and Early Life of Ramaṇa

The study of the lives of the mystics or god-men reveals to us that mystic experience can be attained in two ways. One may attain it by going through a rigorous discipline involving among other things controlling of the modes of the mind, the passions of the senses and the foibles of the flesh. Realizing of oneness of the reality or union with the Divine is the intended culmination of such discipline spread over a long period of time. As distinguished from this there are those who could achieve such experience all of a sudden like a flash of lightning entailing no pursuit of discipline, no following of ascetic practices. Like Boehme in the West, Ramaṇa Maharṣi comes under the second category.

Vēṅkaṭarāman, as the future Maharṣi was named, was born in a south Indian Brahmin family on 30 December 1879 and had his early education in Madurai until his departure on 28 August 1886 to Tiruvannamalai, which became the venue of his life as disclosed to the public. Not very serious in his studies as a boy, he was acquainted with some religious books popular with people, like *Tevāram* (the Saiva hymns) and the psalms of Tāyumānavar, an eighteenth-century Tamil mystic, and also with the Bible, through local schools. It is also reported that the book that he read and enjoyed during this perod was *Periyapurāṇam,* a hagiology in Tamil of the lives and spiritual experiences of sixty-three saints.

Two events in his early life were significant, which transformed the ordinary young boy with no promise, much less of any indication of spiritual worth, into a "knower" of Brahman (*brahma-vid*), the liberated-in-life (*jīvanmukta*), a great sage (Maharṣi).

One day an elderly relative of his visited his home, and Vēṅkaṭarāman inquired of him where he came from. "From Arunācala," came the reply. When the young boy, who was sixteen, wanted to know where Arunācala was, he was informed that Tiruvannamalai was Arunācala. Though at that time Vēṅkaṭarāman did not understand the significance of the word "Arunācala," which refers to the Fire-Hill, signifying supreme Light (*āruṇa*) which is immutable (*acala*) and therefore eternal, symbolizing wisdom in concrete, visible form, it fascinated him and stilled his mind. Recalling this momentous incident later on, the Maharṣi says in his *Eight Verses on Arunācala* (*Arunācala aṣṭakam*),

> O, great wonder! It stands as an insentient hill. Its action is mysterious, past human understanding. From my childhood I had this idea within my mind that Arunācala was something of a surpassing grandeur. But even when I came to know through another that it was the same as Tiruvannamalai, I did not realize its meaning. When it drew me up to it, stilling my mind, and I came close, I found that it was the Immovable." (*CR*, 100)

Another incident took place when he was seventeen. One day all of a sudden fear of death took hold of him. He felt he was going to die. Instead of seeking the help of a doctor or others, he decided that he himself had to solve the problem then and there. With a view to finding out what it was that was mortal, he lay down and made his body stiff like a corpse. Then he realized suddenly that there was death only for the body and not for the Self, the "I" within, which is deathless. Recalling this incident, which took place six weeks before he left Madurai for good, Ramaṇa observed: "From that moment onwards the 'I' or Self focussed attention on itself by a powerful fascination. Fear of death had vanished once and for all. Absorption in the Self continued unbroken from that time on."[2]

Four observations are relevant in this context. First, soon after the second incident stated above there was a radical change in the outlook and behavior of Vēṅkaṭarāman, which was noticed by his elder brother. The young boy became totally indifferent to the things of the world, as though he had renounced the world. Second, the realization of the Self that he attained, though sudden, was not a temporary experience. On the contrary, it stayed with him permanently in a natural and normal way such that he remained as the unchanging Self unaffected by everything else. In other words, he was from that time on in the state of *sahaja-samādhi* (effortless absorption). "In *sahaja*," as the Maharṣi explained to a disciple, "one sees the only Self and sees the world as a form assumed by the Self" (*CR*, 184). When a person is in this kind of *samādhi*, he is calm and composed even during activity and is unaffected by the deeds he performs and by the things of the external world. What the young boy attained and the kind of life he lived thereafter are a vindication of the description that "when all desires that cling to one's heart fall off, then a mortal becomes immortal, and one attains Brahman here" (Kaṭha U 2.3.14).

Third, it is noteworthy that the first problem with which Vēṅkaṭarāman was seized was about death and immortality. It was the fundamental and ever-recurring problem for which the young Naciketas (ibid., beginning of the text) sought and obtained the answer from no less a person than Yama, the god of Death. Vēṅkaṭarāman raised this question and got the answer by himself, even though he was neither acquainted with the teaching of the *Upaniṣad*(s) nor exposed to the philosophy of Advaita. In his case the transition was not from scripture to experience, but the reverse. He did not go through the discipline of scriptural study, rational reflection thereon, and repeated contemplation upon it—what the Upaniṣadic tradition calls the discipline of "hearing-reflecting-meditating" (*sravaṇa-manana-nididhyāsana* BĀU 2.4.5)—before gaining the plenary experience. On the contrary, after attaining the non-dual experience, he elucidated in his own characteristic way to those that sought him, with clarity and cogency and by means of apt illustrations of his own, the philosophy of Advaita and the intricate concepts therein, as if he had studied the texts. It may be stated here that, when he responded to the questions of the disciples, he spoke as an authority and not as a scribe. His authentic experience which was the authority for him corroborated the scriptural teaching of non-duality. It is worth quoting what Ramaṇa Maharṣi said on one occasion (*TR*, 11):

> I had never heard of Brahman, *samsāra*, and so forth. I did not yet know that there was an essence or impersonal Real underlying everything, and that *Īśvara* and I were both identical with it. Later, at Tiruvannamalai, as I listened to the *Rbhugita* and other sacred books, I learnt all this and found that the books were analysing and naming what I had felt intuitively without analysis or name.

Fourth, though the enlightenment flashed on him all of a sudden, it took some time for Ramaṇa to come to what we call "normal outward life." During the early period of his stay at Tiruvannamalai, he was in the state of total Self-absorption without speaking and eating, completely neglecting the body and oblivious of the surroundings. It must be borne in mind that his silence and fasting were due to his absorption in the Self; they were not the *sādhana* for Self-realization. As he moved from place to place—from the great temple of Gurumūrtam, then to the Virūpākṣa cave, and thereafter to Skandāśramam (names of the different spots of the hill)—before finally settling down at what later came to be called Ramaṇāśramam, he was surrounded by devotees and spiritual aspirants who sought his guidance and help in matters spiritual. Very often he was silent; sometimes he spoke to them. At the request of some of the disciples, he explained the contents of the great scriptural works. It means that the transition from inward Self-absorption to outward social life took place over a period of several months; and there emerged a new "person," answering to the picture of a perfected being as entirely *sāttvik* (luminous), free from *rāja*(s) (activistic drive) and *tamas* (inertia-prone), and also free from *vāsanā*(s) or memories, the mind-body surviving, as the tradition would say, like a burnt rope with the form, but not the strength or function, of a rope.

Though Ramaṇa Maharṣi did not philosophize systematically like an academic philosopher, the Hindu tradition looks upon him as an Advaita "philosopher" in the mainstream flowing from the *Upaniṣad*(s) through Gauḍapāda, Sankara, and other illustrious teachers of Advaita. We have to gather his philosophy from his answers to the questions put to him by his disciples, from his talks to and conversations with the spiritual aspirants, from his occasional writings selected and arranged by his disciples, and from the devotional hymns to Arunācala composed by him, which serve as a rich treasure house for the use of scholars and lay people. He was not interested in theoretical discussion and sophisticated analysis of philosophical problems. Nor did he resort to dialectics considering alternative points of view, examining the objections and providing replies to them. He was not interested in theory. Whenever he elucidated any theory, it was with a view to helping the spiritual aspirants in their practice. He discouraged philosophical dispute, as it was not conducive to self-realization: "Can anything appear apart from that which is eternal and perfect? This kind of dispute is endless. Do not engage in it. Instead, turn your mind inward and put an end to all this" (*TR*, 14).

The One and the Many

According to Ramaṇa, reality is one and non-dual, whatever be the name given to it. The *Upaniṣad*(s), as we know, refer to it as "Brahman," "Ātman," "Sat," and so on. It is called Brahman, since it is the self or essence of everything. It is *sat*, since it is existent. Using a significant Tamil expression, Ramaṇa refers to it as *uḷḷatu*, i.e., that which is. Though it is beyond speech and description, we refer to it through expressions such as Brahman, Ātman, Sat, and so on, with a view to showing that it is different from the objects known to us in our day-to-day experience. The purpose of description is not to affirm anything of reality, but to negate the false which passes for reality. Ramaṇa's description of reality, which is the same as the "not this, not this" (*neti neti*) description of the *Upaniṣad* (BĀU 2.4.5) in respect of both methodology and purpose, shows that the real is the substratum of the false and that it is the limit to all negation and speech. Ramaṇa says (*TR*, 16):

> Reality must always be real. It has no names and forms, but is what underlies them. It underlies all limitations, being itself limitless. It is not bound in any way. It underlies unrealities, being itself Real. It is that which is. It is as it is. It transcends speech and is beyond description such as being or non-being.

If there is only one reality, does it mean that the three entities,–God, man, and the world–which are admitted generally in philosophy and accepted by most people on the basis of commonsense do not exist? The answer to this question is both yes and no. According to Ramaṇa, God, man, and the world are not different from Brahman/Ātman. They do not exist independently of it. It is Brahman or the Self that appears as God, man, and the world. From the cosmic point of view, Brahman is God. The Self in man is no other than Brahman. The psychophysical organism of man which is not-Self is not real. Through *māyā* Brahman appears as the pluralistic universe. As long as a person does not realize the truth that there is only one reality, he sees plurality in the form of God, man, and the world and holds that these are distinct, though related, reals. Ramaṇa maintains that the one reality is perceived as three–as God, man, and the world–due to ignorance (*avidyā*). What is to be noted here is that all these three entities appear and disappear together. There is no God without man and the world; man does not exist without God and the world; nor does the world exist in the absence of God and man. According to Ramaṇa, the mystery for the simultaneous appearance and disappearance of the triple principles of God, man, and the world lies in the mind or the ego, the immediately identifiable product or personification of *avidyā*.

Like the traditional Advaitin, Ramaṇa suggests inquiry into the triple states of experience (*avasthā-traya*) to find out the nature of the Self as well as the role of the mind or the ego, which is responsible for our experience of plurality. So long as the ego in a human being persists, the latter experiences plurality. But when the ego disappears at the dawn of right knowledge, plurality vanishes and there emerges the one reality, that which is all the time–past, present, and future. The non-dual reality which exists all the time remains concealed because of the functioning of the ego. It is the very nature of the ego to project plurality. Ramaṇa frequently makes use of the analysis of the three states of experience–waking, dreaming, and deep sleep –to elucidate his point. While the mind functions in the states of waking (*jāgrat*) and dream (*svapna*), it does not function in the state of deep sleep (*suṣupti*), as it has relapsed into its causal state. Sleep is what it is because of the absence of the functioning of the mind. That we experience plurality both in waking and dream states is well known. But in the state of sleep we do not see anything, external or internal. The difference between sleep on the one hand and the other two states on the other arises because of the absence of the mind in the former and its presence in the latter. The obvious conclusion that is drawn from this is that we experience plurality in waking and dream states because of the functioning of the mind or the ego, whereas we do not have such experience in sleep because of the absence of the mind in that state. It means that plurality appears with the mind and also disappears with it. Gauḍapāda, the grand-preceptor of Sankara, declared: "The plurality, comprising everything that is movable and immovable, is perceived by the mind (and is the mind alone). For, plurality is never perceived when the mind ceases to act" (*Māṇḍukya-kārikā* 3.31). In a passage which parallels those uttered by classical Advaitins such as Gauḍapāda, Sankara, and Sureśvara, Ramaṇa observes: "If the ego is, all else is. If the ego is not, all else is not. The ego, verily, is all. . . ."[3]

When a person becomes egoless in the normal waking state, he experiences the non-dual reality. It is a case of discovering the Self, which is the reality, when the veil of plurality projected by the ego gets removed by the disappearance of the ego. One who has discovered the Self remains as the Self and is free from the experience of plurality which is bondage. In the words of the Maharṣi: "All systems of thought postulate the three principles (i.e., the world, man, and God). Only one principle appears as three principles. To say that the three principles remain as three principles is but so long as the egoity lasts. After the destruction of egoity, to remain in one's own state is best."[4]

Grades of Experience: No Grades of Reality

We may speak of two levels or grades of experience—the experience at the level of ignorance and the experience at the level of knowledge. A person who is ignorant not only experiences plurality but also behaves as if plurality is real. On the contrary, one who has known the truth has the non-dual experience. To such a person, everything is Brahman and there is no such thing as the world. According to Ramaṇa, since reality is one and non-dual and since it remains the same without any modification without any addition or loss, there are no grades of reality; and so it makes no sense to speak of Brahman or the Self as more real and the world as less real.[5] There is no question of both Brahman and the world coexisting for the purpose of evaluating their grades of reality. "Being now immersed in the world," says Ramaṇa, "you see it as real; get beyond it and it will disappear, and Reality alone will remain" (*TR*, 38). So it is a case of either Brahman or the world and not of both Brahman and the world. This, however, does not prevent us from speaking about the levels or grades of experience for the *jīva*. Since man is capable of moral and spiritual development, there is the possibility of transition from one level of experience to another, from the state of ignorance (darkness) to the state of knowledge (light), from death to immortality. It is for this reason that Ramaṇa says that we can speak of grades of experience for the *jīva*, though it is absurd to speak of grades of reality.

One of the oft-repeated criticisms against Advaita is that it has written off the world as unreal or illusory. The critic does not pay attention to the *standpoint* from which the world is said to be unreal. Ramaṇa clarifies the position of Advaita in his own characteristic way by providing an apt illustration. He says that according to Sankara the world has no reality apart from the Self or Brahman. The world is unreal as the world, but real as the Self. That is why, observes Ramaṇa, the *Upaniṣad* says, "All this is Brahman." Though it is a fact that we experience the world when we are absorbed in it without seeing the reality behind it, the world as the world disappears when its substratum is seen. So what exists is the Self and nothing but the Self. Ramaṇa provides the following illustration to appreciate the Advaita standpoint. Says Ramaṇa: "Brahman or the Self is like the cinema screen and the world like the pictures on it. You can see the picture only so long as there is a screen. But when the observer himself becomes the screen, only the Self remains" (*TR,* 16). Summarizing the philosophy of Advaita in three propositions, he explains the unreality of the world as follows: "Sankara has been criticized for his philosophy of *māyā* (illusion) without understanding his meaning. He made three statements: that Brahman is real, that the universe is unreal, and that Brahman is the universe. He did not stop with the second. The third statement explains the first two; it signifies that when the universe is perceived apart from Brahman, that perception is false and illusory. What it amounts to is that phenomena are real when experienced as the Self and illusory when seen apart from the Self" (*TR,* 16).

The Self and the Not-Self

The Advaita teaching is that the Self alone is real. A negative way of saying it is that everything else which is not-Self is unreal. According to the hoary Advaita tradition to which Sankara himself makes a reference, the supreme reality which is devoid of diversity (*niṣprapañca*, literally, a-cosmic) can be indicated only by adopting the method of superimposition (*adhyāropa*) and negation (*apavāda*).[6] The Self is not known because of the superimposition of the not-Self thereon; and if the Self is to be known, the not-Self has to be negated. The self-luminous Self will reveal itself when the not-Self which veils it is removed. The purpose of scripture, says Ramaṇa, is to help a person who is ignorant "to retrace his steps to his original source" by giving up the false ideas about the Self and useless accretions (*TR*, 63).

The term "not-Self" as used in Advaita is so comprehensive as to include everything from the mind-sense-body complex to the things of the external world. There is no need to enumerate and analyze the stuff of the not-Self. In the words of the Maharṣi: "Just as one who wants to throw away the garbage has no need to analyze it and see what it is, so one who wants to know the Self has no need to count the number of categories or inquire into their characteristics: what he has to do is to reject altogether the categories that hide the Self . . ." (*CR*, 44).

The Radical Question

Since what is to be known is the Self, Ramaṇa did not encourage the spiritual aspirants to raise questions about God, heaven and earth, and the nature of union with God and the consequence thereof for the simple reason that theoretical discussion and abstract speculation about these problems will not only be not helpful to them but will hinder their spiritual progress by causing doubt and confusion, distraction and loss of faith. He did sometimes answer these questions by exhorting them at the same time to undertake Self-inquiry, which was more important than getting answers for the questions about the choir of heaven and the furniture of earth.

One of the questions which is usually raised is whether man is not different from God. To a theist who is debating with an Advaitin this question is important, as he is under the assumption that Advaita has abolished the distinction between God and man. When once such a question was asked, the Maharṣi replied: "Who asks this question? God does not. You do. So find who you are and then you may find out whether God is distinct from you" (*TR*, 74). Similarly, to the question whether man who is imperfect can know God who is perfect, his answer was: "God does not say so. It is you who ask the question. After finding out who you are, you may know what God is" (*TR*, 47). To a question about the existence of God, his answer was: "Why worry about God? We do not know whether God exists, but we know that we exist. So first concentrate on yourself. Find out who you are" (*TR*, 52). Though he would very often turn the attention of the questioner to the more urgent and immediate problem of Self-inquiry, he would at times answer the question about God–man–world relation. On one occasion he told a disciple: "You now think that you are an individual; outside you there is the universe, and beyond the universe is God. So there is the idea of separateness. This idea must go. For God is not separate from you or the cosmos . . ." (*TR*, 46).

There is a difference of opinion among the Advaitin, Viśiṣtadvaitin, and the Dvaitin about the final state of realization called *mukti*. When a disciple of the Maharṣi wanted to know which of these views was correct, the answer that he gave was: "Why speculate about what will happen sometime in the future? All are agreed that the 'I' exists. To whichever school of thought he may belong, let the earnest seeker first find out what the 'I' is. Then it will be time enough to know what the final state will be, whether the 'I' will get merged in the Supreme Being or stand apart from Him. Let us not forestall the conclusion, but keep an open mind" (*TR*, 49).

From the way in which Ramaṇa Maharṣi answered questions about God and religion, one should not draw the conclusion that the Maharṣi was evasive on theological doctrines and issues. The problem here is whether one raises the right question by answering which every other question can be answered. Ramaṇa was convinced on the basis of his own authentic experience that the discussion on all these matters must ultimately come to the inquiry about the Self. To him the question about the Self is radical. When once the answer to this question is found, there will be no further questions to be answered. On one occasion he said: "People will not understand the bare and simple truth—the truth of their everyday, ever-present, and eternal experience. That is the truth of the Self. Is there anyone not aware of the Self? Yet they do not even like to hear of it, whereas they are eager to know what lies beyond—heaven and hell and reincarnation. Because they love mystery and not the plain truth, religions pamper them—only to bring them round to the Self in the end. Moreover, much as you may wander you must return ultimately to the Self. So why not abide in the Self here and now?" (*TR*, 63).

The "I" as the Pseudo-Self

It is, indeed, difficult to figure out the nature of the "I" which is involved in our day-to-day experience as the *subject* of our knowledge, the *agent* of our action, and the *enjoyer* of the consequences. The Self which is pure consciousness does not say "I." The Self is associated with the mind, the senses, and the body in the waking state; and it is associated with the mind alone in the dream state. But in the state of deep sleep it remains alone free from the adjuncts (*upādhi*(s)) such as the mind, the senses, and the body. It does not say "I" in deep sleep. The senses and the body which are insentient do not say "I." The fact is that the notion of "I" arises only during waking and dream states. Eliminating the Self on the one hand and the senses and the body on the other as not being responsible for the notion of "I," we have to trace it, says Ramaṇa, to the mind or the ego which functions during the states of dream and waking. The mind is nothing but a bundle of thoughts. Of all thoughts, the "I" is the root. Therefore, the mind, declares Ramaṇa, is only the thought "I" (*TR*, 119). The mind with the "I"-notion establishes contact with the world through the body. It may be stated here that the mind is a matrix of relations. If the first person singular exists, then the second and the third persons (i.e., you, he, she, it, and they) exist.[7] In the absence of the "I" no relation is possible. That is why Ramaṇa asks: Apart from the body is there a world? And, apart from the "I" is there a body.[8]

The "I" which appears with the mind and also disappears with it as seen in deep sleep is not, declares the Maharṣi, the Self. It is the pseudo-Self. Considering its work and involvement in our transmigratory existence, the Maharṣi goes to the extent of characterizing it as bondage itself. If it is bondage, then its disappearance is liberation. The Maharṣi assures us that the "I" which is the pseudo-Self, which is a phantom, will vanish into thin air when the real Self, which is its source, is known. In the words of the Maharṣi (*TR*, 121):

> The Self is pure consciousness. Yet a man identifies himself with the body which is insentient and which does not itself say: "I am the body." Some one else says so. The unlimited Self does not. Who does? A spurious "I" arises between pure consciousness and the insentient body and imagines itself to be limited to the body. Seek this and it will vanish like a phantom. The phantom is the ego or mind or individuality. All the *śāstra*(s) are based on the rise of this phantom, whose elimination is their purpose.

The Method of Self-Inquiry

According to Ramaṇa Maharṣi, Self-inquiry is the most direct method for realizing the Self through the removal of the mind or the ego. Since the mind, assuming the form of the "I," is the source of all other forms and thoughts, it is the primary obstacle in the way of Self-realization. While the method of Self-inquiry aims at the extinction of the mind directly from the beginning, other methods retain the mind and make use of it for its removal and thereby for attaining the goal, and so the subsidence of the mind is only temporary and not final in the other methods. The mind, which is the villain of the piece, will not commit suicide of its own accord. In the words of Ramaṇa (*TR*, 112):

> Every kind of path except Self-enquiry presupposes the retention of the mind as the instrument for following it, and cannot be followed without the mind. The ego may take different and more subtle forms at different stages of one's practice, but it is never destroyed. The attempt to destroy the ego or the mind

> by methods other than Self-enquiry is like a thief turning policeman to catch the thief that is himself. Self-enquiry alone can reveal the truth that neither the ego nor the mind really exists and enable one to realize the pure, undifferentiated Being or the Self or the Absolute.

It is a matter of experience that, while the "I" notion does not arise in the state of sleep, it does arise in dream and waking states. It is not difficult to differentiate the gross body from the Self; and so the former can easily be eliminated as not "I." The problem arises only with regard to the mind which raises its head with the notion of "I." Since the mind is subtle and since it passes for a sentient being with the "I"-thought, it is difficult to discriminate it from the Self. It is here that one has to pursue the inquiry relentlessly and ask, "Who am I?" Ramaṇa says (*TR*, 117):

> He who eliminates all the not-I cannot eliminate the "I." In order to be able to say "I am not this," or "I am That," there must be the "I" to say it. This "I" is only the ego, or the "I"-thought. After the rising up of this "I"-thought, all other thoughts arise. The "I"-thought is, therefore, the root thought. If the root is pulled out, all the rest is at the same time uprooted. Therefore seek the root "I." Then all these problems will vanish and the pure Self alone will remain.

The effort in the form of inquiry is required only for the elimination of the "I" through discovering the source of "I." The Self which is real is eternal, and hence it is always realized. However, one thinks that it is not realized because of the veil or obstruction—ignorance—whose concrete manifestation is the "I"-thought. Therefore, through inquiry one should remove the "I"-thought. Once the veil or covering is removed, the Self will shine of its own accord. Un-veiling the Self or dis-covering the Self, is called Self-realization. To one who has realized the Self, there is neither the mind nor the body; and in the absence of the mind and the body, there is no such thing as the world. Such a one has attained liberation.

It is wrong to think that the Self is *known* through inquiry. The truth is that the Self cannot be known in the way in which insentient objects, which constitute the realm of the not-Self, are known. A material object which is not known can be known through the help of the Self. But the Self cannot be known through anything else, for everything other than the Self is insentient and so is incapable of revealing even an ordinary object, much less the Self. The real position is that the Self which is self-luminous does not remain unknown. It reveals itself when the obstruction is removed. That is why the *Upaniṣad* says: "That (Self) is surely different from the known and, again, it is above the unknown" (KU 1.4). The Maharṣi sums up the position as follows (*TR*, 125, 126):

25. Ekmukhalinga, 6th century. Baramula.

> The Self always is. There is no knowing it. It is not some new knowledge to be acquired. What is new and not here and now cannot be permanent. The Self always is, but knowledge of it is obstructed and the obstruction is called ignorance. Remove the ignorance and knowledge shines forth. In fact, it is not the Self that has this ignorance or even knowledge. They are only accretions to be cleared away. That is why the Self is said to be beyond knowledge and ignorance. It remains as it naturally is—that is all.

A word of caution is necessary at this stage to remove a possible confusion that there is no place for mind in the method of Self-inquiry. Ramaṇa does not belittle the importance of the mind for the purpose of Self-inquiry, for only a mind which is pure will turn inward and not outward. He says: "Regulation of diet, restricting it to *sāttvic* food, taken in moderate quantities, is the best of all rules of conduct and the most conducive to the development of *sāttvic* (pure) qualities of mind. These in turn help one in the practice of Self-enquiry" (*TR,* 157). Though the mind by its very nature is pure, under the duress of ignorance it becomes impure and gets agitated, goes outward assuming many forms with the notions of "I" and "mine." The mind acts as if it is real and pretends that it is everything. It is this, says Ramaṇa, that has to be questioned. Instead of accepting its reality, we have to seek its source; and once the source of the mind is found out, everything will be the Self and there will be no mind. As Ramaṇa puts it: "The mind turned outwards results in thoughts and objects. Turned inwards it becomes itself the Self" (*TR,* 113).

In the light of the foregoing explanation it will be possible for us to say what Self-inquiry is not. First of all, Self-inquiry is not introspection. The aim of Self-inquiry is to transcend the mind by finding out its source and not to take stock of and analyze the contents of the mind as in the case of introspection. Second, the method of Self-inquiry is different from the method of psychoanalysis. While the latter probes into the unconscious through an analysis of the contents of the dream, the former aims at transcending both the conscious and the unconscious levels of experience. In the terminology of the *Upaniṣad*(s), the method of Self-inquiry aims at the Self which is called the fourth (*turīya* or *caturtha*), as it transcends the three states of experience—waking, dreaming, and sleep. Third, Self-inquiry is not meditation or contemplation (*upāsanā*). It is well known that without retaining the mind as the instrument meditation cannot be practiced. But Self-inquiry aims at the dissolution of the mind. Moreover, meditation, says Ramaṇa, requires an object to meditate on, whereas in Self-inquiry there is only the subject and no object (*TR,* 112). Fourth, Self-inquiry is not a method of repeating the question "Who am I?" like a mantra. Any amount of repetition of "Who am I?" will not lead to Self-realization. "Who am I?"

is not a mantra for repetition, but a question requiring an answer in terms of the source of the "I." Lastly, Self-inquiry is not a method of mind control. The technique of mind control presupposes the utility of the mind as an instrument. The mind which is subservient so long as it is under control will rebound to its original, chaotic state of restlessness when the control is withdrawn. On the contrary, the method of Self-inquiry aims at the removal of the mind by discovering its source.

Self-inquiry, according to Ramaṇa, is not the only method for attaining Self-realization. There are other methods as well which he commended to the spiritual aspirants. He made it clear that one and the same method may not be suitable to all, as there are differences among spiritual aspirants. Though there are different methods, all of them lead to the same goal by overcoming the mind or by transforming it. The effacement of the ego does take place in all the methods at some stage or other. However, from the beginning the method of Self-inquiry raises the problem of the ego and aims at the extinction of the ego, and hence it has been considered by Ramaṇa to be the most direct method for Self-realization.

Those who are not temperamentally fit for the method of Self-inquiry can follow the path of love and devotion (*bhakti*). The ego can be killed by the act of total surrender to the Lord, which involves the abandonment of "I" and "mine." Though very often Ramaṇa said that there were only two ways for Self-realization, that is, the way of Self-inquiry and the path of surrender, he did not think only in terms of these two paths. He recommended the pursuit of the Yoga discipline to those who were inclined toward it. One can also, according to Ramaṇa, achieve the effacement of the ego through *karmayoga*, that is, through distinterested performance of good deeds and social service. There are critics who wonder whether it is possible to perform any deed disinterestedly. Drawing the distinction between the activities that we do at home and those that we perform in public office, Ramaṇa points out that, while there is attachment in the former, there is detachment in the latter. According to him, it is possible to perform all the activities of life with detachment and regard only the Self as real. It may be of interest in this context to refer to Ramaṇa's view of renunciation (*saṁnyāsa*). Those who are fit for leading the life of a monk may accept *saṁnyāsa āśrama* (the station of a renunciant) and pursue Self-inquiry through dispassion. However, a life of renunciation can be led even by a householder. It depends on how one understands the connotation of the term *saṁnyāsa.* According to Ramaṇa, "*sannyāsa* means renouncing one's individuality, not shaving one's head and putting on ochre robes. A man may be a householder, but if he does not think he is one, he is a *sannyāsin.* On the other hand, he may wear ochre robes and wander about, but so long as he thinks he is a *sannyāsin*, he is not one. To think about one's renunciation defeats the purpose of renouncing" (*TR*, 79). Desire operates on the basis of distinctions (*vikalpa*) and is followed by determination (*sankalpa*) to achieve the object of desire. Distinctions, desire, determination—all these constitute the "family" of a person. *Saṁnyāsa*, according to Ramaṇa, means renunciation of the family of *vikalpa*(s) and *sankalpa*(s).

Self-realization Is Liberation

Like every mystic, Ramaṇa Maharṣi speaks not only about the way but also about the goal. Self-realization is the goal to be attained through Self-inquiry or any other method. It is liberation from bondage. It is the mystic experience of the oneness of reality. It must be borne in mind that one does not get the mystic experience for the mere asking or liking for it. It does not mean on that account that it is something which can be acquired by laborious effort. While asceticism can be acquired, mystic experience cannot, because it is something that is vouchsafed to one through the grace of God or through the grace of guru, who is God in the visible form, human or nonhuman. According to Ramaṇa, both God and guru are the manifestations of the Self. God, who is no other than the Self, appears as a guru, instructs the devotee, and makes his mind turn inward. Once the mind moves inward in search of the source, the Self takes care of the devotee. The guru, declares Ramaṇa, is both outer and inner.

Self-realization is something which cannot be described. Language is quite inadequate to describe that experience, because it is the experience in which distinctions such as the divine and the human, the knower and the known, the natural and the supernatural, the subjective and the objective, vanish. Meister Eckhart described that experience as that in which "all is one, and one is all." "All that a man has here externally in multiplicity is intrinsically one. This is the deepest depth."[9] According to Ramaṇa Maharṣi, it is pure awareness which transcends both knowledge and ignorance. It can only be hinted at through words like peace, bliss, the supreme good, etc.

To see or to realize the Self is to remain as the Self, which is real, one and non-dual. There are, according to Ramaṇa, three ways in which one can see the Self. First of all, one sees the Self in the objects of the world. Here the Self *per se* is not seen. On the contrary, it is seen as the manifest world of name and form. Second, a person who has the benefit of the study of scripture and who is capable of discrimination between the real and the unreal is able to know the Self as different from the objects of knowledge, what the *Upaniṣad*(s) characterize as *dṛśya* (perceived). The Self by its very nature is devoid of qualities and bereft of distinctions. There is nothing like the Self; there is nothing unlike the Self and the Self is also free from internal distinctions (*svagata-bheda*). This is what the Maharṣi calls "seeing the Self as void." Third, one sees the Self as the Self (*TR,* 133). Strictly speaking, there is no seeing, because the seer and the object seen are the same and in the absence of the duality of the seer and the seen there is no seeing. As Ramaṇa puts it, there is no seeing, because seeing is being. It is *the only case* where to know is to be. It will be seen that this position is neither unintelligible nor untenable if it is borne in mind that man is all the time the Self, though he has "I-am-the-body-consciousness" due to his ignorance. Man's body-consciousness is adventitious, because it arises only when the mind functions. It is, therefore, dependent on the mind. The removal of ignorance and thereby the mind through Self-inquiry enables a person to see the Self and remain as the Self. This is what is known as Self-realization.

Liberation Here and Now

According to Ramaṇa, Self-realization which is liberation can be attained here and now, in this life itself. It is not a promise of the future, but an assurance of the present. It is not a would-be state to be attained in a future life after death. On the contrary, it is a state accessible to everyone, irrespective of the distinctions of sex, caste, class, and nationality. Since the Self is one and non-dual, there is no second entity to which the Self can be related. "Without foot or hand, (yet) swift and grasping, he sees without eye; he hears without ear. He knows whatever is to be known. Of him there is none who knows. They call him the Primeval, the supreme Person" (SvU 3.19). When the *Upaniṣad* says that the Self is without feet and hands, eye and ear, it is only in a suggestive way to convey the idea that the Self is bodiless (*asarīra*). The authority of scripture apart, we have the evidence of deep sleep experience which testifies to the fact that the Self is without body.

It is the onlooker who notices the presence or the absence of him as a *jīvanmukta* (liberated-in-life) or a *videhamukta* (liberated from the body) as the case may be. For the enlightened *jñāni* with a body is a *jīvanmukta,* and he attains *videhamukti* when he sheds the body. But this difference exists only for the onlooker, not for the *jñāni.* His state is the same before and after the body is dropped" (*TR,* 107). There is only one liberation. There are neither degrees nor kinds of liberation.

Ramaṇa Maharṣi is of the view that the experience of the highest state, call it Self-realization, or mystic experience, or liberation, is the same to all. Nevertheless, differences such as theistic mysticism and identity mysticism, liberation in the sense of communion with God and Self-realization, arise because of the interpretations of that experience through the mind. Ramaṇa says that "the minds are different and so the interpretations also differ" (*TR,* 61).

Another Exemplar of Advaita Tradition

It is impossible to narrate the cultural history of South India from the beginning of this century without giving an account of the life and activities of Śrī Candraśekharendra Sarasvati, the sixty-eighth Śaṅkarācārya of the Kāñcī *Kāmakoṭi-pīṭha.* Referring to the impact of the sage on the people, William Cenkner writes: "[Śrī Candraśekharendra Sarasvati's] ministry, his administrative acumen and his influence upon the people of Tamil Nadu as head of a religious institution remain unparalleled by any figure of this century."[10] The Śaṅkarācāryas who have come in the lineage of Ādi Sankara are looked upon as *Jagadguru*(s), that is, world-teachers, since their teachings are meant for all sections of society, for the entire humanity. "Even when they are addressed to the Hindus, they are applicable *mutatis mutandis* to the followers of other faiths."[11] The interest of the Sage of Kāñcī is not narrowly restricted to religion and philosophy. On the contrary, the entire spectrum of the creative work which brings out the higher aspects of life and reveals the greatness of man and the glory of God receives his careful attention even to the minutest details. History and archaeology, music and mathematics, politics and public administration, temple worship and architecture–none is outside his scope. He combines in himself an ecclesiastical administrator, a worshiping saint, a mystical seer, a profound philosopher, a perceptive historian, and a marvelous linguist. It is no wonder, therefore, that he is interested in the creative activities of all sections of people. His memory is prodigious. He remembers men and matters. He can easily recall the salient features of the places he has seen; he can identify persons and families even after a long time. As Paul Brunton puts it, "there is behind him such an unusual concentration and such a rare intensity of spiritual force" that his impact on the people is both extensive and deep.[12] He is a friend to the poor, a philosopher to the learned, and a guide to the religious flock of vast dimensions.

Early Life

Svāmināthan was the name given to Śrī Candraśekharendra Sarasvati when he was born as the second child of his parents, Subrahmaṇya Śāstrī and Mahālakṣmī, on 20 May 1894 in Viḻuppuram, about one hundred miles south of Madras. His father started his career as a teacher and then joined the Educational Service. Svāmināthan went to a school first in Chidambaram and continued his studies in Tindivanam following his father's transfer to that place. He discontinued his studies at the Arcot American Mission School in 1907 when he was installed in the celebrated pontifical seat at Kāñcī as the sixty-eighth Śaṅkarācārya. His academic record was excellent. He was a prize winner and a model student.

On the occasion of *upanayanam* (initiation) of Svāmināthan in 1905, the sixty-sixth Śaṅkarācārya of *Kāmakoṭi-pīṭha*, who was camping near Tindivanam, sent his blessing to the boy. Sometime later, Svāmināthan, with a friend of his, visited the camp of the sixty-sixth *Ācārya* and offered his homage to His Holiness. After Svāmināthan left the camp, the *Ācārya* informed two *paṇḍit*(s) (resident scholars) of the *maṭha* of his desire to install Svāmināthan as his successor to the *pīṭha* (pontifical office). The desire of His Holiness was, indeed, prophetic.

When the sixty-sixth *Ācārya* attained *siddhi* (i.e., left his mortal coil) in a place called Kalavai, a maternal cousin of Svāmināthan was installed as the sixty-seventh Śaṅkarācārya of the *Kāmakoṭi-pīṭha*. However, he took ill all of a sudden and attained *siddhi*, leaving the *pīṭha* vacant for Svāmināthan's ascension to it as the sixty-eighth Śankarācārya, when he (Svāmināthan) was a young boy of only thirteen years. The change from the mundane life of thirteen years in a small family to the monastic life of spiritual ministration as the *Jagadguru* (world-teacher) for the uplifting of the larger family of humanity is, indeed, momentous. The loss for the small family of Subrahmaṇya Śāstrī is the gain for the entire humanity. Blessed were the parents for being instrumental in the birth of a *Mahātmā* (great soul) who has been destined to continue the tradition of Ādi Śaṅkara by adorning the sacred and hoary *Kāmakoṭi-pīṭha* in the holy city of Kāñcī.

The *Ācārya* selected a young disciple of nineteen years, by name Subrahmaṇyam, as his successor to the *Kāmakoṭi-pīṭha*, initiated him into *saṃnyāsa āśrama* giving him the *saṃnyāsa* name Jayendra Sarasvatī on 22 March 1954, and trained him for continuing the tradition of Ādi Śaṅkara and also for discharging the responsibilities of the *maṭha*. In 1970 the *Ācārya* placed Srī Jayendra Sarasvatī in charge of the *Kāmakoṭi-pīṭha* at Kāñcī as the sixty-ninth Śaṅkarācārya and began a life of seclusion in different places in Tamil Nadu, Andhra Pradesh, and Maharashtra.

Two Perspectives

Advaita teaches that there is only one reality called Brahman or Ātman and that the world of plurality is no other than Brahman or Ātman. It conveys this teaching by drawing a distinction between two standpoints—the absolute and the relative. The former is called *paramārthika* standpoint, and the latter, *vyavahārika* standpoint. The two standpoints are also referred to as the standpoint of knowledge and the standpoint of ignorance respectively. The Sage of Kāñcī drives home this simple but profound truth by inviting our attention to the example of a doll-elephant made of wood available in the writings of Tirumūlar, the great mystic-saint of the Tamil tradition, and Ādi Sankara. From the perspective of the child who is engaged in play, the doll, the given object, is the elephant; but from the perspective of a carpenter who knows the truth, the doll is wood and nothing else. It means that, when the given object is viewed as an elephant, it is not perceived as wood; and when it is seen as wood, it is no more the elephant. What is true of the illustration—the wood and the elephant—is also true of the illustrated—Brahman and the world. The world is made up of five elements—earth, water, fire, air, and ether. Brahman, the sole reality, which is the source of the world, remains concealed when there is the perception of earth and other elements which constitute the world, and when Brahman is seen, the world disappears.

Complicated metaphysical and epistemological issues are involved both in the illustration and the illustrated. However, the most important question here is whether a person can gain the vision of the non-dual reality. Scriptural texts repeatedly declare that it is possible; and following the lead of scripture the Sage of Kāñcī assures us on the basis of his authentic experience that the vision of the non-dual reality can be gained by everyone, provided there is the right approach to the problem. So long as a person does not realize the truth of non-duality, he functions in the *vyavahārika* realm as the subject of knowledge, agent of action, and the enjoyer of the consequences of his action.[13]

In his own characteristic way, the Sage of Kāñcī shows the relevance of the teaching of scripture to the problems of humanity. It should not be thought that the philosophy of Advaita is high and dry ideally suited for the intellectuals who are off their feet. On the contrary, its teaching is realistic and is extremely relevant to all of us who suffer in empirical existence. When we think that there is a second entity different from us, we develop a desire for or an aversion to it. It is the very nature of desire and aversion to throw us into the wheel of action. A person gets himself involved in action, good or bad, to fulfill his desire and aversion. Through his deeds, good and bad, he acquires merit and demerit, which in their turn lead to birth; and embodiment is suffering. It means that the thought of the existence of a second entity leads to suffering through a series of causal nexuses. Why, then, is there the thought of a second entity? It is because of ignorance. When a person is ignorant of the Self, which alone exists, which is one and non-dual, he thinks of plurality and is caught in the whirlpool of suffering. It is, therefore, necessary for us to detect the root cause and remove it. Unless this is done, there is no cure at all for the disease we suffer from. The Sage of Kāñcī drives home this point through an illustration. He says:

> Take the case of a mound of soft-earth thrown by the white-ants on the (bamboo) roof. We remove that soft earth once in ten days. Once again it will be there thrown by the white-ants. Even though we try to remove it many times, it appears again and again. What shall we do to remove it? Only when we destroy the queen ant which is inside the bamboo, the termites will not build the mound. What is the use of removing the soft-earth many times so long as the queen ant is inside the bamboo?"[14]

Ignorance (*avidyā*) is the queen ant, and it functions through desire and aversion. It can be destroyed only through knowledge of the non-dual Self.

Preservation of the Vedic Spirit

As a spiritual leader of the Hindus, the Sage of Kāñcī has impressed upon his followers the need for the preservation of their religion and also the way to do it by explaining the antiquity of their religion and the conditions under which other religions must have taken their birth. According to the Sage of Kāñcī, the religion of the Hindus was the earliest religion of humanity. While every other religion has a name, the religion of the Hindus has no name. The name "Hinduism" was given to the religion of the people of India by foreigners in recent times. This name was unknown to our ancestors and is also unknown to the common man among us. There was no need for a name for this religion, which was universal. A name is required for the purpose of distinguishing one thing from another when there are more than one thing of the same kind. But when there is only one thing, there is no need to give it a name. The same is the case with the religion of the Hindus, which was the only religion that was prevalent throughout the world. The argument of the Sage of Kāñcī deserves serious consideration by the historians of religions:

> Other religions did not exist before the time of their founders. Ours is a religion which existed long before the founded religions. Obviously, it was the only religion in the world ministering to the spiritual needs of mankind as a whole. There was no second religion from which it was required to be distinguished. Hence, there was no need for a name for it. It was, and even now continues to be nameless.[15]

He supports this view on the basis of the fragments of faith, custom, names, and religious practices similar to those of Hinduism discovered in other parts of the world by explorers, researchers, and anthropologists. When the doctrines and practices of this basic, universal religion declined in other parts of the world and when people became unethical, there took place the advent of great prophets who founded *new* religions. The *Ācārya* draws our attention to the fact that the fundamental moral principles taught by these religious leaders are not different from those of the basic universal religion.

It is not possible to say when this basic religion began. We cannot determine its beginning in time. The truth it stands for is eternal. It is, therefore, said to be *sanātana* (perennial). "The nearest Sanskrit word for religion is *dharma,* though *dharma* signifies much more than religion."[16] If any name is required for this basic, universal religion, which is followed by the people identified as Hindus, then we have the name *sanātana dharma,* i.e., eternal religion. Since the basic authority for this eternal religion is the Veda, it has come to be called "Vedic religion." The Vedas, which are the source for the different religious sects of Hinduism such as Saivism and Vaiṣṇavism, are in Sanskrit. The language of the Vedas today, declares the *Ācārya,* is the same in form and feature as it was in time immemorial "as the Vedic chanting has been so carefully guarded as not to allow any possibility of a lapse or change from its pristine form."[17]

There are many definitions of religion. The explanation of religion which the *Ācārya* gives is simple and forceful. Religion, he says, is the way to inward peace.[18] There is peace in unity; what leads to unity is religion; and so religion is the means to peace. Also, religion may be explained, according to him, as *dharma.* What sustains man and society is *dharma.* The *Ācārya* points out that *dharma* is the means to wealth (*artha*) and pleasure (*kāma*) on the one hand, and liberation (*mokṣa*) on the other. *Dharma* is the means to economic well-being, which in its turn is the means to pleasure. But if *dharma* is practiced without any selfish desire, it leads to *mokṣa.* Inasmuch as economic prosperity and pleasure are not permanent, the *Ācārya* exhorts the people to practice *dharma* disinterestedly as a dedication to God; such a practice is true *dharma* or religion.[19] This advice is intended for all people, Hindus as well as the non-Hindus. Every effort should, therefore, be made to preserve our religion, as it is the means to peace, as it is the way to our freedom which is peace.

A religion can be preserved only if those who profess it follow its tenets and practices. The basic, universal religion which still flourishes in India declined and disappeared elsewhere. When people in those places did not practice its teachings, new religions came into existence in all those places to fill up the vacuum due to the efforts of great spiritual leaders like Jesus, Muhammad, and others. The Vedic religion, the *Ācārya* says, has survived in India as a result of the practice of *bhakti* and *dhyāna*—that is, devotion and meditation—which leads to the purification of the mind.[20] Since the basic teachings of all religions are the same, there is no antagonism between one religion and another. The *Ācārya* declares that there is no danger to one religion from another. He says: "If our religion is in danger, it is not because of other religions. On the contrary, it is due to the lack of religious practices on our side. One gets disease when one is weak. Our weakness is the cause of disease."[21] The Sage is aware of the problem of proselytism that is prevalent in India and other places. However, he makes it clear that the Vedic religion cannot be preserved and spread by following what other religionists do. The Vedic religion did not come into existence through force and propaganda. Bees of their own accord swarm a tree which is full of flowers; there is no compulsion on them by any outside agency. The same is the case with religion, which may be compared to the florescence of a tree. The *Ācārya* suggests that, if we scrupulously adhere to the religious practices, someone among us will become perfect and that the presence of one perfect human is strength and solace to others who live with him or her, and religion will be taken care of. If we are weak, we cannot propagate our religion; and if we are perfect, there is no need to propagate our religion. The way to strength, which is long and hard, lies through moral and spiritual practices (*anuṣṭhāna*).[22]

Also, the Vedic religion can be preserved only by protecting Sanskrit, which is the language of the Veda. The *Ācārya* says that Sanskrit has to be preserved and protected not for the sake of language but for the sake of the Veda which constitutes the basic scripture of the Hindus. In view of the difficulty of translation and also of the danger of distortion of meaning in the process of translation, the *Ācārya* warns us against any attempt to preserve the contents of the Veda by translating them from Sanskrit to other languages. On the contrary, there is advantage in preserving the Veda in the original language itself. Consider, for example, Saivism and Vaiṣṇavism, the two major sects of Hinduism. Both of them owe their allegiance to the Veda. Both of them, despite some minor differences, are *vaidika-matha;* that is, their doctrines are embedded in the Veda. They are not two different religions; however, they have come into existence and function as two different sects, following the lead of certain preceptors who have interpreted the texts of the Veda in two different ways. There is scope for other interpretations as well. This has been and will be possible since the source book is preserved in the original language.[23]

Intra-religious and Inter-religious Harmony

The Vedic religion is both monistic and polytheistic. To the Hindu there is no difficulty in combining these two positions, as they are not mutually exclusive. The one reality which is unborn manifests itself in many forms (*Taittirīya Āraṇyaka* 3.133). Since all the gods and goddesses of the pantheon are manifestations of the one reality, there is no question of superiority and inferiority among them and no hierarchy among them. This, however, does not prevent a person from choosing and being devoted to his "personal god" (*iṣṭa-devatā*). He may even consider his *iṣṭa-devatā* as the highest. The *Ācārya* says that this approach is both intelligible and useful. He elucidates this point by means of an example.

> A bridge across a river has a number of arches. To a man standing under one arch, all other arches will appear smaller than the one he stands under. This arch will appear biggest to his eyes. Even so, to a votary of a particular deity all other deities will appear inferior. But the truth is that all deities are manifestations of the one God. All arches are similarly constructed and have the same dimension.[24]

Brahmā, Viṣṇu, and Śiva, who constitute the Hindu trinity, are entrusted with the work of creation, protection, and destruction respectively. The *Ācārya* shows that there is no hierarchy among these three functions by correlating them with the triple states of experience which everyone undergoes. Deep sleep is comparable to *pralaya,* as there is dissolution of everything in that state. There is *sṛṣṭi* in dream. The state of wakefulness is *sthiti.* Śiva, Brahmā, and Viṣṇu, characterized by the *guṇa*(s) of *sattva, rajas,* and *tamas* respectively, are associated with the triple states of experience—sleep, dreaming, and waking—in the same order. The points to be noted here are that all the three functions alternate like the three states of experience and that there is no hierarchy among the divinities associated with them. There is no justification for quarrel between one denomination and another within the fold of Hinduism.

It is necessary to extend the logic which holds good between one sect and another within Hinduism to the relation between one religion and another. The God of Hinduism and the God of Christianity are not different. However, the mode of worship of the same God may be different between Hinduism and Christianity. The *Ācārya* draws our attention to the prevalence of tradition (*sampradaya*) in each family in the matter and manner of worship within the Hindu fold. In the same way, each religion has its own tradition in respect of the worship of God. An oft-repeated verse which the *Ācārya* quotes in this connection says: "He whom the Saivas worship as Siva, the Vedantins as Brahman, who is worshiped as Buddha by the Buddhists, as the Creator by the Naiyāyikas, as Arhat by the Jains, and as Karma by the Mīmāṁsakas, may that Hari give you the fruits that you desire." The logic which justifies intra-religious harmony equally validates inter-religious harmony.

The Sage of Kāñcī exhorts the people to realize the implication of the idea that the God of all religions and of all religious denominations is the same. First of all, it implies at the denominational level that there is no need to give up one form of worship or worship of one God and adopt another. It is wrong for a Saivite to become a Vaiṣṇavite, and for a Vaiṣṇavite to become a Saivite. Second, it implies that there is no need for a person to change his religion. What is available in one religion is equally available in another religion. Third, the convert to another religion scorns the God whom he was worshiping the previous day. This one thing, says the Sage, is enough for his ruin. Fourth, "invitation to a new religion implies that all who lived before the birth of that religion did not attain salvation and also that salvation is denied to all those who do not belong to that religion. Obviously this is absurd."[25]

Moral and Spiritual Discipline

The purpose of moral and spiritual discipline is to help man attain God-realization or Self-realization and thereby to overcome transmigratory existence. Everyone, advises the *Ācārya,* should endeavor to make the present life the last one by taking full advantage of the opportinuties available in this life for moral and spiritual development. Fortunately for us, we are not left in the lurch in this regard. It is usually claimed that moral development has taken place from customary morality to legal morality, and from legal morality to reflective morality, in which the conscience of the individual is invested with the highest moral authority. That conscience is not always a safe guide as to what is right and wrong is well known. We speak of a good conscience as well as a bad conscience. The deliverances of conscience differ from place to place and from person to person. As Richard III mournfully admits, conscience has "a thousand several tongues, and every tongue brings in a several take" (Shakespeare, *Richard III,* V, III, 194). The *Ācārya* points out that scripture, which is the embodiment of the highest wisdom of the knowers of truth, is our authority about what ought to be done and what ought not to be done. He quotes a text of the BG (16.23) which says that a person who, ignoring the injunction of scripture, acts impulsively can never attain the ends of life; that is to say, he attains neither happiness here nor liberation. It means that the authority of scripture can never be superseded by any other authority, much less by conscience. Working out a hierarchy of moral standards, the *Ācārya* says that the Vedas, which are the primary source of *dharma,* should be considered to be the highest authority. Next to the Vedas comes *smrti.* It means that in the absence of guidance from the Vedas one should be guided by what it taught in *smrti.* The authorities to be accepted in the descending order after *smrti* are the conduct of those who are wlel versed in *smrti,* conduct of good people, and finally one's own conscience. Resort to conscience should be the last, if guidance from the other authorities starting from the Vedas is not available in a particular moral situation. The *Ācārya* deplores the modern attitude of turning upside down the hierarchy of moral standards.

> Nowadays, however, the fashion is to make it all topsy-turvy, to give the first place to what is called one's conscience relegating all the other prescribed guidances to a secondary place, or as is often done, to condemn them as meaningless and irrational. The ancient view, however, about the *pramāna*(s) or criteria of *dharma* has stood the test of time.[26]

According to Ādi Sankara, man had been accorded a special place among all beings by virtue of his competence for scripture-enjoined action (*karma*) and knowledge (*jñāna*).[27] Taking advantage of the scriptural teaching, a spiritual aspirant has to abstain from prohibited acts, but has to perform those which are obligatory in a spirit of dedication to God. One who performs action disinterestedly as an offering to God is said to practice *karmayoga.* In all his discourses the *Ācārya* refers to the importance of *karmayoga.* The practice of *karmayoga* calls for the cultivation of basic virtues such as non-injury, truth-speaking, non-stealing, purity, and control of the senses, which are conducive to the purification of the mind.

The purpose of human birth is to put an end to future birth; and it can be achieved, says the *Ācārya,* by making proper use of the body. To make effective use of the body one has to lead a disciplined life. Of the "eight limbs" of the Yoga discipline, the first two, called *yama* (self-restraint) and *niyama* (observance), are intended to provide a moral foundation for spiritual training. The *Ācārya* reiterates the fact that it is impossible to reach the top of Yoga discipline by ignoring the first two steps, which are designed to help a person overcome the egoistic impulses. He exhorts the people to realize the significance of *aparigraha,* which is one of the five restraints coming under *yama. Parigraha* means owning possessions; *aparigraha* means giving up or disowning of possessions. To make effective use of the body for spiritual progress the minimum needs of food, water, clothing, and shelter have to be taken care of by everyone. However, to own anything more than what is required for the fulfillment of basic needs amounts to theft. According to the *Ācārya*, a person who does not self-impose this restraint when he lives as a member of society commits theft. Improving the standard of living should not be confused with improving the quality of life. The *Ācārya* points out that the former, in which the government and other agencies of planning are interested, leads to increasing the needs one after another beyond the minimum requirement, compelling us to face the insoluble problems of scarcity, price increase, wage increase, inflation, social hierarchy, competition, poverty, and so on. The solution to all these socio-economic problems lies in the scrupulous adherence to the virtue of *aparigraha* by *everyone* in society. How a man governs himself from within is as important as how he is governed from without. The greatest slave is he who is controlled by his own rank selfishness. The *Ācārya,* therefore, suggests a simple living which will ennoble the quality of life on the basis of *aparigraha.* One who does not care for *aparigraha* is antisocial and cannot, therefore, be the beneficiary of the grace of God.[28]

As an important part of basic education, the *Ācārya* recommends "self-help" both for the young and the old in all aspects of life, private as well as public, in the home as well as outside the home—in all such simple things as cooking, washing, purchasing, as it promotes self-culture and self-control, which are indispensable for spiritual development.

According to the Sage of Kāñcī, *karmayoga* includes social service, for which there is scope for everyone. The poor can render social service through physical help and the rich through their wealth. The Sage recommends *free* service to the people by the professionals for some time every day or every week depending on the kind of work they are engaged in. The most important aspect of social service is the protection of the temples where worship is conducted for the benefit of the entire community. The work of public and private institutions engaged in social service will be fruitful only when they take care of the temples also. If they do everything except service to the temples, their efforts will be no better than those of Sisyphus.

The moral discipline must be followed by spiritual discipline comprising *bhaktiyoga* and *jñānayoga. Bhakti* or devotion to God is absolutely necessary for man's spiritual upliftment. *Bhakti* is attachment to God to free ourselves from all other attachments. Through it, the mind, which is drawn to and anchored at the Lord, is made pure and still such that it captures the love and grace, peace and bliss of the Lord who is worshiped. While there is happiness in union, there is unhappiness in separation. Devotion is the link between the devotee and the Deity. Through devotion, the devotee attains union with the Deity. The goal of *bhakti,* says the *Ācārya,* is the annulment of duality (*dvaitabhāva*) and the attainment of oneness (*advaita-bhāva*), which has been beautifully brought out by Ādi Sankara when he addresses the Mother of the universe expressing his longing, "May I become one with You" (*bhavānī tvam*).[29]

When the mind has been made pure and still by the practice of *karmayoga* and *bhaktiyoga,* the scriptural instruction imparted by the guru, followed by reflection and contemplation thereon, enables the seeker of liberation to realize Brahman and remain as Brahman, ever free and never bound. Such a person becomes the liberated-in-life.

Personality, Freedom, and Love

Three features which stand prominently in the case of Ramaṇa Maharṣi and Śrī Candraśekharendra Sarasvati are their personality, freedom, and love. The term "personality" is here used not in the familiar sense of referring to the physical features of a person, not even in the psychological sense, but in the spiritual sense. Personality is an axiological category and is, therefore, the opposite of individuality, which is a naturalistic and biological category. It is the spiritual principle which constitutes personality. The enlightenment which a mystic or a man of God-realization has attained brings about a radical transformation in him and has its impact on others who come into contact with him. The peace and tranquillity which he enjoys are shared by others though for a little while so long as they remain in his presence.

It has been uniformly reported by all those who have come under the spell of the magnetic personality of the Maharṣi that, as soon as they see him and sit in his presence, their questioning mood gives way to quietness and acceptance. The picturesque account given by Paul Brunton of his first meeting with the Maharṣi is worth quoting here. He writes:

> One by one, the questions which I have prepared in the train with such meticulous accuracy drop away. For it does not now seem to matter whether they are asked or not, and it does not seem to matter whether I solve the problems which have hitherto troubled me. I know only that a steady river of quietness seems to be flowing near me, that a great peace is penetrating, and that my thought-tortured brain is beginning to arrive at some rest.[30]

After meeting the Sage of Kāñcī, Seyyed Hossein Nasr said:

> To behold the presence of His Holiness the Jagadguru and to be blessed by the privilege of receiving the refreshing breeze which flows from him and which extinguishes the very fire of existence separating man from God is to realize that the Divine Freedom manifests itself where . . . it wills. . . . In the eyes of the Jagadguru, the silence of Eternity of India which is immutable and eternal like the peaks of the Himalayas shines and penetrates into the very

> centre of the heart where presides the "Throne of God." Through his glance the heart becomes suddenly transmuted alchemically from a piece of flesh into a jewel that reflects the inner light and illuminates the whole from within.[31]

It is very difficult for us even to imagine how Ādi Sankara, the embodiment of scriptural lore and wisdom, led an active life moving from place to place and guiding the people through precept and practice, when travel from one corner of India to another would have been extremely difficult. As Mahadevan says, "Anyone who comes into the august presence of His Holiness cannot but recall to his mind the image of Ādi Sankara, the immaculate sage who was divine and yet human, whose saving grace was universal in its sweep, and whose concern was for all—even for the lowliest and the last."[32]

By virtue of Self-realization both the Maharṣi and the *Ācārya* are the embodiment of freedom; they are the liberated-in-life. Mystic experience of Self-realization is the overcoming of finitude and embodiment. Consequently both of them, notwithstanding their existence in this world, transcend the empirical order of life which requires the functioning of the ego projecting the notions of "I" and "mine." As the ego is absent in them, they are free.

As God-realized persons, both of them act, and yet are inactive. They act for the sake of others without the sense of agency; and so whatever they do does not affect them. They exemplify in their lives the combination of the highest wisdom and unselfish work which sanctify mankind and confer on it the blessings that are lasting. The truth, however, is that they are inactive, for they remain as the Self without body-consciousness. They are the personification of love. Whatever they say and whatever they do are acts of bestowal of grace on others. As benefactors of humanity, they do social service in the true sense of the term. Their spiritual awakening contributes to the transformation of the world. Pleasure and pain and "that unrest which men miscall delight" do not touch them. Remaining as "the still point of the turning world," to those who are in the dark they are the beacons of light; to those who are weak, they are the source of strength; and to those who are afflicted, they are the fountain of joy.

Notes

1. *The Collected Works of Ramaṇa Maharishi,* ed. Arthur Osborne (London: Rider, 1964) 49 (abbreviated as *CR*).

2. *The Teachings of Ramana Maharishi,* ed. Arthur Osborne (London: Rider, 1971) 10 (abbreviated as *TR*).

3. T. M. P. Mahadevan, *Ramana Maharshi and His Philosophy of Existence* (Tiruvannamalai: Śrī Ramanāśramam, 1959) v. 26, p. 98.
4. Ibid., v. 2, p. 39.
5. *Talks with Śrī Ramaṇa Maharshi* (3 vols., in 1; 6th ed.; Tiruvannamalai: Śrī Ramaṇāśramam, 1978) 116.
6. See Sankara's commentary on the *Bhagavadgītā*, 13.13.
7. *Ramana Maharshi and His Philosophy of Existence,* v. 14, p. 78.
8. Ibid., vv. 5–6, pp. 55–60.
9. Quoted by Rudolph Otto, *Mysticism East and West* (London: Macmillan, 1932) 61.
10. William Cenkner, *A Tradition of Teachers: Śaṅkara and the Jagadgurus Today* (Delhi: Motilal Banarsidass, 1983) 123.
11. *Spiritual Perspectives,* ed. T. M. P. Mahadevan (New Delhi: Arnold-Heinemann, 1975) 15.
12. Ibid., 75.
13. See *The Discourses of the Ācārya* (in Tamil) 1957–59, Part IV (1st ed.; Madras: Kalaimagal Office, 1980) 100–106. See *The Voice of Saṅkara* (Madras: Ādi Saṅkara Advaita Research Centre) 309–21, for the English version of this lecture.
14. See *The Discourses of the Ācārya* (in Tamil) 1957–59, Part IV, pp. 100–106; also *The Voice of Śaṅkara,* 6/4: 309–21.
15. Śrī Candraśekharendra Sarasvati, *Aspects of Our Religion* (Bombay: Bharatiya Vidya Bhavan, 1966) 1–2.
16. Ibid., 2.
17. Ibid., 12.
18. Śrī Candraśekharendra Sarasvati, *Hindu Dharma* (Kanchipuram: Hindu Samaya Manram, 1976) 40.
19. Ibid., 44.
20. See *The Discourses of the Ācārya* (in Tamil) 1957–58, Part I (5th ed.; Madras: Kalaimagal Office) 8.
21. Ibid., 80.
22. Śrī Candraśekharendra Sarasvati, *Aspects of Our Religion,* 47.
23. *The Discourses of the Ācārya* (in Tamil) 1957–58, Part I, pp. 15–16.
24. Ibid., 41–42.
25. Ibid., 44.
26. *Aspects of Our Religion,* 20.
27. See Sankara's commentary on the *Taittirīya Upaniṣad,* 2.1.1.
28. See *The Discourses of the Ācārya* (in Tamil) 1957–59, Part III (1st ed.; Madras: Kalaimagal Office) 146–51.
29. *Aspects of Religion,* 26–27.
30. Paul Brunton, *A Search in Secret India* (London: Rider, 1964) 101.
31. T. M. P. Mahadevan, *Spiritual Perspectives,* 17.
32. Ibid., 15.

Bibliography

Sources

Mahadevan, T. M. P. *Ramana Maharshi and His Philosophy of Existence.* Tiruvannamalai: Sri Ramanāśramam, 1959. Contains translation of Ramana's forty verses entitled *Ulladu Nāṛppadu.*

Narasimier, B. V., trans. *Upadesa Sāram.* Madras: C. M. & Sons, 1929.
Osborne, Arthur, ed. *The Collected Works of Ramana Maharishi.* London: Rider, 1964.
Sri Candrasekharendra Sarasvati. *Daivattin Kural* ("The Voice of God"). 4 vols. Madras: Vānati Publishers, 1976, 1978, 1982, 1985.
——. *The Discourses of the Acarya* (in Tamil). 4 parts. Madras: Kalaimagal Office, 1957-59, 1980.
——. *Hindu Dharma.* Kanchipuram: Hindu Samaya Manram, 1976.

Studies

Brunton, Paul. *A Search in Secret India.* London: Rider, 1934.
——. *The Maharshi and His Message.* Tiruvannamalai: Sri Ramanasramam, n.d.
Mahadevan, T. M. P. *Ramana Maharshi: The Sage of Arunacala.* London: Allen & Unwin, 1977.
——. *Spiritual Perspectives.* New Delhi: Arnold Heineman Publishers, 1975.

19

Śrī Ānandamayī Mā: Divine Play of the Spiritual Journey

Bithika Mukerji

It is often said, and with some truth, that India is a land of saints and god-men. Indeed, there are many spiritual teachers renowned the world over even in contemporary India. It will not be right, however, to situate Śrī Ānandamayī Mā amid this company. It is true that she occupied a position of great authority, yet she did so by virtue of her way of being in the world rather than anything else. She professed no philosophy of her own, nor formulated any messages for humanity. On the contrary, she repeatedly declared herself to be quite untutored in the knowledge of scripture or in the kind of spiritual disciplines that characterize the masters of most religious communities. She would say this of herself in a light and good-humored manner to forestall, as it were, any attempt to assign to her the status of a guru.

In spite of her sustained disclaimers about herself and manifest humility in the presence of any person of recognized or even just-claimed spiritual eminence, her own impact on every kind of audience was always overwhelming. Her presence had the unique quality of demanding nothing yet creating an atmosphere of peace which overcame even the most turbulent and unquiet mind. To be in her presence was to be at peace with oneself and with the world.

It is difficult to avoid the use of the word "unique" when referring to Śrī Ānandamayī Mā, just as it is impossible to unravel the mystery of her personality. Generally, the study of the development of a personality reveals many a clue to its nature, but here we meet with an uncontrived spontaneity which is baffling in the extreme. Śrī Ānandamayī Mā, as a child, a young woman, and in her mature years, was completely self-sufficient, with no manifest desires or prejudices and utterly devoid of a will to any particular course of action one could call "worldly." Although she seemed to want nothing for herself, she was not indifferent to the issues that were important for the people around her. Her undefinable air of aloofness was somehow tempered by the delight she took in her surroundings; joy emanated not only from her facial expression but from her entire body. To look upon her radiant form was to shed the cares of the world, at least for the time being. This radiance—or aura of glory, if it may be so called—was seen to be hers from her birth to her passing away.

Although she was seen to be a happy person, the spiritual depth of her joyous way of being in the world was not always appreciated or understood in its full implications. In her childhood and youth her unruffled serenity, not to say cheerfulness, in all situations—even in what the world calls adverse circumstances—made her appear simple-minded to her elders. These impressions were short-lived because at the same time she appeared to be very intelligent and gifted beyond her years. During these years her family and friends thought her to be extraordinarily good-tempered, docile, and unselfish. Gradually it dawned on them that these qualities were not personality traits but the outer manifestation of an inner self-sufficiency which required nothing from the world for its fulfillment.

Not the least of Śrī Ānandamayī Mā's endearing traits was her sense of impish mischievousness. Looking back over the years, it seems that this aspect of her behavior was very important; not only did it counteract the effects of her transhuman aloofness but it effectively dispelled any tendency to a merely sentimental adoration of her. Even the atmosphere of exaltation which was a feature of her presence remained tempered by her humorous appeal to the piquant in almost every situation. She made congregations laugh with her; her joyful talks on the possibility of God-realization in this life, transformed spiritual discipline (*sādhana*) into a balanced way of life suitable for the most ordinary men and women.

Śrī Ānandamayī Mā was considered at times to be an enlightened *yogi* liberated in this life (*jīvanmukta*) or one of stable wisdom (*sthitaprajna*), as the *Bhagavadgītā* puts it; but with the dawning realization that no matter how high she was raised in the estimation of men, something of her remained outside the parameters of human understanding. The word "paradox" is used to indicate that bridge which is the meeting point of opposites—but what words can express an obliteration of not only of the opposites but of all diversities as well? Yet in this obliteration was to be found a resilient affirmation of even the smallest details of life. Her all-embracing vision was in fact a hymn of praise to the wonderful variety of creation rather than its denial. It is well known that she had countenanced all forms of ritual worship of the many deities enjoined in the Hindu scriptures; she had also made it possible to celebrate many of the most arduous Vedic sacrifices under proper conditions. The vast spectrum of possibilities in the Hindu way of life was held together very easily and naturally by Śrī Ānandamayī Mā. She trivialized nothing which had any religious significance and belittled none who showed even the least inclination toward a spiritual way of life. Indeed, her affirmation of people, life, and all creation is just another aspect of that same boundless vision of unity which falls beyond the scope of language.

The most extravagant language, nevertheless, has been used to describe the enigmatic personality of one who remained on this plane of existence for a good eighty-six years. She was widely acclaimed as the living personification on earth of that Being who is called God by the devout, while eminent scholars caught a glimpse in her of the immensity of the vision of the One. Heads of every renowned ascetic order of India, in spite of differences among themselves, assembled on special occasions in reverent recognition of her as the quintessence and the exemplar of the timeless spirit of India.

One of the greatest scholars of our times, Pandit Gopinath Kaviraj, applied his vast learning for many years to interpret the words of Śrī Ānandamayī Mā. On numerous occasions, when controversies arose, her word was accepted as the living voice of scripture by qualified exponents of Hindu law. While Śrī Aurobindo had observed that Śrī Ānandamayī Mā ever abides in the state of the being-consciousness-bliss of the Universal Self (*saccidānanda*), Mahatma Gandhi, when at a loss to answer the spiritual queries of one of his most trusted lieutenants (Jamnalal Bajaj), sent him to Śrī Ānandamayī Mā and took pride that he had found the right guru for this exceptional man.

Philosophers sustain the theory that she is the visible manifestation in the form of a universal master (*jagadaguru*) of that primordial divine power (*ādhyā-śakti*) which pulses at the heart of all that exists. The list of such high estimations of her nature may be lengthened to many pages, but it is not necessary to do so. All those who have seen and heard Śrī Ānandamayī Mā will readily understand that indeed, it adds nothing to her stature. Such descriptions merely indicate the inadequacy of language when it seeks to encompass the dimension of mystery.

Śrī Ānandamayī Mā herself did not choose to unravel the mystery of her presence on earth. To the oft-repeated question, "Who are you," she as often replied, "Whoever or whatever *you* think, that I am," or "Whatever I was at birth, I am now and I shall be hereafter." Once to an importuning devotee who asked this question, she replied: "Why ask such a childish question? Why don't you tell yourself that this body is here in response to man's yearnings for spiritual fulfillment. What more do you need to know about it?"

So perhaps it is not necessary to understand the events of the advent or the passing away of Śrī Ānandamayī Mā; maybe it is sufficient to be receptive, if one is so inclined, to the "message" of her way of being in this world, at this time.

Early Years (1896–1914)

The early years of Śrī Ānandamayī Mā's life were spent in the villages of Bengal, now Bangladesh. On 17 February 1984 a delegation of devotees from India went on a pilgrimage to Kheora, the village where she was born on 30 April 1896. All these years, in spite of the changes of regimes in Bangladesh, the site of the humble shed which had sheltered her as an infant has remained intact, protected by a grove of trees and high walls. The Muslim population accorded a warm welcome to the Hindu devotees. In a public function it was proudly announced: "Although *Mā* was born in a Hindu family, She is also the *Mā* of the Muslims, She is our *own Mā*."[1]

Śrī Ānandamayī Mā was named Nirmala Sundari, which means literally "taintlessly beautiful." She is known to have been a delightfully engaging little girl, fair and ethereal as a fairy, so good and well behaved as to be a little astonishing. Her unquestioning obedience, uncompromising truthfulness, and unimpaired cheerfulness made her dear to the hearts of her playmates and elders. Her willingness to be of service to anyone in need made her a welcome visitor in every household of the village, irrespective of caste or religion. The whole of her village was in fact her home. She also spent parts of her childhood years in the villages of Vidyakut and Sultanpur.

When Śrī Ānandamayī Mā was not quite thirteen, a marriage was arranged for her with Śrī Rāmani Mohan Chakravarti of Atpara. In later years he came to be known as Bholanath, and we shall refer to him by this name in these accounts. The Mahārāja of Tripura, the reigning prince of this region, held her father in high esteem as a devout scholarly Brahmin of exemplary conduct. So much so that on the occasion of Nirmala Sundari's marriage, the Mahārāja as a mark of his respect sent his caparisoned elephants to form a part of the bridal procession. The marriage took place with due pomp and ceremony on 7 February 1909. This simple incident prefigured in a sense the future for Śrī Ānandamayī Mā; this occasion was marked by a quality of plenitude and magnificence which was quite unrelated to her worldly circumstances. This aura of magnificence always surrounded her, somehow without affecting her austere way of life. Moreover, such paradoxes did not seem in any way remarkable in her presence.

The cultural pattern of arranged and early marriages caters to the exigencies of a particular situation. The child-bride is generally left to the care of her own parents till she attains to her years of maturity, or, if it is convenient, she is sometimes accommodated in the family of the bridegroom. In Śrī Ānandamayī Mā's case, she lived on with her parents for another year, after which time she was received into the family of the eldest brother of Bholanath, Śrī Revati Mohan, who in the absence of their parents was the head of the family. She remained with them for nearly four years. Bholanath visited them occasionally, bringing simple gifts for her as well as for his small nephew and niece. He wrote to her more frequently, however; and she replied in respectful tones befitting the manner of a young person writing to an older man.

These years (1910–1914) for her were a time of hard and grueling household work. She was pitchforked into this situation without any preparation, but even so she was not found inadequate or out of her depth even for a day. Although her own mother was not a little anxious regarding her lack of experience, the young bride endeared herself quickly to her new family. They were charmed by her joyful expression, her neatness, her marvelous cooking, and above all the timely performance of her chores. If the servant was absent, she ungrudgingly shouldered the heavy tasks of fetching water and breaking the coal for the stove. She also had the added work of taking care of the two children Ashu and Labanya. These youngsters head a long list of children who remained completely devoted to her as they grew up and when they took up their places in the world in subsequent years.

Śrī Ānandamayī Mā was not always immersed in housework. The neighbors loved to welcome the shyly smiling, charming young girl whenever she had a little leisure. Some of them taught her embroidery, cane-work, and spinning. After the day's work was done, Śrī Ānandamayī Mā devoted some little time to these crafts.

Śrī Ānandamayī Mā's behavior was such that it did not appear that she was overworked, tired, or unhappy—and, in fact, she was not. She, as always, abided in her own state of tranquillity and self-containment. Her tranquillity was not a matter of "endurance," because for her comfort and discomfort were equally acceptable. Even to say this is not enough. Śrī Ānandamayī Mā took as much delight in what the world calls physical discomfort as in any other phenomena. Many times even under dire provocation, she was totally free of resentment. She was loved by all who came in contact with her. The lasting impression left on neighbors was that of a joyous and happy young girl, perhaps a little simple-minded not to resent the hard work which was put on her young shoulders by her elders.

Bholanath's eldest brother, Revati Mohan, passed away in 1913 after a short illness. The bereaved family returned to their village home, Atpara. The other four brothers (including Bholanath) and their sisters, gradually lost touch with each other for want of a central place of homecoming. As it happened, this was restored to them by Śrī Ānandamayī Mā. In later years the brothers, sisters, and cousins were to be reunited under Bholanath's roof as one big family, during the time they spent in Dhaka.

The Divine Play (Līlā) of Spiritual Discipline (Sādhana) (1918–1924)

At the age of eighteen, Śrī Ānandamayī Mā came to keep house for Bholanath at Ashtagram, where he was in service. After about a year and four months, she went to stay with her parents at Vidyakut for some time. While she was in Vidyakut, Bholanath was transferred to Bajitpur. It took him a while to find proper quarters for himself and Śrī Ānandamayī Mā. Finally she came to join him in Bajitpur at the beginning of 1918.

The details of her life as a housewife at Asthagram and Bajitpur are well known. Her painstaking, scrupulous service to Bholanath was on a par with the high standard of housekeeping she had maintained at his brother's house. She anticipated the least of his needs and provided for them beforehand as if she could read his thoughts. Her mother had told her that Bholanath was to be respected and obeyed. Śrī Ānandamayī Mā during Bholanath's lifetime never deviated from the standard of behavior set up for her by her mother. Bholanath was pleased with her childlike, innocent spirit of service. He patiently waited for her to feel some of the sentiments of young womanhood, but in this he found himself to have been completely mistaken. Śrī Ānandamayī Mā, herself, in one of her humorous reminiscences of the incidents of her earlier life said, "In the beginning Bholanath would say 'You are very childlike. It will be all right when you grow up,' but it seems I never grew up!"

Very soon, Bholanath's attention was taken up by a marvelous vista opening out in front of his eyes, because at about this time there arose in Śrī Ānandamayī Mā the conscious intent or *kheyāla* to engage in the divine play or *līlā* of spiritual discipline (*sādhana*). These two words *kheyāla* and *līlā* came to be associated with her gradually as aptly describing her way of being in the world. Although *kheyāla* is similar to the "will" or "wish" or any kind of desire, it is more like a sudden spontaneous thought arising not out of any need in her but because it was just the right idea for the time, place, and people around her. Again, a *kheyāla* is self-caused and requires no ultimate result to justify it. To this must be added that beyond giving expression to a *kheyāla* she did not contrive to bring about results, but, once expressed, it became irresistibly operative. A chain of events would take place so that somehow her *kheyāla* would be fulfilled. In the beginning many of these occurrences were thought to be coincidences, but in time the creative impulse inherent in her intention became sufficiently well defined as to become almost self-evident. Śrī Ānandamayī Mā, when questioned as to why she should have had a *kheyāla* for this, that, or the other, would reply at times, "There is no need for me to explain" ("no rendering of account is necessary," *kaifiyat dewa na*).

Thus, none observed any change in Śrī Ānandamayī Mā during or after the period of her spiritual practice. She remained just as she always was. For this reason, her spiritual practice or *sādhana* came to be known as her play (*līlā*). The word *līlā,* like *kheyāla,* denotes spontaneous disinterested action, pure sport which is an end in itself, although spiritual discipline requires the exertion of effort toward spiritual fulfillment. Thus, in her personal spiritual discipline as in her benevolent intent (*kheyāla*) for others, her work combined in a mysterious way effort with unperturbed tranquillity.

Eastern cultures accept the fact that human beings are born with differing predilections and varying capabilities. Even so, these differences dissolve away in the unifying experience of a yearning for transcendence. When this yearning is translated into love for God, it may be called religion. Religions are the many ways of relating to the One God who is hidden in the deepest recesses of the heart as the supremely beloved One (*iṣṭadevatā*). All forms of loving relationships are possible with Him who is beyond any particular form and all relationships. He may be for us a child, lover, father, mother, friend as well as master, because He alone is the one repository of the entire spectrum of love.

Every possible way which leads to God-realization has been illumined by those who seek Truth. Śrī Ānandamayī Mā's period of spiritual discipline bears witness to the personal experiences of those great men and women who have already traveled down these paths and is an abiding inspiration for those who follow behind. During this period she was a devout and dedicated seeker (*sādhaka*) fully occupied with the manifestations of the inner life, while her outward behavior remained that of a serene and pleasant-spoken young housewife. At the end of the day, she would ask Bholanath's permission to sit for a while to practice the simplest form of devotion, namely, the repetition of God's names (*nāmajapa*). During these evening sessions Bholanath watched amazed as her body assumed various yogic postures and her hands made ritual gestures (*mudrā*) in close coordination with her breathing. She would sink into deep meditation for hours, her body still and motionless, sometimes like a rock, and sometimes limp like a rag doll. Bholanath recognized a few of these yogic postures, but much of what happened was beyond his ken. He knew she had no previous knowledge of Yoga and had no doubt about the spontaneous nature of these manifestations. She became more and more centered on the inner life, until this process of interiorization culminated in an initiation, which in this case was as unique as the spiritual discipline which led up to it.

Śrī Ānandamayī Mā herself narrated this incident in these words:

> On this night of *Rākhi pūrnimā* (3 August 1922) I was sitting as usual in the corner of the room. I watched my finger go through the motions of drawing a mystical diagram on the ground before me, as a mantra issued from within me which inscribed itself, as it were, inside the diagram. As the master (guru) I revealed the mantra; as the disciple (*sisya*) I accepted it and started to recite it. The mantra now replaced the Names of God which I had been repeating earlier, as the realization dawned within me that the Master, the mantra, the Lord (*ista*) and the disciple are One.

Śrī Ānandamayī Mā used to explain the nature of spiritual initiation in these words:

> You wish to attract the attention of somebody you can see but you don't know his name; so you use any words or just a sound to draw his attention. He comes over and says "Did you want me? My name is such and such." Similarly God Himself in the role of the Guru discloses His Name to the pilgrim wandering in search of a guide. In the ultimate analysis the pilgrim is one with the Name and with the Guru. How can it be otherwise? He alone can impart the gift of His Name and none but He Himself can sustain the knowledge of His Name.

After her initiation Śrī Ānandamayī Mā was observed to be in states of profound contemplation frequently. For long hours she would lie on the floor, her face and body bathed in a light marvelous to behold. Few, however, saw her in this state, and this also was as it should be because the deepest spiritual experiences are had in solitude. The why and wherefore of the play of her spirituality were only gradually grasped by scholars and men of discernment in later years by persistent questioning, for this was a subject Śrī Ānandamayī Mā did not discuss. She has, however, disclosed that in six short years (1918–1924) she traversed the paths of all religions and faiths apart from the variety of forms of Hinduism. She had the *kheyāla* to experience, as it were, the trials, hardships, despairs of the pilgrim in search of God and also his state of blissful enlightenment. A vast range of spiritual experience was encapsulated within this short span of time for the benefit of all seekers of truth. Many Buddhists, Muslims, Christians, and others will bear out the truth of this statement from their own experience of dialogue with her about their own spiritual discipline. When asked "Why did you need to traverse these paths like any mortal pilgrim? Surely omniscience renders such labor redundant," Śrī Ānandamayī Mā would say:

> When you come to me, do I not enquire about your welfare and the welfare of your family? You may say that if I am already aware of the answers I should

not make enquiries. Would that please you better? The fact of the matter is that when a pilgrim is struggling to reach the goal, he welcomes the testimony of a fellow-traveller although it is true that, in this case, there was no question of journeying into the unknown. It may be said that the experiences of an intensive spiritual life were highlighted so that all human beings with spiritual aspirations may take heart and feel encouraged to continue on their paths. Are you not reassured when I confirm the validity of the stages of your endeavours and speaking on the basis of a lived experience emphasize that the quest for Self-realization is the only ultimately worthwhile aim in life?

The Gathering of Devotees

In April 1924, Bholanath came to Dhaka in search of a job and was offered a post as the manager of the Shahbagh Gardens, which he accepted. There was a small house on the premises where he resided with Śrī Ānandamayī Mā for nearly four years. Shortly after he took up his post, two of his young nephews came to stay with them and other members of both families began to visit them often. Bholanath was a very hospitable and generous host. He was of an outgoing, robust temperament, very much inclined toward enjoying the good things of life. Śrī Ānandamayī Mā continued to cook marvelous meals for his guests and took care of his household as much as lay within her power at that time.

The Shahbagh years (1924–1928) witnessed a strange and most attractive amalgam of family life and an exalted spiritual atmosphere. The impossible was made possible in Śrī Ānandamayī Mā's presence. When she came to Dhaka, she was frequently in states of introverted contemplation which may be called *samādhi;* she often lay perfectly still on the floor for many hours. Although her body was still, the radiance on her face remained undiminished. It was observed that she was neither unconscious nor in deep sleep. It was rather a state of complete withdrawal from the outside world. Sometimes day would merge into night and the new light of dawn shine before any signs of life or movement could be seen in her body. Under Bholanath's guidance, the family and later her first devotees learned to take care of her physical form at such times. Bholanath had got in the habit of keeping vigil over her on such occasions and at the first signs of returning life, he would gently rub her hands or feet and speak loudly, as if calling a person at a distance. On arising out of these states, Śrī Ānandamayī Mā would in the most natural way smile at the people around her and then gradually take up again her interrupted household duties. It did not seem that she passed from one state to another but rather that both were somehow the same for her.

Bholanath had already accepted unreservedly Śrī Ānandamayī Mā's

26. Mā Ānandamayi.

unworldly childlike attitude toward him. Now he saw in her the manifestations of the most marvelous characteristics of spiritual eminence. He was never frightened nor disbelieved that this was anything but a confrontation with a mighty phenomenon. Throughout his life he never deviated from a disposition to completely trust in her *kheyāla* or her way of life and continued to occupy his position with dignity and kindness toward all as the head of the family of devotees which grew to considerable proportions under his aegis. Scores of devotees bear witness to his open-hearted generosity in welcoming to his hearth and home the unrestful world in search of peace.

The rumor of an extraordinarily divine personality in the guise of a young housewife residing at Shahbagh spread throughout the town of Dhaka. People sought introductions to Bholanath in order to have an audience with Śrī Ānandamayī Mā. The pattern of gatherings around her was set by Bholanath. If he knew the male visitors personally or if they were vouched for by friends, he would usher them in to her presence and wished that she should answer their questions. Women, on the other hand, could effect a more direct approach. Śrī Ānandamayī Mā would greet them with a smile and unroll cane-work mats for them to sit on. She would then converse with them and inquire about their welfare.

Śrī Ānandamayī Mā gave no spiritual guidance unless it was her *kheyāla* to do so. These early devotees wished for nothing better than the privilege of staying in close proximity to her and gazing upon her divine person. For the onlookers the radiance of her countenance and the extraordinary aura which characterized even her most ordinary behavior and speech were nothing short of their idea of divinity. She was hailed as Kali, Durgā, Saraswatī, in accordance with the predilections of her audience.

At about this time, the miraculous became a prominent feature of her life. Śrī Ānandamayī Mā said that yogic powers come naturally to a *sādhaka;* he should not be distracted by them or make use of them for worldly goals. In her case, she hardly made any deliberate use of these yogic powers, although at times their abundance caused them to flow out of her just as water spills out naturally from an overfull pitcher. The world is fascinated by the display of even an infinitesimal part of the spiritual wealth which accrues to a *sādhaka*, and since she was at this time playing the role of *sādhaka*, she naturally created an atmosphere of the miraculous which affected all who came to her.

Śrī Ānandamayī Mā came to be known as the "Mā of Shahbagh," then later "Mā of Dhaka." Then she became simply Mātāji for the rest of India and the lands outside its confines. The small familylike gatherings at Shahbagh expanded into the larger family of the devotees of Dhaka ultimately to include the immense clan of her devotees throughout the world.

Every aspect of Śrī Ānandamayī Mā's life is a complete totality in itself; it spans the full spectrum of her personality. For instance, the healing power of her touch, glance, or word was a constant feature of her personality. Sometimes a spontaneous glance of compassion would be enough to remedy the ills of the body and the mind of a devotee, or his family. The many states of contemplation (*samādhi*) which involved the complete suspension of all bodily activities and functions, coupled with an inner experience of the plenitude of bliss, were as natural to her as playfulness is for a child. In her childhood, these states were regarded as fits of absent-mindedness or daydreamings or just sleep. Nor did these states cease when she was no longer engaged in spiritual discipline. They happened on occasions throughout her life. Moreover, as in her childhood so later as well, she never expressed a desire or wish but always attuned herself to the wishes of the people around her. This "adaptability" remained with her even when her wishes were of great importance to her devotees. Even her closest companion could not say definitely whether he was truly carrying out her wishes, because it was always a personal interpretation of the *kheyāla* of Śrī Ānandamayī Mā.

To divide her life into her childhood, marriage, housekeeping, or *sādhana* is merely a convenient way of dealing with a vast subject. There were no stages in her life. She played the role (*līlā*) of being a little girl, a young housewife, a *sādhaka* with as much delight as she performed the play (*līlā*) of being a tireless wanderer over the land of India in subsequent years. Her "play" (*līlā*) was not just play-acting; she did not just assume a role or pretend to be what she was not; she truly was a child, a young housewife, and later a guide for those who had need of her help in their spiritual endeavors.

The Bird on the Wing

Śrī Ānandamayī Mā sometimes described herself as a "bird on the wing" (*uḍā pākhi*). A bird alights at random on any tree and takes to the air again to perch on some other. Similarly, after leaving Shahbagh, Śrī Ānandamayī Mā began to travel so extensively that it became a way of life for her and her close companions. To be more precise, Śrī Ānandamayī Mā's travels can be described better as aimless wanderings, because no plans were made beforehand or funds provided for the purpose. Like all other events of her life, this mode of existence also came about without any special contrivance on anybody's part. A suggestion would be made to go on a pilgrimage; a party would assemble and the journey would take place. Śrī Ānandamayī Mā on such occasions always took along with her such men and women of her or Bholanath's family who by themselves would never have had the chance to travel out of their villages or towns. Wherever she went, she was always the central figure of a large crowd of men, women, and children. She managed with ease to hold together without tension the life of a thoughtful and kind matron of a large family and a mendicant's life of aimless peregrinations. It is not that this was seen as such by the travelers. In her presence, the hardships of impromptu travel became adventure full of marvelous experiences which enriched the lives of all who took part in it.

For many years her mode of travel was something like this: she would arrive at a railway station and suggest that they board the first train available. This decided the direction of the journey. Somebody in the party would suggest the name of a famous temple, or a holy site *en route,* and they would get off the train to visit it. Arriving at a town, they would proceed to a local inn (*dharamśālā*) for pilgrims where travelers are allowed to stay for three days. If the party was small, Śrī Ānandamayī Mā would stay on the open veranda of a temple, or even under trees in the open. On other occasions more organized parties would form to visit holy towns on the occasion of religious festivals.

Śrī Ānandamayī Mā's companions were not chosen or selected deliberately. All who wished to go with her went along if they were in a position to do so. Sometimes it so happened that people who had come to see her off at the railway station would board the train along with her at the last moment, because they could not tear themselves away or bid farewell to her. It made Śrī Ānandamayī Mā laugh very much to see all the confusion and chaos she seemed to create, but it was she who would then make ingenious suggestions to provide for her fellow travelers so that they could be comfortable while they were away from their homes.

In later years, however, this spontaneous travel was considerably curtailed: programs were announced beforehand and Śrī Ānandamayī Mā's travel itinerary fixed so that people might meet her or know where to go on these special occasions. Provision was made in those towns which she visited regularly for permanent rooms for her to stay in. Ashrams were built all over the country so that she should not be obliged to stay in inns (*dharamśālā(s)*).

Notwithstanding all these efforts on the part of those devoted to her service, Śrī Ānandamayī Mā continued to travel ceaselessly, and mostly at random. She never committed herself to any definite programs. She would say, "We shall see what happens" or "Whatever happens, happens."

To say all this is not even to touch the fringe of the manner of her relating to the world. She was not whimsical or careless of the convenience of others. She was most considerate, kind, and mindful of the requirements of the people around her. The least effort undertaken on her behalf brought forth a showering of blessings and a living acknowledgment which is not easily surpassed. To underscore the same point it may be said that just as she never did or said anything to disturb her families or neighbors, so in later years she demonstrated how perfectly in tune she was with her constantly changing surroundings. New places or outwardly alien cross-sections of society were for her familiar; she was never a stranger or a traveler to distant lands. She said:

> I see the world as a garden. Men, animals, creatures, plants, all have their appointed places. Each in its particularity enhances the richness of the whole. All of you in your variety add to the wealth of the garden and I enjoy the multiplicity. I merely walk from one corner of the garden to the other. Why do you grieve so if I am not visible to you for a while?

The truth of this statement has been demonstrated by the fact that when speaking to individuals or congregations she was never at a loss for a response. With consummate artistry she could endlessly delight any gathering, whether of scholars, businessmen, monks, students, villagers, or sophisticates from the metropolises of the world. The world was home for her, and all people were her own people.

Words of Śrī Ānandamayī Mā

Śrī Ānandamayī Mā attracted to her presence multitudes of people of all age groups and coming from all walks of life. Differences of religions, social status, caste, country, or cultural tradition became fluid in her presence because she respected everyone and gave of herself unstintingly to all who came. In this reciprocity lay the secret of the mystery of her overwhelming attraction, which radiated around her physical presence.

She had her own explanation for this phenomenon, which held in thrall everyone who found himself in her vicinity. In later life she used to say that although her body was aged she was a little child and, as such, was a friend to all children of the world. Their parents were like her own parents. What could be more natural than that children would love their "friend" and all parents would look upon "a child" with loving care, for a child is a natural recipient of love. So it was no wonder that she was a well-beloved friend or a child dear to the heart of all who came close to her.

Śrī Ānandamayī Mā never delivered speeches; how could an "untutored child" presume to teach her elders? If, however, anybody could elicit a response from her, then he was welcome to make the effort. Her body was like a musical instrument which when played emits a resonance. It was for the interlocuter to draw answers from her. Just as the quality of music depends on the skill of the musician, so also her answers were geared to the need of the questioner as well as to his capacity for understanding and assimilation.

The truth of such statements does not belie the fact that Śrī Ānandamayī Mā did have something to say to all those who approached her for guidance. She in general elaborated upon the following theme in countless ways, weaving it into most of her answers to different queries:

> God alone is the one and only truly worthwhile concern for man—all else is pain and in vain (*hari kathai kathā aur sab vrthā, vyathā*).

She did not deny man's right to occupy himself with things other than God, but that is the way to self-forgetfulness. She would say:

> To know himself is the supreme calling for man, to realize that the tabernacle of the world must not be substituted for his true home.

To the question "Should one renounce the world?," she would respond:

> No, why? Where is the place where God is not? The natural way of life itself should be transformed into the spiritual way of life. In fact there is nothing which can be "other" to God; so properly speaking to live in the world is to be on way to Self-realization. Since this perspective has been lost to us we perforce must speak in the language of "otherness to God."

> To realize one's Self means to discover that there is naught else except God. God and God alone is and all else is God only. God's true being cannot be described, for when speaking of "being" there is the opposite of "non-being." When trying to express Him by language, He becomes imperfect. All the same, in order to use words He is spoken of as *sat-cit-ānanda* (being-consciousness-bliss) Because He is, there is being, and because He is Knowledge Itself, there is consciousness; and to be conscious of that being is indeed bliss; this is why He is called *saccidānanda* but in reality He is beyond bliss and non-bliss.

> The human condition is inescapably a state of fragmented existence. This disjointed way of life causes disquietude of the mind and a longing for peace and tranquillity. Man has it in himself to rise from a state of perennial wanting to the everlasting state of Self-realization, for Who indeed are You? You yourself are God!

The following question was put to her by a young Irish journalist many years ago:

> Is there no substance to me as an individual? Is there nothing in me that is not God?

Śrī Ānandamayī Mā answered:

> No. Even in "not being God" there is only God alone. Everything is He. You are now in a state in which God is present in the guise of absence. Contemplate the One present even in the guise of absence![2]

To the question "How should one proceed?," Śrī Ānandamayī Mā sometimes gave the following answer:

> The rhythm of worldly existence is in a way a shadow of the cosmic rhythm in so far as all men are ceaselessly involved in the pursuit of worldly desires, which engender more desires in such a way that there is no relief or respite from this revolving cycle which is the order of time. In order to break this stranglehold, one must put in a thin wedge to check the force. With constant effort this wedge may be widened to envelop the entirety of the circle so that the same rhythm is caught up to the cosmic one. The rhythm from within the time circle may be transformed into the timeless rhythm.

Śrī Ānandamayī Mā herself has described what could be called her special message to the world: she has explained what she meant by the "thin wedge." In the round of twenty-four hours, she requested everyone to dedicate just fifteen minutes to God. Every day at the same hour for fifteen minutes one should take a respite from the world and devote oneself totally to the remembrance of God. Any image or any name of God can be used as an aid for this purpose. It is not absolutely necessary to make a drastic change in one's daily routine. If one is unable to sit alone, and meditate quietly, one may simply turn one's attention inward for that short period of time. The important thing is to choose an hour when one is least likely to be disturbed and adhere to it strictly. The fifteen minutes will gradually expand to fill the entire twenty-four hours and the time cycle will become an unbroken round of recollection or self-containment.

She has developed the same theme in other ways also. In response to a question for specific instructions, Śrī Ānandamayī Mā said:

> Once a month or week, and gradually more frequently if possible, one should make a strong resolve to live only in the sphere of Truth. On that day one should eat moderately, watch one's speech and actions carefully to avoid the least incorrect utterance or unworthy behaviour and the passions and emotions should be controlled. One should look upon one's husband or wife and one's children as manifestations of the Divine and render service to all the members of the family (including servants) in this spirit. Even if there should be occasions for anger, or other provocations, one should respond with calmness and not be jolted out of a tranquil frame of mind. In spite of

> a few or even many failures in the beginning, one should persevere till the goal of perfect control of thought, speech and action is attained. If one member of a family practises this, then the whole family will feel the calming effects of that one day.

Śrī Ānandamayī Mā paused for a moment and added amid laughter:

> Maybe some naughty children will take advantage of you, but it will pass. When you feel confident of yourself then you may increase the number of days you practice this in a week. The aim should be that this become a way of life rather than just a special occasion. On those days some time should be allotted to the reading of scriptures, meditation and the recitation of God's names (*nāmajapa*). In a short time this will enable you to turn inward and be in tune with the rhythm of your own life-breath which links you to the Cosmic Breath (*prāna*). In this way you can hope to realize your own inner Self, because who knows at what auspicious moment one may get caught up in that universal rhythm!

Śrī Ānandamayī Mā untiringly repeated the necessity of restraining the powers of the world which distract the mind and create a sense of want. The secret is to consider everything as belonging to God and oneself as a servant. One should discipline oneself to life in the belief that there is naught else except the Divine Will in operation in the world. She did not encourage anybody to neglect his duty in the world or to take his obligations to his family, society and country lightly, but she continuously sounded the one theme of God-realization like the constant drone of the keynote which fits in with every tune. She stressed the importance of the world as the necessary ground from where the quest for Self-realization begins. She would say, "To aspire to the realization of Truth is all that is worthy of a human being."

It is to be remembered that Śrī Ānandamayī Mā spoke to audiences who were under the influence of the spirit of secularism. She readily entered into discussions regarding problems which were important to modern men. She was fully aware of the crisis situation of our times: her response to a specific question in this context is very typical.

"Will man ever destroy this world and himself?" someone asked; to which she replied:

> Man has certainly not got the power to create, preserve or destroy. In Him whose play all this is, all possibilities are contained. The "destruction" of one's Self virtually amounts to the destruction of the universe. [To live in forgetfulness of one's supreme calling to be in search of the Self is called "destruction."] Where this Self is, there the world exists. To be destroyed lies in the very nature of that which is of the world and therefore perishable; it has always been destroyed, it is being destroyed and it will be destroyed. But where He is and He alone, who is to destroy whom? There the question of destruction cannot arise. Where is He who is That Self? Find out! The Self

> is not subject to destruction. The ceaseless endeavor to know that Self is man's bounden duty.

On another occasion she was approached by a Swāmiji from the Rāmakrishna Mission. He spoke in some anguish regarding the rising influence of the secular in the holy land of Bhāratvarṣa (India). He said, "The Indians are thoughtlessly imitating the West, whereas the people of the West come here on their spiritual quest!" Śrī Ānandamayī Mā said:

> It is in the nature of the world (*jagat*, "that which moves") to undergo change. Whatever was, is not anymore; all that is now will not remain. This coming into being and passing away is the essence of the world. Yet, because of this transience there is stability, permanence.
>
> Did you not say that Bhàratvarsa (India) is holy land? This is indeed true; because that is so, those who seek spiritual solace, are able to find it here. If those you call foreigners find what they are seeking in this land, why should it be a reason for chagrin? Are they not your brothers too? Why "brothers," they are indeed you, yourself. God is disporting himself in countless ways. The ways of His play are infinite. It is now like this, maybe anon it will be different.

The Swāmiji was not satisfied. He asked bluntly, "Can we not hope for the recovery of the glory of India?"

> Don't you say God is all-auspicious? Maybe the change you desire is in the offing because He is manifesting Himself as such thoughts in the minds of many persons such as you.

The Swamiji desisted saying that she had parried his questions but not answered them.[3]

This conversation is indicative of Śrī Ānandamayī Mā's aloofness from engaging in talks about the future. She did not project herself as a savior of mankind. To a direct question such as this: "Why are you in the world?" she replied: "In this world? I am not anywhere, I am myself reposing within myself."

> What is your work?
>
> I have no work. For whom can I work since there is only One?[4]

Inevitably a tiny part of Śrī Ānandamayī Mā's "teaching" could be incorporated in this article. Perhaps it would be more realistic to conclude this section with a variety of her responses to questions from different persons.

> If you have no mission to fulfill or message to give, why do you tell us to worship God?

Śrī Ānandamayī Mā:

> If you do not ask, then I have nothing to say, but if you ask, and if it is my *kheyāla,* then certainly I shall tell you about the better way of life (*śreyas*).
>
> Your sorrow, your pain, your agony is indeed my sorrow; this body understands everything. . . . Whenever you have the chance, laugh as much as you can. By this all the rigid knots in your body will be loosened. But to laugh superficially is not enough. Your whole being must be united in laughter both outwardly and inwardly. Do you know what this kind of laughter is like? You simply shake with merriment from head to foot, so that one cannot tell which part of your body is most affected. What you usually do is to laugh with your mouth while your mind and emotions are not involved. But I want you to laugh with your whole countenance, with your whole heart and souls, with all the breath of your life. In order to be able to laugh in this way you must have implicit faith in the power of the Self and try to bring the outer and inner parts of your being into perfect harmony. Do not multiply your needs, nor give way to the sense of want but live a life of spotless purity. Making the interests of others your own seek refuge at His feet in total surrender. You will then see how the laughter that flows from such a heart defeats the world.
>
> Mā, say that you belong to us!
>
> I belong everywhere and to everybody.[5]

Conclusion

The yearning to find a meaning in life knows no boundaries of time and space, history or geography, but encompasses a wide spectrum of ideals and visions of the true goal of human life. This polarity would seem to comprise the spiritual history of mankind. The experiences of this century have taught us the necessity of paying heed to all expressions of this need to relate meaningfully to a world we ourselves have created so we seek to learn from the inchoate thought patterns of ancient cultures as well as the strident voices of prescriptive ideologies.

In India the quest for this meaningfulness assumes the form of finding ways of relating to its past heritage. This age of progress with its swift and cataclysmic changes is bewildering in its effect of transvaluation of values. India tries to effect a middle way between the forces of modernization and her rooted conviction in the reality of the timeless order of ultimate Truth. Perhaps it is a sign of hope that in India there is no awareness of any lost horizon. The secret of India's continuing resilience to the forces of radicalizations lies in the simultaneity of the two opposing forces which ever remain entwined in the very fabric of her being, namely, pull of the world, where a sense of duty must prevail, evil be suppressed and justice upheld;

this is counterbalanced by the call to renunciation and a striving for that supreme knowledge of the One Reality which liberates.

Rabindra Nath Tagore once wrote that the different characters of the sages Vaśiṣṭha and Viśvāmitra illustrate well the contrast between the development of the East and the West. The former was a recluse, the latter a robust man of action; the former lived away from the world, the latter taught the young prince Rāma how to fight the forces of evil in the world; the former whispered the mantra of renunciation into the young man's ear and the latter told him how to rule his kingdom righteously. The poet wonders if the two sages will ever meet on friendly terms so that the world may witness the unfolding of new vistas in the future.

Can it not be said here that India herself has reconciled the visions of the two seers insofar as both sages spoke to Rāma, who was both an exemplary king as well as an ideal renunciate. India to this day worships Rāma, who paid heed to both his teachers.

It is a fact that Indian spirituality is grounded in its myths and that even modern India does not find it difficult to hold together the teachings of Viśvāmitra and Vaśiṣṭha. Even so there is at present a possibility of a rift between them at a deeper level. In the rarefied atmosphere of scientific clarity, can the ancient gods continue to speak meaningfully and overcome modern skepticism and disbelief? We can observe the beginnings of a separation between religion and spirituality in the sense that it appears possible to be without faith in God and yet strive to merge the human consciousness into a higher consciousness on the cosmic level.

This separation does not belong to the spirit of India. India likes to go on believing in ritualistic worship of her many deities, her religious festivals, her pilgrimages, holy rivers and mountains, sacred animals and trees and shrubs and stones—in fact, her mythology in its entirety. Is it possible to continue to believe in mythos as a dimension of Truth, not in opposition to but in harmony with logos?

Śrī Ānandamayī Mā fully understood the existential implications of the present age of technology and by her way of being in the world put it in a correct perspective for those who wished to see beyond it. That God is as much present in the world given over to scientific research as in the age of "mythology," we may say, is the message conveyed by her sojourn on earth. She made it possible once more to talk meaningfully of the one Reality which as the beauteous unity of vision and resonance was revealed as mantra in the poetic experience of the Vedic seer. Just as a mirror shines like the sun in the light of the sun, so did the tradition of the Vedas, the *Purāṇa*(s), the *Āgama*(s), and the *smrtis* become actual because she lived it as self-evident truth.

Indians think that the soil of Bhāratvarṣa (India) is holy. Once in a while we see in India not merely a teacher or just a saint, but an exemplar of the way of life which is the quintessence of her spirit. India cherishes a coming together of heaven and earth, a commingling of the timeless order and the order of time, a meeting of horizons of the eternal yearning in man and the descent of Grace. Once in a while such a dream is transformed into living experience by the presence of a Teacher who not only awakens the longing for the quest for Truth but enkindles and sustains faith in its ultimate fulfillment.

Such was Śrī Ānandamayī Mā.

Notes

1. *Ānanda Vārtā* 31/3 (July 1984) 231.
2. *Ānanda Vārtā* (May 1966) 34.
3. *Ānanda Vārtā* 16/1 (January 1969).
4. *Ānanda Vārtā* 26/2 (April 1979) 66.
5. All citations in the essay apart from those documented from *Ānanda Vārta,* the official journal published from Srī Ānandemayī Charitable Society, Calcutta, are taken from the multivolume biography of the saint in Bengali by Guru Priya Devi (*Sri Sri Ananda Mayi*).

Bibliography

Sources

Guru Priya Devi. *Sri Sri Ananda Mayi.* Calcutta: Śrī Ānandamayī Charitable Society; vols. 1, 2 in English, 1985, 1986; vols. 2, 3, and 7 to 17 in Bengali; vols. 1, 4, 5, and 6 in Bengali (new ed.), 1986.

Herbert, Jean. *Aux sources de la joie (Sad Vani).* Quebec, Canada: Editions Lucides, 1985.

Studies

Bhaiji. *Mother as Revealed to Me.* Calcutta: Matri Mandir, 1968.

Herbert, Josette. *L'enseignement de Mattnandamayi.* Paris: Editions Abin Michel, 1986.

Lipski, Alexander. *Life and Teachings of Sri Anandamayi Ma.* New ed. Calcutta: Matri Mandir, 1985.

Mukerji, Bithika. *From the Life of Anandamayi Ma.* 2 vols. Calcutta: Matri Mandir, 1972, 1980.

Glossary

abhādita. What is not falsifiable, uncontradicted.

ābhāsa. Light, reflection, resemblance, semblance, appearance.

abhavya. Undevout, ineligible soul incapable of attaining liberation.

abhi-tapas. Concerted brooding, intense meditation.

abhiniveśa. Resolution, determination of purpose, instinctive clinging to worldly life and the fear that one might be cut off from it by death.

abhiṣeka. Consecration, anointing, inaugurating by sprinkling of water, coronation, installation (of kings or religious heads), religious bathing.

abhyāsa. Repeated practice or exercise, continued use.

acala. Steady, immovable, fixed.

Ācārya. Teacher or preceptor, spiritual guide, holy teacher who instructs the pupil in the Vedas; when affixed to proper names, learned venerable (doctor).

acintya. What defies thought, beyond the scrutability of reason.

acit. Non-intelligent, non-spirit, material existence.

ādānam. Accepting, seizing, earning, acquiring.

adharma. Unrighteousness, wickedness, sinful, injustice, an unjust act, a quality pertaining to the soul or mind imperceptible but inferred from reasoning and from transmigration.

adhibhūta. A highest being or spirit or its all-pervading influence; the integrating factor at the level of corporeality or material elements.

adhi daiva, adhi deva. Presiding god or deity, integration *in divinis.*

adhvaryu. One of the four Vedic priests in their roles as functionaries assisting in the performance of the rite of sacrifice.

adhyāpana. Teaching, the causative counterpart of learning (*adhyayana*).

adhyāropa. Superimposition, the initial phase of identification as a heuristic device prior to subsequent recession or de-identification.

ādhyā-sakti. Name of the first or initial-most phase of the operation of *sakti.*

adhyātma. Relating to the spirit, spiritual (*adhi,* "over"; *ātman,* "spirit").

adhyātma vidyā. The science and the art of the discovery of spirit.

ādhyātmika. Integration or unification from the overall perspective of spirit; what originates (e.g., suffering) not from without but from mind, self, or spirit.

adhyayana. Learning, study, learning by rote especially the Vedas, done as a vocation and an obligation.

Advaita. Non-duality, identity, denial of otherness, unitive life; indivisibleness of the web of life and existence, communion of the soul with God.

Āgama. Scripture, testimony from the most reliable source, the Vedas, special scriptures which are foundational texts to specific traditions of Hinduism like Saivism.

aghāti karma. Nondestructive karma which does not obscure or delude but is only responsible for bodily existence in the present life.

Agni. Fire-god of the Vedas presiding over the abode of mortals, the god of the sacrificial rite, its eternal preserver.

agnīdh. One of the four Vedic priests in their role as functionaries or officiants assisting in performing the sacrificial ritual.

Agnihotra. Oblation to Agni, maintenance of the sacred fire and offering oblations to it as part of the brahminical "daily rite."

Agniyādhāna. Lighting of the sacred fire done as part of the rite, performed by a sacrificer and his wife and employing four priests.

aham. I, the first person nominative singular; assertion of superiority, egotism, sense of self, self-love considered as spiritual ignorance, conceit of individuality, pride, also *sakti* or power of self-being, the pure I as the vibration of spirit.

ahamkāra. The ego-making principle which is constitutive of the psyche, the implicit "I" in all assertorial certitude, the self-assertiveness in all assertion, the ego-motive in perception.

āhārah. Fetching, bringing near; good.

āhārya. To be taken, to be brought near; artificial, adventitious; intended; effected by decoration.

ahimsā. Nonviolence, nonkilling as a practice or vow; a spiritual ideal of regard for life and absence of malice; either meaning a total repudiation of force or employing force in an ethical spirit in the line of vindication of "own duty."

āhuti. Offering an oblation to a deity, any rite accompanied with oblation.

Āhvanīya. One of the three fires, namely, the eastern burning at a sacrifice; a consecrated fire taken from the householder's perpetual fire.

ajāti vāda. The theory or doctrine of *ajāti,* i.e., not coming into being of anything; non-creation of the so-called created order.

ajiva. The insentient; non-soul; the nonliving comprising matter, motion and rest elements, space, time, merit and demerit.

ājīvaka. Those professing the doctrine termed *ā-jīva,* "as long as the life-monad." The doctrine is that there can be no realization as long as the life-monad (*jīva*) has not completed the normal course of evolution, which spans a fixed number of inevitable births; a religious sect contemporary to the founders of Jainism and even of Buddhism, treated by them as "heretical" because of the sect's espousal of a thoroughgoing determinism denying the free will of man and his moral responsibility for any so-called good and evil. There is no cause for the depravity of beings or for their purity. Nothing depends on human effort, the varying conditions at any time being entirely due to fate, to the milieu, and to "own nature."

ajñāna. Wrong knowledge; ignorance; nescience; the principle which hides truth, deludes the spirit by presenting reality in a form which it has not, and lures it in the wrong direction.

akincanya. The sense of utter unworthiness or helplessness, the feeling of incapacity to follow the prescribed paths of works contemplation or devotion.

akṣara. The syllable; the imperishable; etymologically, that which pervades (*aśnute*) or that which does not pass away (*akṣarati*) and either way applying to the highest self which pervades all effects and does not pass away or decay; what does not cease to exist until there is knowledge.

āḷvār(s). Tamil word used as proper name to refer to the Tamil saints, twelve in number and belonging to the period between the second and the eighth century of the Common Era. They are God-intoxicated mystics, "divers" immersed in the ocean of ecstatic love for God in his beauteous extraterrestrial form as *Nārāyana* pervading all beings and things and communicating the joy of their communion with him to humanity; their hymns collected under the label "four thousand sacred lyrics" are venerated as "revelation" by the Sri-Vaiṣnava community.

amṛta. Immortal, imperishable, indestructible, eternal; the world of immortality, heaven, the power of immortal light; nectar of immortality, ambrosia of the gods supposed to be churned out of the ocean; antidote against poison; what causes immortality; deity; proper name of the deity; a label for the physician of the gods, the sun, the soul, Viṣnu, Śiva; final beatitude, absolution; one who tastes the sacrificial residue; the nectarlike quality established by drinking the soma-contents obtained from soma-sacrifice.

anadhigata. Previously unacquired; unprecedented.

anala. The fire; the god of fire (Agni), wind, bile.

ānanda. Happiness, joy, supreme bliss, felicity, plenteousness, name of Viṣnu, of Śiva.

ānandamaya. Fullness of bliss, abundance of bliss; predicated of *ātman* either as a label naming its essence or as its attribute; the energy or power of consciousness (*cit-śakti*).

anantaguṇa. Infinity of divine attributes.

ananyatvam. Nonseparateness, the state marked by absence of otherness (*anyatvam*); negation of negation; non-duality.

anāvaraṇakatva. Unveiledness; the state of lifting of the veil (*āvaraṇa*) that has been hiding the real.

anavasāda. Safety, protection; the state of being free of depression, sinking, fainting or sitting down (*avasādah*), being without a sense of ruin, loss, or end; to be free of spiritual exhaustion.

anekānta; anekāntavāda. Being manifold or pluralistic; theory of relative pluralism as against the extreme of absolutism or radical pluralism; the theory that nothing could be affirmed absolutely, as affirmations are true only under certain conditions and limitations; the ontology that things possess an infinite number of predicates from infinite points of view, each of which can be only affirmed in a particular sense.

anilah. Wind; the god of wind; the wind in the body, one of the humors; rheumatism referred to disorder of the wind (according to *Āyurveda*).

anirvacanīya; anirvācya. Indefinability; that which does not contain reality or unreality or both reality and unreality; the status of the phenomenal things of the world, the phenomenality of them being like the illusory, indefinable.

anivṛttīkaraṇa. Nonceasing operation; spiritual striving even after experiencing spiritual tranquillity to ward off possible onset of greed or passions.

annāda. The Eater of food (*anna*). Prajapati's state of "the eater of food" in which a performer of sacrifice aims at establishing himself.

annam. Food; what is made of food; food as representing the lowest form in which Self (*ātman*) is manifest; brahman as represented by food.

anṛta. Falsehood, evil, lying, deception, fraud.

antaḥ. End; aims, limit, boundary, last or extreme point; vicinity, neighborhood; a final syllable or letter of a word.

antahkaraṇa. Internal organ; mind; inner sense or sensorium.

antahkaraṇa vṛtti. The modes or modifications of the inner sense; mental modifications; psychic states either opaque or dense or transparent coalescing with consciousness.

antaranga sādhanā. Spiritual disciplines of an inward kind; inner *praxis* involving withdrawal from the outer; transcendental reflection, contemplation, and absorption.

antārātman. The introverted soul, one which is uninvolved in external things or uninterested in worldly pleasures but meditates on its own nature.

antarikṣa. Middle region.

antarmukhīnatā. Inward disposition; introvertedness.

antaryāmin. Inner ruler; inner self of all beings; Brahman immanent in the self.

anubhava; anubhūti. Experience either of the normal, mediated kind, i.e., sensory and even rational, or some direct experience which becomes realized through special cognitive process; sometimes refers to aesthetic experience (*rasānubhava*) also unmediated as in the case of spiritual experience; used also interchangeably with the content of experience (*anubhūti*).

ānukūlyasya sankalpa. The will or resolution to be in conformity to God's will; a condition or factor necessary for the discipline of self-surrender (*prapatti*).

anupaśaya. What accounts for relief from aggravation due to disease; one of the several factors of Indian pathogenesis (*Āyurveda*).

anuṣtāna. Commencing or undertaking a course of action; practice of religious rites or ceremonies.

anuvyavasāya. Reperception; when a cognition occurs it is objective cognition (*vyavasāya*), e.g., "this is a paperweight," but after this it is again related to the self by the mind as "I know this paperweight." All practical work proceeds as a result of this reperception.

apagaraḥ. One who reviles or says what is disagreeable; censure.

apānah. One of the five life-winds in the body which goes downward and out at the anus; breathing out.

apara. (As a pronoun) another, more, matchless, different; hinder, later, inferior or lower; nonextensive.

aparigraḥ. Nonacceptance, rejection, voluntary destitution, poverty.

aparokṣa. Not perceptible to the senses; not distant or remote; immediate; vision implying participation.

apatha, apatham. Pathless, roadless; a wrong road; deviation, bad or evil course; heretical.

apauruṣeya. Superhuman; not of the authorship of man (or woman); of divine origin; of no origin, authorless.

apavāda. Reproach or blame; evil report; an exception; refutation as of a wrong imputation or belief.

apekṣābuddhi. Awaiting mind; care, attention, heed; respect, deference.

aprākṛta. Not ordinary, extraordinary; not vulgar; special.

aprāmāṇya. Unauthoritative, unwarranted, non-valid; untrustworthy.

apūrva. Not preceded, new, unknown, not first; the remote consequence of an act, like going to heaven as the result of good acts; virtue and vice as the external cause of future happiness or misery.

arcāvatāra. Material image (*arca*) into which the Deity "descends" (*avatāra*) as disclosing his accessible grace to enable worship and communion.

arci. The realm of pure light.

arcirādi mārga. The path of light meant for those who are to be liberated, i.e., not to return to the mortal world again to be reborn.

arhat. The adorable; the omniscient; the ascetic who has conquered passions and the senses through realization of equanimity; one who is absolutely free from the will to live yet has immense compassion for all and wills actively the well-being of every being; one in whom all fetters are destroyed and who consequently realizes *nirvāṇa.*

ārogya. Health; good health.

arpaṇa. Placing or putting upon or in offering, resigning; giving back.

artha. Thing; existence or being of things; the whole range of tangible objects that can be possessed, enjoyed, and lost and which are required for the upkeep of a household and for the virtuous fulfillment of life's obligations; riches and worldly prosperity; business-matter, business affair; end and aim, wish, desire, motive, concern; includes the object of human pursuit, the means of this pursuit and also the needs and the desire suggesting the pursuit; meaning, signification, import.

arthasāstra. The Hindu system or doctrine of *artha;* the authoritative handwork (*sāstra*) of the science of wealth wherein are to be found all the timeless laws of economy, politics, diplomacy, and war; the encyclopedic work known after the name of *Kauṭalya,* the legendary Chancellor of Chandragupta Maurya (fourth century) before the Common Era.

arūpa. Formless; being devoid of visible form (*rūpa*).

asamprajñāta. Without knowledge of any object; descriptive of the last stage of *samādhi* in which the old impressions due to the continued experience of worldly events—objective or even internal—are destroyed and the buddhi becomes pure and transparent like spirit (*puruṣa*).

āsana. Firm posture as a condition which renders possible fixing of one's mind on any object that one chooses; the particular postures of body, hands, and feet prescribed for all spiritual exercises and described in Yoga texts.

asmitā. "I-am-ness"; the egoism supporting my experience, the real essence and foundation of my life subject to *samsāra* or the whirl of worldly existence; treated as the derivative of, as marking the stage of, spiritual ignorance (*avidyā*); lies inherent in the *buddhi* as its particular mode and transmigrates with *buddhi* from birth to birth and is impossible to get rid of without transcendental efforts; also means a state of unifying concentration helping *buddhi* concentrate on pure substance—the being of things as divested of all modifications.

āsava. Intoxicants; depravities; flowing in of karma matter.

āsrava. Influence of the prejudices, intellectual as well as affectional; the influx of karma-particles—infra atomic kinds into the soul.

āśrama. The differentiated stages of a man's lifetime according to the Hindu dharma. The four of them are (1) that of the student who submits to learning, (2) that of the householder marking the period of man's maturity and enactment of his due role in the world, (3) the stage of retirement to the forest for meditation, and (4) the mendicant wandering stage; spiritual liberation (*mokṣa*) is for the latter two and not for the first or second.

āstika. The "orthodox" who regards the Vedas as infallible and sometimes establishes the validity of his belief on their authority; a term of self-interpretation tacitly employed by the Hindu systems of religion and philosophy to define their parameters without overlapping into the "heterodox" (*nāstika*); more generally speaking, it means one who accords recognition to spirit and spiritual (*adhyātma*) and distinguishes him from one who says no to spirit and denies a self as different from corporeality, and its transmigration in accord with the law of Karman or its destiny as one of realizing of its immortality—who, in other words, espouses a philosophy of the mundane.

astitva. Being-ness; the nature of is-ness of things and beings.

asuḥ. Breath; life; spiritual life; life of departed spirits.

asurah. An evil spirit, demon; a general name for the enemies of gods; also used to refer to gods in the Veda meaning supreme life-force.

asvamedha. Horse-sacrifice, a most solemn Vedic sacrificial rite in which a perfect specimen of a horse is first let loose on grazing grounds over the earth for the full cycle of a year, extending its adventurous stroll of conquest as far as it pleased by overthrowing anyone who attempted to obstruct its way, and then escorting it home to be slaughtered sacrificially with the most elaborate rites. This royal sacrifice elevated the king to the position as paramount sovereign.

ātivāhika. The world of wind or atmosphere which the soul leaving the mortal plane traverses before either returning to the mortal world or directly reaching the realm of the supreme God.

Ātman. The individual soul or life-monad; that which makes the universe animate, a living organism by circulating through its (the universe's) limbs and spheres; the life monads contained within and constituting the very substance of corporeal body, ascending and descending through various stages of being, now human, now divine, now animal, now lower, those enjoying the highest states of being possessing five sense faculties as well as the faculties of thinking and speech; self or oneself in which sense it is used reflexively for all three persons and in the singular number, masculine gender or number of the noun to which it refers (indicated by the non-capitalized use of *ātman*); Supreme Soul, Brahman; essence, nature (*ātmaka*); the person of the whole body; mind, intellect; the understanding; reason; form; care, efforts or endeavors (non-capitalized *ātman*).

Ātma-vidyā, Ātma-jnāna. Spiritual knowledge, knowledge or gnosis meaning both theory and practice of *ātman* which as spirit in the subjective sense is interchangeable with Brahman which is spirit in the objective sense.

AUM, om, aum. The addressing name for Supreme Spirit, the declaratory name Brahman itself expressed in an address form and hence enjoined to be meditated on by the old sacred chant which symbolizes it; as a symbol for meditation of Brahman, it is also called *praṇava* as preeminent prayer; by extension it refers to all the Vedas, hence chanted before commencing and after ending recitation of any part of the Veda.

aupāsanā. A ritual term, relating to household fire, a fire used for domestic worship.

auṣadam. Treatment; a medicament; medicine in general; an herb; mineral.

avacceda vāda. Determination-theory, one of the two ways of explaining how the mental modifications (*vṛtti*) partake of pure consciousness underlying mind, the mental modes in their attenuated form being thought to define or determine the indeterminate consciousness more and more clearly like sunlight contributing to the visibility of objects with greater and greater clarity. The alternative theory is that the modes "reflect" pure consciousness like a transparent foil.

avasthā traya. States of experience three in kind: the wakeful, dream, and deep sleep; inquiry into the three states of consciousness is the method whereby one may arrive at the truth of what outlasts them as the "fourth" while also indwelling them.

avatāra. The cult of divine descent or incarnation combining history and mythology, characteristic of the Hindu epics and the Purāṇas; represents according to tradition the concrete manifestations of divine grace and its periodic incursion into all species and into the history of humanity, when evil triumphs over goodness.

avidyā. Ignorance, folly, want of learning; spiritual ignorance or nescience; illusion personified which causes the perception of what does not really exist as inherent in what alone indeed really exists; the counterpositive of *vidyā*, the metaphysical knowledge of the truth (empirical knowledge or learning still falling within the sphere of *avidyā*).

āvirbhāva. Manifestation, counterpositive of de-manifestation (*tirobhāva*); presence, appearance, incarnation.

avyakta. Unmanifest; a term technically applied to Nature (*prakṛti*).

ayodhyā. The place free of conflicts; the abode of Brahma (*Brahmapura*), of the divine manifest in nature; name of the city of the ruling family of Iksvāku (the modern oudh) associated with Rāma and one of the Jaina Tīrthankara.

Āyurveda. Knowledge of life, an ancillary branch of the Atharua Veda transmitted as a science and as treatises bearing the names of the gods, sages and their disciples representing the line of transmission; the general name of classical Hindu medicine.

bahirātman. The extroverted soul which regards external things as its own, as "mine," and is involved in worldly pleasure.

bambha. A Prakrit term meaning truth.

bandhu, bandhutā. A relation, relative in general; kindred, kinsmen taken collectively; affinity.

bhaga. Good fortune, luck, happy lot, happiness; propensity; distinction; glory; beauty; excellence; indifference to worldly objects; strength; omnipresence.

bhagavad, bhagavān. Glorious, illustrious; revered; divine or venerable, applied to gods, demi-gods, and other holy or respectable personages.

bhakti, bhakta. Devotion, attachment, loyalty, faithfulness, reverence, service, worship, homage; a worshiper, devotee, adorer, attendant.

bhakti-mārga. The way of devotion to god regarded as the way to the attainment of final emancipation and eternal bliss.

bhakti-yoga. A yogic scheme of God-realization as the completion of moral and spiritual disciplines; a disciplinary process involving different stages, all of which are dominated by the single aim of seeing God face to face.

bhara-samarpaṇa. Renunciation of the sense of responsibility involved in the saving act; casting oneself on the saving power of grace by which the weight of world-weariness is lifted and a state of being without fear (*nirbhaya*) is accomplished.

bhava. Birth; deed which brings about rebirth; that from which anything becomes, like merit and demerit; what exists in all places and times (Brahman).

bhāva. The internal aspect of action pertaining to motive or intention of one who acts, the purity of which makes the act intrinsically good; positive nature; being, on which depends negation; what generates the cognition "it is."

bhavya. One who is capable of attaining spiritual liberation; that which is future.

bhayankar. Frightening, terrible, fearful; dangerous, perilous.

bheda. Difference; reciprocal negation, dissension, breaking, splitting; rending; dividing, separating; interruption; injury, wound.

bhedābheda. Relation of difference and nondifference; assertion of things being different from each other while also being nondifferent in some sense.

bheda vijnāna. Discrimination; the wisdom of disjunction.

bhīma. Terrible; name of one of the Pāndava brothers.

bhiṣaj. Physician, doctor.

bhoga. Eating, consuming; enjoyment, fruition, possession; suffering, enduring, experiencing, feeling, perception; sexual enjoyment; an object of enjoyment.

bhūta. Become, being, existing, produced, formed; happening; true, right, proper fit; past; any being human, divine, or even inanimate; creature; spirit, ghost, devil; physical element.

bībhatsa. One of eight or nine *rasa*(s), "sentiments," in poetry; disgusting, loathsome, revolting; malignant; mischievous; cruel, ferocious.

bīja. Seed, a germ element, origin, cause; the seed or germ of the plot of a play; the mystical letter forming the essential part of the mantra(s) of a deity.

bimapraribimba. The relation of original and its reflection.

bimba. Archetype of a reflection.

brahmā. Officiating as functionaries in the rite of sacrifice; the creator god.

brahmabhāva. The state of Brahman unaffected by pairs of opposites like merit and sin; description of the station of the true renouncer (*samnyāsi*).

brahmacarya. Celibacy, continence, the life-mode of "walking with" that leads to Brahman.

brahmaloka. The higher world of brahmā, the creator, the plane to which the soul travels after coming out of the body.

brahman. The mystic power pervading the universe; the utterances founded upon the manifestations of the *brahman.*

Brahman. The supreme principle which is the moving force behind the gods; the ground of the universe, the source of all existence; declared as nondifferent from *ātman;* described as unconditioned existence, self-luminous intelligence and unexcellable bliss.

brāhman, brahman. The priestly class and the priestly functionary.

brāhmaṇa. The stratum of texts between the Samhitā(s) and the upaniṣad(s).

Brahma-niṣta. One established in Brahma-realization.

Brahmapura. The abode of Brahman.

brahmarandhra. The point at the center of the head through which the breath of life (*prāna*) leaves the body in the process of being liberated from the body.

Brahma-vid. The knower of Brahman; one who has realized Brahman.

Brahma-vidyā. The science or supreme knowledge pertaining to Brahman, the same as Ātma-vidya.

Brahma yajna. Brahman-sacrifice, the highest rite focused on Brahman, namely, learning and teaching of Brahman.

Brahmayāna. The state of directly reaching the realm of the supreme Godhead.

brahmodya. Ritual priestly debate wherein the enigmatic utterances (*brahman*) become the subject matter.

buddhi. The intellectual faculty of discrimination of which the rational and analytical are only extensions; an instrumentation which is above the plane of mind (*manas*); having a psychological and cosmic aspect related as cause and effect in spiritual realization.

buddhi grāhya. The transcendental bliss contemplatively seized by intellect without the mediation by sense.

buddhi-vāsanā. The mental or intellect's imprints.

buddhiyoga. The integrated intellect which gives focus to an integral yoga.

caitanyam. Consciousness, awareness.

cakra. Wheel, disk; center in the subtle body, six in number through which the cosmic energy lying dormant at the base of the spine uncoils and ascends to the apex of *brahmarandra.*

cakravartin. The virtuous world-monarch who sets the sacred wheel of the world-pacifying monarchy in motion.

candāḷa. Wicked or cruel in deeds; a general name for the lowest and most despised outcaste.

candas. The Vedas, the sacred texts of the Vedic hymns; a meter; metrical science or prosody regarded as one of six "limbs" or auxiliaries to the Veda; chanter of the *sāmaveda;* meaning, intention.

Caraka, Caraka Samhitā. Legendary author after whom are named the collections (*samhitā*) which constitute the most authoritative text on Āyurveda; Caraka and Dradhabala redacted an earlier work and flourished in the pre-Buddhist India; an incarnation of the serpent God Seṣa, Caraka took birth in the family of a learned sage in Varanasi, redacted the above work, and propagated Āyurveda among humanity.

caramasloka. The "last" or the ultimate verse of Krishna's instruction to Arjuna in the *Bhagavad Gītā* to discard all pathways to God-realization but to take refuge in Him and that "he should not grieve" as He will cleanse him of all sins; one of the three formulas (*mantras*) on which authority "surrender" is solemnized.

caraṇa guṇa. Rectitude of the will; practice.

cāturmāsya. The rite of sacrifice performed every four months to which group belong four sacrifices, three of them offered on the full-moon days of the first, fourth, and ninth months of the year and the fourth on the first day of the waxing moon—the first day of the lunar year (between February and March).

caturtha. The fourth, that which has no elements (*a-matra*); pure consciousness of self or spirit.

cayanayāga. A sacrifice requiring the construction of five altar piles next to each other symbolizing the four directions–east, west, south, and north–and shaped like that of a flying hawk. To the head and other parts of the figure, correspond the eye, etc., of the sacrificer. This likewise is the case with the five piles. By performing this rite the ritualist endows the parts with immortality and the nectar of perfect knowledge.

cetanā. Volition; consciousness understood as the decisive factor in confirming the existence or nonexistence of living beings and hailed as the mainstay; the only true constituent of humanity, according to the medical sciences.

cidābhāsa. The reflection of consciousness in the medium of the intellect.

cidambaram. The expanse of Spirit as Light; name of a sacred temple and shrine of South India in the sanctum of which is called the Hall of Ethereal Consciousness (*cid sabhā*), wherein resides the Deity imaged as the Sovereign Dancer (*natarāja*).

cit. Intelligence, consciousness.

citi, cit-śakti. The power or force of intelligence; the dynamic aspect of consciousness displayed in cognitive life.

citta. Memory; the mind-stuff sought to be brought to rest by Yoga; as the participle of the verb *cint,* "to think," it comprises observing, thinking, intending–the functions of both the reasoning faculty and the heart.

citta suddhiḥ. Purification of *citta;* the purging of *citta* of all desires which give it its fitness for reflecting spirit without opacity.

citta vrtti. Mental fluctuations or states which yoga aims at bringing under one's control.

dahara vidyā. Meditation on the Small (*dahara*), the Ether inside the heart-lotus; the "Ether of the heart" is the radiant expanse of consciousness which is the attribute of Brahman.

daivī vāk. Word or language as sourced in the divine.

daksiṇā. On the right or south of, in the southern direction; a present or gift to *brāhmaṇa* at the completion of a religious rite; gift or donation in general.

damaḥ. Taming, subduing; self-command curbing the passions; firmness of mind.

damśana. A Prakrit term interchangeable with *darśana,* meaning philosophy in the sense of a view of ultimate reality, the world, and the self.

dāna. Giving, granting, teaching; handing over; liberality, charity; bribery as an expedient of overcoming one's enemy; purification.

darśana. The enterprise of thinking systematically with a view to accomplishing the goal of vision or direct experience; points of view or perspectives all regarded as aspects of a single, orthodox tradition; valid intuitions from differing points of view; projections apparently and overtly contradictory and yet complementary of one truth on various planes of consciousness.

darśa, darśapūrnamāsa. Darśa is "the day on which the moon is seen only by the sun and no one else"; it has the same sense as *amavāsyā, "the day when the two dwell together"; purnamāsā* means "the moment when the moon is full"; the rite that is performed on these days is the pattern of all other sacrifices.

dāsa. A slave or servant; a man of the fourth caste; the common people; the humblest, used by the speaker as a mark of humility.

dasanāmi(s). The monastic institution marked by recognition of ten orders of *samnyasin*(s); appellation for the Advaita order of ascetics inclusive of *tirtha, āśrama, vana, araṇya, giri, parvata, sāgara, saraswati, bhārati,* and *pūri.* These ten orders are believed to be pupils in succession of the four disciples of Sankara, the first two of Padmapāda, the next two of Hastāmalaka and the next three of Toṭaka and the last three of Suresvara.

dasyu(s). Identical in meaning with *dāsa;* antagonism between *ārya* and *dāsa* is emphasized and prayers offered in the *Rg Veda* to gods for subduing the *dāsa* in favor of the Arya; the antithesis between them is based on cult as well as bodily appearance and color; the *dasyu* is represented as not obeying the ordinances of the gods.

dayā. Compassion, tenderness, sympathy; sentiment of heroic compassion.

deva. Divine, celestial; deity; a divine man, a *brāhmana;* a title of honor used in addressing a king ("your majesty").

devayāna. The way of the gods as a transmigration doctrine meant for those who cultivate faith and asceticism; marks regions of ever-increasing light as stations on the way to the "light of lights."

devi. Goddess; a female deity; a crowned queen who has undergone consecration along with her husband; a respectful title applied to a lady of the first rank.

dhana. Property, wealth, riches, treasure; any valued possession; capital; booty, spoil.

dhāranā. The act of persevering; retentive memory; keeping the mind collected; steadiness; a settled rule, conclusion; continuance in rectitude; conviction.

dharma. Righteousness; goodness; merit; justice, a just act; a quality of the mind or soul imperceptible but inferred from reasoning; the whole context of religious and moral duties; the doctrine of the duties and rights of each in the ideal society and as such the law of all action.

dharmaśāstra. Books of the Law attributed to mythical personages like Manu ("forefather of man") and eminent brahmin saints and teachers of antiquity; earlier works filled with social, ritual, and religious prescriptions intended for one or other of the Vedic schools; the later law books reached out to cover the whole context of orthodox Hindu life.

dharmātmā, dhārmika. One who has made *dharma* his very soul.

dhātu. Bodily juice; body tissues; elements; a mineral, metal; bones; good health.

dhīḥ. Intuition; intellect, understanding, idea, imagination, conception; intention, purpose; prayer, devotion.

dhrti. Attraction

dhūmādi mārga. The smoky path for the departed souls that are to return to this mortal world again for rebirth.

dhvani. Letter-sounds; noise in general; tune, note, tone; the sound of musical instrument; the suggested sense, as different from the expressed, of a passage.

dhyāna. Meditation by deep concentration; one of the accessories–"internal disciplines"–of yoga, marked by the constant repetition of what the mind seeks to fix on.

dhyānaśloka. The initial verse before commencing the recitation of a poem or mantra recapturing the essence of the deity concerned for constantly fixing the mind on it.

dīkṣā. Consecration for a religious ceremony; initiation in general; a ceremony preliminary to a sacrifice; investiture with the sacred thread.

dīkṣita. Consecrated, initiated as for a religious ceremony; a priest engaged in *dīkṣā*; a pupil; a person who or whose ancestors may have performed a grand sacrificial ceremony such as *jyotiṣtoma.*

divyadarśana. Divine vision.

Divya Prabandham. Name for the collection of the Tamil utterances of the Ālvār(s) totalling four thousand hymns held as divine and authoritative for the tradition of *Srivaiṣnavism.*

doṣa. Disorder of the three humors of the body; malfunctioning; weak point; an error; crime, offense; a fault of composition, of definition.

dravya. Substance, thing, object, matter; the substratum of properties; any possession, wealth, goods, property, money; a wager, stake; substantive.

drk. Perceiving principle; consciousness.

drśya. The perceived; the objective content of consciousness.

duhkha. Sorrow; misery; suffering; ill; a feeling-experience of the soul cognate with pleasure (*sukha*) generated as a result of causal operation.

dvaita, dvaitabhava. Duality; the sense of duality and difference; what legitimizes the application of the number two; distinction, otherness.

dvaita vāda. The theory or argument in defense of a dualist ontology.

dvaitādvaita. Combination of duality and non-duality; identity and difference; identity that entails or presupposes difference.

Dvāpara. Name of the third *yuga* of the universe, the copper era that preceded the current "iron age."

dvandva. A couple of any two things; a strife, contention, dispute; doubt, uncertainty; one of the principal kinds of compounds in Sanskrit, in which two or more words are joined together which, if not compounded, would stand in the same case and be connected by the conjunction "and."

dvaya mantra. One of the three sacred truths of Vedanta according to the tradition of Rāmānuja; the mantra incorporating the twofold implications of the supreme truth, namely, as Śriman Nārāyana and Śri initiating the seeker into the dual form of the God typifying the Fatherhood and the Motherhood, majesty and accessibility.

dveṣa. Aversion, dislike, abhorrence, repugnance; enmity, hostility, malignity.

dvija. The twice-born; a man of any of the first three castes, the priestly, warrior, and the mercantile ones; a *brāhmaṇa* over whom the purificatory rites are performed thus rendering him qualified to recite the Veda.

Dyāvāprthviḥ. Heaven (*Dyaus* and Earth (*Pṛthvi*) symbolizing respectively luminous expansion and sheer extension with or without accompanying luminosity; the divine pair viewed as the parent of all beings and gods.

ekāgrata. One-pointedness; an advancement in the steadying of the states of *citta* in which it can concentrate on the object for a long time prior to the stopping of the processes of *citta.*

ekam. One, single, alone, only; not accompanied by any one; not the same; identical.

ekānta. Solitary; apart; one-sided or most extreme view; a false belief unknowingly accepted and uncritically followed (in contrast to *anekānta,* manifoldness of views).

gaṇadhara. Enlightened group teacher.

gārhapatya. One of the three fires with which Vedic rites of sacrifice are to be performed around a circular mound; like the other fires, this one is also to be maintained permanently by the householder.

ghāti karma. Destructive karma, obscuring the natural faculties of infinite knowledge, perception, bliss and power; to be contradistinguished from *a-ghāti* (nondestructive) kind which are only responsible for bodily existence in the present life.

goptrtva varaṇa. The act of seeking the *dayā* of the Lord as the only hope for spiritual liberation; one of the several elements or parts (*anga*) of the scheme of self-surrender (*prapatti*).

gotra. Spiritual genes; the family into which an individual is born; descendants of a common patriarchal ancestor; assemblage or group of persons; closely interwoven with the conception of choosing or invoking the fire in a rite by taking the names of illustrious *ṛṣi* ancestors of a sacrifice; the latter is called *pravara.*

guṇasthāna. The stages of purification marking spiritual development from the lowest to the highest states; classified under fourteen heads.

Guru. Teacher; preceptor; any venerable or respectable person, an elderly personage or relative, the elders; a religious teacher, spiritual preceptor; one who performs the purificatory ceremonies for someone and instructs him in the Vedas; name of Prābhākara, the leader of a school of the Mimamsaka(s).

haṭha-yoga. A particular mode of yoga so-called because it is difficult, involving constant practices of elaborate nervous exercises; it is also associated with healing and other supernatural powers, influenced the development of Tantra.

hetu. Cause, reason, the reason which establishes the conclusion on the strength of the similarity of the case in hand with known examples or negative instances; also a medical term meaning cause which, together with symptom (*linga*) and treatment (*auṣada*), constitutes a whole.

himsā. The intent to kill; injury inflicting harm on any creature.

homa. Offering oblations to gods by pouring anything fit to be offered, like melted butter, into the consecrated fire; one of the fire daily "sacrifices" to be performed by a *brahmaṇa.*

hotā. A sacrificial priest, especially one who recites the prayers of the *Rg Veda* at a sacrifice.

idā. Praise, prayer; worship.

Indra. King of the gods placed in the first rank among the gods (Vedic); in later mythology and epics Indra falls in the rank; one of the names of the Buddha; name of Pārsva, one of the *tīrthankara.*

indrajāla. The net of Indra, i.e., conjuring, jugglery, magic trick, stratagem in war; creation of an appearance of things that do not exist.

indriya. An organ of sense; bodily power or force of the senses; abode of the senses.

indu. The blissful one.

Īśa, īśā, īśvara. The supreme Lord, owning master; name of Siva; powerful, able; a king, ruler.

iṣta devatā. A desired or cherished deity; the worshiper's special tutelary divinity.

iṣti. Sacrifice performed with wife and four priests employed; distinguished from animal sacrifice (*pasu yajna*) and soma sacrifice (*soma yajna*).

jagad guru. The world teacher; title given to the office of the preceptor-founder, like Sankara and his spiritual lineage.

jagat. The universe of becoming; the world as a series of changeful happenings.

jāgrat. The wakeful state.

jāti. Class, caste, the classic role into which one has been brought by birth; the collective.

jayagrantha. The "victorious compositions" of Veda Vyāsa, which include the Purāṇa, *dharmaśastra* and the two epics of *Ramayana* and the *Mahābharata.*

jīva. Life-monad, uncreated and imperishable, intrinsically alike but "tainted" in its perfection through the influx of the non-self (*a-jiva*) constituents of the universe; individual life-monad subject to transmigration but with a transcendent affinity or oneness with God.

jīvan mukta, jīvan mukti. One who becomes spiritually free while continuing in the embodied life; the state of spiritual freedom attained while yet in the body; the Hindu counterpart of arhantship and nirvāṇa.

jñāna. Knowledge; gnosis; wisdom, cognition; intellectual intuition; knowledge of details in contrast to knowledge of things without their details (*darśana*) (both of which obtain in the state of attainment of omniscience).

jñāna cakṣu. The eye of knowledge in contrast to the fleshly eye; enlightened vision.

jñāna lakṣana. Description of *buddhiyoga;* noetic contact of a transcendental nature, by virtue of which we can associate the other perceptions of other senses when perceiving by any one sense.

jñāna mārga. The path of knowledge in contrast to the paths of ritual action or devotion.

jñāna yoga. Knowing of self as finding its true fulfillment in the knowledge of God; the yoga by which is actualized self-knowledge through the knowing of God, the reality of realities; the spiritual apprehension of the real (to be contrasted with the intellectual pathway to perfection) in the non-dual enstasis of immediacy.

jnānendriya. The senses involved in knowing in contrast to doing.

jñāpti. The experience of knowledge-realization; knowing by being.

jñeya. The object of knowing.

kainkarya. Service consecrated to that in whom one takes refuge (*saraṇya*).

kaivalya. Isolation; completeness through integration representing the final state of release which is marked by omniscience, perfection, and beatitude; the state of one who is *kevala.*

kāla. Time in general; fit or opportune time, proper occasion; a portion of time; the supreme spirit regarded as the destroyer of the universe; fate, destiny.

kāla-vipāka, kāla-samprāpti. Time's fruition; temporal precipitation; the transformation of time; a medical concept invoked as the explanation of transformation of food in successive body constituents after food is digested in the stomach and also as explanation of production of disease or its reversal.

kali. The fourth age of the world, the iron age; strife; quarrel, dissension; the side of a die which is marked with one point.

kalyāṇa guṇa. Auspicious qualities characterizing the divine; numinous attributes of the deity.

kāma. Pleasure and love; desire incarnate, the God of love who sends desire quivering to the heart; one of the human ends making its imperious demands on life; the theme of *kāma* literature.

kāmya karma. Motivated activities; deeds imbued with the desire for accomplishing goals of a self-seeking kind; in contrast with "daily" acts or deeds which are done purely with a sense of ought.

Kannada. One of the Indian languages belonging to the Dravidian family and spoken in the southwestern region of Karnāṭaka.

kāraṇa-citta. The causal mind-stuff, i.e., *citta* by itself considered without association with body, when it is all-pervading.

karma. Action, work, rite, performance (from the root *kṛ*, "to make"); the fruits of action reaped or yet to be reaped, here and in the other world; the connecting link between desire and rebirth; a kind of subtle matter produced through the actions of body, speech, and mind, which sticks to the soul (Jainism); three stratifications or kinds of karma: the seeds of destiny stored as a result of former actions but which have not yet begun to germinate, not yet begun to sprout, mature and transform themselves into the harvest of a life; the seeds that would normally collect and be stored if one were to continue in the path of ignorance basic to the present biography; seeds collected and stored in the past that have actually begun to grow, i.e., the karma bearing fruit in the shape of actual events. In the case of a perfected sage freed from ignorance, the first two types of karma do not affect him (or her) any more; the third that have been yielding the harvest of present biography, not being done away, produce the momentum of the continued phenomenal life but not being refreshed will die away presently.

karma caturanga. The four aspects of *karmayoga*, namely, knowledge that all activities are sourced in the divine, selflessness in motivations, continuance of prescribed duties and offering of results at the feet of God.

karma-kartr virodha. The accusative–nominative contrast as mutually exclusive.

karmakṣaya. The withering away of all past deeds so that they are no longer potent to cause more births and deaths, consequent to a vision of God.

karmayoga. The yoga of selfless action proclaimed to all humankind as the doctrine of salvation *in* the world; shedding of selfishness and giving up of the false notion taking the form "I am the doer" and "the world is mine."

kārpaṇya. A sense of total poverty or nothingness of oneself in relation to what one strives after; self-naughting as a prelude to self-realization.

karuṇā. Compassion, pity, tenderness, tender-hearted.

kārya-citta. Mind-stuff in its form as the effect of a cause, in association with body and subject to contraction and expansion.

kauśalam. Excellence; well-being; prosperity; skillfulness.

Kavi. Poet and sage; omniscient; wise; thoughtful.

kevala. Peculiar, exclusive, isolated, alone; pure, simple, unmingled, unattended by anything else, bare, uncovered (as ground)

kevala jñāna. Knowledge isolated from karmic obstruction; infinite knowledge; omniscience.

kevalin. One who has attained *kevala jñāna.*

kleśa. Afflictions of attachment, etc.; sorrow.

kriyā-yoga. Austerity, self-study and devotion to God—these active expressions of the observances (*niyama*) which constitute the limbs of yoga are called *kriyā-yoga*, the purpose being the lessening of *kleśa* and cultivation of *samādhi.*

kratu. Inner energy; mantra in its causal form.

kṣatriya. Noble; warrior class; the kingly administration of the sacred order.

kṣetra. *Prakṛti* and its evolutionary products; the state of the conglomeration of physical body–mind; the field.

kṣetrajna. The knower of *kṣetra,* the living principle of the self without the body–mind complex.

kundalinī yoga. The yoga of arousing of the *kundalinī,* "that which is coiled up," i.e., the great store of potential energy at the base of the spine that is normally all but unused or aroused save for going into sex drives and other physical appetites; when fully aroused by the practice of meditation and other spiritual disciplines, it is said to travel up the spine through the middle passage in the spine called *suṣumnā,* traversing six centers of consciousness, until it reaches the seventh, the center of the brain. The rise of *kundalinī* to the higher centers of the navel, heart, throat, etc., all located within the *suṣumnā* itself, provides various degrees of enlightenment.

laghutva. Lightness, transparency, or thinness as of the psychic states reflecting more of consciousness that underlies it.

laya-yoga. The same as *kundalinī yoga;* called thus on account of stepwise dissolution (*laya*) of all creation in the microcosm. According to Tantra cosmology, the same process is carried out in the macrocosm causing the dissolution of the cosmos (*mahāpralaya*).

līlā. Play or sport used as the descriptive model for explaining divine work or activities cosmic and soteriological; indicative of the indistinction of play and work on the higher level of reference where activity is not compelled by conditions not of one's own choosing.

linga. Symptom, mark, sign; token; emblem, badge, symbol, distinguishing mark; the image of Śiva as expressive of "formless form"; the subtle frame or body, the indestructible original of the gross or visible body.

loka. "That which is seen" (*lokyata*), i.e., this and higher worlds; the created realms; levels of consciousness or spheres of experience.

madhu vidyā. A form of worship and meditation (*vidyā*) having esoteric significance and providing knowledge of the divine; the form in which the sun is contemplated as the honey (*madhu*) of gods, the sky as the beehive; the Vedic hymn, the trees, the sacrifices are the flowers and the offerings of soma, milk, etc., as the honey itself. Divinities like fire and sages live on this honey.

madhyamā vāk. The level of speech occupying the middle position prior to the gross overt level of audible form and succeeding the level of pure "seeing"; what accounts for the silent practice of *mantra.*

Mādhyamika. The Mahayana school of the Middle way which maintains that the ultimate is vacuity-in-itself (*sūnya*) meaning by it that it neither "is" nor "is not" nor both "is and is not" nor "neither is nor is not." Not that there is no reality but that it excludes all conceivable predicates including that of nonexistence.

mahā bhūta(s). The gross elements of earth, water, fire, air, and ether.

mahat. The great; the earliest and the most universal state from which all the rest of the world has sprung forth, all the *buddhi*(s) of individuals and potentially all the matter of which the gross world is formed; also called the sign (*linga*) as the later evolutes give us the ground of inferring its existence, in contrast to *Prakṛti* the non-sign (*a-linga*).

mahātmā. One who has identified completely with One self (*mahat Ātman*); applied to any holy person in the sense of a great soul.

mahāvākya(s). The great formulas of the upaniṣads enunciating identity, like "that thou art," which became the subject matter of discourse and debate in Vedanta.

Mahāvira. The last Jaina savior, the twenty-fourth in the line, a contemporary of Buddha; the foundation of Jainism is attributed to him by occidental historians. The standing attitude, exhibiting a puppetlike rigidity in art representations, denotes inner absorption and splendid isolation.

mala. Dirt; filth; feces; impurity; moral taint, sin; spiritual defilement, ignorance, egoity, and individualistic pride.

manas. The thinking faculty; a constituent of the "inner sensorium" (*antah karaṇa*); what works through the senses, the latter not giving rise to knowledge unless *manas* be in touch with them; source of two movements—indeterminate sensing and conceiving prior to the rise of definitive understanding; coordinates the indeterminate sense materials into determinate conceptual forms as class notions with particular characteristics.

mānasa pratyakṣa. A form of perception in which memories of past perceptions by other senses are associated with a precept visualized at the present moment; the mental perception by which the soul is perceived as the substratum of the notion "I."

mantra. Sacred formula, word-sounds, representing the form of the deity, to be recited and repeated as part of "meditative thinking"; oral repetition of a word or phrase evoking the referent of the word and the spiritual power attached thereto; Vedic hymn or sacred prayer addressed to any deity; earliest Vedic literature; an incantation; consultation, deliberation, secret.

mantra-yoga. The yogic discipline involving recitation of mantra to purify and change human action, speech, and thought; through the particular sound uttered as *mantra;* the *cakra* which forms the proper home of this sound and the functions connected therewith, stimulated in a local, ascertainable way, the corresponding *mantra-caitanya* being awakened.

mārga. Spiritual pathway.

matam. Thought; esteemed; meditated upon; intended; approved; doctrine, tenet, creed, religious belief.

matāntaram. A different view, a different creed, the opinion of the "other."

maṭhah. The hut or abode of an ascetic, a small cell; monastery, convent; seminary, place of learning; temple; cloister.

mātrā. An affix adding to nouns the sense of "measuring as much as," "as high or long or broad as," a measure whether of length, breadth, height, size, space, distance, or number, usually at the end of a syllable, word, or composition; totality; the simple measure of anything, one thing and no more.

māyā. From the root *mā*, "to measure," "to form," the word denotes the power of a god or demon to produce illusory effects, to appear under deceptive masks ("magic" derives from this sense); the illusion superimposed upon reality as an effect of ignorance; the entire visible cosmos is *māyā* as superimposed upon true being by one's deceitful senses and unillumined mind; also a positive cosmological sense as what gives forth the world, the whence and the whither of the evolution of the cosmos.

medhaḥ. A Vedic sacrifice; a sacrificial animal or victim; an epithet of Viṣṇu.

Mīmāmsā, Mīmāmsaka. Generally known as Purva Mīmāmsā and Pūrva Mīmāmsaka, the former naming the Hindu exegetical *darśana* and the latter, one that subscribes to it, its spokesman. From the root *man,* "to think," "rationally reflect," the *darśana* is a systematized code of principles in accord with which the Vedic texts are to be interpreted for purposes of sacrifice—the principles by which one could arrive at a rational and uniform solution for issues like the relation of words in a sentence or their mutual relative importance with reference to the general drift of the sentence; a system of philosophy only in the sense that as preliminary to its objective of Vedic exegesis it speculates about the external world, soul, perception, inference, the issue of verbal meaning and validity; *mīmāmsa* principles of interpretation have legal value even to this day and likewise color consciously or otherwise the general methodological orientation of the Hindu to interpretation and understanding of sacred writings.

mithyā, mithyātva. The false; counterfeit; delusion; falsity, described in various ways as the indeterminable, as appearance and as what is removable by none but knowledge, etc., is used as the defining characteristic of the world.

mithyā dṛṣti. False insights representing the lowest stage from which to take off for advancing in spiritual life; souls incapable of attaining liberation remain at this stage for an indefinite period of time.

moha. Infatuation, affective insensibility; spiritually at the opposite pole of happiness (*sukha*); blinding feeling through ignorance; confusion.

mokṣa, mukti. Spiritual freedom, the fourth of the four aims or human ends of life; the final human good often set over against the first three, namely, *artha, kāma,* and even *dharma;* from the root *muc,* "to loose," "set free," the word imparts rescue, deliverance, emancipation, in the negative but also in the positive sense, described as realizing of sameness of nature with God or identity with the Higher self.

mudrā. Seal, the mystic hand postures playing an important role in Indian ritual and art; fried paddy and the like as are chewed; one of the items in the sacramental fare in certain Tantric rites.

mūlādhāra. The deep place at the root of the spine at which place lies coiled away like a sleeping serpent the divine power asleep; is the seat of the "earth" pictured on a crimson lotus of four petals.

mūlāvidyā. Avidyā that is causal or primal, responsible for the delusions considered as a class. Dependent on it are "derivative ignorances" (*tulāvidya*), which account for individual delusions. The derivate kind is removed by cognition of the respective objects concerned; ignorance about the rope is removable by cognition of the rope. But *mulāvidyā* is removable by knowledge of the supreme reality alone and hence it persists till the onset of Brahman realization.

mumukṣutva. Desire or yearning for freedom in the spiritual sense; the ultimate precondition that truly qualifies for undertaking the quest for Brahman.

naimittika, naimittika karma. What comes to be because of an occasioning factor (*nimitta*); obligatory duty occasioned, say, by the birth of a son is *naimittika karma.*

naiṣtikī cikitsā. Perpetual treatment, where there is complete cessation of disease through body constituents regaining equilibrium as before.

Naiyāyika, Nyāya. A follower or spokesman of the *Nyāya* school of thought. The meaning of the appellation *Nyāya* is "to scrutinize an object by means of logical proof." The *Nyāya* system recognizes sixteen categories (*padārthas*), of which the most significant, reflecting the viewpoint of the system, are the "knowable" and the "means of valid knowledge." Not the things themselves but how they are known and demonstrated is the main concern. The *Nyāya* is logic and also a theory underlying the art of controversy. The syllogism of the *Nyāya* comprises five members and the conception which is its nerve bears the name "invariable association" (*vyāpti*). The ideal of spiritual liberation espoused is that of detachment even of mind from the soul culminating in absolute unconsciousness.

nyāsa. Offering of oneself; surrender.

Nyāya-Vaiśeṣika. The twin systems of logic and cosmology closely allied in their realistic and pessimistic outlook and amalgamated by their exponents themselves. The Vaiśeṣika derives its name from the category unique to the system, namely, "difference" (*viśeṣa*) because it is an atomistic doctrine. The atoms, themselves devoid of extensions, in combination become extensive and visible. The combined school adopted theistic views acknowledging God in addition to souls but who did not, however, create matter. God is never bereft of knowledge or will (unlike the soul in liberation) but has no pain or pleasure, likes or dislikes and, therefore, though ever active, never engages himself in activity for himself. From this picture of perfection it follows that the human being also while alive should become enlightened, refine desire and will and purge them of all selfishness, learn to endure pain and abolish hate.

padārtha. Categories; real thing; the referent of a word (*pada*).

pancāgnividyā. The knowledge of the five fires mentioned in the ChU as imparted by the King Pravahana Jaivali to Gautama and never before taught to any brahmin is the basis of the eschatology of the Vedanta. The five fires are this world, rain, the earth, the man, and woman.

pāñcarātra Āgama. Pāñcarātra rites of sacrifice of the Agama literature of the Pāñcarātra branch of Śrivaiṣnava religion, its distinction consisting of the details of ritualistic worship in temples; thus named meaning "of five nights," perhaps because it deals with the fivefold forms of Lord Vasudeva, *para, vyuha, vibhava, antaryāmin* and *arcā* each succeeding self-manifestation more valuable as more urgent from the perspective of the spiritual seeker. The Brahman and the *antaryamin* of the upaniṣads, the Vāsudeva (*para*) of Pāñcarātra, the Bhagavān of Visnu-Purāṇa, the *avatara* of the epics and the *arca* of whom the Ālvārs sing, are equated in the Ramanuja tradition of Vedanta.

pāpa. Evil, sinful, wicked, vicious, accursed; abandoned; inauspicious; bad fortune.

parā. The supreme word; identified with *sabda Brahman* as the source from which the word as well as the meaning derives.

parā-bhakti. Highest *bhakti* prior to the perceptual awareness of God.

paramā-bhakti. The *bhakti* generated by the direct vision of God; sometimes also spoken of as *bhakti* descriptive of spiritual realization (*sādhya bhakti*).

parama puruṣārtha. The highest human end, namely, spiritual freedom.

paramārtha. The basic reality (*parama,* "paramount"; *artha,* "object") underlying the phenomenal realm; apprehension when the impressions conveyed by the senses to a brain in the service of passions and emotions of an ego no longer delude; the reality that is opened up to the "dis-illusioned"; the knower of the *paramārtha* is the "philosopher."

pāramārthika drṣti. The ultimate or the absolute standpoint in contrast to the perspective of empirical discourse (*vyāvahārika*); the spiritual viewpoint of the "philosopher."

paramātmā. The Supreme Soul, truly free from attachment and aversion; it has conquered all passions and thus may be said to realize its potentialities of infinite knowledge, perceptions, bliss, and power; the highest liberated self; experience as either what comes about by actual climbing upward to the spiritual apex or meditatively contacted by one on the way to siddhahood when he "perceives" a soul in that formless, unfettered state which he is destined someday to reach.

parārtha. For the sake of others (in contrast to what is for one's own sake *ātmārtha*); a being-for-others to be lived out in forbearance and humility like earth.

parātpara. "Beyond the beyond"; employed in reference to Brahman's transcendence as the unspeakable, transcending the transcendent; indicative of the universality of spirit which is the destined goal of the knower freed from name and shape.

pariṇāma. Transformation, modification, evolution; characteristic of the material plane.

parokṣa. Perceptible to the senses; mediate cognition; normal cognitive experience, sensory, conceptual, and linguistic.

paśu, paśu yāga. Animal or cattle; the sacrifice involving slaughtering of animals like horse sacrifice.

paśyantī. The higher knowledge leading to liberation; the initial stage of consciousness marked by unity and freedom from all differentiation and sequence. Meditation aims at raising the level of consciousness to this innermost stage of the word; literally, "seeing."

pathaḥ. The yogic approach to spiritual *praxis,* the "path" described as "sharp as the edge of a razor, hard to traverse, untreadable."

pathya. The medical treatment by which the constituents of the body become even; "that which keeps one in the proper path" (in contrast to *a-pathya*).

pīṭha. The "seat" or center in the name of Goddess for dissemination of sacred learning (*vidyā pīṭha*).

pitr yāna. The way of the ancestor (*pitr*) or, more correctly, of the god-class created to guard the departed ancestors; as a transmigration doctrine, a way to be born again among mortals.

pradhāna prakṛti. The earliest or the first; nature, the matrix or mother of all things by the breaking of which, later on, all modifications take place; name of *prakṛti,* the mutual equilibrium of *guṇas.*

prajñā. Intuition, transcendental insight occasioned by discernment.

prajñāparādha. Offense against *prajñā,* technically the name for disease; offense against a healthy pattern of living consisting in provoking or inhibiting the natural calls in motion and a host of other things listed in medical science.

prākṛta. Natural, common, vulgar, unrefined (in contrast to "well-made or formed" *samskrta*).

pramā, pramāṇa. Valid knowledge, means or verifiers of valid knowledge, sensory, rational, and even revelatory.

prāmāṇya. The validity of valid knowledge understood either as intrinsic to it or occasioned by the presence of a causal excellence and likewise apprehended along with the apprehension of valid knowledge or apprehended by a separate act of knowledge.

prāṇa, prāṇamaya. Bio-motor or, more simply, life force accounting for the vital being of the self; bodily power; self as a personification of the vital function of life.

prapatti. The path of self-surrender as alternative to *bhakti* provided for the weak and infirm, preserving the essentials of *bhakti* but dispensing with its predisposing conditions and omitting the need for ceaseless practice.

prasāda. Divine grace.

pratibhā. Reliable kind of knowledge taking place all the time in us and rooted in ourselves, connecting together the meanings conveyed by the different words of a sentence; intuition arising spontaneously in all beings but occasioned by causes like nature, observing of Vedic prescriptions, practice of yoga, the unseen force generated by previous karma.

pratīkam, pratimā. The Vedic word for symbol, e.g., OM is the *pratīkam* of the Supreme Spirit; when the symbol is visual by consecration (*abhiṣeka*) the symbol becomes an image (*pratimā*); OM works as an image even though it is self-consecrated.

pratiprasava. Counterflow to the ordinary tendencies of *prakṛti*, a "turning around," a reversal of the usual tendencies of the mind so that it can discern its proper relation to spirit.

pratyāhāra. The inward turning of the senses implying withdrawal from external impressions in order to secure the attentiveness of absorption; the culmination of outer accomplishments of yoga.

pravṛtti. "Rolling forward," the cosmic tendency to repeat oneself helplessly (in contrast to waking up to one's true nature, rolling backwards, *nivrtti*); to state the same macrocosmically, continued advance, flow, the outward flowing of the cosmic movement, the correlative of *nivrtti,* the fulfillment of the cosmic play.

prāyaścitta. Expiation; "re-forming" of the *citta* by repentance expressed by means of rites involving sacrifice.

pūjā. Offering of worship with flowers (*pū,* a Tamil word for flower).

Puruṣa. Pure sentience, changeless, eternal, and omniscient, nonactive recipient or enjoyer without being a doer or agent; concluded from the presence in nature of means adapted to the accomplishment of particular ends as that for whom nature exists; the supreme Man, the cosmic Person, pervading the world with only a fourth of himself, whereas the remaining three parts transcend to a region beyond.

Puruṣamedha. The sacrifice performed after due completion of Vedic *yajna*(s), in which the performer consummates his total identification with the entire universe, with all that it contains, thus becoming one with the cosmic Person; the performer deems all things, all creatures, even human beings, as sacrificial animals, thereby expands his identity to cover the entire universe, and inhales the sacrificial fire within himself.

rāga. Attachment (in contrast to antipathy [*dveṣa*]).

ṛṣi. The Vedic seer, the sage, who with his mind's eye directly perceives Truth unfolding through layers of reality, cosmic harmony unfolding within his being.

ṛta. Truth, the eternal path of divine righteousness for all beings (in contrast to what threatens the harmony of human life and nature, i.e., evil "*anrta*").

rtabharā. The truth-ladenness of the insight or *prajnā* in the state of *samādhi.*

śabda pramāṇa. Verbal testimony as a means of valid knowledge cognate and complementary with reason and perception but having a scope that extends beyond them.

śabdapūrva yoga. Yoga or union with the inner, eternal undifferentiated sequenceless word, the purpose of yoga being always to transcend sequence as such, characteristic of the differentiated state; yoga as a means of attaining Brahman, the Word-Principle.

saccidānanda. The anonymity of existence, intelligence, and bliss (*sat, cit, ānanda*) as disclosive of the unitary essence of Brahman; understood as, strictly, the "definition, as it were," of the indefinable.

ṣaḍanga. The six limbs or members of yoga, namely, breath-control, withdrawal of the senses, meditation, concentration, reasoning, and absorption; the six limbs of Veda, namely, the auxiliary disciplines of phonetics, rituals, grammar, etymology, prosody, and astronomy.

sādhanā. Means for the attainment of the goal (*sādhya*); means of fitting the mind for instruction of knowledge; two main paths of *sādhāna,* discrimination and devotion.

sāksi, sāksībhāva, sāksi caitanya, sāksitā. Transcendental consciousness disclosing itself at the stage of cognitive intellect which uniquely defines the human level as "witness" peering through its thin form like the rays of the sun from behind the clouds, as disinterested onlooker; the state of being witness to what is borne witness to (*sākṣya*) as existing or also as not existing when absent, without judgment; symbolizes utter equanimity and impartiality as ingredients of spiritual perfection.

sakti-Śiva. Power, force, symbolized as the "female" energy of the male; male and female as polar manifestations, passive and active, of a single transcendent principle; *sakti* and *Śiva* in essence one though manifest as two.

sama. Calmness, counted as one of the spiritual riches (*sampatti*) necessary for entering spiritual life.

samādhi. Absorption, total perceptual attention which has two forms: with a consciousness of the duality of the perceiver and the perceived and without it, i.e., a non-dual absorption beyond even the exquisite consciousness of the union of the two. While the former is a fully conscious state of absorption founded on an ecstatic identification of two entities which are yet felt to be distinct, the latter is a mergence of the mental activity, the oscillating vitality (*citta vrtti*) of consciousness in the self to such a degree that the distinction becomes dissolved. The first deepens into the second where the two terms of the vision deliquesce in each other, now truly one-without-a-second.

samaiya. A Prakrit word denoting a feeling of equality with fellow beings, rectitude, as well as balanced mental state; indicates the true essence of selfhood.

samatvam, samabhāva. The "sameness" or equanimity of the enlightened sage, which is a reflection of the same unchanging principle within oneself which one sees in the outside world; the principle of changeless Being common to God and humanity.

Sāṁkhya-yoga. The names extremely common in Hindu philosophical literature as indicative of two complementary but distinct methods of approaching the reality of spirit. Sāmkhya meaning "reflection" stands for realizing of spirit through knowledge, and yoga, meaning contemplation, signifies the method of realizing the same by means of steady and persistent meditation; names also the blend of two doctrines sharing a common metaphysical standpoint and the same or similar ideal of life.

samnyāsa. Renunciation of household life, abandoning all ceremonial observances including the worship of the sacred fires; the spirit of renunciation is also said to consist in "renouncing and yet working," i.e., without coveting its fruits.

sampradāya. Tradition, traditional doctrine or knowledge; traditional handing down of instruction; a peculiar system of religious teaching.

samsāraḥ. Course, passage, the circuit of worldly life, mundane existence; transmigratory concourse of life.

samskāra. Impressions of past acts and thoughts serving as causative forces for bringing about further developments; latent impressions of former experience undergone in the present or bygone life, impressions manifesting themselves as propensities to action; *sams-kr* means "to transform something, to decorate" and the verb means to purify a person into a member of the sacramental community.

samyama. Discipline, constraint which when applied to any object leads to a direct perception of it because of the state of special attention that comes to prevail through *samyama.*

saranāgati. Self-surrender; seeking as refuge the feet (*saraṃa*) of the Lord; responsiveness to the operation of grace.

sarīra. Body, corporeality which includes the gross, cellular body subject to constant destruction and creation but also the inner world of forms and experiences—the notions, ideas, thoughts, emotions, visions, fantasies, of the "subtle body."

sat, satya. Being which was declared to be "in the beginning," "one only without a second"; "that being" (*tat*) also declared as the true or truth (*satyam*); the good (in contrast to *adat,* "the wicked").

sāyujyam. Intimate union, identification, absorption into a deity; one of the four states of *mukti.*

siṣya. "He who is to be taught" by the guru.

sraddhā. Faith; attentive reverence.

sthitaprajna, sthira buddhi. The person of steadied wisdom, of *buddhi* in control of the mind, alike attaining to Brahman.

svagata-bheda. Internal distinctions as between a person and his qualities or traits; one of the triple forms of difference alike denied of the differenceless reality of Brahman.

svāmitva. Ownership; proprietary right, lordship, sovereignity.

svarūpa. "Own form"; essence that is identical with and does not merely belong to something; what is intrinsic.

svayam prakāsatā. Self-luminosity; what is unconditional and at the same time immediate, descriptive of Spirit as the light of consciousness and its epistemological independence.

tamas. Inertia; darkness; denseness constitutive of the very substance of the matter of the universe like its two other counterparts, namely, light (*sattva*) and dynamism (*rajas*).

tapas. Penance, religious austerity, mortification; warmth, fire; pain, suffering; meditation connected with practice of personal self-denial or bodily mortification.

tarkaḥ. Argumentation; reasoning, speculation, discussion; the science of logic, reduction to absurdity.

tattvam. True state or condition; true or essential nature of the human soul or the material world; first principle.

tirobhāva. Veiling, unmanifest, concealment.

tulāvidya. Individuated ignorance accounting for particular instances of error and illusion subject to cancellation by knowledge of respective objects; in contrast with *mulāvidya.*

turīya. The fourth (the same as the *caturtham*); the fourth state of the soul in which it is "one" with spirit.

upāsanā. Service, attendance, waiting upon, engaging in; being intent on; worship; adoration; religious meditation.

vahiranga sādhanā. Extrinsic aids of self-training for recovering direct experience of spirit.

vāsanā. From the root *vas,* "to dwell in," the impressions unconsciously left on the mind by past good or bad actions; the subtle body (*sūkṣma sarīra*) is pervaded by *vāsanā* ("fragrance, the subtle residues") of its earlier karma. These *vāsanā*(s) cause *samaskara*(s), permanent scars going from life to life.

vastu. A real or reality, the really existing thing; the thing as it is in itself (in contrast to as it is perceived) (*viṣaya*).

vidhi. Vedic injunction; performance, action, a rule; commandment, any precept enjoining something for the first time.

vijñāna. Plenitude-of-knowledge, *vi* referring to infinity; understanding which is the function of the psyche comprising the subtle body; knowledge from the study of scriptures (in contrast to *prajnā*, "intuitive knowledge").

vijñānamaya. Consisting of or personification of *vijñāna;* description of self as reflective consciousness still short of the final essence of self as bliss.

viṣaya. The object as perceived by a subject; the real but as presented.

viśiṣṭādvaita. The doctrine according to which the relation between the supreme being and the particular things is that of *viśeṣya,* "the substance that is qualified," and *viśeṣana,* "the attribute that qualifies," the relation between the two being termed *viśiṣta;* the advaita or non-dualism of the differenced, as between substance and attribute, soul and its body, the whole and its parts.

vivarta vāda. Doctrine of apparent change; transformation, not actual but only apparent, signifying complete disappearance.

viveka khyāti. Knowledge of discrimination or discernment which permits transcendental insight to come into play.

vrta. Vowed observance; a religious act of devotion or austerity; a vow in general.

vrtti jñāna. Episodic cognition; *jñāna* that arises through mental modifications (*vrtti*); knowledge events as modes of consciousness.

vyavaharika. Literally, the conventional; relative existence; the empirical; the phenomenal; descriptive of the world of experience (in contrast to *paramarthika*).

Contributors

KRISHNA SIVARAMAN is currently Professor Emeritus of Religious Studies at McMaster University, Canada, and is the author of *Saivism in Philosophical Perspective*, coeditor of and contributor to *Revelation in Indian Philosophy*, and author of chapters in *Perspectives on Advaita*, *Modern Indian Responses to Religious Pluralism*, and many articles published in North America and India.

JOHN G. ARAPURA is Professor Emeritus of Religious Studies, McMaster University, Canada. He is the author of *Radhakrishnan and Integral Experience*, *Religion as Anxiety and Tranquility*, *Gnosis and the Question of Thought in Vedanta*, *Hermeneutical Essays on Vedanta Topics*, and numerous articles.

R. BALASUBRAMANIAN is the Director of the Radhakrishnan Institute of Advanced Studies in Philosophy, and Professor of Philosophy, University of Madras, and is the author of several works on Advaita: *The Taittiriya Upanisad Bhasya Vartika of Suresvara*, *Advaita Vedanta*, *Naishkarmya Siddhi*, and the editor of *Indian Philosophical Annual*, University of Madras; also member, Board of Editors and Advisors, World Spirituality.

KALIDAS BHATTACHARYYA was Professor of Philosophy and Vice Chancellor, Visva Bharati Shantiniketan, and authored several books and numerous articles published in the technical journals of Philosophy in India. Some titles of the books are *Philosophy, Logic and Language*, *A Modern Understanding of Advaita Vedanta*, *Presuppositions of Science and Philosophy and Other Essays*, *The Indian Concepts of Knowledge and Self.* Vedantic doctrine of consciousness and the notions of subjectivity, knowledge, and freedom are the pervasive themes of the author's writings, spread over a period of four decades.

S. S. BHAVASAR is Professor and Practitioner of Ayurvedic Studies in the University of Poona and is the author of writings in Marathi and English.

HAROLD G. COWARD is Professor of Religious Studies and Director of Humanities Institute at the University of Calgary, Canada. He has published several books: *Bhartrhari, the Sphota Theory of Language*, *Pluralism: Challenges to World Religions*, *Jung and Eastern Thought*, *Scripture in World Religions*, and numerous articles in the journals of Canada, the United States, and India.

SAGAR MAL JAIN is the Director of Parsvanath Institute of Jaina Religion, Varanasi, and is the author of several books in Hindi on Jainism and editor of journals published from the Institute.

GERTRUD KIEM is practitioner of homeopathic medicine in Mirano, Italy, and is the author of studies in the field of comparative medicine.

KLAUS K. KLOSTERMAIER is University Distinguished Professor and Head of the Department of Religious Studies, University of Manitoba, Canada, and author of *A Survey of Hinduism*, *Mythology and Philosophy of Salvation in the Theistic Tradition of India*, and several monographs in German.

Arun Kumar Mookerjee teaches Philosophy at Jadavpur University, Calcutta, and is the author and editor of books on education and psychology as well as articles on Indian philosophical subjects.

Bithika Mukerji is retired Reader of Philosophy, Banaras Hindu University, and is the author of *Neo-Vedanta and Modernity* and a monograph on Hinduism published in German and English; also member, Board of Editors and Advisors, World Spirituality.

Rajendra P. Pandeya is Professor of Philosophy at Ravishankar University, Raipur, and formerly Professor and Chairman, Department of Philosophy and Religion at Visva Bharati, Shantiniketan, and is the author of a number of articles published in the Visva Bharati *Journal of Philosophy*, including some on the Veda, and of a book with the title *The Problem of Fact.*

K. T. Pandurangi is retired Professor of Sanskrit, Bangalore University, and is the author and editor of Sanskrit works in the fields of Dvaita Vedanta and Purva Mimamsa, including *Brahma Sutra Vyakhyanam, The Wealth of Sanskrit Manuscripts in India and Abroad.*

Kenneth H. Post is Executive Secretary to the President, McMaster University, Canada, and is the coauthor of *The Foundations of Political Order in Genesis and the Chandogya Upanisad* and articles published in India and Canada.

S. S. Raghavachar is retired Professor of Philosophy, University of Mysore, and is the author of books on Ramanuja as well as on the Advaita and the Dvaita traditions. Some of the titles are *Dvaita Vedanta, Sribhasya on the Philosophy of Brahma Sutra, Śri Ramanuja on the Upanisads, Vedartha Samgrah.*

Ravi Ravindra is Professor jointly in the Departments of Physics and Religious Studies at Dalhousie University, Canada. He is the author of essays in such journals as *Religious Studies*, and is coauthor of a chapter entitled "The Dimensions of the Self: Buddhi in the Bhagavad Gita and Psyche in Plotinus" in *Neo Platonism and Indian Thought.*

Arvind Sharma is Associate Professor of Religious Studies at McGill University, Canada, and is the author of several books on a variety of subjects as well as on Hinduism, notably *Gitartha Samgrah of Abhinava Gupta* and *The Hindu Gita*, coauthor, editor/contributor to anthologies and chapters in books edited by other authors; elected as Fellow to the Royal Asiatic Society, London.

Hriday R. Sharma is Senior Lecturer in Vedic Studies in Samskrit Mahavidyalaya at Banaras Hindu University and is the author of essays in Hindi and Sanskrit published in University and other journals, all relating to Vedic ritual.

K. R. Sundararajan is Professor and Chairman, Department of Theology, St. Bonaventure University, New York, and has published numerous articles on such subjects as Incarnation according to Hinduism and Christianity, and Limits of Hindu-Christian Dialogue, in journals of the United States and India.

Wayne Whillier is Associate Professor of Religious Studies and also Associate Dean of Social Sciences, McMaster University, Canada, and author of some articles published in Canadian and Australian journals and a monograph on Vedic Studies awaiting publication.

Photographic Credits

The editor and the publisher wish to thank the custodians of the works of art for supplying photographs and granting permissions to use them. The assistance and cooperation of Dr. Bettina Baumer in the selection and arrangement of the illustrative materials from India is gratefully acknowledged.

1. Mathura Museum.
2. American Institute of Indian Studies.
3. The Cleveland Museum of Art. Purchase from the J. H. Wade Fund 43.72.
4. American Institute of Indian Studies.
5. Kyosuke Ito.
6. The Cleveland Museum of Art. Edward L. Whittmore Fund, 59.132.
7. Kyosuke Ito.
8. American Institute of Indian Studies.
9. Archaeological Survey of India.
10. American Institute of Indian Studies.
11. Dr. Bettina Baumer.
12. American Institute of Indian Studies.
13. American Institute of Indian Studies.
14. American Institute of Indian Studies.
15. Kyosuke Ito.
16. Asian Art Museum of San Francisco. The Avery Brundage Collection, 60.S47+.
17. Asian Art Museum of San Francisco. The Avery Brundage Collection, 66.S8.
18. Archaeological Survey of India.
19. American Institute of Indian Studies.
20. Kyosuke Ito.
21. Archaeological Survey of the Government of India.
22. Kyosuke Ito.
23. The Cleveland Museum of Art. John L. Severance Fund, 69.34.
24. Dr. Bettina Baumer
25. American Institute of Indian Studies.
26. Publications Division, Shree Shree Anand-M-Yee Charitable Society, Calcutta.

Indexes

Subjects

abortion, 100; Brahmin abortion, 96, 98
Absolute, the: positive character of, 293; versus the relative, 380
absolute identity: theory of, 286
adhikāra, xix
adhyātma, xxii
Advaita school of Vedanta, 305
altruism: in Jainism, 165-66
Ānanadamayī Mā, Śrī, 392-412; early years, 395-97; gathering of devotees of, 400-403; spiritual discipline and, 397-400; travels of, 403-5; words of, 405-10
āpaḥ, 11
ascetic: role of, 116
asceticism, xix
ātman, xx, 70
Ātma-vidyā, 69-72
attachment: abandonment of, 153; ego attachment to Vedic words, 223; to sequenced language, 223-24
attributes of God, 312
AUM, 77, 78, 83, 272; as primordial speech sound, 215
avidyā, 304-5
Āyurveda, 344; fundamentals of, 345-47; pathogenesis and, 349-50

being: oneness with the Supreme Spirit and, 74; unity of, 26; in the *Upaniṣads*, 72-76
belief: versus knowledge, 247
Bhagavadgītā: *buddhi-yoga* in, 192-205; Yoga and, 188-89
Bhāgavata Purāna, 322
bhakti, 264-65; concept of, 312-14; stages of, 313
bhakti-yoga, 266, 267-70
bliss, 23-26, 315-16
body: creation by the Supreme Deity, 321; effective use of the, 386; eight wheels of the, 24; manifestations of vitality in, 32; teachings of the, 320
body of God, 328-31
bondage: factors of, 304-5; in Jaina philosophy, 154-55; relationship to matter, 305
"book of nature," 333
Brahmabhāva, 37-38
Brahman, xx, xxi, xxii, 42, 46-47; Ātman and, 70; essence of, 279; identity with, 76; ritual knowledge of, 57; state of, xxxii; truth of the, 56; *Upaniṣads* and, 66-67
Brahman/Ātman, 71-72
Brahman-realization, 278
Brahma-vidyā, 69-72
Brahmin abortion, 96, 98, 100
brahminical spirituality, xxxiv
Brahmin murder, 96, 98, 100
brahmodya, 47-48, 49
brotherliness: model for, 118-20
buddhi, 189; concept of, 192-93; role in *Gītā*, 193-97
Buddhism, xix; *Mahāyāna*, 245; spread of, 152
buddhi-yoga, 196-97; contemporary relevance of, 204-5; integrality of, 202-4; path of, 198-202
Buddist devotional practices, 332

Candraśekharendra Sarasvati, Śrī, 361; on the absolute versus the relative, 379-81; early life, 378-79; on harmony, 384-85; on moral and spiritual discipline, 385-88; on personality, freedom, and love, 388-89; on preservation of the Vedic spirit, 381-83
capital crime, 92-94, 98-101; *dharmasūtra*(s) on, 94-97
Caraka Samhita, 339-40; health in, 347-48; Indian culture and, 340-45

Names

Colophon

Hindu Spirituality: Vedas through Vedanta,

Volume 6 of World Spirituality: An Encyclopedic History of the Religious Quest, was designed by Maurya P. Horgan and Paul J. Kobelski.

The type is 11-point Garamond Antiqua and was set by

The Scriptorium, Denver, Colorado.